The Archaeology of Anglo-Jewry in England and Wales 1656–c.1880

Kenneth Marks

Archaeopress

Gordon House
276 Banbury Road
Oxford OX2 7ED

www.archaeopress.com

ISBN 978 1 905739 76 9

© Archaeopress and K Marks 2014

Cover image: Merthyr Tydfil Synagogue 1872, sold in 1983. Photo by J Marks 2010.

All rights reserved. No part of this book may be reproduced, stored in retrieval system, or transmitted, in any form or by any means, electronic, mechanical, photocopying or otherwise, without the prior written permission of the copyright owners.

Printed in England by Information Press, Oxford

Contents

Acknowledgements xiii

Introduction 1
1.1 The form of this study 2

Brief Summary of Anglo-Jewish History c.1066-c.1880 4
2.1 Pre-expulsion period c.1066-1290 4
2.2 Jewish population growth from 1656-c.1880 7
2.3 Community in London from 1656-c.1880 8
    1800-c.1880 Emancipation 12
    Where did they live in London? 13
2.4 Rise of provincial communities from c.1740-c.1880 14
    2.4.1 Chronological establishment of provincial communities 16
2.5 Concluding remarks 17

Research Aims and Methodology 19
3.1 Research aims 19
    3.1.1 Research Questions 19
3.2 Methodology 20
    3.2.1 Preliminary work 22
    3.2.2 Gathering information 23
        3.2.2.1 Published information and excavation reports 23
        3.2.2.2 Analysis of data collected 23
    3.2.3 The nature of the evidence, methodological problems and limitations 24
        3.2.3.1 Synagogues 25
        3.2.3.2 Cemeteries 25
    3.3.1 Glossary 26
    3.3.2 Gazetteer 26

Living Communities: Synagogues, street and place names with Jewish connections, *mikva'ot* (ritual baths), material culture and artefacts 27
4.1 London communities and synagogues 28
    4.1.1. Bayswater Synagogue W2 30
    4.1.2 Bevis Marks Synagogue EC3 32
    4.1.3 Central Synagogue W1 35
    4.1.4 Creechurch Lane EC3 36
    4.1.5 The Great Synagogue EC3 39
    4.1.6 Hambro Synagogue EC3 43
    4.1.7 The New Synagogue E.C.3 45
    4.1.8 New West End Synagogue W2 46
    4.1.9 Princelet Street Synagogue E1 49

- 4.1.10 Sandy's Row Synagogue EC1 50
- 4.1.11 Western Synagogue WC1 51
- 4.1.12 West London Synagogue W.1 53
- 4.2 Provincial communities and synagogues 55
  - 4.2.1 Bath 58
    - 4.2.2.1 Birmingham 59
    - 4.2.2.2 Birmingham: Singers Hill 60
  - 4.2.3 Bradford 61
  - 4.2.4 Brighton 62
    - 4.2.5.1 Bristol 65
    - 4.2.5.2 Bristol: Synagogue Park Row BS1 established c.1870-still in use 66
  - 4.2.6 Canterbury 68
  - 4.2.7 Cardiff 70
  - 4.2.8 Chatham 70
  - 4.2.9 Cheltenham 72
  - 4.2.10 Coventry 73
  - 4.2.11 Dover 74
  - 4.2.12 Exeter 75
  - 4.2.13 Falmouth 76
  - 4.2.14 Gloucester 78
    - 4.2.15.1 Hull 78
    - 4.2.15.2 Robinson Row 79
  - 4.2.16 Ipswich 80
  - 4.2.17 King's Lynn 81
  - 4.2.18 Leeds 81
    - 4.2.19.1 Liverpool 82
    - 4.2.19.2 Liverpool: Princes Road Synagogue (Grade 1) 1872-still in use 85
    - 4.2.20.1 Manchester 86
    - 4.2.20.2 Manchester: The Great Synagogue Cheetham Hill 88
    - 4.2.20.3 Manchester: Reform Synagogue 89
    - 4.2.20.4 Manchester: Spanish and Portuguese Synagogue 90
  - 4.2.21 Merthyr Tydfil 92
    - 4.2.22.1 Newcastle 93
    - 4.2.22.2 Newcastle: Leazes Park Synagogue 94
  - 4.2.23 Norwich 95
  - 4.2.24 Nottingham 96
  - 4.2.25 Oxford 98
  - 4.2.26 Penzance 100
  - 4.2.27 Plymouth 102
  - 4.2.28 Portsmouth 104
    - 4.2.29.1 Ramsgate 107
    - 4.2.29.2 Ramsgate: Montefiore Mausoleum 109
  - 4.2.30 Sheerness 110
  - 4.2.31 Sheffield 110
  - 4.2.32 Southampton 112
  - 4.2.33 Sunderland 112
  - 4.2.34 Swansea 113
  - 4.2.35 Yarmouth (Great) 114
  - 4.2.36 Synagogues conclusion 114
- 4.3 Street and place names with Jewish connections 116

4.3.1 London ... 116
4.3.2 Provinces ... 117
4.4 *Mikva'ot* (ritual baths), material culture, and artefacts ... 118
    4.4.1 *Mikva'ot* (ritual baths) ... 119
        4.4.1.2 Provinces ... 121
    4.4.2 London material culture and artefacts ... 123
        4.4.2.1 'Delftware' Hebrew Plate c.1720 ... 123
        4.4.2.2 Kosher meat and cloth seals 17th/18th centuries ... 125
        4.4.2.3 Shofar'ot (ram's horns) c.19th century ... 128

Communities in Death (Cemeteries) ... 132
5.1 London cemeteries ... 134
    5.1.1 Sephardi *Velho* (Old) Mile End Road E1 ... 135
    5.1.2 Sephardi *Nuevo* (New) Mile End Road E1 ... 138
    5.1.3 Sephardi Brentwood Coxtie Green CM14 ... 139
    5.1.4 Ashkenazi Alderney Road E ... 140
    5.1.5 Ashkenazi Bancroft Road E1 ... 143
    5.1.6 Ashkenazi Brady Street E1 ... 144
    5.1.7 Ashkenazi Fulham Road SW3 ... 146
    5.1.8 Ashkenazi Lauriston Road E9 ... 147
    5.1.9 Ashkenazi West Ham E15 ... 149
    5.1.10 West London Reform Balls Pond Road N1 ... 151
    5.1.11 Ashkenazi Willesden NW10 ... 153
5.2 Provincial Cemeteries ... 154
    5.2.1 Bath: Bradford Road ... 156
    5.2.2 Birmingham: Witton Old Cemetery ... 159
    5.2.3 Bradford: Scholemoor, Jewish sections ... 160
    5.2.4 Brighton: Florence Place ... 161
    5.2.5 Bristol: St Philip's Cemetery, Barton Road ... 162
    5.2.6 Canterbury: Whitstable Road ... 165
    5.2.7 Cardiff: Highfield Road ... 165
    5.2.8 Chatham: High Street ... 167
    5.2.9 Cheltenham: Elm Street ... 168
    5.2.10 Coventry: London Road ... 169
    5.2.11 Dover: Old Charlton Road ... 170
    5.2.12 Exeter: Bull Meadow ... 171
    5.2.13 Falmouth: Ponsharden ... 172
    5.2.14 Gloucester: Coney Hill ... 174
        5.2.15.1 Hull ... 176
        5.2.15.2 Hull: Hessle Road ... 177
        5.2.15.3 Hull: Delhi Street ... 177
        5.2.16.1 Ipswich: Salthouse Lane ... 178
        5.2.16.2 Ipswich: Cemetery Lane ... 180
    5.2.17 King's Lynn: Mill Fleet ... 181
        5.2.18.1 Leeds: Hill Top ... 182
        5.2.18.2 Leeds: Gildersome Gelderd Road ... 182
        5.2.19.1 Liverpool: Deane Road ... 182
        5.2.19.2 Liverpool: Broad Green ... 185
        5.2.19.3 Liverpool: Green Lane ... 185
        5.2.20.1 Manchester: Brindle Heath] ... 186

5.2.20.2 Manchester: Prestwich Village 187
  5.2.20.3 Manchester: Whitefield Reform Cemetery.. 187
  5.2.20.4 Manchester: Philips Park 188
 5.2.21 Merthyr Tydfil: Brecon Road 189
  5.2.22.1 Newcastle 190
  5.2.22.2 Newcastle: St John's Jewish Section 190
  5.2.23.1 Norwich: Mariners Lane.. 192
  5.2.23.2 Norwich: St Crispin's Road 194
  5.2.23.3 Norwich: Bowthorpe Road (Jewish Section) 194
  5.2.24.1 Nottingham: North Sherwood Street... 196
  4.2.24.2 Nottingham: Hardy Street 197
 5.2.25 Oxford (no cemeteries in period under discussion) 198
 5.2.26 Penzance: Leskinnick Terrace... 198
 5.2.27 Plymouth Hoe: Lambhay Hill 200
 5.2.28 Portsmouth: Fawcett Road 202
 5.2.29 Ramsgate: Upper Dumpton Road 204
  5.2.30.1 Sheerness Hope Street 205
  5.2.30.2 Isle of Sheppey (Jewish section) 205
  5.2.31.1 Sheffield: Bowden Street 206
  5.2.31.2 Sheffield: Waller Road Walkley 207
  5.2.31.3 Sheffield: Ecclesfield 207
 5.2.32 Southampton: Common Cemetery (Jewish Section) 208
  5.2.33.1 Sunderland: Ayres Quay 210
  5.2.33.2 Sunderland: Bishopswearmouth 212
 5.2.34 Swansea: Mayhill Old Jew's Burial Ground 213
  5.2.35.1 Yarmouth (Great): Alma Road 214
  5.2.35.2 Yarmouth (Great): Kitchener Road... 215
 5.2.36 Cemeteries conclusion... 216

A Comparative Approach to Jewish UrbanTopography..218
6.1 London: growth, topography and migration...224
 6.1.1 London: Jewish suburbia..227
  6.1.1.2 London: synagogue membership, growth of working-class suburbs and patterns
  of settlement...228
  6.1.1.3 London: cemeteries 229
6.2 Provinces: growth, topography and migration 230
 6.2.1 Provinces: the early communities 230
  6.2.2.1 Birmingham.. 231
  6.2.2.2 Bradford.. 232
  6.2.2.3 Brighton and Hove.. 233
  6.2.2.4 Bristol.. 233
  6.2.2.5 Hull 234
  6.2.2.6 Leeds... 236
  6.2.2.7 Liverpool 237
  6.2.2.8 Manchester.. 240
  6.2.2.9 North–East England.. 242
  6.2.2.10 Nottingham 244
  6.2.2.11 Oxford... 245
  6.2.2.12 South Wales.. 246
  6.2.2.13 South-West England 248
Conclusion 250

Discussion, Conclusion and Suggestions for Future Research 252
7.1 Topography of Anglo-Jewry 1656-c.1880 252
7.2 Suggestions for future research 257

Glossary, Bibliography and Sources 261

Glossary 261

Bibliography and Sources 263

Gazetteer 271

List of Figures

Figure 1.1 London and 35 provincial communities established prior to 1880 xvi
Figure 2.1 Map of medieval Jewish communities in 12th-13th centuries 6
Figure 3.1 format of summary sheet in gazetteer. 26
Figure 4.1 Jacob Ilive's Map of Aldgate Ward 1756 29
Figure 4.2 Map of London showing Beavis Markes (now Bevis Marks) and Dukes Place the location of the first two custom-made synagogues in London, Dukes Place (1690). 30
Figure 4.4 Bayswater Synagogue: interior in 1863 (contemporary engraving) (Renton 2000, 80) 31
Figure 4.3 Bayswater Synagogue 1863: exterior (Phillips et al. 1963). 31
Figure 4.5 Bayswater Synagogue 1863: the Ark showing dressed Torah scrolls 32
Figure 4.6 Interior of the Spanish and Portuguese Synagogue in Amsterdam, showing the *bimah* (central platform) 33
Figure 4.7 Plan of the ground floor level of Bevis Marks 1701 (Bevis Marks archives) 33
Figure 4.8 The interior of Spanish and Portuguese Synagogue, Bevis Marks EC3 (1812) 34
Figure 4.9 Interior Central Synagogue W1 (1870). 35
Figure 4.10 Conjectural plan of Creechurch Lane EC3 (1657). 36
Figure 4.11 Conjectural plan of extended Creechurch Lane EC3 (1674). 37
Figure 4.12 Plaque in Creechurch Lane EC3 marking site of first synagogue in England 38
Figure 4.13 Ground floor plan of The Great Synagogue EC3 (1690/1692). 39
Figure 4.14 Duke's Place EC3 Gothic archway entrance to The Great Synagogue. 40
Figure 4.15 The Great Synagogue entrance from Duke's Place EC3 early 19th century. 40
Figure 4.16 The Great Synagogue Duke's Place EC3 plan (1788-1790) 41
Figure 4.17 Interior of The Great Synagogue Duke's Place EC3 (1809). 41
Figure 4.18 The Great Synagogue Ark. 42
Figure 4.19 Ruins of the Great Synagogue Duke's Place EC3 destroyed in the *Blitz* 1941. 42
Figure 4.20 Temporary hut in Duke's Place EC3 (1943). 42
Figure 4.21 Plaque marking the site of The Great Synagogue. 42
Figure 4.22 IInterior Hambro Synagogue EC2 (c.1725. 43
Figure 4.23 Engraving of the Hambro Synagogue. 43
Figure 4.24 Hambro Synagogue excavation (2006) showing foundations of one remaining wall 44
Figure 4.25 New Synagogue, Leadenhall Street entrance (1761). 45
Figure 4.26 New Synagogue foundation stone Egerton Road Synagogue N13. 45
Figure 4.27 Interior New Synagogue EC3 (1841). 46
Figure 4.28 New West End Synagogue W2 foundation stone (1877). 47
Figure 4.29 Exterior New West End Synagogue W2 (1878). 47
Figure 4.30 Interior New West End Synagogue W2. 48
Figure 4.31 New West End Synagogue W2, clock with Hebrew letters. 48
Figure 4.32 Exterior Princelet Street Synagogue E1 (1870) 50
Figure 4.33 Interior Princelet Street Synagogue E1. 50
Figure 4.34 Interior Sandy's Row Synagogue E1 (1854). 50
Figure 4.35 Map of the Strand area showing location of Western Synagogue W1 (c.1761). 52
Figure 4.36 Interior Western Synagogue St. Albans Place WC1 (1851). 52
Figure 4.37 Western Synagogue, Alfred Place, Westminster WC1interior 1915 52
Figure 4.38 Western Synagogue doors now in entrance to Montague Road Cemetery N18. 53
Figure 4.39 Entrance to West London Reform Synagogue W1 (1870) 54
Figure 4.40 Interior of West London Reform Synagogue W1 (1870). 55
Figure 4.41 Interior of West London Reform Synagogue W1 (1993). 55
Figure 4.42 Bath: site of Corn Street Synagogue (c.1840) 58
Figure 4.43 Birmingham: The position of the Ark in the former Severn Street Synagogue 1825. 59
Figure 4.44 Birmingham: Singers Hill Synagogue 1856 front elevation (by permission S. Busby)...... 60
Figure 4.45 Birmingham: Singers Hill Synagogue, interior (by permission S. Busby) 60
Figure 4.46 Bradford: Front elevation Bowland Street Reform Synagogue (1880/1881). 61

Figure 4.47 Bradford: Bowland Street Reform Synagogue, interior and Ark... 62
Figure 4.48 Brighton: Jew Street, possible entrance to synagogue? (c.1792).. 63
Figure 4.49 Brighton: Devonshire Place, façade of former synagogue (1825)... 63
Figure 4.50 Brighton: Middle Street Synagogue, foundation stone (1874) 63
Figure 4.51 Brighton: Middle Street Synagogue, façade and entrance (1874) 64
Figure 4.52 Brighton: Middle Street Synagogue, interior.. 64
Figure 4.53 Brighton: Middle Street Synagogue, brass *hanukia* (candle stick)...................................... 64
Figure 4.54 Brighton: Middle Street Synagogue, capital depicting fruit and foliage............................... 65
Figure 4.55 Bristol: location of three early synagogues... 65
Figure 4.56 Bristol: Old House Temple Street Synagogue (1756)... 65
Figure 4.57 Bristol Park Row Synagogue, (1870)... 66
Figure 4.58 Bristol: Park Row Synagogue, *bimah* (central platform)... 67
Figure 4.59 Bristol: Park Row Synagogue, Ark. 67
Figure 4.60 Bristol: Park Row Synagogue, prayer board for Royal Family 67
Figure 4.61 Canterbury: Knights Templar inscription. 68
Figure 4.62 Canterbury: Site of Black Prince Chantry and synagogue (1847)... 69
Figure 4.63 Canterbury: King Street, Synagogue entrance, showing obelisks... 69
Figure 4.64 Canterbury: Synagogue interior, now music room of King's School................................... 69
Figure 4.65 Chatham: High Street, synagogue foundation stone (1869).. 71
Figure 4.66 Chatham: synagogue elevated frontage. 71
Figure 4.67 Chatham: synagogue interior.. 71
Figure 4.68 Cheltenham: Synagogue Lane, synagogue (1837-1839). 72
Figure 4.69 Cheltenham: synagogue interior, showing rattan covered pews and Royal Family 73
Figure 4.70 Coventry: Barras Lane, synagogue (1870)... 73
Figure 4.71 Dover: broken tablet from demolished synagogue (1863)... 74
Figure 4.72 Dover: two tablets from demolished synagogue... 74
Figure 4.73 Exeter: synagogue interior with Georgian Ark (1763)... 76
Figure 4.74 Exeter: synagogue metal-work *bimah* (central platform).. 76
Figure 4.75 Falmouth: former synagogue plaque (1808-1880). 77
Figure 4.76 Falmouth: exterior of former synagogue 77
Figure 4.77 Falmouth: former synagogue plan of interior, surveyed in 1958.. 78
Figure 4.78 Hull: interior of Postengate Synagogue (1780). 79
Figure 4.79 Hull: Robinson Row Synagogue ground floor plan (1826)... 79
Figure 4.80 Hull: Robinson Row Synagogue prior to demolition (1926).. 80
Figure 4.81 Ipswich: 1848 map showing cemetery and synagogue) 80
Figure 4.82 Ipswich: Rope Walk Synagogue (1792)... 80
Figure 4.83 Leeds: interior of Belgrave Street Synagogue, interior (1860).. 82
Figure 4.84 Liverpool: plaque on site of first synagogue and burial ground (c.1750)............................. 83
Figure 4.85 Liverpool: Frederick Street Synagogue and burial ground at rear (c.1794)......................... 83
Figure 4.86 Liverpool: Seel Street Synagogue (1807) 83
Figure 4.87 Liverpool: Seel Street Synagogue, plaque marking the site on Telephone Exchange. 84
Figure 4.88 Liverpool: Hope Place Synagogue (1857)... 84
Figure 4.89 Liverpool: Hope Place Synagogue (1864)... 84
Figure 4.90 Liverpool: Hope Place Synagogue, Jewish district surrounding synagogue........................ 84
Figure 4.91 Liverpool: Hope Place Hebrew School built in 1852 85
Figure 4.92 Liverpool: Princess Road Synagogue Toxteth (1872) ().. 85
Figure 4.93 Liverpool: Princes Road Synagogue, interior... 86
Figure 4.94 Manchester: plan showing Synagogue Alley (1741)... 87
Figure 4.95 Manchester: plan showing first room of prayer and synagogue. 87
Figure 4.96 Manchester: exterior of The Great Synagogue (1858) 89
Figure 4.97 Manchester: exterior of The Great Synagogue interior (1858)... 89
Figure 4.98 Manchester: Reform Synagogue (1858).. 90
Figure 4.99 Manchester: Reform Synagogue interior (1858). 90
Figure 4.100 Manchester: former Spanish and Portuguese Synagogue façade and plaque (1874)........ 91
Figure 4.101 Manchester, former Spanish and Portuguese Synagogue interior...................................... 91

Figure 4.102 Merthyr Tydfil: former synagogue (1872). 92
Figure 4.103 Merthyr Tydfil: former synagogue plaque in English and Welsh. 92
Figure 4.104 Merthyr Tydfil: Welsh dragon on front gable, side window showing Star of David. 93
Figure 4.105 Newcastle: plaque and lintel from first synagogue in Temple Street (1838).................... 94
Figure 4.106 Newcastle: entrance to former synagogue in Charlotte Street (1867). 94
Figure 4.107 Newcastle: former Leazes Park Synagogue (1879). 95
Figure 4.108 Norwich: sketches of first synagogue in Tombland Alley (1828). 95
Figure 4.109 Norwich: possible outside of Tombland Alley Synagogue. 96
Figure 4.110 Norwich: former synagogue in Synagogue Street prior to bombing in 1942.......... 96
Figure 4.111 Norwich: synagogue in ruins after bombing in 1942. 96
Figure 4.112 Nottingham: Chaucer Street Synagogue (1890-1950). 97
Figure 4.113 Nottingham: Shakespeare Villas Synagogue former Methodist Chapel (1854). 98
Figure 4.114 Nottingham: Silver *rimonim* (used to decorate the *Torah*). 98
Figure 4.115 Oxford: plan of medieval Jewry and sites of 18th century synagogues. 99
Figure 4.116 Penzance: plan showing sites of synagogue established 1807 and cemetery.......... 100
Figure 4.117 Penzance: former synagogue exterior, remaining wall. 101
Figure 4.118 Penzance: plan of former synagogue 101
Figure 4.119 Penzance: former synagogue interior and decalogue. 102
Figure 4.120 Plymouth: exterior of synagogue (George111) (1761). 104
Figure 4.121 Plymouth: prayer board to The Royal Family (1762). 104
Figure 4.122 Portsmouth: synagogue Georgian Ark in Portsea Synagogue (1780) 105
Figure 4.123 Portsmouth: synagogue Ark now in Southsea Synagogue. 105
Figure 4.124 Portsmouth: plan showing synagogue and location of premises where Jews lived in Napoleonic Wars.. 105
Figure 4.125 Portsmouth: Royal Coat of Arms (George 111)1843 in Southsea Synagogue 106
Figure 4.126 Portsmouth: 51. Portsmouth Synagogue windows with text of Ten Commandments (1843). 106
Figure 4.127 Portsmouth: synagogue lintel stone dated Portsea Synagogue 5540 (1780)............ 107
Figure 4.128 Portsmouth: foundation and commemorative stones 1780 107
Figure 4.129 Ramsgate: exterior of Montefiori Synagogue (1833). 108
Figure 4.130 Ramsgate: Montefiori Synagogue, vestibule with marble stand showing washing of hands. 108
Figure 4.131 Ramsgate: Montefiori Synagogue interior. 108
Figure 4.132 Ramsgate: Montefiori Synagogue, domed glass ceiling light.................................. 108
Figure 4.133 Ramsgate: Mausoleum of Sir Moses and Lady Montefiori (1862). 109
Figure 4.134 Ramsgate: Montefiori Mausoleum showing stone pillar from the Land of Israel 109
Figure 4.135 Sheerness: interior of synagogue (1811). 110
Figure 4.136 Sheffield: front of former North Street Synagogue (1872). 111
Figure 4.137 Sheffield: Gothic arch and Hebrew inscription 111
Figure 4.138 Sheffield: plan of Jewish area, showing first rooms of prayer and first cemetery 111
Figure 4.139 Southampton: synagogue (1864) demolished 1964. 112
Figure 4.140 Swansea: Goat Street Synagogue (1859). 113
Figure 4.141 Swansea: Goat Street Synagogue, destroyed by bombing in 1941. 113
Figure 4.142 Swansea: Goat Street Synagogue interior. 114
Figure 4.143 London: medieval Milk Street E1 *mikveh* now in Jewish Museum..................... 121
Figure 4.144 Canterbury, *The Old Mikveh* (1851). 122
Figure 4.145 Plymouth: *mikveh* originally c.1750, modernised c.1900?.................................... 122
Figure 4.146 London: Mitre Street EC3 site where 1720 *Chalav* (milk) plate was found in rubbish dump.. 123
Figure 4.147 London: 18th century 'delftware' plate with Hebrew inscription *Chalav'*(milk)............. 124
Figure 4.148 London: Mid 18th century 'delftware' plate with Hebrew inscription *Basar* (meat) 124
Figure 4.149 London: six,17th/18th century *kosher* meat seals found in rubbish dumps 127
Figure 4.150 London:three 17th century *kosher* cloth seals City of London and Hampstead. 128
Figure 4.151 London:c.19th century *shofar* ram's horn, recovered from Thames 1850. 130
Figure 4.153 London: c19th century *shofar* ram's horn, excavated Leadenhall Street EC3 n 130
Figure 4.152 Calibrated dates of *shofar'ot* (rams' horns) Radiocarbon Accelerator, Oxford. 130
Figure 5.1 Map showing London Jewish cemeteries in 17th -19th centuries 132

Figure 5.2 Engravings on tombstones. 134
Figure 5.3 Plaque on the Mile End Road, E1. 135
Figure 5.4 *Velho* (old) Sephardi Old Cemetery E1 (1657). 136
Figure 5.5 *Velho* (old) Cemetery E1 stone inscription (1684) with names of founders of the community. 136
Figure 5.6 *Velho* (old) Cemetery E1 skull and cross bones carvings. 137
Figure 5.7 *Nuevo* (new) cemetery E1 (1733) 138
Figure 5.8 Brentwood Cemetery CM14 entrance gate (1974). 139
Figure 5.9 Brentwood Cemetery CM14 mass burial area of 7500 remains from *Nuevo* cemetery. 139
Figure 5.10 Alderney Road Cemetery E1 plaque to founders of the cemetery (1696). 140
Figure 5.11 Alderney Road Cemetery E1 layout. 140
Figure 5.12 Alderney Road Cemetery E1 line drawings (1993), showing plot positions 141
Figure 5.13 Alderney Road Cemetery E1 chest tombs from 1696 and later. 142
Figure 5.14 Alderney Road cemetery E1 tomb of Rabbi Samuel Falk (d.1782) 142
Figure 5.15 Bancroft Road Cemetery E1 (1810). 143
Figure 5.16 Brady Street Cemetery E1 (1761) view of central mound for in depth burials. 144
Figure 5.17 Brady Street Cemetery E1 back to back tombstones. 144
Figure 5.18 Brady Street Cemetery E1 tombs of Nathan and Hannah Rothschild. 145
Figure 5.19 Brady Street Cemetery E1 obelisk and bust of Miriam Levy 145
Figure 5.20 Fulham Road Cemetery SW3 (1815). 146
Figure 5.21 Lauriston Road Cemetery E9 (1788) chest tombs in the shape of coffins 148
Figure 5.22 Lauriston Road Cemetery E9 decorated tomb monuments. 148
Figure 5.23 West Ham Cemetery E15 (1856). 149
Figure 5.24 West Ham cemetery E15 plan, showing strips of re-interred remains from Old Hoxton Cemetery 150
Figure 5.25 West Ham Cemetery E15 (1707-1878) re-interred remains from Old Hoxton Cemetery ... 150
Figure 5.26 West Ham Cemetery E15 Christian Gothic-style prayer hall 150
Figure 5.27 West Ham Cemetery E15 The Rothschild Mausoleum (1866) 151
Figure 5.28 West London Reform Cemetery N1 (1843) grave off Rabbi Wolf Marks (d.1909) 152
Figure 5.29 West London Reform Cemetery N1 chest tomb of Baronet Goldsmith (d.1859). 152
Figure 5.30 Willesden, Cemetery NW10 1873 *ohel* (prayer hall). 154
Figure 5.31 Willesden, Cemetery NW10 marble enclosure of the Rothschild family 154
Figure 5.32 Bath, cemetery shown on extract from Ordinance Survey Map (1904) 157
Figure 5.33 Bath, topographical plan of Jewish Burial Ground (1986). 158
Figure 5.34 Bath, burial ground. 158
Figure 5.35 Bath, *ohel* (prayer hall) (c.1815) 159
Figure 5.36 Birmingham, Witton Old Jewish Cemetery, memorial obelisk (1869). 160
Figure 5.37 Bradford, Scholemoor Reform Cemetery, *ohel* prayer hall (1877). 161
Figure 5.38 Bradford, plan of Municipal Cemetery, showing two Jewish sections. 161
Figure 5.39 Brighton, Florence Place Burial Ground, *ohel* (prayer hall) (1891/3) 162
Figure 5.40 Brighton, Florence Place Old Jewish Burial Ground. 162
Figure 5.41 Bristol, Barton Road Cemetery, plan showing plot positions (1744) 163
Figure 5.42 Bristol, Barton Road Cemetery, part of burial ground before restoration. 163
Figure 5.43 Bristol, Barton Road Cemetery view of burial ground 164
Figure 5.44 Bristol, Barton Road Cemetery, tomb monuments 164
Figure 5.45 Canterbury, Whitstable Road Jews' Burial Ground, entrance (1760) 165
Figure 5.46 Canterbury, Whitstable Road Jews' Burial Ground). 165
Figure 5.47 Cardiff, Highfield Road Old Jewish Cemetery, donation plaque (1841). 165
Figure 5.48 Cardiff, Highfield Road Old Jewish Cemetery, entrance gates 166
Figure 5.49 Cardiff, Highfield Road Old Jewish Cemetery, tombstones and obelisks. 166
Figure 5.50 Cardiff, Highfield Road Old Jewish Cemetery, decorations on tombstones. 166
Figure 5.51 Chatham, High Street, Jews' Burial Ground (1780s) 167
Figure 5.52 Chatham, High Street, Jews' Burial Ground, obelisk to Lazarus Simon Magnus. 167
Figure 5.53 Cheltenham, Elm Street, Jews' Burial Ground (1824), 1893 plan of cemetery 168
Figure 5.54 Cheltenham, Elm Street, row of oldest surviving graves (c.1870). 169
Figure 5.55 Coventry: London Road Cemetery plan showing Jewish Section (1864) 169

Figure 5.56 Coventry: London Road Cemetery, Jewish section, oldest graves 170
Figure 5.57 Dover: Old Charlton Road Cemetery (1864). 171
Figure 5.58 Dover: Old Charlton Road Cemetery, top row with oldest burials from 19th century. .. 171
Figure 5.59 Exeter, Bull Meadow Jew's Burial Ground, outline plans (1757 and 1827). 172
Figure 5.60 Exeter, Bull Meadow Jew's Burial Ground, showing boundary walls. 172
Figure 5.61 Falmouth: Penryn, Jews' Burial Ground (1780). 173
Figure 5.62 Falmouth: Penryn, Jews' Burial Ground, plan of cemetery. 173
Figure 5.63 Falmouth: Penryn, Jews' Burial Ground, tombstone of Alexander Moses (Zender Falmouth). 174
Figure 5.64 Gloucester: Coney Hill Cemetery, plan showing Jewish section with re-interred remains...175
Figure 5.65 Gloucester: Coney Hill Cemetery, plaque recording 1938 re-internment 175
Figure 5.66 Gloucester: Coney Hill Cemetery, gravestones marking re-interred remains.................... 175
Figure 5.67 Hull: Villa Place Cemetery, entrance to former burial ground (1750?) 176
Figure 5.68 Hull: Villa Place Cemetery, grass covered former burial ground. 176
Figure 5.69 Hull: Hessle Road, 'New' Jewish Cemetery (1812)... 177
Figure 5.70 Hull: Hessle Road, public house with Stars of David in windows....................................... 177
Figure 5.71 Hull: Delhi Street Cemetery, Hedon Road remains of former *(ohel)* prayer hall (1858)..178
Figure 5.72 Hull: Delhi Street Cemetery, tombstones destroyed by vandals and area destroyed 1941. 178
Figure 5.73 Ipswich: Salthouse Lane Jews' Burial Ground, wall with gated entrance (1796). 179
Figure 5.74 Ipswich: Salthouse Lane Jews' Burial Ground, showing some of the tombstones. 179
Figure 5.75 Ipswich: Cemetery Lane, graves in Old Cemetery, Jewish Section (1885). 180
Figure 5.76 Ipswich: Cemetery Lane, plan of burial ground showing Jewish section. 180
Figure 5.77 King's Lynn: Millfleet Jews' Burial Ground, commemorative plaque (c.1811). 181
Figure 5.78 King's Lynn: Millfleet Jews' Burial Ground. 181
Figure 5.79 Leeds: Hill Top Cemetery (1860s), when still in use 182
Figure 5.80 Leeds: Hill Top Cemetery, view of derelict burial ground 182
Figure 5.81 Liverpool: Deane Road, Old Jews' Burial Ground (1837), (1851 O.S. map) 183
Figure 5.82 Liverpool: Deane Road, Old Jews' Burial Ground, extract from Ordinance Survey Map (1893). 183
Figure 5.83 Liverpool: Deane Road, Old Jews' Burial Ground, entrance and gateway (1837)............ 183
Figure 5.84 Liverpool: Deane Road, Old Jews' Burial Ground, outline plans (1837) 184
Figure 5.85 Liverpool: Deane Road, Old Jews' Burial Ground, topographical plan............................. 184
Figure 5.86 Liverpool: Deane Road, Old Jews' Burial Ground, showing red brick boundary wall. ... 184
Figure 5.87 Liverpool: Broad Green Cemetery, re-interred remains from Frederick Street and Oaks Street. 185
Figure 5.88 Liverpool: Green Lane Cemetery (1839)... 186
Figure 5.89 Manchester: Brindle Heath Jews' Burial Ground, (1794) and memorial stone................. 186
Figure 5.90 Manchester: Brindle Heath Jews' Burial Ground,(1794-1840) remaining tombstones.... 186
Figure 5.91 Manchester: Brindle Heath Jews' Burial Ground, Star of David... 187
Figure 5.92 Manchester: Prestwich Village Jews' disused Burial Ground (1841-1914). 187
Figure 5.93 Manchester: Higher Lane Whitefield, Reform Cemetery, *ohel* (prayer hall) (1858-still in use).188
Figure 5.94 Manchester: Higher Lane Whitefield, stained glass window in *ohel* (prayer hall))............ 188
Figure 5.95 Manchester: Higher Lane Whitefield, oldest gravestones (1858). 188
Figure 5.96 Manchester: Philips Park Cemetery, entrance to Dissenters section (1875)...................... 189
Figure 5.97 Manchester: Philips Park Cemetery, Jewish section.. 189
Figure 5.98 Merthyr Tydfil: Brecon Road, Jews' Burial Ground, entrance and *ohel* (prayer hall) (1865).189
Figure 5.99 Merthyr Tydfil: Brecon Road, Jews' Burial Ground, inside of *ohel* (prayer hall) 190
Figure 5.100 Merthyr Tydfil: Brecon Road, Jews' Burial Ground, section of cemetery. 190
Figure 5.101 Newcastle: Elswick Road, St. John's Cemetery, Jewish Section (1857)............................ 191
Figure 5.102 Newcastle: Elswick Road, St. John's Cemetery, desecrated grave stones. 191
Figure 5.103 Newcastle: Elswick Road, St. John's Cemetery, topographical plan of oldest section (1857). 192
Figure 5.104 Norwich: Mariners Lane Cemetery, section of 1885 Ordinance Survey Map. 193
Figure 5.105 Norwich: Mariners Lane Cemetery, section of 1860's Ordinance Survey Map.............. 193
Figure 5.106 Norwich: Quakers Lane Jews' Burial Ground 1813, plaque on outside wall (1840)....... 194
Figure 5. 107 Norwich: Quakers Lane Jews' Burial Ground, showing overgrown graves. 194

Figure 5.108 Norwich: City Cemetery Bowthorpe Road, Jewish section, *ohel* (prayer hall) and plaques (1856). 195
Figure 5.109 Norwich: City Cemetery Bowthorpe Road plan of cemetery, showing Jewish section. 195
Figure 5.110 Norwich: City Cemetery Bowthorpe Road, area for unnamed babies and infants. 195
Figure 5.111 Nottingham: North Sherwood Street Cemetery entrance (1823) 196
Figure 5.112 Nottingham: North Sherwood Street Cemetery, view of burial ground. 196
Figure 5.113 Nottingham: North Sherwood Street Cemetery, broken gravestone of Reverend Goldberg. 197
Figure 5.114 Nottingham: North Sherwood Street Cemetery, sandstone obelisk and slate tablets....197
Figure 5.115 Nottingham: Hardy Street Cemetery (1869)..197
Figure 5.116 Nottingham: Hardy Street Cemetery, remains of *bet tahara* (room for washing the dead).198
Figure 5.117 Nottingham: Hardy Street Cemetery, unmarked children's graves................................198
Figure 5.118 Penzance: Leskinnick Terrace Jews' Burial Ground entrance (1791). 199
Figure 5.119 Penzance: Leskinnick Terrace, topographical plan of cemetery.....................................199
Figure 5.120 Penzance: earliest legible inscription (1791). 199
Figure 5.121 Penzance: view of cemetery and wall Grade II. 200
Figure 5.122 Penzance: grave of Jacob Hart (d.1846)..200
Figure 5.123 Plymouth Hoe: Old Jews' Burial Ground Lambhay Hill, showing location of cemetery (1744) 201
Figure 5.124 Plymouth Hoe: Old Jews' Burial Ground Lambhay Hill, topographical plan of cemetery (1970). 201
Figure 5.125 Plymouth Hoe: Old Jews' Burial Ground Lambhay Hill showing neglect. 202
Figure 5.126 Portsmouth: Fawcett Road (Jews' Lane) Old Jews' Burial Ground and *ohel* (prayer hall) (1749)..203
Figure 5.127 Portsmouth: Fawcett Road, tombstone with carved relief with raised hands (a male Cohen). 203
Figure 5.128 Ramsgate: Upper Dumpton Road Jewish Cemetery, section of cemetery (1872..........204
Figure 5.129 Sheerness: Hope Street Old Jews' Burial Ground, exterior wall (c.1804-1855).............205
Figure 5.130 Sheerness: Hope Street Old Jews' Burial Ground remaining tomb stones. 205
Figure 5.131 Sheerness: Isle of Sheppey, Jewish section (1859)...206
Figure 5.132 Sheffield, Bowden Street Cemetery (1831-1880),prior to being destroyed....................206
Figure 5.133 Sheffield: Rodmoor Mausoleum of Bright family (1831)...207
Figure 5.134 Sheffield: Ecclesfield Jewish Cemetery (1893), remains and tombstones from Bowden Street 208
Figure 5.135 Sheffield: Ecclesfield Jewish Cemetery, *ohel* (prayer hall) (1846)...............................208
Figure 5.136 Southampton, Cemetery Road, late 19th-century *ohel* (prayer hall). 209
Figure 5.137 Southampton: Cemetery Road, mid 19th and early 20th century unreadable tomb stones. 209
Figure 5.138 Southampton: Cemetery Road view of cemetery..209
Figure 5.139 Southampton: Cemetery Road Norman Church of England mortuary chapel). 210
Figure 5.140 Sunderland: Ayres Quay Jewish Cemetery, ground plan (c.1780). 211
Figure 5.141 Sunderland: Ayres Quay Jewish Cemetery, boundary wall..211
Figure 5.142 Sunderland: Ayres Quay Jewish Cemetery, Jonassohn obelisk 211
Figure 5.143 Sunderland: Ayres Quay Jewish Cemetery, broken headstone with jug inscription 211
Figure 5.144 Sunderland: Bishopswearmouth, Hylton Road plan of three Jewish sections 212
Figure 5.145 Sunderland: Bishopswearmouth, Hylton Road view of plot 1,(1856-1899) 212
Figure 5.146 Swansea: High View and Long Ridge, Old Jews' Burial Ground (1768) 213
Figure 5.147 Swansea: High View and Long Ridge, Old Jews' Burial Ground, earliest graves 213
Figure 5.148 Yarmouth (Great): Alma Road Old Jews' Burial Ground, entrance (1851)....................214
Figure 5.149 Yarmouth (Great): Alma Road, Old Jews' Burial Ground, medieval wall and burial plots. ..214
Figure 5.150 Yarmouth (Great): Kitchener Road, entrance and knapped flint walls (1858)................215
Figure 5.151 Yarmouth (Great): Kitchener Road, view of cemetery 215
Figure 5.152 Yarmouth (Great):Kitchener Road, Old Cemetery Jewish section..................................216
Figure 6.1 London and 17 port communities established prior to 1815..220
Figure 6.2 Extract from Statistical Account, Chief Rabbi, 1845..221
Figure 6.3 Estimated size of Jewish Communities c.1850. 223
Figure 6.4 Estimated Jewish community distribution c.1810-1850..223

Figure 6.5 Estimated Jewish community distribution 1880..224
Figure 6.6 Extract 1841-1931 census..225
Figure 6.7 London, total membership of the eight synagogues...228
Figure 6.8 Hull, plaque commemorating immigration 1850-1914..234
Figure 6.9 Hull, immigration hall 1850-1914...234
Figure 6.10 Hamburg, immigrants waiting for clearance to go to Hull?...235
Figure 6.11 Leeds, pattern of settlement 1851 and 1881 236
Figure 6.12 Manchester, pattern of settlement 241
Figure 6.13 Newcastle, synagogues and cemeteries 1813-1914..243
Figure 6.14 Nottingham, meeting rooms and places of worship from 1822......................................244
Figure 6.15 South Wales, Jewish communities late 19th century...247
Figure 6.16 Cardiff, Jewish settlement in the 1850s 247
Figure 6.17 South-West England communities 18th/19th centuries..249
Figure 6.18 South-West England estimated population in 1850. 249

Acknowledgements

I am very grateful for the support that I have received from Professor Andrew Reynolds. In addition to his guidance, in moments of doubt and panic, Andrew encouraged me and spurred me on. Whilst researching my study, I also received advice and help from many people, whom I also wish to thank. Dr Sharman Kadish, her book *Jewish Heritage in England an Architectural Guide 2006* (English Heritage) has been an invaluable help in locating the sites discussed. In Israel, Dr Yoav Alon, friend and senior lecturer at Tel Aviv University, helped me formulate my introduction and methodology. Numerous references have been taken from Transactions of the Jewish Historical Society of England. My sons Saul and Jonathan and daughter-in-law Ilanit helped me with scanning, gazetteer and maps. My son Daniel read the first draft and made several useful comments and alterations. My wife Jean gave me support at every stage and accompanied me on visits to provincial synagogues and cemeteries, taking many of the photographs. I could not have done it without her. My study is dedicated to my family past and present.

I would particularly like to thank Arnold and Carol Lewis in Liverpool for their time and hospitality. Thanks also to Bill Williams in Manchester, who has written the definitive books on the history of that community. Bill met with me at the Jewish Museum, where he is Life President and Historical Advisor, and took me around former Jewish sites in the Old Town of Manchester. Bernard Gingold in Birmingham accompanied me to the Old Cemetery and put me in contact with members of Singers Hill Synagogue and Rabbi Shmuel Arkush all of whom have a specialised knowledge of the Birmingham Jewry. Keith Pearce, whose book 'The Lost Jews of Cornwall' (2000) was an invaluable guide when researching the 17th/18th-centuries communities in Cornwall. Keith spent time with me and my wife in Penzance. In Bristol, I was taken to the synagogue and old cemeteries by Alex Schlesinger, local historian and Sam Silverman, President of Bristol Synagogue. In Hull, I was hosted by Dr. David Lewis, secretary and elder of the Orthodox community. He took me to the 19th-century cemeteries, the former location of the Jewish community in the centre of the City and the local records office.

The most moving experience in Hull was to see the 19th/early 20th-century immigration hut that still stands by the railway station. In Leeds and Bradford, Malcolm Sender, local Jewish historian and archivist took me to the cemeteries, synagogues and records office in Leeds and Bradford. In Newcastle and Sunderland, Dorothy Sadlik spent two days with me visiting the former sites of synagogues and cemeteries in Newcastle and Sunderland and helping me in the local records offices. In Norwich, Barry Leveton provided access to records of Norwich's Jewish community and took me to the old cemeteries and site of the former synagogue. In Oxford, Marcus Roberts walked with me around the streets of Jewish Oxford. In Swansea, Norma Glass M.B.E. and David Factor took me and my wife around the City and cemetery. In Sheffield, Eric Stylises spent two days with me, visiting cemeteries and sites of the earliest synagogues and local records office.

The Spanish and Portuguese Burial and United Synagogue Burial Societies and Board of Deputies of British Jews enabled me to visit disused cemeteries. Mark Williams Cemeteries Manager United Synagogue. The Western Charitable Trust, responsible for the disused cemetery in Fulham Road. Elfes Ltd, Monumental Masons allowed me to include details of tombstone decorative inscriptions. I would also like to thank, Jennifer Marin and Louise Asher, Jewish Museum, Camden Town. Bruce Watson, Senior Archaeologist MoLAS. Adam Corsini and Dan Nessbitt Museum of London Archives at LAARC. Jacqui Pearce, specialist in medieval and later pottery at the Museum of London. Virginia Smithson, Department of Prehistory and Europe in the British Museum and the staff in The British Library Map department. Dr. Gerry Black gave me permission to use eight images from Tymsder Publication. I would like to thank Charles Tucker, archivist of The United Synagogue. His knowledge of Anglo-Jewry past and present is second to none. He read my early draft and made several corrections and useful comments. Thanks also to my friend Rolf Noskwith who many several corrections to the final draft and Gustav Milne, senior lecturer at UCL who encouraged me to get my study published by Archaeopress in Oxford.

Every effort has been made to trace all the copyright holders, but if any have been overlooked they can be added at the first opportunity.

Provinces
Bath: Norman Marks, Friends of Bath Jewish Burial Ground, Richard Sermon, Archaeological Officer, Bath and North East Somerset Council.
Birmingham: Bernard Gingold, administrator Singers Hill Synagogue. Lionel Singer local historian, Stanley Busby for photographs of Singers Hill Synagogue. Rabbi Shmuel Arkush, Rabbi of Birmingham Jewish Community Care Centre and an authority on the history of the Birmingham community.
Brighton: Gordon Franks, member of the community and guide of Jewish Brighton.
Bristol: Alex Schlesinger and Sam Silverman, President of the Synagogue.
Canterbury: King's School, Bursars Office.
Cardiff: Rabbi Wellenberg, who hold keys to the Old Cemetery
Chatham: David Herling, Vice Chairman Chatham Hebrew Community.
Cheltenham: Sam Stone, Chairman of the Community. Michael Webber Hon. Secretary
Coventry: Barry Deitch, President Coventry Reform Congregation.

Dover: Hambrook and Johns Funeral Directors, who hold field survey plans of the cemetery compiled in 1996 and Dover Reference Library.
Exeter: Dr. Paul Newglass, President of the Synagogue.
Falmouth: Eric Dawkins, former Town Clerk of Falmouth.
Hull: Dr. David Lewis, community archivist, Hon Sec. Hull Hebrew Community.
King's Lynn: Dr. Jane Clark, local historian.
Leeds: Malcolm Sender, community archivist and Leeds Jewish historian. Nigel Grizzard local historian
Liverpool: Arnold Lewis, community archivist. Saul Marks, Deane Road Cemetery Project.
Manchester: Bill Williams, historian and one of the founders of Manchester's Jewish Museum.
Newcastle: Dorothy Sadlik, resident of Sunderland and Newcastle with a fund of local knowledge and Joe Gellert, community architect.
Norwich: Barry and Maureen Leveton, local historians and archivists.
Nottingham: David Snapper, sixth generation resident of the City and Rolf Noskwith, Nottingham industrialist.
Oxford: Marcus Roberts, jtrails researcher and historian.
Penzance: Keith Pearce, *Author of the Lost Jews of Cornwall.* Alison Bevan, Curator Penlee Museum.
Plymouth: Dr. Peter Lee, Honorary Treasurer, Plymouth Hebrew Congregation.
Portsmouth: Mr. Klein, senior member of the community and Neil and Donna Miles, curators of the Synagogue and key holders of the cemetery.
Ramsgate Miriam Rodrigues-Pereira, Hon. Archivist Spanish and Portuguese Congregation
Southampton: Martin Rose, President of the Hebrew Congregation
Sunderland: Dorothy Sadlik, former resident of city, now living in Newcastle
Sheffield: Eric Sayliss, senior member of the Hebrew Congregation
Swansea: Norma Glass MBE, David Factor, Chairman Swansea Hebrew Congregation.
Truro: Angela Broom, Curator Truro Museum.
Yarmouth: Town Hall and Records Office.

Most of the Anglo-Jewry community is refugees, descended from refugees or economic migrants. I hope that this study will result in the present community knowing more about the settlement in Britain from the 17th century. This study is also an attempt to create an archive before more of our heritage is lost to neglect. There is a wealth of synagogue and cemetery heritage to be preserved and also topographical and physical evidence of the period 1656-c.1880 and it is increasingly in danger.

I am well aware of the shortcomings in my study, and I shall always be grateful to anyone who lets me know of any errors or omissions.

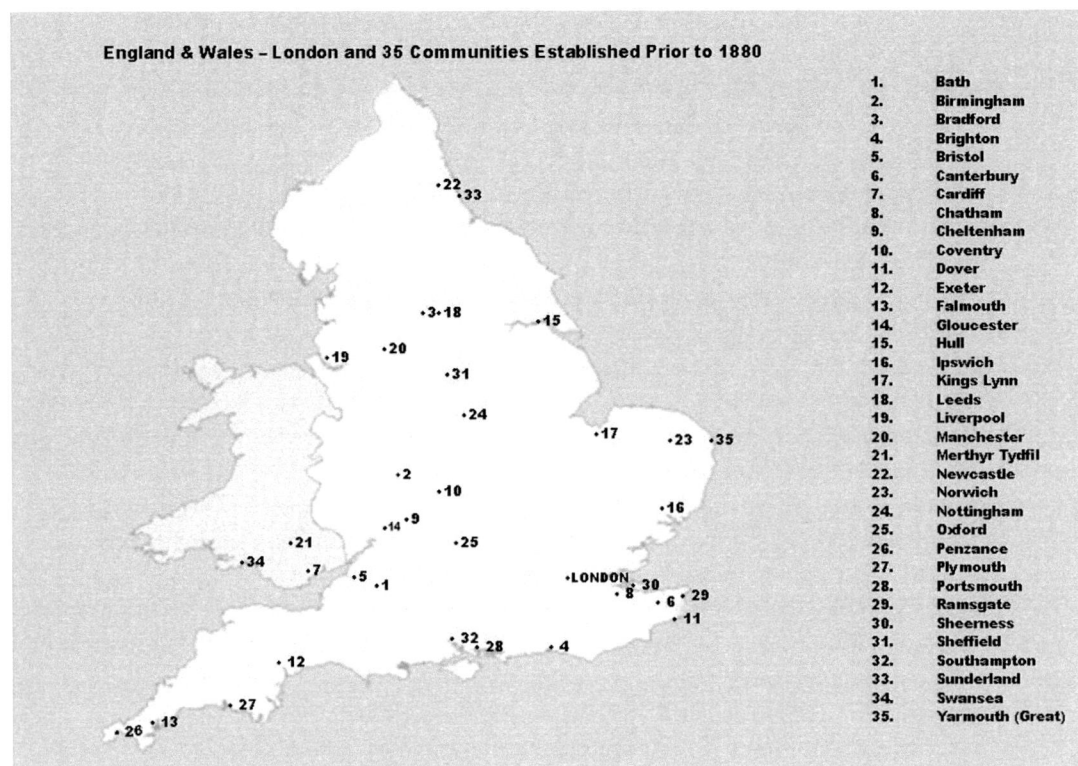

Figure 1.1 London and 35 provincial communities established prior to 1880

Chapter 1

Introduction

From 1656, under Cromwell, during a period when England was a republic, Jews were re-admitted to England after an absence of c.360 years, For around the first 80 years, the community was based solely in London and they could practice their religion openly. In the late second quarter of the 18th century, small communities were established in the provinces. Lipman (1954, 65) states that, '…from a modest beginning, the first Jews numbered around 200 people; the community grew mainly due to the arrival of immigrants from the Continent, so that by 1880 there were already around 60, 000-65, 000 Jews living across the country in around 40 different locations'. Even then, London represented over two thirds of Anglo-Jewry. In one year (1880-1881), the community nearly doubled to around 100, 000, following the arrival of thousands of Jews fleeing from persecution and poverty following the assassination of Alexander II in 1881 and the subsequent anti-Jewish laws (Ibid 85). According to Endelman (2002, 127) 'It is impossible to know the exact number of East European immigrants who settled in Britain. This is in part because the government only began to collect figures of aliens in 1890 and then failed to identify Jews as such'. The history of the Jewish community in England between 1656 and 1880 has been written by several historians, one of the most recent being *The Jews of Britain 1656-2000* (Endelman 2002), with the previous standard work being *A History of the Jews in England* (Roth 1941). The same author wrote several other works, including *The Rise of Provincial Jewry* (1950). Also invaluable has been *Social History of the Jews in England 1850-1950* (Lipman 1954) the approximate size of each community in 1850 is discussed and *The Lost Synagogues of London* (Renton 2000). There are also works on provincial communities such as *Jews in Bristol* (Samuel 1997), *The Lost Jews of Cornwall from the Middle Ages to the Nineteenth Century* (Pearce and Fry 2000), *The Making of Manchester Jewry 1740-1875* (Williams 1976), *Portsmouth Jewry 1730s-1980s* (Weinberg 1998) and a *History of Sunderland Jewish Community 1755-1955* (Levy 1956), *The Jews of Exeter an Illustrated History* (Fry 2013).

This study shows that on the basis of the topography, Judaism is as much a community as it is a religion. Hachlili (2001, 96) states 'The archaeology of Judaism is the term meaning art, archaeology and material culture created specifically for the Jewish community', to this can be added the evidence of burial traditions. As for Jewish archaeology and topography, very little work has been done on these topics, and published works on aspects are few and far between. Moreover, prior to this study, the evidence of urban topography of Anglo-Jewry in the period 1656-c.1880 had not been brought together in a methodical way.

1.1 The form of this study

This study comprises a further six chapters, which cover the topics described below.

Chapter 2 gives a brief historical picture of the pre-expulsion period, prior to 1290, while the main part deals with Anglo-Jewish history between 1656 and 1880. It separates the London and provincial communities, as it was not until c.1742 that Jewish communities were established in the provinces. The basis for the dates when provincial communities were established is discussed, as is the approximate size and growth of the community in this period.

Chapter 3 identifies themes and approaches and sets out the primary research aims and questions, the methodology, methodological problems and limitations. A questionnaire used when visiting each site, in order to bring a uniform approach, is presented, and the structure of the gazetteer is considered.

Chapter 4 examines the physical evidence of 17th-late 19th-century Jewish communities and synagogues. Their location reflects the history and mobility of the community. Each synagogue is listed and first-and-second edition Ordnance Survey Maps (1880-1900) showing their locations are provided in the gazetteer. In a few cases, there were 'Jewries' and street names with Jewish connections that indicate concentrations of Jews, but this was in contrast to cities in Continental Europe, such as in Paris and Venice which had quarters of the city in which Jews were formerly required to live, known as 'ghettos'. The only archaeological evidence of these areas is the surrounding walls, which were built to isolate and also protect the communities and synagogues which were not destroyed by the Nazis.

Chapter 4 also examines the evidence of *mikva'ot* (religious baths), in certain provincial cities; there are none remaining in London from this period. It also discusses material culture in the form of excavated archaeological evidence (only from London) that can be positively identified as being Jewish, such as pottery, *kosher* meat, cloth seals and *shofar'ot* (ritual rams' horns). These were previously discussed in the authors MA dissertation *'The Archaeology of Anglo-Jewry in London c.1070-1290 and 1656-1850'* (Marks 2008). These topics have been expanded to included further evidence.

Chapter 5 examines the second main body of evidence: cemeteries. Differences existed in burial traditions between Sephardi (Spanish and Portuguese Origins) and Ashkenazi (European) Jews, and changes took place over the period in the form of inscriptions, styles of gravestones and monumental architecture. Where they exist, plans of graveyards are shown. First-edition and second-edition Ordnance Survey Maps showing locations of Jewish cemeteries in the 17th-late 19th century are shown in the gazetteer.

Chapter 6 identifies areas of Jewish settlement and examines changes and movements over the 220-year period. This chapter also includes a discussion of settlement and the economic reasons that lay behind it.

Chapter 7 concludes with an appraisal of the key findings set in a wider cultural and social perspective. Suggestions are made for future research.

Part 2 comprises a gazetteer with summary sheets and extracts from Ordnance Survey maps for individual towns and sites.

Chapter 2

Brief Summary of Anglo-Jewish History c.1066–c.1880

Before discussing the evidence and topography of Anglo-Jewry in Britain between 1656 and c.1880, it is necessary to understand the history of medieval Anglo-Jewry, expulsion in 1290 and the impact this had on immigrants coming to England in the 17th century. Unlike the medieval period, when the first Jewish immigrants came from France, the first immigrants from 1656 came mainly from Amsterdam via Spain and Portugal, followed by Jews from Central and Eastern Europe (Roth 1978, 173).

2.1 Pre-expulsion period c.1066-1290

The first Jews to settle in Britain came largely from Rouen in Normandy after 1066, at the invitation of William the Conqueror. Later, following a massacre in Rouen in 1096 by crusading knights (a prelude to the atrocities on the Rhineland, when all who refused baptism were butchered), the Jewish community in England increased with more immigrants from France. According to Roth (1978, 6) '…it is likely that a settled and relatively numerous Anglo-Jewish Community owes its origin to these events, though there is no documentary evidence to support this assumption'.

William previously had business dealings with Jews in France, particularly money lenders. In the middle ages, Christians were forbidden by cannon law to lend money for interest. Thus, Jews provided credit prior to the emergence of banks, and medieval monarchs found it particularly useful that Jews engaged in money lending. According to Black (2003, 10) '…in addition to financiers, French Jewish doctors came and Jewish and Christian merchants and craftsmen, particularly silversmiths and jewellers'.

Unlike on the continent, formal ghettos were never instituted in England. Whilst there were clusters of Jews in distinct quarters, Jews and Christians lived alongside each other, often near the commercial centre or market place, in areas known as 'Jewries'. According to Roth 'The internal organisation of English Jewry in the Middle Ages was very similar to that which prevailed elsewhere in Europe. Life centred about the synagogues' (1978, 117).

In London and the provinces, Jew's houses were sometimes situated near the castle or cathedral for protection against persecution. The more wealthy Jewish traders and moneylenders lived in stone houses, which afforded greater protection and signified status. It was in these houses that some of the more wealthy had a room set aside for communal prayers and sometimes the under croft was adapted for use as a mikveh (ritual bath). Jews were among the first to live is stone houses in London, which later made them the target for being confiscated and taken over by the nobility.

Throughout the 220 years before expulsion in 1290, heavy taxes were imposed on Jewish communities. 'The Exchequer of the Jews' was set up, and its records in the form of tallage returns (record of taxes levied by the King), deeds and pipe rolls (rolled up parchment containing financial records of yearly audits performed by the Exchequer) are now in the Guildhall Library, the Public Records Office in Kew and St Paul's Cathedral Archives. These show that in the period 1263-1273 alone, £420, 000 was collected from a declining and increasingly persecuted community. While in 1264, 1500 Jews were said to have been killed in London, while in 1280, Jews were forced to attend conversionist sermons (Renton 2000, 17). In 1271, Henry III gave the main synagogue in London to the Dominican friars because the Jews made too much noise when praying (Tovey 1738, 104).Taxes were imposed up to the time of expulsion, which bankrupted the remaining community. Those left were no longer a source of revenue, and therefore they had no value to the King. In 1290 Edward I ordered the expulsion of the Jews from England, and any that did not convert to Christianity were put to death. Property was confiscated, often given to Edward's family or favoured members of the court, whilst Jewish cemeteries such as in London, York and Oxford were destroyed, made into gardens or built over. For example, Stow (1598, 261) states 'This plot of land (the London cemetery) remained to the said Jews till the time of their final banishment out of England, and is now turned into fair garden plots and summer houses for pleasure'.

There are no completely reliable figures as to the size of the 13th century community. According to Lipman (1968, 65) 'at the beginning of the 13th century the community may have been as many as 4, 000-5, 000.The number of Jews then expelled was around 15, 000 (Stow 1598, 245). This figure, however, has been shown to be far too high. Black (2003, 17) states that, '... it now seems generally accepted that at peak there were between 5, 000-6, 000 Jews in England', with at least 25 centres with *archaes*, (chests or coffers for the deposit of the records of Jewish financial transactions). After 1253, Jews were only allowed to live in towns with an *archae* (Figure 1). Morris (2008, 227) notes that, 'According to more recent research, by the time of expulsion there were only around 2, 000 remaining in England'. Any medieval Jewish population figures can only be approximate. By the time the Jews were expelled in 1290, many had already gone to France. England was the first country in medieval Europe to expel its Jewish community. Edward's policy was to remove by confiscation and destruction all physical evidence of Jews in England, although as noted above, large numbers of medieval arbitrary tax documents levied

Figure 2.1 Map of medieval Jewish communities in 12th-13th centuries, showing those with archaes (chests or coffers for the deposit of the records of Jewish financial transactions) (Campbell, et al 2009).

by the king, known as tallages, pipe rolls (annual records of the British Exchequer) and deeds relating to the Jews shed light on the topography and chronology of Anglo-Jewry in the medieval period.

The discovery of the medieval Jewish cemetery in Cripplegate following the bombing of the City of London during the Blitz (Honeybourne, 1959) as well as the unearthing of *mikva'ot* (ritual baths) during re-development in Gresham Street in 1986 and Milk Street in 2001 (Blair et al. 2001) are the most important medieval Jewish archaeological finds made in Britain. Evidence for medieval Jewry is known from several towns, including Bristol, Lincoln, Northampton, Norwich, Worcester and York, and there are medieval finds from London, such as four Hebrew tombstone fragments found in Aldersgate and Moorfields (Honeybourne, 1959) and several medieval copper-alloy Sabbath lamps from Bristol and London.

Despite expulsion, destruction and confiscation of property, Jewish life never completely disappeared. Outwardly, remaining Jews known as Marronas, who were forced to convert to Christianity to save their lives and were compelled to attend church, married and were buried as Christians. Roth. 1978, 141 notes show that, 'A number of 'secret Jews' (Marranos) fled to London from Spain and Portugal to escape persecution, joining those who worshipped outwardly as Christians but practised Judaism in secret in unknown private houses'.

This is known from Jewish traders who returned to Amsterdam after attending secret services in London (Ibid, 141). According to Black (2003,18) '…before re-admission in 1656 there is written evidence of Jewish doctors from Continental Europe treating Edward II (1307-1327) and Henry IV (1399-1413)'. When Elizabeth came to the throne in 1558, several Jewish families returned to England' (Ibid, 18). In 1558, 'there were possibly 40 or so families living in London' (Ibid, 19). 'The head of one family was Dr. Roderigo Lopez, the first house physician at St Bartholomew's Hospital. His most eminent patient was the Queen, although he was falsely accused of trying to poison her at the instigation of the King of Spain and executed at Tyburn in 1594' (Roth 1978, 143).

2.2 Jewish population growth from 1656-c.1880

Year	Size of Community	Comments
1656/1657	160	Readmission
1663	219	
1684	414-450	
1695	c.1,000	Census showed 850 within City of London walls
1727/1742	6,000*	Beginnings of provincial communities
1753/1760	6000/ 8,000**	Majority in London
1767	18,000**	
1800	20,000/25,000	
1815	30,000**	c.18,000 in London
1850	c.35,000 ****	c.20,000 in London
1870	40,000	
c.1880	**60,000/65,000****	**(representing c. 0.2 percent of total population)**
1881	100,000***	c. 47,000 in London

Between 1881 and 1914, 120-150,000 East European Jews settled in Britain
*Tovey, 1738   **Roth, 1978   ***Adler, 1970   ****Lipman, 1961
Other figures from A Survey of Anglo-Jewry in 1851 (Lipman, 1951).
N.B. Prior to 1852, no precise figures exist for the size of the Jewish population. There was no Government agency that regulated the entry of aliens.

Jewish population figures can be based only on contemporary estimates and limited demographic information. Official censuses in the 19th century did not classify populations according to religion. In 1880/1881, no passport or police registration was required to enter England, and many immigrants passed through, some staying for a short while to raise money to pay for their journey onto America, Canada and South Africa.

2.3 Community in London from 1656-c.1880

As early as 1630, 26 years before Cromwell's admission edict, merchants with Jewish origins, known as *Marranos* (Christianized Jews) from Portugal, Spain and Italy, joined the few Jews already living in London. These immigrants had adopted Spanish and Portuguese names; their previous medieval name-form was first name, followed by town or street of their habitation, such as 'Aaron of Lincoln' or 'Moses of Milk Street'. One such immigrant, Fernandez Carvajal, was a native of Portugal who, according to Roth (1978, 159) 'was to become among the most prominent merchants in London'. Black states (2003, 210) that, 'It was to Carvajal that Cromwell gave the assurance of the right of Jews to remain in England'. He is referred to again later.

The Jews of Spain fled from the Inquisition in 1492, moving first to Portugal, then to Amsterdam, where they could openly practice their religion. Amsterdam subsequently became one of the world's leading trading centres with a thriving Jewish community that posed little threat to the Protestant community (Roth 1978, 158). Cromwell, a devout Puritan, aimed to copy the commercial success of Amsterdam and re-establish London as a major trading centre, the re-admission of the Jews was key to this. In 1656, he authorized re-admission after the absence of a community for 366 years. According to Renton (2000, 21) 'The re-admission was based on English financial and commercial interests, as well as on the Puritan study of the Old Testament, allied with a desire for the ultimate conversion and redemption of The Jews'. 'There was also a belief amongst Dutch and English Puritans that the Second Coming of a Messiah would only happen when Jews were present all over the world' (Roth 1978, 157).

In 1665, after 10 years of negotiations during which clergy and merchants opposed the idea, Jews were officially allowed to settle. Certain terms were imposed. At first, Cromwell only allowed entry to merchants and their families, and they had to live in London. The topography of the earliest re-resettlement community is to be found in the City of London, within the area known as the 'Square Mile'. The early settlers were not allowed either to proselytize or speak against Christianity, nor could they publish religious books in English. Furthermore, the community had to be self-dependent and support its own poor. They were, by and large, Dutch of Spanish and Portuguese origin (Sephardim), joined later by a small group of German and Polish origin (Ashkenazim). The Sephardim considered themselves to be superior to the Ashkenazim as they came from a social class in Holland that was assimilated and moneyed, whilst the Ashkenazim came from the more insular and poorer communities in Germany and central Europe.

Cromwell permitted a small group of about 40 or 50 merchants and the families of Portuguese Jewish merchants already living in London to meet for prayers in private houses and to acquire a cemetery in Mile End in the east of London. Black (2003, 19) notes that, 'synagogue services were held privately in a house owned by one Alvaro Mendes in Creechurch Lane, Aldgate'. In 1657, the first synagogue following re-admission was opened in this street, large enough to hold the entire community at that time. Endelman (2002, 29) writes that, 'In 1660 there were about 35 Sephardim living in London, by 1684 this had increased to 90'. Creechurch Lane was extended in 1673 to hold 250 congregants, by end of the 17th century the London community had grown to over a 1, 000 persons (Black 2003, 24/25). Creechurch Lane survived the Great Fire in 1666 and was in use until 1701. There are no surviving remains, but there are documents and conjectural plans in the Bevis Marks Synagogue archive that give a full description. The first Ashkenazi synagogue was opened in 1690 in Duke's Place, EC3 in the City of London.

Land for the first Sephardi cemetery was purchased in 1657 in Mile End E1. in an orchard in a corner of a field. Records from Bevis Marks Synagogue Burial Register show that prior to 1660, five tombstones had been placed in this cemetery known as the 'House of Life' (*Bet Chajim*), later known as the *Velho* (Old) Cemetery of the Spanish and Portuguese Jews. At that time, Mile End was a village, situated one mile from the City. The *Velho* cemetery is the oldest post re-settlement Jewish cemetery in Britain and was in use until c.1742. A second Sephardi cemetery opened in 1733, also in Mile End, is known as the *Nuevo* (New) Cemetery of the Spanish and Portuguese Jews. In 1697, the first Ashkenazi (Jews from Central and Eastern Europe) cemetery was opened in Alderney Road adjacent to the *Velho*.

From 1656, Jews were allowed to practice their religion and live openly with rights of residence, but were not allowed to buy freeholds of property. In 1656, they were mainly living around the parish of St Olave, Hart Street, which was within walking distance of Creechurch Lane Synagogue. On August 22nd 1664, the Privy Council issued the first written statement that '….. *the residence of the Jews in England was authorised*' (Roth 1978, 171). A list of Jews in 1660 identifies Jewish families living in Duke's Place, Creechurch Lane and Bevis Marks (Lipman 1970, 43). 'The newcomers took up residence not in Old Jewry (the centre of the medieval community) but in the area of Houndsditch, Duke's Place Petticoat Lane (then called Hog Street) and Jewry Street, all on the edge of the City' (Black 2003, 23). This area was to be associated with the growing community for the next 200 years.

Roth notes that, 'Following Cromwell's death in 1658, his son Richard petitioned for the Jews to be banished and their property confiscated' (1978, 167). This petition received powerful support from the merchants in The City of London who were concerned about trading competition from the new immigrant merchants or 'intruders'. Roth also notes that, 'The petition did not succeed neither did a second petition in 1660 when Charles II came to the throne. The second petition was thrown out in 1664 by the Privy Council' (1978, 176).

From around the 1680s and 1690, the early Sephardi community who were mainly from Spain and Portugal were joined by Ashkenazi immigrants from Holland, Germany and France (Roth 1978, 173). The community now included not only merchants, but also commodity brokers, precious stone dealers and doctors, in addition to pedlars and beggars, who, as was the custom, relied on help from wealthy Jews. Overall, the poor are reckoned to represent around half of the community (Black 2003, 25); this partly accounts for discrepancy in the later census figures, as many were vagrant pedlars. When Carvajal died in 1660, we know from his will that he bequeathed £30 for the relief of the poor (Wolf 2002, 11).

Where many new immigrants lived can be identified by their names in the 1695 census. They appear in six adjoining parishes: St James' Duke's Place, St Katherine Cree, St Andrew Undershaft, St Katherine Undershaft, St Katherine Coleman and St Helen's Bishopsgate (Figure 4.1). Jews lived and moved in complete freedom, although they tended to live near each other.

By 1690, there were two synagogues in London, one Sephardi in Creechurch Lane and one Ashkenazi in Duke's Place. At first, the Sephardim and Ashkenazim shared one cemetery. There would have been at least one *shochet* (ritual animal slaughterer), who also performed administrative functions. Ritual animal slaughtering was also sometimes carried out by the rabbi, who also may have acted as a *mohel* (one who performs the rite of circumcision).

It is still evident that the poor and infants were buried without head stones. Cemetery evidence will show that sometimes burial records were not accurate. Written records and scarce evidence from inscriptions that can still be read on head stones show that by 1660, and there was an organised and structured community, for example the title 'Rabbi' is evident on restored tombstones (personal observation 2009).

In the late 17th century, in addition to around 1, 000 Jews already settled in London, new immigrants, mostly poor and unskilled, were arriving from Central and Eastern Europe. They dealt in used clothes and peddled, and some opened small shops (Black 2003, 25). Until 1692, many new immigrants met for prayers in private houses occupied by Ashkenazi Jews, not with the Sephardim in Creechurch Lane. The principal reason for this is that Ashkenazim and Sephardim had a different cultural background and retain a different pronunciation of Hebrew with a different form of synagogue service. In 1701, the Sephardim opened a larger synagogue around the corner from the original synagogue in Creechurch Lane. Bevis Marks gets its name from *Buries Markes* from the Court of the Abbots of Bury (St Edmunds), the old name signifying the area where the Abbot held jurisdiction (Hyamson 1951, 75). According to Black (2003, 28) 'The design of Bevis Marks was loosely based of the main synagogue in Amsterdam'. Many of the original members of the London Sephardi community came from Amsterdam. Bevis Marks is the oldest surviving synagogue in Britain with services held every day and is Grade I listed by English Heritage.

From c.1720, the Jewish community numbered about 5, 000 to 6, 000, virtually all based in London. 'In the period 1720-1735 around 1, 500 poor Sephardim arrived in London fleeing from the Inquisition in Spain and Portugal. In the second half of the century more Sephardim arrived from Holland, Italy, North Africa and Gibraltar' (Endelman 2002, 168-170). Even with Sephardi immigration, by the 1720s, the Ashkenazim outnumbered the Sephardim. The late 17th and early 18th-century, during the reign of William III (1694-1702), marked the consolidation and acceptance of Jews into society.

Until c.1740, the early history and physical evidence of the Jews of Britain is only found in London. From around 1740, there were two social groups, rich and poor.

Itinerant peddlers returned to London or the nearest provincial town at week-ends, where there were Jews residing, or to be with their families, and to restock with goods for selling the following week. For the poor, trying to make a living in London was difficult, as there were too many peddlers plying their trade in a fairly limited area. Some took to the road selling second-hand clothing, jewellery and other small items that could be carried from town to town. According to Endelman (2002, 41) 'prior to 1740 there would have been itinerant peddlers and long-time vagabonds who travelled the length of the Diaspora'. Roth (1950, 15) notes that, 'some settled in towns where there was a market, others in sea ports, although it was not until c.80 years after re-admission that communities with cemeteries and rooms for prayers were established in the provinces'.

The acquisition of land for a cemetery and the availability of a mikveh (ritual bath) characterised towns where Jews lived, unless they could bathe in the sea or there were facilities in public baths. Rabbis forbade Jews to establish new communities without a mikveh. A mikveh is considered more important than a synagogue, as communal services can be held in private houses. Whilst little hard evidence remains of the early re-settlement *mikva'ot* (plural), documentary evidence reveals *mikva'ot* at synagogues or in houses occupied by Jews. It is necessary to understand the importance of *mikva'ot* in Jewish religious life. A mikveh (singular) is used by both men and women and involves total immersion: Orthodox Jews consider physical purity as a powerful metaphor for spiritual purity. Kadish (1996, 101) states that, '… since temple time and indeed before, the mikveh literally 'a gathering of water' or ritual bath has played an essential role in the practice of Judaism'.

Religious objects such as *Torahs* (parchment scrolls hand-written in Hebrew containing the first five books of the scriptures), silver objects to decorate them, silver candle sticks, prayer books and the congregation itself make a room or synagogue holy. Evidence of synagogues prior to 1880 comprises mainly documentary narratives and illustrations. As communities moved or needed larger synagogues, original buildings were converted to other uses or destroyed. When communities dwindled in size and could no longer support a synagogue, services were held in hired hall or private houses.

'By 1790 the London community had grown to around 18,000 and a larger Ashkenazi synagogue was erected in Duke's Place, later to be called 'The Great Synagogue' (Black 2003, 29). It was destroyed during the London Blitz on 11th May 1941 and replaced by a temporary hut (Figure 4.20). Roth (1987, 241) states, 'By 1800 the total community in Britain had increased in number to around 20,000' due to a new wave of pogroms in Eastern Europe leading to thousands of fugitives fleeing persecution'. By the end of the 18th century, there were four important synagogues in London: Bevis Marks, the Great Synagogue; the New Synagogue which opened 1761 at Leadenhall Street and the Hambro, which was opened in a house and extended in 1725. Of these, only Bevis Marks remains. In the 19th-century, there were a number of smaller synagogues, mostly in houses or rented halls. Amongst these were Sandy's Row (established 1851), Princes (Princelet) Street (established 1870) and Whites Row (established 1860), which served Dutch, German and Polish immigrants. The overwhelming majority of Jews who settled in England during the 18th and early 19th century came from traditional Jewish communities, in Poland, Germany and Holland.

Throughout the 18th century and the first quarter of the 19th century, the bulk of the community in London remained in the eastern part of the City. Due to lack of space, it began to spread further east, but remained within walking distance of the main synagogues and street markets. Subsequently, the more established immigrants started to move out of the City and east London. From synagogue records, according to Lipman (1972, 44), 'First, two small Jewish settlements of mostly shopkeepers and craftsmen sprang up in the West End, around Covent Garden, St James and Southwark'. In theory, Jews were not allowed to be retailers, as this trade was limited to freemen of the City of London who could take the Christological oath. Outside the City, this practice was ignored. The second development was that 'the richest Jews while keeping their homes in the City in order to be near their businesses were acquiring 'country' seats in Stanmore, Totteridge, Watford, and Highgate' (Ibid, 44).

1800-c.1880 Emancipation

By the beginning of the 19th century, the majority of the Jewish community were either poor immigrants or children of immigrants. By 1880, this had changed and many were now 'middle-class'. More immigrants came from Holland, Germany and Poland, and according to Black (1978, 241), 'By 1830, there were about 30, 000 Jews in total living in Britain, 20, 000 in London and 10, 000 in the provinces'. These immigrants were received and supported by religious and voluntary associations in an established community with an institutional framework: most of them could not speak English (Englander 1994, 64). Some made enough money to pay their sea fare to the United States, Canada and South Africa. By the middle of the 19th century, there were now three classes of Jews: rich merchants and bankers, the growing middle class, and the poor. Over the 200-year period from the re-settlement, the community now reflected wider society in England.

It was not till 1858, however, that a Jew (Baron Lionel de Rothschild) became a Member of Parliament, as the previous Oath of Allegiance had excluded Jews from sitting in the House. By 1870, there were eight Jewish Members of Parliament. Also, they could not be called to the Bar, which required them to take the oath according to the forms of the established church, nor attend university in Oxford or Cambridge, and they were therefore excluded from many professions, such as law. The establishment of University College in London in 1826 was a landmark for the Jewish community, as it was non-denominational and accepted students from all religions. In 1830, the Common Council in London enacted a new rule that '…any person who took up the freedom could make the necessary oath in a form agreeable to his religious convictions' (Roth 1978, 254). This allowed Jews to become freemen of the City, members of the livery companies and to engage in trade. In 1830, Moses Montefiore, a philanthropist, became sheriff of London and was knighted by Queen Victoria. He was the first Jewish knight since Solomon de Medina in 1700. By

1880, there were 200 families who had made their fortunes from banking and other financial activities, who were the main supporters of charitable institutions such as care homes for the Jewish poor and schools' (Black 2003, 77). The election of a Jewish Member of Parliament, a Jew appointed a sheriff of London and knighted, demonstrates their acceptance into the wider society

The London community was to change from 1880, the year recognised by the later community as the great divide for Anglo-Jewish history. Between 1881 and 1914, 3, 000, 000 Jews fled from oppression and poverty, of which 100, 000/150, 000 settled in Britain. This watershed marks the end point of this study.

Where did they live in London?

European Jews have always been urban in their orientation. Throughout the medieval period, over half of the Jews in England lived in London. According to Hillaby (1990, 90), 'A distinct area of Jewish settlement can be traced to an early date. Historical documents in St Paul's refer to a *vicus Judeorum* in about 1130 in all probability 'Old Jewry'. Evidence, such as tallage books, deeds and pipe rolls reveals Jewish settlement in 10 London parishes by the 13th century. First, they were not far from 'The Cheap' the principle marketing area of the city if not the kingdom' (Ibid, 92). Second, they were close to the Tower of London, where the royal Constable was responsible for the administration and protection of the Jewry. On re-admission, they did not settle around the Guildhall (the location of five medieval synagogues), as this area had been rebuilt, and the City fathers did not want 'intruders' to live amongst them (Roth 1978, 168). As they were not freemen of the City, Jews were not allowed to open shops there. However they were free to open shops and market stalls on the eastern fringe. Lipman (1956, 52) states 'The eastern borders of the City attracted other foreigners such as the Huguenots as this area contained zones that were immune from various trade regulations and taxes'. Up to the end of the 18th century, the majority of London Jews lived in the east of London, around Spitalfields. Jews who lived in the City were both rich and poor. According to Lipman, 'The more wealthy members of the community started to move from the area to Hackney and Finsbury around the 1830s (1962, 78-102). The very rich, such as members of the Rothschild, Montefiore, Goldsmid and Mocatto families, moved to the West End. In the 1860s, some of the new middle class moved to Bayswater, Notting Hill and Shepherds Bush. In the 1880s, some moved to the Maida Vale area where according to Black (2003, 64) '20 per cent of Maida Vale's 10, 000 residents were Jewish'. Hackney, at this time a village, was within reach of the City, became a new residential area for the growing 'middle class'.

These changes in demography resulted in new synagogues being established and old ones being abandoned. Synagogues, as well holding religious services, acted as community centres and schools. In the early 19th-century, Orthodox or traditional families who had moved westwards from the City, and even out of the West End, were separated from their synagogues and had to walk four or five miles on a Sabbath or High Holidays to attend services. In the West End in 1841, The West London Reform Synagogue, near to Marble Arch was established in 1870. The previous small buildings being in Burton Street WC1 and Margaret Street W1, but it did not attract those who wished to worship in the traditional and unReformed way. In 1862, the foundation stone for an Orthodox synagogue was laid in Bayswater off the Harrow Road, 'a pleasant suburban neighbourhood' (Renton 2000, 79).

The development of London Jewish suburbia from 1830s or early 1840s accelerated with the growth of railways in the mid-19th century, when the rich and middle class were moving out of the East End, although the vast majority of London's 20, 000 Jews were still living in east London (Ibid, 79).

Following the severe winter of 1848/9, the standard of living of the poor deteriorated and more charities were established by the communities' voluntary agencies. Black (2003, 73) writes, 'Their primary function was to save the aged poor from starvation and exposure on the streets or having to endure the terrible conditions of the work-house, and to allow them to practise and die in their faith'. There is little physical evidence of these early 19th-century establishments in the east of London, as from 1880/1881, the 'Genesis' period of Anglo-Jewry, new enlarged facilities were needed, such as soup kitchens, hospitals and schools, and the original establishments were abandoned.

By c.1880, the poor still were mainly living in the east and East End of London that at the end of the century was overcrowded, with poor sanitation, polluted air and dirty streets. The middle classes had moved out to the north, north-west and west, with the very rich were living in the heart of the West End. Even with this demographic and urban topographical change, the wealthiest of the community supported the poor and new immigrants arriving from Eastern Europe. The topography and migration of the community in London and the provinces in the 18th and 19th centuries is discussed in Chapter 6.

2.4 Rise of provincial communities from c.1740-c.1880

For the first 80 years or so following re-admission, there were no communities in the provinces. It is not always possible to establish the exact date that a provincial community was established. Individual Jews settled in provincial towns mainly for commercial purposes, and when there were 10 men over the age of 13 who had been *bar-mitzvahed* (the religious initiation service into manhood), they could then hold full services, usually in a private home or a hired room.

The infant provincial communities were for the most part Ashkenazim, who were poorer than their Sephardi brethren. For economic reasons, there needed to be a community large enough to afford a rabbi, who sometimes acted as the *shochet* (ritual slaughterer) and *mohel* (circumciser). When they could afford to open a synagogue, the dedication was recorded by plaques or in synagogue records. A more accurate date is when land was purchased for a cemetery and the first interment noted in the synagogue burial register. Most early burial registers no longer exist and many middle 18th-century tombstones have not survived. Responsibility for the upkeep of old Orthodox cemeteries is mostly with The Board of Deputies of British Jews. Many rely on volunteers, the local community, local heritage or archaeological societies. In *'The Rise of Provincial' Jewry'* (1950). Roth makes the point that Jews are rooted in this country and briefly sets out to 'provide some of the elements that this may be established'. He continues 'I hope that this concentration of material will further stimulate research by persons with greater local qualifications and conveniences' (Ibid, 11). Lipman (1951, 26) states that, 'It is from around 1851 that the first reliable sources are available. *The Jewish Chronicle*, the major Jewish newspaper dating from this time, is also a reliable source of information. Several provincial historians have written books that detail the establishment and growth of their communities. Local histories include *The Making of Manchester Jewry 1740-1875* (Williams 1976), *Jews in Bristol* (Samuel 1997) and *'The Lost Jews of Cornwall'* (Pearce and Fry 2000). Unpublished works include *A History of Birmingham Jewry* (Chesses 2003), and *Swansea Hebrew Congregation 1730-1980* (Glass 1980).

By the late 18th century, communities were established in about 20 cities and towns outside London, 13 were in ports. Many navy agents, ship's chandlers and sailors' outfitters were Jews, providing provisions and equipment for the ships. Three of the earliest communities were Portsmouth (1730), Birmingham (c.1730) and Falmouth (1740). Roth (1950, 94) states that, '….local tradition ascribes the foundation of the community (Portsmouth) to the 1730s and the cemetery was acquired in 1749'. Endelman (2002, 12) notes that 'Portsmouth at this time had the largest community outside London with around 50 families'.

By the 1850s, and after the end of the Revolutionary and Napoleonic Wars, the importance of the naval towns such as Portsmouth, Falmouth, Plymouth and Sheerness began to decline, as the British Navy was reduced in size by nearly 80%. By the end of the 18th century, small groups of Jews formed communities in market towns, such as Canterbury, Exeter, Gloucester, Norwich and Oxford and spa towns such as Bath, Brighton and Cheltenham. There is no longer a community in Bath, Canterbury, Dover, Falmouth, Gloucester, King's Lynn, Penzance, Sheerness or Great Yarmouth. Roth states 'The history of the majority of these defunct Jewries will probably never be written, from sheer dearth of material' (Jewish Chronicle 1933). However since 1933, the history and evidence of the communities in Bath, Canterbury, Falmouth, King's Lynn and Great Yarmouth have been written but not always published. They all have been examined by the author.

In the 1830s and 1840s, several thousand more German Jews settled in Britain. Many were businessmen with contacts with merchant houses in Germany, particularly dealing in textiles where cities like Manchester and Nottingham were pre-eminent. As previously noted, by 1850, when the total Jewish community had reached c.35, 000, over 20, 000 were in London. This situation was due to improvements in communications, the coming of the railway, the decline in market towns during the years 1760-1820 and the growth in industrial towns such as Liverpool, Manchester, Nottingham, Leeds and Glasgow, but London remained predominant.

In 1845, a community survey titled *A Statistical Account of the Congregations In The British Empire 1845 (5606)* (Figure 6.2) was conducted for the Chief Rabbi's office and lists the number of seat holders present on the day the survey was taken, usually around 10% of the community. The Account notes if there was a mikveh (ritual bath), *mikva'ot* (pl.) in the community as discussed in Chapter 5. According to Lipman (1972, 187/188) 'By 1851 there were thirty six towns which had organized communities with at least another dozen or so with a handful of Jewish families each'. Endelman (2002, 80) reports that 'In 1851 there were about 1, 500 Jews in Liverpool, 1, 100 in Manchester and 780 in Birmingham'. These numbers are discussed below, as they are relevant to the topography of the communities in these cities. Smaller communities had also been established in Coventry, Glasgow, Leeds, Nottingham and Sheffield. Hull became a stopping port on the way to the United States, Canada and South Africa. Small communities were also established in seaside resorts and spas such as Brighton, Bath, and Ramsgate. The rise, and in some cases fall, migration and topography of the provincial communities is discussed in the chapters that follow, with the historical and physical evidence.

In summary, Jews who lived in the provinces, particularly ports and market towns chose to live there for a number of reasons, particularly the commercial opportunities. Towards the mid 19th century, in the new industrial age, several provincial communities declined or ceased to exist, particularly in the ports and market towns on the south coast. The younger generation were attracted to London and the large industrial cities of the north, and some emigrated.

2.4.1 Chronological establishment of provincial communities

PORTSMOUTH	1730/1740	BATH	c.1800*
BIRMINGHAM	1730	BRIGHTON	1800
FALMOUTH	1740*	COVENTRY	c.1800
PENZANCE	1740*	YARMOUTH GREAT)	1801*
KINGS LYNN	1740*	HULL	1810
CHATHAM	1750	NORWICH	1813
LIVERPOOL	1750	LEEDS	c.1820
PLYMOUTH	1752	NOTTINGHAM	1822
BRISTOL	1753	CHELTENHAM	1824
CANTERURY	1760*	NEWCASTLE	1830
EXETER	1763	RAMSGATE	1833
SWANSEA	1768	SOUTHAMPTON	1833
DOVER	c.1770*	SHEFFIELD	1838
MANCHESTER	c.1780	CARDIFF	c.1840
SUNDERLAND	1781	OXFORD	1841
GLOUCESTER	1784*	MERTHYR TYDFIL	1848*
SHEERNESS	1790*	BRADFORD	c.1873
IPSWICH	1792*		

36 communities including London, England and Wales listed are discussed, 18 are in ports. Scotland, Ireland and Jersey have been excluded.
*11 towns where there is no longer a community.
Dates have been compiled from The Rise of Provincial Jewry. Roth, C. 1950. The History of the Jews in Great Britain. Margoliouth, M. 1851. Jewish London an Illustrated History. Black, G. 2003. Local community records and histories.

2.5 Concluding remarks

The brief history of the Jewish medieval community (1070-1290) provided at the beginning of this chapter, contrasts in many ways with the history of the growing community in the period 1656-c.1880. The medieval community at its peak in the early 13th-century numbered around 5, 000, although lack of records makes it difficult to establish more exact figures. The community was mostly based in London, with around two-thirds of the total, and by the early 13th-century, there were small communities, many only with a handful of Jews in around 70 towns (Figure 2.1).

Following re-admission, less than 10 of these towns were resettled by the middle of the 19th century. Lincoln, Winchester and York were not populated with Jews following re-admission; the reason being that other than London, the commercial centres had moved as the community no longer needed the protection of the King or his Lords. In the case of York, the massacre in 1190 had an almost permanent effect. In Lincoln, there is the restored medieval prayer room in 'Jews House and Jews Court', and it is sometimes used by the 30-40 Jews who live in Lincoln or nearby. Overall, there is little Jewish archaeological evidence remaining of the medieval period. Archaeological evidence other than cemeteries for the early urban re-settlement period is also limited, because community centres of habitation moved with their synagogues within cities. There was also a demographic shift out of city centres, for example in London out of the east of the City to the suburbs. Early communities in the industrial cities such as Birmingham, Liverpool and Manchester also moved from city centres and poor districts to the suburbs.

In the City of London, only one synagogue remains from the 18th century: Bevis Marks. In the provinces, only two synagogues remain from the Georgian period in Exeter and Plymouth, where services are still held. The 18th century Great Synagogue in London was destroyed during the Blitz in 1941. The middle/late 18th-century synagogues in Dover, Norwich and Swansea were destroyed or badly damaged in wartime bombings. Large areas of the East End of London where the Jews lived in the period under discussion have been redeveloped, as have the early settlement areas in cities such as Birmingham, Leeds, Liverpool, Manchester, Plymouth and Portsmouth and Swansea. Place and street names with Jewish connections are discussed in Chapter 4.

As Kadish states (1996, 1), '…a great deal, far too much, of Jewish architectural heritage in Britain has been lost, and what survives is extremely vulnerable'. No pictorial, architects plans or contemporary illustrations survive' During the past 20 years, several of the books referred to in this study have in some cases revised the historical record of Anglo-Jewry, but the archaeological and physical evidence, other than cemeteries and the few remaining synagogues from the 18th and 19thcenturies, whilst not neglected, receives comparatively little attention. In Britain, unlike certain countries in Europe such as Italy and France there were never ghettos where Jews lived enclosed in walled areas. This was done not only to protect them but also to control their movements. Little identifiable evidence remains of these other than Venice. In Britain following readmission Jews were permitted to live and travel where ever they wished.

In summary, the history, archaeological and topographical evidence of Anglo-Jewry from re-admission to the end of the 19th century is entirely based on Jews who lived in towns and cities. By bringing this evidence together, with a social perspective of the lives of Anglo-Jewry in the 17th-late 19th centuries it is possible to increase our knowledge of Jewish life in this period and to recognise the frugality of a diminishing archaeological resource.

Chapter 3

Research Aims and Methodology

3.1 Research aims

This study aims to bring together in a comprehensive, comparative and standardized way the archaeological evidence, cultural setting and topography of urban Anglo-Jewry in England and Wales, starting in London from 1656 and the provinces, from c.1742 prior to the mass immigration starting in 1881. It identifies the location and demographic origins of the community in different phases of its development from histories, records, synagogue membership and first-and-second edition Ordnance Survey Maps. This is linked with other documentary evidence throughout England and south Wales, and to examine the effect that settlement had on urban topography. Although small communities resided in Scotland and Ireland in the period under discussion, they are beyond the scope of this study, as are those small communities in England with less than 50 persons c.1850.

3.1.1 Research Questions

Several research questions provide a methodological template for the study of the growth and topography of Anglo-Jewry in the period 1656-c.1881.

> First: What evidence is there of the establishment and movement or closure of the early synagogues, both in London and the provinces, as communities expanded, moved from ports and city centres or declined?
> Second: What evidence exists in towns of *mikva'ot* (ritual baths), material culture and artefacts, and place and street names with a Jewish association?
> Third: What were the locations and dates of the establishment, use and then closure of the 17th-19th-century cemeteries and the evidence for this?
> Fourth: What can we learn from gravestones, their inscriptions, style and design, as well as monumental architecture, about increasing prosperity and integration of Jews into wider society?
> Fifth: What evidence is there of the movement of communities within the major cities, the rise and decline of the early communities mainly in ports on

the south coast and market towns, and the growth of the communities in the industrial cities of the Midlands and North? How does this compare with other immigrant/non-conformist groups in relation to wider English social situations?

Summary data is recorded, and a pro-forma for each of the sites visited in London and 35 cities and towns studied. These are presented in the gazetteer, together with Ordnance Survey Maps (1880s-1900) and 1858 health maps from South Wales.

3.2 Methodology

The archaeology of Anglo-Jewry in London is in part based on the author's' MA dissertation (Marks 2008). Briefly discussed in the dissertation are artefacts found from excavations which can be identified as Jewish, in the London area, which includes, two 19th century *shofar'ot* (rams horns), a 1720s *chalav* (milk plate) and 17th-18th century lead meat and cloth seals with Hebrew writing. The dissertation also included two synagogues, Bevis Marks 1701, The Great Synagogue 1690 and three cemeteries, the *Velho* (Old) and *Nuevo* (New) Sephardi cemeteries and the first Ashkenazi cemetery in Alderney Road. This has been expanded in the study to include 12 London synagogues and 11 cemeteries

The study has been expanded from the dissertation to investigate the movement and growth of the community into the suburbs from the east of London. Every site in London and the provinces discussed has been visited. In the provinces, research was carried out town by town using historical data as the starting point and visiting the cemeteries and synagogues where they still exist. Visits were made with members of the local community and Heritage committees, with their specialised knowledge. Before visiting some of the disused cemeteries, special permission was arranged with local contacts. Contact was also made with local museums, reference libraries, records offices and archaeological societies.

The synagogue is the most important communal institution in Jewish society, not only as a place for prayer, but also for the conduct of other religious practices such as *bar mitzvahs* (the celebration when a boy reaches the age of 13 and is considered ready to take on the responsibilities of manhood) and weddings. Funeral services are generally not held in synagogues, but at the cemetery. Synagogues and prayer halls functioned as meeting places and schools. Because of the need to observe the Sabbath, Orthodox Jews will only walk to synagogue. Therefore its location had to be at the heart of the community. Thus, unlike cemeteries, which, once purchased and opened, remained intact; synagogues and their movement or closure can give a clear picture of the dynamics of the community. In other words, locations of synagogues form a pattern of resettlement which can be analyzed in relation to urban topography.

Many synagogues of the period under discussion have been identified. Some are still in use whilst others have been converted into mosques, churches, apartments and warehouses. Some are in a poor state of repair. Others, particularly in the City of London, to the east of London and in port cities, were destroyed during World War II, with few, if any, surviving records. Synagogues from this period have also been demolished during redevelopment.

Maps, records, illustrations, photographs have been consulted. The exterior elevations of some of the early synagogues were designed by local non-Jewish architects several with the appearance of non-conformist chapels. Inside, they were uniform in design, with a *bimah* (central platform), and an upper gallery for the separation of men and women, the Ark, which holds the *Torah* scrolls, where possible, pointing eastwards towards Jerusalem. It is known from synagogue records that local architects and craftsmen contributed towards individual features, such as stonework and wood being crafted for the seats and benches. By the middle of the 19th century some of the larger communities outside London, such as Birmingham, Liverpool and Manchester, had established 'cathedral' synagogues demonstrating the increasing wealth and confidence of the community.

In archaeological research, material culture normally forms an important source, although in this study a paucity of evidence poses a severe obstacle. *Mikva'ot* (ritual baths) are discussed, although none from this period have yet been identified in London. Occasionally there is physical and archaeological evidence for *mikva'ot* from this period, such as in Canterbury, Exeter, Hull and Plymouth. Most of the religious artefacts, whether used in the synagogue or home would have been taken from the old synagogue to the new or handed down by the family to the next generation. Many artefacts such as *Torah* scrolls, silver candlesticks, if not still being used in newer synagogues, are now in museums, private collections in Britain or abroad or lost.

In the provinces, there is a limited amount of material culture, such as at Portsmouth, where the foundation stone of the synagogue was moved from an earlier building. In the Jewish Museum Camden Town, there is a wooden panel, a Decalogue and lamps with Hebrew writing from the early 19th century, from the Falmouth and Penzance Synagogues. These were rescued when the synagogues closed.

Certain areas in London and the provinces are known by historical evidence to have had a Jewish presence. In some cases, street-names are now the only evidence with names like Old Jewry, Jewry Street, Synagogue Place or Jewish Fields, where a cemetery is located in Penzance. Identifying these names can assist in drawing a more complete picture of the Jewish presence in England.

Perhaps paradoxically, the main body of evidence of archaeological evidence for Jewish life is derived from cemeteries. Where there was a Jewish community, a cemetery was established, sometimes before the synagogue (as prayers could be held in private houses or rented halls). The cemetery was a crucial component of every Jewish community. According to Orthodox Jewish law, the body of the deceased after burial should be left undisturbed. Furthermore, because of the same tradition, cemeteries have survived. Jewish cemeteries represent an important source of information. Moreover, where there are plans, records of burial dates and position of the plot of the deceased, rich information can be revealed. Some of these plans are included. Unfortunately there are few, and research has shown that many have been destroyed or lost.

Around 60 Jewish cemeteries around England and Wales have been identified and visited. It was not possible to gain access to four of them. For each cemetery, a data sheet was prepared (see gazetteer) in order to gather information in a coherent form (site of cemetery, date of first and last burial), and evidence, if any, of an ohel (prayer room). Headstones were examined in order to identify significant inscriptions. An effort was also made to identify names and origins of some of the deceased, as well as clues to their social and economic standing. Censuses from 1695-1871 serve as a tool for investigation; the 1695 census reveals important information about the Jewish presence in London at the end of the 17th century. It helps to determine the geographical spreading of Jews, as it locates them by their distinctive names in six London parishes. It also reveals the makeup of the early community which was almost entirely of Sephardic (Spanish and Portuguese) descent. Of considerable value has been the Statistical Accounts of the Congregations in the British Empire (1845), issued by the Chief Rabbi's office, which gives details membership of synagogues, mikva'ot, cemeteries and education facilities in 42 cities and towns. The original archive is held and was examined by the author in the London Metropolitan Archives. It is not a complete picture of the Jewish community at that date, as it does not detail the Sephardi community and the small Reform Community formed in 1840. Some congregations in London, such as Sandy's Row Synagogue, although Ashkenazi and Orthodox, were also not included in the census, as they were independent of the authority of the Chief Rabbi. The census only details paid-up members of Ashkenazi synagogues. It does not take into account itinerant pedlars with no fixed abode, who attended services on the Sabbath, and the poor who were not paid-up members. The numbers can only be approximate. However, the 1845 Statistical Account does give a picture of the demography of Jews in the mid 19th century and is regularly used by students of the period. Lipman's (1954) Social History of the Jews in England, lists 40 communities, with an estimate of the population in each in 1850. It is the first reasonably accurate statistical survey of the entire community.

3.2.1 Preliminary work

All the sites visited are or were religious, and there are accepted customs of behaviour. For example, when entering a synagogue, a head covering should be worn by men, and women should have their shoulders covered and not wear shorts. It is not considered respectful to step over or walk on a grave. In Jewish law, it is traditional not to disturb grave sites; excavation is forbidden. However, cemeteries or sections of cemeteries have been relocated and re-interment of remains is then permitted, such as the Hoxton Cemetery, London (5.1.9), which was re-interred in West Ham Cemetery. In Brentwood, Essex, 7500 remains have been re-interred from the Sephardi Nuevo Cemetery in Mile End (5.1.2). On leaving a cemetery, one should wash ones' hands if running water is available.

It has not been possible to detail every tombstone inscription in the cemeteries visited. In most cemeteries, inscriptions that can be read have already been recorded. Some of particular significance or unusual features are noted. Having collected the evidence by city or town, it is then brought together by category, synagogues, place names, *mikva'ot*, artefacts and cemeteries, each in separate chapters and summarised in the gazetteer. In the gazetteer are extracts from first and second edition Ordnance Survey Maps (1880-1901) showing the location of synagogues and cemeteries.

3.2.2 Gathering information

3.2.2.1 Published information and excavation reports

In addition to historical narratives, there are numerous, publications on Anglo-Jewry in the 17th-19th centuries. Amongst the most important being *Transactions and Miscellaneous of the Jewish Historical Society (THJE)* which has been published continuously since 1893. In the Transactions, there are occasional archaeological articles, sometimes reproduced from publications such as *The London Archaeologist, The Lost Synagogues of London* (Renton 2004) and *Jewish Heritage in England, an Architectural Guide* (Kadish 2006). These publications have been invaluable in research for this study. Several excavation reports deal with Jewish finds from the medieval period, such as *Two Medieval Jewish Ritual Baths-Mikva'ot found at Gresham Street and Milk Street in London* Blair et al. (2001) and *The Jewish Burial Ground at Jewbury (York)* (1994) Lilly et al. A number of published London excavation reports deal with artefacts from the 17th century onwards; so far only four, 'a delftware plate' in *Post-Medieval Archaeology* (Pearce 1998), *kosher* meat seals in *Lead Cloth Seals and Related Items in the British Museum* (Egan 1995), *shofar'ot* (rams' horns) in *London Archaeologist* (Chase et al. 2008), and *Excavations at Lloyd's Register, 71 Fenchurch Street City of London, (The Hambro Synagogue)* (Bluer et al. 2006). In Liverpool, there is the excavation report of the first Jewish cemetery, *Memorials of Liverpool* (Picton, 1873).

3.2.2.2 Analysis of data collected

A pro-forma questionnaire was prepared for each of the sites and towns and these can be found in the gazetteer. Information collected included the following:
1. When the community was established
2. When the first and subsequent synagogues were established and, where relevant, closed
3. Size and topography of communities in 17th/18th/19th centuries
4. Jewish place and street names.
5. The presence of a mikveh
6. Material culture, including religious and domestic objects

7. The first and subsequent cemeteries with any plans
8. Ordnance Survey Maps c.1880-1901

3.2.3 *The nature of the evidence, methodological problems and limitations*

There is considerable written evidence for the topography of the community in the period under discussion, but much less physical evidence of synagogues and cemeteries. Other limiting factors are:

During the 20th century, much evidence for Jewish life was destroyed. The City of London and the east of London was heavily bombed during the Blitz in 1941. After World War II, many of these areas were redeveloped and not reoccupied by Jewish families. They had moved further east or to the north and west of London. This also occurred in the provinces. The early Jewish area in Portsmouth for example being near the port was subject to heavy bombing and later redeveloped. The remaining community moved to Southsea. The dock area of Liverpool, where the first Jewish immigrants settled was also bombed during the war. In Birmingham, the area settled by Jews was also redeveloped. Many streets shown in these towns on late 19th-century Ordnance Survey Maps no longer exist.

Only in the last few years has there been a growing awareness of the danger of the physical history of the Jewish community being lost. Several synagogues and parts of cemeteries have now been scheduled by English Heritage, but this does not prevent them from being at risk. The Jewish community in England is in decline from a peak after the War in 1945 of over 400,000 to around 270,000 in 2011. This is due to emigration, marrying 'out' and Jews no longer attending synagogue and practising their religion. This places severe financial burdens on communities and institutions, such as The Board of Deputies of British Jews, in the preservation and upkeep of cemeteries and synagogues. In some cases, awareness of Jewish Heritage has come too late.

Census figures of 1695 record around 1,000 Jews in London. Jewish names of Sephardi extraction can easily be identified. The census of 1850 has been studied by researchers and is considered to give a reasonably accurate picture of the Anglo-Jewish community at that date. However even up to c.1880, the figures are only be a guide and not completely accurate.

This is due to four reasons:
a: religion cannot be identified from the census. Only the 2001 census included a voluntary question on religion. b: in the early period, there were large numbers of itinerant pedlars of no fixed abode. c: many Jews changed their family name in order to become more anglicised and pronounceable. d: there are no completely reliable population figures, as immigrant Jews in the 19th century did not require passports to enter England. Jewish population size can be based only on contemporary estimates and a limited range of demographic information. The following highlights some of the problems according to each category of research data.

3.2.3.1 Synagogues

1. As previously stated, in London, only one synagogue has survived from the early 18th-century, the Bevis Marks Synagogue in the City of London. There were three other 19th-century synagogues in the City of London. Other 19th-century synagogues outside the City in London are discussed. There is a clear relationship in this period between the location of synagogues and where Jews lived. There were also many small rooms or halls of prayer for those Jews who did not want to pray in a large synagogue and preferred to be in a small congregation, often with fellow refugees from the same homeland, two of these in Princelet Street E1 and Sandy's Row EC1 have been examined.
2. In two smaller provincial communities, Exeter and Plymouth, there remain two functioning Georgian synagogues from the middle of the 18th century. There are 19th-century 'cathedral' synagogues in the major provincial cities, such as Birmingham and Liverpool, which still function even though the community has moved to other areas of the cities. Other synagogues from this period have sometimes been converted to other uses such as mosques and apartments and access to them is limited.

The centre of family life has always been the home. In the Jewish tradition, before Sabbath evening and meal (Friday), a service is held in the home. Some of the festivals, such as Passover (commemorating the Exodus from Egypt) and Chanukah (the festival of lights) are also celebrated in the home rather than the synagogue.

It is rarely possible to identify from physical evidence the actual house where Jews lived, even if the building has survived. Unlike the medieval period, where there is evidence of *mikva'ot* in private Jewish houses, in the period under discussion *mikva'ot* were often established as communal facilities, sometimes in the synagogue. Communal baths or the sea were also used, this is discussed later. Lastly, many of the Jews in England in the 17th and 18th centuries were poor and trying to trace their numbers in life and death is not always possible. It is the evidence of 17th-19th cemeteries and the establishment of synagogues, followed by their relocation and then closure that form the greater part of the research for this study

3.2.3.2 Cemeteries

Research into cemeteries faces several problems:
1. Many of deceased from poor families could not afford a headstone. In most cases, babies and infants were interred without marker stones and without burial records. Babies and infant deaths were as high as 40% of those buried.
2. Some disused cemeteries have become overgrown and neglected.
3. Only granite, slate and some later marble headstones have survived weathering and acid rain. Many gravestones are broken or destroyed.
4. Some cemeteries in the east of London were damaged by bombs in World

War II. There are burial records, but the remains were reburied in a different cemetery in unmarked mass graves.
5. Burial records that survive are often in poor condition, and, from the author's own experience, in some cases' it is difficult to establish a link between the burial records, cemetery and actual burial plot.

In spite of these difficulties, the gazetteer brings together this important resource for the topography of Anglo- Jewry in the period 1656-c.1880.

3.3.1 Glossary

Hebrew words and titles are used in this study. In order to make them understandable, they are written in English rather than Hebrew, with translations taken from several sources, such as glossaries in quoted books. *The New Oxford Dictionary of English* (1998) has a number of the most commonly used Hebrew words

3.3.2 Gazetteer

All quoted references and sources have been included. These include primary and secondary sources, in addition to extracts from Ordnance Survey and Public Health maps which show place names with Jewish connections, the locations of synagogues and cemeteries discussed.

LOCATION	CHAPTER	SITE	DATE ESTABLISHED	IN USE TO	DATE OF VISIT	GAZETTEER NUMBER

ADDITIONAL NOTES

NOTABLE GRAVES

BIBLIOGRAPHY

OTHER SOURCES

FIGURE NUMBERS

NUMBER OF BURIALS

Figure 3.1 format of summary sheet in gazetteer.

Chapter 4

Living Communities
Synagogues, street and place names with Jewish connections, *mikva'ot* (ritual baths), material culture and artefacts

The destruction of Jerusalem and the Temple in AD70 was the main event that created synagogues. This destruction created and changed the customs, ritual practices and brought about the style of architecture of synagogue buildings at that time. Public worship by study and prayer was now the cult of the synagogue (Hachlili, 2001, 4). Synagogues provided a building to house the Alter and *Torahs* (the first five books of the Hebrew Bible) on a wall oriented to Jerusalem (Ibid, 97). The synagogue, as to-day became a meeting house as well as a hall of prayer.

The name by which a synagogue is known is indicative of its function. The word synagogue is of Greek origin; the equivalent in Hebrew is *beth ha knesset* (the House of Assembly or meeting place). The synagogue plays an integral role in recording the life of a community. The orientation of synagogues, where possible, is east-west, with the Ark at the eastern end facing Jerusalem. The Ark contains the Scrolls, usually in an elevated cupboard on a raised platform reached by steps, giving the Scrolls a position of prominence where they can be seen by most members of the congregation wherever they are sitting. The doors or gates to the Ark are usually covered by a curtain. The Ark is opened during Sabbath and High Holiday services and the Scrolls are removed. Above, many synagogues have a Hebrew text, which states (in English):

'Remember before Whom you stand'

Ornaments on the eastern wall include a depiction of two tablets inscribed with Hebrew characters, indicating the Ten Commandments. In Orthodox synagogues, marble or wooden plaques with prayers in Hebrew and English for the royal family are also placed on the eastern wall. In earlier synagogues, when new kings and queens were enthroned, previous royal family names were changed or over-painted, examples of this are discussed.

The *bimah* (raised platform with reading desk) is situated in Ashkenazi synagogues in the centre of the building. In Sephardi synagogues, it is placed at the opposites end to the ark. In Reform synagogues, there is no central *bimah;* the Scrolls are read from a raised platform in front of the Ark. During the service, the Scrolls are taken from the Ark and placed on a desk on the *bimah,* after they have been undressed for the reading of the Law, which is sung or read in Hebrew. Examples of *bimas* are shown in this study. They are usually square or oblong, with railings of wood or metal with candelabra or lights placed at each corner. The earliest synagogues, such as Bevis Marks, had wooden benches for the congregation. Seats could be opened, where the holder could place his prayer books and *tallit* (prayer shawl with fringes attached). In some synagogues, such as Exeter, there are seats attached to the side of the *bimah*. Renton (2000, 185) suggests 'that these seats were apparently for the privileged and had better lighting from the candles on the *bimah*'.

In Orthodox synagogues it is still the custom for women to sit in the gallery separate from men. In early synagogues, such as Creechurch Lane and The Great Synagogue in Duke's Place, women sat in a gallery behind a latticed grill. This chapter examines written and physical evidence of early prayer rooms, halls and the establishment of synagogues. This is followed by the evidence of site relocation as communities migrated or declined. In London, several of the early synagogues in the east of London were destroyed during World War II. Out of 12, 18th/19th century London synagogues discussed, only one 18th century synagogue survives, Bevis Marks in the City. Congregation members had to be within walking distance of their synagogue.

As the demography changed, new synagogues were established. In some cases, declining communities became unviable resulting in amalgamation, with buildings being put to other uses or destroyed. In chapter 6, the social and cultural implications of these changes in spatial patterns are examined. This chapter also discusses *mikva'ot* where there is documented but no physical evidence in London of these. *Mikva'ot* are still evident in some of the early provincial communities. Place and street names with Jewish connections are examined, along with Jewish artefacts found during excavations.

4.1 London communities and synagogues

The first Jewish re-settlement from 1665 took place in London with Sephardi Jews from the Netherlands, Italy, North Africa, Spain, Portugal, and a few Ashkenazim from central and Eastern Europe (Hyamson 1951, 11). The location of synagogues, often with their communal buildings used for schools and community activities, form a pattern of resettlement that can be analysed in relation to urban topography. There are three conditions for the establishment of a Jewish community: a house of prayer, a consecrated burial ground and a mikveh (ritual bath).

From the 1695 Census lists, 850 out of the 1,000 Jews who lived in London can be shown to have lived within the walls of the City, towards the Tower of London (Roth 1978, 190). The law at that time did not allow Jews to buy property freeholds in London, and the merchants in the City of London, concerned about competition, objected to Jews leasing property near the Guildhall and St Paul's, which had been the central area of London's Jewish medieval life. Black wrote 'This time the newcomers took up residence not in the Old Jewry but in the area of Duke's Place (now Duke Street, Houndsditch and Petticoat Lane (then called Hogg Street) on the Edge of the City' (2003, 23). It was within the walls of the City of London that the first synagogues were established (Figures 2, 3). The first synagogues in London began in the City and later were established eastwards. They then spread north, south, west and further east as the community in London moved. The establishment of a room of prayer and then a synagogue was essential in bringing a community together. The location of these synagogues reflects the history, mobility and topography of the community.

London synagogues

4.1.1. Bayswater Synagogue W2	established 1863 demolished 1966
4.1.2. Sephardi Bevis Marks EC3	established 1701-still in use
4.1.3. Central Synagogue W1	established 1855-1941*
4.1.4. Sephardi Creechurch Lane EC3	established 1657-1701
4.1.5. Great Synagogue EC3	established 1690-1941*
4.1.6. Hambro Synagogue EC3	established 1707 demolished 1892/3
4.1.7. New Synagogue EC3	established 1761-1911**
4.1.8. New West End Synagogue W2	established 1879-still in use
4.1.9. Princelet Street Synagogue E1	established 1870-1962
4.1.10. Sandy's Row Synagogue E1	established c.1870-still in use
4.1.11. Western Synagogue W1	established 1761*-1991
4.1.12. West London Reform Synagogue W1	established 1870-still in use

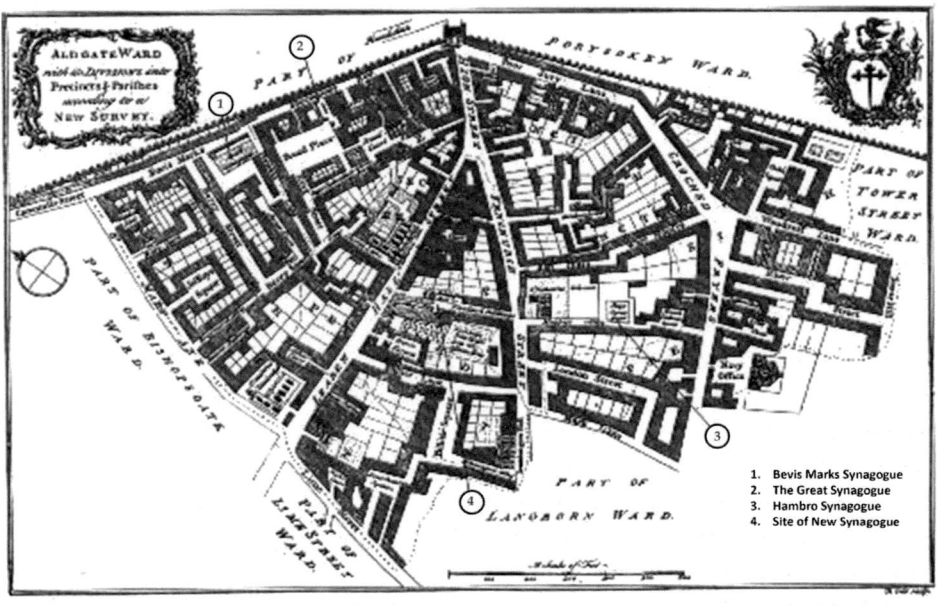

*Destroyed during the Blitz in 1941
**New congregation established in 1958 in N16

Figure 4.1 Jacob Ilive's Map of Aldgate Ward 1756 showing the first four City of London synagogues (Renton 2000, 26).

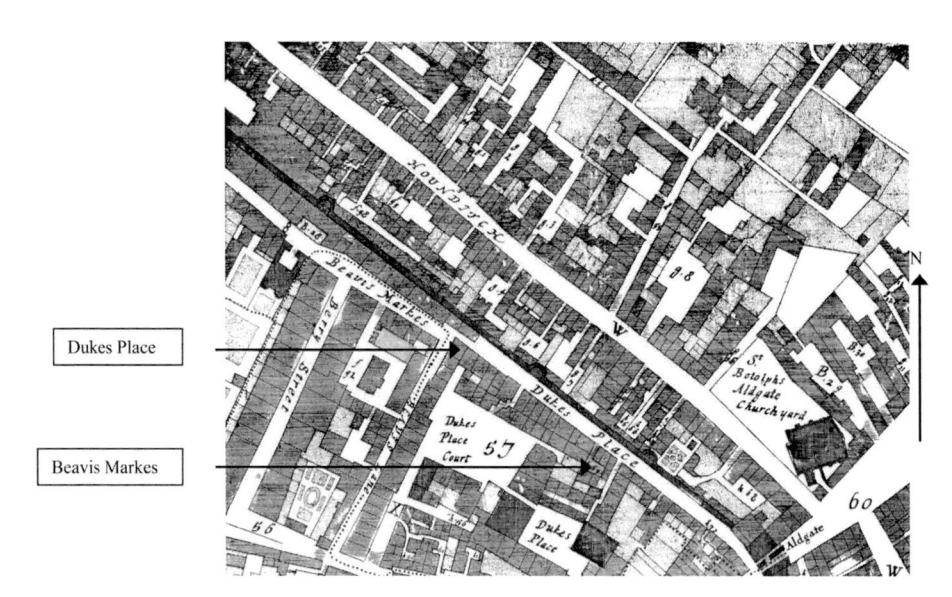

Figure 4.2 Ogilby and Morgan's Map (5ft to a mile) of London showing Beavis Markes (now Bevis Marks) and Dukes Place the location of the first two custom-made synagogues in London, Dukes Place (1690), Bevis Marks (1701) (London History Folios 85. 22/1676).

Resettlement even at the beginning of the 18th century was not without opposition: Roth (1978, 19) quotes from a Treatise first published in 1709 (author unknown) in the reign of Queen Anne (1702-1714):

'For, with submission, it is but a very slender sign of expelling Immorality and Prophaneness, and a less Sign of Reformation or Religion, to see a Synagogue erecting in Duke's Place within the Heart of the Great City of London, for Jewish Rabies, and such like, to pour out their Blasphemies'.

4.1.1. Bayswater Synagogue W2 [1]

Bayswater Synagogue was established 1863 (Figure 4.3) and demolished in 1966 to make way for motorway development. A new synagogue was established in Andover Place W2 in 1971/2 but closed in 1984. According to Phillips et al., (1963, 2) 'Families who had moved westwards from the City were separated from their synagogues. Sabbath or Festival attendance meant either a four or five mile trudge or suffering the discomforts of the City hotels'. Renton (2000, 79) states that, '… Bayswater could hold 341 male members on the ground floor and 334 women in the Ladies' Gallery' (Figure 4.4).

The establishment of this synagogue illustrates the movement of the better off members of the community westwards. Prior to Bayswater's establishment, at the High Holiday periods, when synagogues in the City could not accommodate all their

Figure 4.3 Bayswater Synagogue 1863: exterior (Phillips et al. 1963).

Figure 4.4 Bayswater Synagogue: interior in 1863 (contemporary engraving) (Renton 2000, 80)

members or visitors who only attend services on these days, hotel rooms or halls were used as overflows. The parent synagogue (The Great) supplied silver ritual objects, such as the *yadayim* (pointers) used when reading the *Torah* (the five books of Moses) so that the handwritten scroll on parchment is not touched, and the *rimonim* (silver plates and bells), which are hung and placed on the *torah* scrolls once they have been

Figure 4.5 Bayswater Synagogue 1863: the Ark showing dressed Torah scrolls (Phillips et al.1963, 27).

dressed (Figure 4.5). According to Phillips et al., '…..from 1864 there was a mikveh adjacent to the synagogue, which remained open until the 1930s (Ibid, 12). *mikva'ot* (pl.) are discussed in Chapter 4.4.

Bayswater Synagogue was established by an upper-middle-class community, including members of the Rothschild family, whose female members helped to clothe poor children attending the local Jewish School. Rufus Isaacs, later the first Marquis of Reading, was thought to have had his *bar mitzvah* ceremony (the age of religious majority for a boy) at Bayswater Synagogue.

4.1.2   Bevis Marks Synagogue EC3   [2]

By 1701, when the Sephardi community had grown to around 500 persons, a larger synagogue was built to replace Creechurch Lane (discussed 4.1.4). The first purpose-built Sephardi synagogue after the readmission was positioned around the corner from Creechurch Lane (the previous synagogue was in a converted house). It is situated in a discreet back alley site off the main road in Plough Yard in Houndsditch EC3. Bevis Marks was the first purpose-built synagogue in England since the 13th-century. The site was located in the easternmost ward of the City of London. The street name, Bevis Marks is a much-corrupted version of 'Buries Marks', the residence of the medieval Abbot of Bury St. Edmunds (Hyamson 1951, 75). The synagogue is on the site of the Abbot's residence and is Britain's oldest surviving synagogue. According to the synagogue records, the freehold was acquired in 1749, nearly 50 years after it was opened (Kadish et al. 2001, 2). Until recently, it was the only Grade-I-listed synagogue in Britain. In 2008/2009, two further synagogues were listed as Grade I: New West End, St Petersburgh Place Bayswater W.2 (1877-9) (4.1.8), London and Princes Road, Liverpool L8 (1872-4) (4.2.19.2). Bevis Marks is the oldest English-speaking synagogue in the world and is for the most part unaltered since it was opened in 1701. The exterior was designed to be 'low key' so as not to offend the Gentile community, with arched windows on every side providing maximum natural lighting. From outside, it has the appearance of a non-conformist chapel (personal observation 2009). Kadish (2006, 3) writes, 'This is not surprising as the architect was a Quaker master builder, *Joseph Avis,* a church builder who had previously worked with *Christopher Wren*'. There is also documented evidence in the

Figure 4.6 Interior of the Spanish and Portuguese Synagogue in Amsterdam, showing the bimah (central platform) (photograph K. Marks 2007).

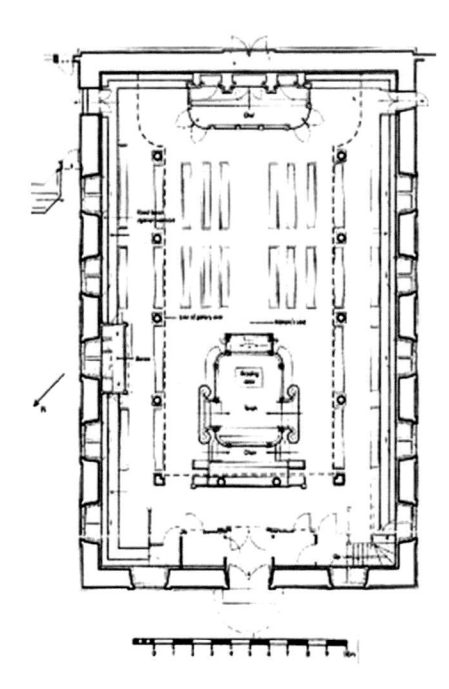

Figure 4.7 Plan of the ground floor level of Bevis Marks 1701 (Bevis Marks archives).

synagogue archives that he over-estimated the cost of the building, which was less than 3, 000 pounds and returned some of his payment, as he considered it wrong to make a profit on a religious building (Ibid, 3).

The Ashkenazi Great Synagogue (1671) and the Spanish and Portuguese Great Synagogue (1674) in Amsterdam became the prototypes for synagogue architecture throughout Britain. The interior design of the Sephardi Bevis Marks Synagogue was loosely based on the synagogue in Amsterdam (Figure 4.6).

Bevis Marks is rectangular in shape and measures 80x50ft (Figure 4.7), with 12 columns supporting the gallery representing the Twelve Tribes of Israel. Seven candelabra light the building; six are the same size, the seventh in the centre is larger and representing the Sabbath (Saturday) (Figure 4.8). According to Hyamson (1951, 76) one of the candelabra was a gift of the Amsterdam Sephardi Community and was

*Figure 4.8 The interior of Spanish and Portuguese Synagogue, Bevis Marks EC3 (1812).
By Isaac Mendes Belisario (Bevis Marks, Samuel 2006: xv11)
(reproduced by permission Spanish and Portuguese Congregation 2009).*

brought from Holland. Ten brass candlesticks symbolise the Ten Commandments. Kadish (1996,59) states that, 'Bevis Marks' plan combined aspects of the Great Synagogue in Amsterdam (built 1674-5) with Wren's Church designs and that this directly influenced the Great Synagogue (Ashkenazi) in London' which is discussed in 4.1.5. There are wooden benches from the original 1657 synagogue and an entry in the congregation's minutes for November 1701 'recorded that 2s (shillings, 10p) were paid for carrying the benches across the road to the new synagogue' (Ibid, 14).

Bevis Marks contains rare 17th-18th century *Torahs,* ritual silver and embroidered textiles. The Ark which houses the *Sifrie Torah* (scrolls containing the hand-written text of the Pentateuch), is in the shape of an ornamental screen that covers the back wall and is placed on the east wall, roughly in the direction of Jerusalem. The Hebrew inscription over the ark reads in English '*Know before whom thou standest*', an adaptation of *Ethics of the Fathers 3:1*. As will be seen with the other synagogues discussed, these features are frequently found in synagogues of the later period.

There is a legend, unsupported by documents or detailed examination that an oak beam used in the roof was presented by Princess Anne (later Queen Anne). Roth (1978, 185) states that, 'This beam had supposedly been used in one of the ships of the Royal Navy'. Kadish (1966, 3) states that, 'Bevis Marks stands testimony to the longevity of the Jewish presence in England'. With the movement of some of the community westwards in 1853, a small number of Sephardim who lived in the West End opened a branch of Bevis Marks in Wigmore Street, W1, which no longer exists.

4.1.3 Central Synagogue W1 [3]

The establishment of the Central Synagogue in Great Portland Street W.1 illustrates the growth and prosperity of the community and its movement to West London from the beginning of the reign of Queen Victoria. The minutes of a Great Synagogue meeting in 1848 resolved *"that it being considered of the utmost importance that a place of worship in connection of the Synagogue be established at the West End of the Metropolis"* (Renton 2000, 73). This synagogue was under the management of The Great Synagogue in Duke's Place in the City. In 1855, the first synagogue in Great Portland Street was consecrated, with 212 seats downstairs and 144 in the gallery (Ibid, 73). Newman (1976, 216) states that, 'By 1870 it had a membership of nearly 300 seat-holders and by 1880 had nearly 400, making it the second largest community after The Great Synagogue at that time'. This indicates the growth of the Orthodox community in the West End of London by the middle of the 19th century. In 1870, a new and larger building was erected in Great Portland Street, with seating for over 800; it was destroyed by bombing May 10th 1941.

In 1870, the United Synagogue was created with four other synagogues, the Great, Hambro, New and Bayswater. Figure 4.9 shows the grand interior of the Great Portland Street building, built according to the Orthodox tradition, with the *bimah* (platform) in the centre and galleries for the women on the long sides. There are no surviving plans; however, the depiction of the interior shows some important features. The interior is highly ornate, with a mixture of forms from different Jewish cultures. Renton (2000, 73) quotes from Künzl, who wrote on the Islamic architectural style with arches meeting at

Figure 4.9 Interior Central Synagogue: r in 1870 The interior as depicted after opening in Old and New London, Vol. IV (Westminster and the Western Suburbs) by Wellford, (Black 2003, 58).

the apex of 19th and early 20th century synagogues. '*The Gothic elements can only be seen in the vault and the tracery of the windows. Undoubtedly, the Islamic elements are the pr-eminent and a strong similarity to the Synagogue in Leipzig*'. Roth (2004, 75) states that, 'The Central Synagogue in 1872 had amongst its members, five Members of Parliament, six Barons, two Aldermen of the City of London, the Solicitor General and a Royal Academician'.

In the early 1870s, the total Jewish community in England was c.40, 000 with half still living in the east of London. In the 1850s, Mills judged that just over half of London's Jews were 'lower class' (1853, 257). By the 1870s/1880s, although the community was disproportionately middle-class, there were a number of very wealthy families living in the West End of London, some of whom were members of the Central Synagogue Great Portland Street. Black (2003, 70, 71) states that, 'In 1870 of the eight Jewish members of Parliament, five were members of the Central Synagogue'. Following World War II, Great Portland Street was to become the centre of the fashion industry in England, with a high proportion of Jewish traders. The present synagogue was rebuilt on the site in 1958. The Central Synagogue represented a rise in social status of part of the community, with its movement from the east of London to the West End. Members living in the West End, Regents Park, around Marble Arch and Park Lane were now more easily able to walk to synagogue on the Sabbath and High Holidays.

4.1.4　　　　　　　Creechurch Lane EC3　　　　　　　　　　[4]

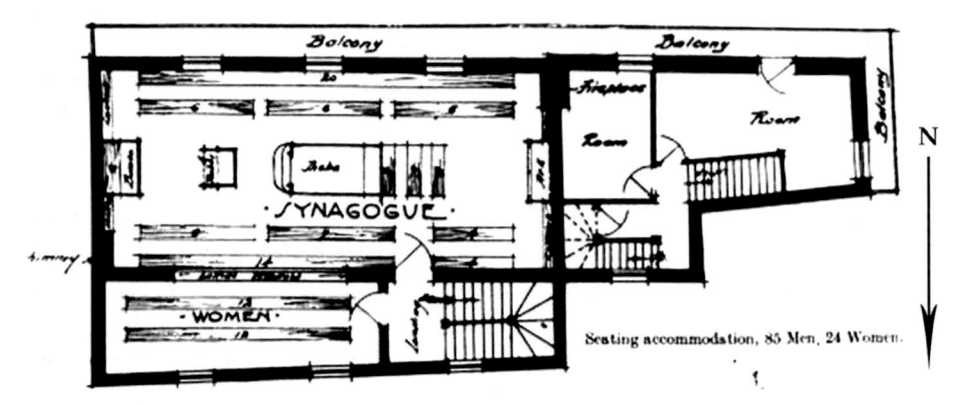

Figure 4.10 Conjectural ground plan of the 1657 synagogue in Creechurch Lane, Aldgate EC3 with a notional seating plan. (Reproduced from the article by W. Samuel by permission of the Jewish Historical Society of England) (Renton, 2000) and Spanish and Portuguese Congregation (2009).

In 1656, a house was acquired in Creechurch Lane in the parish of St Katherine Creechurch, Aldgate, in the City of London (Hyamson 1951, 14). As recorded in the entrance of St Katherine's Church 'Creechurch recalls the priory of Christ Church from 1108' (personal observation, 2009). Renton (2000, 188) writes that, 'In 1657

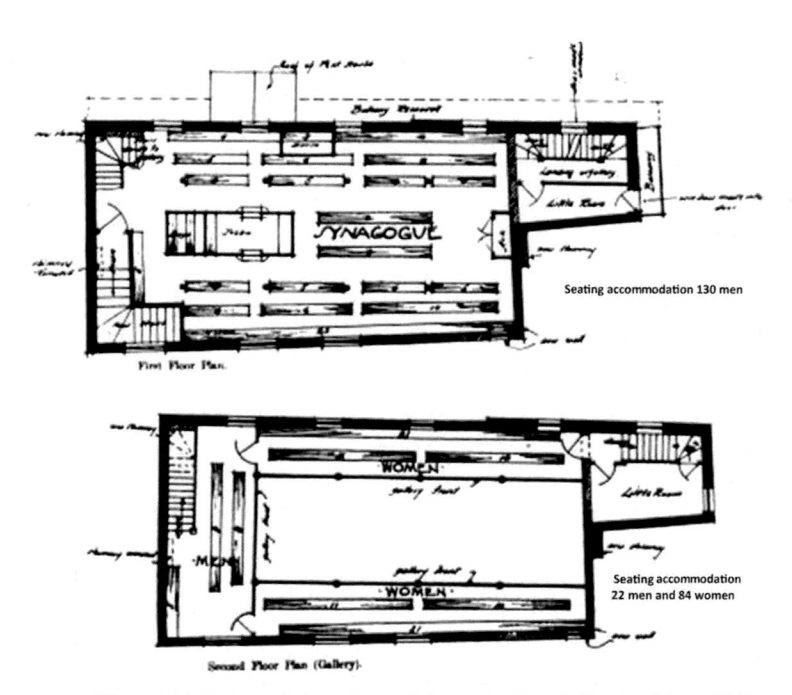

Figure 4.11 Conjectural plans of ground floor and gallery of Creechurch Lane EC3 after reconstruction in 1674 (Reproduced from t article by W. Samuel by kind permission of the Jewish Historical Society of England) (Renton.2000) and Spanish and Portuguese Congregation 2009.

the first synagogue of the re-admission period was opened. The house had been converted, with the room of prayer on the first floor large enough to sit around 85 men and 24 women, in total 109 congregants'. The acquisition of the house in Creechurch Lane would only have happened if the Jews were confident that they could now live openly in England with freedom to worship. There is no evidence remaining of this building, but there are detailed conjectural plans. 'These plans are deduced from correspondence from 1662, now in the British Museum and are quoted in full by Renton' (Ibid, 188) (Figure 4.10). Samuel (1924, 20) states that 'The Churchwardens Accounts for the years 1650 to 1656 contain many references to Carvajal….he was one of the largest ratepayers in the parish', also that 'Carvajal…. had taken a lease on the building in 1656' (Ibid, 29). (Carvajal is referred to in Chapter 2). Sixteen years later in 1673/4, it was extended to hold 170 men and 84 women (Renton 2000, 23) (Figure 4.11). Renton states that 'The neighbouring brick-built house belonging to a merchant was used for this purpose' (Ibid 21). According to Black (2003, 25) by 1700, 'the London community had grown to over 1,000 persons, half of whom depended on charitable relief from the community' Creechurch Lane Synagogue was in use until 1701 (Ibid, 75). After closure, Creechurch Lane was used as a domestic house before becoming the parish workhouse and was demolished in 1857. The site was rebuilt after the 1939-1945 war and is now the offices of the Cunard Shipping Line. The definitive research and publication of this earliest synagogue is by Samuel (1924), based on documents and deeds preserved in Bevis Marks, British Museum and the Guildhall archives. Samuel (1924, 4) states that:

> 'Now there are in the Bevis Marks archives to-day three deeds which treat of an early Synagogue of the re-settlement, and it seems to me that they are the only documents there which provide us with any sort of view-albeit an imperfect and incomplete one of the Meeting House in Creechurch Lane'.

The interesting words in this extract are 'Meeting House', which suggests that prior to becoming a synagogue, the house in Creechurch Lane would have been a secret meeting place of Jews or Marranos (Christianised Jews) before re-admission. The earlier of two leases, preserved in Bevis Marks indicate that the grantors of the lease are the two Churchwardens of St Katherine Creechurch and six other church wardens. This indicates that the freehold of the property still belonged to the church. It is significant in contrast to the late medieval pre-expulsion period, when the Church was at the forefront of ensuring that no 'unbelievers' were resident in their parish, that the 17th-century churches were prepared to lease property to Jews. Jamilly (1953/5, 128) states that 'In old congregational records, the sites of synagogues are often found to be held by non-Jewish Trustees or leased on short terms' This could also indicate that in the early days of re-admission the first settlers were reluctant to spend large sums of money on long leases for new and elaborate synagogues, as there was still the threat that they maybe expelled. This threat was removed in 1664 under Charles II (Hymanson 1946, 74).

Plans of Creechurch Lane

The seating plan (Figure 4.10) shows that the congregants sat on wooden benches, some of these being used in the later (1701) synagogue at Bevis Marks. Men and women were separated, sometimes by a wood or iron grid window. Separation of the sexes is still practised in Orthodox synagogues. The reason being that men should not be distracted by their women while they were praying and also that the women should not be distracted by the men. To get to the women's section, stairs from the ground floor lead to a gallery. The central platform (*bimah*) was for the rabbi and members of the congregation when they were called upon to read from the *Torah* (the first five books of the Hebrew Scriptures). The *bimah* faced the Ark where the *Torah* scrolls were kept,

Figure 4.12 Plaque on the Cunard building in Creechurch Lane in the City of London, EC3 marking the site of the Sephardi synagogue established in 1657 on the re-admission of Jews to England under Cromwell (photograph K.Marks 2007).

with the Ark pointing towards Jerusalem. The second plan shows the larger building following its reconstruction in 1674. Black (2003, 24) states that 'It was extended in 1673/4 to hold 250 congregants when the London community had grown to over 1, 000 persons'. 'The estimated cost of the extension scheme was £222 'a big sum in those days' (Renton 2004, 22).

The basic interior design of all synagogues following re-admission has not changed radically in over 300 years (Figure 4.11). All that remains to indicate where the synagogue was located is a plaque (Figure 4.12). Religious objects from this period, such as the *Sefer Torahs* (the hand-written scrolls containing the five books of Moses), silver ornaments and candle sticks are either used or are in the vaults in Bevis Marks.

4.1.5 The Great Synagogue EC3 [5]

Renton (2000, 30) notes that, 'From 1620 there was increased immigration of Ashkenazi Jews from Germany. The Ashkenazi community originally rented a house and then opened their first synagogue in Duke's Place (now Duke Street) Aldgate in 1690 with a membership of 200' According to Jamilly (1953/5, 75) 'Apart from the importance of its foundation, this building was of little architectural significance. In all probability a large room was used plain and poor in its furnishings'. Ashkenazim use a different form of service and pronunciation of Hebrew from the Sephardi which brought about separation. Roth (1950, 11) reports that, 'the earliest records (until 1722) of the Great Synagogue have been lost' although the traditional date for the establishment of the first 'German' Synagogue is 1690/2'.

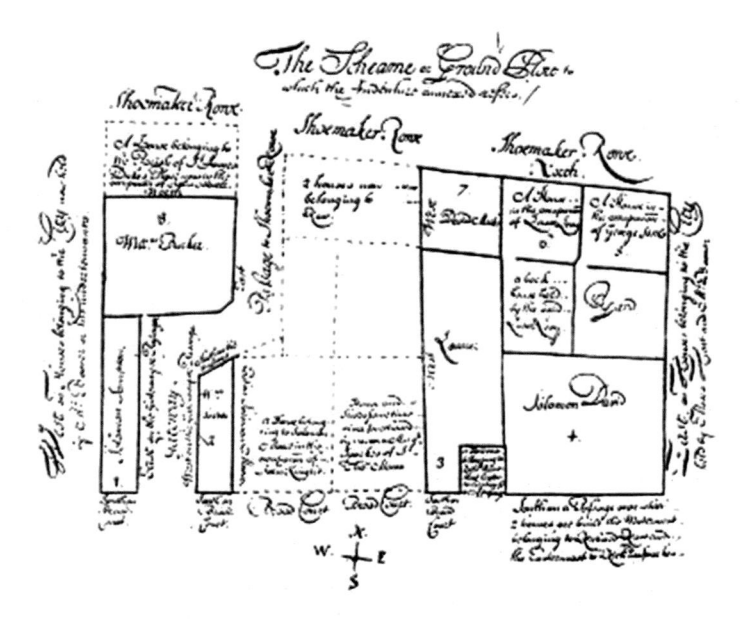

Figure 4.13 Ground Plan of the Great Synagogue established 1690/1692 (From a deed of 1721-2) (Roth, 1950).

The total cost was £2,000, donated by Moses Hart, leader of the Ashkenazi community in London at that time (Renton 2000, 50). Figure 4.13 shows the area that was demolished to make room for the synagogue, although no plans exist of the 17th century building. In the medieval period, the area was occupied by the Priory of the Holy Trinity. Up to the end of the 19th century, access was through a Gothic archway (Figure 4.14).

Figure 4.14 Duke's Place EC3. Gothic archway entrance in the 18th Century (From an engraving) (Roth, 1950).

Figure 4.15 The Great Synagogue entrance from Duke's Place EC3 early 19th century (From a wash drawing in the Jewish Museum London) (Roth 1950).

In 1722, the Ashkenazi community had some wealthy members but, in contrast to the Sephardi community, the majority was poor and uneducated. The poor were mostly unskilled and many became street traders, peddlers and small-scale shopkeepers. Roth (1950, 225) notes that, 'by 1760 the total Jewish community in England was estimated to be between 6,000-8,000, the overwhelming majority of whom lived in London'. By 1767, ten communities had been created in the provinces, with a total Jewish population in England of around 18,000. It is difficult to establish exact figures, as some immigrants would not have been members of a synagogue. Many of these immigrants were practising Ashkenazi Jews, and a larger synagogue was built in 1790 (Renton 2000, 30). Whilst other Ashkenazi synagogues were being opened in London, this remained the 'cathedral' of the community. The Great Synagogue and its congregation became the parent body of the Ashkenazi community in Britain, and its rabbi was considered to be the spiritual head (The Chief Rabbi) of the total community in Britain and throughout the 'Empire'. The Great Synagogue not only became a reflection of material success, but this community was also instrumental in the creation of several major charitable organisations that helped the poor from birth to death. In 1696, the Ashkenazi community purchased land for a cemetery in Alderney Road adjacent to the Sephardi cemetery.

The Architecture of The Great Synagogue

The site was on the corner of Shoemaker Row and Duke's Place, now Duke's Street and 'tenants moved with the added persuasion of a monetary payment' (Renton 2000, 50). In September 1722, on the eve of the Jewish New Year, the synagogue was dedicated. In the years ahead, the building was reconstructed and extended four times, reflecting the increasing wealth of some of the members, with the last reconstructions being in 1790 (Figure 4.17). Kadish (1996, 65/6) notes that, 'The Great Synagogue became the biggest place of worship in London, exceeding Bevis Marks and even larger than the Parish Church of St James, Duke's Place' (Figures 4.17/18). Newman (1976, 216) states that, 'By 1880 it had 400 male seat holders, by far the largest congregation in England'. The interior design of the Great Synagogue (Ashkenazi) was basically the same as Bevis Marks (Sephardi), with the exception being the position of the *bima* (central platform), which in the Sephardi Synagogues was more to the rear of the ground floor, rather than in the centre.

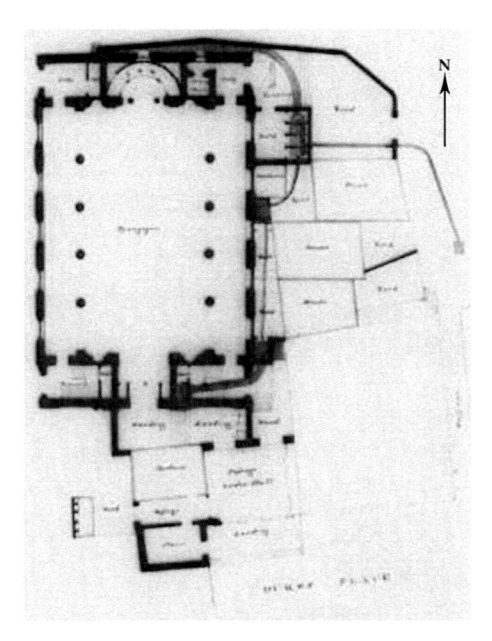

Figure 4.16 The Great Synagogue 1788-90 plans of the synagogue, the hall and adjoining houses Greater London Record Office (now London Metropolitan Archives) (Kadish 1996)

Figure 4.17 Interior of The Great Synagogue EC3 (1809) Print by A. Pugin and T. Rowlandson. From Ackerman's Microcosm of London (Reproduced by permission of Spanish and Portuguese Congregation 2009).

*Figure 4.18 The Great Synagogue Ark (*The Diaspora in Palestine Exploration Quarterly *1937).*

Figure 4.19 The Great Synagogue EC3. Service of intercession held in 1941 in bombed ruins (Renton 2000).

Figure 4.20 Duke's Place EC3. A temporary hut erected in 1943 in cleared grounds of The Great Synagogue: in use during and after World War II (Renton, 2000).

Figure 4.21 Plaque marking the site of The Great Synagogue in Duke's Place EC3.destroyed May 1941, not September 1941 as indicated on the plaque (photograph. K. Marks 2007).

On 11th May 1941, during the Blitz, The Great Synagogue was completely destroyed (Figure 4.19), and replaced by a temporary hut (Figure 4.20). During World War II this area of London was so badly damaged by repeated bombings that many of the City population were evacuated, never to return. In 1958, the hut was closed as there were insufficient members. Nothing remains of the original structure, although in Duke's Street there is a plaque marking the site (Figure 4.21).

4.1.6 Hambro Synagogue EC3 [6]

The name 'Hambro' may be a corruption of 'Hamburg' (Renton 2000, 39). Lindsay (1993, 47) notes that 'the founder of the community was Marcus Moses, who had come from there'. The prayer hall in a house in Magpie (Magpye) Alley, Fenchurch Street opened in 1707. At the same time, the community acquired a site for a cemetery in Hoxton, which is discussed in 5.1.9. A purpose-built synagogue was erected in the garden of the house in c.1720. It was the first independent, synagogue in London. According to Endelman, the Jewish establishment both Sephardi (Bevis Marks) and Ashkenazi (Duke's Place) tried to prevent its opening which would have resulted in them losing members (2002, 52). Renton notes that, '1718 was a milestone in the acceptance of Anglo-Jewry, as from this date English-born Jews were allowed to own freeholds' (2000, 40). The earliest cartographic appearance of this synagogue is on the Rocque map of 1746 (Bluer et al. 2006). (Newman 1976, 216) states that, 'In 1870, the Hambro Synagogue had 161 male seat-holders and, in spite of the overall growth in the Jewish community, in 1880 had the same number'. These figures show that the Orthodox community did not count women towards the number of seat holders; a community of this size was not economically viable. According to Lindsay, the total seating was for 218 men and 55 women (1993, 45) and '....it

Figure 4.22 Interior of The Hambro Synagogue, Fenchurch Street 1725-1893 (Roth 1940, 65).

Figure 4.23 Engraving of The Hambro Synagogue in Magpie Alley EC3 prior to demolition in 1893 (Guildhall Library, Corporation of London).

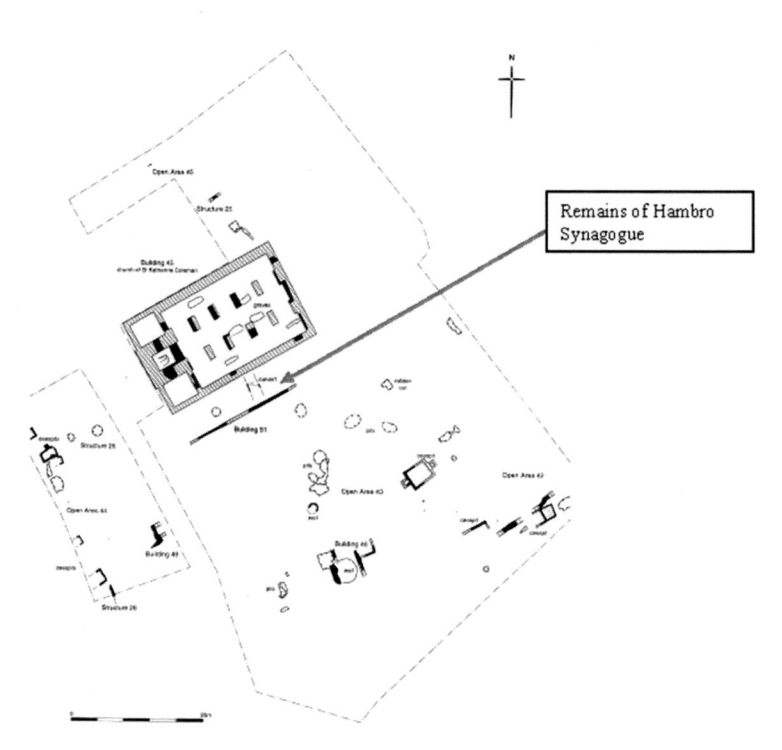

Figure 4.24 Hambro Synagogue, excavation (Building 51) Bluer et al.2006. (MoLAS)

appears to have been similar in design to the Spanish and Portuguese Synagogue' (Bevis Marks) (Ibid, 45). Roth (1950, 114) discusses how, 'The synagogue moved for the last time in 1893 from a site adjoining the church of St Katherine Coleman on the east side of Church Row, Fenchurch Street'. The *Jewish Chronicle* of 1886 quotes from the meeting of the General Council of the United Synagogue as follows '.... The Hambro Synagogue with a large financial deficit.... should be closed' (Ibid, 40).

The site of the Hambro synagogue is well attested from documentary sources and maps. It was eventually closed in 1892/3 sold by auction and pulled down to make room for city improvements. Excavations at Lloyd's Register, 71 Fenchurch Street in 2006 (MoLAS Monograph 30) revealed the remains of one wall of an addition to the 1725 building, can be dated to the late-19th century by the brick work (Bluer et al. 2006).

In 1899, a new Hambros Synagogue was opened in Adler Street Whitechapel E1. Adler Street is named after the Chief Rabbi Herman Adler (1891-1911). With the movement of the community, the Hambro Synagogue was closed in 1936 and amalgamated with The Great Synagogue (Ibid, 41). This synagogue was established as a break-away community from The Great Synagogue. The immigrant members were mainly German speaking, some coming from small communities in Germany, where they had small synagogues and did not feel comfortable in the large 'cathedral' synagogues in London. They were also unfamiliar with the form of service of the established community.

4.1.7   The New Synagogue E.C.3   [7]

Lindsay (1993, 89) states that, 'The New Synagogue began as one of the three City of London synagogues serving Ashkenazi Jews in the early years of the 18th century'. The first 'New Synagogue' was established in 1761. It was formed by mostly German immigrants and former congregants from The Great and Hambro synagogues. More synagogues were needed as the community grew, and there appears to have been some falling out amongst members of The Great and Hambro synagogues, the latter of which were dissatisfied with the English ways of the Great Synagogue (Ibid, 89). The prayer hall was above an inn in Bricklayers' Hall, Leadenhall Street and was used until 1838 (Figure 4.25). In 1761 this community established their burial ground in Brady Street (Stepney) as discussed in 5.1.6.

A *shofar* (ram's horn) used on High Holidays in synagogues was recovered from a waste heap in 1855 from Leadenhall Street and is discussed in Chapter 5.1.3. In 2008, the dating of the *shofar* was established by radio carbon dating. As it was found in 1855, the late-18th century or early-19th century is the probable date. Whilst the *shofar* has been dated, there is the possibility, but no evidence, that it may have had some connection with the New Synagogue, but it has no significance to the dating of this community.

Figure 4.25 Entrance to New Synagogue in Bricklayers Hall 1761 (or Bucklers Hall), Leadenhall Street.EC3. The symbols of the craft are seen outside the door to the side of the inn. The gentleman emerging from the door wears a tricorn-hat; presumably he is Jewish (Renton 2000, 44).

Figure 4.26 New Synagogue: Foundation stone in the New Synagogue, Stamford Hill N13, and showing dates of former synagogues (photograph K. Marks 2010).

In 1761 this new congregation purchased their own burial ground in Brady Street (Stepney), which contains several special features which are discussed in 5.1.6. In 1837/8, the congregation moved from Leadenhall Street to a new and larger synagogue in Great St Helens, Bishopsgate (Renton 2000, 44) (Figure 4.27).

In 1880, the New Synagogue had over 350 male seat-holders, while the 1895 Ordnance Survey Map shows that it had a capacity of 570. By the late 1880s the number of congregants was in decline, as many wealthy members who supported the synagogue financially had moved to the West End of London. The 1895 Ordnance Survey Map shows the building still as a synagogue, but by this date it was occupied by the Jewish Literary and Scientific Institution (Ibid, 46). Figure 4.27 is the only engraving to have survived that shows the interior of the synagogue.

Figure 4.27 the interior of the New Synagogue in Great St. Helens, Bishopsgate EC3. (Steel engraving by H.Melville, after T.H. Shepherd from London Interiors, 1841) (Renton 2000,46).

The site was eventually sold, nothing now remains. However in the Cheltenham Synagogue, which is discussed (4.2.9), as reported by the *Jewish Chronicle* (1999), there are the '*the light oak Ark, bimah, benches and reading desk, now over 230 years old, were a gift from the New Synagogue, when it moved, in 1837, from Leadenhall Street to Bishopsgate*' (Ibid, 46). The final move was in 1915 to Egerton Road N6; this synagogue is still in use. It can be seen that some of the interior fittings were brought from St Helen's, including the lamps on the *bimah*, the curtains and silverware, as well as the Ark. Of these four London synagogues (Bevis Marks, The Great, Hambro and the New) from the early re-settlement period, only Bevis Marks remains. Some of the interior fittings of the others have been moved to other functioning synagogues or are in museums.

4.1.8 New West End Synagogue W2 [8]

The architect of St Petersburgh Place Victorian Synagogue was George Audsley (1838-1925), the same architect that designed Liverpool's Princes Road Synagogue, which is discussed in (4.2.19.2). There are similarities in features between the two

Figure 4.28 The New West End Synagogue, St. Petersburgh Place Bayswater. W2. Foundation stone (1877) (photograph K. Marks 2010).

Figure 4.29 The New West End Synagogue, St Petersburgh Place W2 (The Builder July 1878).

buildings with Audsley using some of the Liverpool firms who had worked on Princes Road (Kadish 2006, 39). Jamilly (1996, 201) writes that, 'Audsley, who was not Jewish, worked with a Nathan Joseph, the clerk of the works, who administered the contract and advised on liturgical aspects'. The New West End membership indicates the migration of the Ashkenazi Orthodox community who were middle and upper class and the social 'elite' away from the East End of London in the middle-to-late 19th century to the West End; this is discussed below in 6.1. Members lived in Bayswater, Notting Hill, Kensington and Hammersmith. Amongst the membership and major donors for the building of the new synagogue were Leopold de Rothschild and the banker Samuel Montagu. The New West End Synagogue was upgraded by English Heritage in 2008 from Grade 11 star to Grade 1; making it one of only three synagogues in England with Liverpool and Bevis Marks to be Grade 1 listed. The synagogue is described by English Heritage (News Release 2007) as, 'being among the top 3% of the countries most architecturally and historic important buildings'. The foundation stone was laid in 1877 (Figure 4.28), and the building was consecrated in 1879. The inscription on the foundation faces inwards.

It was suggested by one of the members of the community that at some time it was turned inwards to avoid vandalism (personal contact 2010).

The outside of the synagogue is made of red brick and Mansfield stone and terracotta dressings with a slate roof. Kadish (2006, 39) describes the style of the building as 'combining Gothic, Romanesque, Assyrian and with Moorish elements'. The frontage and façade of the building is a three part composition with corner turrets and a central section that has a large rose window set within a cusped horseshoe arch (Figure 4.29) (Ibid,39). According to Jamilly (1996, 201), 'Joseph rejected neo-classical styles and Gothic as essentially Christian'. The basilica-shaped prayer hall is approached through the foyer containing memorial and donor tablets and a war memorial with two staircases leading to the ladies' gallery.

The interior was originally lit by gas and converted to electricity in 1894, although, some of the original gas fittings still survive (personal observation 2010). The stained glass windows were added in the early 20th century; they were not part of the original building. Kadish states that, 'The rose window over the Ark was added in 1935' (Ibid, 39). It incorporates Jewish symbols such as a *Sefer Torah* (Scrolls of the Law) *Luhot* (Tablets of the Law), *menorah* (candelabrum), *shofar* (ram's horn trumpet, blown in synagogue to mark the Jewish New Year) and others. Kadish also notes

Figure 4.30 Interior of The New West End Synagogue, St. Petersburgh Place, Bayswater, W2 interior, showing the Ark and later rose window (photograph K. Marks 2010).

Figure 4.31 The New West End Synagogue. St Petersburgh Place Bayswater W2 Unusual clock in vestibule with Hebrew letters showing the hour (photograph K. Marks 2010).

that, 'the gilded and turreted Ark, Assyrian in inspiration, is set beneath a large horse shoe arch. Many of the elaborate interior features were added after the building was first used, all paid for by members of the congregation; this includes the present colour scheme of alabaster, green and gold carried out in 1895' (Ibid, 39).

The name of major donors for the building of the synagogue and the subsequent improvements are inscribed on the donor tablets in the entrance hall. According to Kadish (2006, 137), the *bimah*, which is unusually placed slightly towards the rear of the ground floor, was made by *Norbury, Upton and Paterson* of Liverpool, and was installed in 1907. No two capitals around the bimah are of the same design (personal observation 2010).

The outside of the building and the opulent additions to the interior, with its mosaic floor, glass rose front window, alabaster and marble walls, suggest that no expense was spared when this 'cathedral' synagogue was built. The New West End Synagogue represents the increased prosperity and confidence of West London Orthodox Jews from the end of the 19th century.

4.1.9　　　　　　Princelet Street Synagogue E1　　　　　　　　[9]

Princelet Street, although no longer used for services is the last remaining small synagogue of the 19th century in the East End of London. The original Georgian terraced house was built in 1719. In 1743, it became the house and workplace of a Huguenot (French Calvinists) weaver, as did most of the houses on this street. The Huguenots came to England from France fleeing Catholic persecution. Many of the roof lines of the houses in Princelet Street still have wide attic windows in order to give maximum light to the interior weaving rooms (personal observation, 2010). In 1826, following the collapse of the silk industry, the Huguenots moved out and assimilated with the local population. Irish immigrants then came into Spitalfields.

In 1869/70 when the Jewish community in London had reached over 20, 000, the building was purchased by a group of Polish Jews fleeing Eastern Europe. They formed the Loyal United Friendly Society, with a membership of 120 (Renton 2000, 173). Lindsay notes that 'The congregation mainly consisted of poor Jews who worked in the tailoring and garment trade' (1993, 61). The main prayer hall was built in the back garden of the house. The ladies' gallery was on three sides and reached by an internal staircase. Donor boards are still evident with the amounts given by each of the contributors (personal observation 2010). With the decline of the Jewish East End after World War II and the movement of the community, mainly to North London, the synagogue was eventually closed in the 1960s. It is now partly restored and is the Museum of Immigration, dedicated to the immigrants of the district: Huguenots, Jews and Bengalis.

Princelet Street is the last remaining of over 100 small synagogues and prayer halls of the period under discussion, and it was in use into the 20th century in the East End of London. Princelet Street was one of many prayer halls and meeting places of poor Jews who did not want to be members of the established synagogues.

In the small synagogues such as Princelet Street, Jews could pray and meet with fellow refugees from the same culture and who spoke the same language. At this time the building is mostly closed to visitors due its poor state of preservation.

Figure 4.32 Princelet Street Synagogue 1870 Now Museum of Immigration (photograph K.Marks 2010).

Figure 4.33 Princelet Street now Princelet Street Synagogue: interior view. (Lindsay 1993, 59).

4.1.10 Sandy's Row Synagogue EC1 [10]

Figure 4.34 Sandy's Row Synagogue E1 1854 interior (photograph K.Marks 2009).

According to Kadish (2006, 10), the original Sandy's Row Dutch immigrant community came to England in c.1854. These immigrants worked mainly in the tobacco industry and set up their own independent congregation (Ibid10). They later established the synagogue and formed a religious Friendly Society in Spitalfields using small rooms in the Spitalfields district. Sandy's Row was originally a Huguenot church and was then used by a number of Protestant and Baptist groups before being acquired for use as a synagogue in 1870. It is one of the earliest examples of a chapel conversion for Jewish worship in Britain (Ibid, 10). Regular services are still held there, and it is the oldest Ashkenazi congregation in London. Like many synagogues, the outside has no special significance. The inside, modelled on The Great Synagogue in Duke's Place, has the same basic interior design as all synagogues of this period. However, the interior has a unique feature. For this, one must look to the origins of the community, Holland, as the synagogue is decorated in orange and white, the Dutch national colours (Figure 4.34).

From a cultural perspective, this shows that although the immigrants had left their native country, they wanted to retain their link with their homeland. In view of the historic and cultural significance of this, English Heritage and the Lottery Fund have awarded a grant of £250, 000 towards much-needed repairs and decorations, which has to be at least matched by funds raised by the community. In the basement are the synagogue archives, which will be included in a new heritage museum.

4.1.11   Western Synagogue WC1   [11]

Lindsay (1993, 67) reports that, 'Westminster in the 18th century was a very different place from the overcrowded City of London and in particular the East End with its unpaved streets and lack of sanitation'. According to Mathias Levy (1897) in his history of the Western Synagogue, it was established in 1774. According to Renton (1993, 67), 'a later history by the Revd Arthur Barnett who was a minister of the congregation considered a more likely date would have been c.1765'. The synagogue records show that the congregation moved buildings over 10 times in its 200-year history before it finally closed in 1991 and amalgamated with Marble Arch Synagogue. This exemplifies the movement, growth and increasing prosperity of its members, who came from a Polish culture rather than the Spanish and Portuguese of Bevis Marks and German of The Great Synagogue. The first room of prayer (1761) was in a private house in Great Pulteney Street W1, the second was established in 1765 in the locality of the Strand in Denmark Court (Figure 4.35). The Strand was more convenient for those who were living in Westminster than having to walk on Saturdays and High Holidays to the City. The site was demolished in 1830, and from the Ordnance Survey Map would appear that it is today the location of the Strand Palace Hotel. Following demolition, the congregation moved to an empty theatre nearby but still in Denmark Court (Ibid, 50). According to Renton 'the lease for this building was signed by members of the congregation living in the Covent Garden and Strand area (Ibid, 51)'. When the lease expired, the next move in 1826 was to St Alban's Place, Haymarket SW1 which was in use to 1914 (Figure 4.36). A temporary premises was used in Whitfield Street W1 and in 1915, there was a further move to Alfred Place Westminster (Figure 4.37) (Ibid, 52). By the 1880s, the Western synagogue membership included some of the most eminent members of the Jewish community in England: Sir Samuel Montagu, MP (Lord Swaythling); Sir Stuart Samuel, MP; Hannah de Rothschild; and Lady Rosebery, wife of the fifth Earl who became Prime Minister (Lindsay 1993, 68).

Alfred Place Synagogue was destroyed during the Blitz in 1941; all that remains apart from religious artefacts are the doors, which are now used at the entrance of the prayer hall of the Western Synagogue Cemetery, Montague Road, Edmonton (Figure 4.38) (Ibid, 55). Later synagogues of this congregation from 1943 onwards

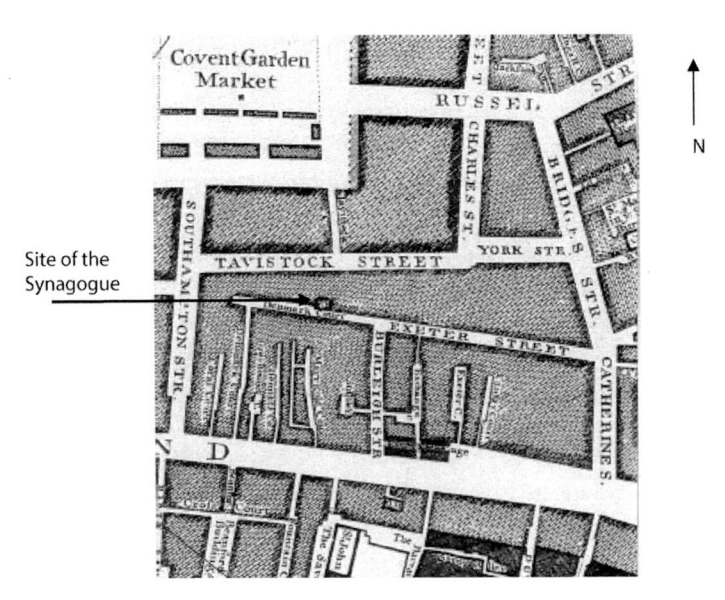

52   THE ARCHAEOLOGY OF ANGLO-JEWRY IN ENGLAND AND WALES 1656–C.1880

Figure 4.35 A map showing location of Western Synagogue in The Strand at Convent Garden W1 (c.1761) and Denmark Court. Detail from the Map of Georgian London *(London Topographical Society Publication No 126, 1982).*

Figure 4.36 Western Synagogue interior St. Albans Place WC2, service celebrating the re-consecration (Illustrated London News 1851).

Figure 4.37 Western Synagogue, Alfred Place, Westminster WC1 interior 1915 (Renton 2000, 54).

Figure 4.38 Doors from the Western Synagogue Alfred Place, used for the entrance to the prayer hall of the Western Synagogue Cemetery in Montague Road Edmonton N18 (Renton 2000, 55).

are not discussed here. The Western Synagogue community, which was a secessionist congregation from The Great Synagogue purchased their own cemetery in Bancroft Road, Mile End E1 in 1815 and later opened a new cemetery in Fulham Road SW3 both of which are discussed later in (5.1.5. and 5.1.7).

Migration from the early areas of London Jewish settlement began in the middle of the 19th century. Transport became more widely available with the introduction of the horse bus, later followed by tram and train services. Renton (2000, 26) notes that, 'By 1824 prayer books were distributed to over 20 synagogues in areas of London outside the East End in areas such as the West End and north London and that the life span of a Jewish congregation seems to be around 50 to 70 years, from the foundation of a synagogue to its eventual decline'.

4.1.12　　　　　　West London Synagogue W.1　　　　　　[12]

The Reform movement began in Germany in 1819, but emerged in Britain in 1842. It developed from the need for religious changes. Unlike the Orthodox, services are held in a mixture of Hebrew and English. At first women sat separately from men, later men and women sat together. Unlike the Orthodox women can now also be rabbis. The definitive book on the Reform Movement is *'Tradition and Change, A History of the Reform Movement in Britain1840-1995' (Kershen et al. 1995)*. This study informs us not only to the Reform Movement but also makes some comparisons with the Orthodox community.

The West London Reform Synagogue was formed by Sephardi Jews living in the West End of London, who broke away c.1842 from the Sephardi Bevis Marks congregation in the City. Lipman (1954, 15) observes that, 'The first congregation included 19 Sephardim and 5 Ashkenazim families. The first synagogue was in Burton

Figure 4.39 West London: Reform Synagogue: Entrance in Upper Berkeley Street W1 (Lindsay 1993, 7).

Street, Bloomsbury WC1'. No pictures or plans exist of this building, and by 1849, it was too small, and the community moved to a larger building at 50 Margaret Street W1, near Oxford Circus. In the following 20 years, the community continued to grow. In 1870, the congregation moved to its current location in Upper Berkeley Street W.1. The West London Synagogue is the 'cathedral' synagogue of Reform Judaism and the oldest and largest Reform synagogue in Britain. The first congregation lived to the west of the City of London and in the West End, in Bloomsbury, St Marylebone, Mayfair and Westminster. Members of the Reform Movement were not allowed to be buried in Orthodox cemeteries and their marriages were and are still not recognised by the Orthodox. This led to the first Reform cemetery in London being established in Balls Pond Road in 1843 (discussed in 5.1.10).

West London Synagogue is an outstanding example of a synagogue in Byzantine architectural style; this style is a form of Orientalism, associated with the architecture of the eastern Mediterranean. Black (2003, 69) notes how, 'the magnificent interior of the present building reflects its origins. The strong Moorish influence in the great arches of the interior and cupola above the Ark are eloquent reminders of the Sephardi background of the founding fathers of the synagogue'. Until 1897, the *bimah* was in the centre of the prayer hall (Figure 4.39). It was later moved in front of the Ark, which is typical of other Reform synagogues. Lindsay (1993, 73) reports that 'The ark is notable for its open grill work through which the *Sifrei Torah* (the Scrolls of the Torah) can be seen by members of the congregation throughout the services'. In front of the Ark is a 'Moorish' everlasting oil light, which is suspended on a chain from the domed ceiling. The gallery was for women only until the mid 20th century, when it was decided that men and women should sit together. Over the entrance to the ladies gallery are inscriptions in Hebrew, with the opening and closing verses from Proverbs 31:10-31. These read in English as follows:

'Who can find a noble wife?
She is worth far more than rubies
Her husband trusts her completely
She gives him all the important things he needs'

Figure 4.40 West London Reform Synagogue Illustrated London News (June 1872).

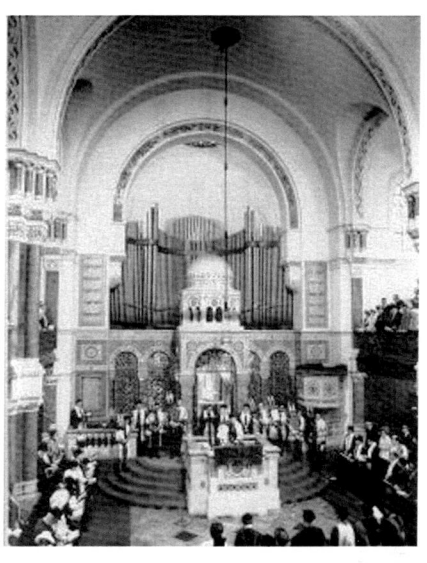

Figure 4.41 West London Reform Synagogue: later interior view taken when ordination of rabbis' service was taking place, showing bimah now in front of Ark. (Lindsay 1993, 74).

This is part of the traditional prayer praising the Jewish wife and is said or sung on Friday evening at the Sabbath table. Entry to the gallery is by two staircases at the end of a panelled vestibule. At the base of the staircase is a pair of bronze lamps brought from the previous Reform synagogue in Margaret Street, as was the brass *hanukiah* (candelabra), which is to the side of the Ark. The main prayer hall is dominated by the Ark and the organ behind the *bimah*. Kadish (2006, 42) observes that, 'West London is the only synagogue in England that an integrated pipe organ which is situated behind a grill behind the Ark with the choir'.

4.2 Provincial communities and synagogues

A brief history of provincial Jewish communities from c.1740-1880 is provided above in Chapter 2.4. In the 35 cities and towns studied, Jewish cemeteries remain, whilst evidence of synagogues is more limited. In cities such as Exeter and Plymouth, the original 18th-century Georgian synagogue buildings still function. Where small Orthodox communities once existed in towns such as Coventry, Falmouth and Merthyr Tydfil, disused synagogues can be recognized by Heritage plaques, Hebrew inscriptions on the porticos, or Stars of David on the windows. Several synagogues are now boarded up or used for other purposes. In Canterbury, the former synagogue is now used as the music centre of Kings' School. In larger cities where there is a community that has moved to the suburbs, such as Hull and Sheffield, the outside of the abandoned synagogue in the city centre is stll evident.

Jewish presence in 12 of the provincial towns researched can be traced back to the early/middle18th century, though the communities have moved from the areas where they first settled, in some cases the community no longer exists. For example, the former synagogue building in Penzance, where there is no longer a community, can only be seen from the rear (Figure 4.117), where original windows are evident. Otherwise, there is no means of recognizing the building other than from town community records and 19th-century Ordnance Survey Maps. In Birmingham, the 1809 Synagogue building is now a Masonic Hall. In Manchester, which has the largest Jewish community outside London, out of three 18th and 19th 'cathedral' synagogues in Cheetham Hill only one building remains, the Spanish and Portuguese former synagogue established 1874; it is now the Jewish Museum. The Great Synagogue in Manchester established 1780 went out of use as the community moved away from Cheetham Hill; the building became derelict and demolished in 1986. The Reform Synagogue, also in Cheetham Hill, was destroyed by bombing in 1941. In Nottingham, although the community was established in 1822, the earliest synagogue remaining is from 1889 in a former Methodist chapel. In the case of small congregations, that at first held services in halls or private houses, no physical evidence of these buildings remain, with locations of a few only known from synagogue records.

In cities such as Birmingham, Liverpool, Leeds, Manchester and Newcastle the first immigrants settled in the poor areas. As some prospered, they moved to more affluent areas, but they were always within walking distance of their synagogue. With this migration and demographic change, synagogues were either destroyed or closed or used for other purposes. In the case of these cities, the research sets out the evidence by which this can be established from documents and First-and-Second Edition Ordnance Survey Maps (1880s/1901).

The Statistical Account of the Jewish Congregations in the British Empire (1845) (Figure 6.2) collected by the Chief Rabbi's Office lists provincial Orthodox Ashkenazi communities with supporting data, such as number of members, whether there was a cemetery and whether there was a mikveh. Roth (1950, 13) notes that in 1851 a religious census was carried out, '… which provided among other things the approximate date of the construction of the synagogue'. By 1840-1850, the era of the railway had begun, and the communities in the industrial provincial cities were growing in number, but they were yet not numerically preponderant. Out of the first 23 communities established by 1815, 17 were in ports. By the end the 19th century, many of these had declined and in some cases ceased to exist. Religious artifacts from closed provincial synagogues such as Falmouth and Penzance have been recovered from local antique dealers and are now in museums.

4.2.1	Bath*:	Community established c.1800: synagogue closed 1901
4.2.2.1	Birmingham***:	Community established 1730: synagogues prior to Singers Hill
4.2.2.2	Birmingham***:	Singers Hill Synagogue 1856-still in use
4.2.3	Bradford***:	Community established c.1873: synagogue: 1880-still in use

4.2.4.1	Brighton****:	Community established 1800: synagogues prior to Middle Street
4.2.4.2	Brighton****:	Middle Street Synagogue 1874: now closed for regular services
4.2.5.1	Bristol***:	Community established 1753: synagogues prior to Park Row
4.2.5.2	Bristol***:	Park Row Synagogue 1870-still in use
4.2.6	Canterbury****:	Community established 1760: synagogue closed 1931
4.2.7	Cardiff***:	Community established c1840
4.2.8	Chatham***:	Community established c.1750: synagogue 1869-still in use
4.2.9	Cheltenham**:	Community established 1824: synagogue 1837-still in use
4.2.10	Coventry****:	Community established c.1800: synagogue 1870-2008
4.2.11	Dover**:	Community established c.1770: synagogue bombed in 1941-no community remains
4.2.12	Exeter**:	Community established 1763: synagogue 1764-still in use
4.2.13	Falmouth**:	Community established 1740: synagogue1808-1880-no community remains
4.2.14	Gloucester**:	Community established c.1784-no community remains
4.2.15.1	Hull***:	Community established c.1810: early synagogues
4.2.15.2	Hull***:	Robinson Row Synagogue 1826-1902
4.2.16	Ipswich***	Community established 1792: synagogue in use to 1877-no community remains
4.2.17	King's Lynn***:	Community established 1747: synagogue in use to 1846
4.2.18	Leeds***:	Community established c.1820: first synagogue 1850
4.2.19.1	Liverpool**:	Community established c.1750: early synagogues
4.2.19.2	Liverpool**:	Princes Road Synagogue established 1874-still in use
4.2.20.1	Manchester***:	Community established c.1780: early synagogues
4.2.20.2	Manchester***:	Great Synagogue established 1858-demolished 1986
4.2.20.3	Manchester***:	Reform Synagogue established 1858-destroyed 1941
4.2.20.4	Manchester***:	Spanish and Portuguese Synagogue 1874-now The Jewish Museum
4.2.21	Merthyr Tydfil***:	Community established 1848: synagogue1872-1983-no community remains
4.2.22.1	Newcastle***:	Community established 1830: early synagogues
4.2.22.2	Newcastle***:	Leazes Park Synagogue 1879-1987
4.2.23	Norwich***:	Community established 1813: synagogue established 1835: destroyed 1942
4.2.24	Nottingham***:	Community established 1822: synagogue 1889
4.2.25	Oxford***:	Community established 1841: synagogues 1847-1884
4.2.26	Penzance**:	Community established 1807: synagogue 1807-1892-no community remains
4.2.27	Plymouth**:	Community established c.1752: synagogue 1761/2-still in use
4.2.28	Portsmouth/ Southsea**:	Community established c.1730: present synagogue 1936 (previous building 1780-1936 in Portsea)
4.2.29	Ramsgate****:	Synagogue 1833: still occasionally used-no community remains
4.2.30	Sheerness***:	Community established 1790: synagogue 1811-1887-no community remains
4.2.31	Sheffield****:	Community established 1838: first synagogue 1851
4.2.32	Southampton****:	Community established 1833: synagogue1864-1964
4.2.33	Sunderland***:	Community established c.1781: 1861-1928
4.2 34	Swansea***:	Community established 1768: synagogues 1740-1941
4.2.35	Yarmouth Great***	Community established 1801: 1847-1892-no community remains
4.2.36	Conclusion	

* visited 2008   ** visited 2009   *** visited 2010   **** visited 2011

4.2.1 Bath [13]

Roth (1950, 27) notes that, 'the first mention of Jews in Bath was 1736. Jews frequented Bath for the waters at a relatively early date'. The traditional date for the establishment of the community is c.1800 (Ibid, 110). The community in the 19th century would have been small. The Chief Rabbi's questionnaire of 1845 shows that there were four householders, five paying seat-holders, a *chazzan* (reader to the congregation) and a *shochet* (ritual slaughterer), 15 males, 12 females and 23 children. Services would have also been attended by Jewish visitors taking the health-giving waters. The reader to the congregation, Solomon Wolfe, served the community for 50 years (c.1815-1865), as recorded on his headstone in Bath cemetery (5.2.1) (personal observation 2008).

No Jewish community remains in Bath, nor is there any evidence of the 19th century synagogue, earlier halls or houses used for prayers. According to Lipman (1954, 185) in 1850 the community was reckoned to be around 50 persons. The community comprised mostly shopkeepers and tradespersons scattered around the centre of the town and provided services connected to the spa (Brown et al, 136/137). The Bath and East Somerset Council Monument Full Report (2008) states that '…in 1812 a school moved out of a building in Orchard Street and although a private dwelling it was used as a synagogue'. Prior to opening in Corn Street (Figure 4.42), services had been held in three different halls. Brown (1986, 146) notes that 'The clue to the whereabouts of the first synagogue lies in the history of Bath theatres'. These buildings would have been suitable for use as a synagogue. Brown continues 'In 1842 the synagogue moved to Corn Street and was in use until c.1880s' (Ibid, 146). It was closed in 1901. According to Roth (1950, 28), 'there is no remaining evidence for any of these buildings, the Corn Street building was subject

Figure 4.42 Bath: The building on the bend in the road is the Corn Street Synagogue (Brown et al, 1982-6, 149).

to flooding'. They were destroyed by bombing in World War II. The one advantage that the Bath community had over many others was that it had a natural mikveh, the Roman baths. With its ample supply of spring water, *The 1845 Statistical Account of the Congregations in the British Empire* (Fig.6.2) shows that the public baths were used for ritual bathing. There are today a few Jewish families living in or near the city, who mainly join the community for services in Bristol, 12 miles away.

4.2.2.1   Birmingham   [14]

The urban topography of the community in Birmingham is discussed in Chapter 6.2.1. Roth (1950, 110) notes that, the 'traditional foundation or first mention of community was c.1730'. Documents and physical evidence from this period do not exist. Roth continues '....it is impossible to go into great detail regarding the community's origin' (Ibid, 32). The first two synagogues were in private houses and were established c.1780. The area known as the 'Froggery' was the location of the synagogues. The Froggery was demolished in the middle of the 19th century and is now New Street Railway Station. The synagogue prior to Singers Hill was in Severn Street, established in 1809 near to Hurst Street and Inge Street, both known Jewish areas.

In 1813, there were Dissenter riots when several churches and the synagogue were attacked and looted. Kadish (2006, 121) states that, 'the synagogue was rebuilt in 1825-7'. This building still exists and is now a Masonic hall. In addition to the Masonic regalia decorating the walls, in the rear section there is a banqueting hall with *Magen David* (Star of David) decorations on wall brackets as well as *Magen David* stars engraved in the fire- place (personal observation 2010). The former Ark surround has fluted Doric columns. Other than these decorations, there is nothing remaining which identifies the building as previously being a synagogue. For a brief period from 1853-1855, there was a schism within the community, and a breakaway synagogue was founded in Wrottesley Street. This did not last; the building was sold, later to be converted to a chapel. The Wrottesley congregation joined with the members of Severn Street to form the Singers Hill Synagogue, established in 1856.

Figure 4.43   Birmingham: The position of the Ark in the former Severn Street Synagogue 1825, now Masonic Hall (photograph Birmingham City Council X713554/15).

4.2.2.2 Birmingham: Singers Hill

Figure 4.44 .Birmingham: Singers Hill Synagogue 1856 front elevation (by permission S. Busby).

Figure 4.45 Birmingham: Singers Hill Synagogue, interior (by permission S. Busby).

Singers Hill Synagogue is over 150 years old and is the oldest 'cathedral Synagogue' in England; it holds services every day. Kadish (2006, 117) observes that, 'it was designed by a local architect Henry Thomason (1826-1901) who was later responsible for the building of Birmingham's Council House and Art Gallery buildings which are within walking distance of the synagogue'. Levy (1984, 15) states that, 'When it was built the site held a commanding position from which could be observed the distant fields of Edgbaston, there being at that time no houses in between'. The outside is built of red brick with stone dressings. The entrance is through a courtyard, where on either side there were houses for the resident ministers (Figure 4.44). Kadish (1996, 149) states that, 'there is no mikveh, the mikveh at this date is recorded as being in the public bathhouse in Kent Street, where there was a natural spring'. According to Rabbi Arkush, special baths with their own piping were installed by the local authorities to ensure that the mikveh was *kosher* (conformed to Jewish law).

The main prayer hall, which can hold a congregation of a 1, 000, is built to a basilica plan, with the central part of the building separated from the side aisles by arcades. There is a gallery, mainly for women, on three sides supported by columns of Bath stone. At the top of the columns are Corinthian capitals. Originally there were ornamental grid wrought-iron balustrades fronting the gallery, which have since been removed. The mahogany Ark is set in the east wall, facing Jerusalem (personal observation 2009).

4.2.3 Bradford [15]

Figure 4.46 Bradford: Bowland Street Reform Synagogue 1880/1881 Grade 11 front elevation (photograph K. Marks 2010).

Cecil Roth in *The Rise of Provincial Jewry* (1950) *1740-1840* does not include Bradford, even though it is known by local historian Nigel Grizzard that there were Jews in the city from 1820s. Neither is Bradford included in *the 1845 Statistical Accounts of the Congregations of the British Empire* (Figure 6.2), issued by the office of the Chief Rabbi. The reason for this is that the first community and synagogue in Bradford was comprised of Reform Jews who were not recognized by the Orthodox authorities.

According to Kadish (2006, 165), 'Bradford is unique (in England) in that it boasted a Reform synagogue before it acquired an Orthodox one'. 'The architects of the building were the *Healey Brothers and Francis,* known for designing several churches in West Yorkshire' (Ibid, 165). However, the design of the outside of Bowland Street Synagogue, with its distinctive architecture, could be mistaken for an Islamic temple (personal observation 2010) (Figure 4.46). 'Constructed in local Bolton Stone with red sienna and cream stone the building employs a technique known as *ablaq* in Arabic' (Ibid, 165). Gizzard (personal contact 2010) suggests

Figure 4.47) Bradford; Bowland Street Reform Synagogue, interior–the Ark (photograph K. Marks 2010).

that the outside is Moorish (inspired by Spain and North Africa) as the architect realized he was not designing a church and wanted to use a distinctive style to signify the difference. The Hebrew inscription above the main west door is from Isaiah 26:2, which translates in English as: *'Then you will be called the City that does what is right. You will be called The Faithful City'*. The inscription is decorated with a Star of David. There are four large front traceried windows. Along the front roofline there is a row of crested shapes, which add to the Islamic style of the façade. Above this, and beneath the central Star of David, is the main Hebrew inscription from Genesis 28:17 which in English is:

Jacob was afraid. He said, 'How holy this place is! This must be the house of God; this is the gate of heaven' (personal observation 2010).

The interior is dominated by the Ark, again in the Islamic style, framed by a cusped and lobed arch (Figure 4.47), on top of which is a dome with a Decalogue with the first words of the Ten Commandments. Under this in Hebrew is the first line of the *Shema* prayer (Deuteronomy 6:4), which in English reads *'The Lord is our God, The Lord is One'*. The Ark is made of wood, painted white and gilded.

Unlike Orthodox synagogue prayer halls, the *bimah* is in front of the Ark facing the congregation at the east end. Unlike the Reform synagogue in Upper Berkeley Street London (1869), there is no women's gallery, the first synagogue to be built in this way; men and women would have been seated on different sides of the prayer hall. There is an organ, which was the custom in continental Reform synagogues. The Bowland Street Reform Synagogue is mostly unchanged from when it was originally built by wealthy German immigrants who came to Bradford in the 19th century to trade wool. Bradford was to become the world centre of the woolen industry. Unfortunately, the synagogue is in urgent need of repair (personal observation 2010). In 2013 it received a major grant from English Heritage to make repairs.

4.2.4 Brighton [16]

There were individual Jews in Brighton from 1766. The community was established c.1800 (Roth 1950, 110). Spector (1968/9, 42) dates the first community from 1782.

Figure 4.49 Brighton: façade of former Devonshire Place. Regency synagogue in use 1825-1875. (photograph K. Marks 2011).

Figure 4.48 Brighton: Jew Street, wall with bricked up stone entrance possibly part of the synagogue? c. 1792 (photograph K. Marks 2011).

Figure 4.50 Brighton: Middle Street Synagogue, foundation stone 1874 (photograph K. Marks 2011)

Brighton: synagogues prior to Middle Street

The first room of prayer in Brighton to c.1792; it was in Jew Street, a narrow alley in the centre of the town (Spector 1968/9, 43) (Figure 4.48). Around 1808, the community moved to Poune's Court (now demolished) off West Street. In 1825, with growing numbers (c.100 persons), a new synagogue was built in Devonshire Place, now converted into apartments. The facade remains with the words *'Jews' Synagogue'* just below the pediment (Figure 4.49) (personal observation 2011). The foundation stone for the new synagogue was laid in 1874 with the building consecrated in 1875. Brighton: Middle Street Synagogue established 1874-in use to c.2005.

The façade is built in the Italian Romanesque style, using polished Aberdeen granite for the main columns with Portland stone bases (Kadish 2006, 73). There is a wheel window in the gable. On the façade above the entrance there is a carved inscription from Genesis 28:17, which in English reads, *'How holy this place is. This must be the house of God. This is the gate of heaven'*. The chronogram in Hebrew letters establishes when the building was opened, 1875. A stone tablet above the gable in the shape of a *Torah* (Five Books of Moses) scroll bears more biblical references and an abbreviated form of the Ten Commandments (personal observation 2011).

Figure 4.51 Brighton: Middle Street Synagogue 1874, façade and entrance (photograph K. Marks 2011).

Middle Street was the first synagogue in Britain to have electric light. According to Spector (1974, 48), 'The synagogue benefited from the generosity of the Sassoon family'. Baroness Rothschild and Hannah Rothschild gave the congregation a magnificent candelabra. Sir Moses Montefiore presented the congregation with a *Sefer Torah* (scrolls with the Five Books of Moses) There are two stained glass windows dedicated to Hannah Rothschild (d.1890), wife of Lord Rosebery. There is a 1845 brass *hanukiah* (lit during the Festival of *Hanukah*) which was brought from the Regency Synagogue in Devonshire Place (Figure 4.49). The interior is splendid, Kadish states (2006,73) that, 'it is basilican (a large oblong hall with colonnades) in plan and a riot of marble, brass, mosaic stencilling, gilding and stained glass'. Unique in England, the Ark is set within a polygonal apse, lit from the top by a decorated glass semi-dome. The brass pulpit was donated by Sir Albert Sassoon (Kadish 2006, 74) (Figure 4.53).

Figure 4.52 Brighton: Middle Street Synagogue, showing bimah *(central platform) and view towards the Ark (photograph K.Marks 2011).*

Figure 4.53 Brighton: Middle Street Synagogue, 1845 brass hanukiah *(used on the festival of Hanukah, commemorating the rededication of the Temple (photograph K. Marks 2011).*

Figure 4.54 Brighton: Middle Street Synagogue, one of the capitals depicting fruits and foliage from the Holy Land (photograph K, Marks 2011).

4.2.5.1 Bristol [17]

The traditional date of the foundation of the Bristol community was c.1753 (Roth 1950, 110). *The 1845 Statistical Accounts of the Congregations in The British Empire 1845,* show Bristol with one of the largest Jewish communities in the provinces with c.150 male adult synagogue members, three paid officials, a rabbi, *shochet* (ritual slaughterer)

Figure 4.55 Bristol: Ashmead's map of Bristol showing location of the three early synagogues (Bristol Records Office).

Figure 4.56 Bristol: Old House in Temple Street, known as the Stone Kitchen, which housed the Synagogue from 1756-1786 (drawing by H. O'Neil, collection: Bristol City Museums and Art Gallery).

and one other official. It also notes that by this date there were two burial grounds and a mikveh. Lipman (1954, 186), estimates that the total number of Jews in Bristol in 1851 was c.300. By the middle/end of the 19th century Bristol, became less important than Liverpool as a port. This is reflected in the size of the Jewish trading and manufacturing community at that time of c.300 against Liverpool c.3, 000 (Ibid, 187). Figure 4.55 shows locations of the first three synagogues.

According to Samuel (1997, 11), 'The first Bristol Synagogue was in an old alehouse in Temple Street' in use from 1756-1786 (Figure 4.56). The Rate Book Summary shows that the Parish of Temple between 1750 and 1800 had the greatest concentration of Jews (21 names) compared with the other nearby Parishes in Bristol City' (Ibid, 46).

In 1786, the growing community moved to larger accommodation in the former Weavers Hall, in Temple Street, the vacated premises of a Bristol guild (Ibid, 63). This Synagogue was demolished in 1868/1870 when Temple Meads Railway Station was built. The ceremonial 1786 silver, the curved mahogany Ark doors, the wrought iron work which surrounds the Ten Commandments above them and four brass pillar-candelabra, placed on the corners of the *bimah* were moved to the 1870 Synagogue in Park Row (Ibid, 67).

4.2.5.2 Bristol: Synagogue Park Row BS1 established c.1870-still in use

Figure 4.57 Bristol: entrance to the 1870 Park Row Synagogue (photograph K. Marks 2010).

The present Bristol Synagogue is built on a hill on an elevated site of a former quarry. It was designed by the London-based Jewish architect Hyman Henry Collins, who also designed the Victorian Chatham Synagogue discussed in 4.2.8. 'The exterior is dressed in local rubble stone in Collins' favorite Italianate style' (Kadish 2006, 97) (Figure 4.57). Entry is via raised steps through an arched porch, with iron entrance gates dated to 1921 (Ibid, 97). In the stone band under the parapet is an inscription in Hebrew from Isaiah 2.5 which reads in English:

'People of Jacob, come. Let us live the way the Lord has taught us to'.

To the right of the entrance is the former the rabbis' house (Figure 4.57). There is no evidence of a mikveh in or near the synagogue and its location is unknown, although its existence is proven by the *1845 Chief Rabbis Statistical Accoun*t (Figure 6.2). Inside, the prayer hall runs at right angles to the entrance to preserve the correct orientation, with the Ark pointing to the east. Above the Ark is an inscription in Hebrew which in English reads, *Know before you stand'*. The main interests internally are the fixtures and fittings brought from other closed synagogues (Figure 4.58). The re-use of Jewish religious and ceremonial artifacts as synagogues closed and new ones are established, indicates why other than London, there is virtually no below-ground archaeological evidence of Jewish material culture.

Figure 4.58 Bristol: interior of Park Row Synagogue with four brass pillar-candelabra at the corners of the bimah brought from Weavers Hall Synagogue (closed 1868/70) (photograph, K. Marks 2010).

Figure 4.59 Bristol: Interior of Park Row Synagogue with curved mahogany Ark doors from Weavers Hall Synagogue (closed 1868/70) (photograph K. Marks 2010).

Figure 4.60 Bristol: Park Row Synagogue. Prayer board to the Royal Family from the former Ramsgate Synagogue 1833, with the over painting of new sovereign's inscription (photograph K. Marks 2010).

4.2.6 Canterbury [18]

There was a Jewish community in Canterbury in the medieval period, which was expelled in 1290. Cohn-Sherbok (1984,14) writes, 'There is a Royal charter in the Cathedral Archives of 1291 granting the Jews' land in Canterbury to the priory and lists the names of the Jewish land owners'. There is still a Jewry Lane, the site of the medieval Jewish quarter near to the old synagogue (personal observation 2011). Following re-admission, the first mention of Jews in Canterbury is c.1750, and the traditional foundation of the community was 1760 (Roth 1950, 110). The *History of Canterbury* records that there was a small community in the town c.1730 (Hasted 1799, 40). This would make it one of the earliest post re-settlement provincial communities in the provinces. According to Lipman (1954, 185), the Jewish population in the City in 1850 was 100, making it the second largest community in the South-East after Chatham In the second half of the 19th century, the community gradually began to decline (like many other smaller communities in market towns).

According to Cohn-Sherbok (1984, 33), the first synagogue, prior to the Old Synagogue in King Street in the 1750s, was in a temporary building in the St. Dunstan's area on the corner of High Street and Sour Street. In c.1762 a second synagogue was erected in St Dunstan's Street. Hasted (1799, 40) noted, 'that at present the habitations of Jews, who are numerous in this city and its suburbs, are mostly in the parish and street of St Peter's, and in the suburb of Westgate, in which they have a synagogue, and at some distance further westwards, a burying ground'. Cohn-Sherbrook (1984, 15) writes, 'that in 1845, the Canterbury community received notice that, the synagogue would have to be taken down because it stood in the way of the construction of a new railway line'. It was closed in 1846. The site is being archaeologically excavated in 2011.

Old Synagogue: King Street CT1: 1847/8-1931 Grade 11

Figure 4.61 Canterbury: Knights Templar stone inscription by the front gate to the synagogue (photograph J. Marks 2011).

In 1846, the community appealed for funds in order to help with the construction of a new synagogue. Rabbi Cohn-Sherbok notes from the synagogue records that other synagogues contributed, including Bevis Marks, The Great Synagogue in London, and the Great Synagogue in Manchester, as well as synagogues in Portsea, Brighton, Plymouth, Sheerness, Dublin and Montego (Ibid, 18). In addition to the donations received from the Jewish community, 'various city officials of Canterbury and non-Jewish citizens donated money, freehold land was purchased in King's Street in the parish of St Alphege' (Ibid, 18). Ironically, this site was formerly the medieval Knights Templar (Figure 4.61) adjoining Edward the Black Prince's Chantry (4.62), who expelled the Jews in 1290. The small front garden and path is bordered by medieval walls (personal observation, 2011).

The Chief Rabbi (Nathan Adler) attended the consecration in 1847 with Sir Moses Montefiore and his wife. Sir Moses was a major contributor to the synagogue's establishment and is discussed in 4.2.29. Canterbury Synagogue is the only example of Egyptian Revival architecture in England and is 'one of a small number worldwide'

Figure 4.62 Canterbury: Site of the synagogue (Cohn-Sherbok 1984, 22).

(Kadish 2006, 63). The design is clearly avoiding the use of Gothic architecture, because of its association with medieval persecution. It could be suggested with its obelisks and columns that it was influenced by Solomon's Temple in Jerusalem.

The local architect was instructed by the community to avoid the building looking like a church because '…. because of its unhappy association with persecution by the

Figure 4.63 Canterbury: 1847 synagogue entrance path showing obelisks and ornamental columns (Cohn-Sherbok 1984).

Figure 4.64 Canterbury: synagogue interior showing the former space for the Ark, with lotus- leaves capitals (Cohn-Sherbok 1984).

medieval church' (Ibid, 64). The entrance path is through two obelisks and a small garden (Figure 4.63). The front, street-facing is built in imitation granite and has a pyramid form, with two columns. On this exterior wall are two projecting rectangular columns with lotus-leaf capitals (Figure 4.63). This design is repeated inside on the Ark surround (personal observation 2011). The Ark itself is worked in imitation veined marble (Figure 4.64). The building tapers to the roof with Egyptian motifs, two obelisks with palmettes (ornaments of radiating petals like a palm leaf). The only original furniture is the gallery pews, and the synagogue held around 100 persons.

The synagogue was restored in 1889 and was in use until 1931(Ibid, 64). In 1982, it was sold to The King's School and is now used as a music room. Next to the entrance is the 1851 mikveh discussed in Chapter 4 which is now used as the office of the music master..

4.2.7 Cardiff [19]

The Community was established c.1840, 70 years later than Swansea and earlier than Merthyr Tydfil (1848). The first mention of Jews in Cardiff is c.1797 (Roth 1950, 110). Lipman (1954, 244), estimates the size of the community in 1850 as between 50-100, making it smaller than the communities in Merthyr Tydfil and Swansea. Cardiff now has the largest Jewish community in South Wales with two congregations, Orthodox and Reform. The first synagogue was in a rented room in Trinity Street in the old part of the city, near to the market (Dennis 1951, 30). As the community grew, Bute Street near to the docks became the focus of settlement. In 1858, the first custom-made synagogue was opened in East Terrace overlooking the canal (Henriques 1993, 230) and was demolished c.1949. The synagogue was near to Bute Road (later Bute Street). In Chapter 6, the topography of the community in Cardiff is discussed, and the location of the synagogue is shown. In the beginning, the community lived and traded near to the port; as it grew and prospered, some of its members moved away from the slum dock area, a trend which continued into the early/mid-20th century.

4.2.8 Chatham [20]

There was a Jewish community in Chatham in the medieval period that was expelled by 1290. The present Chatham community (established 1750) is one of the oldest in the country. Chatham and Rochester, being major ports, traded with the Baltic, North European and Low Countries and attracted Jews to settle. According to Lancaster (1998, 1) 'In the 18th and early 19th centuries, many were engaged as naval agents, ships chandlers, or military tailors'. The present synagogue was built in 1869 on the site of the original 1750 building. It is unique in Britain as it is the only synagogue with its burial ground at the rear and side of the prayer hall. Chatham Memorial Synagogue is so named as it was under the private patronage of a wealthy local naval agent, Simon Magnus, who dedicated the synagogue in memory of his son Captain Lazarus Simon Magnus, Mayor of Queensborough, a town on the Isle of Sheppey, who died in an accident aged 39. His memorial obelisk is discussed in 5.2.8. The style of the interior and some of the other grave stones lying flat would indicate that the original congregation was mixture of Sephardi and Ashkenazi Jews.

The former Orthodox synagogues in Gravesend, Isle of Sheppey, Sheerness and Canterbury have ceased to exist, and thus, Chatham is now the only Orthodox synagogue in mid-Kent. The foundation and memorial stone on the front of the building gives the date when the synagogue was established (1869) (Figure 4.65). The synagogue has a north front faced with Kentish ragstone and Bath stone with columns and decoration (Figure 4.66). The building is at 364, High Street, and on this street in the early 19th century there were at least 14 Jewish traders including pawnbrokers, slop sellers (old clothes), silversmiths and watchmakers (Green 1982/1986, 97-123). The synagogue and cemetery were thus at the centre of the community in this period.

The interior is Romanesque-inspired in style, with round arches and massive vaulting, heavy piers, walls with small windows and with decorations of flora found in Israel, such as vines, pomegranates, olives, wheat, bulrush and lily (personal observation 2010). The floor is of colored tiles. The Ark wooden doors have the inscription in Hebrew: (in English) reads:

Figure 4.65 Chatham: synagogue foundation stone 1869 (photograph K. Marks 2010).

Figure 4.66 Chatham: elevated frontage of synagogue (photograph K.Marks 2010).

Figure 4.67 Chatham: Ark and bimah *(central platform) (photograph K. Marks 2010)*

'Know before Whom you stand'.

In the Ark is a *Sefer Torah* over 200 years old, which, when opened, can be seen to be written in the Sephardi style of Hebrew letters, which are rounder than Ashkenazi (personal observation 2010). The small ladies' gallery is at the rear.

4.2.9 Cheltenham [21]

Figure 4.68 Cheltenham: exterior of synagogue showing Roman Doric pilasters. (photograph J. Marks 2009).

Prior to the present synagogue opened in 1837/9, services were held in temporary premises in the upper room at the St George's Place, on the corner of what is now Chelsea Square (Tarode 1999, 31). In the early part of the 19th century, 'traveling Jewish merchants took full advantage of the many business opportunities which they found in the new town, as did many established circuit traders and professionals' (Ibid 27). The building is situated in Synagogue Lane. The frontage is of white stucco with Roman Doric pilasters forming a fake portico (Figure 4.68). From the outside, it gives the appearance of being a non-conformist chapel (personal observation 2009). There is a glass ceiling dome, one of the principal ornaments of the synagogue. There are two non-matching stained glass windows either side of the Ark. The synagogue can hold 100 men and 30 women in the gallery. The 1845 Chief Rabbi's census shows that the Cheltenham community had over 100 members, swelled at the High Holidays and fashionable seasons by visitors to the spa to take 'the healing waters'. The present Orthodox community numbers less than 50.

What is exceptional about this synagogue are the fixtures; they are older than the building. Much of the furniture, fixtures and fittings, such as the Ark and the *bimah* came from the New Synagogue in Leadenhall Street, London, which is discussed in 4.1.7. The Synagogue archives contain a bill that shows that local carriers were used to transfer the furnishings from London:

7.9.1838 Tanner and Baylis Warehouse, to carriage one case of pictures from London: £2.1.6d and one wagon load of fittings for the synagogue: £86.0.0d (1838)

The date of the invoice, coincides with the date of relocation of the New Synagogue from Leadenhall Street to the new larger synagogue in Great St Helen's, off Bishopsgate. Leadenhall Street had donated its redundant furniture dating from 1761 to the new synagogue in Cheltenham. This makes the furniture, including the *bimah* in Cheltenham Synagogue, the oldest surviving Ashkenazi furniture still being used in the UK. The oldest surviving Sephardi furniture is in Bevis Marks, London (1701). The *bimah* and pews in Cheltenham are covered in original rattan upholstery, some of which is badly worn, with the wooden seats underneath evident. There is no other synagogue in the U.K. with this style of furniture (Figure 4.69).

The Royal family prayer board (Figure 4.69) is on the south wall; on the opposite wall is a matching board with prayers said on *Yom Kippur* (Day of Atonement; the holiest day in the Jewish religious calendar). According to Sam Stone, Chairman of the Synagogue, paint analysis in 1998 revealed the over- painted name of George II (1727-60). However, the makers of the board were *Cole and King*, who went out of business in 1730 (Kadish 2006, 101), 30 years before Leadenhall Street was established. If this is the case, the Royal Prayer Board could only have come from The Great Synagogue (established in 1690) or the Hambro (established in 1725). This would make the Royal Prayer Board the oldest example in the country.

Figure 4.69 Cheltenham: synagogue interior showing rattan covered pews and Royal Family prayer board, originally dating from George II (1727- 60) (photograph J. Marks 2009).

4.2.10 Coventry [22]

The first mention of Jews in Coventry is c.1775, with the traditional date of the foundation of the community being c.1800 (Roth 1950, 110). It is no longer possible to gain access to the Victorian synagogue established in 1870. According to Roth (1950, 53), 'prior to its establishment services were held in as private house in Trinity Passage'. The outside is in red brick in Romanesque style, with

Figure 4.70 Coventry: Barras Lane Synagogue (1870) now closed (photograph K. Marks 2011)

Bath stone dressings (personal observation 2011). According to Barry Deitch (President of the Reform Community), interior fittings have been removed to the newer Orthodox community in Solihull (personal contact 2011). The building is now boarded up and shows signs of neglect. The recent closure of Coventry synagogue is another example of a small provincial Orthodox community, which due to declining membership no longer survives.

4.2.11 Dover [23]

According to Roth, Dover 'appears to be the oldest seaside community' (1950,54). The synagogue in Northampton Street Dover was badly damaged during World War II, when the area near the docks was subject to heavy bombing. Northampton Street no longer exists. It was demolished in 1950, when the whole area was reconstructed. Most of the community left the City in 1941 as Dover was only 32km across the Channel from France and was thought to be a likely landing place for the German invasion. The Jewish community was never re-established. Jones (1916, 215) states, 'A Jewish Synagogue at the top of Northampton Street the successor of one in Hawkesbury Street was built in 1862 and opened in 1863'. *The 1845 Statistical Account of the Congregations in the British Empire* (Figure 6.2), compiled prior to the opening of the new synagogue, shows that Dover synagogue had 31 members and used the sea for ritual purification. Jones continues, 'the style is Greek, the edifice is designed to accommodate 250 persons and the cost was 1, 000 guineas. The consecration ceremony was performed by the Chief Rabbi, Dr Adler on 10th August 1863' (Ibid,

Figure 4.72 Dover: tablets from the demolished synagogue on wall of cemetery (photograph K.Marks 2009).

4.71 Dover: broken tablet from demolished synagogue in cemetery. (photograph K. Marks 2009).

215). The size of the seating accommodation is interesting, and it appears likely that during the summer months and High Holidays that the number attending services was increased by Jews on holiday in Dover or living outside the town, who only came to synagogue to celebrate the New Year and attend on the Fast Day.

Figures 4.71 and 4.72 show plaques located, respectively, next to or on the wall to the north of the cemetery in Old Charlton Road. These are the only remains of the synagogue, brought to the cemetery for preservation. Although now difficult to read, it is still possible to make out the inscriptions. One tablet reads:

> *This memorial tablet is erected to the memory of the Rev R I. Cohen of Sussex [House] Dover who died in Liverpool Dec 3rd 1885 in the 62nd year of his age. He conceived the idea of building this synagogue and by his great personal exertions and by the respect[t] which his good name carried with it [am] ong all the classes of the Jewish community He was mainly instrumental by collecting sufficient funds for its erection while its maintenance in piece and honor was the pride of and delight of his life by Gods permission this synagogue was made the closing scene of his earthly labours for the last act of his failing health allowed? him to accomplish was the reading of the prayers o[n]the Day of Atonement 5626 soon after which [it] pleased God to take him* (personal observation, 2009).

The second tablet is in appreciation of Rabbi Cohen and the third has a prayer to the Royal Family in English with the heading in Hebrew (personal observation 2009).

4.2.12   Exeter   [24]

The first mention of Jews in Exeter is 1735 (Margoliouth, 1851). The first Jews to settle in Exeter were from Italy (Roth 1950, 59). Exeter's synagogue opened in 1763-4, one year after Plymouth, the only other Georgian synagogue that still survives. It holds regular services with the community numbering around 100 persons, including 25-30 children (personal contact 2009). Unlike, other former synagogues in Devon and Cornwall, the front lane opens directly onto a street, named 'Synagogue Place'. In 1977, a Land Certificate granted ownership of this lane to the congregation (personal contact 2009). The entrance is flanked by two Doric columns, which were added in 1835 (Kadish 2006, 92).

Originally the building had no windows, being lit from above by a curved window or lantern on top of a dome (personal contact 2009). Now, there are four brass chandeliers hanging from the ceiling. According to *The Statistical Accounts of the Congregations in the British Empire (1845)* (Figure 6.2), the community numbered around 175 (c.35 families). Only Liverpool, Birmingham and Plymouth had larger communities. There is no evidence of the second floor, which suffered bomb damaged during World War II and there is a ladies' gallery in a poor state of repair (personal observation 2009). The downstairs prayer hall is small, which ensures that no matter how few worshippers come to pray, there is a feeling of intimacy and contact (personal observation 2009). The Ark (Figure 4.73), although elaborate, is

Figure 4.73 Exeter: synagogue interior, the Georgian Ark (1763) (photograph J. Marks 2009).

Figure 4.74 Exeter: synagogue bimah (central platform) with a balustrade with interlocking curved metalwork (photograph J. Marks 2009).

simpler than that at Plymouth. It has the same inscription in Hebrew, painted on the cornice between the two tiers (extract from Psalm 5:7) which in English reads as follows:

'With deep respect I will bow down towards your holy temple'

As at Plymouth, some of the letters have been highlighted to yield the date 5524, corresponding with 1763-4, the year the synagogue was opened.

There are a number of other special features to the interior. First, the Gothic/Regency interlocking curved metal work around the *bimah* is unique in design in England (Kadish 2006, 93) (Figure 4.74). Second, the seat benches are known by the synagogue records to have been made by local carpenters; these seats can be seen to have been altered when the orientation of the Ark was corrected in 1836 from the north side to the south-east. Third, the small box pews have prayer book rests, hinged at the back, which can be tilted when the congregant is standing (personal observation 2009).

4.2.13 Falmouth [25]

The first settlers came to Falmouth c.1740 (Margoliouth 1851). The founder was Alexander Moses, known as 'Zender Falmouth', who is buried in the Falmouth cemetery, where his tombstone and that of his wife still survive (Figure 5.63). Alexander Moses,

Figure 4.75 Falmouth: former synagogue plaque 1808-1880 (photograph J. Marks 2009).

Figure 4.76 Falmouth: exterior of former synagogue (photograph J. Marks 2009).

with his wife Phoebe, set up a silversmith in Falmouth about 1740 (Jacobs 1951, 64). According to the *Falmouth and Penryn Directory and Guide* of 1864, a synagogue was established in c.1766, this building no longer exists. The present building was erected in 1808 with a capacity of 80 people, including a ladies' gallery. It was in use until 1880 (Figure 4.75). The restored and converted brick building (Figure 4.76) is rendered along the sides; the roof is slate (personal observation 2009).

In 1842, the community numbered 14 families, around 50 persons, and prospered by supplying the packet boats which harbored in the bay (Roth 1950, 62), which may be one of the reasons that the synagogue is situated on Smithick Hill overlooking the harbour. Even on the Sabbath, the worshippers could keep a watchful eye on ships arriving and leaving the port. Pearce states that 'as late as 1970 pipe marks on the outside wall could be seen leading to the stone surround of the mikveh in the undergrowth, and the stone steps which led down to it, but the area has since been covered over with tarmac'(2000,293).

The building was surveyed by Edward Jamilly in 1958 when it was a furniture depository. The survey shows two slender columns supporting the ladies' gallery at the back of the synagogue on the west wall opposite the Ark, one of which remains (4.77). In common with many synagogues, there was no direct entrance from the front street; the main access was at the rear of the building. There are two possible reasons for this. First, it made the building more secure from unwanted visitors, and second, it enabled more people to be seated along the long walls. The frontage faces east where the Ark would have been placed. From around 1850, with the decline of trade coming from packet ships, and with ships using other ports along the south coast, the Falmouth community declined, and by 1880, no longer functioned as such.

The painted *Luhot* (Ten Commandments) formerly over the Ark is now in the Jewish Museum, London. A *Torah* (Five Books of Moses) scroll deposited by the widow of the last member Samuel Jacob is deposited in the Truro Museum. The scroll is labeled with the words: *'Scroll of the Law formerly used in the Jews Synagogue Falmouth'*

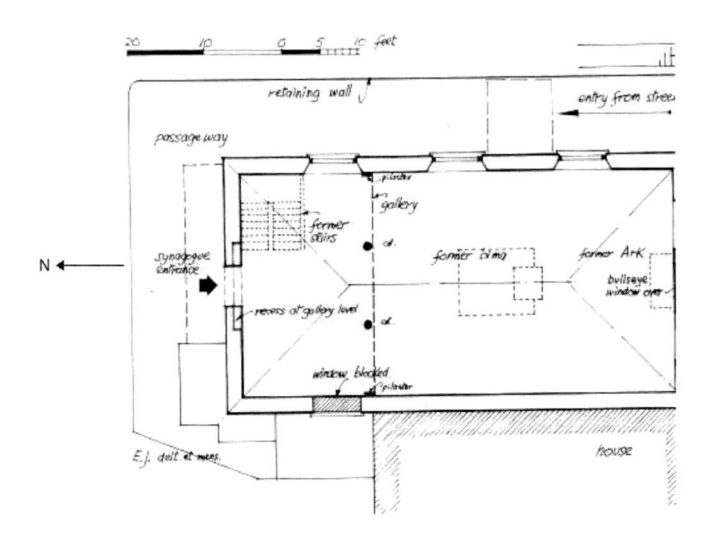

Figure 4.77 Falmouth: plan of interior of former synagogue, surveyed in 1958 by Jamilly (Courtney Library, Truro).

(personal contact 2009). Roth (1950, 62) notes that, 'a Cornish oven, formerly in the synagogue and perhaps used for baking *Matzoth* (unleavened bread) on Passover was preserved in the Falmouth Museum'. However the museum no longer exists and according to the curator of the Maritime Museum in Falmouth, the contents, including articles from Darwin's collections, were sold off. The whereabouts of the clay oven is unknown (personal contact 2009).

4.2.14 Gloucester [26]

Gloucester had a Jewish community in the medieval period. Post re-admission, the first mention of Jews in Gloucester is c.1765, and a community was established in 1784 (Roth 1950, 110). There are no synagogue records, although Kadish (2016, 101), details a synagogue in 1792. 27 tombstones and remains dating from c.1807 were re-interred in 1938 from the city centre cemetery into the Coney Hill Municipal Cemetery (5.2.14). From c.1850, there was no longer a Jewish community in Gloucester. The synagogue building does not survive. It was near to Lower Southgate Street, but is not marked on the 1882 Ordnance Survey Map, that is in the gazetteer.

4.2.15.1 Hull [27]

Community was established c.1810 (Roth 1950, 110), although according to Finestein (1996/8, 34) (a local historian), the first synagogue and community was established in 1780.

Figure 4.78 Hull: Interior of Roman Catholic Chapel in Postern Gate, destroyed in the Gordon riots. Rebuilt as a synagogue in 1780 (Diocese of Middlesbrough).

First synagogue: Postern Gate c.1780-1809

The premises were originally a disused Roman Catholic Chapel, sacked in the Gordon riots by a mob in 1780. The chapel was rebuilt to hold 20/30 persons (Finestein 1996/8, 35/36) (Figure 4.78)

Second Synagogue: Princess Dock, Paradise Row 1809-1826
Princess Dock Synagogue was a secessionist congregation from Postern Gate that closed when the two congregations amalgamated. No plans or drawings exist of this building. Princess Dock no longer exists, as it was destroyed when the docks were extended in 1829 (Finestein 1996/8, 33).

4.2.15.2 Robinson Row

Figure 4.79 shows a plan of the frontage and ground floor. The *bimah* (central platform), as is traditional in Orthodox synagogues, is placed in the centre of the hall, facing the Ark pointing to the east. Towards the rear, can be seen a low partition separating men from women, who would have sat in the three rows of benches. The 1856 Ordnance Survey Map shows that Robinson Row had seating room for 250 men and women, including 50 'free seating places' for non-paying Jews who attended the synagogue. Finestein suggests that the Hull community which had a membership of around 400 persons, made allowances for immigrants, who were passing through Hull who would not travel on the Sabbath (Saturday) or High Holidays. By 1871 Robinson Row was too small to accommodate the community and the immigrants passing through (1996/8, 34).

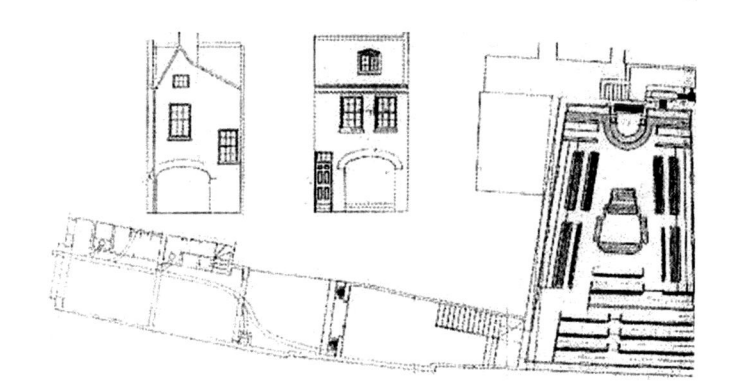

Figure 4.79 Hull: Ground floor plan of Robinson Row Synagogue (1826) (no scale) (By permission Hull City Archives).

The *Jewish Chronicle* on 8th September 1871 reports that:

'No town of a similar size in the United Kingdom has a larger number of foreign Jews direct from foreign climes'. For the High Festivals in 1875, *The Jewish World* reported '....that as many as 500 people attended the additional services in the hall of the Mechanics' Institute'.

Finestein (1996/80, 520) states that, 'the desire for larger premises was further fostered by the widening acknowledgment that Robinson Row was no longer in an area favoured by fashion'. Figure 4.80 shows the rear of Robinson Row Synagogue prior to demolition in 1926. The 1856 Ordnance Survey Map in the gazetteer shows the location of all three synagogues to be within walking distance of the community established between 1780 and the late 19th century.

Figure 4.80 Hull: Robinson Row Synagogue prior to demolition in 1926 (By permission Hull City Archives from Dalais 2010).

4.2.16 Ipswich [28]

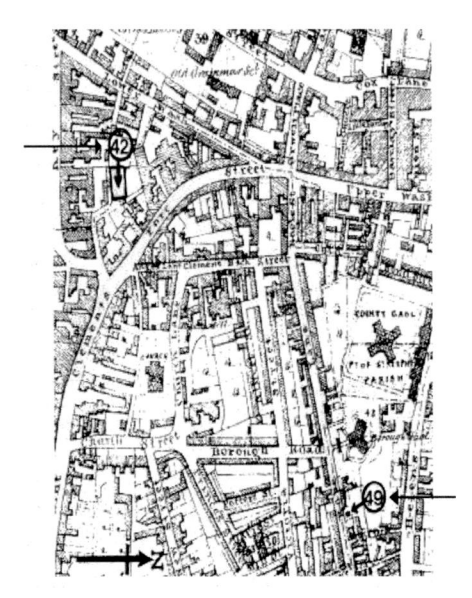

Figure 4.81 Ipswich: cemetery, no 42, upper left and synagogue no.49, lower right. (Detail from Edward Monson's map of 1848) (scale 1:26)

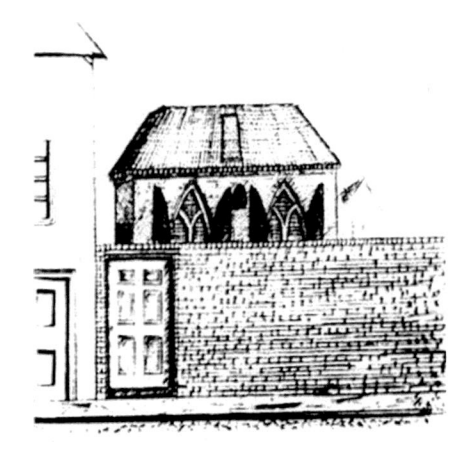

Figure 4.82 Ipswich: The synagogue in Rope Walk (1792), Clarke's History and Description of Ipswich 1830. 'Reproduced by kind permission of Suffolk Record Office Ipswich branch'.

Roth (1950, 72) attributes the founding of the community to 1792, but according to Margoliouth (*History, 1851*) there were Jews in Ipswich from around 1750. Roth (1950, 72) noted that: 'At first a room was hired in St Clements for the purpose of divine worship'. It is in the parish of St Clements that the first Jewish cemetery was established, marked 42 (Figure 4.81). According to Clark (*History of Ipswich 319/320*), the foundation stone of the synagogue was laid on August 18th 1792 and held no more than 100 persons The synagogue was in Rope Walk (Figure 4.81, marked 49), and the only record of the building is a drawing (Figure 4.82). The community in 1830 was estimated by Lipman (1951, 182) to comprise no more that 50, rising to around 75 in 1851. The synagogue was demolished in 1877.

4.2.17　　　　　　　　　King's Lynn　　　　　　　　　[29]

The medieval community in King's Lynn was massacred in 1190. The founding of the re-admission community dates to c.1747, but it had ceased to exist by the middle of the 19th century (Roth 1950, 8). King's Lynn was not included in the 1845 Statistical Account of the Congregations in the British Empire, confirming that there was no community remaining by this date. The early synagogue was in Tower Street, and in 1811 it became a Methodist chapel, and the synagogue was destroyed. The 1886 Ordnance Survey map shows a Methodist Chapel on the site. There was a small community numbering 25 to 50 persons, who held their services in a house or hall until 1826, when a new synagogue was opened in a yard at the rear of 9 High Street, which existed to 1846 (Tuck 1987, 4). Nothing is known of the appearance of either building (Kadish 2006, 109).

In the 18th century, King's Lynn was one of the most important ports in England. Situated on the mouth of the River Ouse, with trading links to north European ports, King's Lynn was also connected to the network of inland waterways. With the Industrial Revolution and, the later coming of the railways, combined with the fact that the port was not deep enough to take large ships, King's Lynn went into recession and by the middle of the 19th century had became depopulated; many of the Jewish traders left. As with many of the early communities in port towns, no physical evidence remains other than Millfleet Jews' Burial Ground which is discussed in Chapter 5.2.17.

4.2.18　　　　　　　　　Leeds　　　　　　　　　　[30]

The first three synagogues in Leeds were Back Rockingham Street Synagogue, 1850-1860, The Great Synagogue Belgrave Street, 1860-1930 and New Briggate Synagogue, 1869-1930. None of these synagogues survives, there is no synagogue still in use in Leeds older than 40 years. Stained glass windows and the *bimah* (central platform) were removed from The Great Synagogue and placed in the new synagogue when it was built in 1970 (Sender, personal communication 2010).

Freedman (1992, 3) states that, 'the 1841 census reveals that the community in

Figure 4.83 Leeds: Interior of Belgrave Street Synagogue (1860) (photograph Leeds Community Archives by permission M. Sender, 2010).

Leeds was made up of less than 60 souls… most of whom would have been itinerant hawkers'. By the 1850s, Leeds had developed into an industrial centre with a population of over 170, 000. The factories in the city were mainly producing industrial and agricultural equipment and were involved in transport services. Leeds was the centre of an already well-developed system of communications, with links to Hull, Liverpool, Birmingham, Newcastle Manchester and London. It was not until the end of the 19th century that the clothing industry developed, and this marked the beginning of large-scale Jewish immigration into the city. Before Back Rockingham Street synagogue was established in 1850, services were held in private houses in the Leylands. According to Krausz (1964, 2), the congregation in 1850 was small, with around 100 people of whom only 18 were paying seat holders. The officiating minister combined the offices of minister, *mohel* (one who performed circumcisions) and *shochet* (ritual slaughterer).

Back Rockingham Street was replaced in 1860 by a larger synagogue 'The Great Synagogue' in Belgrave Street (Figure 4.83). This synagogue was known locally as the 'Englisher Shool' (synagogue), as its members comprised those that were already established and were considered by the new immigrants to be more anglicized (Ibid, 9). In 1869, the New Briggate Synagogue was founded. New immigrants tended to stick together and hold services where the order of service and ritual was familiar. There were also several small rooms of worship, which catered for the needs of each of these smaller congregations. In the last quarter of the 19th century, there were at least 12 places of worship for the growing community, none of these survive.

4.2.19.1　　　　　　　　　　Liverpool　　　　　　　　　　[31]

Wolfman (1986, 37) states that, '…prior to the opening of the Victorian synagogue in Princes Road the earliest synagogue in Liverpool dates from the middle of the 18th century, around 1753', the first in the North of England. The first synagogue was established in a private house in Cumberland Street (1753-1775) near the port area (roughly on the site of the former post office (Ibid, 37). The synagogue lay at the end of a cul-de-sac named Synagogue Court, near Stanley Street (4.84). The front faced towards Whitechapel, then known as Frog Lane. According to city records, the area of the synagogue and field was 26 yards on the east and west, 14 yards on the north and 9 1/2 yards on the south. Benas (1899, 49), describes the house as 'little better than a corner cottage with a small garden used as the burial ground'.

In 1775, the growing community moved from Cumberland Street to Turton Court, near Canning Place by the dock gates and Custom House on the south side of the Old Dock (where Canning Place now is) (Ibid, 38). In 1778, the synagogue moved again, to a house in Upper Frederick Street, adjacent to the burial ground. According to Williams (1987, 2), 'it was capable of holding 70 worshippers'. The community acquired a second cemetery in 1789 at 133 Upper Frederick Street (near the docks), which is discussed in 5.2.19.2. The Upper Frederick Synagogue was in use to 1807. In 1807, the foundation stone of a purpose-built place of worship with seating capacity for 169 men and 121 female worshippers was laid in Seel Street (Ibid, 2) (Figure 4.86). The topographical implication of these relocations of Liverpool's synagogues is discussed in Chapter 6.

(c. one meter square)
Figure 4.84 Liverpool: Plaque in Met Quarter Shopping Mall near to the site of Liverpool's first synagogue and burial ground in Synagogue Court, Cumberland Street 1753 (photograph K. Marks 2009).

Figure 4.85 Liverpool: Frederick Street, house used as a synagogue with burial ground at rear, Old Hebrew Congregation 1794 (Ettinger 1930, 17).

Figure 4.86 Liverpool: Seel Street Synagogue 1807-1870, first purpose built synagogue (by permission Merseyside Jewish Community Archives at Liverpool Records Office).

84   THE ARCHAEOLOGY OF ANGLO-JEWRY IN ENGLAND AND WALES 1656–C.1880

Figure 4.87 Liverpool: Plaque on wall of Telephone Exchange marking the site of the Seel Street Synagogue (1807-1870) (photograph K. Marks 2009).

Figure 4.88 Liverpool: New Hebrew Congregation in Hope Place Synagogue (1857-1874) (Ettinger 1930, 9).

Williams (1987, 3) writes, 'Seel Street Synagogue was designed by a local architect, Thomas Harrison of Chester…and was fronted with an elegant façade of Ionic columns; this synagogue was a clear symbol of the community's growing stature and acceptance'. In 1857, with the social diversity of the growing community, a 'New Hebrew Congregation' was formed in Hope Place as a breakaway congregation from Seel Street, now known as the 'Old Hebrew Congregation'. This building was adjacent to a Jewish school, where according to

Figure 4.89 Liverpool: Watercolour of Hope Place in 1864, including Hope Place Synagogue and Hope Place School (by permission Merseyside Jewish Community Archives at Liverpool Record Office).

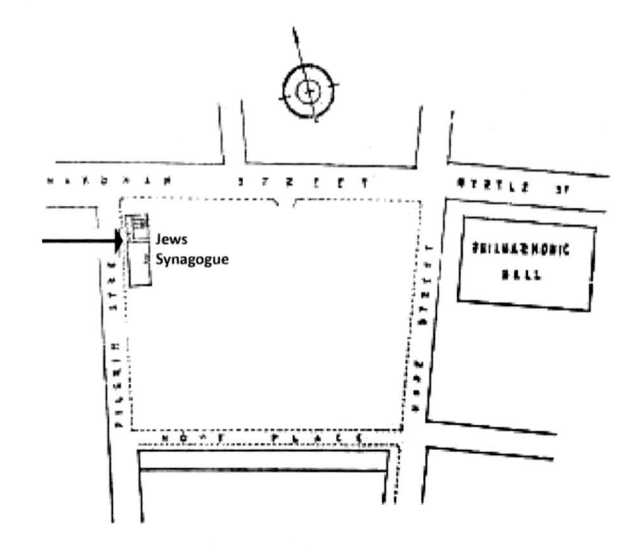

Figure 4.90 Liverpool: The district surrounding Hope Place Synagogue, "Mount Zion" no scale. (Ettinger 1933, 6).

Williams 'in 1873 the school was attended by 300 boys and girls' (Ibid, 4) (Figure 4.91). The only evidence of these early synagogues and the school are plaques in new shopping centers and on buildings now put to other uses. They demonstrate the topography, expansion and movement of the community from the port area to the more affluent city suburbs. By 1872, the Liverpool Jewish community numbered around 3, 000 people (Ibid, 5).

Figure 4.91 Liverpool: Hope Place Hebrew School built in 1852 (photograph K. Marks 2009).

4.2.19.2 Liverpool: Princes Road Synagogue (Grade 1) 1872-still in use

The outside of Princes Road Synagogue is made from red brick and stone. Originally, there were six decorative minarets (Figure.4.92) that were removed in 1960, as they were considered unsafe. The entrance under corner turrets is through a deep-arched portal under a large wheel window set within an arch. Inside the doorway at ground level is a brass plate on the foundation stone, detailing the officials of the synagogue at the date when the stone was laid (1872) (personal observation 2009). There is a lavish marble *bimah*, presented by David Lewis, the founder of England's first departmental store, Lewis's, which traded in Liverpool until June 2010 (Figure 4.93).

This Grade I-listed synagogue was designed by Scottish-born Liverpool architects, the Audlsey brothers, who later (1877) designed the New West Synagogue in Bayswater, London. (4.1.1) the front is almost identical to Princes Road. The lavishness and size of Princes Road

Figure 4.92 Liverpool: Princess Road Synagogue Toxteth (1872) (Liverpool Community archives, by permission Arnold Lewis, community archivist)

Figure 4.93 Liverpool: interior of Princes Road Synagogue bimah *(central platform) (left); turreted gilded Assyrian Ark (right) (photograph K.Marks 2009).*

Synagogue demonstrates several aspects of the growth in numbers, movement and increase in prosperity of many of Liverpool's community.

In a little over 100 years, from when the first small community used a room in a house for prayers, many had moved to the lavish 'cathedral' synagogue in a building designed by British architects. Not all Liverpool's Orthodox community were members of Princes Road, which has seating capacity for nearly 450 men and over 350 women. In 1872, the total community numbered around 3, 000, not all of whom would have attended synagogue. Immigrants from c.1870s/1880s formed a number of small religious societies (*chevroth*) where they could pray and meet with former fellow countrymen who shared the same language and culture from their former homelands in Eastern Europe. These rooms of prayer no longer survive.

4.2.20.1   Manchester   [32]

Williams (1976, 10) states that 'Although direct evidence of Jewish commercial and professional activity in Manchester in the boom years of the 1770s and 1780s is lacking, the town was occasionally visited by anonymous itinerant dealers in which Jewish hawkers specialized'. There is a town plan of Manchester and Salford, published in 1741 (Figure 4.94) with an alley named 'Synagogue Alley'.

There being no synagogues in Manchester at this date, Williams (Ibid, 3) suggests, that there was a building in the alley used by a group of hawkers, who met occasionally to replenish their stocks, exchange communal gossip and make up a quorum (*minyan*) of 10 men in order to worship. In the late 1780s and early 1790s, a small group of hawkers and small shopkeepers previously based in Liverpool established the community, with the first synagogue and settlement in the congested streets and cramped courts radiating from Miller Street, Shudehill and Long Millgate (Ibid,12) (Figure 4.95). In 1794, the first burial ground was acquired in Brindle Heath

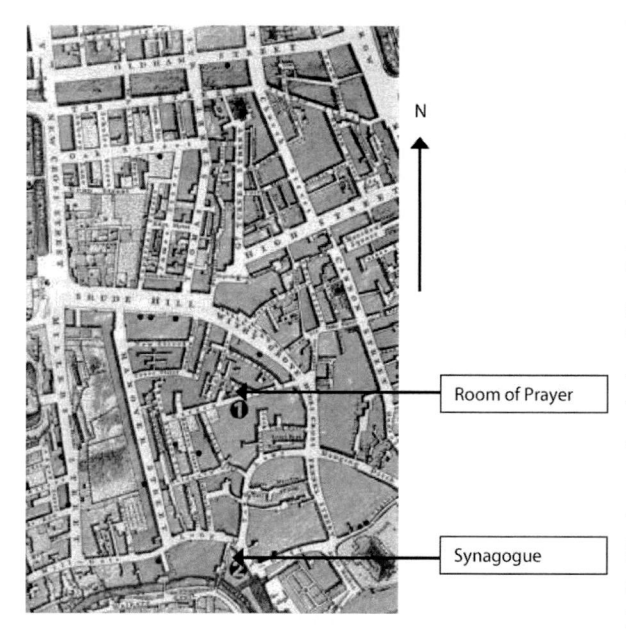

Figure 4.94 Manchester: Section of Casson and Berry's Plan of the town of Manchester and Salford, 1741 Showing Synagogue Alley (Williams 1976, 4) (no scale available)

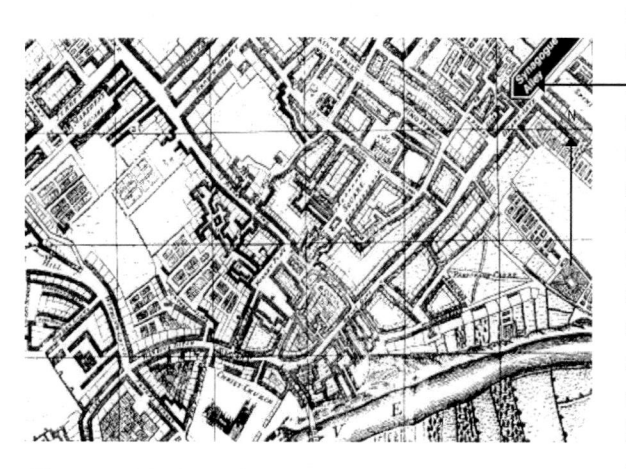

Figure 4.95 Manchester: Section of C.Laurent's Topographical Plan of Manchester and Salford, 1793 (Scale 1:5069). (1) The warehouse where the community first worshipped; (2) the synagogue in Ainsworth's Court (Williams 1976, 13).

Pendelton and is discussed in 5.2.20.

Little remains of this area, except the street sign and the old post office which was being demolished in 2010 (personal observation). The community in 1790 numbered c.60 persons and by 1824-1825 had expanded to c.600 with a new synagogue built in Halliwell Street that held 61 seat holders' (Williams 1976, 50). As there was no other synagogue it can be assumed that services were held in private houses. There was a small school attached. As with the other growing provincial Jewish communities, the move from a prayer hall, often in a house or hall, to a custom-built synagogue represents an important step in the development of a community. First, there had to be enough members to pay for the building and running costs, which might also include a rabbi. The rabbi sometimes also acted as the *shochet* (ritual slaughterer). Second, there had to be community leadership. Third, it demonstrated growing confidence that the Jewish community was firmly established in Manchester's business and communal life. *The Statistical Account of the Congregations in the British Empire 1845* (Figure 6.2) shows that Manchester by 1845 had become the third-largest community in the provinces, only Birmingham and Liverpool were larger. Halliwell Street close to Victoria Station was to become the main point of entry and transit of later immigrants. Some stayed in Manchester, while the vast majority passed through on their way to Liverpool, then on to America, Canada and South Africa. In 1848, Manchester's Town Council announced that to build a major new road (Corporation Street) giving improved access to the town centre, the Halliwell Synagogue was compulsorily purchased and demolished (Ibid, 24/25).

By 1858, the community had grown to 2,000 and was now larger than Birmingham and Liverpool. Many had become prosperous and began to move northwards out of the Halliwell area up to Cheetham Hill, which is discussed in section 6.2.2.8. With this change in topography of the community and the demolition of the Halliwell Synagogue, two new synagogues were established in 1858. The reason for two new synagogues was a split between the Reformers and the traditional Orthodox. Despite the split, when it came to charity and looking after the poor and needy Jews in Manchester, they co-operated. The Manchester Congregation of British Jews (Reform Congregation) was smaller than the Orthodox one and according to Williams, '….was made up substantially of wealthier Manchester merchants, engaged in overseas trade' (Ibid, 27). The size and architecture of the two new synagogue buildings (which were erected a few hundred yards from one another), demonstrated the confidence and security of the community. The Reform Synagogue was destroyed by bombing in 1941. The Orthodox Great Synagogue was in use until 1974 the congregation having moved further out to the suburbs of Manchester and the building was subsequently destroyed. The only remaining synagogue in Cheetham Hill from this period is that established in 1874, the Spanish and Portuguese Synagogue, is now Manchester's Jewish Museum.

4.2.20.2 Manchester: The Great Synagogue Cheetham Hill

The Halliwell Street congregation was known as the 'Old Congregation', while the new house of worship established in Cheetham Hill was called 'The Great Synagogue'. As the community moved out of the Halliwell area, Cheetham became the hub of the Jewish community in Manchester. The architect of the synagogue was Thomas Bird of Manchester, who also designed Cheetham Town Hall. The foundation stone was laid in 1857. Architects' drawings (no longer existing) or later photographs show that the exterior was neo-Classical. Steps leading up to the entrance doors are flanked by two Corinthian columns, almost giving the outside appearance of an entrance to a Classical temple (Figure 4.96). William describes it as 'Manchester Baroque' (Ibid, 26), and it was City's 'cathedral' synagogue. Williams (1976, 256) notes that '…the architect describes the façade as possessing an 'Italian character', with a flight of twelve steps 40ft in length, led up to a row of columns of polished stonework which formed the entrance to a covered loggia'.

'The interior had space for '372 gentlemen, 9 boys or pupils, and 60 free sittings' (Ibid, 256). No mention is made of the number of seats in the ladies' gallery. The wings of the loggia led to the staircases to the ladies gallery. The interior was arranged in traditional style around the *bimah*, with the seats arranged laterally below the ladies' gallery (Figure 4.97). Five steps on either side led up to the Ark at the east end of the synagogue. Williams states that 'The pedestals, the curved doors of the Ark, an imposing pulpit, the desk and the presidential box, were all beautifully carved out of Spanish polished mahogany. The synagogue was lit by gilt chandeliers and the Persian carpets were supplied by one of the congregation' (Ibid, 256). The opulence and extravagance of the Great Synagogue demonstrated the status and confidence of Manchester's Orthodox community. There are no architects plans or drawings of this synagogue or community archives. The building was demolished in 1986, despite a Grade II listing (communal records). The mikveh in this synagogue went out of use in 1939 (Kadish 1996, 151). All the other *mikva'ot* in Manchester, date from the early 20th century.

Figure 4.96 Manchester: Exterior of The Great Synagogue Cheetham Hill Road 1858 (Williams 1976, 247).

Figure 4.97 Manchester: Interior of The Great Synagogue Cheetham Hill Road 1858 (photograph by permission of Jewish Heritage UK and the Glyn family).

4.2.20.3 Manchester: Reform Synagogue

Williams (1976, 246) writes that, 'The break-away Reform Synagogue (Figure 4.98), smaller than The Great Synagogue, was built to hold 400 men in the nave and 250 women in two galleries above'. At that time in Reform synagogues, women and men sat separately. It was designed by Edward Solomons (1828-1906), who also designed the Spanish and Portuguese Synagogue in Cheetham Hill Road' A photograph shows a simple arch at the east end that framed an octagonal apse, the Ark was placed in this, and before it was the reader's desk (Figure 4.99). Kadish(2011,114) writes that Manchester's Reform Synagogue was the first in the history of synagogue

Figure 4.98 Manchester: exterior of Reform Synagogue of Manchester Congregation of British Jews Cheetham Hill Road 1858 (photograph by permission of Jewish Heritage UK and the Glyn family).

Figure 4.99 Manchester: interior of the Synagogue of Manchester Reform Congregation of British Jews Cheetham Hill Road established 1858 (photograph by permission of Jewish Heritage UK and the Glyn family).

architecture in Britain to adopt the Oriental style. Unlike the layout of Orthodox synagogues, the reader's desk was placed before the Ark, and not in the centre of the nave. Williams notes that there was an organ in the west gallery (Ibid, 247). The separation of the growing Manchester community in 1858 demonstrated the divide that had taken place on matters of theology, liturgy and synagogue design. The building was destroyed by German bombing in 1941, no plans or drawings exist.

4.2.20.4 Manchester: Spanish and Portuguese Synagogue

During the 1850s and 1860s, Sephardi textile merchants from Corfu, Gibraltar, Greece, Morocco, Tunisia and Turkey settled in Manchester, the 'Cotton City.' According to Williams (2008, 39), 'the new settlers were engaged in overseas trade sending goods, mainly textiles to South America, Mediterranean coastlands and the Far East'.

At first, some of them worshipped in private houses and the Ashkenazi Synagogue in Halliwell Street. Williams (1976, 321) notes that, 'at the time of the 1861 census most of the early Sephardi immigrants were living in lodgings with Jewish families in Strangeways and Cheetham Hill' (The first Sephardi Synagogue in Manchester was the former Jew's School at 78 Cheetham Hill Road). By 1874 there were three 'cathedral' synagogues in Cheetham Hill, The Great, the Reform and the Sephardi, all a short distance from each other. Manchester from 1874 became the only provincial city that had congregations representing all three sections of the Jewish community in England, Ashkenazi, Sephardi and Reform. The Sephardi community, according to Williams 'accepted the prayer book and usages of Bevis Marks in London (4.1.2) ….. and placed itself under the religious jurisdiction of the *Haham* the Sephardi equivalent of the Chief Rabbi' (Ibid.38/39). The former

Figure 4.100 Manchester: Façade of the former Spanish and Portuguese Synagogue, now the Jewish useum (left); plaque by the entrance to The Jewish Museum (right) (photograph K. Marks 2010).

Spanish and Portuguese Synagogue is the oldest surviving synagogue in Manchester.

The building was designed by Edward Solomons, who, as mentioned, also designed the Manchester Reform Synagogue. The façade is of red brick with a central projecting gable (Figure 4.100). The entrance is framed by a horseshoe arch, repeated in the five windows above. On the right-hand side of the entrance is a plaque which describes the building as having 'Spanish and Saracenic (Muslim style) motifs' (Figure 4.100). This style had been used in medieval synagogues in Spain and in the Mediterranean countries where the Sephardim had settled. The architecture of the synagogue reflected the roots of the congregation, many coming from the Iberian Peninsula.

Figure 4.101 Manchester: interior showing ark from ladies gallery (left); interior column returned to its original state in 1980's (right). (photograph K.Marks 2010).

'The *Ehal* (Ark) being classical in style is of marble, pink granite and alabaster, but framed within a bold and cusped horseshoe arch' (Figure 4.101) (Kadish 2006, 143). During restoration work in the 1980s, one of the columns was returned to its original state, showing the stencilling and gold paintwork. The balustrade to the gallery is also painted in gold, having been inspired by Egyptian mosques (Ibid, 143).

4.2.21 Merthyr Tydfil [33]

In the 19th century, the three major communities in South Wales were Swansea, Cardiff and Merthyr Tydfil. The latter established in 1848. Kadish (2006, 203) reports that, '....the first and second synagogues were established in John Street in 1848 and 1852 and were demolished in the 1990s'. The third synagogue up the hill from the city centre was built in 1872 and still exists. There is no longer a community in Merthyr Tydfil. The outside is double-turreted with the Welsh dragon on the front gable (Figure 104) with a plaque on the stair wall recording when the synagogue was established (Figure 103). On a side wall in one of the windows, there is a Star of David (Figure 104). The building was sold in 1983 and is now in a poor state of repair (personal observation 2010). It is the oldest and one of the most important purpose built synagogues still standing in Wales.

Figure 4.102 Merthyr Tydfil: former synagogue(1872) front view (photograph J. Marks 2010).

Figure 4.103 Merthyr Tydfil: 'The Jewish Synagogue' 1872 Bryntirion Road (photograph J. Marks 2010).

Figure 104 Merthyr Tydfil: Bryntirion Road. Welsh dragon on front gable of the synagogue (left); ynagogue side window showing Star of David (right) (photograph J. Marks 2010).

4.2.22.1 Newcastle [34]

The first mention of individual Jews in Newcastle is 1775 with the foundation of a community in 1830 (Roth 1950, 111). The first room of prayer opened soon after the community was established in a private house in Pilgrim Street, which no longer exists. According to Olsover (1980, 18), 'The congregation migrated from place to place, worshipping in Bigg Markey, Pudding Chare, Carliol Street and elsewhere, sometimes even in public houses'. In 1835, 250 square yards of land nearby were purchased in Thornton Street for a burial ground, which is discussed in 5.2.22.

The first synagogue near to Thornton Street was established in Temple Street in 1838 but was subsequently destroyed c.1867 (Guttentag 1973, 15). The synagogue contained a mikveh. Olsover suggests that there was a subterranean passage connecting the synagogue with the cemetery, but this may have been a pathway or narrow lane (Ibid, 18). No plans or illustrations exist of this synagogue. By 1845, around six years after the synagogue was founded, the congregation consisted of 33 adults and 33 children (Ibid, 20). By 1864, the building was too small for the growing community and it was enlarged. In the grounds of the Gosforth Synagogue, which was established in 1954, there is a plaque and remains of the lintel from Temple Street, which are all that remains of Newcastle's first synagogue (Figure 4.105).

ENTABLATURE
Of the first purpose-built
SYNAGOGUE
AT TEMPLE SREET IN THIS CITY
ERECTED1838-5598
'REMEMBER THE DAYS OF OLD'
DEUT. 32.7

Figure 4.105 Newcastle: Plaque and lintel from Temple Street Synagogue (1838), now in Gosforth Synagogue (photograph D. Sadlik 2010).

Figure 4.106 Newcastle: Entrance to former Charlotte Street Synagogue 1867-1879 (photograph K. Marks 2010).

In 1867, there was a split in the congregation, and new premises were found in Charlotte Square. Figure 4.106 shows the remaining front entrance of the synagogue (personal observation 2010). In 1879, following discussions between the two communities, they agreed to come together and acquired a new synagogue large enough to hold the two existing congregations and new immigrants who had settled in the city. By 1879, there were c.750 Jews in the community which was still growing. A site was purchased in Albion Street near to Leazes Park and Elswick Road, which was the Jewish area, the synagogue was consecrated in 1880.

4.2.22.2 Newcastle: Leazes Park Synagogue

This synagogue was the 'cathedral' synagogue of Newcastle Jewry. All that remains is the frontage constructed of Newcastle sandstone. Stars of David are still evident in the heads to the upper-floor windows (personal observation 2010). Kadish (2006, 187) notes that 'the frontage, not symmetrical, with a tripartite and gabled central range with entrance doors in the wings at either end featuring decorative lobed arch surrounds'. According to Olsover (1981, 280), 'The building provided for about 350 men on the ground floor and the galleries held between 200 and 300'. The synagogue conformed to Orthodox traditions, with the *bimah)* in the centre of the ground floor and the orientation of the Ark at the east end. Olsover describes 'an Oriental and Byzantine feeling, freely drawn upon in the interior décor' (Ibid, 30). Prior to its closure, the community was moving out of the area, and only the old and infirm remained within walking distance of the synagogue. 30 years ago it was closed. None of the interior remains, and the building has now been converted into apartments (personal observation 2010).

Figure 4.107 Newcastle: Former Leazes Park Synagogue 1879 (photograph K. Marks 2010).

4.2.23 Norwich [35]

'The first mention of individual Jews in the city dates to c.1750 and the establishment of the Norwich community is dated to 1813' (Roth 1950, 111). As with other small communities at that time, prayers would have been held in private houses. Two synagogues existed before the present one in Earlham Road opened in 1968 (not discussed). According to Leveton (2009, 10) 'The first synagogue opened in 1828 was in Tombland Alley close to Norwich Cathedral'. Brown (1990, 221), describes the synagogue as '...a modest prayer hall, a top lit room...notable mostly for its privacy, tucked away as it was at the end of an extremely narrow passage off Tombland'. Tombland Alley was also the approximate location of Norwich's medieval Jewry.

At that time, the synagogue

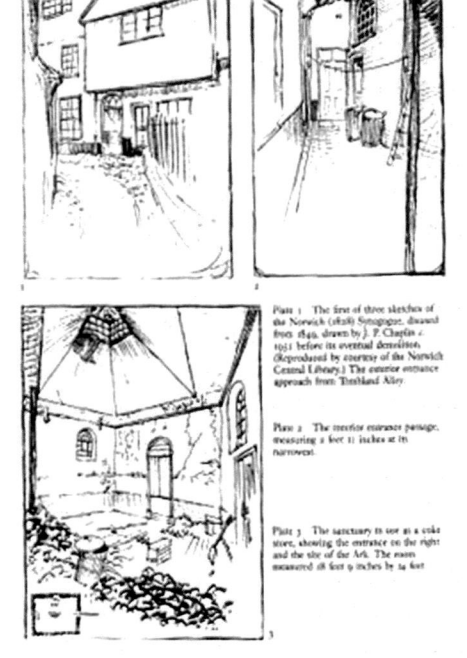

Figure 4.108 Norwich: Sketches showing the first synagogue Tombland Alley (1828). (Norwich City Library).

Figure 4.109 Norwich: recently restored Regency houses in Tombland Alley, near the Cathedral, possibly to have contained the Regency synagogue (by permission Maureen Leveton).

Figure 4.110 Norwich: St. Faith's Lane later Synagogue Street. Synagogue prior to bombing in 1942 (Norwich City Library).

Figure 4.111 Norwich: St. Faith's Lane, later Synagogue Street. Synagogue, in ruins after bombing in 1942 (Norwich City Library).

records show that 29 families were members, suggesting that in total there were around 75 Jews in Norwich. This is the size of the 1851 community identified by Lipman (1951, 23). In 1835, a new synagogue was erected in St Faiths Lane, later renamed Synagogue Street, which was destroyed by bombing in 1942. As with many small provincial communities, most of the physical evidence of Norwich's 19th century community comprises the cemeteries (discussed in 5.2.23).

4.2.24 Nottingham [36]

Roth (1950, 111), attributes the establishment of the Nottingham community to 1822 and according to Lassman et al., (1944, 17), 'there is documented proof of there being a handful of Jews in the City from 1763'. The first cemetery was established in 1823 in North Sherwood Street, this cemetery is discussed in 5.2.24.1. Kadish (2006, 130) suggests that, 'the first synagogues (rooms in private houses) were used from c.1827'. In 1845, there were no more than 50 Jews living in the town (Roth 1950, 87). Fisher (1998, 33) suggests that this would have only been the number of observant and affiliated members and that the community by this date 'must have run into several hundreds'.

Between 1822 and 1890, services were held in 10 different private homes and hired meeting rooms. It was not until 1890 that the first purpose-built synagogue was built in Chaucer Street (Ibid, 43). The houses or rooms of prayer no longer exist except for one wall of the 1820s Barker Gate prayer hall (not examined) (Ibid, 43). Figure 6.13 shows the location of eight of these meeting rooms and places of worship, which are discussed in Chapter 6.

Chaucer Street, Nottingham's first 'handsome and commodious synagogue' (Ibid, 46), held 180 in the main body of the hall and 100 in the galleries, large enough at that time to hold the entire community on the High Holidays. The community moved to the new synagogue in Shakespeare Villas in 1954. Chaucer Street was demolished in 1991, when the area was re-developed. The Jewish community peaked in the 1950s with around 1, 000 persons.

Figure 4.112 Nottingham: Chaucer Street Synagogue 1890-1954 (Fisher et al.1998, 44).

Nottingham: Hebrew Congregation Shakespeare Villas NG1 Grade11. 1954-still used

The present synagogue was a former Wesleyan Methodist chapel erected in 1854. The restored 19th-century building houses the red, grey and cream granite and marble (4.113). On the front of the building is inscribed above the front entrance '*Enter Into His Gates With Thanksgiving*'. This inscription dates to 1854 and was considered by the Jewish community to be as appropriate as much as it was to the Wesleyans (personal contact 2010). The Ark screen is from the Chaucer Street Synagogue (Figure 4.113).

In Nottingham Castle Museum is a set of *rimonim*, (silver breast plate, bells and pointer) used to decorate the *Torah* (scrolls of the law), on loan from the Congregation. Donated to the Nottingham Hebrew Congregation c.1913 (personal contact David Snapper), the reason why it is in the museum and not in the synagogue is that the community cannot afford to pay the insurance. The set was made in Germany in the

Figure 4.113: Nottingham: Hebrew Congregation Synagogue,(former Methodist Chapel); Ark moved from Chaucer Street Synagogue (right). Shakespeare Villas NG1 (photographs K. Marks 2010).

18th century and consists of: a pair of *Torah* finials with bells, made of parcel gilt silver in Berlin in c.1750, the finials used to decorate the tops of the two poles around which the scrolls are wound: a silver *Torah* Shield, made in Hamburg c.1716, the shield or breast plate hangs in the front of the scrolls, that are draped in a mantle of silk or velvet and then removed for the reading of the scroll and a *Torah* pointer *(yad)* made in Sweden in 1913 (personal observation 2010).

Figure 4.114 Nottingham: Shakespeare Villas Synagogue: 18th-century silver rimonim *(used to decorate the* Torah, *now in Nottingham Castle Museum) (photograph K. Marks 2010).*

4.2.25   Oxford   [37]

Roth (1950, 111), attributes the foundation of the Oxford community to 1841; the first mention of individual Jews in the City is 1733. Lewis (1992, 1) states that, 'As Anglo-Jewish provincial communities go; Oxford was a relatively late arrival and has not been of great importance in itself'. *The 1845 Statistical Account of the Congregations in the British Empire* (Figure 6.2), shows that there were 20 individuals attending payers, but there was no synagogue, with prayers being held in a private room. In 1851, the national census included a question on religious buildings, which indicates that the first synagogue was established c.1849. There are no remains of Oxford's 19th-century synagogues.

Prior to Paradise Square, there was no synagogue in Oxford. Lewis (1992, 17) states that, 'We cannot place the synagogue in it (Paradise Square) with any certainty, although we may suspect that it was at the north end, where the Zacharias family were living in 1851'. The synagogue was near to Oxford Castle and also near to the main area of Jewish occupation. It held 30 seats, of which six were reserved for members (Ibid, 18). Compared with churches, chapels, colleges and halls in Oxford, it would have been a modest hall of prayer, with its members being tradesmen, not involved with the academic life of the University, due to the exclusion of Jews until c.1869.

'St Aldate's was the second synagogue to be established above a warehouse, possibly no.12 or 13' (Ibid, 20). Lewis quotes from *The Jewish Chronicle* of 1870 report on High Holidays thus: *'The attendance of the synagogue in Oxford was very good, 25 persons attending on each day of the holidays (Ibid, 20), as the small community could not afford a rabbi, the services would have been led by the shochet (ritual slaughterer) or a member of the congregation.*

The third room of prayer or synagogue was situated over stables. Lewis quotes from an undergraduate who attended services on the High Holidays, as follows:

> *'The entrance was thoroughly dirty, and, after having entered, there faces us a washhouse and stabling, and other things not pleasant to behold. '…. there was no provision whatever for the religious education of the young. On Yom Kippur (the Fast Day) the Jews met in an untidy room for divine service, and only some of them appeared on that day'* (Ibid, 26).

Later, the site became the Old Fire Station, which still exists. In the 1880s, the Oxford congregation applied to become members of the United Synagogue. According to Newman (1976, 30) this was rejected as at that time as only London

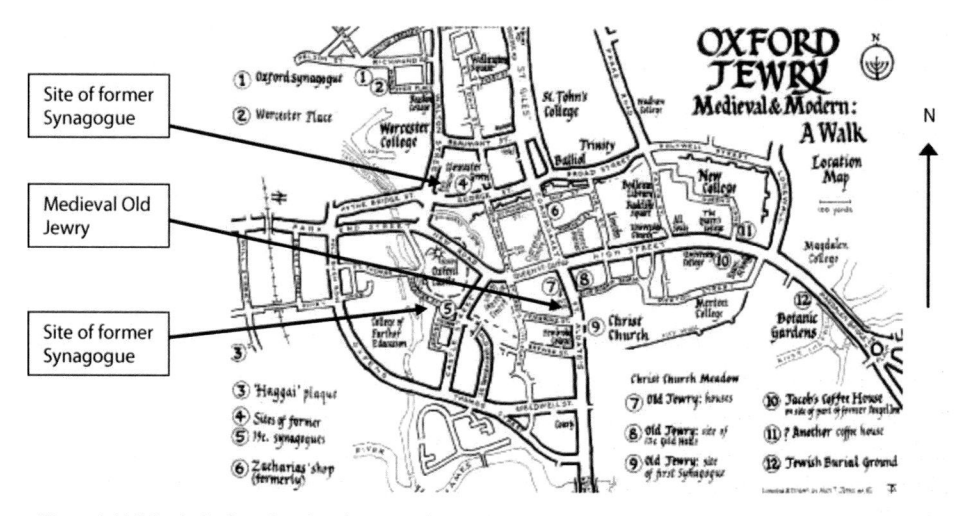

Figure 4.115 Oxford: plan of medieval Jewry and sites of synagogues and coffee house owned by Jews in 18th century (Lewis 1992, preface).

synagogues were to be included in the membership for financial reasons. The Chairman of the Executive Committee, argued also 'that Oxford was placed in a peculiar position, in that it was as much carried on for the benefit of the students at the University…..in fact the synagogue was only kept open during term time, since there were not sufficient Jews to form a *minyan* (ten men over the age of thirteen) in the vacations. In 1893, a new synagogue was consecrated by the Chief Rabbi, at that time Rev. Dr Adler. It was large enough to hold the growing community and Jewish undergraduates. In 1894, a burial ground was consecrated in Oxford (not discussed, as it was first used after the period under discussion). This was Oxford's second Jewish cemetery, the first being seven centuries before, opposite Magdalen College, when there was a sizeable community in the city.

4.2.26 Penzance [38]

The first records of this community began in 1807 Roth (1950, 111) but individual Jews were known to have lived in the town from the first half of the 18th century. Figure 4.116 shows the location of the synagogue and cemetery which overlooks the harbour. All that remains of the 1807 synagogue is the rear east wall (Figure 4.117). The building's front has been absorbed into the Star Inn on Market Jew Street (discussed in 4.3). According to Roth in *The Jewish Chronicle* of 1933, 'the synagogue was sold in 1906, the proceeds being devoted to the upkeep of the cemetery' (discussed in 5.2.26). Nothing remains of the interior, which would identify the building as a former synagogue. Unlike Falmouth, there is no commemorative plaque on the outside wall.

The community formed about 1740, with the first synagogue, perhaps in a house or other temporary accommodation, opened in c.1768 (Margoliouth 1851),

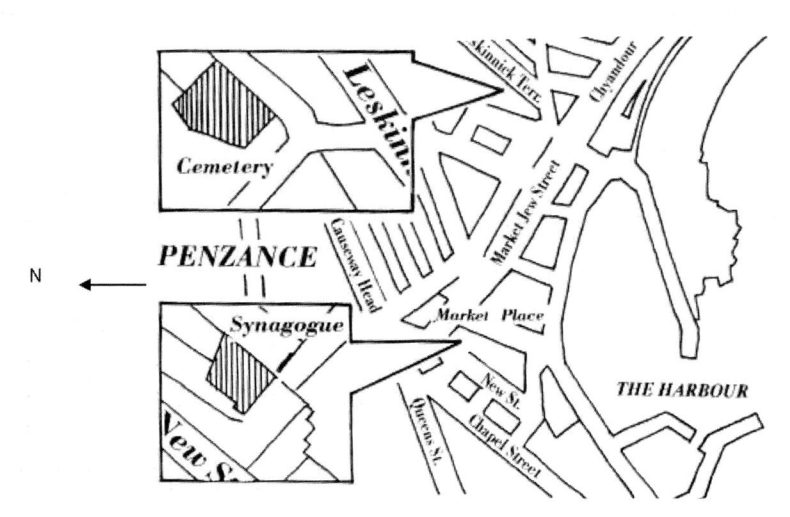

Figure 4.116 Penzance the sites of the synagogue and Jewish cemetery (map by permission of Bill Smith in Pearce et al. 2000, 74 (no scale).

on the same site as the 1807 synagogue (Figure 4.116) on land leased from the local Bramwell family. At that time Jews were not permitted to own the freeholds of property. The first settlers were ships chandlers and merchants. Their names, in the community records and on tombstones, indicate that they came mainly from Germany and the Low Countries (Belgium and Holland). According to Roth, 'at this date the community was no more than six householders, about 25 persons, supplemented on the Sabbath by itinerant peddlers and other poor congregants who could not contribute to the upkeep of the synagogue' (Ibid, 72).

Figure 4.117 Penzance: Former synagogue remaining eastern wall (photograph J. Marks 2009).

The survey carried out by the Chief Rabbi's office in 1845 shows that the community in Penzance numbered around 50 people (Figure 6.1), but then it declined so that by the end of the 19th century it was no longer viable, the synagogue was closed in 1906.

The remaining east wall has two arched windows, now boarded up. The building was surveyed in 1958 by the architect Jamilly (Fry et al, 2000). His drawing (Figure 4.118) shows the street entrance on New Street leading into a small courtyard, the door to the synagogue being on the west wall opposite the Ark. The railed Ark was on the east wall placed between the two remaining arched windows. The *bimah* was in

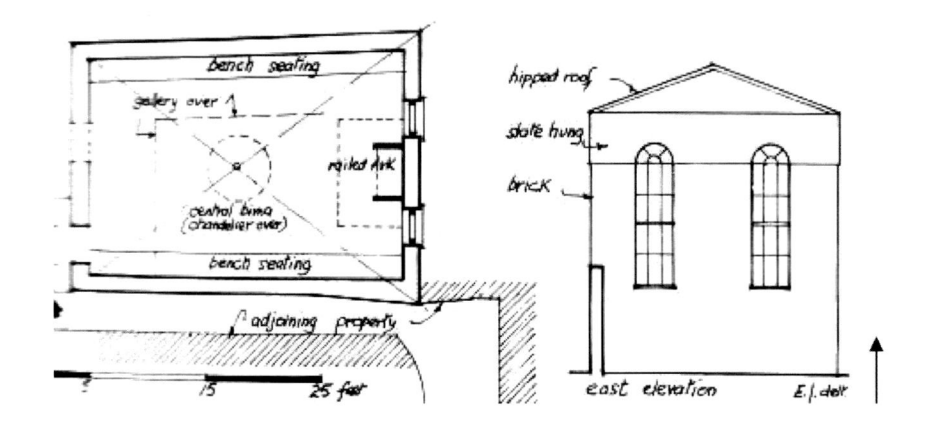

Figure 4.118 Penzance: plan of former synagogue, surveyed in 1958 by Jamilly (Fry et al, 2000, 23).

Figure 4.119 Penzance: Former synagogue The interior showing the ladies gallery c.1970 and Decalogue (Courtesy: David Giddings) (Pearce et al. 2000, 297).

the centre of the synagogue with a chandelier above it. There was bench seating for men on two sides, with a ladies' gallery on the north and south walls.

Fry records that, 'two snapshots were taken in 1960 of the interior, when the building was as a church for the Plymouth Brethren' (Ibid, 23). One of these survives and shows part of the original interior, Decalogue (Ten Commandments) and ladies' gallery still remaining (Figure 4.119). The Decalogue is now in the Jewish Museum, Camden Town. The *Luhot* or Decalogue (the Ten Commandments) would have been placed over the Ark. No other artifacts from this disused synagogue have yet been traced.

One of the main shopping streets in Penzance is 'Market Jew Street'. There are several other Cornish words connected with the mining industry, such as 'Jew's House', which was a particular type of disused smelting works and 'Jew's leavings', which was tin mixed up with mine refuse. Again, there is no evidence that these were connected to Jews. Although it is known that Jewish traders had shops in this street in the late 19th century (Pearce 2000, 247), the use of the word Jew is derived from the Cornish language and has nothing to do with the Jewish community (Ibid, 16). There is no physical evidence of the mikveh, which, according to Pearce (personal contact 2009), was in a private house belonging to Hyman Woolf (c.1810) in Causeway Head and is noted in the records of the congregation and discussed in (4.4.2).

4.2.27 Plymouth

Plymouth's synagogue is the oldest surviving Georgian architectural style Ashkenazi synagogue in the English-speaking world. Roth (1950, 91), notes that 'the first mention of Jews being in Plymouth is 1740 and tradition has it that the date of the foundation of the community was 1752-1756'. The synagogue was built in 1761-2. Prior to this, services were held in private homes or in rented rooms. The first account of Jews in Plymouth is in *A Picture of Plymouth* (1740) (Ibid, 91). At that time there were seven persons; two dealers in naval stores, two silversmiths, a grocer, a general merchant and a slop-seller (old clothes) (Ibid, 91).The early community was mainly from Holland and Germany. Rabbi Bernard Susser (1972, 5) who was Rabbi to the community (1961-1965), reports that 'by around 1762, the community numbered some 30-50 families' and bought the freehold of the synagogue in 1834

(Plymouth Synagogue records). *The Statistical Accounts of the congregations in the British Empire 1845* (Figure 6.2), shows Plymouth with 205 members, at that time one of the largest provincial communities, with only Birmingham, Bristol, Liverpool, Manchester and Portsmouth larger,

The synagogue is tucked away on a side street. The exterior is whitewashed stone roofed with Cornish slate. From the outside, the building has the appearance of a non-conformist meeting house (personal observation 2009). The Ark faces towards Jerusalem, with the front door at the rear. Two large round-headed windows can be seen from Catherine Street and are on either side of the Ark (personal observation 2009); they were added in 1874 (personal communication Dr. Peter Lee 2009).

At the rear of the synagogue building is a Victorian vestry house; the keystone in Latin characters over the door indicates that it was built in 1874. According to Dr. Lee, the vestry was built on the site of the 18th century mikveh (personal communication 2009). In the early 18th century Catherine Street was marsh land, providing a natural source of fresh water for ritual bathing. During 2007, the Victorian (1874-c.1930s) basement mikveh was uncovered by the caretaker Jerry Sibley; it is discussed in Chapter 4.4. In the Victorian period the vestibule was floored with Minton terracotta (personal observation 2009).

The windows on the left-and-right hand side of the hall are original (synagogue records). The stained glass windows were added in the 20th century, replacing plain glass. According to Kadish (2006, 91/92), 'The two windows on either side of the Ark were cut into the wall after 1874; most of the interior fixtures and fittings are original'. The lavish Ark dominates the interior and is described by the Working Party on Jewish Monuments in the UK and Ireland (1999) 'as the only full blooded Baroque Ark surviving in this country, complete with shadow painting of the Hebrew characters'.

Kadish states:

> *With its broken pediment, fluted Corinthian pilasters, carved finials and urns and oversized blue and gold Luhot (around the Ten Commandments), the Plymouth example, perhaps made in the Netherlands or German Lands, has been likened to the baroque Arks of the synagogues of Venice* (Ibid 91).

The Hebrew inscription on the cornice separating the two sections of the Ark is from Psalm 5:7, the English translation being *With deep respect I will bow down towards your holy temple'.* Some letters have lines above them, indicating the Hebrew date 5522, corresponding to 1761-1762 and confirms the date when the synagogue was built.

The hall is plastered and whitewashed, and this focuses the eye onto the Ark and the large wooden *bimah* topped by tall brass candlesticks. Around the corners of the *bimah* are curved benches, which are most unusual. These perhaps provided additional seating space at High Holidays, when the synagogue would have been full, or used by the elders of the congregation.

The Prayer Board to the Royal Family, which was a feature of many synagogues, hangs in the vestibule. The names of King George V (1910-1935) and Queen Mary

Figure 4.120 Plymouth: George III synagogue exterior from Catherine Street (1761/2) (photograph J. Marks 2009).

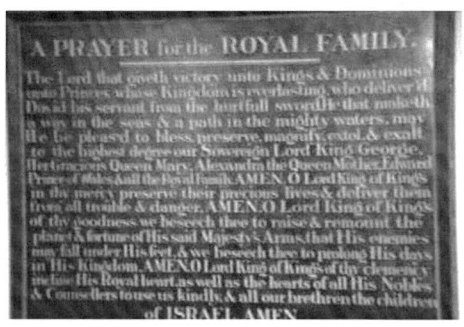

Figure 4.121 Plymouth: 1762 over painted George V and Queen Mary prayer board to the Royal Family. (photograph J. Marks 2009).

would have been over painted on the original board, which according to the synagogue records, dates from the synagogue consecration in 1762 (Figure 4.121). Kadish (2006, 91) states that, 'The original ladies' gallery lay on the west side facing the Ark, and as the community expanded it was extended along the sides to match the original'.

4.2.28 Portsmouth [39]

Portsmouth was the first provincial community established in England following re-settlement in 1656. Jewish traders were engaged in trades relating to servicing the fleet and supplying the Royal Navy which was at that time the world's greatest fleet. The first community was established c.1730 in Portsea, near to the docks and in the centre of the city's commercial area. A plan exists (Green 1982, 107) (Figure 4.124) taken from community records, and shows the locations of where some of the Jews had shops or lived during the Napoleonic Period. Roth (1935, 158) notes that, '…the first synagogue opened in 1780 on the corner of Queen Street and White's Row (now Curzon Howe Road), near to the Royal Docks. The 1780 synagogue was constructed on the same site as an earlier hall of prayer' (Ibid, 181).

Portsmouth Jewry was at its peak during the economic boom of the Napoleonic wars. In 1812 the community is estimated at between 400-500 people, probably the most substantial in the provinces (Weinberg 1998, 10). Following the end of the Napoleonic wars by 1850, the community declined to around 300, many leaving to go to London and the industrial towns in the north or other parts of the Empire (Ibid, 11). The size of the community increased during the mass immigration, following the Russian pogroms starting c.1880. The *Jewish Year Book* records the Jewish population in 1896 as 500.

In 1842, White's Row synagogue was reconstructed and enlarged (Figure 4.122). The community and synagogue moved to Southsea before World War II (4.123), and the current building was consecrated in 1936 and contains the original Ark from the

LIVING COMMUNITIES 105

Figure 4.122 Portsmouth: White's Row 1780-1936 Ark moved to new synagogue in Southsea. (A reconstruction by George Lukomski) (Roth, 1935.

Figure 4.123 Portsmouth: the 1780 Georgian Ark at Portsmouth Synagogue from White's Row Synagogue now in Portsea Synagogue (Kadish, 2006, 82).

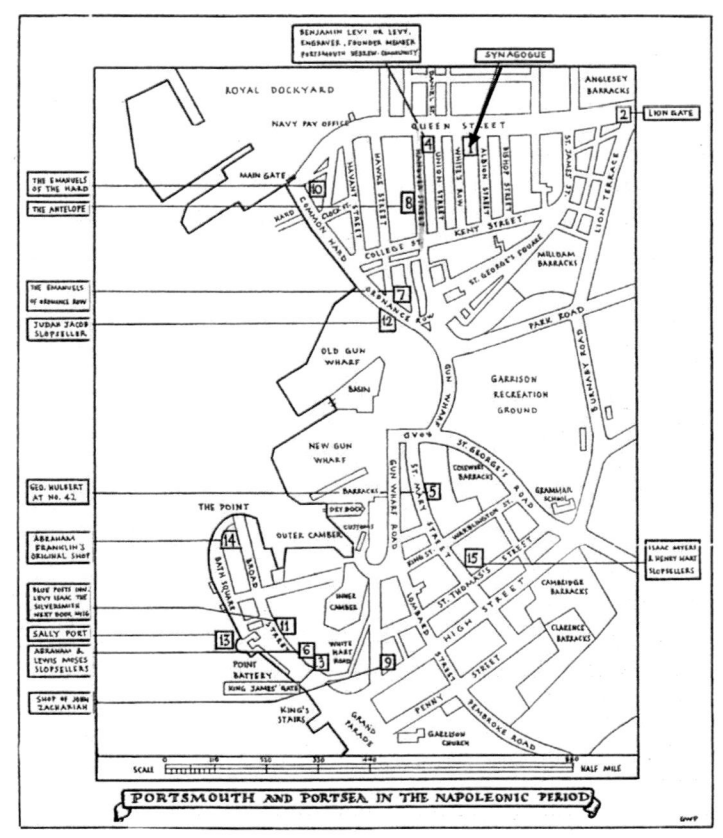

Figure 4.124 Plan of Portsmouth and Portsea, showing the synagogue and location of houses where Jews lived and traded during the Napoleonic Wars (Green 1982, 107).

106 THE ARCHAEOLOGY OF ANGLO-JEWRY IN ENGLAND AND WALES 1656–C.1880

Georgian (1780) building (Figure 4.122). Large parts of the docks in Portsea, including the old synagogue site were destroyed by bombing in World War II.

Removed from above the White's Row Synagogue clock is the coat of arms of George III, demonstrating loyalty to the Monarch (Figure 4.125). This coat of arms is unique, as it more usual to have a prayer board to the Royal Family, as in other synagogues such as Cheltenham. Another unusual feature is the pair of large round-headed windows on either side of the Ark, dated to 1843, and also moved from the old synagogue in Portsea. The windows contain the full text of the Ten Commandments in both Hebrew and English (Figure 4.126).

Figure 4.125 Portsmouth: Southsea synagogue, Coat of Arms of George III (1843) (photograph K. Marks 2009)

A foundation lintel stone, preserved from the synagogue in White's Row and painted in blue, has been set in the wall of the vestibule or *succah* (a hut or booth where part of the Feast of Tabernacles is celebrated) (Figure 4.127). The date 5540 is shown (corresponding to 1780), the year the first synagogue was established.

Figure 4.126 Portsea: Southsea:Synagogue windows (1843) on either side of the Ark, with text of Ten Commandments (photograph K. Marks 2009).

The Hebrew translates as follows:

> *'For now the Lord God has opened before us a great country and made this house provide strength to the newcomer as to the founders- unto each one'.* There is a quote from Haggai 2:9 *'The new temple will be more beautiful than the first one'* and a second quote from 1 Kings 8:13. *'Then Solomon said......As you can see, I've built a beautiful (house) for you. You can live in it for ever'.*

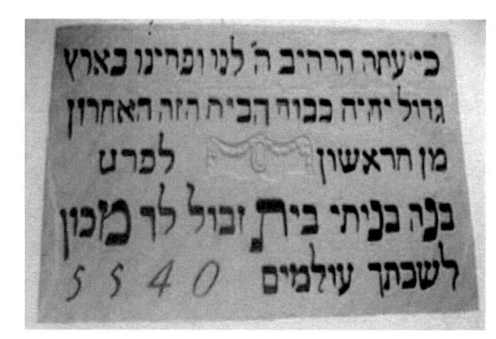

Figure 4.127 Portsmouth: Portsea lintel stone dated 5540 (1780) (photograph K. Marks 2009).

In the stairwell behind the Ark are further stones (Figure 4.128), one detailing the leaders of the congregation when the foundation stones of the first synagogue were laid: Benjamin Levy, Abraham Woolfe and Gershom ben Benjamin on Lag b'Omer 5540 (corresponding to 23rd May 1780). The second commemorates the official foundation-stone-laying ceremony one month later on 10 Sivan 5540 (13th June 1780) lead by David Tevele Schiff, Rabbi of the Ashkenazi Great Synagogue in London and the second Chief Rabbi (1765-1791), and the Sephardi *Haham* (Chief Rabbi), Moses Cohen D'Azevedo. The fact that both the Chief Rabbi of the Ashkenazi Community and the Chief Rabbi of the Sephardi Community were at the dedication of the synagogue reflects the importance of the Portsmouth community at that time.

Figure 4.128 Portsmouth: foundation and commemorative stones removed from the 1780 synagogue in Portsea (photograph K. Marks 2009).

4.2.29.1 Ramsgate [40]

Roth (1950, 111), attributes the date of the foundation of the Ramsgate community to c.1833, although individual Jews lived in Ramsgate from 1786. According to Lipman (1954, Appendix) the community numbered around 45 members in 1850. Before the synagogue was established, the nearest congregation was in Canterbury. The establishment of the synagogue was due to Sir Moses Montefiore (1784-1885), Anglo-Jewry's most important 19th-century philanthropist and a devout Jew.

Montefiore Synagogue

Designed by a Jewish architect, David Mocatta, it was the first purpose-built synagogue in Britain designed by a Jew and was located on the Montefiore's estate, which no longer exists. According to Rodrigues-Pereira (1984, 1) 'The first bricks placed in the foundations were from Jerusalem' (1954, Appendix). The synagogue still holds occasional services. Kadish (2006, 59) describes the building as 'based on a rectangular plan with canted corners plus a semicircular apse at the back to accommodate the Ark'.

The exterior is finished in cream-painted stucco. On entering the small lobby, there is a marble washstand decorated with a hand holding a water jug, which is reminiscent of the inscriptions on tombstones indicating that the deceased was a Levi washing the hands of the priests (Figure 4.130). In contrast with other

Figure 4.129 Ramsgate: exterior and entrance of The Montefiore Sephardi Synagogue 1833 (photograph J. Marks 2011).

Figure 4.130 Ramsgate: marble washstand in synagogue vestibule showing jug and the washing of hands, before entering the synagogue (photograph J. Marks 2011).

Figure 4.131 Ramsgate: Interior view of Montefiore Sephardi Synagogue from balcony showing original brass candelabras with candles, Ark and plaques (photograph J. Marks 2011).

Figure 4.132 Ramsgate: Montefiore Sephardi Synagogue, showing original domed ceiling light of clear and red glass (photograph J. Marks 2011).

synagogues there are no Hebrew inscriptions or Jewish symbols in the interior; two plaques was affixed at a later date show the Montefiore coat of arms. Sir Moses' own chair is near the Ark, while there is Lady Montefiore's seat in the gallery. Brass candelabras were originally lit with candles, although only one in front of the Ark is lit in this way. An additional source of light would have come from the octagonal central skylight of clear and red glass.

The synagogue held around 100 men and 50 women (personal observation of numbered seats 2011). Still endowed by the Montofiore Trust, membership is free and open to all, whether Orthodox, Sephardi or Reform. The few Jews who settled in Ramsgate were mainly trade people. During the summer and High Holidays, the number of Jews attending Sabbath services would have increased, as Ramsgate was a popular holiday resort in the mid-to late-19th century.

4.2.29.2   Ramsgate: Montefiore Mausoleum   [86]

The mausoleum next to the synagogue is a replica of Rachel's Tomb on the road between Jerusalem and Bethlehem, which is still a place of pilgrimage for both Jews and Moslems. Sir Moses visited the tomb in 1839 and paid for its repair. The mausoleum in Ramsgate contains Sir Moses, who died in 1885 when he was 101 and his wife, who died childless aged 78 in 1862. The Montfiores were regular visitors to the Middle East and, were responsible for the building of one of the first Jewish neighborhoods outside the walls of the Old City of Jerusalem. Above the entrance to the mausoleum, in Hebrew, is an extract from the last verse of the Hymn '*Adon Olam*' (Master of the Universe). The tombs, of red granite, face east (towards

Figure 4.133 Ramsgate: mausoleum of Sir Moses and Lady Montefiore (1862) (photograph J. Marks 2011).

Figure 4.134 Ramsgate: rear of the mausoleum showing stone pillar from the Land of Israel (photograph J. Marks 2011)

Jerusalem). There are no decorations inside; however, there is a permanently lit memorial candle. Behind the mausoleum is a pillar on a plinth. According to Kadish 'it was reputedly brought back from the Land of Israel and perhaps alludes to the mausoleum built over the grave of the Patriarch Jacob's wife' (Ibid, 61).

4.2.30 Sheerness [41]

Figure 4.135 Sheerness: Isle of Sheppey, interior of 1811 synagogue (Sheerness Heritage Centre).

Roth (1950, 111, dates the foundation of the Sheerness community to 1790. Prayers prior to the establishment of the synagogue in 1811 would have been held in a private house. The first synagogue of this small community was built on the corner of Kent Street and Sheppey Street, Blue Town, Isle of Sheppey. Blue Town is so called because the small wooden houses near the Naval Dock Yard were painted navy blue, which can still be seen today on the few remaining buildings from this period (personal contact 2010). Blue Town was the centre of the early community, before some moved to the Sheerness. Blue Town, being near to the docks, was built on reclaimed marshland and was subject to the unruly life that existed around 19th century navel installations. According to Lipman (1954, 185), '....by 1850 the size of the community had declined to around 75'. The synagogue was dismantled in 1887 (Roth 1950, 98). Little is known about this synagogue. Some religious objects were sent to other communities, such as Stroud (which no longer exists), and the candelabrum used for *Chanukah* (The Festival of Lights) was given to the Mocatta Museum and were on display in the Jewish Studies Library in UCL(some have now been sold). No Jewish community remains in the Isle of Sheppey or Sheerness.

4.2.31 Sheffield [42]

Roth (1950, 111), attributes the foundation of the Sheffield community to 1838 noting individual Jews there from c.1774. The first to be identified with certainty were brothers Isaac and Philip Bright who settled in the city from 1786 (Ballin 1986, 3). The first room of prayer (1820s) was behind a tailor's shop in Pinstone Street (Figure 4.138/3), followed by further rooms of prayer from 1842 (Figure 4.138/5). In 1851, a small synagogue was opened in Figtree Lane in the city centre (Ibid, 13). The exact location is uncertain, as the lane on one side was mostly demolished during redevelopment. In 1872, the first custom-built synagogue was established in North Church Street with seating for 227 persons (Figures 4.136/137). North Church Street, in the city centre, and in use until 1930, was bombed during World War II. West Bar and Scotland Street were areas of Jewish settlement with cheap housing. Many Jews became prosperous in the cutlery and silverware industries moving to Broomhill and Nether Edge. They later moved away from the city centre to the suburbs in Ecclesall where the community remains in a state of decline.

Old Hebrew Congregation: North Church Street S1
Figure 4.136 shows the front of the former red-brick synagogue which is now offices. The inscription in Hebrew above the front doorway reads (in English):

Figure 4.136 Sheffield: front of former North Church Street Synagogue 1872 (photograph K. Marks 2011).

Figure 4.137 Sheffield: detail of the Gothic arch inscription above entrance to former synagogue (photograph K. Marks 2011).

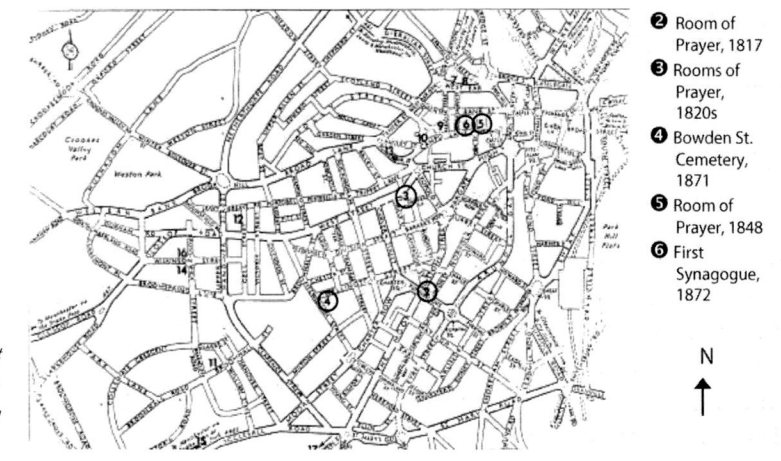

Figure 4.138 Sheffield: Jewish area showing first rooms of prayer and first cemetery (Ballin, 1986).

❷ Room of Prayer, 1817
❸ Rooms of Prayer, 1820s
❹ Bowden St. Cemetery, 1871
❺ Room of Prayer, 1848
❻ First Synagogue, 1872

N ↑

> *1.Kings. Chap.8.V.33*
> *They pray to you in this temple*
> *Synagogue*

The text contains a chronogram confirming the date in the English equivalent for the establishment of the synagogue as 1872. This building is the only surviving synagogue in England built in the early English Gothic style (Kadish 2006, 171), and was built by a local church builder, Mitchell Withers, Senior. There was originally a mikveh, which was closed along with the building in 1930 (Ibid, 171).

4.2.32 Southampton [43]

According to the census return of 1851, the Southampton community was established in 1833, although there were individual Jews there from around 1782 (Roth 1950, 111). As with other Jewish communities in port towns, hawkers and peddlers increasingly settled after the Napoleonic Wars, becoming small shop keepers, and then left as its boom ended (Kushner 2002, 96). Lipman (1954, 243), estimates the size of the community in c.1850 as 75 as compared with Portsmouth's 300. Southampton was apparently an offshoot of Portsmouth (personal contact Martyn Rose 2011).

Figure 4.139 Southampton: synagogue consecrated in 1864, demolished 1964 (Southampton Jewish News 2008).

The first room of prayer, in use from 1833, was in East Street off the High Street. There is no record of where it was in the street, which at the time comprised small houses and shops. The early community was shopkeepers and tailors, who made and sold uniforms to the navy. It can be assumed that the room of prayer was either in a house or above a shop. The first permanent synagogue, Italianate in style, was completed and consecrated in 1864 in Albion Place (Figure 4.139). The synagogue backed on to the City walls and was in use until 1962; it was demolished in 1964. Wooden pews were moved to the new synagogue in a former Methodist chapel, established in 1964, as were the six *Sefer Torahs* (scrolls with the Five Books of Moses). Southampton was not a city of major Jewish settlement, but rather a major transit port for Jews on their way to The New World.

4.2.33 Sunderland [44]

The foundation of the Sunderland community dates to 1781 (Roth 1950, 111). The first synagogue was a room of prayer in a private house in Vine Street, where the rabbi lived. By 1850, membership had dwindled, and the synagogue closed in 1860. The torah scrolls and other the religious objects from the synagogue were sold to the Sunderland Hebrew Congregation for use in a new synagogue in Moor Street. A second synagogue consecrated in Moor Street in 1862 in the East End of Sunderland, close to the Wear Estuary, was demolished in 1928. The third synagogue in Sunderland opened in 1928 in Ryhope Road (Grade II) and closed in 2006. The community, numbering 2,000 in the 1950s, declined to just over 100 in 2001 and now has less than 20 persons. Other evidence of the early community in Sunderland is the two cemeteries (discussed in 5.2.33.1, 2).

4.2.34　　　　　　　Swansea　　　　　　　[45]

The foundation of the Jewish community in Swansea dates to 1768, making it the oldest community in Wales, with the first mention of individual Jews in the town being in 1731/1741 (Roth 1950, 111). The first room of prayer was in a house in Wind Street in use from 1740-1788/9. The second room of prayer, in the Strand, was in use from 1788-1818. The first purpose-made synagogue was erected in Waterloo Street, in use from 1818-1857, large enough to hold 60-70 persons. According to Glass, the Waterloo Street Synagogue was the third house of prayer of the community (1980, 31). *The Statistical Account of the Congregations in the British Empire 1845* (London Metropolitan Archive ACC/2805/1/1/107) (Figure 6.2), shows 133 individual members, making the Swansea community at that date one of the largest in the provinces. By 1857, the Waterloo Street Synagogue was too small for the community,

Figure 4.140 Swansea: Entrance to Goat Street Synagogue (Glass 1980, 45; West Glamorgan Archives).

Figure 4.141 Swansea: Goat Street Synagogue destroyed by bombing in 1941 (Glass, 1980, 57; West Glamorgan Archives).

Figure 4.142 Swansea: Goat Street Synagogue (West Glamorgan Archives). (Glass 1980, 65)

which had grown from four or five families in 1818 to 30 families. A new synagogue was opened in Goat Street in 1859 with room for 228 persons, 120 men and 108 women (Figure 4.141) It was destroyed by bombing in 1941 (Figure 4.141). Unlike other provincial ports, such as Hull and Liverpool, Swansea was not on the immigrant route, and so Jewish settlement came late. It was during the late-19th century that South Wales Jewry expanded, with the industrializing of the largest coal exporting port in the world and the growth of the railway, and the trading opportunities this also brought about in the valley communities. The topography of the three main Jewish communities in the 19th century (Cardiff, Swansea and Merthyr Tydfil), all in South Wales is discussed in Chapter 6.

4.2.35　　　　　　　Yarmouth (Great)　　　　　　　[46]

The Great Yarmouth community was founded in 1801, although there was a small number of Jews in this port town c.1760 (Roth 1950, 111). The only remaining physical evidence of the community are the two cemeteries discussed (5.2.35). Roth's date assumes that a place of worship existed in Chapel Street at the same time as the cemetery was established in 1801. The site later became a Masonic Hall. The synagogue was eventually transferred to a lane off George Street, traditionally known as 'Jew's or Synagogue Row'. In 1846, a new synagogue was constructed on the same site, perhaps the smallest in England with capacity for no more than 60 people. The total size of the community was 48 persons (Ibid, 107). Lipman (1954, 21) states that, '… by 1850, Yarmouth, mainly a fishing port, had a small community of perhaps 75 souls, dating from the beginning of the century; its synagogue had been rebuilt three or four years before'. Yarmouth declined as a community from about this time and by the end of the 19th century had disappeared (Ibid, 161). A few Jews still remain.

4.2.36 *Synagogues conclusion*

In summary, in all of the provincial communities discussed, prayers were held in private houses or hired halls before there was a large enough community to establish a purpose-built synagogue Early synagogues, like the places of worship of Christian Non-Conformists, were mostly in side streets or alleys, with the entrance often being to the side or rear of the building. This made them more secure and gave them a form of protection. From the outside, many looked like Non-Conformist chapels. The exterior of the early synagogue buildings were often designed by Christian architects who had experience in designing chapels and churches. The first purpose-built synagogue after the re-admission was Bevis Marks (1701). It was the creation of a carpenter, Henry Ramsay, who prepared the study model, and then built by a Quaker master-builder, Joseph Avis, who also worked on St Bride's in Fleet Street (Jamilly 1996, 193). The interior was based on the Sephardi Synagogue in Amsterdam, and the interior layout has set the basic design for Orthodox synagogues ever since. The New Synagogue in Great St. Helens, London EC3 (4.1.7), was a landmark in synagogue design. Opened in 1838, it was one of the largest and most celebrated in London (Ibid, 198). The architect of this 'cathedral' synagogue was again a non-Jew, John Davis who was a Non-Conformist chapel designer. The 17th/18th-century synagogues in London were founded in the City and later spread to the East End. They then spread north, south, west and east as the community grew and became more affluent.

Most early London synagogues no longer exist being either destroyed during the war, demolished or used for other purposes such as temples, offices and apartments. The number of synagogues demonstrates the diversity of the early London Jewish community. Immigrants settled in cities and towns, joining Jews already settled. They came from different backgrounds with different traditions within Judaism; London synagogues reveal these movements and 'sects' ranging from Orthodox to Reform.

Provincial synagogues, although varying in size, were also built to a standard plan, based on Creechurch Lane and other Orthodox synagogues in London. The *bimah* was always on the ground floor, in a central position facing the Ark, which pointed east, towards Jerusalem. In front of the *bimah*, there was usually a pew for the wardens. There were balconies for the separation of women from men. In front of the balconies, lattices were made in wood, brass or wrought iron. Over time, the height of balconies was reduced, so that today in Orthodox synagogues, although women and men are still separated, there is no longer a lattice gallery front. Interior lighting was provided by natural light, sometimes from the ceiling and windows to the side or rear of the building, and brass candelabras hanging from the ceiling with light fittings round the *bimah*. Early synagogues were lit by candles. The Ark was set into a cupboard covered by curtains and/or doors, like the altarpiece of a church, and was the focal point. It contained the *Torahs* (The Five Books of Moses), with the Decalogue (Ten Commandments) above. Seating consisted of wooden straight-backed benches, usually with lockers underneath to hold prayer books. Full members of the synagogue were 'seat holders' who had their own regular places as long as they paid their annual fees. Jamilly (1953/5 75) states that, 'Rabbinical teaching laid no great store on the building; it is merely a place in which to worship and although there is some merit in size, it is good to worship the Lord in the sight of a multitude; a room in a private house will do equally well'.

Synagogues were the centre of communal life. With the gradual movement of the community out of poor city centers or port areas where they first settled to more congenial and healthier parts of cities and towns, synagogue buildings were left behind. Limitations of space have precluded discussion of the numerous small synagogues in London and the provinces that in the main no longer exist.

Out of the 35 communities discussed, 10 are now defunct. It is doubtful if a further six will survive for longer than five to ten years, due to ageing and the younger generation moving mainly to London, Manchester and overseas. The 21st-century declining Anglo-Jewish community is concentrated more and more on London and Manchester.

4.3 Street and place names with Jewish connections

Street and place-names with Jewish connections can be divided into two periods, medieval (1066-1290) and re-admission (1656-c.1880). From the medieval period, there are still names such as Old Jewry, Jew's Street and Jewry Street, in London and Winchester. In Lincoln, there is Jew's Court and Jew's House. The medieval street names indicate where there was a concentration of Jews living, always close to the town centre and near to the castle and under the protection of the King or local lord. In Norwich, the medieval Jewry area was destroyed in the Blitz. Currently being redeveloped, representation has been made by the community to have the street name 'Synagogue Street' reinstated. From the 18th century and later, there is a Synagogue Lane and Synagogue Place in Cheltenham and Exeter on side streets where the synagogues are located. Jew's Lane in Portsmouth, leading to the Jewish cemetery, is still known by this name but has been renamed. There are streets named after prominent Jews, mostly in London and Brighton, and these are listed below.

4.3.1 London

Adler Street E1: Dr Nathan Adler was Chief Rabbi 1845-1890.
Disraeli Road E7, W5, NW10 and SW15: four roads named in commemoration of Benjamin Disraeli (1804-1881).
Henriques Street E1: Jacob Henriques was one of the founders of The Reform Movement and was involved in charitable works.
Jews Row Wandsworth SW18: site of Jews' House, now demolished, owned by Jacob and Rachel Da Costa in the late-18th century.
Jew's Walk Sydenham SE26: not known why it has this name.
Jewin Street and Jewin Crescent EC2: streets now under the Barbican, destroyed in the Blitz in 1941. These streets were on the site of the medieval Jewish cemetery.
Montagu Road Cemetery N18: named after Samuel Montagu and a Liberal M.P. for Whitechapel. He later became Lord Swaythling.
Old Jewry EC2 and Jewry Street EC3: streets in the City of London where there was a concentration of Jewish inhabitants in the medieval period. A synagogue once stood in Old Jewry, at the north-west corner. The street is still named.
Old Montague Street E1: Samuel Montague. Lord Swaythling. Liberal MP
St. Lawrence Jewry EC2: site of church on the edge of the medieval Jewry.

4.3.2 Provinces

BATH
Jews Lane.

BRADFORD
Moser Avenue and Moser Street: named after Jacob Moser, one of the founders of Bowland Street Synagogue and Lord Mayor of the City.

BRIGHTON and HOVE
Jew Street: site of first synagogue c.1792-1800.
Coleman Avenue: Reginald Coleman-Cohen, brother of Lord Cohen.
D'Avigdor Road: after Sir Osmand D'Avigdor Goldsmid and Julian Road: (after Sir Julian Goldsmid)
Goldsmid Mews and Road: eminent Jewish philanthropist
Montefiore Road: (after Sir Moses Montefiore).
Osmond Road and Gardens: after Sir Osmand D'Avigdor Goldsmid.
Palmeira Square/Avenue: after the Portuguese title of Sir Isaac Goldsmid. Sir Isaac was the first Jew to be created a Baronet.
Somerhill Road/Avenue/Court: after the Somerhill Estates of D'Avigdor Goldsmid
n.b. Brighton and Hove have more streets named after prominent 19th-century Jews than any other city in Britain.

BRISTOL
Jews' Lane: in the former medieval Jewish quarter, still exists.

CANTERBURY
Jewry Lane: in the former Jewish quarter in the medieval period, still exists.

CHELTENHAM
Synagogue Lane: off St. James's Square GL50, location of synagogue.

EXETER
Synagogue Place EX2: Mary Arches Street. Synagogue entrance is on this Street.

LINCOLN
Jews' House and Jews' Court: Steep Hill (Grade 1).
Possibly the only medieval synagogue remaining in Britain.

LIVERPOOL
Balm Street: named after the balm of Gilead invented by a Dr. Solomon.
Shalom Court: street leading to Greenback Drive, synagogue, now closed.
Solomon Street: Dr. Solomon, who made a fortune in 19th-century inventing a balm that claimed to cure all ills.
Synagogue Court: street with first synagogue, later known as Cumberland Street.

MANCHESTER
Synagogue Alley: location of synagogue to mid-18th century, no longer exists.
Torah Street: named after adjacent Talmud Torah School (1895).

NORWICH
Synagogue Street: location of synagogue, destroyed in 1942.
NOTTINGHAM
Jews' Lane: now St Nicholas Street.
OXFORD
Old Jewry: medieval street where Jews lived, no longer exists.
Jew's Mount: possible medieval fortification of the Jews.
PENZANCE
Jews' Fields and Jerusalem Row: area of cemetery, now renamed Leskinnic Terrace.
Market Jew Street: no connection with the Jewish community.
PLYMOUTH
Synagogue Lane: leading to the synagogue entrance.
PORTSMOUTH
Jews' Lane: now Fawcett Road, Old Jewish Burial Ground.
SUNDERLAND
Jews' Street: now Crescent Row, Old Jewish Burial Ground.
WINCHESTER
Jewry Street: medieval street where Jews lived, still named.
YARMOUTH (GREAT)
Jews' or Synagogue Row: situated off Market Place.
YORK
Jubbergate: medieval name, street near market and shambles, still exists.

4.4 *Mikva'ot* (ritual baths), material culture, and artefacts

A mikveh is a bath used for ritual purification, often by Jewish women after their monthly period. The word mikveh is Hebrew for 'a collection of water'. *Mikva'ot* (pl.) was located sometimes in private houses, in or near synagogues or close to the Jewish community. Therefore, the documented evidence of location of *mikva'ot* indicates that there was nearby an area of Jewish settlement. So far no *mikva'ot* have been found in London from the period under discussion, but there is documented evidence, and this is discussed. As well as documents, there is a number of *mikva'ot* and possible *mikva'ot* in the provinces from this period, no longer used. Baptism in a font plays an important part in Christian life; it maybe that this ritual of immersion and purification re-interprets the Jewish ritual and has found its way into Christianity. The Greek root meaning for baptism is immersion.

Jewish artefacts
Jewish artefacts have been found in London during excavations, some are now in museums, and there are objects from extant synagogues now in museums or in use in later synagogues. Some Jewish archaeological objects have been discussed in the author's MA dissertation (Marks 2000). They are considered here in their wider social context. Considering the length of the period under discussion, around 220

years, very few objects have been found. Only objects that are conclusively Jewish are included, and these are identified from Hebrew lettering, religious symbols, Jewish names or Jewish ritual functions.

4.4.1 Mikva'ot *(ritual baths)*

No evidence remains of 17th-19th-century *mikva'ot* in London, although there are a few examples in the provinces. The reason for this lack of archaeological evidence is discussed, as well as the importance of the mikveh in Orthodox Jewish life. The mikveh was originally a purifying bath used to prepare men and women for Temple ritual. In modern times, it is used to prepare women for sexual encounters with their husbands, after two weeks of abstinence caused by their monthly period. *Mikva'ot* have been found on sites in Israel, for example Jerusalem, and from the Second Temple period (c.AD 70) at Masada and Herodium (c.AD 66). Others have been found from the medieval period in the Rhineland (Worms and Cologne), possibly in France (Rouen), in the Iberian Peninsular and in the Pinkas Synagogue in Prague (Kadish 1996, 104). The presence of a mikveh indicates the level of religious observance of a community. According to Kadish 'It is believed that the Christian rite of baptism is derived from the mikveh' (1996, 101).

Two medieval *mikva'ot* have been found in London, one in 1-6 Milk Street in 2001 and the other in 81-87 Gresham Street in 1986 (Blair et al 2000). The Milk Street remains, which are more complete than those in Gresham Street, were installed in The Jewish Museum, Camden Town (2010). There is an extant mikveh in Canterbury. There is also a possible medieval mikveh in Bristol (found 1987). More recently, the site is considered to be a *'bet tahara'*, a cleansing house for washing the deceased before burial (Kadish 2006, 98). In the period under discussion, the first documented evidence of *mikva'ot* is in the Chief Rabbi's Survey of 1845. Of the 39 communities who completed the survey, 20 reported that they had a mikveh. Some of the very small communities, such as Dover and Yarmouth, indicated that the sea was used. Others such as Bath and Southampton used public bathing facilities. Kadish (1996, 135) states that, 'as early as 1850, the Birmingham and Hull municipalities provided a 'kosher bath' in the local bath houses'. Until the 20th century Kadish indicates her findings show '….that the majority of *mikvaot* were built under private auspices and were not situated in communal buildings, in cellars or outhouses of synagogues, as was the practice on the Continent' (Ibid,135). Orthodox Jews consider physical purity as a powerful metaphor for spiritual purity, Kadish states, 'Since Temple time, and indeed before, the mikveh (pl. *mikva'ot*; literally a gathering of water) or ritual bath has played an essential role in the practice of Judaism (Ibid, 101). The Jewish law that applies to their construction is derived from Leviticus 11:36: '*Only a spring and a pit, a gathering of water, shall be clean*. The key words are *'only a spring'*. There are a number of requirements to meet the religious laws. Amongst which are the following:

First, that there was a source of fresh running water and the capacity of the bath contained a minimum of 200 gallons of water. Physical evidence shows that early *mikva'ot* mostly in private houses were built using artesian wells that supplied the house with water. Rainwater *mikva'ot* came later in 18th century. Kadish states that, 'A rainwater mikveh must contain at least 40 *se'ah* of water, calculated at between 80 and 200 gallons (24 cubic feet). 40 *se'ah* is traditionally taken to be the about twice the volume of the average man.' (Ibid, 102). Secondly, that the bath was completely sealed so that there were no leaks. Thirdly, the mikveh must be built directly into the ground or be an integral part of a building attached to the ground (Ibid, 102). The rabbis of the *Talmud* (commentaries on the Divine Laws in the Bible) considered the presence of a mikveh essential to the establishment of a new community. Once a month, married religious women go to the ritual baths, where they submerge themselves in the water, say a blessing and emerge spiritually cleansed.

Mikva'ot are rarely present in the written and physical evidence of the early re-admission communities. Where there is evidence of *mikva'ot*, as at Canterbury, Portsmouth (Southsea) and Plymouth, they have been out of use for decades. *Mikva'ot* are expensive to maintain and the lack of demand, combined with declining communities, has rendered them redundant. This lack of information may be that the subject was considered 'taboo' given its association with sexuality. According to Orthodox Jewish law (as noted above), there is a requirement of ritual monthly immersion by married women. It could be that the Christian rite of baptism originates from the mikveh.

LONDON

Documented evidence of *mikva'ot* (Kadish 1996 146-148)

Creechurch Lane Synagogue EC3	extant 1664
1 and 2 Mitre Square, Aldgate (Great Synagogue)EC3	before 1854-66
2½ Heneage Lane (Bevis Marks Synagogue) EC3	extant 1853-1900
8 Sussex Place, Leadenhall Street EC3	extant1854
12 Camomile Street Bishops Gate EC3	extant 1856
28 Stewards Street, Brushfield Street EC1	extant 1897-1916

WEST LONDON

Leicester Square WC2 21 Little Newport Street, (one of two private *mikva'ot* attached to the Maiden Lane Synagogue)	c.1824-54
Western Synagogue W1 (private establishment)	extant 1845
Bayswater Synagogue W2 9 St. Germain's Terrace	1866+

EAST LONDON

19 Church Lane, Whitechapel E1 1879-85
Approximately 16 other *mikva'ot* post date 1880, all except one are extant.

NORTH LONDON
Approximately 20 *mikva'ot* post date 1880, many still in use

NORTH-WEST LONDON
9/10 *mikva'ot* post 1880 still in use

SOUTH LONDON
One mikveh post 1880-still in use

Figure 4.143 Medieval mikveh,*(ritual bath) Milk Street during excavation in 001(LAMAS Vol.52, 2001) (left);* mikveh *now in Jewish Museum, Camden Town 2010 (right) (photograph K. Marks 2010).*

4.4.1.2 Provinces

Extract from Statistical Account of the Congregations in the British Empire 1845 (5606) London Metropolitan Archive ACC/2805/1/1/107.

YES		ALTERNATIVE
BIRMINGHAM	BATH	SPA
BRIGHTON	CANTERBURY*	PUBLIC BATHS
BRISTOL	CARDIFF	NO
CHATHAM	CHELTENHAM	PUBLIC BATHS
EXETER	DOVER	SEA
FALMOUTH	IPSWICH	NO
HULL	LYNN NORFOLK	NO
KINGSTON-UPON HULL	NEWCASTLE	PUBLIC BATHS
LEEDS	NOTTINGHAM	PUBLIC BATHS
LIVERPOOL(2)	OXFORD	NO
MANCHESTER (2)	SOUTHAMPTON	PUBLIC BATHS
NORWICH	YARMOUTH	SEA
PENZANCE		

PLYMOUTH
PORTSMOUTH
NORWICH
SHEERNESS
SHEFFIELD
SUNDERLAND
SWANSEA

Data taken from *Statistical Account of the Congregations in the British Empire 1845 (5606)* London Metropolitan Archive ACC/2805/1/1/107
*There was a *mikveh* in Canterbury (dated 1851) (Figure 4.144).

Canterbury:

Figure 4.144 Canterbury: The Old Mikveh *(1851) (no longer in use) (Cohn-Sherbok 1984, 35).*

The Canterbury mikveh, next to the former synagogue, is the only example found of a 19th-century mikveh in a stand-alone building (Figure 4.144). It is no longer in use as a ritual bath. The pool is no longer evident, as it has been covered over. The building has been preserved and is used by Kings School Canterbury as the music master's office. It was built in 1851 in matching style to the synagogue, with obelisks at the front entrance.

Plymouth:
Plymouth Synagogue established 1761/2, is discussed in 4.2.27; the mikveh predates the synagogue, and according to Dr Lee (Hon. Treasurer) can be dated to c.1750. At this time, the location of the synagogue and mikveh was on marsh land, where there was a natural spring. The water from this spring would have supplied the bath. From the tiles, it appears to have been modernised and repaired in the Victorian period (personal observation 2009), but there are no documents to confirm this. The mikveh went out of use in 1925. At the time of visiting, it had been uncovered by the caretaker, Jerry Sibley and infills of rubbish removed (Figure 4.145). This is a rare example of an 18th century mikveh, *in situ* adjacent to an 18th-century synagogue.

Figure 4.145 Plymouth: mikveh *(ritual bath) (originally 1750) showing six steps into pool (photograph K.Marks 2009).*

4.4.2 London material culture and artefacts

4.4.2.1 'Delftware' Hebrew Plate c.1720

The 'Delftware' plate was examined by Jacqui Pearce at MoLAS (Museum of London Archaeological Service) in her paper '*A Rare delftware Hebrew plate and associated assemblage from an excavation in Mitre Street, City of London*' (1998, 95-112). The remains were found in Mitre Street, in the former precinct of Holy Trinity Priory, Aldgate. Figure 4.146 identifies this area as being within the City walls, towards the Tower of London, and from the 1695 census returns, it was an area with a concentration of Jewish inhabitants. Figure 4.146 shows the location of the find in Mitre Street and the location of three nearby synagogues;

(1) Creechurch Street where the first Sephardi synagogue was established (1657), (2) The Great Synagogue (Ashkenazi), (1690) and (3) near to the Spanish and Portuguese Sephardi Synagogue in Bevis Marks, (1701). The 1695 census indicates that the main tenant of 12-14 Mitre Street where the plate was found was a Sephardi Jew, Moses Capadocia. Pearce also states that, 'there were two other families, probably also Jewish. Thus it is possible that the Alley contained a Jewish residence in the decades that followed' (Ibid, 96).

Excavations in 1984, by the then-Department of Urban Archaeology (DUA) of the Museum of London revealed 'A large assemblage of ceramic and other finds dating to the mid 18th century recovered from the fill of a brick-lined domestic rubbish/cess-pit' (Ibid, 95). Pearce indicates that 'all the pieces from Mitre Street date to the

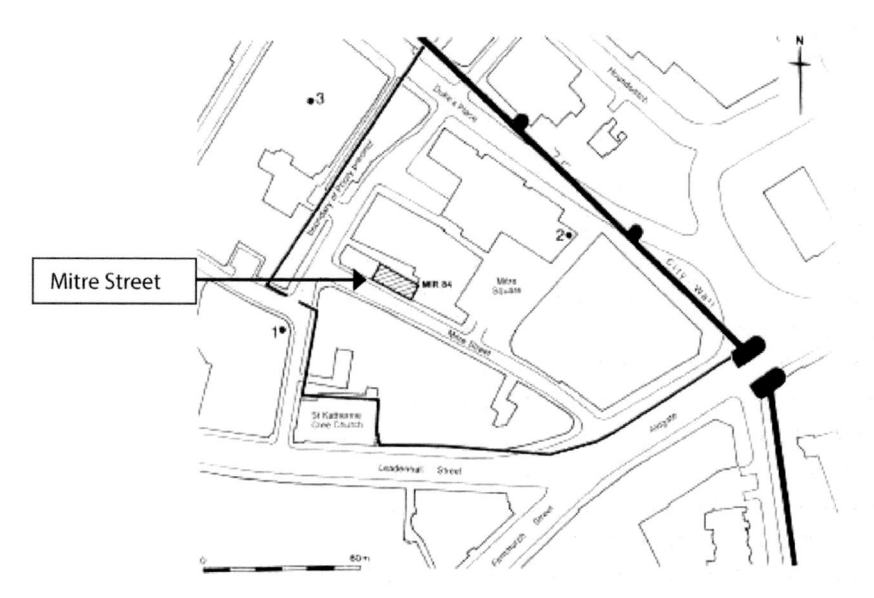

Figure 4.146 Map of the site of 1720 plate in Mitre Street EC3. 1. The Spanish and Portuguese Synagogue, Creechurch Lane; 2.The Great Synagogue; 3. The Sephardi Synagogue in Bevis Marks (Post-Medieval Archaeology 1998)

Figure 4.147 early 18th century 'delftware' plate with Hebrew inscription. chalav indicating that it was used for milk-based meals (Museum of London).

Figure 4.148 mid 18th century 'delftware plate' with Hebrew inscription basar indicating that it was used for meat-based meals (Jewish Museum, London).

late 17th or first half of the 18th century, and were probably made in London at factories in Lambeth and Southwark'(Ibid, 98). Among the 165 sherds from a total of 43 pottery vessels was an almost complete delftware plate with a Hebrew inscription with the word *chalav* (milk) (Figure 4.147). Pearce describes it as a 'find without parallel in excavated material from London' (Ibid, 95). She might have said that it was a find without parallel in England, as so far as the writer is aware, no other inscribed Hebrew plate from this period has been found during excavations. There is an unprovenanced plate of similar design and colour in The Jewish Museum in Camden Town inscribed in Hebrew with basar (meat) (Figure 4.148).

The *chalav* (milk) plate, although found in 1984, was not written up until 1995, as it was in an unsorted bag in storage at MoLAS with other pottery finds from this site. It was only after re-examination that the significance of this almost-complete find became clear. This tin-glazed earthenware plate is 22cm in diameter, and the lettering is in the centre of the plate. The border, which Pearce (Ibid, 102) describes as 'Chinese inspired', can be paralleled with patterns common during the 1720s. Following further enquiries with Jacqui Pearce in 2007 to help confirm the dating, she stated that, 'The border is rather loosely painted compared with the care lavished on the Hebrew inscription, but this and the form of the plate combined help to provide a chronological context' (personal communication 2007). The plate was also examined by Michael Archer at the Victoria and Albert Museum, who confirmed the date. Pearce also states 'that the decoration and shape indicate Lambeth as the most likely source of manufacture' (Ibid, 102)

Orthodox Jews use separate utensils for milk and meat. Mixtures of milk and meat are prohibited according to Jewish law. This dietary law central to *kashrut* (being kosher) is based on a verse in the Book of Exodus which forbids 'boiling a kid (goat) in its mother's milk' (Exodus 34:26). Milk and meat are never mixed, nor do the Orthodox eat dairy products and meat at the same meals.

The inscription *chalav* ensures that there is no danger of any members of the household, particularly non-Jewish servants, getting the plates mixed. The plate would have come from an observant home, either Sephardi or Ashkenazi, but the writing style is more in the Ashkenazi tradition and was most likely part of a specially commissioned service. It could also indicate that it came from a high- status home, as it is unlikely that a poor family would have been able to afford a specially made service. Pearce states '….it is highly unlikely that any Hebrew–speaking painters were employed in the Lambeth factories. Templates for the inscriptions would need to have been provided at the time of ordering' (Ibid, 101).

There is no evidence that any Jews were employed in making pottery. The fact that the plate was archaeologically excavated as part of a closed assemblage of domestic pottery and other artefacts 'gives it a social and historical context which is lacking for the delftware plate in the Jewish Museum' (Ibid, 107). It provides further evidence of the Jewish community in the Aldgate area of London during the first half of the 18th century. The plate was put on permanent display in The Museum of London in 2011.

4.4.2.2 Kosher *meat and cloth seals 17th/18th centuries*

Kosher meat seals
Orthodox communities have access to a *kosher* butcher. Orthodox Jews will only eat meat bought from *kosher* butchers, where they know that the meat has been slaughtered according to religious law. In the period under discussion, lead seals were attached to the butchered meat or chicken with the name of the *shochet* (ritual slaughterer) and/or the supervising rabbi, with possibly the date when the animal was slaughtered and the word *kosher*. There are six *kosher* meat seals in the Department of Medieval and Later Antiquities in the British Museum. According to The British Museum these seals can be dated to the 17th-18th centuries although, some may be of later date. Unfortunately, they have no provenance, and none of them come from archaeologically excavated contexts; they were found in rubbish dumps in and around London. There are three other lead seals in the Museum of London, Archaeological Archive and Research Centre, Eagle Wharf Road N1.

Kosher meat seals, The British Museum
Registration no: 1895, 0721.9 PRN: MCB842. Curatorial Area: Byzantine
Description: Double seal; lead; a Jewish Butcher's 'seal of purity': connected by a bar and passed through a plain clip; the seals are inscribed on each side with Hebrew characters.
Inscription details: Inscription in Hebrew in Hebrew script. (worn, difficult to read Hebrew letters *dalet* (d) *resh* (r?)

Length: 4.40cm. Length: 3.10cm (clip)
Period: Jewish
Found/Acquired: Europe, United Kingdom, England, Greater London, London

Registration no: 1895, 0721.10PRN: MCB8 Curatorial Area: Byzantine. Collection
Description: Double seal; lead; a Jewish Butchers 'seal of purity' connected to
a bar; the seals are inscribed on each side with Hebrew characters.
Inscription details: Inscription in Hebrew in Hebrew script (Hebrew letters; *aleph*(a),
bet (b), *dalet* (d), another *aleph* and *dalet*

Registration no: 1987, 0607.5 PRN: MCB854 Curatorial Area: Post-Med Collection
Description: Seal; lead; two-lobed; inscribed; probable used for labelling chickens.
Inscriptions details: Inscription (obverse and reverse in Hebrew in Hebrew script.
Translation: *KOSHER*
Length: 4.50 cm
Jewish
Production Date: 17th/ /18th C (?)
Made in: USSR (USSR)

Registration no: 1987, 0607.7 PRN: MCB854 Curatorial Area: Post-Med Collection
Description: sealing; lead two–lobed, only one remains, inscribed; probably used for
labelling chickens.
Inscription details: Inscription (obverse and reverse) in Hebrew in Hebrew script
Hebrew letters; *aleph* (a), *bet* (b), *dalet* (d),
Translation: *KOSHER*
Length: 1.50 cm
Period: Jewish
Production date: 17thC (?)
Production date: 18th C (?)
Made in; USSR (USSR)

Registration no; 1987, 1607.7 PRN; MCB854 Curatorial Area: Post-Med Collection
Description; sealing; lead; two lobed, only one survives; inscribed; probably used for
labelling chickens.
Inscription details; Inscription (obverse and reverse) in Hebrew in Hebrew script
Translation *KOSHER*
Length: 1.50cm
Production date: 17th C. (?)
Production date: 18th C (?)
Made in: USSR (USSR)

Registration no: S44 PRN: MCN 9066 Curatorial Area: Post-Med Collection
Description: *Kosher*–seal; lead; used for labelling meat; strip cut off; (1) and (2);
inscribed.

Inscription details: Inscription (obverse in Hebrew script
Transliteration: *KOSHER*
Inscription details: Inscription (reverse) in Hebrew script
Transliteration: MEIR THEIR [THUR]
Diameter: 17.00mm (disc one) Diameter: 18.mm (disc two), 17th C?

Lead *Kosher* Cloth Seals in Museum of London
Site record: FRY98. Ferry Lane, Brentford
Description: *Kosher*-seal; used for labelling cloth
Site record: BGP92 Hampstead Heath, NW3
Description: Two *Kosher*-seals used for labelling cloth

Two of the seals in the British Museum have lettered discs riveted and connected by a bar, which would have been used to attach the seal to the meat or chicken (Figure 4.149). Due to wear, they are difficult to read, although it is possible to distinguish some of the Hebrew words under a magnifying glass (personal observation 2009): *kosher* is on all of them and one bears the name Meyer Shur. Egan (1995, 123-4) speculates 'that he was the ritual slaughterer'. There are individual Hebrew letters, which may indicate the day of the week when the animal was slaughtered or prepared. According to Pearce (1998, 107) '…the former Jewish Quarter of Amsterdam is particularly rich in such finds which can be associated with the Jewish community'. Amongst these were numerous lead seals marked *Kosjer (kosher)* on one side. Some of the seals found in Amsterdam were still attached to the leg bones of chickens. These seals confirm that there were *kosher* butchers in London during the 17th-18th centuries.

Figure 4.149 Six Kosher *meat seals found in rubbish dumps in London now in the Department of Medieval and Later Antiquities, British Museum Photographed by the British Museum Company Ltd. 2009).*

Kosher cloth seals, Museum of London

In the Museum of London, there are three *kosher* lead seals that could have been attached on the end of fabric rolls. These certify that when the cloth was manufactured, only dyes from vegetables were used, not from animals; also that the cloth was not made by using a mixture of yarns such as cotton with wool. One was found in The City of London (M.O.L.FRY98) and two on Hampstead Heath (M.O.L.BGP92) (Figure 4.150). According to Egan, 'Sephardi Jews were prominent in London trade in dyestuffs from the late seventeenth century; their connection with textile finishing provides possible circumstances for devising this alternative use of seals of the present form' (1995, 124).

M.O.L.FRY98	M.O.L.BGP92
No Accession numbers 10/11 (2 seals)	Accession number 10
Site Ferry Lane Brentford	Site British Gas Pipeline
Middlesex TW8	Hampstead Heath NW3

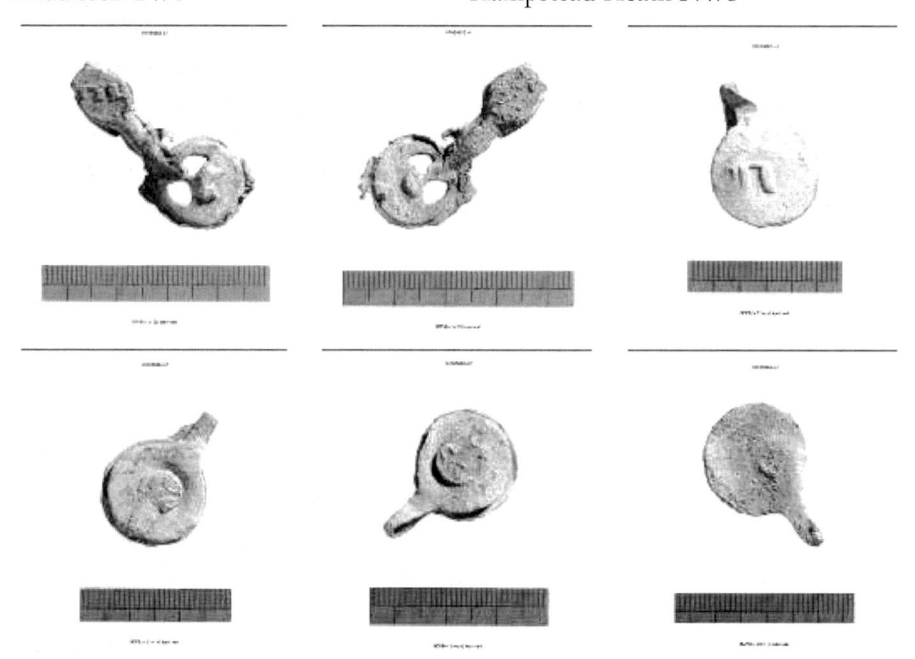

Figure 4.150 Three 17th century kosher *cloth seals found in London, now in Museum of London Archaeological Archives. (photograph by Museum of London, 2009).*

4.4.2.3 Shofar'ot *(ram's horns) c.19th century*

Two *shofar'ot* were discovered in London in the mid 19th-century; one was recovered from the Thames; the second was found in a rubbish dump in Leadenhall Street EC3. Both are now in museums, the Cuming Museum, Southwark and the Jewish Museum, Camden Town. In 2008, they were both labelled as being possibly medieval, pre-dating the expulsion of the Jewish community in 1290. The author of this study, in collaboration with Bruce Watson at the Museum of London, Jennifer Marin at the Jewish Museum and Tamara Chase at the Cuming Museum, organised the radiocarbon dating of both *shofar'ot* in order to give these two artefacts a chronological provenance and to be able to discuss their usage and cultural context. The results were published in *The London Archaeologist Vol.12 No. 1. 2008* (Chase et al, 2008) and also in *Transactions Vol. 42 2009 of the Jewish Historical Society* (Ibid, 2008). The *shofar'ot* have been included in this study, as they are important archaeological finds, which, up to the time of these publications, had not received proper recognition.

The *shofar* (plural *shofar'ot*) is the oldest musical instrument in the world still used. It is blown in synagogue on the most important and solemn days in the Jewish calendar, Rosh Hashanah (The New Year) and Yom Kippur (The Day of Atonement). It was used in ancient Israel to announce the New Moon and therefore, the start of the new month. It is mentioned in the Old Testament 69 times and translated in the English versions as 'trumpet'. The first mention is in *Exodus* (19:12 and 16:19):

> *'They may go up to the mountain only when the rams horn gives out a long blast' (19:12) and 'A thick cloud covered the mountain. 'A trumpet gave out a very large blast. Everyone in the camp trembled' (19:16). 'The whole mountain trembled and shook. The sound of the trumpet got louder and louder. Then Moses spoke. And the voice of God answered him' (19:19).*

These quotes help to illustrate the significance of the *shofar* and its symbolic use in synagogue. The *shofar* is described by the rabbis as 'a musical instrument of antiquity of God's own making'.

Radiocarbon dating of the two London *shofar'ot*.
The *shofar'ot* were taken to the Research Laboratory for Archaeology and History of Art (Radiocarbon Accelerator Unit) at the University of Oxford. It is 95.4% certain that the *shofar'ot* date from the period 1680-1939, and within this range there is a 63.3% probability date from 1800–1939. As they were found in 1850, this date range can be narrowed to c.1680-1850, indicating that they were discarded during the 18th century (Chase et al, 2008).

The *shofar* in The Cuming Museum was recovered from the Thames near Vauxhall, presumably through dredging (Figure 4.151). On personal contact in 2008, it was explained by the curator that, due to lack of space and not realising its significance, it had been put in storage. The radiocarbon dating result for this *shofar* showed that it also postdates the medieval period as it can be narrowed to c.1680-1850, indicating that it was discarded during the 18th century' (Ibid, 2008).

The intriguing question is why it should have been thrown into the Thames? It is the Jewish custom that disused or damaged Jewish religious objects, including prayer books, are buried rather than discarded. It may be that the Vauxhall *shofar* was deliberately discarded in the Thames as a form of burial.

Figure 4.151 c.19th century shofar *(ram's horn trumpet) recovered from the Thames off Vauxhall 1850. Colour brown, shape: trumpet, hollow but flat with points carved at end (Reproduced with permission of the Cuming Museum, Southwark London, 2008).*

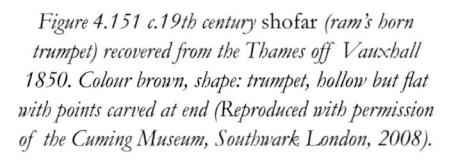

Figure 4.152 c.19th century shofar *from Jewish Museum recovered from Leadenhall Street Colour brown, shape: trumpet hollow but flat (Reproduced with permission of the Jewish Museum, Camden Town London 2008).*

The *shofar* from the Jewish Museum was found during excavation in Leadenhall Street in 1855. According to Chase, (personal communication) nothing is known about the circumstances of its discovery. The radiocarbon date for the Leadenhall *shofar* reveals that it has a 95.4% probability of dating from 1680-1939, and that within this date range, there is a 63.5% probability that it dates from 1801-1939. The New Synagogue, Leadenhall Street EC3 is discussed in 4.1.7. It notes that it was founded in 1761 in Bricklayers' Hall in Leadenhall Street (4.152). It is possible that that this *shofar* had some connection with the New Synagogue; however, there is no explanation as to why it would have been discarded. Both *shofar'ot* are of very similar dates. Both *shofar'ot* are similar in style and size, both are shaped liked a trumpet, hollow but flat with points carved at the ends. Both are approximately 30x115x15mm, and both show signs of damage. This may have occurred during shaping, which would have affected the purity of the sound. This is a possible reason why they were discarded. The results of the radiocarbon date the *shofar'ot* to the middle to late-18th/ middle 19th centuries.

In order to summarize this Chapter: Jews do not need a synagogue to pray or hold services. As long as there are 10 men who have been *bar mitzvahed* (over the age of 13), services can be held in houses or even outside. The conclusion that one reaches after having examined the evidence, or lack of evidence of synagogues in

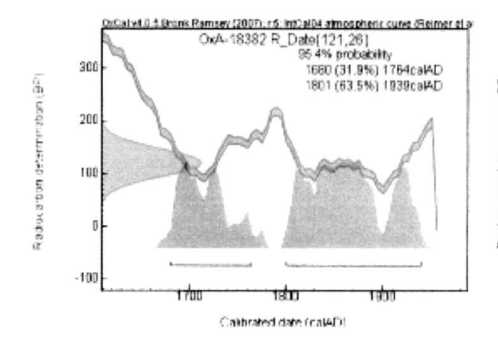

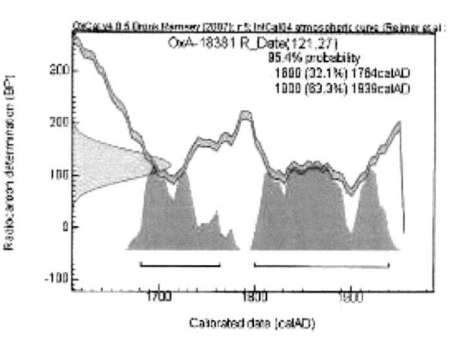

Figure 4.153 Radiocarbon accelerator calibrated dating of shofar'ot *from Vauxhall and Leadenhall Street (Research Laboratory for Archaeology and History of Art University of Oxford 2008).*

the period under discussion, is that the early communities were regularly on the move, and when they moved, they established new prayer halls or synagogues and took their religious objects with them. The buildings themselves were not important; it was the congregation and the religious artifacts that made a community.

Synagogues were meeting places both to pray and study, and when the congregations declined, many were sold and the proceeds used to fund new synagogues or used for the upkeep of cemeteries. The following chapter discusses cemeteries, most of which are no longer used, but which remain a testimony to the communities following re-admission in 1656.

Chapter 5

Communities in Death (Cemeteries)

This chapter discusses both London's early Jewish cemeteries and those in the 35 provincial cities and towns under study. Most early cemeteries are no longer used; in the main, they have been left undisturbed. Based on the Biblical idea that all human beings are created in the image of God, Jewish tradition insists that the dead be treated with holiness and respect and that a cemetery is an eternal resting place, which should always be maintained. However, some cemeteries are in poor condition, overgrown with unreadable tombstones due to damage and weathering from acid rain. Tombstone inscriptions that can be read and are of particular significance are discussed, as is the difference in the style of memorial stones between Sephardi and

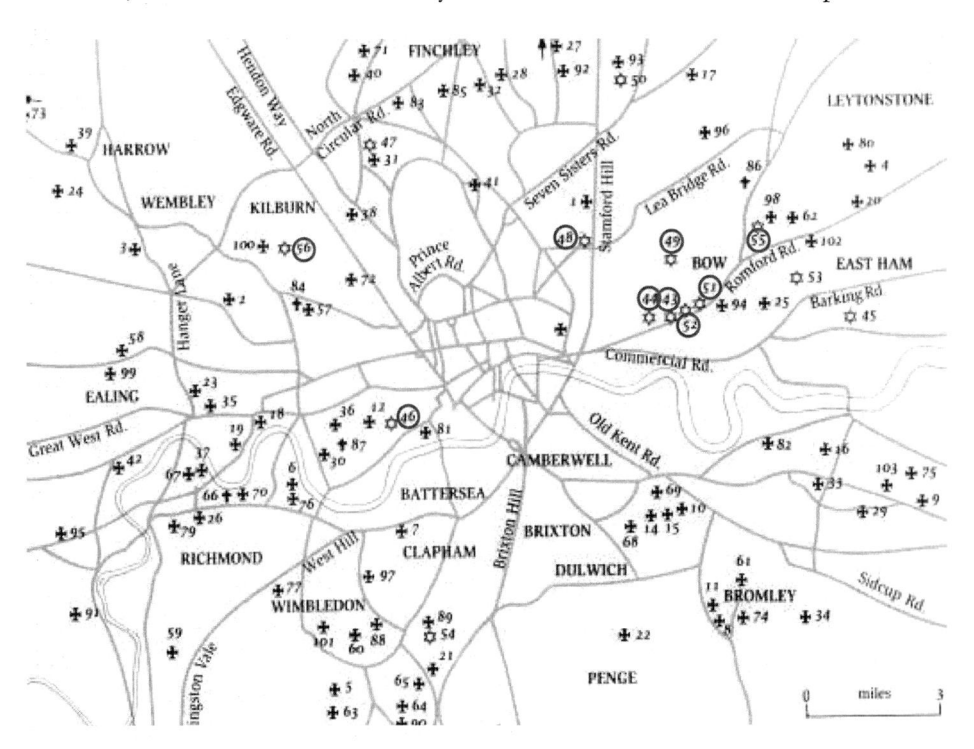

Figure 5.1 London's Jewish burial grounds in the 17th-19th centuries are Nos. 43, 44, 46, 48, 49, 51, 52, 55, 56 (Clout 1991, 166).

Ashkenazi cemeteries. Also discussed is the change over the centuries in tombstone inscriptions and monumental architecture.

The 17th-19th centuries saw the growth and consolidation of the Jewish community throughout Britain, with an increasing number of cemeteries. Jewish cemeteries provide a unique historical and social perspective of Jewish life in England in the 17th-19th centuries. Archaeological evidence of Anglo-Jewry of this period is in fact mostly based on cemetery evidence and burial records. At the end of the 17th century, according to the 1695 census, there were about 1,000 Jews in Britain all of whom lived in London. By the end of the 18th century, the entire community had grown to around 20,000, of which more than half were in London; the remainder were spread over 21 towns, each with their own cemeteries.

There are now 22 Jewish cemeteries in London (including Brentwood), 11 of these, north of the River Thames, fall within the period under discussion (Figure 5.1). There are distinct differences between Sephardi and Ashkenazi cemeteries. Sephardi tombstones are laid horizontally, whilst Ashkenazi tombstones are in the main vertical. The names of the deceased who died in this period are often evidence of origins. Spanish and Portuguese for the Sephardim, such as Pereira and Mendoza and middle and eastern European names for the Ashkenazim, such as Aronovsky, Jacobovitz and Woolf. It is not the custom to lay flowers or plant shrubs in Orthodox cemeteries, which can give them a dignified starkness. For both the Ashkenazi and Sephardi tombstones, most inscriptions, particularly the earlier ones, are mainly in Hebrew, although when the community became more integrated, English is more in evidence. Unlike the first burials after re-admission, where, in the main, the tombstones are modest, in the 19th century the wealthier people had elaborate tombstones and monuments. Some later Ashkenazi tombstones have decorated engravings (see Figure 5.2), and it is evident that 18th/19th-century elaborate tombstones and monuments are symbols of status.

No matter how wealthy or poor, it is Jewish custom for burials to take place in a plain, undecorated coffin, without handles, with the deceased washed beforehand and then buried in a shroud. Men wear their *tallith* (fringed shawl traditionally worn by men at prayer). In comparison with Christian burials, Houlbrooke (1999, 193) states, 'that in the 18th century, the wealthy (Christians) went to their graves in increasingly elaborate grave clothes and coffins covered with fabric, fitted with grips and adorned with engraved plates'. In the 19th century before the general establishment of cemeteries, Christian corpses were buried underneath the church or in the church-yard. Chatham burial ground discussed in 5.2.8 is the only Jewish burial ground in England adjoining a synagogue. Nearly all Jewish cemeteries established in this period were outside city limits; there is a Jewish view that you don't bury the dead within city walls, for hygienic reasons and ritual purity. However, the main and practical reason for this being the availability of land; the further from the inhabited areas the more burial space was available.

Some poor Jews would have sometimes been buried in unmarked, unrecorded graves, possibly not in Jewish cemeteries, as the estimated Jews of the period cannot be reconciled with the number and size of known burial grounds in the period. Some

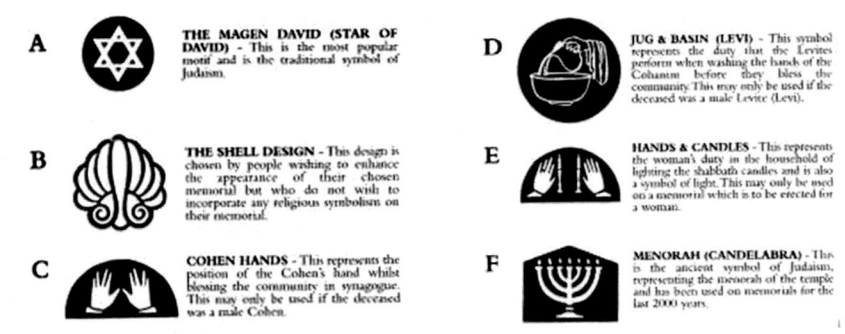

A — **THE MAGEN DAVID (STAR OF DAVID)** - This is the most popular motif and is the traditional symbol of Judaism.

B — **THE SHELL DESIGN** - This design is chosen by people wishing to enhance the appearance of their chosen memorial but who do not wish to incorporate any religious symbolism on their memorial.

C — **COHEN HANDS** - This represents the position of the Cohen's hand whilst blessing the community in synagogue. This may only be used if the deceased was a male Cohen.

D — **JUG & BASIN (LEVI)** - This symbol represents the duty that the Levites perform when washing the hands of the Cohanim before they bless the community. This may only be used if the deceased was a male Levite (Levi).

E — **HANDS & CANDLES** - This represents the woman's duty in the household of lighting the shabbath candles and is also a symbol of light. This may only be used on a memorial which is to be erected for a woman.

F — **MENORAH (CANDELABRA)** - This is the ancient symbol of Judaism, representing the menorah of the temple and has been used on memorials for the last 2000 years.

Figure 5.2 engravings on tombstones. (Reproduced with permission of A. Elfes Ltd. Monumental Masons).

cemeteries no longer have burial records. The integrity of any Jewish population and burial figures has to be questioned, as the early Ashkenazi community, according to Black (2003, 40) '…had their fair share of vagrants, beggars, the destitute, the unemployed and homeless boys and girls roaming the streets'.

5.1   London cemeteries

The history of the Britain's Jewish community in the 17th and 18th centuries is intrinsically bound to that of the East of London. Within a small area around the Mile End Road, outside the City walls, five of the first Jewish cemeteries can be found. The first Jewish cemetery in England following re-admission was the Sephardi cemetery in Mile End in 1657. This was followed by Ashkenazi burial grounds in Alderney Road in 1696, Hoxton (no longer exists), Brady Street and Lauriston Road, and Hackney in the 18th century. In the early 19th century, Jewish cemeteries were established in other parts of London. The 11 London cemeteries discussed are:

5.1.1	Sephardi *Velho* (Old) Mile End E1*	1657-1742
5.1.2	Sephardi *Nuevo* (New) Mile End E1*	1733-1918
5.1.3	Sephardi Brentwood CM14***	
	Re-interred remains from *Nuevo*	1974
5.1.4	Ashkenazi Alderney Road. E1*	1696-1853
5.1.5	Ashkenazi Bancroft Road E1**	1810-1895
5.1.6	Ashkenazi Brady Street. E1**	1761-1858
5.1.7	Ashkenazi Fulham Road SW3**	1815-1886
5.1.8	Ashkenazi Lauriston Road E9**	1788-1886
5.1.9	Ashkenazi West Ham E15**	1856-c.1973
5.1.10	West London Balls Pond Road N1**	1843-1897
5.1.11	Ashkenazi Willesden NW10**	1873- still in use

* Visited 2007   **Visited 2008   *** Remains from Mile End c.1733

All these cemeteries had and have reserved spaces for family members who died at a later date.

5.1.1 Sephardi *Velho* (Old) Mile End Road E1 [48]

Hymanson (1951, 24) states that: '….from 1656 to c.1740 the only Jewish community in England was in London. In March 1656 Jews petitioned Oliver Cromwell for leave to purchase a burial ground, permission was granted and the first cemetery was established in 1657, one year after readmission'. The area purchased was an orchard on the north side of Mile End Road, E1. Mile End was a hamlet and, as its names implies, a mile from the City of London. According to Diamond (1955, 168) 'The total area which included the Jewish hospital was about one and half acres'. Bell (1923, 254) states: 'that it was a small plot, little more than an acre in extent, that stands behind No 253, Mile End Road in the rear of the Beth Holim, the Jewish Hospital for healing'. It is known as the *Velho* (Old) Cemetery of the Spanish and Portuguese Jews. The burial register of the Spanish and Portuguese Congregation published by the Jewish Historical Society (1962) contains some 1700 entries, including over 700 small children, known as *'El Angeletos'* (little angels). A few memorial stones on the top have winged cherubs, indicating that the deceased was a child (personal observation 2007).

Some of the original purchase documents and title deeds are preserved in the archives at Bevis Marks Synagogue. According to Margoliouth (1851, 20) these show that the lease was for 999 years. One of the signatories was Antonio Carvajal, referred to earlier. The synagogue accounts show that the annual rent was £10 per annum. Diamond (1955, 170) states 'This indicates that as might be expected, the lessors knew the purpose for which the land was acquired, and Carvajal and De Caceres (one of the other signatories) had to pay a fancy price to get it'. Later Carvajal (d. 1659), and his wife were buried in this cemetery. His tomb was restored in 1925 with a memorial plaque. On the Mile End Road that fronts the cemetery there is a plaque, which marks the site of the first Jewish hospital established in 1665, which states:

> '…*for sick, poor and lying-in women*' and continues '*and was located on this site in front of the burial ground of the Spanish and Portuguese Jews' congregation. The first cemetery acquired after their re-settlement*' (Figure 5.3).

Figure 5.3 plaque on the Mile End Road E1 in front of Velho (old) cemetery established 1657 (photograph K. Marks 2007).

The limestone and marble gravestones, most of which have not survived the ravages of time, are mostly illegible (personal observation 2007). Many grave slabs no longer exist. The earliest inscriptions that can be read are in Portuguese or Spanish and Hebrew; the later inscriptions are tri-lingual Portuguese or Spanish and Hebrew and English (personal observation 2007). According to Black (2003, 24) among the first burials were 21 victims of the Great Plague in 1665.

As noted above, Sephardi tombstones are horizontal (Figure 5.4), unlike Ashkenazi, which are mainly vertical. According to Rabbis, there are a number of traditional reasons given for this. The first being that in Spain and Portugal, where the deceased originated, the Church wanted to differentiate between Christian and Jewish burials, with Christian tombstones being upright. The second being that horizontal tombstones symbolize that in death, all are equal, whether rich or poor. Furthermore, Sephardic Jews from Spain and Portugal originally placed their tombstones flat, from the time when Jewish cemeteries were sometimes located in swampy ground or areas subject to earthquakes.. Laying the tombstone flat would help to keep the stone in place (personal contact The Spanish and Portuguese Burial Society 2007).

At the rear of the cemetery, to the north, is a stone inscription dated 1684 that gives the names in Portuguese of founders of the community. This stone is decorated with a winged cherub, described in the biblical tradition '*as attending to God*". One of the few grave stones that can be read is that of the Sephardi Chief Rabbi known as the *Haham,* Yehoshua Da Silva. His stone was renewed by the Sephardi Burial Society in 1978 (memorial plaque). Among the most notable persons buried in this ground is Dr Fernando Mendes, physician to Charles II and Moses Athias, the first

Figure 5.4 Velho *(old) Sephardi Old Cemetery established 1657 in Mile End E1. (photograph K. Marks 2007).*

Figure 5.5 Stone inscription in Velho *(Old) Mile End Cemetery E1 dated 1684 with names of founders of the community and decorated with cherub (photograph K. Marks 2007).*

rabbi of the Sephardi community (records of The Spanish and Portuguese Burial Society).

It is evident from some of the rows and spaces in the cemetery that they were children's graves, as the burial plots are half the size of the adults; often children were buried without grave markers. Diamond (1955, 184) states that 'the mortality of young infants was so high in this age and burial space so precious, that the community could not give them burial in a six–foot grave with a gravestone, he estimates that the mortality rate of infants could have been nearly half of the total average burials in each year'.

Roth (1978, 141) states, 'Not all the first resettlement Jews were buried in this cemetery, some of the Marranos (Christianised Jews) although they were a minority and members of Bevis Marks, some were buried (with their families) in non-Jewish burial grounds'. Therefore, there are no accurate figures of the Jewish population of London in the 17th century. There was also a rule that if a Marrano man had not been circumcised, his case for burial in the *Velho* would have to be brought before the community elders. If buried in a Jewish cemetery he may have been interred in an unmarked grave near the walls and not in a central position. 'The burial rules for Marranos and where their plots are situated can be identified and shows a cultural rejection by the community, they were regarded as renegades. They were also rejected by some Christians as Jews of impure blood' (Ibid, 179). Diamond (1969, 184) estimates that, the Jewish population in London had grown from around 167 in 1657 to around 1, 000 by 1711. This concurs with the 1695 census return. A second difficulty in establishing exact figures is the death rate of infants.

Propped up on the north rear wall are two stone panel carvings of skull-and-crossbones probably from tombs (Figure 5.6). Kadish (2006, 29) notes 'These are unusual in Jewish cemeteries in England, however similar carvings are found in the Amsterdam Sephardi cemetery' It is against Jewish tradition to have human images carved in stone; skulls represented mortality. These images would have been carved by non Jewish monumental masons.

Figure 5.6 Skulls and cross bones carvings in the Velho *(Old) Cemetery in Mile End, E1 (photograph K. Marks 2007).*

5.1.2 Sephardi *Nuevo* (New) Mile End Road E1 [49]

The *Nuevo* (New) Sephardi Cemetery was established in 1733 (Figure 5.7) to the east of the *Velho* (Old) Cemetery, which was in use until 1742 and enlarged to the east in 1849-1853 to three acres. The burial ground originally contained 10, 300 graves about 40% of them children (The Spanish and Portuguese Burial Society Records, 1962). The cemetery still contains around 2, 000 graves. Part of the west wall, originally in the south-east corner of the cemetery, probably dates from the establishment of the cemetery; the plain wall ended in a gate pier, for one of the two cemetery gates, since rebuilt, bares traces of a structure abutting its internal face, probably a mortuary chapel removed in the 1960s (Maloney el al. 2008).

Some of the tombstone inscriptions are in Portuguese, Hebrew and English. The names indicate the foreign origins of the deceased, such as Abecassis, Castro, Costa, Castello, Mendoza, Mendes, Ramos and Sassoon (personal observation, 2007). The only readable stones are those made of granite, which only the wealthy could afford. There are a number of family plots (personal observation, 2007), and a paved area with a central plinth inscribed with 30 names, possibly indicating the original number of graves in this area, which no longer bear individual marker stones, due to World War II destruction, wear or vandalism. On a number of graves are small piles of stones (personal observation, 2007), a traditional way of showing that a relative or close friend had visited the grave to pay their respects and pray for the deceased. It is known from the Spanish and Portuguese synagogue records that there were direct descendents of the 18th-century community alive in the 19th century who were buried in the *Nuevo*.

Part of the cemetery was destroyed in the Blitz in 1941, with the loss of many of the graves. In 1973 some of the ground was controversially sold to Queen Mary

Figure 5.7 The Nuevo *(New) Sephardi Cemetery in Mile End Road. E1 established 1733. At the rear can be seen part of Queen Mary College (photograph K. Marks 2007).*

College and the remains of 7, 500 persons who died before 1813 were re-interred in a field in Brentwood. This burial ground is discussed in 5.1.3. As previously mentioned, in the Jewish tradition, it is not usually permitted for graves to be excavated; remains of the deceased should not be disturbed, waiting for the day when the Messiah comes and the deceased souls will rise to heaven and the dead will be reborn. Traditionally, Sephardi cremation is not allowed for the same reason in the Ashkenazi Orthodox community, as the Orthodox believe that one day the departed soul will be united with their physical remains.

5.1.3   Sephardi Brentwood Coxtie Green CM14   [50]

This cemetery contains around 7, 500 remains re-interred in 1974 in four mass graves from the Georgian (1733) section of the *Nuevo* cemetery in Mile End Road, E1. There are no individual tombstones from the original burial ground as they were destroyed. In the archives of Bevis Marks and The Spanish and Portuguese Burial Society Records is the list of the deceased. The cemetery is located in a secluded walled field between Weald Park Golf Club and Oakhurst Farm. Entrance is through a low red-brick gate entrance (Figure 5.8).

There are four plaques either side of the gate; two in Hebrew, two in English. The exterior plaques indicate that the cemetery belongs to the Spanish and Portuguese Community. The interior plaques state the following in Hebrew and English:

> *The remains here remembered were removed in 1974 from the greater part of the Nuevo Cemetery of the Spanish and Portuguese Jews at Mile End London. Where they had originally been buried mainly between 1734 and 1876.*

Figure 5.8 Brentwood Cemetery 1974: entrance gate (photograph K. Marks 2010).

Figure 5.9 Brentwood: mass burial of 7500 remains from Nuevo *Cemetery (photograph K.Marks 2010).*

5.1.4 Ashkenazi Alderney Road E1 [51]

Prior to the opening of this cemetery in c.1696, London's mainly poor Ashkenazi or immigrants from eastern Europe, were buried in the Sephardi *Velho* Cemetery, but as their numbers increased the Ashkenazi community needed their own burial ground. As stated by Susser (1997, 4) in his archive of the inscriptions in Alderney Road, the Sephardi authorities were particularly concerned 'as to the number of poor dead who were a charge on the communal funds'. The Ashkenazi community bought a plot of garden land with a 999-year lease adjoining the *Velho* to the south-east, in Alderney Road. Susser states, 'Within this cemetery lie the mortal remains of the founders, lay leaders and rabbis of the community' (Ibid, 8). Alderney Road is the oldest Ashkenazi cemetery in England. It holds around c.4, 000 graves, of which c.40% are children, buried in unmarked graves. The original cemetery keeper's house still stands with a resident keeper.

Roth states that 'Benjamin Levy who was an employee of the congregation purchased the burial ground' (1978, 175), was buried there in 1705 next to his second wife, although there is no record of where they were buried or any trace of their graves. Many of the grave stones have suffered from acid rain and are now illegible. There are now three sections in the cemetery, the original area, and the extensions which were purchased in 1749, fronting onto Alderney Road. This additional land gives the cemetery an unusual shape, with the old and later plots narrowly joined at one corner and a path enabling one to walk from one side to the other.

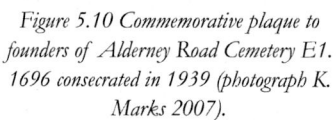

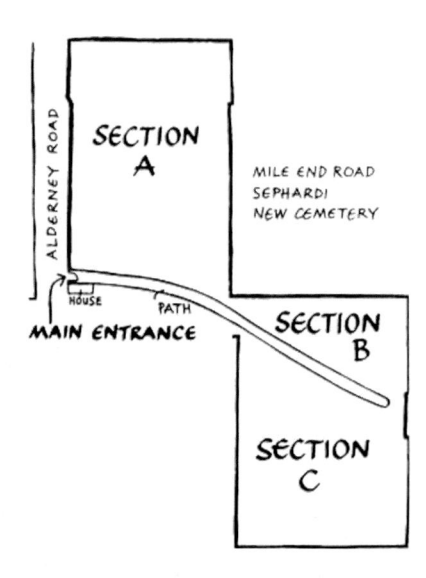

Figure 5.10 Commemorative plaque to founders of Alderney Road Cemetery E1. 1696 consecrated in 1939 (photograph K. Marks 2007).

Figure 5.11 Layout of the Alderney Road Cemetery E1 Drawn by Yael Turner and Paula Palumbo (Susser, ed. 1997, 7).

Alderney Road, now under the authority of the United Synagogue, is the only United Synagogue cemetery in London surveyed in detail with a plot plan and an index of inscriptions, where they could still be read (Figure 5.11). This exercise was carried out in 1997 under the supervision of Dr. Sharman Kadish, Charles Tucker, Archivist of the Chief Rabbi's Office, Tina Murdoch of ICOMOS UK and Rabbi Bernard Susser, who died just before publication of the survey.

The cemetery was in use until 1852/3. By 1753 the Jewish population in England was 6, 000, mostly in London, with the Ashkenazi community constituting around 4, 000 (Roth 1978, 197).

Susser states (1997, 67):

> 'To-day the cemetery is like an oasis in a world of bustle and modernity. It is beautifully kept by the United Synagogue and it radiates an atmosphere of peace and tranquillity. This cemetery, and the adjoining one of the Sephardim, are not only part of the history of English history, but are now part of the history of England'.

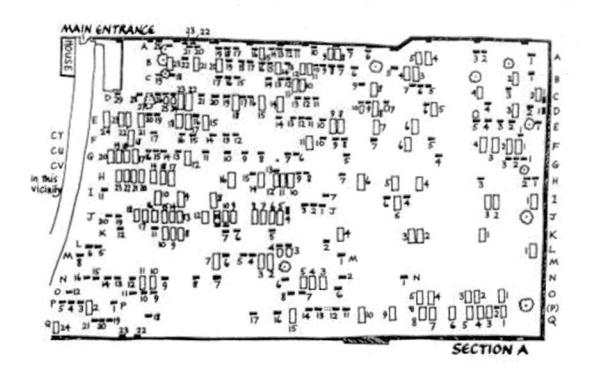

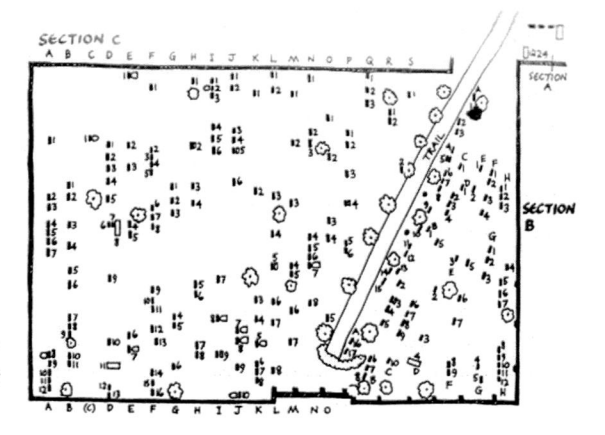

Figure 5.12 1993 Line drawings of Alderney Road Cemetery E1. 1696 Drawn by Yael Turner and Paula Palomba (no scale available) (Susser ed. 1997, 8/9). n.b. Any plot or date of death details that are not shown is because they are not in the burial register or evident in the cemetery.

Figure 5.13 Alderney Road E.1 chest tombs in Ashkenazi cemetery from 1696 (photograph K. Marks 2007).

Ashkenazim grave stones are mainly vertical, unlike the Sephardi ones and some of the more prominent and richer members have elaborate tombs and chest monuments (5.13), with birth and death dates and sometimes a special dedication or a quote from the Old Testament. Among the funereal motifs used in this cemetery are engravings, such as flowers when the deceased was an unmarried girl, images of cut trees for young men. Motifs, such as priestly hands, raised in prayer, indicate that the deceased was a Cohen (i.e. descended from the Biblical priestly tribe). These Cohen's graves are sometimes found buried near the walls of a cemetery. A jug and basin indicates that the deceased was a Levy. There are also funereal non-Jewish motifs, such as drapery and hour glasses, that are typical of contemporary Christian cemeteries. Some of the stones are similar in design, which suggests that the families of the deceased purchased stones from monumental masons that were pre-designed

Figure 5.14 Alderney Road E1 tomb of Rabbi Samuel Falk d. 1782; visited every week by the ultra Orthodox followers. Memorial stone renewed by The Chief Rabbi (1997) (photograph, K.Marks 2007).

or in stock, and then the stone mason would add the name of the deceased with an individual dedication. There are also a few Eastern European motifs, such as a pair of hands and an open book (a learned man). Some of the tombstones can give insight into the origins of the deceased, indicating they came for example, from Bohemia, Hamburg or Prague. Many of the poor and children were buried without a marker-stone (personal observation 2007).

Amongst the graves are the following:

Moses Hart (d.1756), he financed a large part of the building of the original Great Synagogue.
Elias Levy and his wife, benefactors of The Great Synagogue (Plot AJ11).
Judith Levy (d.1803) at 98, she was the daughter of **Moses Hart.** She was known as the 'Queen of Richmond Green', and was a major donor to the reconstruction of The Great Synagogue (Plot AJ10).
Rabbi Hayim Samuel Jacob de Falk (d.1782) (Figure 5.14). The tomb is visited every week by his followers. It is a place of pilgrimage. On *Tisha B'Av,* the Jewish festival that commemorates the destruction of the Temple in Jerusalem in AD69 by the Romans, several hundred Chassidic and Ultra Orthodox followers come to pray at his memorial (Plot AF1).
Rabbi Aaron Hart, first Chief Rabbi (served 1709-1756) (Plot AQ22).
Rabbi David Tevele Schiff second Chief Rabbi (served 1765-1791) (Plot AE18). The original headstone was replaced in 1997 as the original is no longer legible.
The earliest inscription that can still be read is from 1705. The name of the deceased is **Joseph D'Azevedo,** which is a Sephardi name and not Ashkenazi.

5.1.5   Ashkenazi Bancroft Road E1   [52]

This cemetery around the corner from Alderney Road Cemetery (5.1.4) was used by the Maiden Lane Synagogue. According to Roth, this congregation, due to differences with the Western Synagogue (4.1.11) (some members preferring an independent synagogue), broke away c.1813 (1932, 127). It is estimated by Charles Tucker, the United Synagogue archivist, that there could have been 600-700 graves in area of c.1, 600 square yards. The graves are closely packed. In 1895 the cemetery was stated to be full. Only 11 tombstones remain upright (personal observation, 2009),

Figure 5.15 Bancroft Road Cemetery (photograph, K.Marks 2009).

although some outlines of some graves remain, without marker stones. At the time of visiting the burial ground was in a poor state. In 1944, the grounds were damaged by flying bombs and all records were destroyed when the Western Synagogue was bombed in 1941. The remaining area does not appear on the Clout cemeteries map (Figure.5.1).

5.1.6　　　　　　　　Ashkenazi Brady Street E1　　　　　　　　[53]

Brady Street Cemetery was established in 1761 and closed in 1858, although special permission was given for one burial in 1990, which is discussed. Black (2003, 47) states, 'By 1800 there were around 18, 000 Jews in London, the community was still expanding, albeit at a slower rate'. In this period this cemetery was used by both the New Synagogue (4.1.7) and subsequently the Great Synagogue (4.1.5). The 1780 *ohel*, near the entrance no longer exists but is shown on the 1871 Ordnance Survey Map in the gazetteer. The map also shows that almost adjacent to the cemetery there were almshouses and manure works. Brady Street contains more than 3, 000 burials and has unusual features. By 1790 it was full, so the burial and synagogue authorities put a four-foot thick layer of earth over part of the ground, using this area for two and possibly up to four layers of graves, creating a flat-topped mound. Because of the layers, the gravestones were placed back to back, similar to the famous Prague Jewish cemetery. This cemetery is the only one in London with this feature. 'This area is known as 'Strangers Ground', so-called as it was intended for those Jews who

Figure 5.16 View of part of Brady Street Cemetery E1 established 1761: central mound for in depth burials. (photograph K. Marks 2007).

Figure 5.17 Brady Street Cemetery 1761 showing back to back tombstones, (photograph K.Marks 2007).

Figure 5.18 Brady Street Cemetery E1. Marble tombs of Nathan and Hannah Rothschild, Nathan Rothschild a descendent is buried with a pink granite memorial outside the railed area. (photograph K. Marks 2007).

Figure 5.19 Brady Street Cemetery E1 obelisk and bust of Miriam Levy (photograph K. Marks 2007).

did not belong to a synagogue' (Beach 2006, 171). The total number of burials is unknown, although according to Charles Tucker (personal contact 2010) there are several thousand.

Some Georgian tombs survive, mostly upright, but many are illegible, particularly those lying flat and covered in moss (personal observation 2007). The elaborate and railed off tombstones with classical pediments (Figure 5.18) of Nathan Meyer Victor Rothschild (1777-1836) and his wife Hannah (1783-1850) are well preserved. New marble plaques with their names have been fixed to their chest tombs (personal observation, 2009). Nathan Rothschild was the founder of the London branch of the great banking house. Rothschild, amongst others, funded the government during the Napoleonic wars. It was he who brought Prime Minister Lord Liverpool the news of the victory at Waterloo before he had had the dispatches from Wellington. Although the cemetery was closed in 1895, an act of Parliament was passed to allow a descendent also named Nathan Victor 3rd Sir Baron Rothschild (1910-1990) to be buried alongside his ancestors. Sir Victor's burial in 1990 protected the Brady Street burial ground from destruction for 100 years, as burial grounds cannot be sold until 100 years after the last burial.

Another rare feature in the middle of the cemetery is the bust of Miriam Levy (1801-1856) (Figure 5.19), placed on top of a square obelisk decorated with figurative reliefs. It is against Jewish tradition to have an image of a person, but Miriam Levy was an exceptional person in the community, a welfare worker who started the first soup kitchens for the poor in Whitechapel in the East End of London (Kadish 2006, 26).

The Brady Street tombstones and monuments demonstrate Jewish influence and assimilation in 18th-century England. While the earliest inscriptions are in Hebrew, after about 1825, both Hebrew and English appear. Whilst the deceased were buried in the Jewish tradition (in a plain coffin and wrapped in a shroud with no grave goods), status is evident from the size and elaborateness and quality of the tomb stones, and in the case of the Rothschilds, elaborate memorials. Richer and more prominent persons had more conspicuous plot positions, sometimes with chest tombs and obelisks. As with other Jewish cemeteries, however, the rich, famous, middle class and poor are buried near to each other. However, post 1810 privileged members were buried in the north-west section; the size and shape of many of these memorials being similar to contemporary non-Jewish headstones.

5.1.7 Ashkenazi Fulham Road SW3 [54]

Fulham Road cemetery was the most important burial ground in West London and belonged to the Western Synagogue in Denmark Court, Strand (Levy 1897, 41). Situated in the Fulham Road, next to the Royal Marsden Hospital, the ground was purchased in 1813 and was in use until 1886 with a few later burials in reserved places. The first burial was c.1815, with subsequent family members buried later in reserved places. According to the administrator of this cemetery Mr Garcia, (personal contact 2009) (Western Charitable Foundation), virtually all records have been lost.

The *ohel*, used for receiving the corpses, prayers and the service prior to burial, no longer exists. Levy (1897, 39) states '…..a small building of two stories had been erected at the entrance to the burial ground; the lower part was called the hall, for receiving the corpses'. Roth (1933, 151) notes that 'This area of the cemetery was later sold for shops and offices, one body being removed'. It is evident from the elaborate upright stones that this was, in part, a high status burial ground. Most inscriptions are unreadable, but amongst them on a granite obelisk is Solomon Hart. R.A, the first Jewish Royal Academician and an obelisk for the Dowager Dame Cecilia Solomons, married to the first Jewish Lord Mayor of London, Sir David Solomons. Another

Figure 5.20 Fulham Road Cemetery SW3. Royal Marsden Hospital in background (photograph, K.Marks 2009).

notable grave is that of Zadoc Jessel, father of Sir George Jessel, Master of the Rolls (1873-1883)

Among the trees there is a mature mulberry, a reminder that originally the burial ground was part of a park, where according to the Borough of Chelsea records, 2,000 mulberry trees were planted in 1719. Following closure, members of the Western Synagogue from 1884 were buried in Edmonton Cemetery N18, which is not discussed. Roth (1933, 156) states 'In 1886 the Home Office issued an order closing the Brompton ground with the exceptions being in favour of some reserved spaces'.

5.1.8 Ashkenazi Lauriston Road E9 [55]

As individuals prospered, they moved from the east of London to the suburbs. In the late 18th century, Hackney was a village and convenient for those working in the east end and the City was a mile and a half away. A reason for this migration, not only to Hackney but also other suburbs of London was provided by Lipman (1962-7, 78-102) 'the desire of the largely English-born Jewish middle class to assimilate to their environment'. In the late 19th century Hackney was one of the first areas of London to be populated increasingly by the 'lower middle' class. The village of Hackney '…was a place selected for retirement by many of that *respectable* class in society' (Robinson 1842, 24).

Lauriston Road Cemetery was their village burial ground in the late 18th and 19th centuries (Ibid, 25). The Hambro Synagogue Burial register, compiled from 1807, details 373 burials in this, their second cemetery. The graves are numbered on the burial register, but there is no cemetery plan. According to Tucker (United Synagogue archivist, personal contact 2010), the cemetery holds 400-500 graves but there are no sectional plans. Many elaborate tombstones reflect the wealth of some of those buried; many of the sandstone and slate head stones are illegible. There is a group of Victorian memorials (Figure 5.21) in the shape of coffins, where the inscription can be read, and two other graves with a matching pair of elaborate columns decorated with urns (Figure 5.22). These memorials are railed off, which indicates a family plot. Were it not for the Hebrew inscriptions on the monuments and tombstones, one could be in a prosperous Christian Victorian cemetery (personal observation 2009).

The *ohel* (prayer room) or wash house no longer exists, but its position near the front of the cemetery is evident from the remains of the foundations still in place (personal observation 2009). As was the custom, not only in Jewish cemeteries, night watchmen made sure that grave robbers would not interfere with the newly dug graves. At the front, to one side, is the caretakers' house. The position of the grave plots in Lauriston Road cemetery combined with the burial register, indicates a step change from the earlier London cemeteries, for example Brady Street (1761-1858). There is a distinct difference in the prominence of the graves of the wealthy with their elaborate tombstones.

Synagogues had, and still have, to be self-supporting, with wealthy members

Figure 5.21 Lauriston Road Cemetery 1788, chest tombs in the shape of coffins (photograph K. Marks 2009).

Figure 5.22 Lauriston Road Cemetery 1788, unusual and elaborately decorated tomb monuments, topped with decorated urns (photograph K. Marks 2009).

subsidising the poor and needy. Upkeep of the buildings and cemetery, religious education and the salary of the rabbi were paid by synagogue members. The *Ba'alei Batim* (corresponding to the Vestry men in the English parish), were the founders, officials and distinguished members of the Hambro Synagogue (4.1.5). Their plots are prominently positioned near the centre of the cemetery or near the main pathways. The seat holders, strangers, guests and poorer members have simpler and less ornate burial stones, placed in less prominent positions, some near the walls. The two classes of members have separate sections or separate rows.

The Hambro Synagogue no longer survives, although the Lauriston Road Cemetery is an indicator of social and status difference among the members of this synagogue in the late 18th and 19th centuries; it is also evident that certain 'virgin plots' were reserved so that families could be buried together, such as the plot of Yehiel Preger, the first burial in 1788, whose wife was buried next to him in 1798 (personal observation 2009). Details and surnames on certain grave stones indicate origins of the deceased. Anglicised names, such as Hart (grave 35) and Norden (76), indicate assimilation taking place during the 18th and 19th centuries. There are headstones indicating town or country of residence which then became the family name. For example: Akiba Portsmouth (37) Nathan Liverpool (57) Abraham Oxford (86), Jacob Frenchman (288). Getz Whitechapel (82). German and other origins and former towns of residence of the deceased also became surnames, such as Samuel Mannheim (31). Occupations sometimes became family names, such as Joseph Schneider (tailor) (18). A number of the tombstones are inscribed not only with the name of the deceased, 'Lewis Cohen (d.1868), and date of death and also with his address Clifton Gardens, Maida Vale and of New York U.S.A' (personal observation 2009). They echo upper class memorials in churches from c.1800 and middle class headstones used in commercial cemeteries from c.1840.

5.1.9 Ashkenazi West Ham E15 [56]

In the 1850's The New Synagogue's (Great St Helens) first cemetery in Brady Street (5.16) was becoming full. This five-acre West Ham cemetery was acquired in 1856 and closed in c.1972 (4.1.7). Holding around 15, 000 graves (personal contact Tucker, 2010). Burials of former members of The Great Synagogue (4.2.5) also took place. The 1896 Ordnance Survey Map shows the location of the cemetery designated as 'Jews Burial Ground'. The site was on farm land, now the West Ham Christian Cemetery, shown as Cann Hall, Trevelyan Road, on the 1896 Ordnance Survey map

Nothing remains of the *ohel* or caretaker's house, which was on the left of the original west entrance, the land having been recently sold. Whilst the location of these buildings is evident from the ground-level foundations (personal observation 2009), all that remains are vacant areas where these buildings once stood. The former entrance is bricked up, so that entry now has to be made through a side gate (personal observation 2010). The cemetery is dominated by the Rothschild Mausoleum (Figure 5.27).

Whilst West Ham's adjacent Christian and other denominations cemetery is well maintained with grass, trees and flowers, the Jewish burial ground is bleak, other than the Rothschild mausoleum. There are decaying monuments, hundreds of graves with no marker stones, and grave stones, particularly from the 19th century which are in sandstone and limestone, rather than granite or marble, these have been weathered by acid rain. Many, once upright are now lying flat and broken and can no longer be read (personal observation, 2009) (Figure 5.23). There is a number of headstones with metal plates with the name and date of death of the deceased attached, which partly cover the original inscription. Still evident are the graves of two eminent personalities, Lord Mayors of London, Sir David Salomons (1797-1872) and Sir Benjamin Philips (1810-1889).

When this cemetery opened in 1858, large numbers of mainly poor immigrants from Eastern Europe were settling in the East End of London. The community had a duty to bury anyone known to be Jewish. West Ham, although in the

Figure 5.23 West Ham Cemetery E15 1856, (photograph K. Marks 2009).

countryside, near to Stratford and the east of London, was used as the burial ground. Poverty is reflected by the fact that many of the graves have no markers; London's acid rain and neglect has taken its toll (personal observation 2009).

Behind the Rothschild Mausoleum, near the rear (north) of the cemetery, between rows of graves, are two strips marked by *plaques* stating that in *'1960 remains from the Old Hoxton Cemetery, members of the Hambro Synagogue had been re-interred when the Hoxton site was destroyed for re-development'* (Figure 5.24). No individuals are recorded *in situ* but according to Charles Tucker there are burial records in The London Metropolitan Archives (Figure 5.25), although there are some tombstones from Hoxton, one of which dates to 1794.

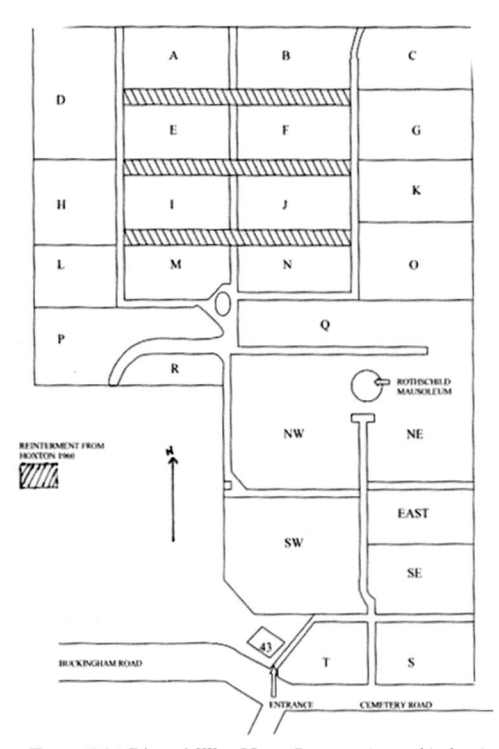

Figure 5.24 Plan of West Ham Cemetery (no scale) showing strips of re-interred remains from Old Hoxton Cemetery (1960) and site of the Rothschild mausoleum (United Synagogue Burial Society).

Figure 5.26 West Ham 19th century Christian Cemetery showing Gothic-style prayer hall, similar to the ohel (prayer hall) in Willesden Jewish Cemetery (5.1.11) of similar date (photograph K.Marks 2009).

Figure 5.25 1960 Re-interred remains from the Old Hoxton cemetery (1707-1878) (photograph K. Marks 2009).

The Rothschild Mausoleum

The centrepiece of the cemetery is the Renaissance-style white marble rotunda of the mausoleum of Eva (Evelina) de Rothschild (1839-1866) and her husband, Ferdinand de Rothschild (1839-1898) (Figure 5.27). Eva died in childbirth at the age of 27, less than a year after being married. The exterior of the rotunda is decorated with elaborated Corinthian columns inscribed with Eva's name. Inside are two chest tombs with inscriptions on the rear wall they read as follows:

> *'If I ascend up into heaven thou art there. If I lie down in the grave behold I find thee Even there thy hand leads me and thou right hand supports me. 'She opened her lips with wisdom and in her speech was the law of kindness.'*

Figure 5.27 West Ham Cemetery E15: The Rothschild Mausoleum 1866 (photograph K.Marks 2009).

Underneath is a separate plaque with the words *'My darling wife'* (personal observation 2009). The mausoleum was built by Ferdinand to mark the tragic end to a brief, but happy marriage In addition to becoming the MP for Aylesbury, he devoted his life to philanthropy. He built Waddesdon Manor in Buckinghamshire in memory of his wife, he never re-married. Why did Ferdinand de Rothschild choose this cemetery. One reason may be that Brady Street, where his ancestor Nathan was buried, did not have sufficient space in 1866 for an elaborate mausoleum. Willesden Cemetery, where several of the Rothschild family were later buried with elaborate tombstones and monuments, was not established until 1873.

5.1.10 West London Reform Balls Pond Road N1 [57]

The West London Congregation of Reform Jews was formed in 1841. The first Reform cemetery in England was opened in 1843. Most of the graves, where one can still read the inscriptions are from the second quarter of the 20th century. Burial records indicate that c.900 persons are interred. The Reform community was formed in the middle of the 19th century, when there was a growing wealthy and upper middle-class community in the West End. It was a mixture of Ashkenazi and Sephardi Jews, as evidenced by tombstone inscriptions. The names, such as David Mocatta (d.1883), inscribed in English, state that he was 'one of the first Jews who were members of the Institute of British Architects' and also one of the founders of the West London Synagogue (personal observation 2009). Mocatta designed the Montefiore Mausoleum in Ramsgate (4.2.29). There are graves of members of the Montefiore and Henriques' families and a Toledano, a Sephardi name, but his tombstone is upright in the Ashkenazi tradition. These names indicate Spanish and Portuguese origins. Victorian memorials in Portland stone, granite and marble with highly decorated inscriptions, mainly in English sometimes include the address of the deceased. A granite column dedicated to the first Rabbi of West London Synagogue of British Jews, Reverend Professor David Wolf Marks D.D. (1811-1909), and his wife, Sarah, inscribed with psalms, almost impossible to read although it is also almost entirely inscribed in English (Figure 5.28).

One of the most impressive tombstones is that of Sir Isaac Lyon Goldsmid, Bart. (d.1859), the first Jewish Baronet (1841). In addition to his financial undertakings in the City, he was one of the founders of U.C.L. The inscription reads *'all without distinction or creed could receive the advantages of a superior education'* (personal observation 2009). He was a major benefactor to U.C.L. Hospital and many other charitable organisations. He was also instrumental in repealing the civil disabilities of the Jews in England, where many professions were barred to them. On one side of the

Figure 5.28 West London Reform; Balls Pond Road Cemetery N1: granite column marking the grave of Rabbi Wolf Marks D.D. (d.1909) and his wife Sarah (photograph K. Marks, 2009)

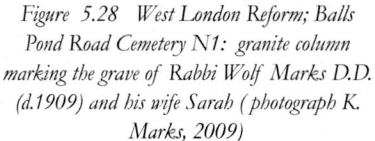

Figure 5.29 West London Reform Balls Pond Road Cemetery. Chest tomb of Baronet Goldsmid.(d.1859) with coat of arms (photograph K. Marks 2009).

monument is the dedication in English and on the other is the same inscription in Hebrew, much damaged (personal observation 2009).

The tallest obelisk monument (over three meters high) is dedicated to George Elliot Johansson (d.1874 at the age of 11). His father David, who came from Sunderland, is also buried in this cemetery. This family is discussed in 5.2.33.1. In a corner of the burial ground there are a number of unmarked graves of infants and children who died in the late-19th century, There is no trace of an *ohel*. The predominant use of English for the inscriptions indicates assimilation of part of the upper-middle-class community in the 19th century. The cultural mix of Ashkenazi and Sephardi tombstones reflects the early founders of the Reform Movement. This cemetery was in use until c.1895, when Golders Green Reform and Sephardi cemeteries were opened and a few later tombstones (up to 1952) mark where relatives had reserved plots.

5.1.11   Ashkenazi Willesden NW10   [58]

Willesden cemetery, established in 1873, was the first major project of the Ashkenazi United Synagogue with five constituent synagogues, with the rabbi of The Great Synagogue recognised as being the Chief Rabbi. The five synagogues were the Great, Hambro, New, Bayswater and Central. From 1873 their deceased members were buried in Willesden. It is now one of the largest Jewish cemeteries in Britain. According to Charles Tucker (archivist of the United Synagogue), there are over c.20, 000 adult graves and many hundreds of unmarked children's graves in a total area of around 40 acres (personal contact 2009). From its establishment, Willesden became the most important and prestigious Orthodox Jewish cemetery in Britain.

The design of the *ohel* and the stylistic development of later tombstones and monuments show the influence of assimilation and increasing prosperity and status of many of those buried. Unlike the tombstones in early London cemeteries, many have elaborate inscriptions and decorations, and some are in marble. Rather than the main body of the inscriptions being in Hebrew, English is more evident. There is clearly evidence of wanting to be more 'English'. The original Gothic-style *ohel* remains (Figure 5.30) and resembles a non-conformist chapel. Built of Kentish ragstone (Kadish 2006, 51), the leaded and tinted glass arched windows and archways inside are in the Gothic style.

The earliest burial is that of Samuel Moses JP. He was buried on 2nd October 1873 the day that the cemetery was consecrated by the chief rabbi. The tombstone gives Moses' address in Regents Park, London, followed by the address of his second home, Boa Vista, Tasmania (personal observation 2009). Other memorials from this period also give the address of the deceased and in many cases the address shows movement from the east of London to the west and north. Buried here are 12 members of the Rothschild family in family enclosures (Figure 5.31). These enclosure were originally in the family mausoleum, built 1890's, but were removed following damage and dilapidation during World War II.

Figure 5.30 Willesden: cemetery ohel (prayer hall) opened in 1870 (photograph K. Marks 2009).

Figure 5.31 Willesden: cemetery one of the white marble enclosures of the Rothschild family (photograph K. Marks 2009).

According to Kadish (2006, 51): 'Willesden contains some of the finest Jewish memorials in the country, many belonging to the 'Cousinhood' of leading Jewish families'. In addition to the later graves of two chief rabbis are other leading figures in Anglo-Jewry from the City of London, including Lord Bearstead and Robert Waley-Cohen (Former Lord Mayor). There are several other graves of interest including that of Benjamin Hall (Big Ben was named after him). Another unusual feature is the wide turning area near the main entrance, which according to Elkan Levy (personal contact 2009), enabled horse drawn carriages to make a turn to exit the cemetery grounds.

5.2   Provincial Cemeteries

In all of the 35 provincial towns researched, the 18th-century Jewish cemeteries were outside ancient city walls; possible reasons for this practice are examined. Some have been destroyed as cities have expanded, and as a result, some later cemeteries contain re-interments in mass graves, sometimes with tombstones from old cemeteries or a memorial obelisk, such as in Birmingham (Witton Old Cemetery), or a plaque as in Gloucester (Coney Hill, Jewish Section Municipal Cemetery) and Sheffield (Ecclesfield Jewish Cemetery).

In the period under discussion, the establishment, and then decline of some of the smaller provincial communities is evident from the dates and number of burials. Other than cemeteries examined, there is a paucity of physical and documented evidence in many of the early post re-admission provincial Jewish communities.

There is comparable evidence across communities, such as tombstones and monuments, their stylistic changes and inscriptions. Early tombstones are simple, in local stone such as limestone, sandstone and slate. Both in London and the provinces, early inscriptions, where they survive, are in Hebrew, while the later (19th century) inscriptions have both Hebrew and English. In addition to the date of birth and death of the deceased on tombstones, gravestones sometimes detail the country or town where the deceased came from, an invaluable source of demographic information.

This section discusses 15 Jewish provincial cemeteries established by the end of the 18th century and a further 38 by c.1880, in 35 cities and towns, comprising 53 cemeteries in total.

5.2.1	Bath*	Bradford Road: 1812-1921
5.2.2	Birmingham***	Witton Old Cemetery: 1869-1937, re-interred remains from 1766 and 1823 burial grounds
5.2.3	Bradford ***	Scholemoor, Jewish Sections: 1877-still in use.
5.2.4	Brighton****	Florence Place Old Jewish Burial Ground 1826-c.1920.
5.2.5	Bristol***	St. Philips Jewish Cemetery Barton Road: 1744-1944.
5.2.6	Canterbury****	Whitstable Road in use 1760-1870 (one burial 1916)
5.2.7	Cardiff**	Highfield Road Old Jewish Cemetery: 184-still in use.
5.2.8	Chatham***	High Street: 1780-1940.
5.2.9	Cheltenham**	Elm Street: 1824-still in use.
5.2.10	Coventry****	London Road, Jewish Section 1864-still in use.
5.2.11	Dover**	Old Charlton Road: 1864-still in use.
5.2.12	Exeter **	Bull Meadow: 1757-still used
5.2.13	Falmouth**	Ponshardon c.1789-1868
5.2.14	Gloucester**	Coney Hill: re-interred remains from c.1780 burial ground.
5.2.15.1	Hull***	Villa Place: 1780-1812.
5.2.15.2	Hull***	Hessle Road: 1812-1858.
5.2.15.3	Hull***	Delhi Street: 1858-still in use.
5.2.16.1	Ipswich***	Salthouse Lane: 1796-1854.
5.2.16.2	Ipswich***	Cemetery Lane: 1855-1985.
5.2.17	Kings Lynn***	Stonegate Street: 1811-1846.
5.2.18.1	Leeds***	Hill Top: 1873-1990.
5.2.18.2	Leeds***	Gilderssome: 1850-still in use.
5.2.19.1	Liverpool**	Deane Road: 1837-1904.
5.2.19.2	Liverpool**	Broad Green: 1904 re-interred remains from 1789 and 1902 city centre burial grounds-still in use

5.2.19.3	Liverpool **	Green Lane: 1839-1921.
5.2.20.1	Manchester***	Brindle Heath: 1794-1840.
5.2.20.2	Manchester***	Prestwich Village: 1840-1914.
5.2.20.3	Manchester***	Whitefield (Reform): 1858-2005
5.2.20.4	Manchester***	Philips Park: 1865-1953.
5.2.21	Merthyr Tydfil***	Brecon Road: 1865-1999.
5.2.22.1	Newcastle***	Thornton Street: 1835-1853.
5.2.22.2	Newcastle***	St John's Cemetery, Jewish Section: 1857-1950.
5.2.23.1	Norwich***	Mariners Lane: c.1750-1826.
5.2.23.2	Norwich***	Quaker's Lane: 1813-1854.
5.2.23.3	Norwich***	Bowthorpe Road: 1856-still in use.
5.2.24.1	Nottingham***	North Sherwood Street: 1823-1869.
5.2.24.2	Nottingham ***	Hardy Street: 1867-1947.
5.2.25	Oxford ***	First cemetery: established 1894.
5.2.26	Penzance**	Leskinnick Terrace: 1791-2000.
5.2.27	Plymouth Hoe**	Lamhay Hill: 1744-c.1860.
5.2.28	Portsmouth**	Fawcett Road: 1749-still in use
5.2.29	Ramsgate****	Upper Dumpton Park Road 1872-still in use.
5.2.30.1	Sheerness***	Hope Street: c.1804-1855.
5.2.30.2	Sheerness***	Isle of Sheppey, Halfway Road: 1859-1899.
5.2.31.1	Sheffield****	Bowden Street: 1831-1880.
5.2.31.2	Sheffield****	Walkley Jewish Cemetery 1873-1900
5.2.31.3	Sheffield****	Ecclesfield Jewish Cemetery 1873-still in use.
5.2.32	Southampton****	Southampton Common (Old) Cemetery, Jewish Section: 1846-still in use
5.2.33.1	Sunderland***	Ayres Quay: c.1780-1856
5.2.33.2	Sunderland***	Bishopswearmouth: Jewish Sections 1856-still in use.
5.2.34	Swansea***	Mayhill Old Jews' Burial Ground: 1768-1965.
5.2.35.1	Yarmouth (Great) ***	Alma Road: 1801-1885.
5.2.35.2	Yarmouth (Great)***	Kitchener Road: 1858-1936.
5.2.36	Conclusion	

*visited 2008   ** visited 2009   ***visited 2010   ****visited 2011

5.2.1 Bath: Bradford Road [59]

The deeds to this burial ground were examined in Bath Records Office. The cemetery was established outside the city limits in the suburbs of Bath, in Coombe Down. The deeds show that the land was purchased in 1812. The first burial took place in 1815 (Brown et al. 1982-6, 144), and as the community grew in numbers the cemetery was enlarged in 1862 to its present size (100ft x40ft).

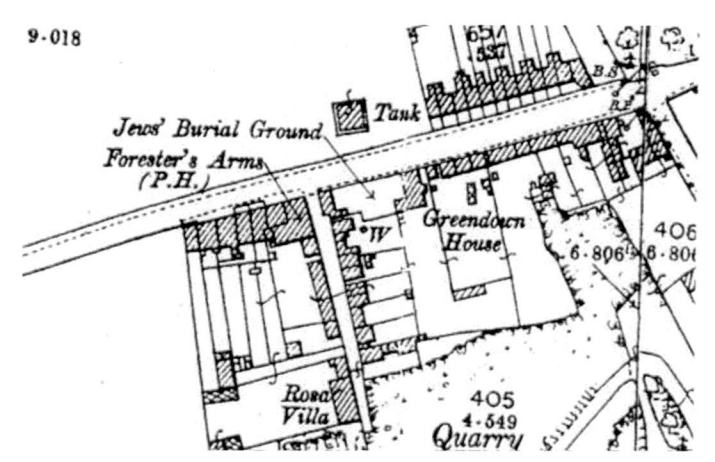

Figure 5.32 Bath: cemetery shown on extract from 1904 Ordnance Survey Map (5ft to a mile) (Bath Records Office)

The cemetery is surrounded by high Pennant stone walls. No original records survive, but the tombstones were identified when the site was surveyed by Judith Samuel and Bernard Susser in the 1980s and 1990s. A plan was made of 51 graves (Figure 5.33), 38 with tombstones. The styles of the tombstones reflect local Christian styles, even though they are inscribed in Hebrew and English. Local Christian monumental masons' names are evident on some of the head-stones (personal observation 2008). Many of the inscriptions have deteriorated and can no longer be read due to weathering (personal observation 2008).The latest gravestone is 1921. Grave stones 33 and 36 are flat compared with other upright grave stones. This could suggest that the deceased were Sephardi of Spanish and Portuguese origin. Brown et al. gives details of some of the Sephardim known to have lived in Bath. The small Bath community was mostly Ashkenazi, so only one Jewish burial ground was needed. Until recently, the cemetery was in a poor state, overgrown with vegetation, but thanks to the Coombe Down Heritage Society, the initiative of the few remaining Jews living in Bath and the newly established Friends of Bath Jewish Burial Ground, it has been cleared (personal observation 2008) (Figure 5.34). Graves of interest were examined, where the deceased can be linked to the surviving pictures of Bath houses known to be occupied by Jews in the 19th century.

1. Daniel Rees d.1842 (plot No.13), lived with brother, Abraham d.1845. Address 20, Bathwick Street (Figure 5.33). Abraham, according to Brown et al., was a London tailor who retired to Bath (Ibid, 144).
2. Myer Fishel d.1861 (plot No.2), formerly a silversmith of 6, New Bond Street London. No address in Bath is given.

These graves would seem to indicate that a number of Jews retired to Bath, perhaps to take advantage of the health-giving waters. A number of Jewish doctors, dentists and owners of shops selling heath products are also noted by Brown et al. Reverend. Solomon Wolfe d.1866 (plot No.18) was reader of the Bath Hebrew Congregation for 50 years. According to Brown et al., (1982-1986, 151) soon after his death the number attending synagogue declined and services were no longer held on a regular basis The title Reverend indicates that he was not an ordained rabbi but was a *chazzan* (reader to the congregation). As well as conducting marriages and *barmitvahs,* when a boy reaches the age of 13 and is called to read from the *Torah* (the first five books of the Old Testament), the Reverend would more than likely have been qualified also to serve as the *shochet* (*kosher* butcher) and also a *mohel* (qualified to perform circumcisions).

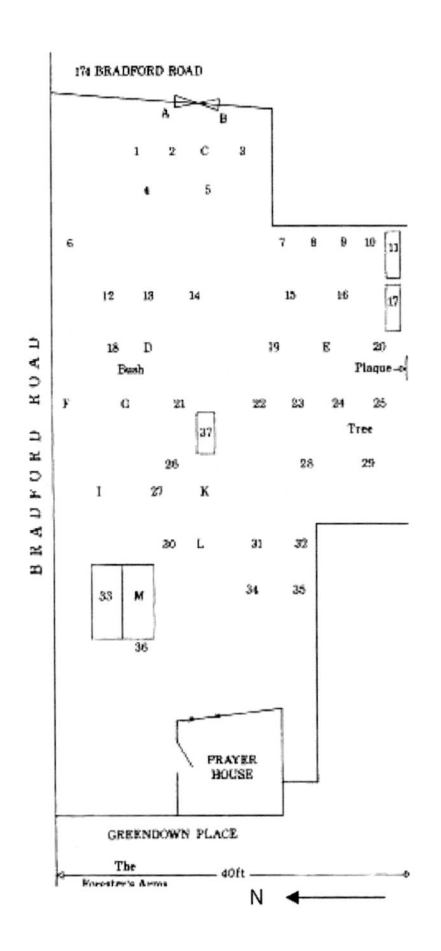

Figure 5.33 Bath: topographical plan of Jewish Burial Ground (Samuel, J and Susser, B.1986).

Figure 5.34 Bath: Jewish Burial Ground c.1815 (photograph K. Marks 2008).

The *Ohel* (prayer room) Grade II

This early 19th-century *ohel* is one of few standing from this period, albeit in a poor state of preservation (personal observation 2008) (Figure 5.35). Constructed of Bath stone, with a chimney stack and the remains of a fireplace inside, this feature suggests that it was occupied, perhaps by persons responsible for the upkeep of the cemetery. No survey of this historic building at the time of writing this study has yet been carried out, although this was approved in 2010 with funding from English Heritage for survey and repairs.

Figure 5.35 Bath ohel *(prayer hall) (c.1815) Grade II listed (photograph K. Marks 2008).*

5.2.2 Birmingham: Witton Old Cemetery [60]

In 1869, two-and-half acres of land south of College Road were acquired by the Jewish Community from the Birmingham Corporation to establish Witton Old Jewish Cemetery. The Witton New Cemetery, located opposite, was established in 1938. The old cemetery contains 2,718 burials, including 657 children (Singers Hill Synagogue records). Only 15 children's graves are marked. According to the cemetery manager (personal contact 2010), there are no plans or records still surviving which show the plot positions or details of the deceased.

Witton Old Jewish Cemetery remained in use until 1993 and contains the re-interred remains from two earlier cemeteries in Birmingham, Granville Street Cemetery (c.1766-1825) and around 30 tombstone fragments from the Betholom Row Burial Ground (1823-1872). Nothing remains of these burial grounds. A granite obelisk (Grade II) erected in 1876 marks the re-interment in a mass grave of Granville Street Cemetery (Figure 5.36). The memorial which is enclosed by iron railings marks the area of re-internments. The inscription on the west face of the base of the obelisk (in English and Hebrew) reads as follows in English:

> '*This monument marks the place where the bodies removed from the Jewish Cemetery near Granville Street were re-interred in 5636-1836*'. The Hebrew inscription repeats these words, with the addition of an acronym for '*May his/her soul be bound up in the bond of life*' (personal observation 2010).

Figure 5.36 Birmingham: memorial obelisk in Witton Old Jewish Cemetery (1869), marking re-interred remains from Granville Street. (photograph Birmingham Synagogue Archives).

The *ohel* in Witton Old cemetery has been demolished, although its hexagonal foundations have been preserved (personal observation 2010). Granville Street and the local area no longer exist. The synagogue records show that two cottages with grounds for a cemetery were acquired in October 1766 and fell into disuse c.1825.

Granville Street cemetery was in the garden of a house in the Froggery, the first Jewish area in Birmingham, now the location of the New Street Railway Station. In 1874, the Birmingham West Suburban Railway Company 'raised the level of Granville Street adjoining in order to construct a bridge'. Litigation followed and the property was sold in 1876 and '…a further sum of £300 was paid in full satisfaction and compensation for the trouble and expense incurred by the Trustees in removing the bodies and tombstones' (synagogue records 31/33). Stacked against the wall behind the obelisk on the east wall are c.30 fragments, mostly unreadable, from Bethlehem Row Burial Ground (1823-1872). Synagogue records show that by 1872, 500 internments had taken place. All that remains on the site, which is inaccessible, is a memorial tablet which reads 'Jews Burial Ground' and the tombstone fragments noted above. Levy (1984, 20) notes that 'until the end of the 19th century Witton Old Cemetery served as the burial ground of Jews from all over the Midlands, where there were small communities who did not have a burial ground, such as Leicester and Walsall'.

5.2.3   Bradford: Scholemoor, Jewish sections   [61]

There are two Jewish sections in the Municipal Cemetery; to the North of the burial ground is the Reform section acquired in 1877, where the founders of the Bradford Reform community are buried. The smaller Orthodox section was established 10 years later in 1886 at the entrance in Neocropolis Road. In between are sections for the Muslim community. The Reform *ohel* is made from sandstone bricks and was erected before the first burial took place in May 1877 (Figure 5.37). All the early memorials are in York Stone, with the more recent headstones in granite and marble, which became more fashionable in the 20th century. In the Reform section there are c.200 graves.

Figure 5.37 Bradford: Scholemoor Reform Cemetery and ohel *(prayer hall) (1877) (photograph K.Marks 2010).*

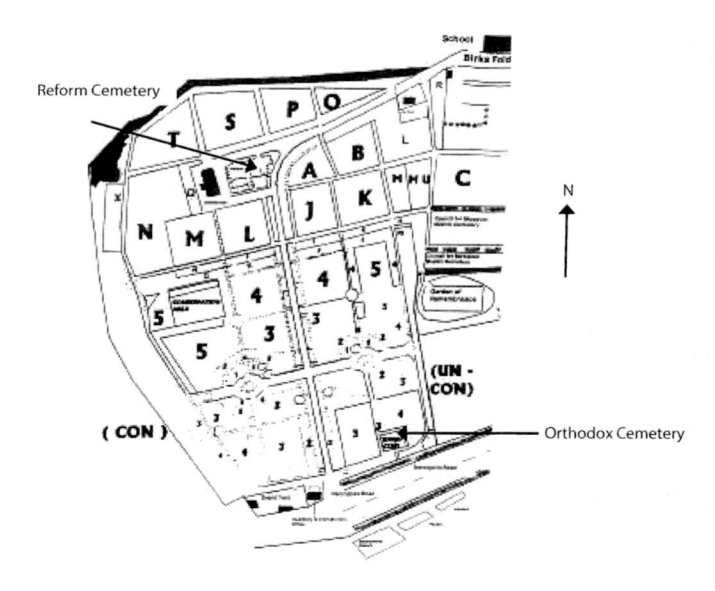

Figure 5.38 Bradford: Plan of Scholemoor Municipal Cemetery, showing two Jewish sections, Orthodox and Reform (Bradford Municipal Burial Society).

5.2.4 Brighton: Florence Place [62]

This was Brighton's first Jewish burial ground. Spector (1968/9, 47) notes: 'that Jews who died in the town before 1826 were mostly buried in London cemeteries'. The original *ohel* no longer exists and was replaced in 1891/2 by the current terracotta hexagonal structure (Kadish 2006, 79). The cemetery, no longer used, is partly overgrown on a slope with the oldest graves to the rear. There are around 350 graves (personal observation 2011).

Figure 5.39 Brighton: Florence Place, Old Jewish Burial Ground terracotta ohel *(1891/3), (photograph K. Marks 2011).*

Figure 5.40 Brighton: Florence Place, Old Jewish Burial Ground (photograph K. Marks 2011).

5.2.5   Bristol: St Philip's Cemetery, Barton Road   [63]

St Philip's Jewish Cemetery, Barton Road, established in 1744, is the first of Bristol's Jewish cemeteries with over 150 graves, according to Tobias et al. (1997, 1). The earliest identified tombstones date from 1762. In the middle of the 18th century, there were restrictions on Jews owning land, so it was leased before being acquired by the Bristol Jewish Community in 1859. In 1901 there was a fire in an adjoining building, and the firemen, in order to gain access, demolished one of the cemetery walls. In the process, a number of graves stones were toppled and not replaced *in situ* (Ibid, 5). Figure 5.41 shows a plan of the cemetery, and Figure 5.42 shows part of the cemetery in 1986 before restoration and clearing of rubble and rubbish.

From 1814-1880, a small cemetery existed in Rose Street in part of the garden of a private house owned by Lazarus Jacobs, an eminent glass maker. According to Tobias et al., in 1913, the site was acquired by the Great Western Railway to extend the goods yard at Temple Meads Station (Ibid, 3). In 1924, 27 graves and tombstones were removed and remains reburied in the new Ridgeway Cemetery (1898) (not discussed) (Ibid, 16). Inscriptions on many of the Barton Road Cemetery grave stones are so worn that they cannot be read (personal observation 2010).

Comprehensive records with photographs taken by the Bristol Jewish Cemetery Committee in 1997/1999 exist also for the remains from Rose Street Cemetery. Early inscriptions are mostly Hebrew, but by the middle 1800s, there is more English than Hebrew, with the date of death is sometimes in English only. Later tombstones have both Hebrew and English (Figure 5.44), further indicating the process of assimilation of the Bristol Orthodox community.

COMMUNITIES IN DEATH (CEMETERIES)   163

JEWISH BURIAL GROUND, BARTON ROAD, BRISTOL
Row numbers

	131	130	129	128	127	126	
132							125
133							124

PATH   123

XIII	111	112		CC	113	114	115	DD	116		117		EE	FF	GG		131
XII	110	BB	109	108	AA	107	106	105	Z	104	103	102	101	100	99		120
XI	90	W	91	92	93	94	95	96	X			97	Y	98			119
X	89	88	V	87	86	85	84	U	T	S	R	Q	83				118
IX	N	O	77	78	79	80	81	82	P								

PATH

VIII	76	75	74	73	72	71
VII	61	62	63	J	64	65	66	67	68	69	70	L	M
VI	60	59	58	57	56	55	I	54	53	52	51	50	49
	47
V	33	34	35	36	G	37	38	39	40	41	42	43	44	45	46	H

PATH (right side: 48)

| IV | 32 | 31 | F | 30 | 29 | 28 | 27 | E | 26 | 25 | 24 | 23 |
| III | 12 | 13 | 14 | 15 | A | B | 16 | 17 | C | 18 | 19 | 20 | 21 | D |

22

PATH

| II | 11 | 10 | 9 | 8 | 7 | 6 |
| I | 1 | 2 | 3 | 4 | 5 |

GATE to Barton Road   SITE of PRAYER HOUSE

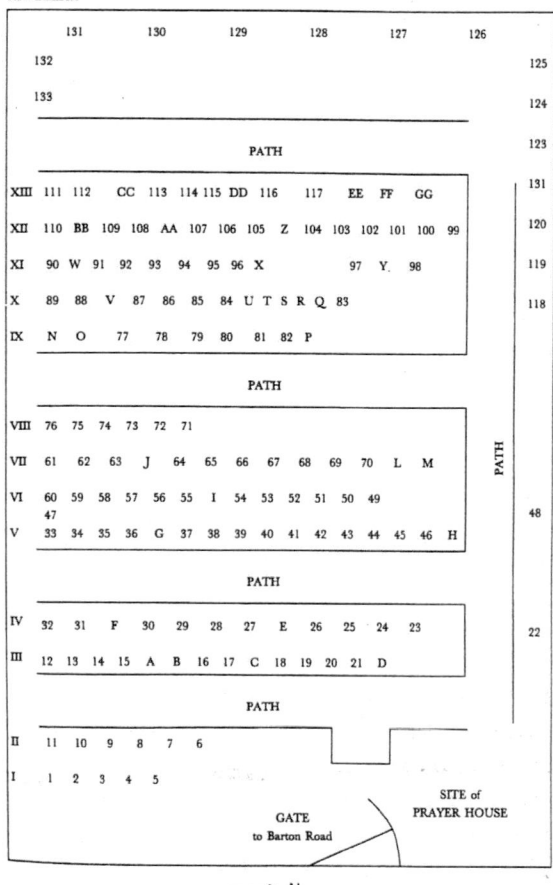

→ N

Figure 5.41 Bristol: Plan of Barton Road Cemetery: (1744), showing entrance on Barton Road, site of prayer house/ house and plot positions (Samuel 1997, 215). Site measurement is c.800m × 100m.

Figure 5.42 Bristol: Barton Road Cemetery, showing the dereliction and neglect of part of the burial ground and site of former ohel (prayer hall) before restoration (photograph, Benjamin Price 1986).

164 THE ARCHAEOLOGY OF ANGLO-JEWRY IN ENGLAND AND WALES 1656–C.1880

Figure 5.43 Bristol: Barton Road Cemetery View of burial ground (photograph K.Marks 2010).

Figure 5.44 Bristol: Barton Road Cemetery, some of the tomb monuments showing the change that takes place over time in the use of Hebrew and English on the inscriptions (Tobias et al. 1997, 10). n.b.03&04, 05&06 identical? (Taken from Tobias et al 1997)

5.2.6 Canterbury: Whitstable Road [64]

Whitstable Road burial ground was in use from 1760, it is outside the medieval town walls and before the first Canterbury synagogue was opened in 1762/3 (Roth 1950, 46). It was the first Jewish burial ground in Kent. Entrance is through a narrow alleyway off the road, through a curved archway with a Star of David above the gate in Egyptian style (personal observation 2010). There are approximately 200 grave stones (Figure 5.46), many of which are now illegible (personal observation (2010); Kadish (2006, 65). notes that partial records survive from 1831-1870.

Figure 5.45 Canterbury: Whitstable Road, Jews' Burial Ground (1760), later entrance. (photograph J. Marks 2011).

Figure 5.46 Canterbury: Whitstable Road, Jews' Burial Ground (photograph J. Marks 2011).

5.2.7 Cardiff: Highfield Road [65]

Prior to the establishment of Cardiff's first Jewish cemetery in 1841, Jews who died in Cardiff were mostly sent to Bristol for burial (Henriques 1993, 12). The Cardiff cemetery is surrounded by high stone walls, with a later gated entrance, decorated with two Stars of David (Figure 5.48). A plaque indicates that the land was donated by the Marquis of Bute in 1841, although this cannot be verified (Figure 5.47), (Kadish 2006, 201).

A number of obelisks (Figure 5.49) and ornate tombstones are decorated with well-preserved inscriptions, such as raised hands, indicating that the deceased was a male *Cohen* (descended from the priestly tribe) (Figure 5.50). A hand holding a jug pouring water to wash

Figure 5.47 Cardiff: Old Jewish Cemetery Highfield Road, (1841), plaque showing that the land was donated by the Marquess of Bute (photograph. K.Marks 2009).

the hands of the *Cohanim*, indicates that the deceased was a male Levy (descended from the Tribe of the Levites) (Figure 5.50). A flower indicates that the deceased was a young girl (Figure 5.50).

Figure 5.48 Cardiff: Old Jewish Cemetery Highfield Road, entrance gates (photograph K. Marks 2009).

Figure 5.49 Cardiff: Old Jewish Cemetery Highfield Road: tombstones and obelisks (photograph K.Marks 2009).

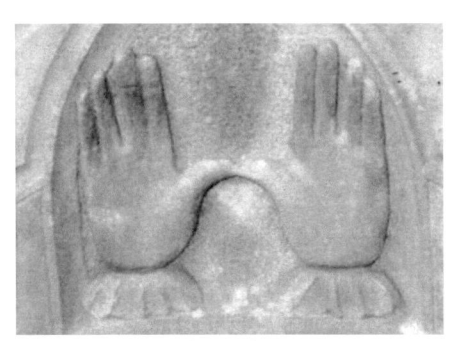

Figure 5.50 Cardiff: Old Jewish Cemetery Highfield Road: top left: decorations on tombstones such as raised handd, indicating that the deceased was a Cohen top right: tombstone with a hand pouring water over the priestly hand, indicating that the deceased was a Levite bottom: tombstone with flower, indicating that the deceased was a young girl (photograph K.Marks 2009).

5.2.8   Chatham: High Street   [66]

This cemetery is unique in Britain as the only Jewish burial ground adjacent to a synagogue, a common practice for Christians who buried their deceased buried in churchyards. Most Orthodox cemeteries in Britain come under the authority of the *Beth Din* (Jewish Court of Law). Sephardi and Reform synagogues have their own burial societies, with burial grounds some distance from synagogues. Chatham Synagogue, at one time affiliated to The United Synagogue, had from its beginning a separate law, so that the cemetery was not under the authority of The United Synagogue. This allowed the cemetery to be placed behind and adjacent to the original c.1750 synagogue.

The present synagogue was established c.1865 on freehold land acquired by Simon Magnus, a local businessman and philanthropist, from St. Bartholomew's Hospital, which overlooks the cemetery. According to David Herling (local community), another unique feature of this cemetery is a strip of land, one yard wide on the west side of the cemetery, which was not included in the freehold purchase. This was used as a passageway from the river landing place opposite to the hospital by lepers and people with other infectious illnesses, such as cholera. The synagogue still pays an annual rent of 5p to the hospital (personal contact 2010).

The cemetery measuring 31yards x27 yards holds between 150-200 graves (personal observation, 2010) and is dominated by the obelisk and memorial to Captain Lazarus Magnus the son of Simon Magnus, who founded the synagogue. According to Lancaster (1998, 1)'....the Deed of Trust states that the memorial has

Figure 5.51 Chatham: High Street Cemetery (1780s) with St Bartholomew's Hospital at the rear (photograph K. Marks 2010).

Figure 5.52 Chatham: Memorial obelisk to Lazarus Simon Magnus (photograph K. Marks 2010).

to be visible from the road'. This is still the case, with the more recent extension of the synagogue in front having glass windows so that there is a view from the High Street of the obelisk (personal observation 2010). Simon Magnus, the father of Lazarus Magnus is buried at the rear of the cemetery. Unfortunately the site is suffering from neglect, with some headstones no longer *in situ,* some no longer readable and others missing.

5.2.9 Cheltenham: Elm Street [67]

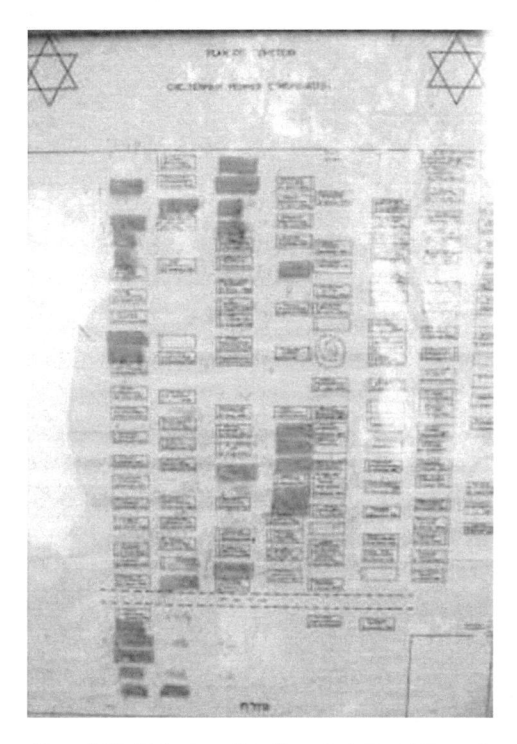

Figure 5.53 Cheltenham: Elm Street Jew's Burial Ground (1824), plot plan from 1893 on wall in ohel *(prayer hall) (photograph J. Marks 2009).*

According to the synagogue records the Cheltenham burial ground was acquired in 1824 (Tarode 1999, 82). This is also the date that Roth (1950, 110) cites for the establishment of the community According to Susser (1996, 159), further ground was acquired in stages over the years 1835, 1839, 1845, and 1860, when a row of cottages fronting onto Elm Street was knocked down; the cemetery reached its present size in

c. 1892. The entrance is through a modern *ohel* (prayer hall) in the high red-brick buttressed wall. The grounds are well kept by the caretaker, David Cook (personal contact 2009). The earliest legible stone is dated 1841, although there is a commemorative wall plaque to a four-month-old baby (d. May 1822). The oldest stones are along the east wall. There remain three wall-mounted stone plaques and two others are leaning against the wall. In all, there are over 70 legible inscriptions from the 19th century (personal observation 2009).

There are no burial records with plot details before 1893, although there is the register of deaths from 1870. There are the tombstones of Sarah Mendes da Silva, aged 86, and Sarah Baruh Lousada, aged 93, their names are Sephardi, the tomb stones are laid flat in the Sephardi tradition. It was common in the smaller communities for Ashkenazi and Sephardim to be buried in the same cemetery. Up to c.1872, the register shows that burials took place in Cheltenham cemetery of Jews who lived in Gloucester, Hereford, Ross on Wye, Stroud and Wales. There is a plan of the grounds on the wall in the *ohel* that shows plots which are filled and where there are vacant spaces (Figure 5.53). This records the deaths of Hester Sterheim of Stroud, 25th August 1879, aged 29, and her two newly born children, aged 12 and 15 days. There is also the tombstone of Walter Levason, aged 9, of Hereford, who drowned in the River Wye in 1852. Burials still take place of members of the Cheltenham's declining Orthodox community.

Figure 5.54 Cheltenham: Elm Street Jews' Burial Ground, row of oldest surviving graves from c.1870 (photograph J. Marks 2009).

5.2.10 Coventry: London Road [68]

Prior to the establishment of this cemetery, Jews who died in Coventry were buried in Betholom Row Cemetery in Birmingham (Kadish 2006, 125) (5.2.2). The Jewish cemetery is in three sections on the edge of the Municipal Burial Ground (Figure 5.55). The first and oldest section is on a steep slope alongside a main road and near the railway line (Figure 5.56). The inscriptions on the stones (approximately 50) can no longer be read. According to Barry Deitch (local resident), there are no burial records of this early section. The second and later section for the Orthodox community is on a grassy slope, separated by a hedge from a small section for Reform Jews. Both of these sections are still in use.

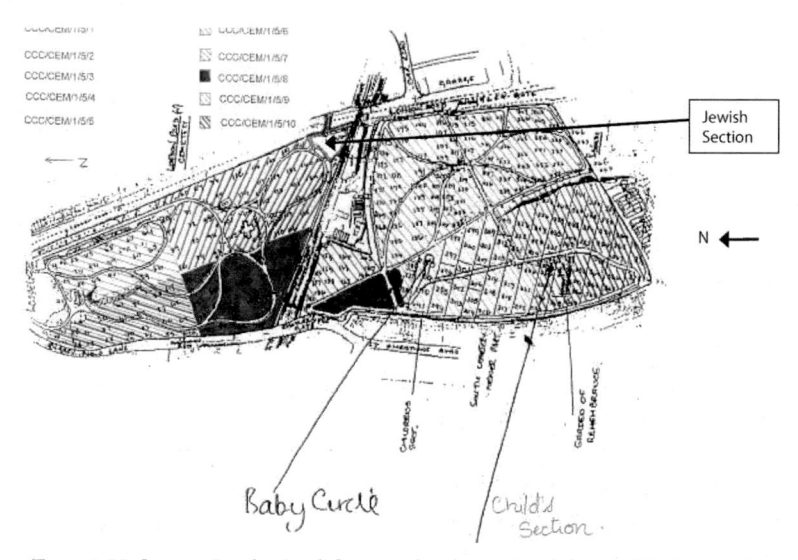

Figure 5.55 Coventry: London Road Cemetery plan showing Jewish Section (1864), (no scale) (History Centre Coventry).

Figure 5.56 Coventry: London Road Cemetery, Jewish Section (1864) oldest graves from 19th century (photograph K. Marks 2011)

5.2.11   Dover: Old Charlton Road   [69]

This cemetery is situated between the town's churchyard cemeteries of St Mary's and St James, and early maps (Dover Records Office) show that it was built on land of little value. The entrance is on Old Charlton Road, and a plaque on the outside wall indicates that it is under the care of the United Synagogue (personal observation 2009). On the north side, a number of plaques taken from the synagogue which was damaged and closed during World War II, are discussed in 4.2.11. Near the entrance are the foundations of the *ohel*, which was 'apparently burnt down' (Kadish 2006, 65).

Roth (1950, 110) quotes Margoliouth's History of 1851: 'that the first mention of Jews in Dover was in 1762 and that the traditional founding of the community was in 1770' The first burial (Catherine Isaacs) is recorded in 1868, so there is a gap of nearly 100 years from the founding of the community and the first burial. There are burials in the Canterbury cemetery of Jews who lived in Dover in this period, and this is noted on their tombstones (personal observation 2011). According to Roth, 'Some Jews living in Dover in the middle of the 18th century had their main residence in London and were members of The Great Synagogue and therefore could have been buried in London cemeteries' (Ibid, 54). There is one chest tomb in the middle of the cemetery of Blooma Cohen, wife of Rabbi Raphael Cohen (d.1865). The other graves are at the top of the hill in rows of 18-20, with a total of c.135 graves facing north-west towards the road. The earliest burials are in the back row at the top of the hill. At least 12 of the 42 in the back rows are unmarked, which show on the 1996 survey as unknown children. Only a quarter of the cemetery is used (person observation 2009) (Figure 5.57). A tablet on the wall of the cemetery reads:

Figure 5.57 Dover: Old Charlton Road Cemetery (1864), view uphill. The gravestone on its own to the front is that of Blooma Cohen, wife of the Rabbi (photograph K. Marks 2009).

Figure 5.58 Dover: cemetery view of top rows of oldest burials from 19th century (photograph K. Marks 2009).

'This tablet…..glory of the Rev.R.I. Cohen Sussex House. Who died in Liverpool December 1865. It was by his rementality, that the new synagogue in Dover was built and this burial ground was formed in respected…. Of his last wish that there might be a final resting place in Dover for members of the community, he loved so well and among whom he spent years of a long and useful life.' (Transcribed by Webster, M. 1996).

5.2.12   Exeter: Bull Meadow   [70]

The cemetery is just outside the Roman City walls of the city near the South Gate. The original lease is in the Devon Record Office. Exeter Synagogue Archives shows that it was acquired from the brothers and sisters of the house or hospital of lepers of Saint Mary Magdalene, without the Southgate of the City of Exeter.

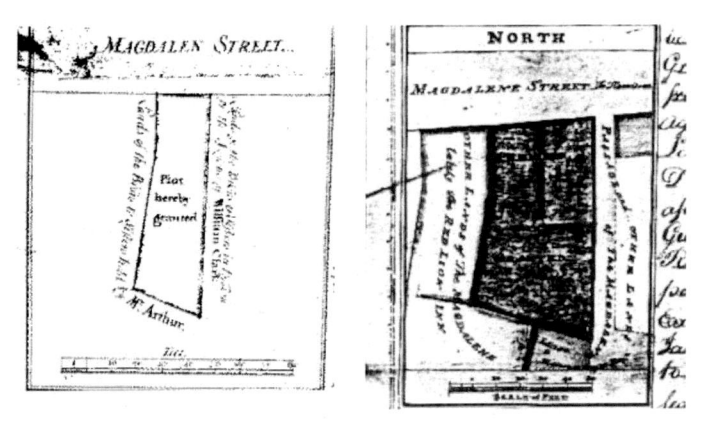

172   The Archaeology of Anglo-Jewry in England and Wales 1656–c.1880

Figure 5.59 Exeter: cemetery outline plan 1757 (left); cemetery outline plan 1827 (by permission Jewish Communities and Records).

Figure 5.60 Exeter: showing cemetery boundary walls (photograph J. Marks 2009).

The two gated entrances have been renewed; one is an entry into the *ohel*. The 18th century wall and arched entrance is Grade 11 listed. On one wall in the reconstructed *ohel* is a stone Decalogue from the closed Torquay synagogue (personal observation 2009). A second entrance leads to the burial ground. Plans in community records date from 1757, 1807, 1827 and 1851, and show the increase in size in all directions which, by 1851, had doubled the original area. This is the size of the present burial ground (Figure 5.60). The earliest tombstones are in the centre of the burial ground. All tombstones are of similar size and some have similar decorations, suggesting the same local stone masons.

5.2.13   Falmouth: Ponsharden   [71]

The Falmouth burial ground is outside Falmouth at Ponsharden, on the Penryn Road and is partially walled. There is no remaining evidence of the *ohel*. The cemetery is situated on a hill (Figure 5.61), next to a neglected and derelict Congregational cemetery. According to Kadish (2006, 96) 'All the tombstones in this cemetery are broken or no longer *in situ*. Both cemetery plots were presented to the two

Plan of Falmouth Jewish Cemetery

```
Row 1.      1 2 3 4  5*  6  7*  8   9* 10* 11*
    2.       1*  2*  3  4  5*6*7*8*  9* 10* 11* 12*
    3.  1  2  3  4 5 6*7*  8   9* 10  11    12   13*
    4.  1 2      3 4      5 6  7  8   9     10
    5.  1 2      3 4  5
    6.  1*  2                    ⟶ N
```

Figure 5.61 Falmouth: Penryn Cemetery (from 1789), view of Jews' Burial Ground (photograph J. Marks 2009).

Figure 5.62 Falmouth: Penryn Cemetery plot plan (by permission Pearce et al. 2000, 129).

communities by Sir Francis, Lord de Dunstanville c.1780'. In fact several of the tombstones are still intact and upright (personal observation, 2013)

According to Pearce et al., (2000, 103) 'there is no burial register however there are records from surveys, the first being c.1870'. The survey in question lists those buried. Tombstones are missing and some inscriptions can no longer be read. Tombstones made from Cornish slate are in better condition than those made from local fine-grained sandstone (personal observation 2009). The earliest tombstone that can be read is dated 1790. Over a period of 140 years until the last burial in 1913, around 50 burials took place (Figure 5.62). The earliest burials from c.1780 are in Rows 1 and 2 (personal observation 2009).

Pearce et al. (2000, 129) states that, 'The asterisks mark the location of graves either unmarked, without a headstone, or marked with a damaged displaced, or illegible headstone' Eric Dawkins, retired Town Clerk of Falmouth is the joint author of the introduction to the chapter on this cemetery in the *'Lost Jews of Cornwall* (Pearce et al. 2000) and has studied Falmouth and district burial grounds of all denominations.

One of the most important tomb stones of slate and Grade II listed, is that of Alexander Moses, known as 'Zander or Zender Moses', the founder of the community (Figure 5.63): The inscription in Hebrew, translated into English reads as follows:

Alexander Moses ("Zender Falmouth")
Died 24th Nisan 5551 (28 April 1791) Plot No.3.
May his soul be bound up in the bond of eternal life. Here dwells and takes delight a faithful man, a leader and guide; a shield to his generation with his body, his blood and his flesh. His house was open and his table laid for all. He stood righteously until the Lord, in whom he trusted, gathered him. Alexander the son of Moses. Died on the 24th and was buried on the 25th Nisan 5551 (April 1791)
(Pearce et al 2000, 108).

Figure 5.63 Falmouth: Penryn Road, tombstone of Alexander Mose (Zender Falmouth) (photograph J. Marks 2009).

There are a number of interesting features to this inscription. As is usual for early inscriptions, it is all in Hebrew. As is traditional, Zender was buried on the day following his death. Although his name was Alexander Moses, to new arrivals and itinerant peddlers, Zender Falmouth would have been the name that he was perhaps best known. Roth (1933, 71) writes '…. In those days any Jew settling down within a town and having certain respectability amongst Jews had the name of the town attached to his first name'. As noted in 5.21, in the Lauriston Road Cemetery in London, a number of deceased adopted their home town name as their surname. Roth (1950, 62) quotes from the *Records of My Family*, by Israel Solomon (New York, 1887, 26): there is an account of how he (Zender) set up Jewish peddlers in trade, on condition that they would return for the Sabbath (Friday evenings) to attend prayers. This helped to ensure that there was a *minyan* (10 male adults), for a full service.

Alexander's wife, Phoebe, buried in Row 2.3, is described on her tombstone as a '*women of worth*', part of a quotation from Proverbs (31:10), which continues '*she is worth far more than rubies*'. One of the other graves is of Esther Elias, who died 1780, and may have been the first person to be buried in the Falmouth cemetery (Pearce 2000, 111).

5.2.14 Gloucester: Coney Hill [72]

In the north-west corner of Gloucester's Municipal Cemetery is a small hedged section where remains from the c.1780 city centre Jewish burial ground have been re-interred (Figure 5.64). According to Margoliouth's History (1851), the first mention of Jews in the City is c.1765, and the traditional date of the founding of the community was 1784. From c.1850, there was no longer a community. In the *1845 Chief Rabbi's Statistical Account,* Gloucester was the only community of 40 at that time not to complete the return (Figure 6.1).

According to Torode (1999, 22) 'the 18th century cemetery was in Organ's Passage or Gardener's Lane off Barton Street and served persons from Ross, Hereford, Stroud as well as Gloucester' The land was bought in 1780 from the rector of St Michael's Parish and measured about 12 x 9 yards (Ibid, 22). According to Fowler, when describing a visit to the burial ground in 1889, the plot was almost wholly occupied by headstones bearing Hebrew inscriptions. The remains of a Watch

House could be seen, where the dead were washed before burial and where prayers before internment were recited. The last dated stone, of 35 in existence, is dated 1887 (Ibid, 22). At that time, only 16 could be read and were recorded by Fowler. The burial ground in the town centre was closed in 1938.

A plaque at the entrance of the Jewish section reads as follows (Figure 5.65):

> *'Here lie the remains of a number of persons of the Jewish faith formerly interred in the old Jewish cemetery adjoining St. Michael's School, and removed here in April 1938, when that cemetery was given by the Jews of this county as a playground for the children of Gloucester'.*

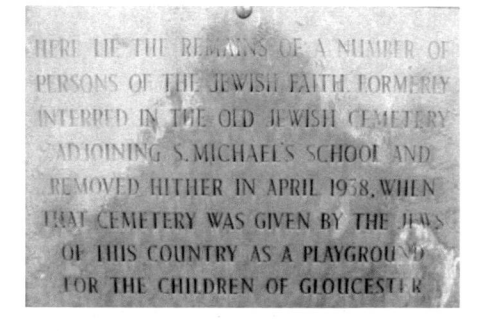

Figure 5.65 Gloucester: plaque (c.1metre × 50cms) recording the 1938 re-internment of 18th century remains (photograph J. Marks 2009)

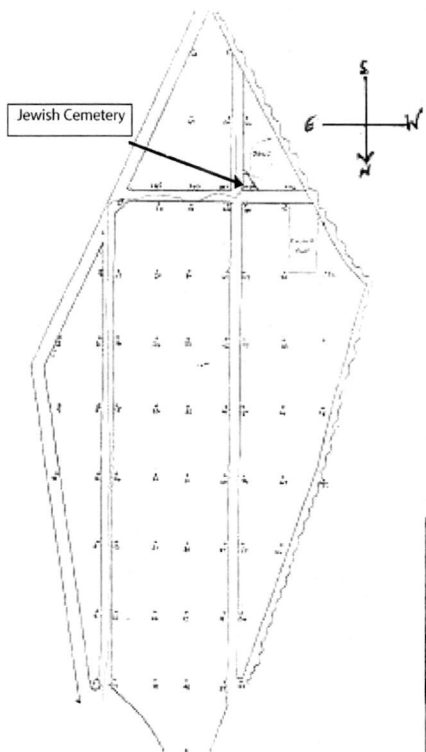

Figure 5.64 Gloucester: Rough plan of Municipal Cemetery, showing position of re-interred Jewish remains from 18th century burial ground (Gloucester Cemetery Burial Office 2009).

Figure 5.66 Gloucester: Jewish Cemetery gravesstones marking re-interred remains (photograph J. Marks 2009).

5.2.15.1   Hull   [73]

There are three Jewish cemeteries in Hull from the period under discussion. The earliest two being Villa Place, with documented evidence of around 50 burials, and Hessle Road with 75-100, the third, Delhi Street was in use from 1858 contains c.1300 graves and is still in use.

Hull: Villa Place

Figure 5.67 Hull: Villa Place Cemetery, 1750? Entrance to burial ground. (photograph K.Marks 2010).

This extant cemetery was bombed during World War II. According to Dr Lewis (local archivist) (personal contact 2010), in 1946, Hull City Council started to re-develop the area, with bulldozers removing headstones. This activity was stopped, as was the proposal to re-inter the remains in one of the other Jewish cemeteries in the city. The entrance gate to the only Jewish burial ground in England under the authority of the National Health Service (Figure 5.67) and displays the dates 1750-1812. According to Dr Lewis, the synagogue records show the date when first used should be 1780 not 1750, although 1780 still makes it one of the oldest provincial Jewish cemeteries in England.

According to the synagogue records, the original graveyard held c.50 burials, although the names of only four or five persons buried are known from the archives. The area of the burial ground is marked by a low fence shaped to the outline of the cemetery (Figure 5.68).

Figure 5.68 Hull: Villa Place grass covered burial ground (1750?) (photograph K. Marks 2010).

5.2.15.2 Hull: Hessle Road

Situated c.250 metres from Villa Place Cemetery, on the south side of Patrick's Ground Lane, according to Kadish (2006, 176) the lease can be traced to 1812 although the register of burials is lost. According to Lewis (personal contact 2010), the names and dates of death are known of 24 Jews buried in Hessle Road, with a further 17 unknown, who died in Hull between 1812 and 1858. In total 34, graves can be identified, although the cemetery holds 75-100 graves of which most of the stones are no longer in place (Figure 5.69). The cemetery was also used by Jews who lived outside Hull from towns with no Jewish cemetery, such as Scarborough (personal contact Dr. Lewis 2010). This cemetery was one of many closed for hygienic reasons by the Privy Council 1858 Burial Act.

Figure 5.69 Hull: Hessle Road New Jewish Cemetery (1812) broken headstones placed around the perimeter (photograph K. Marks 2010).

Figure 5.70 Hull: Hessle Road Cemetery, adjacent public house, with Stars of David on windows (photograph K. Marks 2010).

The adjacent public house, the Alexander Hotel has Stars of David on the ground and first-floor windows (Figure 5.70). According to the publican, oral tradition holds that the rooms were used for prayers before and after a burial. There is also a possibility that Sabbath services were held here for immigrant Jews passing through Hull on their way to Liverpool and then on to America, Canada, South Africa or other cities in England. Orthodox Jews would not travel on the Sabbath. They would have been given dispensation for this while they were on the ships. There is no documented evidence for either of these suggestions.

5.2.15.3 Hull: Delhi Street

This cemetery was established in 1858 and contains c.1300 graves (personal observation 2010). It is still occasionally used. The ground is divided into two sections, the 'Old' section for the Hull Hebrew Congregation and the 'New' for the Hull Western

Figure 5.71 Hull: Delhi Street Cemetery (1858) foundation stones of former ohel *(photograph K. Marks 2010).*

Figure 5.72 Hull: Delhi Road Cemetery, section of grassed area destroyed by bombing 1941 and some of the tombstones destroyed by vandals in 2002 (photograph K. Marks 2010).

Synagogue, from 1903. There were two prayer halls for the two congregations; neither exists but the foundation stones for the later *ohel* (1908) are evident (Figure 5.71). In 1941, a German bomb destroyed part of the oldest section fronting Hedon Road (Figure 5.72). Part of the cemetery was desecrated by vandals in 2002 (Figure 5.72). In Delhi Road Cemetery are buried one Jewish mayor and three lord mayors, indicating the tolerance of Hull's citizens and the involvement in Hull's commercial and communal life of the Jewish community (personal observation 2010).

5.2.16.1　　　　　　　　Ipswich: Salthouse Lane　　　　　　　　[74]

The first Ipswich Jewish Cemetery (Georgian) is in the former Salthouse Lane and is unmarked on Ordnance Survey Maps. According to Kadish (2006, 117)

Figure 5.73 Ipswich: Salthouse Lane Jews Burial Ground (1796), high red brick wall with gated entrance (photograph J. Marks 2010).

Figure 5.74 Ipswich: Salthouse Lane Jews Burial ground interior, showing some of the tombstones (photograph K. Marks 2010).

'The cemetery dates from 1796' Gollancz (1894/5, 2) states 'that it is situated in St Clements's Parish, in an out-of-the way corner of the town, apparently in a very poor and wretched part'. Enclosed by a high red brick-wall, partly rebuilt (Grade II). The entrance is through a narrow iron gate in the south wall (Figure 5.73). On the east wall is a St Clements's Parish boundary stone. Nearby Fore Street was where a small number of Jews lived in the early 19th century near to the port.

There are now seven rows of tombstones, while Gollancz (1894/5, 3) notes eight rows with 24 legible inscriptions (mainly in Hebrew). The cemetery contains about 35 headstones, plus fragments. Some of the stones give details of where the deceased lived outside Ipswich, such as Harwich and Bury St Edmunds.

Lipman (1954, 187) writes 'In 1850 this would have been the only Jewish cemetery in the area as Ipswich was a small community with around 50 congregants'.

5.2.16.2 Ipswich: Cemetery Lane

Figure 5.75 Ipswich: Old Cemetery, Cemetery Lane Jewish Section (1885) showing graves in grassy hollow (photograph K. Marks 2010).

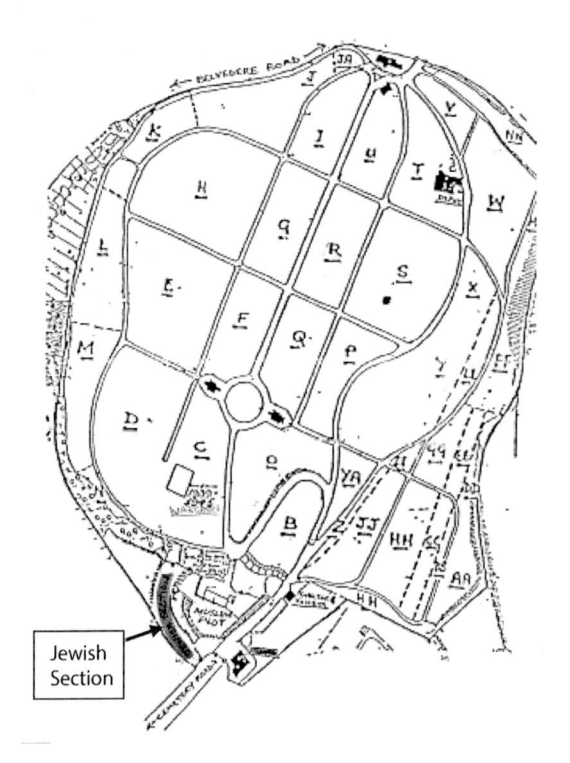

Figure 5.76 Ipswich: Old Cemetery, Cemetery Lane (1885), outline plan of burial ground showing Jewish section in public cemetery, not drawn to scale (Old Cemetery Administration Office).

Although there was no Jewish community in Ipswich after 1885, a few individuals remained. The Synagogue in Rope Lane (Figure 4.43) was demolished in 1877 (personal contact Elizabeth Sugarman 2010), although inscriptions attest to burials between 1877 and 1985 (Figure 5.75). Graves where inscriptions can still be read are of Rabbi Solomon Schiller-Szinessy (1821-1890) born in Budapest and his wife Sarah (d. 21 April 1901 aged 70). He was firstly a rabbi in Hull and then became rabbi to the Reform movement in Manchester (discussed in 4.2.20). He later became Reader in Rabbinics at Cambridge University. Four tombstones are flat (the inscriptions can no longer be read), suggesting that the deceased may have been Sephardim (Figure 5.75). According to Charles Tucker, the municipal authorities have a full list of burials (personal contact 2012).

5.2.17   King's Lynn: Mill Fleet   [75]

This small burial ground is documented in the Town records from 1830, but according to Kadish (2006, 109) burials go back to 1811, with a community dating from 1747 (Roth 1950, 111). The cemetery was established on the south bank of the old river Mill Fleet. King's Lynn declined as a trading port after the river had silted up by the middle of the 19th century. A plaque on the south wall of the cemetery (Figure 5.77), states that:

'*Within these walls is the cemetery of Dutch Jews who lived in Lynn c1750-1846*'.

Jews who died before the cemetery was in use were probably buried in nearby towns where there was a Jewish cemetery, such as Norwich or in a local non- Jewish burial grounds. The cemetery measures c.18m x 10m and is enclosed by a three-metre high wall, which is heavily restored (Figure 5.78) (personal observation 2010). Entrance is through a locked wooden gate on the north side of the burial ground. Nine tomb stones are *in situ*, while three further stones and a number of illegible fragments are placed against the rear south wall. A plaque in the south wall can no longer be read.

Figure 5.77 King's Lynn: Millfleet Jew's Burial Ground commemorative plaque (c.1811). (photograph K. Marks 2010).

Figure 5.78 King's Lynn: Millfleet Jew's Burial Ground (photograph J. Marks 2010).

5.2.18.1 Leeds: Hill Top [76]

This burial ground was purchased by the New Briggate Jewish congregation in 1873 and was shared by at least five Leeds synagogues. The ground is subsiding into a possible mineshaft, and is now closed to the public (personal contact 2010) tomb stones in some cases are falling over. There are no records prior to 1917 (Kadish 2006, 170).

Figure 5.79 Leeds: Hill Top Cemetery (1860s), when still in use (photograph M. Sender).

Figure 5.80 Leeds: Hill Top Cemetery, view of no longer in use burial ground (photograph M. Sender).

5.2.18.2 Leeds: Gildersome Gelderd Road

This is the larger of Leeds' two Jewish Orthodox cemeteries, first used by the Leeds Great Synagogue, Belgrave Street (c.1850) which is no longer in existence. Originally there were three entrances, but two have been closed. It is one of the largest Jewish cemeteries in England, with over 3, 000 burials, and there is enough unused space to last for at least another 100 years (personal communication M. Sender, 2010). There were two *ohelalim*, the oldest having been demolished. The remaining building dates from the 1860s.

Unusual is that the tombstones of the two communities, the United Hebrew Congregation and the Beth HaMedrash Congregation, are in two different sections of the cemetery, with the tombstones facing in different directions. There is a separate section for the important members of the community.

5.2.19.1 Liverpool: Deane Road [77]

Deane Road Cemetery is Liverpool's oldest surviving Jewish Burial ground, the fourth of Liverpool's Jewry from c.1750, and the property and responsibility of Liverpool's Old Hebrew Congregation (Princes Road Synagogue). Extract from

COMMUNITIES IN DEATH (CEMETERIES)   183

Figure 5.81 Liverpool: 1851 Ordnance Survey map of Deane Street (later Deane Road Old Jew's Burial Ground). 25" to a mile

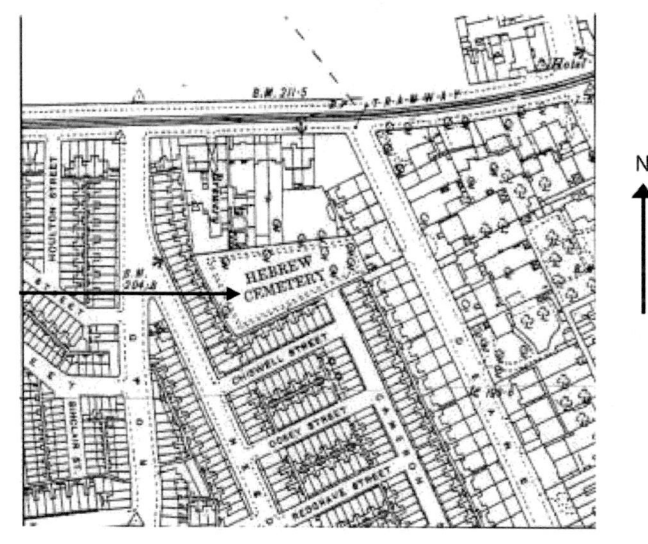

Figure 5.82 Liverpool: 1893 Ordnance Survey map of Deane Road Old Jew's urial Ground.

Figure 5.83 Liverpool: entrance and gateway to Deane Road Old Jews' Burial Ground (1837) (photograph K. Marks 2009).

the Ordnance Survey Map of 1851 (Figure 5.81) shows that Deane Street (later Deane Road) prior to development in the 1880s and 1890s was in the rural area of Liverpool, known as Kensington. At that time, the cemetery was outside the city boundary in open fields. The 1893 Ordnance Survey Map shows the cemetery as it is today in the middle of a built up area (Figure 5.82).

According to Marks (2006, 1), '....until recently the cemetery suffered from neglect and had lain derelict for a century'. Parts have now been restored to bring order to the rows of graves. Entrance is from a railed semi-circular driveway off Deane Road. The entrance, facing east, is through an ornate Greek style archway in a screen made of brick and rendered in stucco and is Grade II listed (Figure 5.83) Above the entrance on the architrave, in both Hebrew and English, is the inscription, *'Here the weary are laid to rest'* (personal observation 2009). The boundary walls are of red brick (Figure 5.86).

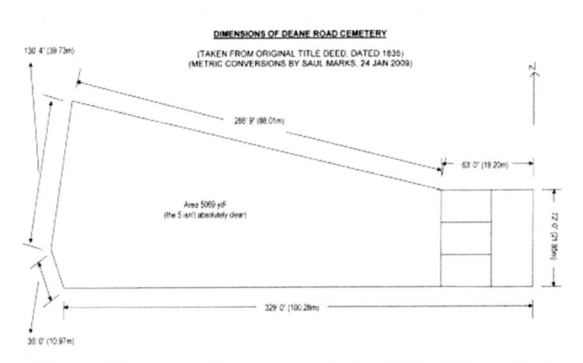

Figure 5.84 Liverpool: Outline plan (scale 1:200) of Deane Road Cemetery.

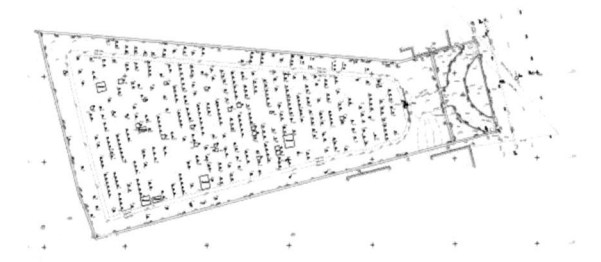

Figure 5.85 Liverpool: topographical plan (1:200) of Deane Road Cemetery (Formby Surveys, by permission Saul Marks).

Figure 5.86 Liverpool: view of Old Jew's Burial Ground Deane Road Showing red brick boundary wall (photograph K. Marks 2009).

On the left-and right-hand side, near the entrance, are the remains of the *ohel* and the caretaker's cottage (personal observation 2009) which according to Marks (personal contact 2009) were demolished in 1952. There are c.1, 700 graves, of which c.900 are children, mostly in unmarked graves (personal observation, 2009), indicating that they either died before they were named or were children from poor families. The early gravestones are of York stone and slate; the later and more elaborate stones from the late 19th century include marble and granite. Some can no longer be read, due to weathering, and some of the inscriptions in lead lettering have fallen out (personal observation 2009). The first burial in

1837 was of 'a distinguished member of the congregation named Henry Hyams, who had been Warden and Treasurer'; this is shown on his tombstone. The earliest legible tombstone on the back wall is of Rebecca Lyon (d.1838). One of the most eminent occupant of the cemetery is David Lewis (d.1885), founder of Lewis's Departmental Stores, the first departmental store chain in Britain. Also buried in the cemetery is Moses Samuel (d.1860), founder of H. Samuel jewellers and Charles Mozley, Liverpool's first Jewish mayor (d.1881). A clear statement is being made by the monumental grave stones and prominent positions of rich and important members of the early Liverpool community.

In contrast to 18th-century Liverpool, when many of the immigrant Jewish community were poor and lived in the dock area and other poor districts, the middle-to-late 19th century tombstones and their inscriptions, combined with burials records, indicate that many male members of Liverpool's Old Hebrew Congregation '.... had been born in England and were successful businessmen, including silversmiths, watchmakers, shipping brokers or bankers' (Marks 2006, 1).

5.2.19.2 Liverpool: Broad Green

Whilst this cemetery is outside the period under discussion, it contains the re-interred remains from two earlier burial grounds, which no longer exist. The first are from the burial ground at 133 Upper Frederick Street (1789-1902), which were re-interred in 1902 and the second is 127 burials from Oakes Street Jewish cemetery (1802-1837) which were re-interred in 1923. A plaque marks the re-interment area. The original badly weathered grave stones removed to this site are laid flat and, in most cases, cannot be read (Figure 5.87). The *ohel* at the entrance is still used. Built at the beginning of the 20th century, it has the appearance of a Non-Conformist chapel (personal observation 2009).

Figure 5.87 Liverpool: Broad Green Jewish Cemetery (1904), area of re-interred remains from Frederick Street and Oakes Street (photograph K. Marks 2009).

5.2.19.3 Liverpool: Green Lane

This cemetery is derelict, the gates are boarded up and the grounds cannot be visited (personal observation 2009). It was used until 1921 by the breakaway New Hebrew Congregation. In the front wall facing Green Lane is a small gap, through which it is just possible to see the overgrown burial ground. Kadish (2006, 141) notes that 'the earliest tombstone, (noted from a photograph in 1930) was that of Lyon Marks (d.1842)'.

Figure 5.88 Liverpool: Green Lane Jewish Cemetery (1839) (photograph K. Marks 2009).

5.2.20.1 Manchester: Brindle Heath [78]

Figure 5.89 Manchester: Brindle Heath Jews' Burial Ground (1794), memorial stone (photograph K.Marks 2010).

Figure 5.90 Manchester: Brindle Heath Jews' Burial Ground (1794-1840) (photograph K. Marks 2010).

Brindle Heath Cemetery, Pendelton is the oldest Jewish burial ground in Manchester. The community purchased a small plot of land in Pendelton in 1794 for the sum of £43 8s 9d, with an annual peppercorn rent from a Methodist silk dyer, Samuel Brierly (Williams 1976, 120). This burial ground was in use until 1840, when a second plot was purchased in Prestwich, Pendelton was closed. 15 out of 29 of those known to have been buried in the cemetery are listed on a memorial stone in front of five surviving tombstone fragments, which are no longer in *situ* (personal observation 2010) (Figure 5.90). One legible stone commemorates Rabbi Isaac, who died in 1795. This is the earliest dated

Manchester tombstone that can still be read (Figure 5.90). The area is surrounded by an iron railing in front of which is a *Magen David* (Star of David) outlined in stone and laid into the tarmac.

Figure 5.91 Manchester: Brindle Heath Jews' Burial Ground, Star of David, possibly indicating area of burial ground (photograph K. Marks 2010).

5.2.20.2 Manchester: Prestwich Village

Following the closure of Brindle Heath, Prestwich Village cemetery was established in 1841 as the main Jewish cemetery in Manchester. It was shared by the three later synagogues, The Manchester Great (1874), the Manchester New (1889) and the Spanish and Portuguese (1874). Burial records (not examined) show 500 graves. By 1884, the burial ground was full and it was closed except for reserved places. It is not possible to enter the burial ground due to its poor state (Figure 5.92). The Gothic-style *ohel* was demolished in 1951 to make space for a *'Peace Garden'* (Kadish 2006, 152). From the gate, it is possible to view part of the cemetery (personal observation 2010).

Figure 5.92 Manchester: Prestwich Village Jews' disused burial ground (1841-1914) (photograph K. Marks 2010).

5.2.20.3 Manchester: Whitefield Reform Cemetery

The Manchester Reform Synagogue Cemetery is the oldest Reform Movement cemetery outside London. Surrounded by a high red-brick wall, on the right hand-side of the entrance is the Victorian *ohel* with a pitched slate roof (Figure 5.93). At each end under the gable, there is a large round stained glass window (Figure 5.94). The oldest tombstones (mid-19th century) are located at the back of the cemetery (personal observation, 2010) (Figure 5.95). Amongst the headstones is an obelisk monument topped with an urn, dedicated to: *'The memory of HENRIETTE relict of the late Jacob Magnus of Hamburg'*. Many of the founding members of the Reform community originated from Germany. There is a list of some of the burials in the Manchester Reform office (personal contact 2010).

Figure 5.93 Manchester: Whitefield Reform Cemetery (1858-still in use), Victorian ohel (photograph K. Marks 2010).

Figure 5.94 Manchester: Whitefield Reform Cemetery original stained eight petal flower design glass window in ohel (photograph K. Marks 2010).

Figure 5.95 Manchester: Whitefield Reform Cemetery oldest grave stones (1858) at rear of cemetery (photograph K. Marks 2010).

5.2.20.4 Manchester: Philips Park

The entrance to the burial ground is in the northern part of this municipal cemetery. To one side of the entrance gates an inscription reads: *'Catholic Entrance'*; the other states:*'Dissenters Entrance'*. The Jewish burial ground is in the Dissenters section (Figure 5.96).

Figure 5.96 Manchester: entrance to municipal cemetery Dissenters section Philips Park (1865-1953) (photograph K. Marks 2010).

Figure 5.97 Manchester: Philips Park Cemetery, view from outside of the wall of the Jewish section 1865? showing some graves where there are no longer have tombstones (photograph K. Marks 2010).

The Manchester Great Synagogue records show an earlier burial ground in Miles Platting, however the records commenced in 1865. The South Manchester Synagogue (not discussed) purchased part of the Dissenters section of the first municipal cemetery in Manchester (1866-7) (Kadish 2006, 156). Some tombstones were removed for safe keeping to the Crumpsall Cemetery, established in 1884 (not discusse) (Manchester Jewish Museum records).

5.2.21   Merthyr Tydfil: Brecon Road   [79]

This cemetery was established in c.1865. No Jewish community remains in Merthyr Tydfil, the last remaining Jew died in 1999. A survey in 1978 revealed c.400 burials (Jacobs and Saffer 1978). The cemetery is on the side of a hill, with the entrance through a high stone wall (Figure 5.98). The gate leads to the *ohel* built in 1898, donated by a member of the community; a dated plaque commemorates its opening. The oldest tombstones are in

Figure 5.98 Merthyr Tydfil: Brecon Road c.1865, entrance to cemetery and ohel *(prayer hall) (photograph J. Marks 2010).*

Figure 5.99 Merthyr Tydfil: Inside of ohel *(prayer hall) (photograph J. Marks 2010)*

Figure 5.100 Merthyr Tydfil: section of Jewish cemetery and old municipal cemetery in the background (photograph J. Marks 2010).

the middle part, with a number of children's graves from the 1870s (personal observation 2010). This cemetery was also used by smaller communities in the Valleys who did not have a Jewish cemetery, evidenced by tomb stone inscriptions noting towns from which the deceased derived, including Aberdare, Aberaman, Brynmaur, Dowlais and Tredegar.

Other towns noted are Birmingham, Falmouth and Northampton (personal observation 2010). Also buried are persons who had left Merthyr Tydfil who wanted to be buried with their families (personal observation 2010). These show where they lived before they died.

5.2.22.1 Newcastle [80]

Newcastle: Thornton Street

The first burial ground of Newcastle Jewry is situated outside the City walls near to the former Temple Street Synagogue in Thornton Street, (discussed in 4.65). At some time, 'the two sites were apparently linked by a private passageway' (Kadish 2006, 188). The entrance is fronted by the Chinese Cultural Centre, now closed. In the remaining area are five weathered sandstone tombstones which have survived, although not all *in situ*. An area originally 250 square yards is now 50 five square yards (Ibid, 188). According to the synagogue records, it originally held 210 persons. It was not possible to get access.

5.2.22.2 Newcastle: St John's Jewish Section

This Victorian Jewish cemetery is separated from the Christian cemetery by a low wall. The Jewish section is one acre with over 1, 000 graves. Section D, the oldest,

Figure 5.101 Newcastle: St John's Cemetery Jewish Section, Elswick Road (1857) showing mid- 19th gravestone in sandstone (photograph K. Marks 2010)

Figure 5.102 Newcastle: St John's Cemetery, Elswick Road Jewish Section, showing some of the c.100 graves desecrated in 2005 (photograph K. Marks 2010).

is near to the gate on St John's Road (Figure 5.101). Memorial stones are mostly of local Doddington sandstone, but can no longer be read, (personal observation, 2010). There is no *ohel*. Burial records are held at the City Council Offices and at the Discovery Museum in Newcastle. A field survey carried out in 2000 shows the location and graves; unmarked plots in this section appear to be from around middle 19th century. Figure 5.103 shows Section D.

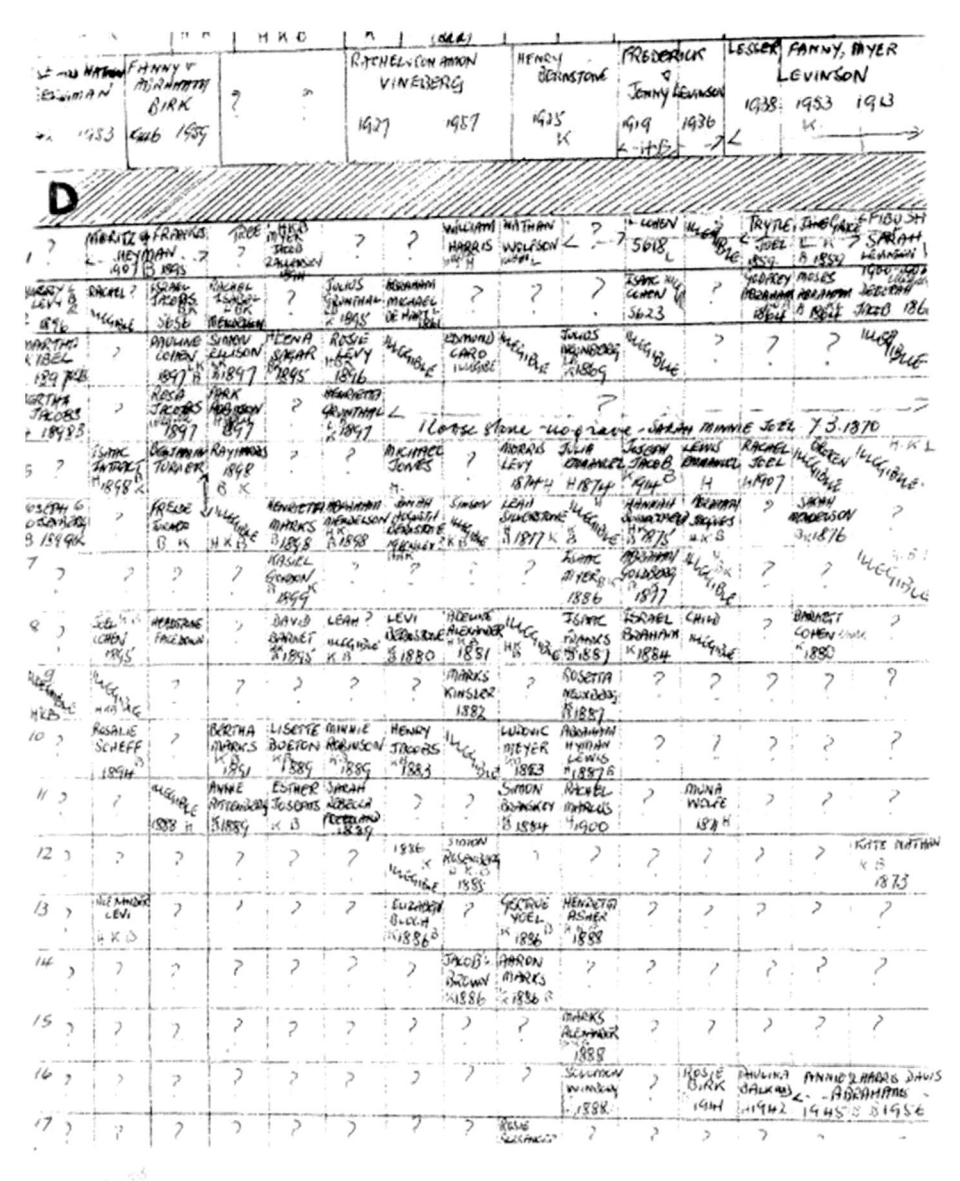

Figure 5.103 Newcastle: St John's Cemetery, Elswick Road Jewish Section, topographical plan (not to scale) of section D with burials dating from 1857 (plan from J. Gellert, community architect and cemetery archivist). The plots marked with a ? are of unknown persons, over half of those buried.(Plans are held in City Council Offices).

5.2.23.1　　　　　　　　Norwich: Mariners Lane　　　　　　　　[81]

Nothing remains of Norwich's first Jewish cemetery in Mariners Lane, and no detailed plans exist. The first plan of the area of the cemetery (1860s) shows 'formerly a Jews Burial Ground now a garden'. The 1885 Ordnance Survey Map shows the area that

COMMUNITIES IN DEATH (CEMETERIES)   193

became the cemetery as a garden with trees (Figure 5.104); it is now a concreted car park covering the same area (personal observation 2010).

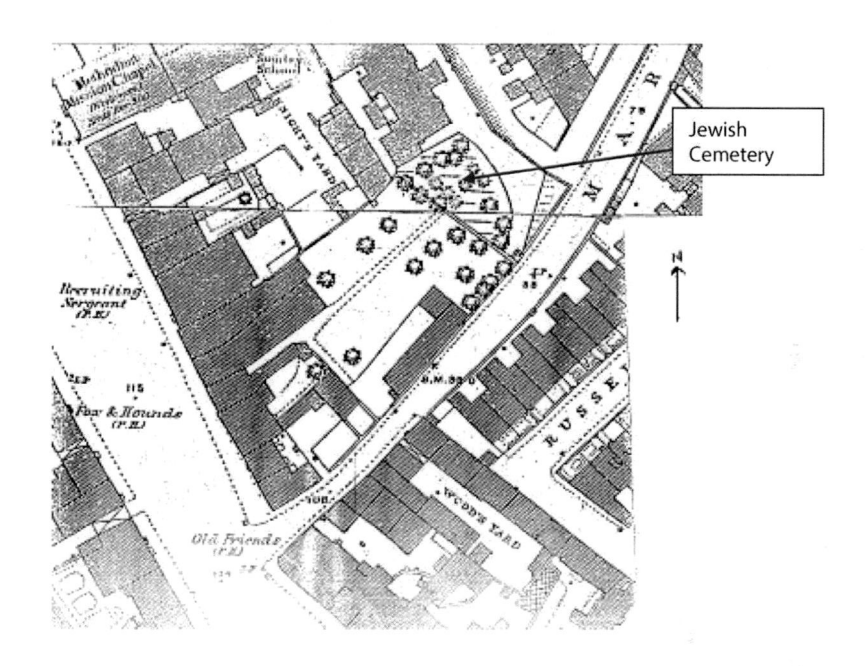

Figure 5.104 Norwich: Mariners Lane Cemetery Ordnance Survey Map 1885, showing the cemetery as a garden with trees (scale 1:500).

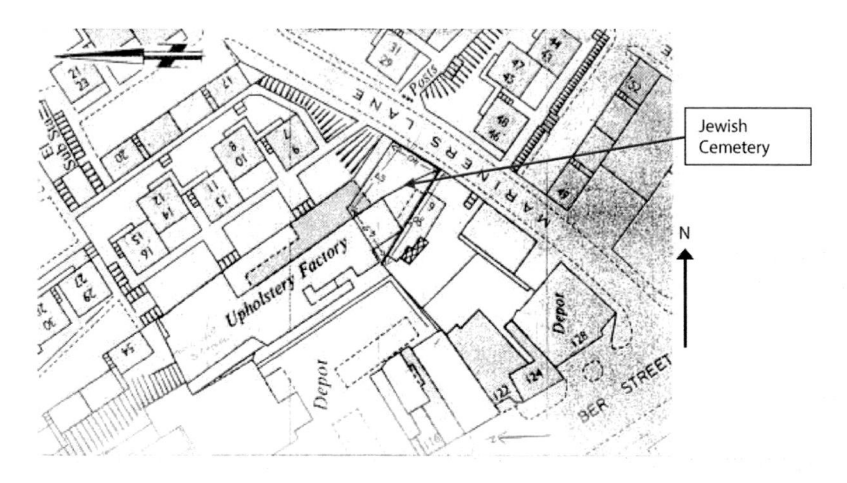

Figure 5.105 Norwich: Mariners Lane Cemetery, Ordnance Survey map 1860s (5" to a mile) outline map of the Former Jewish Burial Ground

5.2.23.2 Norwich: St Crispin's Road

No records survive, although a document in the possession of Barry Leveton, historian of Norwich's Jewish Community, shows that in 1869 there were 39 graves. By 1965 only c.20 graves could be identified, with eight spaces indicating former burials, but with no marker stones (personal contact Barry Leveton 2010). The site is approximately 10m x 15m, enclosed by high walls. A plaque on the wall facing St Crispin's Road (Figure 5.106) reads *'the cemetery is the property of the Hebrew Congregation'* and is dated 5640 (1840). Today the site is neglected, with only two upright stones.

Figure 5.106 Norwich: Quakers Lane Jews Burial Ground (1813) 1840 plaque on outside wall (photograph J. Marks 2010).

Figure 5.107 Norwich: Quakers Lane Jews' Burial Ground, showing overgrown graves and one of the two stones still evident (photograph J. Marks 2010).

5.2.23.3 Norwich: Bowthorpe Road (Jewish Section)

The entrance to the hedged-off Jewish section of Norwich Corporation's City Cemetery is through a grilled gate on the Bowthorpe Road. The 1856 *ohel* is on the right, as one enters, and is built of red and yellow brick with a tiled roof (Figure 5.108), it is still used for services prior to burial. The earliest graves are in the north-east section and face west. All records of early burials were destroyed when Norwich Synagogue was bombed in 1942. Later burial records are with the local council. Unusually, a row of small memorial plaques indicate that the deceased had been cremated. The practice of cremation is recognised by Reform and Liberal Jews but unusual amongst Orthodox communities. The only other example examined in this study, being in the cemetery in Exeter (5.60), where a compromise was reached between the Orthodox and local Non-Orthodox members, that they could be buried in their local Jewish cemetery.

COMMUNITIES IN DEATH (CEMETERIES) 195

Figure 5.108 Norwich: City Cemetery, Bowthorpe Road (1856), Jewish Section showing ohel *(prayer hall), grave stones and memorial plaques (photograph J. Marks 2010).*

Figure 5.110 Norwich: City Cemetery Bowthorpe Road, Jewish Section, showing chained off area for unnamed babies and infants photograph J. Marks 2010).

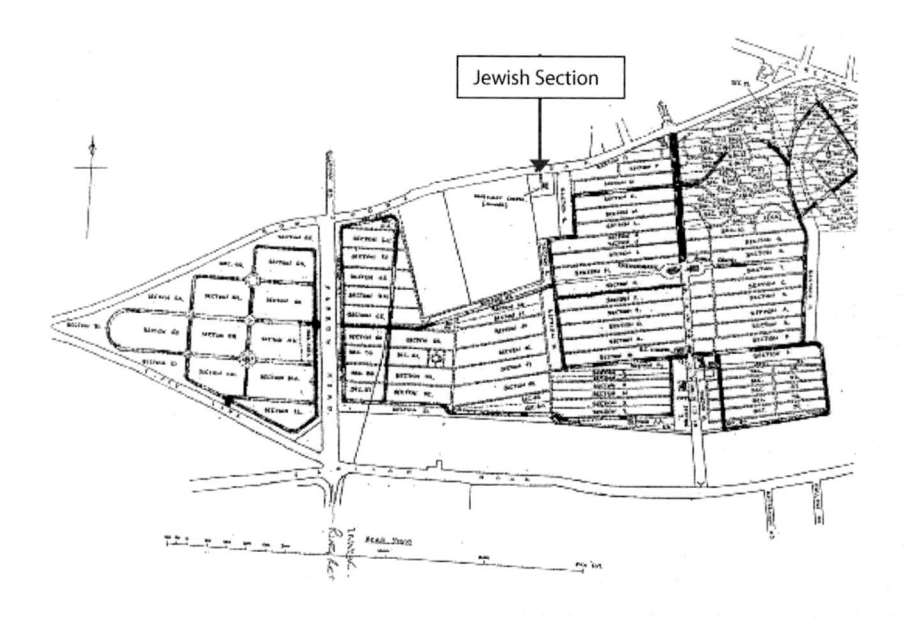

Figure 5.109 Norwich: City Cemetery, Bowthorpe Road, plan of the entire cemetery and Jewish section with no plot details (Norwich City Records Office).

5.2.24.1   Nottingham: North Sherwood Street   [82]

Figure 5.111 Nottingham: entrance to North Sherwood Street Cemetery (1823) (photograph K. Marks 2010).

Figure 5.112 Nottingham: North Sherwood Street Jewish Cemetery established 1823 (photograph K. Marks 2010).

The only remains of Nottingham's 19th century community are two cemeteries, both no longer used. There are no burial records or any outline plan of the North Sherwood Street Cemetery, which is the earlier of the two (personal contact 2010). This small cemetery holds c.50 graves (Figure 5.111) (personal observation 2010). Above the front entrance on a high stone wall is an engraved plaque (not original) in Hebrew and English which states that, *'the cemetery was established in 1823 and the land was purchased from the Nottingham Corporation'* (1946) (Figure.5.111).

There is no trace of an *ohel,* if one ever existed. Only 15 slate and sandstone tomb stones remain upright, with little or no decoration; the remainder, mostly all in Hebrew, lie broken on the ground (Figure 5.112). There are grave mounds with no tombstones (personal observation 2010). Of the broken stones that can still be read, one belongs to the great-great-grandfather of David Snapper, who escorted the author to the cemetery. He was the *Rev. David Goldberg* (Minister1850-1858), who died falling off a ladder while fixing a *mezuzah* (parchment inscribed with religious texts and attached in a case to the doorpost of a Jewish house as a sign of faith) (Figure 5.113).

According to Snapper (personal contact 2010), Reverend Goldberg's wife is buried in Australia, as two of his daughters emigrated there in the late 19th century. At the rear of the cemetery is an unusual small sandstone obelisk. At some time, these slate plaques were attached to the obelisk, as the former position can be identified by inset spaces, but now the plaques are lying alongside it. These are in German and identify the deceased as *Bertha Nathan,* born Westphalia, 1821, it states *'that her date of death was uncertain'.* Her remains were cremated, which is not customary in the Orthodox community (Figure 5.114).

Figure 5.113 Nottingham: North Sherwood Street Cemetery: broken grave stone of Reverend Goldberg. (photograph K. Marks 2010).

Figure 5.114 Nottingham: North Sherwood Street Cemetery; sandstone obelisk with inscriptions on slate tablets (photograph K. Marks 2010).

4.2.24.2 Nottingham: Hardy Street

The entrance to this second cemetery is through an iron gate off Hardy Street. The cemetery is enclosed by high stone walls, with an internal wall dividing the site into two. There are no plans, but there is a burial list in the synagogue (not examined). This cemetery was the successor to North Sherwood Street (1823), with around 250 adult graves and an unknown number of children's graves. (Figure 5.115).

Figure 5.115 Nottingham: Hardy Street Cemetery (1869) (photograph K. Marks 2010).

Alongside the front wall are the remains of a *bet taharah* (a room used for washing the deceased prior to burial), which can be identified by white tile fragments attached to the outside wall (Figure 5.116) and fragments of a white sink in a corner of the cemetery (personal observation 2010). Along the front wall are a number of children's graves, mostly with no marker stones (Figure 5.117). In sharp contrast to the earlier North Sherwood Street Cemetery, many gravestones are granite and marble; there are also several obelisks. The cemetery gives a clear indication of the increasing wealth and status of some members of the community. Engravings on tombstones reveal burials of Jews from Derby, Leicester and Lincoln, who at this time did not have a Jewish cemetery. A number of graves can be identified by mounds of earth without header stones. One isolated gravestone near to the west wall marks the plot where, according to Snapper there is an unnamed person who committed suicide. Up to c.1873 Orthodox communities did not bury in the main body of the cemetery. persons who took their own life.

Figure 5.116 Nottingham: Hardy Street Cemetery: remains of bet tahara *(room used for washing the dead prior to burial) (photograph K. Marks 2010).*

Figure 5.117 Nottingham: Hardy Street Cemetery: unmarked children's graves (photograph K. Marks 2010).

5.2.25 Oxford (no cemeteries in period under discussion)

There were individual Jews in the city from 1733 (Roth 1950, 111), although no cemetery existed in Oxford until 1894. The community was established in 1842. For over 50 years, when a member of the Oxford community died, their body was taken to a Jewish cemetery in London or to other cities in the provinces with a Jewish burial ground. In Lauriston Road Cemetery, London (5.1.8), graves of Abraham Oxford and his wife, who both died in 1795 (cemetery records of the Hambros Synagogue), can be found. In 1844, at 9 St Ebbe's Street, a house where Aaron Jacobs and his wife lived was destroyed by fire. The bodies were taken by train for burial in Brady Street Cemetery in London (Ibid, 15). According to Marcus Roberts, local historian, bodies were also taken to Witton Old Jewish Cemetery in Birmingham (5.2.2). In the medieval period, there was Jewish cemetery opposite Magdalene College, which was destroyed when the Jews were expelled in 1290. By the entrance gate, there is a plaque and monument indicating that the site was the Jews' medieval burial ground and when it was destroyed (personal observation 2010).

5.2.26 Penzance: Leskinnick Terrace   [83]

This cemetery is situated in a back alley of Penzance enclosed by high stone walls that were probably built in 1844-5 (Kadish 2006, 95). The cemetery was use before this date, as the oldest broken stone that can still be read is dated 1791 (personal observation 2009). Kadish also states that it is 'One of the best preserved Georgian Jewish burial grounds in Britain, with almost 50 tombstones, many of Cornish slate' (Ibid, 95); only four grave stones cannot be read. One of the earliest inscriptions on a broken tombstone with the date in Hebrew is equivalent to 30th January 1791 (personal observation 2009). There is rare evidence of the *ohel* (prayer hall) by the entrance, perhaps marked by fragments of the floor inside the gate (personal observation 2009) (Figure 5.118).

Fry et al. (2000, 23) provides a transcription of an anonymous headstone bearing the date 1741 Simmons et al (2000, 130) give a full description of the purchase of the land acquired c.1740 which was then extended in stages as more space was needed. 'By 1827 the whole area around the cemetery had become known as the 'Jews Fields' (Ibid, 132). Canon Rogers, whose family owned the lease to the area 'agreed to the further development of Leskinnick Terrace which became known locally as 'Jerusalem Row' and granted building leases for plots in the 'Higher Jews Burial Ground Field'' (Ibid, 132).

One of the most interesting tombstones is that of Jacob James Hart (1848) consul to the Kingdom of Saxony (Figure 5.122). His uncle, Lemon Hart was an importer of rum from Jamaica. He supplied the Royal Navy in the early 19th

Figure 5.118 Penzance: Leskinnick Terrace Jew's Burial Ground (1791) inside the entrance, the area of the possible former ohel *(prayer hall) (photograph J. Marks 2009).*

Figure 5.119 Penzance: topographical plan of Jewish Cemetery (by permission Pearce et al. 2000, 154).

Figure 5.120 Penzance: earliest legible inscription dated 1791 (photograph J. Marks 2009).

Figure 5.121 Penzance: view of cemetery and wall (Grade 11) (photograph J. Marks 2009).

Figure 5.122 Penzance: grave of Jacob Hart (d.1846) (photograph J.Marks 2009).

century. Lemon Hart later moved his business to London; however, his connection with Penzance was of considerable importance to the community. He was the first president of the new synagogue and was also involved with the wider non-Jewish society in Penzance. His nephew's tomb is covered with a coffin-shaped slab stone, unlike any other Jewish grave sites seen in Devon and Cornwall. It would suggest that this stone copied London fashion at that time. One tombstone has the name Scott, a local stonemason (Pearce, 2009).

The most remarkable aspect of this Georgian cemetery is that in spite of there being no Jewish community in Penzance for nearly 100 years, most of the tombstones are intact (Figure 5.121).

5.2.27 Plymouth Hoe: Lambhay Hill

Susser (2000, 130) notes that 'This cemetery was originally part of the garden belonging to one of the members of the community, Mrs. Sarah Sherrenbeck' (1972, 5). In the small early re-settlement communities, Jews could be buried in a garden leased to a fellow Jew (Ibid, 5). Kadish reports that 'This was the beginning of Plymouth Hoe Cemetery established in c.1726, first used in 1744' (2006, 93) (Figure 5.123). The Plymouth synagogue post-dates the cemetery and was established 1761-1762.

Mrs. Sherrenbeck later transferred more land to the Plymouth community (Susser 1972, 5), and in the middle of the 18th century, adjacent ground was sold to three London merchants, securing the future ownership of the burial ground. According to Susser ' … in 1811 a further piece of ground was required, this time the land was conveyed to three Plymouth Jews, two listed as shopkeepers and one an optician. The fourth signatory was a John Saunders of Plymouth (a non-Jew) and described as a '*gentleman*' (Ibid, 5). This was a legal precaution, as Jews were still not allowed to own the freeholds of land.

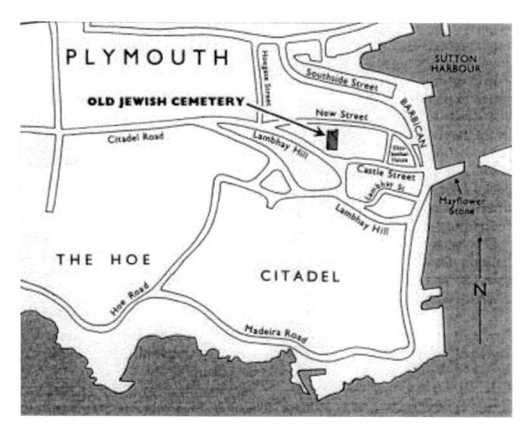

Figure 5.123 Plymouth Hoe: location of Old Jewish Cemetery (1744), (not to scale) (Susser 1972, 4).

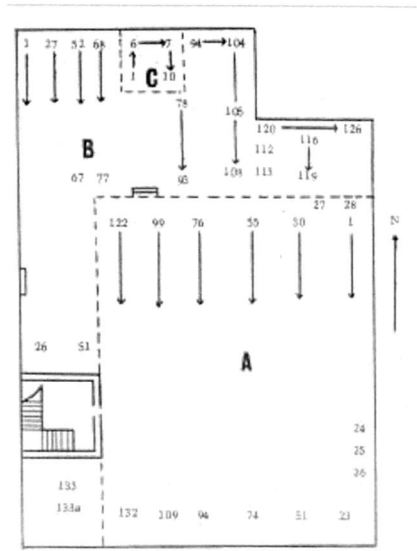

Figure 5.124 Plymouth Hoe: topographical plan of cemetery (Susser, 1970, 3).

PLAN OF HOE CEMETERY

The Plymouth Hoe burial ground functioned until the middle of the 19th century, when a new cemetery in Compton Gifford near Central Park was bought in 1868 (not discussed). The purchase of this new cemetery indicates that there was no more space in the Hoe burial ground and that further land adjacent to this site was not available. The entrance is through a small gate in a high stone wall. Behind the gate is a stone staircase leading down to remains of the ohel which no longer exists (personal observation 2009). The middle portion of the burial ground (A) is sunken and is overgrown and neglected. Rabbi Susser recorded the site in 1970 and refers to transcripts of 95 inscriptions made in 1900. From these, he made a plan of the grounds (Figure 5.124). The Minutes of the Plymouth Congregation at that date indicate that parts of the cemetery were covered with earth in the early 19th century so that a second layer of burials could take place. According to Jewish law, coffins can be interred on top of each other as long as there was 'six hand breadths of earth between them'. This situation can also be observed in the Brady Street Cemetery, London (5.15). A stone set into the wall commemorates the gift of £157 to the Plymouth Congregation to complete the purchase of the ground. It is no longer possible to read the date (personal observation 2009).

The plan shows three sections with grave locations; A, numbered 1-133; B, numbered 1-116; and C, numbered 1-7. Section C; and was for the Joseph family leaders of the community between 1760 and 1860 (Susser 1972, 7). Abraham Isaac *ben* (the son of) Joseph was the first family member buried in this plot alongside his wife Rosy. Susser notes that Rosy's grandfather, Michael Moses, lived in Creechurch Lane, London. Creechurch Lane Synagogue (discussed in 4.1.4) was in the centre of the 1656 Jewish re-settlement in London. According to Roth (1950, 92) 'Abraham

Figure 5.125 Plymouth Hoe: section A of cemetery showing steps and neglect (photograph J. Marks 2009).

Joseph was the leading Jew in his day in the south-west of England. He was agent to the Duke of Clarence (later William IV), and was known popularly as 'the King of the Jews'. The higher-level B was reserved for important members of the community, including the president and wardens of the synagogue. The fronts of the memorial stones in this section are in Hebrew, although some have the English name on the reverse. Susser (1970, 7) states that '…there are many mistakes in the Hebrew, due to masons who are ignorant of Hebrew'.

From these inscriptions and synagogue records, it is possible to build a picture of some of the late 18th-century and 19th-century Plymouth community. Many of the deceased came from Germany and Poland, as indicated by their names. Homelands and trades are sometimes inscribed on the tombstones. These include ship's chandlers, exporters to the ports of the Spanish Peninsula not occupied by the French (Ibid, 7). Others were jewellers, silversmiths and watchmakers. Women are listed as being dressmakers, seamstresses and hat makers. Addresses in the burial register show that the community was spread throughout the city. The cemetery is neglected and receives few visitors (Figure 5.125). In 2010, an auction at Bonhams in London sold some of the synagogue's 1745 silver to raise money for the upkeep of both the synagogue and cemetery.

5.2.28   Portsmouth: Fawcett Road   [84]

In the 18th and early 19th centuries, during the Napoleonic Wars, many Jews in Portsmouth acted as naval agents. Kadish (2006, 83) writes that 'by 1812 Portsmouth was probably the most influential Jewry outside London and was the fourth largest as late as 1851'.

The cemetery was acquired in 1749 (Roth 1950, 94), in what was then known as Lazy Lane, later to become Jew's Lane (now Fawcett Road). Land was leased by four Jews from a non-Jew, Richard Anham, Roth was able to identify one gravestone dating to 1763 (Ibid, 46). According to Weinberg, 'In 1800 a further piece of land, adjoining that of the original, was granted under a 1000 year lease, with further pieces added in 1844 and 1882' (1998, 19). Burial records kept in the synagogue, survive from 1835. Weinberg states that '….no early records of grave places have been maintained' (Ibid, 19). A few burials still take place for members who have reserved spaces to be buried near their families.

Figure 5.126 Portsmouth: Old Jews Burial Ground (1749) and ohel
(photograph K. Marks 2009).

Portsmouth's Old Burial Ground is the oldest Jewish cemetery still in use in England. The present *ohel* dates from 1881; inscriptions inside that indicate the present building is the third on the site since 1768 (personal observation 2009). This 18th-century *ohel* is unique in that before the occasional burials that still take place, the deceased are washed prior to burial in the prayer hall by members of the synagogue known as the *Chevra Kadisha* (Charitable Society for preparing the dead for burial) (personal contact 2009).

The oldest tombstones are near the *ohel* (Figure 5.126). The oldest tombstone and probably first burial is 'The child Alexander, son of Isaac' (d.1763). A few tombstones have carved reliefs, such as raised hands giving the priestly blessing, denoting that the deceased was a male Cohen (Figure 5.127).

Several other tombstones with Levitical motifs (jug and basin), indicate that the deceased were male Levite. Some tombstones have inscriptions on two sides, Hebrew on the side facing inwards with the English equivalent on

Figure 5.127 Portsmouth: Jews' Burial Ground, tombstone with carved relief depicting raised hands (a male Cohen) (photograph K. Marks 2009).

the side facing the road. This practice is most unusual and may have social significance, as the view from the road could give the impression that the cemetery was Christian or Non- Conformist; only the Hebrew inscriptions betray the religious affiliation of the deceased (personal observation 2009). A number of tombstones belong to Navy Agents and merchants, for example Joseph Levy, a Navy Agent (1814-1819). David Barnard, as well as being a Naval Agent, was a pawnbroker; synagogue records show that he lived in Hanover Street, Portsea, close to the original synagogue. A further stone inscription is for Benjamin Levi, one of the founders of the Portsmouth Community. A plan of Portsmouth and Portsea in the Napoleonic period shows the concentration of Jewish merchants and ships chandlers round the port area (Figure 4.84).

One of the most interesting inscriptions in the cemetery is that of Samuel Emanuel, who died in 1795 aged 64, the only survivor of a disaster in 1758, when a number of Jewish traders who had carried goods to H.M.S. Lancaster were blown off course on their return journey and their ship overturned. Roth (1935, 164) writes that, 'five bodies were never recovered: four more were picked up with all signs of life extinct: two persons died after they were brought on board'. Six victims of the disaster were buried without a tombstone. The names of the 11 who died are still recalled once a year at a memorial service in the synagogue. This list of names is the oldest surviving name roll call of Portsmouth Jewry.

'By 1770 the community had grown to between 30-40 substantial householders' (Ibid, 166), suggesting a community of around 150 people including children. Names from the inscriptions indicate that the majority came from Germany and, as was the practice in other communities at this time, the place of origin was appended to the name, such as Benjamin ben Jacob Levy of Wiesbaden, one of the founders of this community.

5.2.29 Ramsgate: Upper Dumpton Road [85]

Figure 5.128 Ramsgate: Upper Dumpton Road Jewish Cemetery (1872), view of part of the burial ground showing Sephardi and Ashkenazi grave stones (photograph J. Marks 2011).

This cemetery contains flat grave stones of Sephardi Jews and upright tombstones of Ashkenazi Jews. Prior to the establishment of this cemetery, Kadish (2006, 63) states that, '....the Sephardim would have been buried in the Nuevo Cemetery in Mile End Road London (5.1.2) and the Ashkenazim in Canterbury (5.2.6)'. It contains around 250 graves, with room for more. According to the caretaker, the burial register, which is lodged at Lauriston Road Cemetery does not include the earliest burials (5.1.8) (personal contact 2011).

5.2.30.1 Sheerness Hope Street [86]

There are two Jewish cemeteries in Sheerness and the Isle of Sheppey. The first is in the centre of Sheerness in Hope Street, the second is a small plot in the municipal cemetery on the Isle of Sheppey nearby. Roth (1950, 97) writes 'The small community reached its peak during the Napoleonic Wars (1799-1815) declining rapidly after 1815'.

The community in Sheerness was established from c.1790s (Roth 1950, 111). Kadish (2006, 68) writes, that 'The synagogue was built in 1811 and dismantled in 1887 when there was no longer a community'. The cemetery measures 60feet x 25 feet and is long neglected, with the front wall and entrance in poor condition (Figure 5.129) (personal observation 2010). There are 11 standing stones but they are illegible, and most of the ground is overgrown (Figure 5.130).

Figure 5.129 Sheerness: Old Jews' Burial Ground (1804) Hope Street ME12 1804-1855 (photograph K. Marks 2010).

Figure 5.130 Sheerness: Old Jews' Burial Ground Hope Street, remaining tombstones (photograph K. Marks 2010).

5.2.30.2 Isle of Sheppey (Jewish section)

Of all the Jewish burial grounds examined in this study this is the smallest, being a plot in the north-east corner of the municipal cemetery. It contains 11 headstones in two rows facing west (Figure 5.131). This was originally a commercial cemetery which went bankrupt and was then taken over by the local council. The stones are named after two families, Levi and Jacobs, although all records are lost (Kadish 2006, 68).

Figure 5.131 Sheerness: Isle of Sheppey Cemetery (1859) Jewish Section (photograph K. Marks 2010).

5.2.31.1   Sheffield: Bowden Street   [87]

By 1831, leases for two Jewish cemeteries had been signed, one of which was for a small cemetery in Bowden Street, near the centre of the city (Ballin 1986, 6). According to community records, the lease was for 800 years for a plot measuring 220 square yards. At that time, the community numbered around 10 families, and by 1851 had doubled (Roth 1950, 99). There are no records or burial plot plans. However on

Figure 5.132 Sheffield: Bowden Street Cemetery, in use from 1831-1880, prior to being destroyed. (Photograph Sheffield Hebrew Congregation, archives).

a visit to the present synagogue, in the archives the author came across a photograph of the cemetery taken prior to it being destroyed as a result of a compulsory purchase order in 1975, when Bowden Street was widened (Figure 5.132). The photograph shows 12 standing stones of which one is for a child. When full, the cemetery would have held c.50 graves. Remains from Bowden Street were re-interred in the Ecclesfield Cemetery (discussed in 5.2.31.3).

Figure 5.133 Sheffield: Rodmoor Mausoleum (1831) of the Bright family (Sheffield Synagogue Archives).

A second cemetery was acquired in 1831 in Rodmoor, near Sheffield in a private burial ground for the Bright family. Isaac Bright married a non-Jewish woman who was a member of a wealthy steel-making family. Isaac wished to be buried alongside his wife, who could not be interred in a Jewish cemetery. It was also used by other Jewish members of the Bright family. According to Eric Sayliss, senior member of the community, the beehive-shaped mausoleum is now derelict and cannot be visited. Its design is unique in Britain (Figure 5.133) (personal contact 2011).

5.2.31.2 Sheffield: Waller Road Walkley

This cemetery, no longer in use is located on a steep slope between the Church of England and Roman Catholic Cemetery at Walkley. Entrance to this small ground is through a narrow gate, and there is a public pathway through the cemetery, overgrown with ivy and brambles (personal observation 2011). There is no evidence of there having been an *ohel,* which is unsurprising as the cemetery is a small one. At that time, the deceased would have been brought to the cemetery by a hearse pulled by horses, a difficult task up the step incline (personal observation 2011). There are no plans, but from the estimated size it would have held c.250 graves, plus a children's section with no tombstones (personal observation 2011). The cemetery was used by Sheffield Benevolent Society, an offshoot of the breakaway Sheffield New Hebrew Congregation, when the mass immigration from Eastern Europe began in the late 19th century.

5.2.31.3 Sheffield: Ecclesfield

This cemetery is divided into two parts, on either side of Colley Road and contains the remains of 2, 000 persons (personal contact Eric Sayliss 2011). In the main cemetery is a railed section with 12 tombstones re-interred from Bowden Road Cemetery (5.2.31.1) (Figure 5.134). The entrance to the older section used by the

Sheffield Old Hebrew Congregation is dominated by the 1931 *ohel*, although it is later than the period under discussion. The northern part of the cemetery is of later date (1931) and is thus not discussed.

Figure 5.134 Sheffield: Ecclesfield Jewish Cemetery (1873) 12 tombstones and re-internments from Bowden Street (1831) in railed section (photograph K. Marks 2011).

Figure 5.135 Sheffield: Ecclesfield Jewish Cemetery ohel (prayer hall)entrance (photograph K.Marks 2011)

5.2.32   Southampton: Common Cemetery (Jewish Section)   [88]

This small cemetery contains approximately 250 graves in a hedged off section of the municipal cemetery. According to Kadish (2006, 85) 'Southampton Common Cemetery was itself one of the earliest landscaped cemeteries in England opened in 1846'. There are three halls of prayer within sight of each other (personal observation 2011). The *ohel* (Figure 5.136), no longer used has been converted into living accommodation next to the entrance lodge. Nearby are Non-Conformist and Church of England mortuary chapels. All three were designed by the same architect, F.J.Francis (Kadish 2006, 85). The *ohel* is in the Tudor style whilst the Church of England Chapel is Romanesque and the Non-Conformist Chapel Early English-Gothic (Ibid, 85). The earliest Jewish burial dates from 1854, and the earliest memorials are large stones, most of which can no longer be read (Figure 5.137). The older part of the cemetery is overgrown. The newer stones near to the *ohel* are smaller, as the Council now stipulates their size. A large number of burial plots have no headstones. According to Martyn Rose, there are no records of the earliest burials (personal contact 2011).

COMMUNITIES IN DEATH (CEMETERIES) 209

Figure 5.136 Southampton: Cemetery Road (1846) ohel (prayer hall) late-19th century (photograph K. Marks 2011).

Figure 5.137 Southampton: mid-19th and early 20th century unreadable Jewish tombstones (photograph K. Marks 2011).

Figure 5.138 Southampton: view of the cemetery with 19th-century graves stones to the rear and 20th century. to the front. (photograph K.Marks 2010).

Figure 5.139 Southampton: English Norman Church of England mortuary chapel (photograph K. Marks 2011).

5.2.33.1 Sunderland: Ayres Quay [89]

This long-abandoned and overgrown cemetery is the oldest in the north-east of England and is reputed to have contained at least 500 burials, including 250 who died in the cholera outbreak in 1851 (community records). The ground is so neglected that the number of plots is impossible to ascertain (personal observation 2010). Figure 5.140 shows the ground plan from the original deed. The area was less than one acre. There is a boundary wall (Figure 5.141). From personal observation (2010), there are six remaining broken tombstones and one broken obelisk, none *in situ*. The obelisk in Hebrew and English commemorates David Jonassohn (Figure 5.142), a local colliery owner and eminent member of the Sunderland Jewish community. Levy indicates that the cemetery was at one time a private plot belonging to the Jonassohns (1956, 50). David Jonassohn died in 1859, a year after the cemetery was closed, so there could have been a reserved area allocated to him to be next to his wife Charlotte who died in 1829. Her stone can be partly read. However, Jonassohn is actually buried with his son in the West London Reform Synagogue Cemetery in Balls Pond Road (discussed 5.1.10).

In 1953, an extract from a letter in the Sunderland *Echo* states:

'More than one hundred years ago, David Jonassohn, a member of Sunderland Jewish Community, built for his Usworth employees, at his own expense, a church for the communicants of the Church of England, and a Chapel for the Dissenters' (Ibid, 311).

Of two broken headstones, one records that the deceased lived in Durham, where there was no Jewish cemetery. The other features a jug, indicating that the deceased was a Levy (a descendent of the Hebrew tribe of Levites) (personal observation 2010). According to Dorothy Sadlik, former resident of Sunderland, during the development of the Ayres Quay area remains were re-interred in Bishopswearmouth Cemetery (personal contact 2010).

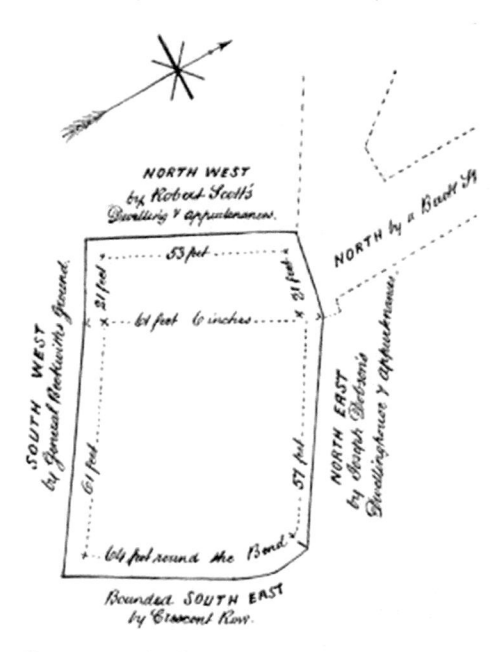

Figure 5.140 Sunderland: Ground plan of Ayres Quay Jewish Cemetery c.1780s (Levy 1956, 28).

Figure 5.141 Sunderland: Ayres Quay Jewish Cemetery, showing part of overgrown boundary wall (photograph K. Marks 2010).

Figure 5.142 Sunderland: Ayres Quay Cemetery, Jonassohn obelisk before vandalism (Levy 1956, 302).

Figure 5.143 Sunderland: Ayres Quay Jewish Cemetery, broken headstone

5.2.33.2 Sunderland: Bishopswearmouth

Three Jewish sections in this cemetery cover the periods 1856-1899, 1899-1926 and 1929 to present. Figure 5.144 shows the plan of plot one, which falls into the period under discussion. County burial records cover the entire cemetery from 1836. There are over 100 graves in plot one, including 19 unmarked spaces containing unnamed infants. Two headstones, one of 1861, indicate that the deceased lived in Hartlepool, a community that no longer exists. There are no monuments, suggesting that the local burial authorities controlled the size of tombstones. An *ohel* from the later period is not discussed.

Figure 5.144 Sunderland: Bishopswearmouth Jewish Cemetery, general view of graves and tombstones in plot 1. 1856-1899 (photograph K. Marks 2010)
(Not to scale)

(Not to scale)

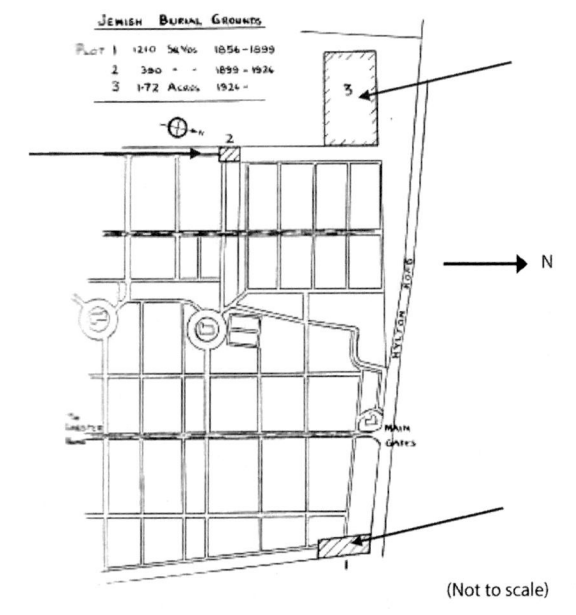

Figure 5.145 Sunderland: Bishopswearmouth, Jewish Cemetery: three Jewish sections (Levy 1956, 79).

5.2.34   Swansea: Mayhill Old Jew's Burial Ground   [90]

This is the earliest Jewish burial ground in South Wales. The 1879 Local Board of Health Map shows the cemetery situated on Town Hill (now Mayhill), overlooking Swansea Bay (personal observation 2010). Originally a quarry and gravel pit, the burial ground has been extended several times over the last 200 years. The original area by the entrance has an eight-feet-high rubble stone wall on three sides; the remains of the fourth wall enclose the original cemetery. Enlarged in 1878 the 1969 Ordnance Survey Map shows the extended area, which contains at least 500 graves, many unmarked. There are no complete burial records earlier than 1862 (Kadish 2006, 202). Evident in the wall next to the entrance are the remains of the *ohel* in red brick, which has been demolished (Figure 5.14.6). Many of the tombstones are carved from Welsh slate. Some indicate that the deceased lived outside Swansea, for example at Llanelli, where there was no Jewish cemetery It went out of use in 1965.

Figure 5.146 Swansea: Old Jews' Burial Ground (1768) original 18th-century section showing 1768 wall and section of the entrance. The grassed area marks the area of the ohel *(photograph J. Marks 2010).*

Figure 5.147 Swansea: earliest graves stones to the front and remains of wall of original cemetery (photograph J. Marks 2010).

5.2.35.1 Yarmouth (Great): Alma Road [91]

The first of Yarmouth's two cemeteries from the period under discussion lies just outside the walls of the medieval town, close to one of the former entrances to the City known as the 'Garden Gate'. The inner side of the wall is that of the former Black Friars Monastery (Figure 5.148). Alma Road Cemetery is one of the few examples in England of Jews being buried next to the medieval city walls. There are four head stones and seven upright headstones placed against the boundary wall. The semi-legible headstones are in two rows, with the three headstones to the front dated 1846. The earliest headstone is 1803, and the inscription reads:

Simon Son of Naphtali Died on Friday Night and Buried Sunday 7 Shevat 5563 (30 January 1803).

Roth (1950, 105) identifies Simon Son of Naphtali as Simon Hart, the pioneer settler in Great Yarmouth. A silversmith and a resident there for 40 years, who rented the burial ground.

Figure 5.148 Yarmouth (Great): wooden gated entrance to Old Jews' Burial Ground (1851) Alma Road next to iron gated entrance of former medieval monastery (photograph J. Marks 2010).

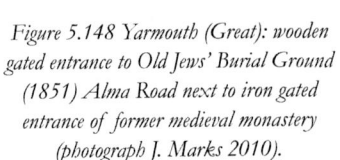

5.149 Yarmouth (Great): Old Jew's Burial Ground, View of medieval wall, burial plots (photograph J. Marks 2010).

5.2.35.2 Yarmouth (Great): Kitchener Road

The second Jewish Cemetery in Kitchener Road is known as 'The Old Jewish Cemetery'. A knapped flint wall separates the Jewish section of the municipal cemetery, which has its own locked entrance at the north end. This burial ground is in a part of the cemetery reserved for 'Non-Conformists'. At the south end of the ground is the partly legible headstone of David Cohen (d. August 1858), the earliest head-stone that can partly be read. In all, there are around 20 standing headstones (personal observation 2010). According to Kadish (2006, 85) 41 burials are recorded in the registers, the last on 29 January 1936'. There is no longer a community in Great Yarmouth.

Figure 5.150 Yarmouth (Great): Old Cemetery (1858) Kitchener Road entrance through knapped flint wall (photograph J. Marks 2010).

Figure 5.151 Yarmouth (Great): Old Cemetery, Kitchener Road View of cemetery (photograph J. Marks 2010). (no scale)

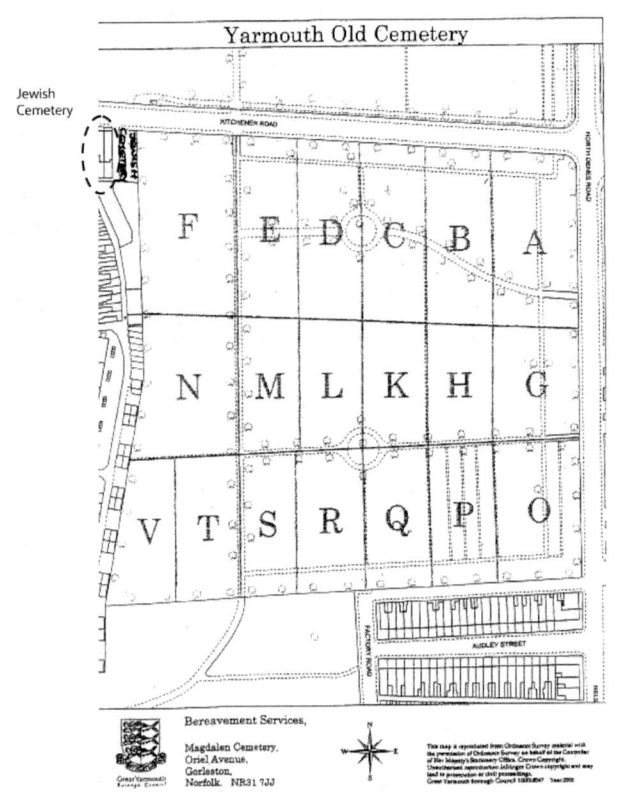

Figure 5.152 Yarmouth (Great): Plan of Municipal Old Cemetery, showing Jewish section in north-east of burial ground (10.6 acres, no plan to scale) (Great Yarmouth Bereavement Services 2006).

5.2.36 Cemeteries conclusion

This study has examined 60 Jewish cemeteries in England and Wales established prior to c.1880. Four of these, in Leeds, Liverpool, Manchester and Newcastle could not be entered as they were not accessible or dangerous for visitors. Cemeteries are the principal body of evidence for the cultural heritage of the early community. The earliest three cemeteries in London from the middle-18th and early-19th century, are the Sephardi, *Velho* (Old) and *Nuevo* (New) in Mile End and the Ashkenazi Cemetery in Alderney Road. The earliest provincial cemeteries examined that survive, are in Bristol (1744), Canterbury (1760), Chatham (1780), Exeter (1757), Falmouth (1780), Hull (1780), Ipswich (1796), Manchester (1794), Norwich (1750), Penzance (1791), Plymouth (1744), Portsmouth (1749) and Swansea (1768). Out of 13, 18th-century provincial cemeteries, 10 are in port cities, reflecting the early settlement of the community.

A number of provincial cemeteries discussed are in, or adjacent, to municipal burial grounds. These include Bradford, Coventry, Dover, Gloucester, Ipswich,

Manchester, Merthyr Tydfil, Newcastle, Norwich, Sheerness, Southampton, Sunderland and Yarmouth (Great). These cemeteries all date from middle-late 19th century when Municipal Christian and other Non–Conformist burials grounds were established following the Burial Acts of the mid-1800's, after which city and town centre cemeteries were no longer used.

The Jewish sections are separated from Christian and Non-Conformist burial grounds by hedges or walls with their own entrances. A few *ohalim* (prayer halls) survive in municipal cemeteries, such as Bradford, Merthyr Tydfil, Norwich and Southampton. Cemeteries located in municipal burial grounds are well kept, even though the earliest tombstones have deteriorated. Orthodox cemeteries, not under the care of municipal authorities, are under the authority of The United Synagogue Burial Society, Spanish and Portuguese Burial Society, Board of Deputies or local community. The two Reform cemeteries discussed, London and Bradford, are looked after by their own burial societies.

Outside London, some of the early cemeteries in Liverpool, Manchester, Norwich, Plymouth, Sheffield and Sunderland are overgrown and neglected. There are no burial records, so it is not possible to know how many graves were in these burial grounds, but it can be estimated that there were between 850-1,000 burials per acre. In all of the cemeteries examined, the earliest tombstones, where they survive, are simple and made in local sandstone, limestone and slate, with the inscriptions entirely in Hebrew. Most of them can no longer be read due to weathering and many are broken or have fallen over. There is evidence that many of the deceased were buried without tombstones with the plot only marked by mounds of earth or border stones, many have been destroyed, mostly through neglect, although some through vandalism. Nearly all newborn babies and infants were buried without gravestones in a separate area, close to cemetery walls. Re-interment is not usually allowed by Jewish law, but there is evidence of re-interments having taken place, mostly due to city re-generation projects. From the beginning of the 19th century, marble and granite was used on tombstones, the inscriptions are both in Hebrew and English. Some tombstones bear inscriptions indicating the country or town from which the deceased came. Status is more evident, with family plots, chest tombs, obelisks, and for the wealthy few, mausoleums.

Within the next ten years, several of the smaller provincial communities will no longer exist. Responsibility for the upkeep of Orthodox cemeteries will fall on the Jewish Board of Deputies, with possible help from English Heritage if they are listed and if any have features that have special significance, such as original walls and historic memorials. Negotiations with English Heritage are currently in progress for several of these sites.

Chapter 6

A Comparative Approach to Jewish Urban Topography

A brief history of the Jews into Britain from c.1656 was presented in Chapter 2. It is not until the early-to-middle 18th century, that there is evidence for changes in the urban topography of the community. This chapter examines the changing topography, growth, population movement and dispersal of the community in the period from c.1740 to c.1880, prior to the mass immigration that began in 1881. In that year, the community nearly doubled in size from c.60, 000 to c.100, 000 persons (Roth 1978, 270).

Anglo-Jewry has traditionally concentrated in the larger urban centres, London being the focal point throughout the history of the community. Outside London, wherever Jewish immigrants settled in major provincial English and Welsh cities, such as Birmingham, Bristol, Leeds, Liverpool, Manchester and Swansea, there were clusters of Jews who lived alongside their non-Jewish neighbours, sometimes also immigrants from other countries, such as Ireland (Clout 2004, 136).

Other than the Sephardim and a few more wealthy Ashkenazi merchants, Jewish immigrants tended to live in the poorest areas in the city or near to ports. For example, Whitechapel in London, the Froggery (no longer existing) in Birmingham, Red Bank and Strangeways in Manchester, the Leylands (no longer existing) in Leeds, and near the ports in Chatham, Falmouth, Hull, Ipswich, Liverpool, Penzance, Portsmouth, Sheerness, Swansea and Great Yarmouth. The Jewish area was where they lived and worked, with synagogues, shops and small workshops at the centre of their religious, cultural and working lives. This is confirmed by both documented and mapped evidence of the first synagogues, many of which are shown in the gazetteer.

Changing settlement patterns are also seen in the need for geographically accessible synagogues. Jewish immigrants gradually moved from slum and poor districts as they became more prosperous. New immigrants arrived to take their places, but those who moved remained amongst Jews.

With the exception of the few wealthy banking families, and compared with the Sephardi (Jews originally from Spain and Portugal) community who were traders, particularly in textiles, Ashkenazi Jews (Jews originating in Germany, Poland and

Russia) were mainly pedlars, tradesmen, shopkeepers and low paid factory workers. In spite of the growth of provincial communities, the London Jewish community, with new immigrants coming in throughout the period, represented around two-thirds of the total community in England at any one time. Roth (1950, 17) notes '...the most ample source of information for the early history of the expansion from London, is the membership roll of The Great Synagogue'. In London, whilst there was movement of some of the community (from early-mid 19th century) to the west, north and east and also out to the suburbs and to the provinces, many kept their synagogue membership in the City; as noted in synagogue membership rolls, burial registers and charitable lists. This was done in order to retain their burial rights in London cemeteries. There are also archives and marriage registers in the United Synagogue and a circumcision register in the British Museum, which contain home addresses (Ibid, 17). Religious affiliation was not required on a census form. However Jewish-sounding names from a number of censuses (1841, 1851, 1861 and 1871) give an indication of where Jews were living and their numbers. They are an important source of topographical information.

Endelman (1979, 9) states 'The transformation of Anglo-Jewry at all levels of the social ladder took place largely in terms of new patterns of behaviour rather than new lines of thought'. This transformation took place when Jews could afford to move out of the poor area of the cities where they had first settled and when some adopted non-Jewish patterns of life, including changing their surnames to English and pronounceable names. Children also assumed English as their first language. Most dressed as their non-Jewish neighbours, men sometimes became clean shaven.

Movement out of The City of London and East End, and, rise of Jewish suburbia and topography in London is mirrored in the major provincial cities. The first Jewish residents of all the major provincial cities lived in the poorest districts. Immigrants, most of whom could not speak English, tended to live near each other, but unlike the period from 1881 when mass immigration was in full flow, there were no ghettos. From c.1800, archives of membership and burial registers have survived in some provincial synagogues and in local Aliens' Registers, for example, Penzance, Plymouth and Portsmouth. The *Jewish Chronicle* from 1844 advertised deaths, sometimes recording place of residence. Unfortunately, many early records have been lost or were destroyed during World War II.

Some tombstone inscriptions include the former country of residence of the deceased; sometimes they record their place of residence in Britain, if they did not live in the town where they were buried. It is evident from synagogue records and censuses, that during the period under discussion, Jews were scattered throughout England and Wales with communities distributed from Yorkshire in the North to Cornwall in the South.

Between 1750 and 1815, the Jewish community in England and Wales more than trebled from c.8, 000 to c.30, 000 (Roth 1978, 225/241) writes that '....in this period, thousands of Ashkenazim came from Continental Europe, mainly from Germany, the vast majority settled in London to be with their fellow Jews' Those with trades,

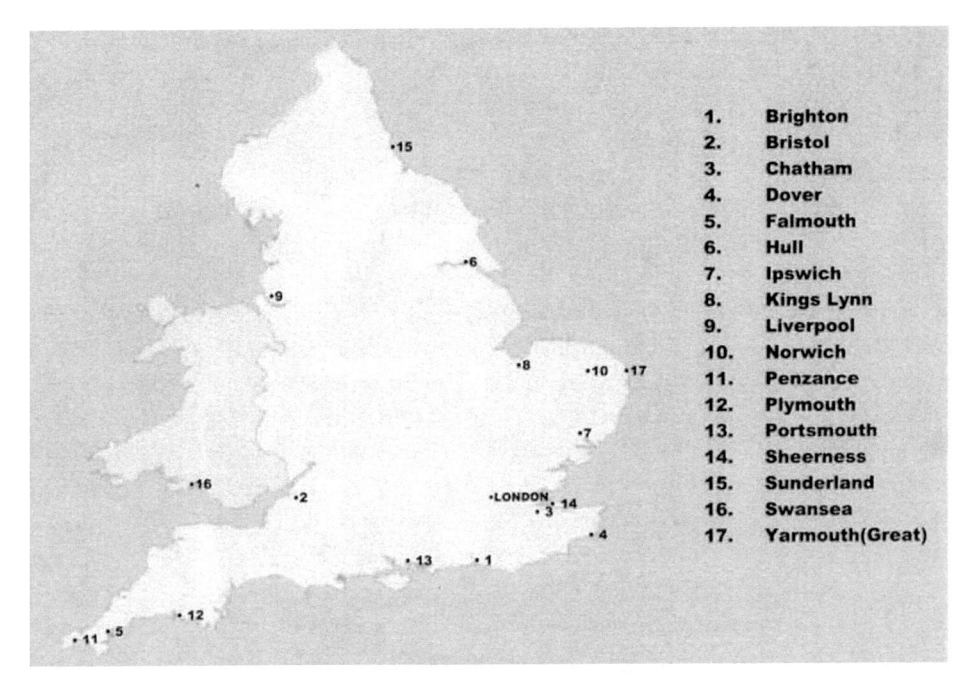

Figure 6.1 London and 17 port communities established prior to 1815.

such as tailors, cabinet makers and cigarette makers, lived not far from their places of work. As Jews were precluded from opening shops or selling from market stalls within the City of London, trade was controlled by Christian Guilds; Jews would not take the Christian sacrament (Ibid1978, 192). For the same reason, they could not become apprenticed to a trade or join professions, such as law and architecture. Many poor and uneducated Ashkenazim became pedlars in order to make a living.

In early-mid 18th century, London pedlars moved to provincial towns where there were commercial opportunities, namely sea ports such as Portsmouth (1730s), Falmouth (1740), Chatham (1750), Liverpool (1750), Plymouth (1752) and Bristol (1753) and industrial cities such as Birmingham (1730s) and Manchester (1780s). Manchester and Birmingham became the most important provincial communities; the communities in these industrial centres were thus now taking precedence (Lipman 1956, 54). In the early-19th-century communities were established in spa and market towns such as Bath (1800), Brighton (1800) and Cheltenham (1824). In some places where they came as pedlars, were able to open shops then followed by wholesale premises, small factories and workshops. When they were sufficiently numerous they formed a congregation. Cemeteries and *mikva'ot* were then established, sometimes before a synagogue. By the middle of the 19th century over 30 congregations outside London were the focal point of Anglo-Jewry for the communities' religious and social life.

This chapter examines the topography of the community in London and major industrial cities in the North and Midlands, such as Birmingham, Leeds, Liverpool,

CITY	seat holders	individuals	paid officials	synagogue	mikveh	burial ground
LONDON:						
Duke's Place*	480	800	3	y	0	1
Hambro*	150	170	6	y	0	1
New*	266	(not known)	7	y	0	0
Western*	210	c.950	7	y	private	1
Maiden Lane*	150	0	3	y	private	1
PROVINCES:						
Bath	5	50	1	y	public baths	1
Birmingham	99	679	4	y	yes	1
Brighton	32	150	2	y	yes	1
Bristol	46	c.150	3	y	yes	2
Canterbury	4	106	1	y	public baths	1
Cardiff	0	9	1	y	0	1
Chatham	40	189	1	y	yes	1
Cheltenham	8	96	2	y	public baths	1
Dover	0	31	1	y	sea	0
Exeter	8	c.175	2	y	yes	1
Falmouth	3	50	1	y	yes	1
Gloucester	(no return)					
Hull	0	65	1	y	yes	1
Ipswich	3	9	1	y	0	1
Leeds	0	17	2	y	yes	1
Liverpool 1	131	c.650	6	y	yes	1
Liverpool 2	12	327	3	y	yes	1
Lynn Norfolk	0	5	0	0	0	1
Manchester Old	33	0	5	y	yes	2
Manchester New	19	57	1	y	yes	1
Newcastle	0	66	2	y	public baths	1
Norwich	3	0	1	y	yes	1
Nottingham	1	6	1	y	public baths	1
Oxford	0	20	1	no return	0	0
Penzance	0	51	1	y	yes	1
Plymouth	33	205	2	y	yes	1
Portsmouth	20	2	2	y	yes	1
Ramsgate	(no return)					
Sheerness	10	13	1	y	yes	1
Sheffield	2	56	1	room	yes	1
Southampton	7	0	1	y	public baths	0
Sunderland	0	30	0	2	yes	1
Swansea	13	133	2	y	yes	1
Yarmouth	0	48	1	y	sea	1
Total:		5365				
Not included:						
Dublin	21	150	1	y	public baths	1
Edinburgh	16	107	1	y	yes	1
Glasgow	9	108	2	y	yes	1
Jersey	5	47	1	y	sea	1
Kingston Jamaica	115	450	5	2	yes	1

Figure 6.2 Extract from Statistical Account of the Congregations in the British Empire 1845 (5606) London Metropolitan Archive ACC/2805/1/1/107.

Manchester and Newcastle It also examines the growth of the community in market towns and some seaports (1755-1855) and then the decline of some communities from early/middle 19th century, following the end of the Napoleonic Wars in 1815, in ports such as such as Portsmouth, Plymouth and Penzance. Figure 6.1 shows that out of the 23 provincial Jewish communities established before 1815, 17 were in ports. With the decline in the importance of sea ports, particularly on the south coast, some communities ceased to exist. Synagogues were sold, put to other uses or destroyed. New communities arose in the industrial North-East, West Midlands and the mining towns of South Wales. Hull from 1850 became the second-largest port after London for immigrant arrivals (Finestein 1996/8, 33).

The 1845 Statistical Account of the Congregations in the British Empire was completed by the Office of the Chief Rabbi (London Metropolitan Archive ACC/2805/1/1/107) (Figure 6.2). These figures do not include children, Orthodox communities independent of the Chief Rabbi, Jews who were not paid-up members of a synagogue or members of the Sephardi community and Reform Movement established in London c.1840. Nevertheless the census still provides a picture of the bulk of the community at that time and includes those attending a Saturday service (roughly 10% of the membership). Travelling pedlars would attend Saturday and High Holiday services, but they were not included as they were not members of the synagogue. The *Statistical Account* shows whether there was a *mikveh* and the number of paid officials (including a rabbi). These figures are discussed by Roth (1950) and amended by Lipman (1954) and shown in Figure 6.2. London and 32 provincial communities and three others shown on the *1845 Statistical Account* are examined in this study. Not included in this study, although they are included in the survey are Scotland, Ireland, Jersey, and Kingston Jamaica, which at that time also came under the authority of the Chief Rabbi. The 1850 community figures (Figure 6.3) discussed by Lipman are considered by Jewish historians to be as accurate as is possible.

Provinces	Size of community	Provinces	Size of community
Bath	50	Merthyr Tydfil	50-100
Bedford*	25	Newcastle	100
Birmingham	800	Norwich	75
Brighton	150	North Shields*	50
Bristol	300	Nottingham	50
Cambridge*	25	Oxford	50
Canterbury	100	Penzance	75
Cardiff	50-100	Plymouth	200-250
Chatham	200	Portsmouth	c.300
Cheltenham	75	Ramsgate	45
Coventry	50-100	Sheerness	75
Dover	50-100	Sheffield	50-60
Dudley*	50-100	Southampton	100-150
Exeter	175	Sunderland	150
Falmouth	150	Swansea	100-150
Gloucester	with Cheltenham	Tynemouth*	50-100
Hull	200	Wolverhampton*	50-100
Ipswich	50	Yarmouth Great	75

King's Lynn	25-50	Dublin*	150-200
Leeds	100	Edinburgh*	100-150
Liverpool	c.2,500	Glasgow*	100-150
Manchester	2,000		
*not discussed		**Total Provinces**	**15,000**
		London	**18,000-20,000**
		Total Gt. Britain	**c.35,000**

Figure 6.3 estimated size of Jewish community c.1850 (Lipman 1954).

ESTIMATED JEWISH COMMUNITY DISTRIBUTION c.1810
(Total c.20,000 adults, including Scotland and Ireland)

- London c.14,000
- Birmingham c.500
- Portsmouth c.500
- Liverpool c.400
- Bristol c.150
- Plymouth c.150
- Manchester c.150
- Others c.4,000 (23 Communities with 100 or less)

ESTIMATED JEWISH COMMUNITY DISTRIBUTION 1850
(Total c.35,000 adults, including Scotland and Ireland)

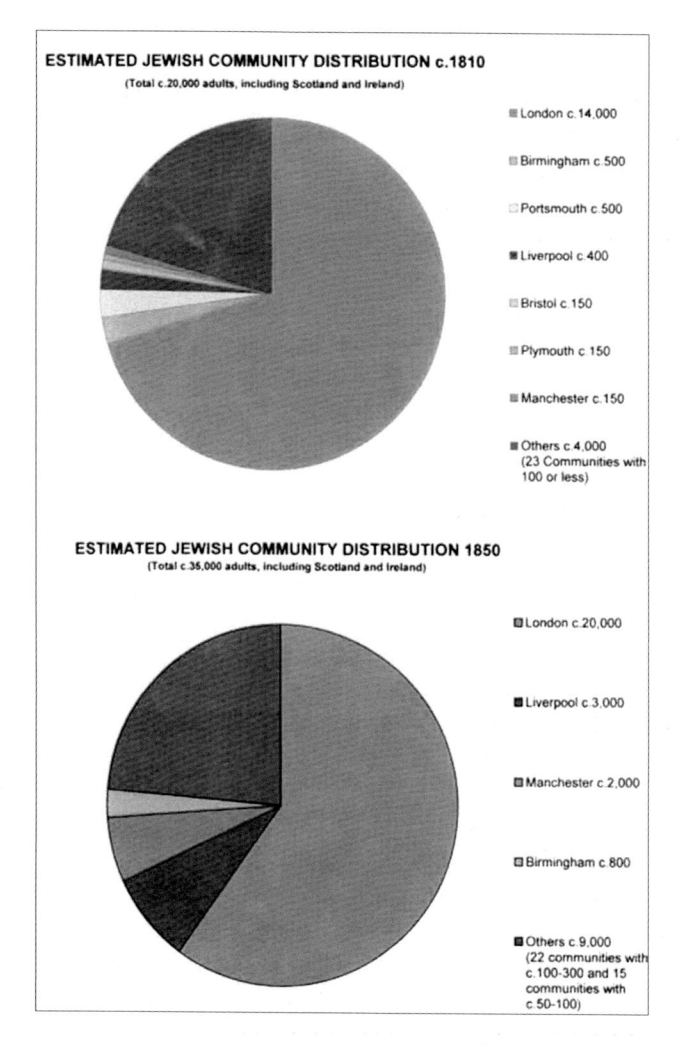

- London c.20,000
- Liverpool c.3,000
- Manchester c.2,000
- Birmingham c.800
- Others c.9,000 (22 communities with c.100-300 and 15 communities with c.50-100)

Figure 6.4 estimated Jewish community distribution c.1810 and 1850.

ESTIMATED JEWISH COMMUNITY DISTRIBUTION 1880
(Total c.60,000 adults, including Scotland and Ireland)

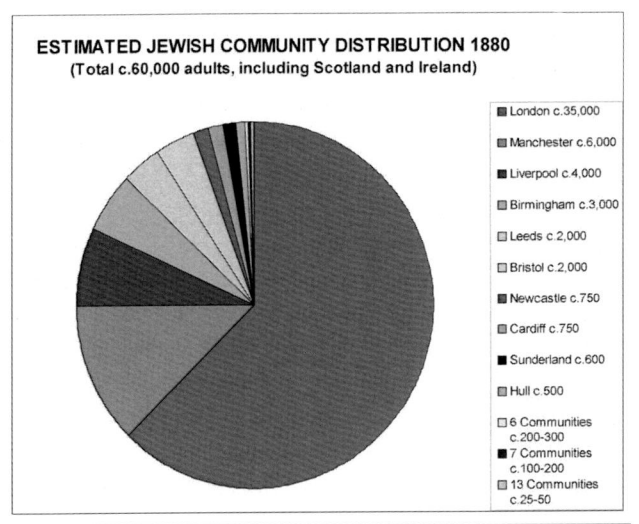

- London c.35,000
- Manchester c.6,000
- Liverpool c.4,000
- Birmingham c.3,000
- Leeds c.2,000
- Bristol c.2,000
- Newcastle c.750
- Cardiff c.750
- Sunderland c.600
- Hull c.500
- 6 Communities c.200-300
- 7 Communities c.100-200
- 13 Communities c.25-50

Total Jewish Community in Britain post 1880	
1881	100, 000 (London 47, 000)
1914	300, 000 (London 180, 000)
1947	400, 000 (London 260, 000)
2007	270, 000 (London 195, 000)

Figure 6.5 Etimated Jewish community distribution 1880 and community size 19th / 21st centuries

6.1 London: growth, topography and migration

According to Gutwirth (1979, 136) 'we know from the census list of 1695, that by that date there were c.600 Jews in East End parishes'. Lipman (1954, 11) states that '…the London Jewish community at the start of the 18th century was c.850 persons. By the end of the century it had increased to c.11, 000 and by 1850 was c.20, 000. Almost all lived east of The City of London. Endelman states that '…the east of London and East End where around 60%-70% settled, was an area where they could join fellow Yiddish-speaking Jews; the language used in Central and Eastern Europe, where they mostly came from' (Ibid, 81). The East End is traditionally an area of poor immigrant settlement starting in the 1600s, when the Huguenots were fleeing French persecution; 200 years later it was the major area of settlement of Eastern European Jews fleeing Russian pogroms.

Before discussing the growth, migration and topography of the London community, it is helpful to understand where the majority of Jews lived prior to mass immigration to England in 1881. Where exactly was the area known as the 'East End'? Kalman (1981, 3) states 'The East End of London is not really a geographical concept; there is no such borough, postal district or telephone exchange, nor will you find it on any Ordnance Survey Maps'. Certainly, it begins to the east of The City of London, with its southern border being the Thames, but how far did it extend to the north and where did it end to the east? According to Lipman (1981, 17) 'the topographical connotation of the term changed as London expanded'. To the east of the city, there was a concentration of Jews in the wards of Aldgate and Portsoken (Ibid, 18). According to Lipman, 'by about 1850, two-thirds of London Jewish population lived in these two parishes' (Ibid, 26). This area changed as London expanded, as did areas of Jewish settlement.

Although Jews could not trade within the City walls, there was nothing to stop them trading outside. According to Roth (1933, 17) '….retail there (in the City) was restricted to Freemen: and the Freedom of The City of London was jealously reserved for Protestants'. This resulted in Whitechapel becoming the heart of the Jewish community in the mid-19th century. Lipman shows changes in Jewish population that formed the 'Jewish East End' (1954, 94). Whilst the figures are small they give an indication of migration out of the City. The City of London in 1840 included a considerable residential area but this migration, not only of Jews, initiated the decline of the City as a residential area. The three remaining congregations weakened, leaving the elderly and poor, who could not afford to move. The movement of the Jewish population from the City left the three largest Ashkenazi synagogues (The Great, Hambro, The New) with less members as they were no longer within walking distance of their homes. As the City declined as a residential area, Jewish settlement in the East End expanded. Jews settled in clusters for religious and social reasons.

Year	City of London	Stepney	Bethnal Green	Bow
1841	129	224	74	5
1851	128	239	90	75
1861	112	237	10	12
1871	76	275	130	26
1881	51	263	127	37
1931	11	225	108	37

Figure 6.6 Extract from 1841-1931 censuses showing decline of The City of London as Jewish residential area.

Although not representative of the entire Jewish community, as religion and religious affiliation was not shown on census forms, Figure 6.6 from censuses taken every ten years were based on individuals with Jewish-sounding names and addresses of members of synagogues. They show, by 1881, the decline and virtual elimination of the City as a Jewish residential area. Roth (1956, 226) quotes Picciotto in his *Sketches of Anglo-Jewish History* (1932):

> '…the city Synagogues having flourished, and their congregations having grown larger and richer, it was found advisable for many Jews in trade to dwell beyond the boundaries of the City; principally in those districts where the rich, the idle and the fashionable meet and lounge and flirt together'.

From the first quarter of the 19th century, there was movement of some 'middle-class' Jews to the West End of London. This started a division in the London community between immigrants and those living in the east and East End, whose natural and first language was Yiddish, and those now living in the West End, where English became their first language. Endelman (2002, 94) states that 'starting in c.1800, wealthy Sephardim started to move out of the east of London and its adjacent streets to Kennington, Islington, Bloomsbury, Kensington and Belgravia'. With increasing prosperity and the rise of the middle class Ashkenazi Jews in the period 1825-1850 saw the start of a steady but persistent migration from the overcrowded east and 'East End' of London to more congenial and prosperous centres, such as Bloomsbury, Westminster, the Strand, and Pall Mall (Lipman 1954,14). From c.1825 wealthy Ashkenazim, such as Nathan Rothschild (1777-1836), moved to Piccadilly and Sir Moses Montefiore (1784-1885) relocated to Green Street (off Park Lane), then to Park Lane itself, and Isaac Goldsmith (1778-1859) moved to Regents Park (Endelman 2002, 94). From the 1830s and 1840s 'well-to-do families moved northward to Finsbury Square and Finsbury Circus and westward to Bloomsbury and Marylebone' (Ibid, 94). From the 1831 census, Jewish-sounding names and obvious names such as Cohen and Levy indicated where London Jews were living. The main axis of transport ran westwards from and to the City. Bloomsbury, near the British Museum, became a residential area, with new synagogues established such as the first Reform West London synagogue WC1 (c.1842) (4.1.12) and the Orthodox Ashkenazi synagogue established in Great Portland Street W1 (1855) (4.1.3). These residential districts were for the 'upper-and-upper middle class'.

Parallel to the move to west of London, Jews settled in Islington. According to Lipman (1962/1967, 85), Jewish-sounding names living in this area can be identified from the 1848 Post Office Court Directory. Renton (2000, 24) states that '….migration from the City began in the middle of the 19th century aided by the development of horse buses and subsequently by trains'. He continues that from this date, the 'lower-middle class' and less affluent started to move to Stepney and Bethnal Green and Bow to the north-east, and the 'lower-middle class' to Hackney and Dalston to the north (Figure 6.7). The 1851 census shows that 'around Gower Street WC1, the area supported Jewish butchers, publishers and University College and its School, attracted Jewish students who lived in Jewish boarding houses' (Ibid, 24). The 1860s/1870s saw well–to-do families moving further west to the Bayswater area, north of Hyde Park and Kensington (Ibid, 25). An Orthodox Ashkenazi synagogue was established in Bayswater W2 in 1863 (4.1.1). From 1870/1880 middle-class families who wanted to move out of the east of London moved northwards to Cannonbury, Highbury, St. John's Wood, Maida Vale and West Hampstead.

Jews and Christians moved out of the east of London as their statuses improved in the social hierarchy. Even when they moved, Jews still clustered together. In the 1860s and 1870s, there was further movement of the wealthier to the west, to Bayswater, north of Hyde Park and Kensington, followed by St. John's Wood, Maida Vale and West Hampstead (Endelman 2002, 96). This migration led to the middle-class Jewish community comprising a smaller percentage of the population where they had newly settled, which lead to a cultural change, Most Jewish children had previously attended Jewish schools but now these were not always available in the new areas of settlement. By attending a non-Jewish school, their religious education was confined to classes at synagogues. Endelman (2002, 99) states that:

> *'The spread of secondary education reinforced the Englishness of English Jews, even those educated in all–Jewish schools. It exposed them to early and mid-Victorian middle class values and to think of themselves as 'English', as well as Jewish, as rooted in the life of the country, rather than tossed onto its shores by circumstance'.*

6.1.1 London: Jewish suburbia

London's Jewish suburbia dates from the 1830s or 1840s. Moving to the suburbs, 'introduced into the social structure a new class, the 'suburbians' (Lipman 1954, 81). The evidence for a move out of the City and the east of London can be found in census returns, synagogue membership, marriage registers and burial records. Wealthy Jews, a small minority of the London community, had country houses and mansions in 'villages' within easy reach of London, such as in Isleworth, Mortlake, Richmond, Roehampton and Teddington. Jews also settled in the north-west, in Highgate, Stanmore and Watford, and the north-east in Stamford Hill and Stoke Newington (Ibid, 80), convenient for working in the City.

According to Endelman (2002, 79) 'by the early/middle 19th century the Jewish middle class were largely English born. They dressed and became more 'English' and wanted to assimilate into their environment'. The movement of the middle-classes of all religions to the suburbs changed London, where by the end of the 19th century the population had risen from 4 million to 6.5 million' (Ibid, 130). At that time the residential expansion was lateral as most people lived in houses rather than apartment blocks. Lipman (1962/7, 81) reports that, 'London's population increased by 20% or more every decade from 1830'. With the extension of the underground, it was not until the 20th century that new areas of Jewish settlement were established in Golders Green, Hampstead, Edgware and Finchley. Upon migrating out of east London, the younger generations of the Jewish 'lower-middle and middle class' did not want to become pedlars or work in so called 'sweat shops of the East End' (Endelman 2002, 143).The number of Jews living in the 'East End' still did not decline from c.1880 onwards, as there was a mass influx of new, mainly poor, immigrants. Between 1880 and 1881, the community in Britain nearly doubled in size from c.60, 000 to c.100, 000, more than half of whom lived in the east of London. 1880 marked the beginning of a new era for Anglo-Jewry; the majority of the community had attained political emancipation and was largely English born or had been living in England for several years. This enabled the communities to support their poor and to absorb newcomers.

6.1.1.2 London: synagogue membership, growth of working-class suburbs and patterns of settlement

From 1870-1880s and the development of railways and horse tramways, working-class suburbs developed north of the Thames. Lipman (1962/7, 90), states 'With these new and regular forms of transport, it was now possible to commute to work in the East End from areas such as Edmonton, Tottenham, Walthamstow, East and West Ham'. New communities were established in these 'suburbs' but were mostly post-1880. Settlement south of the Thames was scattered, with the first synagogue established in Stockwell in 1875, which closed through lack of members in 1877 (Ibid, 91). New synagogues south of the Thames were not re-established until the early 20th-century.

Tracing this pattern of settlement and topography for the majority of Jews outside the East End starting in the 1860s shows that it tended to be to move outwards with easy access to the City and East London, where most people worked or had businesses. It was easier to move home, rather than offices, factories or shops. In the mid-to-late 19th century, the London Jewish middle classes tended to rely on public transport. They spread in clusters, as evidenced by the establishment of new synagogues and the availability of horse-buses, then trains, followed by the underground network. The evidence of changes in London's Jewish urban topography has not provided archaeological evidence. The Bayswater Ashkenazi Synagogue, a branch synagogue of the Great was founded at this time (1863) (4.1.1). As new communities were established, synagogues were opened, and redundant synagogues closed; these buildings were put to other uses or destroyed. Religious artefacts, such as silver ornaments for the *Torah* scrolls (the five Books of Moses), were moved from redundant synagogue to the new. Surplus artefacts were sold to collectors or museums in order to raise funds to support the poor and upkeep of the cemeteries. Few London Jewish artefacts have been excavated in the City of London; these are discussed (4.4.2). They can be identified from their Hebrew inscriptions. From 1850/1, by taking records of membership of the synagogues both in London and the provinces, which show births, marriages and deaths, combining this with Jewish names on the 1851 census and historical narratives from Roth, Lipman, Endelman and provincial historians, it is possible to arrive at a reasonably accurate number of the Jewish population in London.

London: Jewish Population in 1850 (from synagogue membership lists)

Bevis Marks	3,000
Great	2,500
Hambro	1,000
Maiden Lane	500
Market Street, Southwark and Borough	300-400
New	2,000
Western	1,000
West London	500

Figure 6.7 total of the membership of these eight London Synagogues in 1850 c.11, 500 (Lipman 1954, 185).

The estimated size of the total Jewish population in London arrived at by the Chief Rabbi's Office as a result of the statistical inquiries in 1851 was c.18, 000.

6.1.1.3 *London: cemeteries*

Synagogues with their burial societies are a major source of topographical evidence. Burial records indicate where the deceased lived and when they died. Some burial grounds have no detailed area or plot plans, having been lost or destroyed. Locations of cemeteries are shown in the gazetteer on first/second edition Ordnance Survey Maps, mostly dated 1888-1901. From the middle 19th century, new cemeteries were established in the east, north and north-east of London and Fulham. In a number of cases, there is evidence (such as in West Ham and Brentwood) of re-interments from closed cemeteries. Later tombstone burial dates indicate that families reserved burial places in closed cemeteries to be alongside their deceased forebears (personal observation 2009). Individual London cemeteries and the Brentwood cemetery in Essex, connected with London through re-interment are discussed (5.1).

For present-day researchers of old Jewish cemeteries, there are several problems. For most of these older cemeteries, no plot plans exists that show the position of individual graves linked to the burial register if the register still exists. Also, over two or three centuries, acid rain and weathering have taken their toll on the headstones, with most early inscriptions no longer legible. As has been shown, many headstones are broken and not replaced. The only 18th/19th century headstones that can be read are those of granite, marble or slate. In a few cases, metal plates with details of the deceased have been attached to the head stone. In Sephardi cemeteries and Sephardi burials in Ashkenazi cemeteries, such as in the Reform Cemetery in Balls Pond Road N1, tombstones laid flat, (unless made of granite) are completely illegible. Poor Ashkenazim, could not afford headstones, and in many cases, particularly children's graves are marked only by ground-level border stones with no names and dates or nothing (personal observation 2009).

Two cemeteries in and near London have re-interred remains, Hoxton Cemetery N1 (in use 1798-1878) are now in West Ham E15, all their records have been lost. The original land sold for development (5.1.9) (Figure 5.2.4). Re-interment areas in West Ham are marked with inscribed stones. There are no individual markers. In Brentwood Sephardi Cemetery CM14 (5.1.3), according to the Spanish and Portuguese Burial Society who keep the burial register, there are some 7, 500 burials from the Georgian (1733) Mile End Nuevo Cemetery, E1. (discussed 5.1.2). These were re-interred in 1974 when the Sephardi community sold off part of the land. There are no individual tombstones (personal observation 2010). During the Blitz in 1941 a number of cemeteries such as Bancroft Road E1, were damaged and partly destroyed, and there is still evidence of this destruction (personal observation 2009).

6.2 Provinces: growth, topography and migration

6.2.1 Provinces: the early communities

There can be no precise dates for when provincial communities were established. Roth (1950, 16) states 'In a broadsheet of 1689, *The Case of the Jews*, it was specifically stated that there was no Jewish settlement in the country outside the capital at this date'. The statement is repeated in *Anglia Judaica* by D'Blossiers Tovey; recognised as the earliest Anglo-Jewish historian in *A History of the Jews* in *England* (1738). It is not until the late 1730s and 1740s, that small provincial communities were established. During the 1730/60s, 12 provincial communities were founded, the earliest being Portsmouth (1730s), closely followed by Birmingham (1730s). It is generally accepted by Jewish historians that Portsmouth was established before Birmingham, followed by Falmouth (1740), Ipswich (1741), Kings Lynn (1747), Chatham (c.1750), Liverpool (c.1750), Plymouth (1752), Bristol (1753), Canterbury (1760), Exeter (1763) and Swansea (1768) (Roth 1950, 110/111). By 1800 there were 21 communities. By the accession of Queen Victoria in 1837, there were around 31 communities in Britain, of which 17 were in sea ports and several in market towns such as Canterbury, Gloucester and Norwich. Roth writes that '…in 1837 around 10 towns had communities of less than 50 people' (1950, 24). In the 19th century, the manufacturing centres such as Leeds, Manchester, Newcastle and Nottingham became important as Jewish centres. Communities were also established in resort towns such as Bath and Cheltenham.

Pearce (2000, 235) notes that:

> '…by the end of the 19th century some of the early communities such as Falmouth and Penzance no longer existed, as these port towns no longer benefited from the considerable trade arising from supplying the English Fleet during the Napoleonic Wars. For example, in Penzance, Lemon Hart (1768-1845), the first president and one of the founders of the Penzance Synagogue (1808) had been appointed a victualler supplying rum to the Royal Navy'.

Roth (1950, 15-26) observes that 'From c.1818 the majority of provincial Jews lived in 25 communities, although Jewish pedlars were to be found in every part of the country, many of them setting up shops in towns such as Hull (1810), North Shields (1818), Chester (1820), Preston (1821), Doncaster (1825), Hanley (1825), Newcastle under Lyme (1830), Sheffield (1838) and Leeds (1840/1850)'. By 1837, the number of communities outside London had grown to around 40. It is within London and cities such as Birmingham, Bristol, Leeds, Liverpool, Manchester and Newcastle that a dynamic movement of the community is evident. There were small clusters of Jews in the South West, (Devon and Cornwall), South Wales, and the North East,. These are also relevant, although the topography of provincial towns is only discussed in larger centres. Not discussed are towns where there was a community of less than 50, before the mass immigration starting in 1881.

6.2.2.1 Birmingham

The history of Birmingham's community is contained in two volumes edited by Zoe Josephs *Birmingham Jewry 1749-1914'* (1980) and *Birmingham Jewry more aspects 1740-1930 (1984)*. Minutes of the Birmingham Hebrew Congregation, one of the oldest in the provinces, only date back to 1832. *The Statistical Account of the Congregations in the British Empire 1845 (5606)* (Figure 6.2) shows that Birmingham had a Jewish community of c.679. In 1845 only Liverpool was larger.

A descendent of a Mr. M. Stern who lived in Birmingham at that time and quoted by Levine (1956, 4) states:

> *...the whole town reeked of oil and smoke and sweat and drunkenness... but it had its other attractions, a stranger might commence a sort of business with the goods produced in the place, even with a small capital, whether as a shopkeeper or hawker. Dissenters, Quakers, heretics of all sorts were welcomed and undisturbed as far as religious observances were concerned.*

Birmingham in the mid-19th century attracted Jewish immigrants from Poland and Germany. Pedlars and hawkers used Birmingham as a centre for restocking their wares when they returned from selling their goods in Midland small towns and villages (Chesses, 2003, 1).

The first recorded synagogue was erected as early as 1780 with the garden used as a place for burials. in a district known as the 'Froggery' (Ibid,10). Jews lived in streets and courts between Holloway Road and the Bull Ring, which was in this low-lying swampy area, to be swept away in 1845 by the building of New Street Station (Josephs 1980, 10). The Froggery, which was aptly named, was known to have artesian wells, which settlers would have used to supply fresh water to the *mikveh* (personal contact Rabbi Arkush, Birmingham). Meetings for prayers were also held in private residences. By the early 19th century, many Jews had moved out the Froggery, up hill to the Severn Street area where the streets around Hurst Street and Inge Street housed the largest Jewish settlement. A new synagogue, in a private house was established in Hurst Street in 1791, followed in 1809 by a synagogue in Severn Street itself (Ibid, 4) it is now a Masonic Hall. The Froggery was demolished in the mid-19th century to make way for New Street Station (1846-1854).

The present synagogue in Singer's Hill (4.2.2), around the corner from Severn Street, was consecrated in 1856 and accommodates c.1, 000 seat holders (personal observation 2010). Severn Street and Singer's Hill Synagogue were within walking distance of the crowded back-to-back streets and courts in the Hurst Street and Inge Streets areas, where there were Jews and, immigrants from other counties including Ireland. By 1875 no less than 45 per cent of Birmingham's 170, 000 people lived in back-to-back houses in 20, 000 courts (National Trust 2004, 3). These houses sometimes contained small workshops, producing items such as metalware, jewellery, slippers, boots and cigars. Back-to-back houses had two or three rooms, lit by candles with no running water and toilets that were outside in the courtyards. In the courts, 12 or more houses faced onto a tiny yard; in the low-lying areas were often pools of stagnant filth (Josephs 1980, 12).

Community records, censuses and histories of the back-to backs, identify actual houses where Jews were living. For example, in '1851 the Levy family and their four children lived in Court 15 and it is likely that he used part of the house as his workshop' (National Trust 2004, 19). Settlement around Inge Street, Hurst Street and Thorpe Street is described by Josephs (1980, 11) as 'The heart of the Jewish quarter' Here, the immigrants set up their own small prayer halls known a *'steibels'*, where they could pray and meet with fellow Jews. Even though there were no ghettos, they clung to their previous way of life. Many could not speak English, learning instead from their children who went to local schools.

By the middle of the 19th century, there were some prosperous Jewish merchants, acting as importers from the Far East, jewellers, tailors and prominent members of Birmingham's City philanthropic organisations (Levine 1956, 9/10). The 1871 census shows that by this date, Jewish homes were moving uphill to the area around Singers Hill Synagogue, on the edge of Edgbaston; this was the fashionable suburb of Birmingham. The move to Edgbaston demonstrates the increase in wealth of some of the community.

From 1871, the community became more scattered. The 1871 census, which includes occupations, shows that out of 1, 000 persons listed as jewellers nearly 10% were Jews, although Jews numbered less than 1% of the total population at that time (Ibid, 3). From 1858 the Birmingham community flourished, even with the influx of poor immigrants from 1880/1. In the late 19th century many immigrants, mainly from Germany and Russia, were not comfortable in the 'cathedral' synagogue in Singers Hill, as the form of service was unfamiliar to them (Ibid, 1). This situation eventually led to the creation of two new Orthodox synagogues, the Central and the New. There were also a number of *stiebls* (small prayer rooms), although these are not discussed. In summary, from the addresses of synagogue members, charitable donations, burial lists and the censuses of 1841-1871, it is possible to trace the topography of Birmingham's Jewish community from its establishment in the early–mid 18th century to end of the 19th century.

6.2.2.2 Bradford

The first mention of Jews in Bradford is c.1823. There are records of a travelling salesman named Jacobs who sold jewellery; among his customers was the Earl of Harewood (Grizzard 2008, 1). From the 1820s Jews settled in Bradford, a community established before Leeds (1840/1850). Bradford was a small community in the period under discussion, but it was different from any other community at the time. Jews who came to Bradford from 1820/1830 were middle-class educated merchants from Germany. Rather than fleeing persecution, they came to Bradford as it developed into the wool capital of the world. In the 1870s the Jewish population numbered between 200-300 persons. In the 1880s it grew to 100 families (c.400-500 persons) (Ibid, 3). They were not Orthodox but were successful middle-class traders and educated Reform Jews, products of the German Jewish Enlightenment, who saw themselves as both German and Jewish (Ibid, 1). The first synagogue in Bradford was Reform (4.2.3); their services included prayers in English, unacceptable to the Orthodox who travelled to Leeds to attend High Holiday services. The Reform Synagogue in Bradford was the only synagogue established specifically for German Jews. From 1881, poor, mainly Orthodox, Russian immigrants settled in the town. At first they attended the Bowland Street Synagogue, before opening their own building in 1906. This building is now a *Madrassa* (Islamic school) (personal contact 2010). The Orthodox synagogue was closed in 2012.

6.2.2.3 Brighton and Hove

The Brighton community was founded c.1800 and is discussed in 4.2.4, by the later 20th century it was the fifth-largest provincial community after Birmingham, Glasgow, Liverpool and Manchester. The foundations for this growth were set in the 19th century. According to Spector (1968/9, 43), 'coach traffic increased between London and Brighton with as many as 60 coaches a day'. Brighton became a fashionable seaside resort and watering place, convenient and popular for Londoners, and the beach pedlars and hawkers were mainly Jewish (Ibid, 50). Middle Street Synagogue had several rich and philanthropic members, such as the Goldsmids, Montefiores, Rothschilds and Sassoons. This is one reason why Brighton and Hove has more streets named after prominent Jews than any other city in Britain (Ibid, 50). These are shown in 4.3.2 and in the gazetteer.

6.2.2.4 Bristol

There are two histories of the Bristol Jewish community, *Jews in Bristol,* (Samuel, 2007) and *The Jews of Bristol and Liverpool 1750-1850: Port Communities in the Shadow of Slavery,* (Cesarani, 2006). Previously Alex Schlesinger, a Bristol resident, had written a brief summary of Bristol's Jewish history in the '*Save our Shul*' (Synagogue) (unpublished brochure 1971). In the 18th century, Bristol was Britain's second-largest city, trading with the West Indies in slaves, tobacco and sugar; these were exchanged for goods produced in Bristol such as glass and porcelain. Whilst there is no evidence that Jews were directly involved in the slave trade, Jewish traders would have benefited from it, as would have all traders in the city. Shipbuilding and coal mining were also important Bristol industries, while the Jews were small traders mostly selling clothes, jewellery and clocks (Samuel 2007, 50).

The foundation of the Bristol synagogue and burial ground in 1753 (Roth 1950, 110), indicates acceptance by the wider community, even though in that year, The Society of Merchant Venturers petitioned Parliament for the repeal of the Act for the Naturalization of the Jews.

6.2.2.5 Hull

The history of Hull's community was written by Judge Israel Finestein (1996/8) in *The Jews in Hull, between 1766 and 1880*, as well in a paper by Lewis, D. (2002), *Hull's Six Jewish Cemeteries*. These are invaluable works and form the basis for research into the Hull community. Hull was never a major Jewish centre, but it is significant in the study of the topography of Anglo-Jewry.

Hull was the second-largest port after London for Jewish immigration from 1850-1915. During this period, 2.2 million immigrants, mostly from Eastern Europe, passed through the port and railway station, of which according to Lewis c.500, 000 were Jewish (personal contact 2010). A plaque in Hull station commemorates this immigration (Figure 6.8), the immigration hall still stands (Figure 6.10). The community grew from c.40 persons in 1793 to c.200 in 1835 (Finestein 1996/8, 34).

Figure 6.8 Hull: plaque in Hull Station commemorating immigration of 2.2 million people through the station 1850-1914 (photograph K. Marks 2010)

Figure 6.9 Hull: immigration hall 1850-1914, (photograph K.Marks 2010).

*Figure 6.10 Hamburg, immigrants waiting clearance to go to Hull?
(c.1900) (By permission archives D. Lewis).*

Figure 6.10 shows Jews in front of immigration officials in Hamburg, possibly to sail to Hull (c.1900). Boats from Europe were sailing to England nearly every day and there was intense price competition between sailing companies. According to Finestein '….it was some times cheaper to sail to Hull and Grimsby then take the train on to Liverpool, than to make the journey direct from European ports to America (Ibid, 35). The vast majority of immigrants were in transit on to America, Canada and South Africa. Some immigrants stayed in Hull for a few days until the authorities were satisfied they had sufficient funds to continue their journeys. As a result, there were at least three *kosher* hotels or lodging houses near to the arrival area (personal contact Lewis 2010). A few stayed in Hull where, according to Finestein, the community between 1850 and 1880 doubled in size from c.300 to 500-600 (Ibid, 34).

Hull was the largest port in the north-east of England and also a market town. According to Finestein (1996/8 33) '….it was an important outlet to the Baltic and elsewhere for the manufactured products of the Midlands and North and attracted Jewish itinerant pedlars to the city'. In 1780 the first cemetery was acquired in Villa Place (5.2.15). The first synagogue, in Postern Gate was in a poor district, near to the harbour and also near to Market Place which was to become the centre of the community. Two later synagogues have been discussed in 4.2.15. Traders are listed in the local directory as jewellers, watchmakers and pawnbrokers (Ibid, 49). Following the end of the Napoleonic Wars (1815), unlike the ports of the south coast, such as Falmouth and Penzance, the community grew in size. By 1826 more wealthy members of the community had moved out of Market Place towards the suburbs. From the 1830s most of the early immigrants who settled in Hull came from Germany; the later immigrants from the 1870s came mostly from Poland and Russia. In 1840 a railway line was established linking Hull to the main railway lines in England, including London, which resulted in Hull no longer remaining isolated on the north side of the Humber.

6.2.2.6 Leeds

The first mention of individual Jews in Leeds is c.1750, with the foundation of the community in c.1820 (Roth 1950, 111). From later records, it is generally accepted by local historians such as Krausz (1964) that it was established in 1840/1850. The community at that time was small with c.50 persons compared with Birmingham (c.800) and Liverpool (c.3, 000) and was one of the last Jewish communities to be established in the mid-19th century. Today, Leeds is the second largest communities in the provinces after Manchester, with approximately 7,000 Jews; at its peak in the 1930s it was c.20, 000 (personal contact M. Sender).

The first cemetery was acquired in 1840 in Gelderd Road. Before 1840, Jews who died in Leeds were buried in Hull (Hull burial records). The community saw little growth until about 1870, jumping to 2, 000 members by 1880/1 (Krausz, 1964, 5). From 1851 onwards, most of the Jewish immigrants settled in the district know as the Leylands (Figure 6.11), which extended from Regent Street on the East to North Street on the West and from Byron Street to the north to Lady Lane in the south. This district, about 50 acres in extent, was a slum area containing back-to-back houses in narrow cobbled streets and yards (Ibid, 21). According to Vaughan (2001, 2), 'The Leylands was specially segregated from the city and historical evidence shows that up to the 1860s Irish immigrants had settled this district, but by the time this became a Jewish area, the main core of Irish immigrants had moved elsewhere'. Many new immigrants were tailors attracted by the city's growing men's clothing industry (Freedman 1992, 3). From c.1880, Leeds became, after London, the centre of men's clothing production, employing most of the community. In the

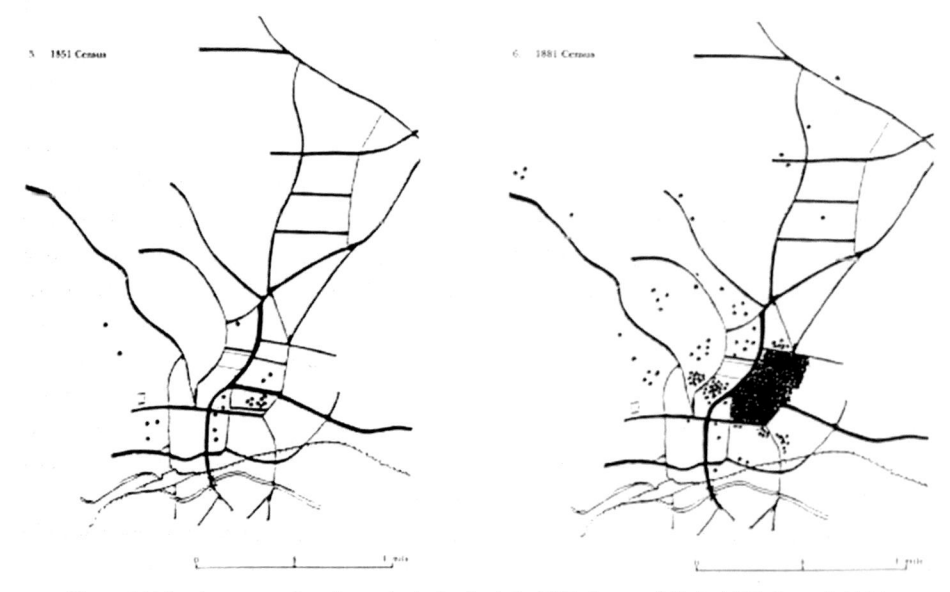

Figure 6.11 Leeds: pattern of settlement in the Leylands in 1851 Census (left); in 1881 Census* (right)
*Each dot on these maps represents a Jewish family (Freedman 1992, 2)

early 20th century, Leeds was to become only second in importance to the East End of London as a centre of the Jewish 'rag' trade. Described by Krausz (1963, 21) as a 'Ghetto' this is the only example of a 19th-century cluster of Jews being described in this way. According to Vaughan (1963, 21), 'The reason being that by 1881 the Leylands Jewish inhabitants as a percentage of the total Leylands population was 33% rising by 1891 to 59% with a community of over 5, 000'. One or two schools in the Leylands had nearly 90% Jewish children (personal contact 2010). The exodus from the Leylands started in 1907, when Jews were already moving towards Chapeltown. The community then spread further the north out of the City toward Chapel Allerton and Moortown. The only 19th-century physical evidence of the Jewish presence in Leeds is two cemeteries.

In summary, the topographical history of the Leeds community begins towards the end of the period under discussion. The better off moved out to the city suburbs, followed later by the remainder: slum clearance from 1930s saw the demolition of the Leylands.

6.2.2.7 Liverpool

The history of Liverpool's Anglo-Jewry has been comprehensively written by two authors, Benas in his *Records of the Jews in Liverpool* (1899) and Bill Williams in his *Liverpool Jewry a Pictorial History* (1987). By the middle-19th-century Liverpool had the largest and most influential community in the provinces (Benas 1899, 1). According to synagogue records, the growth, movement and increased prosperity of some of the community indicates that the early immigrants started to move out of the poor dock area to more prosperous areas of the city and then into the suburbs (personal contact 2010).

The Princes Road Synagogue in Toxteth (4.92) was opened in 1872. This synagogue is described by Kadish (2006, 135) as 'The most lavish High Victorian 'orientalist' synagogue in England, a jewel in the crown of Europe's 'Capital of Culture 2008' is discussed in 4.2.19. She also describes Princes Road as a 'fashionable tree-lined boulevard in the up-and coming Toxteth district' (Ibid, 135). Along Princes Road, grand churches and halls of worship were built in mid-19th century for Liverpool's new prosperous middle classes. Many early settlers in Liverpool intended to immigrate to the New World, but did not have the financial resources to make the journey (Ibid, 48). Of those who remained, many were poor. Wolfman (1987, 35) states that '… many of the Jews made their living from supplying the trade that flowed through the port'. Some became agents for collecting prize money, used this as collateral to lend money to sailors who were irregularly paid'. From these businesses banking and overseas trade developed.

Williams (1987, 1) states '…leading Jewish families emerged who were not only involved with the Jewish community but who also forged links with the wider non-Jewish society'. In Liverpool, as elsewhere in the provinces, continuing expansion and social diversification led to synagogal division and dispute. Whilst there was still only an Orthodox community these splits were political and social within the community, rather than religious (Ibid, 3). When it came to charitable work, the community was united. The result of these changes in dogma is evident in the location of the city's synagogues, which also served as centres of education and charitable work.

Archaeological evidence of the first synagogue, with its contiguous burial ground and some tombstones, has been noted by B.L. Benas (1899). Excavations between Derby Street, Cumberland Street and Upper Stanley Street at the corner of Whitechapel were conducted by Sir James Picton (1805-1889), an eminent local archaeologist and antiquary, these revealed 'a few tombstones with Hebrew inscriptions' (Ibid, 45). Sir James had intended to preserve them for a local museum, but a workman reused them in a wall. According to Benas, 'they were never found again' (Ibid, 45). Picton also notes that on the south side of Cumberland Street and Upper Stanley Street in the business district, stood a small synagogue, between the town hall and the docks. A *History of Liverpool* (1810) (anonymous) indicates that the building was taken over by a sect of Scottish Presbyterians (Sandemanians or Glassites), and by 1803 it had disappeared.

'In 1775 the congregation left the Upper Stanley Street Synagogue and moved to a small house in Turton Court, by the dock gates on the south side of the Old Dock (now Canning Place)' (Wolfman 1987/88, 38). It moved again in 1778, although why so quickly is not recorded. According to Benas 'The reason may have been that the third synagogue, in a house at 133, Frederick Street fronted a yard which was already being used as a burial ground' (1899, 51). According to Kadish (1996, 150) 'There was a *mikveh* in Frederick Street the first in Liverpool'. By the 1780s/1790s, the community in Frederick Street, with its cemetery and *mikveh,* had all the necessary elements to serve a congregation, which numbered 100 in 1789, increasing to over 400 in 1810 (Williams 1987, 2). Picton (1873, 323) writes 'A few hundred yards above St Thomas's Church on the east side of Frederick Street… there exists, at the back of the houses (Figure 4.85) an old Jewish cemetery, of course no longer used, but still containing monuments of departed worthies of the Hebrew race'. These remains were transferred in 1923 to the Broad Green Cemetery (5.2.19) when Frederick Street was redeveloped. The first book of rules of the Frederick Street congregation indicates the origins of its members. Benas (1899, 52) states 'that the laws were written in a 'Yiddish-Hebrew-Polish-German jargon, suggesting that the writer was probably of Lithuanian or Russian origin'. At the end of the 18th century, there is sufficient information to make it possible to draw up a plan showing where the majority of the Jewish community lived.

The 1790 Liverpool Directory records names and addresses of 19 households and shops as being Jewish. Shopkeepers at that time mainly lived above their premises. Wolfman (1987, 40) writes that 'By the beginning of the 19th century new arrivals were coming to Liverpool, some from the ports of Bristol, Falmouth, Hull Penzance, Plymouth and Yarmouth and other provincial towns'. In 1807 the first purpose-built synagogue was dedicated in Seel Street (Figure 4.86), with room enough to hold the majority of the community. 'This was to be the place of worship of the highly Anglicised highly respectable bourgeoisie of the community for nearly 70 years when the community grew (in 1850) to be the largest in the United Kingdom outside London' (Ibid, 40). In 1872 , when the congregation known as 'Old Hebrew Congregation' moved to Princes Road, Toxteth, Seel Street was sold and the synagogue demolished. Previously in c.1856, secession took place, and a new purpose-built synagogue was opened in Hope Place (Figures 4.88&4.89), less than one mile from the harbour. This community became known as 'Liverpool New Hebrew Congregation'. Hope Place was closed as an Orthodox synagogue in 1935. Vestiges of the arcade of the original porch still exist, as does the façade (personal observation 2009).

Princes Road Synagogue (discussed 4.2.19.2) is the oldest existing community and place of worship for Jews in Liverpool. Arnold Lewis (personal contact 2009) the archivist of the community states '…the anglicized Princes Road community were generally prosperous, cultured, English speaking and relatively lax in their religious practises'.

It is evident from the location of the first synagogues and the names extracted from *Liverpool Directory* of 1790, that most of the early community lived in an area south of Old Dock and east of Salthouse Dock opened in 1753 and Bridge Street and Bromfield Street (Wolfman 1987, 32). This is the area now bounded by Canning Place and Blundell Street. He continues that 'these houses, at first respectable, became in course of time, the lowest haunts of vice and profligacy in connection with seaman frequenting the docks' (Ibid, 32). In the *Commercial Directory* of 1816-17, out of 28 silversmiths, 17 were Jewish (Ibid, 35). By the end of the 19th century small tailoring workshops developed, later producing army uniforms.

Prior to the 1880s, most of Liverpool's community lived within two miles of Princes Road and Hope Place, with new immigrants from Eastern Europe, settling in cheaper housing around Brownlow Hill, Paddington, Crown Street and Islington. Although not a ghetto, the settlement area could be described as 'Liverpool's Jewish Quarter' (Ibid, 33). New immigrants, who were highly observant, shunned the 'cathedral' synagogue in Princes Road. They would have formed their own small communities, praying and meeting fellow–countrymen who spoke Yiddish and were from the same cultural background in Eastern Europe. They would have felt uncomfortable attending services in Princes Road Synagogue as they were poor compared with middle class members who, by the late 19th century, were generally prosperous and English speaking. These meeting places and synagogues for the new immigrants date mostly after 1880.

In summary, the first synagogue in Liverpool was established in Cumberland Street c.1753, followed by moves to Frederick Street (1778), Seel Street (1807), Hope Place (1857) and finally Princes Road (1872). The small *stiebls* (prayer rooms for new immigrants) have not been discussed. From the evidence of closure and then establishment of synagogues, with lists with addresses of synagogue members, charitable lists and census returns it is possible to trace the urban topography of Liverpool's Jewish community in the period under discussion.

6.2.2.8 Manchester

The history of the Manchester's Jewish community has been written by Williams in *The Making of Manchester Jewry 1740-1875* (1976) and *Jewish Manchester an Illustrated History (2008)*. Manchester's Jewish community dates from c.1780 (Roth 1950, 111). This was the time that Manchester was evolving as a centre for production of cotton cloth from yarn shipped in from countries like India, and the export of cotton textiles (Williams 2008, 13). The first area of settlement was in the Old Town, in a circular area of streets inside Miller Street, Shude Hill and Long Millgate (Figure 4.95) (Ibid, 12). This was one of the poorest areas in Manchester, with narrow streets, lanes and courts sharing outside toilets, as the houses had no running water. This was also the market centre that Williams describes as a 'district of low-lying, decaying seventeenth-century property, engulfed and overshadowed by the smoke and clamour of new factories and warehouses' (Ibid, 12). The first synagogue was in a converted warehouse in Ainsworth Court off Long Millgate c.1806 (Figure 4.95). At the beginning of the 19th century, when the total population of the Manchester was over 100, 000, the Jewish community did not exceed 15 families or perhaps 75 persons (Ibid, 16).

Throughout England in this period, there was little growth in the total number of the community as immigration had been held back due to the Napoleonic wars. Trade resumed with Channel ports after the Continental blockade was lifted in 1815. From this date, German-Jewish merchants dealing in cotton cloth and yarn settled in Manchester and exported textiles to Germany and elsewhere (Ibid, 22). Pedlars settled in Manchester, mainly in the Old Town, and opened shops and businesses in areas such as Church Street, Exchange Street and Market Street. By 1815, there were only 25 Jewish families in Manchester or perhaps 150 persons (Ibid, 250). In 1824, as the Manchester community grew with more immigrants, a new and larger synagogue was built in Halliwell Street, still in the Old Town near Victoria Station. The Manchester Synagogue records show that there were members who had shops in nearby towns such as Bury, Bradford and Huddersfield, towns where they were individual traders, but Manchester was their community. According to Williams (1976, 32/33), 'Manchester, in particular, was a market for hawkers, a staging point for transmigrants, a source of commodities for export, a target for criminals, and finally, a place of permanent settlement and trade'.

By 1834, the community had increased in size to around 400. 'At this time there were hundreds of immigrants who stayed for a short time, passing through Manchester on their way to Liverpool and then on to America and Canada' (Ibid, 33). The export of cotton goods and shopkeeping, particularly clothes and jewellery, were the main source of income. In the 1840s, the first Sephardi merchants arrived in Manchester as agents, and from the 1860s opened warehouses in central Manchester. Wealthier members of the community started to move out of the polluted and disease-ridden Old Town. This was the beginning of the Jewish migration to the inner suburbs of north Manchester, Higher Broughton and rural Cheetham Hill.

The 1841 Census shows that the community had grown to over 600, with over 200 still living in the Old Town and over 200 living above their shops and in lodging houses in the central commercial districts of Manchester and Salford (Ibid, 126). Also in 1841 the rail route across the north of England was completed, joining Hull, Manchester, Leeds and Liverpool. The topography of the community was now changing, and although some still settled in the Old Town, the majority settled in a new Jewish area on Red Bank. 'Red Bank was a high sandstone ridge which fell away from the area of middle-class settlement on Cheetham Hill down to the railway in the valley of the Irk' (Ibid, 176). This was again a poor area, with people living in cramped and polluted conditions. Red Bank was within walking distance of the synagogues in the Old Town, but the construction of Victoria Station in 1844 and the demolition of many streets to make way for Corporation Street, led to a deterioration of the area. The centre of the Jewish community moved, leading to a social decline of the slums in Red Bank. The area was demolished in 1938-39.

With the demolition of Halliwell Street, Cheetham Hill Road became the focal point of the middle-class community, with The Great Synagogue established in 1858 (4.2.20), the Reform Synagogue nearby was also established in 1858 (4.2.20.3), and the Spanish and Portuguese in 1874 (4.2.20.4). Williams (2008, 27) states that 'The building of the two new Manchester synagogues in 1858 marked the local communities' 'coming of age, both socially and politically'. In the late 1860s some 20 members of The Great Synagogue had moved to South Manchester. In 1873,

Figure 6.12 Manchester: pattern of settlement 1841 (left); 1861 (right) Each dot represents a Jewish family (Williams 1976, 366/368)

the South Manchester Synagogue was consecrated by the Chief Rabbi with an initial membership of 40 (Ibid, 36). By 1875, the Jewish population in Manchester had reached c.7, 000, with half living and working in the Red Bank slums. As the Reform synagogue was too anglicised and the Sephardi synagogue had a different form of service and pronunciation of Hebrew, the new Yiddish-speaking immigrants formed their own small *chevroth* (small societies) where they could meet, worship, and get financial help if it was needed (Ibid, 271). In the late 19th century, the community spread to Prestwich, South Manchester and South and West Didsbury.

In summary, the urban topography and growth of the Manchester community from the early 1790s to c.1880 can be traced by the location of the cities' synagogues and the 1841-1871 censuses. Maps (1841&1861) (Figure 6.12), based on census data, show clusters of Jews living at first mainly in the Old Town and then spreading to the more congenial suburbs to the north, to Cheetham Hill and Higher Broughton. The 1861 map shows the growth to the north of the city but also a small cluster of Jews living in South Manchester. Most of the original area of Jewish settlement in the 18th century in the centre of Manchester no longer exists. Cemeteries from this period are still in existence but little evidence remains due to neglect, weathering and destruction of tombstones. Manchester now has the largest Jewish community in Britain outside London, with c.35, 000 Jews (over 10% of the total community).

6.2.2.9 North–East England

Of 11 communities in North East England, only two are discussed (Newcastle and Sunderland), as the others were very small (less than 50) or have ceased to exist, with the exception of Gateshead, established in the 1880s, with its ultra-Orthodox *yeshiva* (school for teaching the *Torah* or Pentateuch). The relevant communities are: Newcastle (1830), North Shields (1856), South Shields (1880s), Gateshead (1880s), Sunderland (1768), Durham (1888), Hartlepool (1850's), Middlesbrough (c.1865), Stockton (1884) and Darlington (1884) (Kadish 2006, 183-192). The history of the communities in the North-East has been written by L. Olsover (1981) *The Jewish Communities of North-East England 1755-1980 and A.* Levy (1956) *History of the Sunderland Jewish Community 1755-1955,* which is acknowledged by historians as the most important study of this North-East community.

Newcastle and Sunderland

No records exist of Jews resident in Newcastle before 1830. Both Olsover (1980, 17) and Roth (1950, 111) indicate that the first mention of Jews being in the city goes back to 1775. Mackenzie (1827, 408), stated that: 'There are in Newcastle a few Jews, Universalists and freethinking Christians, but they do not assemble as distinct bodies'. According to Olsover (1980, 173), 'When the first Jewish immigrants came to Newcastle they settled in the poorest part of the city near the River Tyne and not far from Central Railway Station completed in 1850'. The majority of these

Newcastle upon Tyne Jewish Synagogues and Cemeteries (1830-1914)

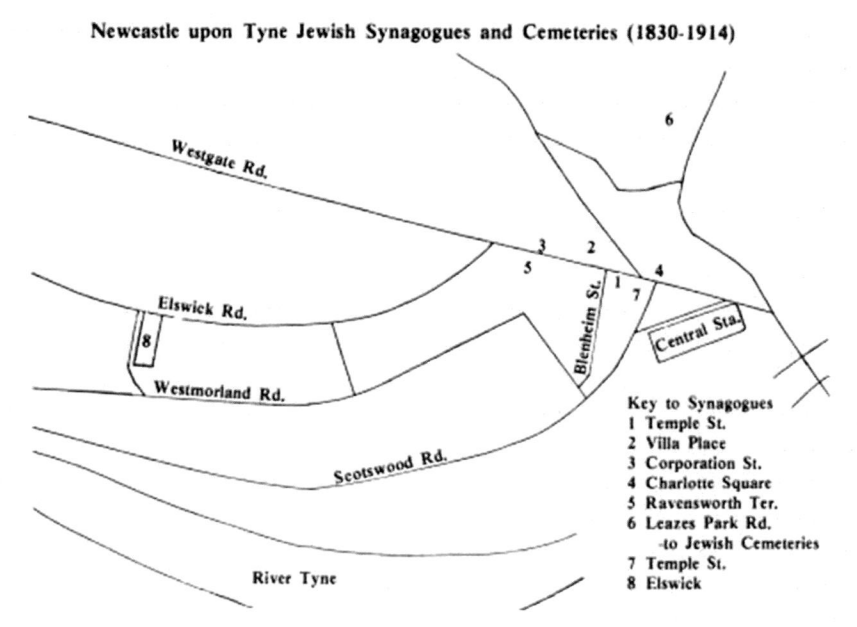

Key to Synagogues
1 Temple St.
2 Villa Place
3 Corporation St.
4 Charlotte Square
5 Ravensworth Ter.
6 Leazes Park Rd.
   -to Jewish Cemeteries
7 Temple St.
8 Elswick

Figure 6.13 Newcastle: synagogues and cemeteries (1813-1914) (Olsover 1980 172). (not to scale)

immigrants settled around Westgate Road, Westmorland Road, Elswick Road and Scotswood Road and adjacent streets. The synagogue was in Temple Street. In 1867, a schism occurred in the community, and a second synagogue was established in Charlotte Square. Figure 6.143 shows the location of these and later synagogues, all in a cluster, a short distance from the Central Railway Station. As the community became more settled and affluent, there was a movement up the hill towards the more desirable area of Jesmond, and then northward towards Rye Hill, Gosforth and Kenton. Leazes Park Synagogue (1879), the successor to Temple Street was still not far from the original Jewish area and became the 'cathedral synagogue' of Newcastle (discussed in 4.2.22.2), This synagogue was closed in 1978 (personal contact 2010).

In 1880 the Newcastle community numbered c.750; at the beginning of the 20th century it numbered c.2, 000 persons peaking at c.3, 500 in the 1940s. The only Orthodox synagogue in Newcastle today is in Gosforth, where the bulk of the remaining community live. Today, the declining community numbers c.500 as it becomes more elderly, with the younger generation moving to London, Manchester and overseas.

The foundation of the Sunderland community dates to 1871, making it the oldest community in the North–East of England (Roth 1950, 111). The first community were merchants from Bohemia who came from Holland; they were joined later in the 18th century by ultra-Orthodox Polish Jews fleeing from persecution via Danzig, where there were frequent direct sailings to England. Tyne and Wear was booming on account of the coal trade (Ibid, 36). According to Roth (1950, 101), the arrival of the 'Polish' Jews who were used to a different form of service than the 'Israelite' first immigrants resulted in a split in the community in 1781, with two centres for prayer, one in Vine Street, the other in a private house near to Bishopswearmouth Cemetery As discussed in 4.2.33, the community numbering 2, 000 in the 1950s now has less than 20 persons (personal contact 2010).

6.2.2.10 Nottingham

The history of Nottingham's Jewish community has been written by local authors Lassman, Spungin and Millett (1944), *in a History of the Jews of Nottingham and* Fisher (1998*) Eight Hundred Years.The Story of Nottingham's Jews.* It is evident from these histories that the community was never more than 1, 000 persons when it peaked in the 1950s, and Fisher (1998, 57) suggests that, it was never more than a few hundred. From c.1822 Jews concentrated round the Chaucer Street area, near the synagogue (Figure 4.112). This area prior to establishment of the synagogue in 1890 had 10 rooms of prayer in private houses and hired halls. The first congregations were mostly pedlars, general dealers, tailors, watchmakers and jewellers (Fisher 1998, 40). These places of worship have been identified by Lassman (1944, 195) (Figure 6.14):

Barker Gate from 1820s, Glasshouse Street* from 1827, Clare Street from c.1826 and 1863, Friar Lane from 1840, Park Street 1849-1857, Broad Street 1855/8-1860, Balloon Court 1860-1863, Beck Lane from1868, Lincoln Street from 1873, Greyfriars Gate 1880-1890, Chaucer Street 1890-1954, first purpose-built synagogue.

Nottingham has been discussed as it is one of the few provincial cities that has a record of where there were 19th century rooms and halls of prayer.

There appear to be discrepancies in the dates quoted by Lassman (1944) and Fisher (1998). Up to 1890, the community was not large enough to be able to afford to build a synagogue. In 1890 there was an influx of immigrants from Russia and Poland, but it was not until after World War II that the community began to scatter,

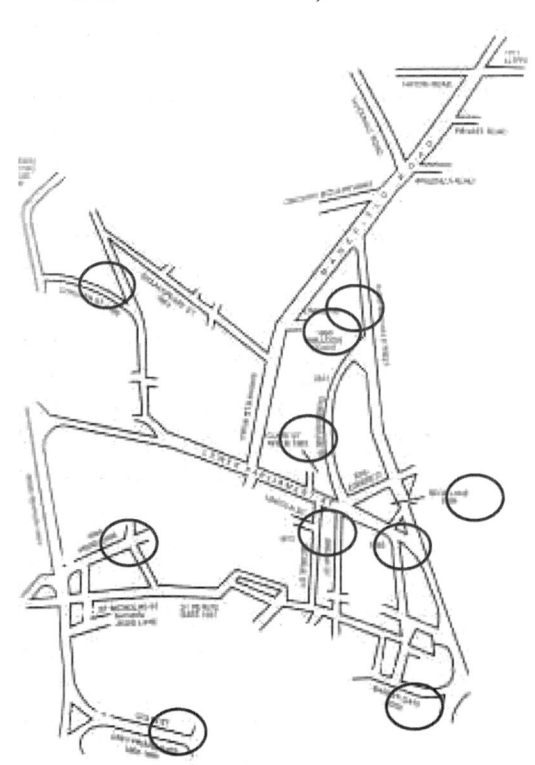

Figure 6.14 Nottingham: places of worship from 1822 (Fisher et al. 1998, 195).

moving away from the Chaucer Street area, which was being redeveloped, to the suburbs of Nottingham, including West Bridgeford, which is two and a half miles south of Nottingham (Ibid, 41). The community was no longer living within walking distance of the synagogue, and had to use transport to get to Shakespeare Villas Synagogue (personal contact, 2009).

6.2.2.11 Oxford

A history of Oxford's community has been written by D. Lewis (1992) in *The Jews of Oxford*. As noted in 4.2.25, the small Oxford community was established in 1841. Initially, Jews were not allowed to live within the 'liberties' of the city and they lived with other non-conformists across the river outside city walls in St. Clements (personal communication Marcus Roberts, 2010). The first cemetery was established in 1894 (discussed 5.2.25). Lewis states 'that even though Oxford was a market town, it had no great draw for Jews' (1992, 1). The city was dominated by the university and only Jews who had converted to Christianity were allowed to teach Hebrew (Ibid, 1). The teaching of Hebrew and study of divinity were an integral part of the ecclesiastical curriculum. The first city community was Ashkenazim, mainly trades' people dealing in old clothes (Ibid, 12). As with other communities this trade, provided clothes for the 'lower classes'. By the middle of the 19th century, Jews in Oxford became sellers of watches, jewellery and tobacco-dealers (Ibid, 12).

London synagogue registers with addresses indicate that both Bevis Marks and The Great Synagogue had members living in Oxford. Lewis notes 'that in 1797 Henry Isaacs by order of the Oxford Council, was to cease carrying on any sort of trade within the liberties of the city' (Ibid, 9). Henry Isaacs lived and died in Ship Street in 1812. As Oxford had no cemetery at this time his remains were sent to London as discussed in 5.2.25. At that time, there were more opportunities for Jewish shopkeepers in Cheltenham and Bath (Ibid, 9).

By the early 19th century, Jewish Hebrew teachers were less inclined to convert to Christianity, and Lewis notes that there was a Selig Newman who taught Hebrew in Oxford whilst being a Minister to the Plymouth's community (1992, 11). The 1841 census shows that there were only three Jewish families in Oxford. These families would constitute the nucleus of the Oxford community for the next 20 or 30 years (Ibid, 12). Harry and his wife Anna (Hannah) Levi and family lived in Queen Street. Isaiah Wo(o)lf lived nearby in Pensons Gardens, and the Harris family lived at 54 St. Ebbe's; all these homes were located a short distance from the synagogue in Paradise Square (Ibid, 11).

With the extension of the railway to Oxford in 1844, the community started to increase in size, so the 1851 census includes 22 Jewish adults and 14 children (Ibid, 17). Lipman (1954, 186) gives the number of Jews who were members of the synagogue in 1850 as 50. Lewis (1992, 27) writes that, in 1878, Oswald Simon, a former undergraduate at Balliol wrote to the *Jewish Chronicle*:

The position of the Oxford Jews is a peculiar one, and perhaps unlike that of their brethren in any other provincial place. They live under the immediate observation of a great world of intellect and culture. The notion of cultivated men regarding Judaism and the Jews are often formed by their Oxford experiences…….. Therefore, in Oxford the Jews are especially responsible for the honour and credit of the House of Israel'.

6.2.2.12 *South Wales*

The first Jewish community in South Wales was Swansea in 1768, followed by Cardiff (c.1840) and Merthyr Tydfil (1848). 'By the late 19th-century and early 20th -century there were 30 small communities in the Valleys' (Figure 6.16) (Henriques 1993, 46); these small communities are not discussed in detail as most had less than 50 Jews, they no longer exist. The reason for settlement starting in the late-19thcentury is discussed as it is relevant to settlement topography of the Welsh Jewish community and Anglo-Jewry as a whole. It was in the mid-19th century when the Irish also arrived in South Wales in large numbers due to the famine of 1846-1849, later to be joined by small numbers of Italians fleeing from poverty in Italy (Ibid 1993, 5). Glaser et al. notes that 'Immigrant Jews, most of whom came from central and Eastern Europe went to the valley towns in the main to trade due to the growth of the coal, iron and steel industries in the Rhondda and Cynon valleys from the mid 1870s to the end of the century' (1963, 46). When later these industries declined, Jewish traders moved on, mainly to London and the industrial cities outside Wales.

According to Lipman (1954, 187), 'The first of the Valley communities was Merthyr Tydfil, established 1848, which in 1850 had around 100 Jews, equal in size at that time to Swansea'. Glaser et al. state that, 'as early as 1830 when the total town (Merthyr's) population was approximately 24, 000, six out of the seven dealers in old clothes listed in the trade directory bore Jewish names (1963, 47). In Pontypool, north of Newport, four out of five furniture brokers were Jewish. Newport community, established c.1859, still has a small congregation who use the *ohel* in the cemetery for prayers. According to Kadish (2006, 203), 'By the 1850s there were Jewish shopkeepers resident in Aberdare, Tredegar, and Pontypridd, who opened a room of prayer in 1867 and in 1895 a small chapel like synagogue which was open until 1979. In Pontypridd, the community was founded in 1867 and a synagogue opened in 1895, closed in 1979 and converted into flats (Ibid, 203). By the end of the 19th century in *Kelly's Directory* of Aberdare, 25 business premises were under Jewish or probable Jewish names (Glaser 1963, 49), their main occupations being pawnbrokers and jewellers.

Merthyr Tydfil, discussed in 4.2.21, had the largest community in the Valleys, the cemetery contains Jews who lived in some of the small towns shown in Figure 6.15. According to Kadish (2006, 203), 'the Jewish quarter in Merthyr Tydfil was in Thomas Town near to both the first synagogue in John Street (no longer exists) and the disused synagogue that still stands at the top of Church Street. Thomas Town with its terraces of miners' cottages is a short distance from the High Street where the Jewish traders had their premises'.

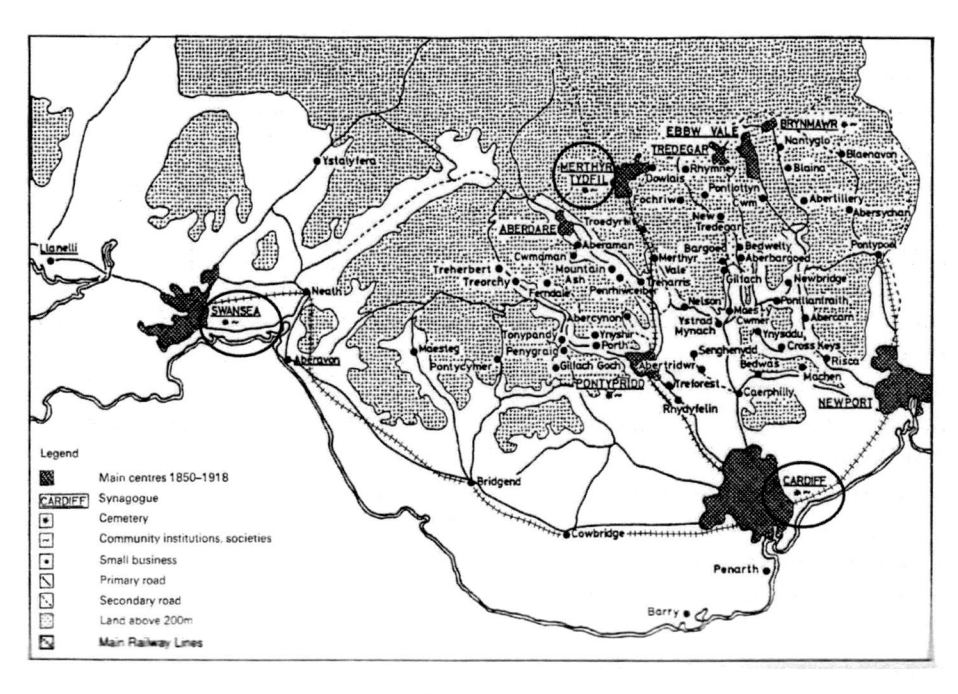

A COMPARATIVE APPROACH TO JEWISH URBAN TOPOGRAPHY   247

Figure 6.15 Jewish Communities in Industrial South Wales late 19th century (Glaser et al. 1963, 46).

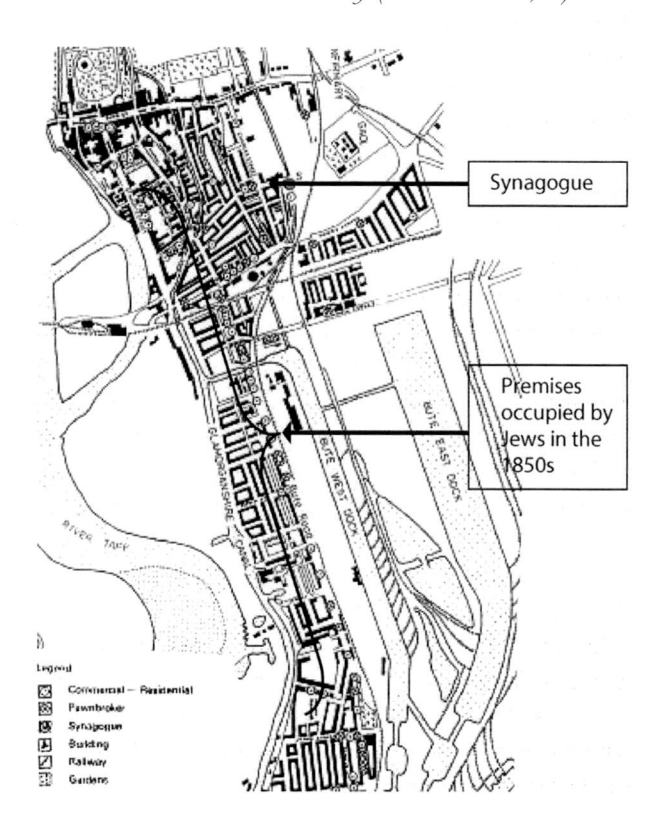

Figure 6.16 Cardiff: Jewish Settlement in Cardiff in the 1850s (no scale) (Glaser et al. 1963, 10)

By the beginning of the 20th century, there were nine synagogues in the Valley towns, but not one remains. South Wales was not on the main immigrant route, even though Swansea was an important sea port and the largest port for the exportation of coal in the world. Swansea's synagogues and cemetery are discussed in 4.2.34 and 5.2.34. Although the Swansea community was small, c.100 persons in 1850, there was a clear area of Jewish settlement near the synagogues.

In summary, most of the early community in Cardiff settled in Bute Road (now Bute Street), near to the former Bute West Dock, which has now been redeveloped. Figure 6.16 shows the synagogue and over 50 premises, houses and shops, occupied by Jews or owners with Jewish-sounding names. Bute Road in 1850 would have held nearly the entire community. From a peak of c.5, 000 Jews in south Wales in the 1930s, there are today c.500 Jews in Cardiff, 50 in Swansea and none in Merthyr Tydfil. Cardiff community, established in 1840, and the largest in South Wales, has two synagogues, Orthodox and Reform.

6.2.2.13 South-West England

In the period under discussion, there were four principal communities in the South–West of England: Falmouth (1740), Penzance (1740), Plymouth (1752), and Exeter (1763). There was also a handful of Jews (50 or less) in 15 towns in Devon and 12 in Cornwall (Figure 6.18). These small communities are not discussed and mostly no longer exist.

One of the reasons for the settlement in the South-West, starting in the mid 18th century was Jews were now allowed to travel and live anywhere in England in order to conduct their business. Itinerant pedlars settled in Falmouth, Penzance and Plymouth, trading with the Royal Navy and ships from the West Indies. Later a community was established in Exeter (Pearce et al. 2000, 53), states '… that in Falmouth (4.2.13) by 1766, there were sufficient Jewish settlers to buy a building on the sea front for use as a synagogue'. Synagogue records show that the first Ashkenazi settlers in the main came from Germany and Bohemia (Susser 1993, 31), states 'It may be surmised that in the early 1750s there were some 29 or 30 families who settled in Exeter'.

Plymouth also had an established community by this date. Plymouth must have had at least a dozen families in 1745 (Ibid, 31). Evidence for this is discussed in 5.2.27. In Plymouth, prior to the synagogue being established in 1761/1762, Jews held small, but organised services in a rented room in Broad Hoe Lane. In the early 1740s, the synagogue account book of 1759, which was in possession of the late Rabbi Susser reveals 52 male members' (Ibid, 31).

Immigration of Jews to the South-West (Figure 6.16) followed the same pattern as it did throughout the country. When immigrants arrived, they mostly joined or settled near to their families or friends. Susser (1993, 33), states 'that in the Plymouth Aliens list (1798-1803) for example, it is possible to identify at least seven, possibly eight sets of brothers, representing sixteen or eighteen heads of families'. This

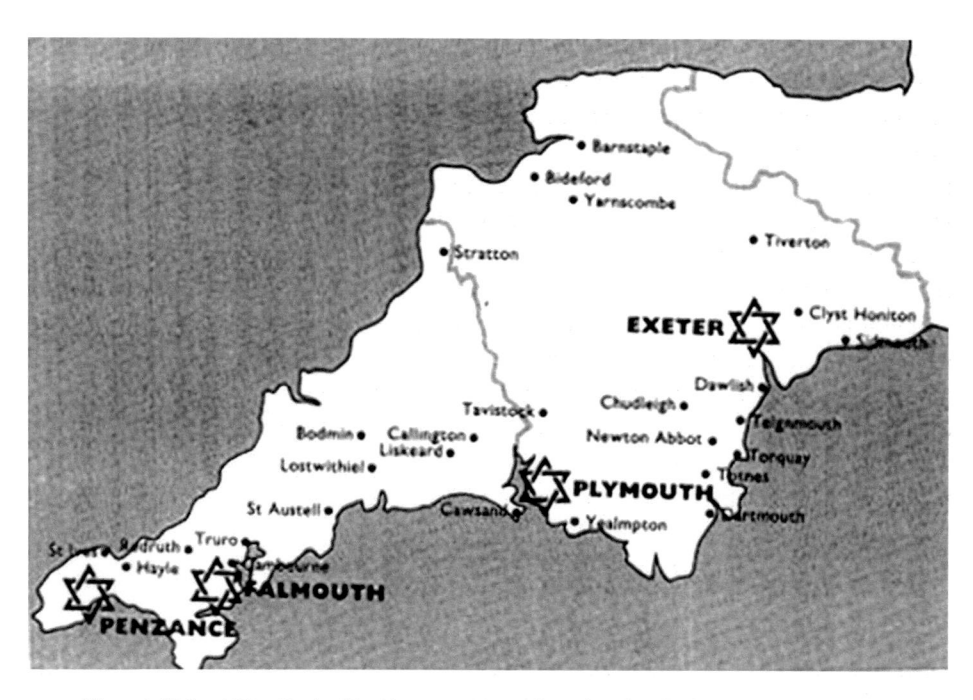

Figure 6.17 South-West England Jewish communities in the 18th and 19th centuries (Susser 1993, 50).

suggests that some of the newly arrived immigrants made their way direct from London, Harwich, Dover and Gravesend to Devon and Cornwall, in order to be with their families. Although the bulk of the immigrants were Ashkenazim, there was also a small number of Sephardim, but never enough to form their own community. Sephardim joined in prayer with the Ashkenazim and were buried alongside them (personal observation 2009). The Sephardim in the main settled in London and Manchester.

Susser (1993, 36) estimates that by the 1760s, the Jewish population of Devon and Cornwall was c.500 persons, which represents c.5% of all the Jews living in England. This was based on the number of seats in the synagogues. Falmouth-50, Penzance-50, Plymouth-142, Exeter-100, A total of c.340 excluding children (1993, 36).

By 1850 the population in the South-West had increased as follow:

Falmouth	150
Plymouth	200-250
Exeter	175-200
Penzance	75
Total	c.550-700

Figure 6.18 South-West England estimate of population in 1850 (Lipman 1951, 28).

These population figures suggest that between 1760 and 1850, unlike the rest of England, there was virtually no increase in the size of the Jewish population in South-West England, with immigrants mostly settling in London and the major industrial cities. The expansion of the railway system from the late 1870s lessoned the need for itinerant peddlers. Isolated small clusters of Jews could travel to their nearest town.

In summary, Falmouth Synagogue closed in 1880 (4.2.13), Penzance in 1906 (4.2.26), and the building were sold. According to Susser (1993, 41), 'the size of the Falmouth community declined from around 50 individuals in 1845 to three families in 1874. From the mid-19th century. Plymouth benefited from new immigrants from Eastern Europe. The majority of immigrants preferred to stay in London or other major cities, such as Birmingham, Liverpool and Manchester. Some moved to Portsmouth, where they had business and family connections, whilst others moved to South Wales to join the growing communities trading with the coal and steel towns and some emigrated abroad. This movement lead to the permanent decline in the Jewish communities in Devon and Cornwall.

Conclusion

By 1870 the Anglo-Jewry community, numbering c.40, 000, was well integrated into English life. By 1880, before the mass immigration started in 1881, the community numbered c.60, 000, with c.35, 000 in London and five provincial cities accounting for a further c.18, 000 (Manchester 7, 000, Liverpool c.4, 000, Birmingham c.3, 000, Leeds c.2, 000, Bristol c.2, 000). The remainder lived in 35 communities spread over Britain (Lipman1954). As they prospered, they moved out of the poor inner city and port areas where they first settled to more congenial areas, still to be with other Jews but were more thinly spread.

As they moved, new synagogues were established, and old buildings sold and used for other purposes or destroyed. Several of the early small seaport communities declined following the end of the Napoleonic Wars in 1815 and by 1880 had ceased to exist, with communities moving to London an the industrial cities in the midlands and north, or some families relocating overseas (Endelman 2002, 80).

The purchase of ground for a cemetery is often used as the traditional date when a community was established. The first cemeteries in London were to the east of London. As cities grew over the course of over 250 years, a number of cemeteries were destroyed during city centre redevelopment, with the remains re-interred in mass graves, surviving tombstones were moved to these later cemeteries. This study has discussed the changes that took place over the period with regard to memorial stones, shifting from local stone, such as sandstone and limestone to granite and marble, as well as the changes to style of inscriptions. Early tombstones are simple and all in Hebrew, but from the 19th century both Hebrew and English are evident.

The Sephardi community have complete records, which are with the Spanish and Portuguese Burial Society and the Metropolitan Archives in London. In the case of the early Ashkenazi cemeteries, there are mostly no records, as they were lost or destroyed.

Unlike London, no archaeological sub-surface Jewish material culture from c.1656-c.1880 was in evidence in any of the provincial cites and towns discussed. This chapter has shown that the urban topography of Anglo-Jewry during the period 1656-c.1880 changed with growth of the community from c.1, 000 in 1695 to 60,000-65,000 in 1880. With the growth of the total population in London and the industrial cities in the midlands and north, new commercial opportunities were offered. The first reliable figures showing the size of the community in London and the provinces are from 1850 (Lipman 1951/1952). The census returns and community records such as synagogue membership and burial records at this date (where they exist) show that around two thirds of the community lived in Greater London, with the majority in the East End. When they could afford to do so, they moved to the northeast, with some moving to west. The growth of the middle class was accompanied by dispersion both in London and the provinces.

The establishment of provincial communities from 1730s/1740s at first was mainly concentrated in seaports, when itinerant pedlars began to settle and start business near the ports or in the marketplaces. This was the beginning of the spread of the community out of London. As more immigrants arrived, they went to towns where there were already some Jews. Most of the Jewish poor in the 1880 were not descendants of early-19th-century immigrants but were new arrivals fleeing from poverty and persecution. It was until the middle of the 19th century that Jews were admitted to all universities to obtain degrees that allowed them to become lawyers, architects and other professions.

Chapters 4 and 5 discussed the establishment of the first cemeteries, many of which still exist, and the cultural change that took place in the style of headstones and memorials. The fact that under Jewish law (except in a few cases), cemeteries should not be disturbed, has resulted in present day researchers being able to establish the presence of the major communities in this period.

Chapter 7

Discussion, Conclusion and Suggestions for Future Research

7.1 Topography of Anglo-Jewry 1656-c.1880

No Jewish community remained in England following the expulsion in 1290. As discussed, before readmission there were an unknown number of Marranos, assimilated Christianized Jews who professed conversion in order to avoid persecution, but practised their religion in secret. In 1656, Jews were re-admitted to England after the absence of more than 350 years.

By 1700 the community numbered around 1, 000 persons; the census of 1685 identifies 850 people with ascribable Jewish names living in the City of London. This study has also discussed provincial communities that were established from c.1730-1740. Of 35 of these communities established prior to 1880, 18 were in ports such as Bristol, Hull, Liverpool, Plymouth and Portsmouth, with Jewish traders supplying the British Navy, particularly during the Napoleonic wars (1799-1815).

In the early stages of the re-settlement there were a number of Sephardi wealthy merchants, bankers and skilled craftsmen who were encouraged by Cromwell to settle in England. From the beginning of the 18th century, the majority of the immigrant community were poor and unskilled Ashkenazim. By 1800, the total Jewish community in England had grown to c.25, 000, with around two-thirds living in London. 'By 1880, the community had grown to c.60, 000, with c.40, 000 in London and the remainder spread over around 40 provincial cities and towns' (Lipman 1954, 65). At that time the largest provincial communities were: Birmingham, Liverpool and Manchester.

Mass immigration of Jews from Eastern Europe started in 1881. The size of the communities in England and Wales that are discussed can only be approximate, as there were no immigration controls at that time. Many Jews fleeing Europe passed through London, Manchester and Liverpool on their way to America, Canada and South Africa. Some stayed for a short period, some settled in England. The figures for the size of the community from 1850 (Lipman 1954) using synagogue, birth, death, marriage and circumcision records (where they existed) are accepted by Jewish scholars and historians as being as accurate as is possible. The topographical research for this study is based not only on the physical evidence of settlement, migration and movement of communities, but also upon historical data and census returns, where Jewish names have been identified.

Jewish immigrants, as did other immigrants, preferred to settle in cities and towns. Research into patterns of Jewish immigration and settlement has consistently indicated that certain areas, particularly poor slum districts near to city centres, docks and railway terminals, were prone to settlement, forming a spatial pattern. The movement of Jewish communities (mostly Orthodox) in every one of the major cities discussed is reflected in the changes of location of synagogues, which in the first years of settlement were shown to be in private houses or rented halls. This was before communities were large enough to afford a synagogue.

This research has also shown that in larger cities and towns, those who came to England and Wales as immigrants or their descendants, gradually moved out of the slums or near the ports where they first settled, to the more congenial areas of the city and suburbs. Even then, for practical and economic reasons, there was a time lag before the establishment of their synagogues. The congregation had to be self-supporting with enough members to ensure that there was a *minyan* (10 men over the age of 13 who had had their *bar mitzvah*). As the congregation grew, they would appoint a reader, later perhaps a rabbi, who not only led services but, acted as *mohel* (performed circumcisions) and *shochet* (ritual slaughterer). Virtually all small synagogues in the period under discussion no longer exist, although some are marked on Ordnance Survey Maps (1888-1901) and are shown in the gazetteer. In cases where the synagogue is not marked, the street is known but not exact location. This research has also shown that the density and location of synagogues changed over time, so that population distribution and movement demonstrates a clear physical impact on urban topography and landscape.

In London, by the 1850s, the community had spread eastwards, westwards and northwards from the original area of settlement to the east of the City. From the 1850s-c.1880, six new important London synagogues were established, and, numerous small prayer rooms, halls and minor synagogues. The major synagogues were Sandy's Row (1854) (4.1.10), Great Portland Street (Central) (1855) (4.1.3), Bayswater (1863) (4.1.1), Princelet Street (1870) (4.1.9), West London Reform (1870) (4.1.12) and New West End (1879) (4.1.8). In 1876, St John's Wood Synagogue was established in a temporary building until 1882, when the purpose-built synagogue was constructed (not discussed). Lipman (1954, 75) states that '….in 1870, there was in East London at least 20 minor synagogues with in total over 2,500 seat-holders'. It has been shown that the beginning of the geographical dispersion of the community lay between 1850 and 1880. Picciotto (1956, 432) observes that 'by 1876 the Jews of England had achieved a high degree of integration into English life'.

In London, both historical and physical evidence reveal that the first community settled near around Dukes' Place and Bevis Marks in the City of London. At first,

Jews who were considered to be aliens were not allowed to own freeholds of land or property. They gradually expanded east, with Whitechapel by the late 19th century becoming the centre of the community. Until the end of the 19th century, there were no ghettos, such as in Venice and Paris, where Jews lived in segregated areas. In Britain, Jews lived in clusters to be within walking distance of their synagogues, and also near to Jewish schools and shops selling *kosher* food. Most immigrants with their distinct appearances, the men with beards and head coverings, in the late 19th century could not speak English. Some were not happy to pray in the 'cathedral' synagogues and thus set up *chevrot* (communal halls and rooms of prayer) in order to pray and meet with fellow countrymen. In London, they settled in the east, where there was the opportunity to get poorly paid work, either in 'sweat shops' making clothing or in factories making products such as cigars and furniture. Factories in the east of London were often owned by established Jews, who understood that their Jewish workers could not work on the Sabbath (Saturday) or any of the major Jewish Festivals.

During the Blitz (1941), one-third of the City and much of East London was destroyed or badly damaged, so that the physical evidence of much of London's 17th-19th-century Anglo-Jewry was destroyed. Synagogues, such as The Great, with their irreplaceable records, were completely destroyed also some cemeteries in the east of London were badly damaged. In the provinces, port areas where Jews first lived, such as Cardiff, Hull, Liverpool, Plymouth and Portsmouth were bombed, as were areas of Jewish concentration in city centres, such as Norwich and Swansea.

Throughout the history of Anglo-Jewry, London has always been the main port of entry for immigrants. This research has shown that following the end of the Napoleonic Wars (1799-1815), sea ports, particularly of the south coast, could no longer sustain a community. Provincial communities in port towns such as Falmouth, Ipswich, King's Lynn, Penzance and Great Yarmouth declined or no longer existed after 1815, as did those in the inland market towns of Bath, Bedford and Canterbury. Lipman (1954, 66) reports that '....of the port communities which survived, Plymouth, Southampton, Dover, Chatham, Ramsgate and Portsmouth became less important compared to the great provincial communities of the late 19th century, Birmingham, Glasgow, Leeds, Liverpool and Manchester'. When the Jewish community declined, they left behind cemeteries. Some are now cared for by local residents, Jewish and non-Jewish alike, who consider these and other old Non-Conformist cemeteries as part of their local heritage.

Other than items that can with certainty be identified of Jewish origin few objects can be discussed in an archaeological context. The main reason being that Jewish material culture mainly used for religious purposes is handed down from one generation to the next. When a synagogue closes the *Torahs* (Five Books of Moses), scrolls written on parchment, with their covers and silver ornaments and *Kiddush* cups are passed on to a new community, or go to private collections and museums. In some cases, the Ark, seating and ornaments were moved from the synagogue being closed to a new synagogue.

It has been observed that many of the early synagogues that survive are in side streets rather than main thoroughfares. In the 17th and early 18th centuries Jews were not allowed by law to build synagogues on main roads. Entrances were often constructed to the rear or side of the building, making it safer for congregants when entering or leaving.

In this period, Jews were not allowed to qualify as architects. Many synagogue exteriors were designed by Christian architects with previous experience of designing churches. This has resulted in the exterior looking like non-conformist chapels, for example Bevis Marks (1701), Cheltenham (1837), and Plymouth (1761). In Hull, the first synagogue was a former Roman Catholic chapel. Some of the later synagogues, such as Nottingham (1954) and Southampton (1964), were converted from Wesleyan Methodist chapels.

Cemeteries are the main source of physical evidence of 17th-19th-century communities. They are identified on Ordnance Survey Maps and can be found in the gazetteer. Jewish cemeteries were located outside city walls, unlike 17th/18th-century Christian burials, which up to 1858, are in city cemeteries or church-yards. There is one exception: Chatham. This cemetery adjacent to the synagogue was privately administered, beyond the authority of the United Synagogue. Small, early 18th-century city cemeteries, for example, Birmingham, Gloucester and Liverpool, were in the gardens of the original synagogues. They no longer exist, remains have been re-interred. In the provinces, a few cases of re-interment have been discussed. In London, following bomb damage there were remains reburied in later cemeteries. This study has observed that in Birmingham, Bristol, Liverpool, Manchester, Newcastle and Sheffield, there are tombstone fragments from earlier cemeteries found during redevelopment of the city centres. In these examples, there are mass re-interred grave sites marked with an obelisk or marker stones but no individual headstones. Only in the Jewish section of Gloucester Municipal cemetery are remains from the city centre buried with named head stones. No scientific examination of Jewish burial remains from the 17th-19th centuries has taken place in England.

Reconciling the number of burials in the cemeteries examined, with documented size of the community at that time is thwarted by a discrepancy between the estimated number of burials and estimated size of the community. This may be explained by the fact that poor and non-observant Jews resident in a given town and itinerant pedlars, who were not members of a synagogue, could have been buried in Christian or Non-Conformist burial grounds. During plagues, Jews were buried in unmarked mass graves. For certain small communities with less than 50 members, there is evidence from inscriptions on headstones that the deceased lived in a nearby small town or village. Where 17th/18th-century headstones were examined, many cannot be read due to weathering, vandalism and neglect. Later granite and some marble headstones have survived better. In Cornwall and Wales, many 18th-century tombstones are in local slate, all in Hebrew, simple and undecorated. 19th-century headstones and monuments are in Hebrew and English, with English gradually becoming more predominant.

By the middle 19th century, social distinction and assimilation is evident with some of the more prosperous members having elaborate funereal monuments, such as obelisks, not only in local stone, but also granite and marble, which became more fashionable, and a sign of increased prosperity. In all cemeteries examined, there are a substantial number of graves with small, unnamed stone markers, and it is possible that the families of the deceased were too poor to afford head stones. In all the cemeteries examined there are areas of unmarked babies and infants graves, children's deaths in this period accounted for a high proportion of the total burials, sometimes as high as 40%-50%, there are no records of children's names or dates.. A sad reflection on the present community is that many cemeteries that are no longer used are in a poor state of repair.

Mikva'ot have been discussed in Chapter 4.4, but it is surprising just how little evidence remains of these baths, which were an essential component of Orthodox Jewish communities. *The Chief Rabbi's Statistical Account of the Congregations in the British Empire* (1845) was the first record of *mikvaot (pl.)* and shows that half of the communities that conformed to Jewish law did not have a *mikveh*. Some, such as Bath, Cheltenham, Hull and Nottingham used public baths, and others in seaside towns, such as Dover and Yarmouth washed in the sea. Kadish (1996,135) states that, 'Our findings show that, until the 20th century the majority of *mikvaot* in this country were built under private auspices and were not situated in communal buildings, or in cellars or outhouses of synagogues, as was the practice on the Continent, especially in Germany'. This would account for the fact that there is almost no evidence remaining of 17th-19th century *mikva'ot*, having been destroyed with the buildings, one of the few exceptions being the former *mikveh* in Canterbury, now King's School music rehearsal room.

The objective in this study has been to bring together the physical evidence of at least 80% of the Jewish community in England and Wales in the period 1656-c.1880 and use this evidence to trace the topography of the immigrant community.

Until around 1740, London was the only community. In order to earn a living, Jews became pedlars, selling items that were easily portable, such as jewellery and old clothes. It was these pedlars who formed the first communities in the provinces. When they could afford to do so they opened shops, many in port and market towns. When they began to settle in the major cities in the Midlands and North, they congregated in the poorest areas, such as in Birmingham, one of the first towns to be settled with a Jewish community (1730/1740), (there is no more precise date). There they lived in an overcrowded area, the Froggery, in back-to-back houses with poor sanitation (National Trust, 2004, 3). This area has been identified and discussed, as has the movement out the Froggery to the more congenial area in the direction of the suburb of Edgbaston. As the community moved, it has been shown that synagogues moved. Such movement out of the poor areas has been revealed in the other major provincial cities discussed, such as Leeds, Liverpool, Manchester and Newcastle.

Between 1870 and 1880, when the community increased in size from c.40, 000 to c.60, 000, immigrants who came to England settled in cities and towns where there was already a community, to be with their family and friends and also to have the benefit of the established charitable organisations. However, they were a burden on communal funds; editorials in the *Jewish Chronicle* of 1846 'urges Jews to contribute generously to Jewish charities', and in 1854 with the start the flow of immigrants from Poland and Russia; 'asks for special donations to an East End soup kitchen who were unable to handle the great influx of Polish Jews' (*Jewish Chronicle* 30 October 1846 and 3 March 1854).

Most of the immigrants who came from Europe from the early 18th century onwards were poor and remained so, but many of their descendents did not remain poor for more than two generations. By the late 19th century, some of the early immigrants who had come during the Georgian period (1714-1830) had become 'middle class'. Poverty was not a permanent state for all of them. Endelman (2002, 79) states that 'On the basis of this ascent from poverty to respectability, Jewish legal status, communal organisation, and religious life also were transformed, and Jewish identity reshaped'. In comparison to the experience of Jewish communities in Europe, living in England during the 17th-19th centuries was free from persecution. Movement due to economic reasons was natural: there were no movement restrictions. The only restrictions were before the mid-Victorian years when Jews, unless they converted, could not enter the ancient universities, such as Oxford and Cambridge, nor could they have careers in professions, such as the law and architecture. Following 'emancipation' in 1858, Jews entered Parliament. Endelman states that. 'From 1880 Anglo-Jewry included about 200 professionals (architects, barristers, dentists, doctors and solicitors), as well as a few university teachers, civil servants and army officers' (Ibid, 165).

In conclusion, to quote B. Travers Herford (1860-1950), a non-Jewish Hebrew scholar in *The Ethics of the Talmud: Sayings of the Fathers*:

> *'The local Community is the real unit of Jewish life, the group of persons living in close proximity to each other having its centre and focus in the Synagogue.... So long as the Community could hold together there was haven of refuge for its harassed members, there they could find solace and strength of their religion and live their own life unmocked by the hard and cruel world. The Jew found the only freedom for the higher life of the spirit in the Synagogue'.*

It is evident that during the period 1656-c.1880, the settlement pattern and topography of the community was not stable, with movement from city centres and ports into the suburbs and the smaller port communities moving to London and the industrial Midlands and North. In 1880/1881, the beginning of mass immigration into Britain transformed the community and 1880 marked the end of one period in the settlement topography of Anglo-Jewry and the beginning of a new era of freedom in Britain for Jews.

7.2 Suggestions for future research

No attempt has been made to discuss every aspect of the topography and physical evidence of Anglo-Jewry in the period under discussion. Each of the larger communities could be the subject of further research and analysis. As a result of the author's research, there are still as many questions still to be answered as have been discussed. The following are considered some of the most important areas where further research would be useful.

1. The topography of approximately c.80% of the community in 1850 has been examined. Still to be researched is Scotland and Ireland, they were beyond the scope of this study. Also a number of small communities (less than 50 persons) established prior to 1880 have not been examined, such as Aldershot (1864), Hartlepool (1850s), Leicester (1866), Newport (1859), North Shields (c.1860), Pontypridd (1867), Stoke on Trent (1873), Stockton (1870s) and Wolverhampton (1830s?). There were also a number of small communities that were established c.1880-1900, such as Blackburn (1880s), Durham (1888), Grimsby (c.1885), Preston (1882), Reading (1886), Southport (1900), South Shields (1880s) and Stroud (1888), there may be others that would also repay further study. Before more is lost, research should be carried out to determine what if any, physical evidence remains of these 17th-19th centuries communities.

2. Suggestions for future work could also be to compare the archaeology and topography of Anglo-Jewry with communities in Western Europe, particularly France and Italy in the 17th-19th centuries.

3. Place-names with Jewish connections have been discussed in 4.3. Some date from the medieval period. Considering the size of the community at any one time (less than half of one percent of the total population), it is remarkable that these exist at all. They tend to be concentrated in London and Brighton. It may be that there are more to be noted.

4 As far as the author is aware, it is only in Leeds and Manchester that a scientific analysis of the formation and spatial pattern of the community has been carried out (Waterman et al. 2003 and Williams 1976). The potential exists for scientific topographical research of other major cities of Jewish settlement such as London, Birmingham and Liverpool.

5. As noted in Figure 2.4.1, in the Chronological Establishment of Provincial Communities, out of 24 communities established by the end of the Napoleonic Wars in 1815, 17 were in ports. The British Navy had the largest fleet in the world; at this time. Jews settled in the port towns in order to take advantage of the considerable trade that came from supplying and refurnishing the ships and also trading with the sailors. Figure 4.123 shows the synagogue and location of houses in Portsmouth and Portsea where Jews lived and traded during the Napoleonic Wars (Green 1982, 6). To the best of the author's knowledge, this is the only example where early settlement in the port towns has been so clearly documented. Cesarini (2006), Finestein

and Kushner (2002) and Weinberg (1998), have written individual histories of port communities. Further studies of the total settlement, rise, decline (in some cases) and topography of port Jews throughout Britain would add to our knowledge of the topography of 18th/19th-century communities.

6. Synagogues have been discussed individually. In several cases other than the 'cathedral' synagogues such as Liverpool and St Petersburgh Place, London many of the architects are unknown and are assumed to have been built by local master builders who had experience of building churches and Non-Conformist chapels. Interiors were designed to conform to Jewish tradition and again would have been constructed by local craftsmen mainly using local materials. Some examples of this, such as Plymouth have been discussed in the study. Sharman Kadish in her recent book *The Synagogues of Britain and Ireland, An Architectural and Social History* (2011), written with the support of English Heritage and several academic institutions such as the University of Manchester, individual researchers, the Jewish Museum and many others is without doubt the most comprehensive and in depth survey yet carried out of synagogue architecture in Britain. This study combined and compared with the evidence of the other minority faiths in Britain would add to the architectural history of sacred buildings. It touches on the issue of gendered space, the separation of men and women in the synagogue. This topic could be developed with the religious and social implications.

7. The main body of evidence is cemeteries. Other than the two 18th/19th century Spanish and Portuguese cemeteries in London (5.4 & 5.5) and Alderney Road Ashkenazi Cemetery (5.12), the remainder of the early London cemeteries do not appear to have detailed plot plans. Many records were destroyed when synagogues holding records were bombed. In the provinces, if they exist, few detailed plot plans were examined. Some are held by synagogues, or detailed in local histories or records such as at Bath, Falmouth and Newcastle, whilst others have been deposited with the local archive offices. The most comprehensive catalogue examined was that of the *'The Jewish Cemeteries of Bristol'* (Tobias et al. 1997). He lists and shows the tombstones and grave numbers of Bristol's three Jewish cemeteries dating from c.1762 (5.25). It reveals the cultural changes that have taken place over this period and is a valuable record of the Bristol community. There is also a topographical Plan of the Deane Street Cemetery in Liverpool (Marks, 2007) (5.2.19.1). As far as the author is aware most Jewish cemeteries in England and Wales have not been explored with images, photographs and plans in such depth as the Kadish book. The recent exception being Leeds who have completed a survey and recorded their cemeteries, with images and plot details. There needs to be a central archive for catalogues and plot plans of cemeteries. Further research needs to be carried out and more catalogue and photographic archives made for future generations. This will help to inform our understanding of the cultural heritage of Jewish burial customs.

8. Other than London, there is no evidence of sub-surface archaeological material culture from the period under discussion. It has been shown that religious objects are rarely discarded, but instead passed on from one community to the next or handed down through the family. If surplus to requirements, as the communities decline, they are placed in museums or sold to collectors. The archaeology of the material culture of Anglo-Jewry could be a subject for further work. There might be more than that has been discussed, also looked at in a wider context compared with other minority communities.

This study has brought together for the first time, a comprehensive study of the evidence for the urban topography of Anglo-Jewry in England and Wales 1656-c.1880. There is still more to be researched.

Glossary, Bibliography and Sources

Glossary

Archaes: medieval chests or coffers for the deposit of the records of Jewish financial transactions.
The Ark: contains the *Sefer Torah* (the five books of Moses-Genesis to Deuteronomy).
Ashkenazi (m) (pl.): Jews of Germany and northern France and Eastern Europe.
Ba'alei Batim: corresponding to the Vestry men in the English parish.
Bar Mitzvah: when a boy reaches the age of thirteen and considered to be a man and is entitled to read the Torah in Synagogue.
Basar: Hebrew, meat.
Bet Tahara: a cleaning or washing house for washing the deceased before burial.
Bima(h): the central platform in the synagogue, from which the Torah is read aloud to the congregation, (derived from the Hebrew-elevated place).
Chalav: Hebrew, milk.
Chazzan: reader to the congregation.
Chevra Kaddisha: Charitable Society with special responsibility for the sick and the dying, for preparing the dead for burial and caring for their dependants.
Chevra (chevrot, pl.): brotherhood.
Cohen (Cohanim.pl): descended from the priestly tribe.
Haham: a spiritual leader among Sephardic Jews.
Hazzan: The cantor or reader, who leads the prayers in the synagogue.
Hehal or Ehal: The Ark in which the Sefer Torahs (scrolls with the five books of Moses) are kept
Kosher: fit to eat according to the dietary laws.
Levi (Levite): a member of the Hebrew tribe of Levi, especially that part of it which provided assistants to the priests in the worship in the temple in Jerusalem.
Luhot: panels or stained glass windows containing the first word of each of Ten Commandments.

Magen David: a hexagram used as a symbol of Judaism. (Shield of David).
Marranos: Christianized Jews who practised Judaism in England in secret till 1656.
Matzo: crisp biscuit of unleavened bread traditionally eaten by Jews during Passover.
Mezuzah: parchment inscribed with religious texts and attached in a case to the doorpost of a Jewish house as a sign of faith.
Mikveh (Mikva'ot pl.): a ritual bath constructed in accordance with Jewish law.
Minyan: a quorum of ten men over the age of thirteen required for traditional Jewish public worship.
Mohel : one who performs the rite of circumcision.
Orhim: strangers or guests.
Rabbi: teachers of Torah who had been ordained.
Rimonim: decorative plate and bells used on the cover of the *sefer torah*.
Rosh Hashanah: the Jewish New Year festival marked by the blowing of the *shofar*.
Sephardi(Sephardim, pl.): the Jews of Spain and Portugal who were expelled in the fifteenth century. They settled in North Africa, Turkey and Italy. Some later went to Amsterdam and England.
Shofar (Shofar'ot, pl.): ancient ritual Jewish musical instrument often made from a ram's horn.
Sefer Torah: scrolls containing the hand-written text of the Pentateuch (Five books of Moses).
Synagogue: a place of worship, in Hebrew known as a 'House of Study'.
Tallit: a fringed shawl traditionally worn by Jewish men at prayer.
Talmud: containing the commentaries by the Rabbis on the Divine laws of the Bible.
Tisha B'Av: a time of mourning over the destruction of the Temple in AD69.
Torah: the first five books of the Hebrew Bible.
Yad (Yadayim, pl.): literally hand, pointer used by the reader of the *sefer torah*.
Yom Kippur: a day of fasting, the most solemn religious fast day of the Jewish Year.

Bibliography and Sources

Ainsworth, R. 2009/2010. *A Century of Wurst: The Origins of Liverpool's Jewish Heritage.* Merseyside Jewish Representative Council Year Book. Raycross Liverpool.

Alderman, G. 1974/1978. The Jew as Scapegoat? The Settlement and Reception of Jews in South Wales before 1941. *Transactions of the Jewish Historical Society* 26, 62-70.

Ballin, N.D. 1986. *The Early Days of Sheffield Jewry 1760-1900.*

Beach, D. 2006. *London's Cemeteries.* Metro Publications London.

Bell, W. 1923. *The House of Life and Jew's Old Burial Ground.* The Daily Telegraph.

Benas, B.L. 1899. Records of the Jews in Liverpool. *Transactions of the Historic Society of Lancashire.* 1, 45-66. New series XV.

Black, G. 2003. *Jewish London. An Illustrated History.* Breedon Books Publishing Company Ltd. Derby.

Blair, I. Hillaby, J. Sermon, R. Watson, B. 2001. Two Medieval Jewish Ritual Baths-Mikva'ot found in Gresham Street and Milk Street in London. *Transactions of the London and Middlesex Archaeological Society* 52, 127-137.

Bluer, R. Brigham, T. Neilson R. Roman and later development east of the forum and Cornhill. Excavations at Lloyd's Register, 71 Fenchurch Street. City of London. *MoLAS Monograph 30.* Museum of London Archaeological Service.

Brown, M. Samuel, J. 1986. The Jews of Bath. *Transactions of the Jewish Historical Society of England* 28, 135-159.

Brown, M. 1990/1992. The Jews of Norfolk and Suffolk before 1840. *Transactions of the Jewish Historical Society of England* 23, 219-235.

Campbell, M. 2009 ed. *A British Perspective. The Black Death, Treasure Hoards and Anglo-Jewish Material Culture.* In Treasures of the Black Death. The Wallace Collection. Reunion des Musees Nationaux. Paris.

Cesarini, D. 2006. *The Jews of Bristol and Liverpool 1750-1850 : Port Communities in the Shadow of Slavery.* Vallentine Mitchell London

Chase, T. Marin, J. Marks, K. Sheffield, J and Watson, B. 2008. The Radiocarbon Dating of Two London Shofarot. *The London Archaeologist* 12 No 1.14-15.

Chesses, A. 2003. *A History of Birmingham Jewry.* Unpublished Singers Hill Synagogue Birmingham.

Clout, H. 2004. *History of London.* Harper Collins London.

Cohn-Sherbok, D. (Rabbi) 1984. *The Jews of Canterbury 1760-1931.* Yorick Books Canterbury.

Diamond, A. 1955. The Cemetery of the Resettlement *Transactions of the Jewish Historical Society of England* 19, 163-190.

Diamond, A. 1969. The Community of the Resettlement *Transactions of the Jewish Historical Society of England* 23, 134-150.

Englander D. 1994. *A Documentary History of Jewish Immigrants in Britain 1840-1920* Leicester University Press.

Endelman, T. 2002. *The Jews of Britain 1656-2000* University of California. U.S.A.

Ettinger, P. 1930. *Hope Place in Liverpool Jewry.* T. Lyon. Liverpool.

Finestein, I. 1996/8. The Jews in Hull 1766-1880. *Transactions of the Jewish Historical Society* 35, 33-91.

Fisher, N. 1998. Eight *Hundred Years. The Story of Nottingham's Jews.* The History of Nottingham Jewry Research Team.

Fowler, J.T. 1890. *The Jews' Burial Ground at Gloucester,* Gloucester Notes and Queries Vol 4 1753.

Freedman, M. 1992. The first 100 years. *Jewish Historical Society (Leeds Branch).*

Fry, H. and Friedlander. 2000. *Synagogues and Cemeteries in the South-West* in *The Jews of Devon and Cornwall.* Hidden Legacy Foundation. Bristol.

Gartner, L. 1973. *The Jewish Immigrant in England 1870-1914*, 2nd edition.

Glaser, l. 1963. *The Jews of South Wales* in *The Jews of South Wales-Historical Studies.* Henriques, U.1993.ed. Cardiff University Press.

Glass, M. 1980. *Swansea Hebrew Congregation 1730-1980.* Unpublished.

Gollancz, H. 1894/5. A Ramble in East Anglia. *Transactions of the Jewish Historical Society of England* 2, 106-140.

Green, G. 1982/6. Anglo-Jewish trading connections with officers and seamen of the Royal Navy (1740-1820). *Transactions of the Jewish Historical Society of England* 29, 97-116.

Grizzard, N. 2007. *Jewish Heritage Trail* printing.com Leeds

Guttentag, G. 1973-1975. 'The Beginnings of the Newcastle Jewish Community' *Transactions of the Jewish Historical Society* 22, 124.

Gutwirth, E. 1979. Stepney Jews in the 1670's. *London and Middlesex Archaeological Society Transactions* 30, 135-137.

Hachlili, R. 2001. *The archaeology of Judaism in Archaeology and World Religion,* Insoll, T. ed. Routlidge London.

Hasted, E. 1799. *History of Canterbury* (publisher not known).

Henriques, U. 1993. *The Jews of South Wales, Historical Studies.* Cardiff University of Wales Press.

Henriques, U. 1993. *The Valleys Communities in The Jews of South Wales, Historical Studies.* University Press of South Wales.

Herford, T. R. 1962 *The Ethics of the Talmud: Sayings of the Fathers.* Schoken Books

Honeybourne, M. 1959. 'The Pre-expulsion Cemetery of the Jews in London'. *Transactions of the Jewish Historical Society of England* 20, 145-159.

Houlbrooke, R. 1999. *The Age of Decency in Death in England. An Illustrated History* Jupp, P and Gittings, C eds. Manchester University Press.

Hymanson, A.1951. *The Sephardim Of England.* The Spanish and Portuguese Jews' Congregation London.

Jacobs, A. 1951.The Jews of Falmouth 1740-1860. *Transactions of the Jewish Historical Society of England* 17, 63-72

Jamilly, E. 1953/5. Anglo-Jewish Architects and Architecture in the 18th and 19th Centuries. *Transactions of the Jewish Historical Society of England* 18, 127-141.

Jamilly, E. 1996. *All Manner of Workmanship: Interior Decoration in British Synagogues* in *Building Jerusalem Jewish Architecture in Britain.* Edited and introduced by Kadish, S. Vallentine Mitchelle London.

Jones, J.B.1916. *Annals of Dover. History of Religion.* Dover Express Works.

Josephs, Z.1980. *Birmingham Jewry 1749-191.* Singers Hill Synagogue Birmingham Unpublished.

Kadish, S. 1996. *'Eden in Albion' A History of the Mikveh in Britain'.* In *Building Jerusalem. Jewish Architecture in Britain.* Valentine Mitchell. London.

Kadish, S. Bowman, B. Kendall, D. 2001. *Bevis Marks Synagogue 1701-2001.* English Heritage

Kadish, S. 2006. *Jewish Heritage in England an Architectural Guide.* English Heritage.

Kadish, S. 2011. *The Synagogues of Britain and Ireland. An Architectural and Social History.* Yale University Press New Haven and London.

Kalman, R. 1981. The Jewish East End –Where Was It? In The Jewish East End 1840-1939. *Jewish Historical Society of England* 28, 2-8.

Kershen, J.& Romain, J. 1995 *Tradition and Change, A History of the Reform Movement in Britain 1840-1995,* Valentine Mitchell, London.

Klein, J. S. 2006. *La Maison Sublime l'Ecole rabbinique & le Royaume juif de Rouen* Communaute d'Agglomeration Rouennnaise. France.

Krausz, E. 1964. *Leeds Jewry Its History and Social Structure.* Heffer and Sons Ltd. Cambridge.

Künzl, H. 1984. *Islamische Stilemente im Synagogenbau des 19, und fruhen 20 jahrhunderts.* Peter Lange, Frankfurt-am Main.

Kushner, T. 2002. *A Tale of Two Port Jewish Communities: Southampton and Portsmouth Compared Port Jews. Jewish Communities in Cosmopolitan Maritime Trading Centres 1550-1950.* D, Cesarini,ed. Frank Cass, London.

Lancaster, G. 1998. *A Venerable Jewish Community in Kent. A Brief History of Chatham Memorial Synagogue.* Unpublished.

Lassman, A., Spungin, J. and Millett, B.1944. *History of the Jews of Nottingham.* Unpublished.

Leveton, M. 2009. *The Jews in Norwich 11th-21st Century.* Norwich and Israel and Social Society.

Levine, H. 1956. *History of the Birmingham Hebrew Congregation 1856-1956.* Unpublished typescript in the Local Studies Department, Birmingham Central Library.

Levy, A. 1956. History of Sunderland Jewish Community. MacDonald, London

Levy, M. 1897. *The Western Synagogue. Some Materials For Its History.* Barber, G. London.

Levy, R.E. 1984. *The History of the Birmingham Hebrew Congregation 1829-1914*. Birmingham Jewish History Research Group.
Lewis, D. 1992. *The Jews of Oxford*. The Alden Press, Oxford.
Lewis, D. 2002. *Hull's Six Jewish Cemeteries*. Jewish Communities and Records.
Lilley, J. M. Stroud, G. Brothwell, D. Williamson M. 1994. *The Jewish Burial Ground at Jewbury*. York Archaeological Trust.
Lindsay, P. 1993. *The Synagogues of London*. Vallentine Mitchell and Co Ltd. London.
Lipman, V. 1951/2. A Survey of Anglo-Jewry in 1851. *Jewish Historical Society of England* 17, 171-188.
Lipman, V. 1954. *Social History of the Jews in England 1850-1950*. Watts and Co London.
Lipman, V. 1956. *A Volume to Commemorate the Tercentenary of the Re-Settlement of the Jews in Great Britain*. Vallentine Mitchell. London.
Lipman, V. 1962/7. The Rise of Jewish Suburbs. *Jewish Historical Society of England* 21, 78-102.
Lipman, V. 1968. The Anatomy of Medieval Anglo-Jewry. *Transactions of the Jewish Historical Society of England* 21, 65.
Lipman, V. 1972. *The Development of London Jewry in a Century of Anglo-Jewish Life. 1870-1970*. Levin, S. Ed. United Synagogue London.
Lipman. V.1981. *Jewish Settlement in the East End 1840-1940. The topographical and Statistical Evidence*. Jewish Historical Society of England.
Lipman, V. 1990. *A History of the Jews in Britain since 1858*. Leicester University Press.
Mackenzie, A. 1827. *History of Newcastle and Gateshead. Vol. 2 Note on Ecclesiastical Establishment in Newcastle*. (publisher unknown).
Maloney, C. Hotrod, I. London Fieldwork and Publication Round-up 2008. *London Archaeologist* 12, Supplement 2 (2009).
Margoliouth, M. 1851. *The History of the Jews in Great Britain*. Richard Bentley. New Burlington Street. London.
Marks, S. 2006. *Birth of a Cemetery: The Story of Deane Road*. Unpublished M.A. dissertation on Liverpool Jewry. Liverpool University.
Mills, J. 1853. *British Jews*. London.
Morris, M. 2008. *Edward I A Great and Terrible King and the Forging of Britain*. Hutchinson London.
National Trust 2004. *Back to Backs in Birmingham*. National Trust.
Newman, A. 1976. *The United Synagogue 1870-1970*. Routledge & Kegan Paul. London.
Olsover, L.1980. *The Jewish Communities of North-East England 1755-1980*. Ashley Mark Publishing Co. Gateshead, Tyne and Wear.
Pearce, J. 1998. A rare delftware Hebrew plate and assemblage from an excavation in Mitre Street, City of London. *Post-Medieval Archaeology* 32, 95-112.
Pearce, K and Fry, H. ed. 2000. *The Lost Jews of Cornwall. From the Middle Ages to the Nineteenth Century*. Redcliffe Press Ltd. Bristol.
Picton, J. 1873. *Memorials of Liverpool. Including a History of the Dock Estate*. Longman, Green and Co. Liverpool.

Phillips, O.S. and Simons, H.A. 1963. *The History of the Bayswater Synagogue 1863-1963*. Stationers' Hall London.

Picciotto, J.1956. *Sketches of Anglo-Jewish History in The Centenary Year of the Resettlement of Jewish England*. Soncino Press. London.

Renton, P. 2000. *The Lost Synagogues of London*. Tymsder Publishing. London.

Robinson, W. 1842. *The History and Antiquities of Hackney*. Greater London Record Office.

Rodrigues-Pereira, M. 1984. *Sir Moses Montefiore's Religious Foundations at Ramsgate*. Montefiore Endowment Committee. Spanish and Portuguese Jews' Congregation.

Roth, C. 1933. *Records of the Western Synagogue 1761-1932*. E, Goldstonand Son Ltd. London.

Roth, C. 1933. *The Jews of Penzance 1720-1913. The Decline and fall of an Anglo-Jewish Community*. Jewish Chronicle Supplement.

Roth, C. 1935. The Portsmouth Community and its Historical Background. *Jewish Historical Society of England* 13, 157-187.

Roth, C. 1950. *The Great Synagogue London 1690-1940*. E. Goldston and Son Ltd. London.

Roth, C, 1950. *The Rise of Provincial Jewry. The Early History of the Jewish Communities in the English Communities 1740-1840*. The Jewish Monthly, Woburn House WC1.

Roth, C.1978. *A History of the Jews in England*. Clarendon Press Oxford.

Samuel, J. 1997. *Jews in Bristol*. Sansom and Co. Bristol.

Samuel, W. 1924. *The First London Synagogue of the Resettlement*. Spottiswoode, Ballantyne and Co. Ltd. London.

Simmons, G. and Pearce, K. 2000. *The Jewish Cemetery, Penzance in The Lost Jews of Cornwall*, Redcliffe Press Ltd. Bristol.

Spector, D. 1968/9. The Jews of Brighton. *Transactions of the Jewish Historical Society* 22, 42-50.

Susser, B.1965. *Notes for the Visitor to the Plymouth Synagogue* (Unpublished).

Susser, B. 1993. *The Jews of South-West England* in Building Jerusalem Vallentine Mitchell London.

Susser, B. 1996. *Jewish Cemeteries in the West of England in Building Jerusalem*, Kadish, S. ed. Valentine Mitchell London.

Susser, B. 1997. *Alderney Road Jewish Cemetery, London E1, 1697-1853: Anglo-Jewry's Oldest Ashkenazi Cemetery*. United Synagogue Publications.

Susser, B. 1970. *An Account of the Old Jewish Cemetery on Plymouth Hoe*. Bro-Cards of Plymouth.

Stow, J.1598. *A Survey of London*. Sutton Publishing Ltd. London.

Tobias, A and S, Samuel, J. Greenwood, A. Sutton, M. Simon, H. Silverman, S. Nirenberg, S, Hill & Hill, M. 1997. *A Catalogue of the Burials in the Jewish Cemeteries of Bristol*. Unpublished.

Torode, B.1999. *The Hebrew Community of Cheltenham, Gloucester and Stroud*. Unpublished, Cheltenham Synagogue.

D'Bloissiers Tovey, 1738. *Anglia Judaica A History of the Jews in England*. Edited and retold by Pearl, E.1990. Weidenfeld and Nicholson. London.

Tuck, W. 1987. *A Biography Relating to the Jewish Sons King's Lynn*. Unpublished.

Vaughan, L. and Penn, A. 2001. *The Jewish 'Ghetto'-Formation and Social Structure*. Institute for Jewish Policy Research.

Weinberg, A. 1998. *Portsmouth Jewry 1730s -1980s*. Subscribers Edition Portsmouth Synagogue.

Williams, B. 1976. *The Making of Manchester Jewry 1740-1875*. Manchester University Press.

Williams B. 1987. *Liverpool Jewry-A Pictorial History* Merseyside Jewish Representative Council.

Williams, B. 2008. *Jewish Manchester an Illustrated History*. The Breedon Books Publishing Company Ltd. Derby.

Wolf, L. 2002. Jewry of the Restoration. 1660-1664.*Transactions of the Jewish Historical. Society* 5.

Wolman, J. 1986. *Liverpool Jewry in the Eighteenth Century* Merseyside Jewish Representative Council.

Sources

Bath Records Office, Birmingham Central Reference Library, Birmingham Jewish Recorder 1939, British Library Map Department, British Museum Library and Department of Prehistory and Europe, Coventry History Centre, Cuming Museum Southwark, Dover Records Office, English Heritage, East Sussex Records Office, Glamorgan Archives (Cardiff and Merthyr Tydfil), Gloucester Archives Office, Isle of Sheppey Heritage Centre, Hull Archives, Illustrated London News various editions, Jewish Museum Camden Town, Jewish Studies Library U.C.L. Jewish Year Books (1909-2004), Kent County Archives Service, King's Lynn Records Library, Leeds Central Library, Liverpool Records Office, London Metropolitan Archives, *Statistical Accounts of the Congregation the British Empire 5606/1845* (Chief Rabbi's Archive.ACC/2805/1/1/107), Manchester Records Office, and Research Laboratory for Archaeology and History of Art, Newcastle Discovery Museum, Norwich City Records Library, Nottingham Records Library, Oxfordshire Studies and Central Library, City of Plymouth Archives and Records, Sheffield Records Office, Society of Antiquaries of London, Southampton Reference Library, Spanish and Portuguese Jew's Congregation Archives Office, Sunderland Records Library, West Glamorgan Archive Service (Swansea), Yarmouth Central Library and Records Office.

First and Second Edition Ordnance Survey Maps of London, 1871-1879 and 1888-1901. 1888/1923 Ordnance Survey Maps of provincial cities and towns and 1852 Welsh Board of Health Maps. 1850-1995 extracts from local maps (some Ordnance Survey).

The Jewish Year Books 1909-2004 have been used as a guide to the size of community which are shown in the gazetteer over the period 1880-2004. JCR-

UK, Jewish Communities and Records have also been an invaluable source also of identifying the sizes of the communities discussed.

Visiting all the London cemeteries discussed; walking the streets in the City and East End of London. Visiting and researching every one of the provincial towns, synagogues, and cemeteries, archives and records offices detailed in this study.

London contacts

Personal contact with Jacqui Pearce, Museum of London, Bruce Watson, MoLAS, Jennifer Marin, Jewish Museum, Camden Town, Tamara Chase, Cuming Museum. Southwark London, Mark Williams, United Synagogue Burial Society, who made it possible for me to visit the closed United Synagogues Cemeteries, in London and in the provinces. Miriam Rodrigues-Pereira, Honorary Archivist to the Spanish and Portuguese Jew's Congregation, London. Reuben Ezekiel, Western Charitable Fund. Elkan Levy, Anglo-Jewish Historian, Rev. Malcolm Wiseman, Former Minister of the Small Jewish Communities.

Provincial contacts
Bath: Norman Marks, Bath resident, Richard Sermon, Archaeological Officer Bath and North East Somerset Council.
Birmingham: Rabbi S. Arkush, Bernard Gingold, Singers Lane Synagogue administrator, Lionel Singer, local historian, Stanley Busby, photographer.
Bradford: Nigel Grizzard, local historian
Brighton: Gordon Franks, member of the community
Bristol: Alex Schlesinger, Chairman of the Friends of Bath Cemetery, Sam Silverman President of Bristol's Hebrew Congregation.
Canterbury: Kent County Archives Service and King's School Canterbury
Cardiff: Rabbi Wellenberg**,** Alan Schwartz
Chatham: David Herling, Vice-Chairman Chatham Memorial Synagogue.
Cheltenham: Sam Stone, Synagogue Chairman, Michael Webber, Sec.
Coventry: Barry Deitch, President of Reform Community
Dover: Hambrook and Johns Funeral Directors.
Exeter: Dr. Paul Newgass, President Exeter Synagogue.
Falmouth: Eric Dawkins, Former Town Clerk
Gloucester: Sarah Aitken, Gloucester Archives
Hull: Dr. David Lewis, archivist, Hon. Secretary of Hull Hebrew Congregation.
Ipswich: Elizabeth Sugarman, local archivist.
King's Lynn: Dr. Jane Clarke, local Jewish historian.
Leeds: Malcolm Sender, community historian and archivist. Bobby Caplin O.B.E. Leeds industrialist
Liverpool: Saul Marks, Deane Street Cemetery. Arnold Lewis, Liverpool's Jewish Archivist.

Manchester: Bill Williams, Historian and Life President and Historical Adviser Manchester Jewish Museum.
Newcastle: Dorothy Slotnik, a member of many of the committees involved in communal activities, with a fund of local knowledge.
Norwich: Maureen and Barry Leveton, local Jewish historians and archivists.
Nottingham: Rolf Noskwith, Nottingham industrialist, David Snapper, former Member of Nottingham's History Research Team Research Team.
Oxford: Marcus Roberts, JTrails.
Penzance: Keith Pearce, Historian Jewish Community in Cornwall and Alison Bevan Curator Penlee Museum.
Plymouth: Dr. Peter Lee Hon, Treasurer Plymouth Hebrew Congregation.
Portsmouth: Aubrey Weinberg, Synagogue Warden.
Ramsgate: Miriam Rodrigues-Pereira, Hon Archivist Spanish and Portuguese Congregation
Sheerness: D. Buttenshaw, local estate agent
Sheffield: Eric Sayliss, senior member of the Sheffield Hebrew Congregation.
Southampton: Martyn Rose, President Southampton Hebrew Congregation.
Sunderland: Dorothy Slotnick, lived in Sunderland, James Nelson local businessman
Swansea: Norma Glass MBE member of the Board of Deputies of British Jews. David Factor, Chairman Swansea Hebrew Congregation
Truro: Angela Broom, Curator Truro Museum.
Yarmouth (Great): Records Library.

Gazetteer

SUMMARY SHEETS AND ORDNANCE SURVEY MAPS

London synagogues
[1]	Bayswater Synagogue
[2]	Bevis Marks Synagogue
[3]	Central Synagogue
[4]	Creechurch Lane Synagogue
[5]	The Great Synagogue
[6]	The Hambros
[7]	The New Synagogue
[8]	New West End Synagogue
[9]	Princelet Street Synagogue
[10]	Sandy's Row Synagogue
[11]	Western Synagogue
[12]	West London Synagogue

London cemeteries
[48]	*Velho* (Old)
[49]	*Nuevo* (New)
[50]	Brentwood
[51]	Alderney Road
[52]	Bancroft Road
[53]	Brady Street
[54]	Fulham Road
[55]	Lauriston Road
[56]	West Ham
[57]	West London
[58]	Willesden

Provincial synagogues and cemeteries

[13]	[59]	Bath	[31]	[77]	Liverpool
[14]	[60]	Birmingham	[32]	[78]	Manchester
[15]	[61]	Bradford	[33]	[79]	Merthyr Tydfil
[16]	[62]	Brighton	[34]	[80]	Newcastle
[17]	[63]	Bristol	[35]	[81]	Norwich
[18]	[64]	Canterbury	[36]	[82]	Nottingham
[19]	[65]	Cardiff	[37]		Oxford
[20]	[66]	Chatham	[38]	[83]	Penzance
[21]	[67]	Cheltenham	[39]	[84]	Portsmouth and Southsea
[22]	[68]	Coventry	[40]	[85]	Ramsgate
[23]	[69]	Dover	[41]	[86]	Sheerness and Isle of Sheppey
[24]	[70]	Exeter	[42]	[87]	Sheffield
[25]	[71]	Falmouth	[43]	[88]	Southampton
[26]	[72]	Gloucester	[44]	[89]	Sunderland
[27]	[73]	Hull	[45]	[90]	Swansea
[28]	[74]	Ipswich	[46]	[91]	Yarmouth (Great)
[29]	[75]	King's Lynn			
[30]	[76]	Leeds			

NB: In the gazetteer some of the microfilms of extracts of Ordnance Survey Maps from the British Library are scratched and in poor condition. In a few cases such as Bath, Cardiff, Falmouth, Merthyr Tydfil and Norwich, not all Ordinance Survey Maps are available to copy, photograph extracts were taken.

LOCATION	CHAPTER	SITE	DATE ESTABLISHED	IN USE TO	DATE OF VISIT	GAZETTEER NUMBER
LONDON	4.1.1	BAYSWATER SYNAGOGUE W2	1863	1966	*	[1]

ADDITIONAL NOTES

Chichester Place, W2

*demolished in 1966 for construction of The West Way
Branch of The Great Synagogue. One of the original five synagogues of the United Synagogue formed in 1870

BIBLIOGRAPHY

Newman, A. 1976 *The United Synagogue 1870 - 1970*

Phillips et al. 1963 *The History of the Bayswater Synagogue 1863 - 1963*

Renton, P. 2000 *The Lost Synagogues of London*

OTHER SOURCES

FIGURE NUMBERS   4.3-4.5

MEMBERSHIP

Date	Male Members
1870	359
1880	318
1890	377

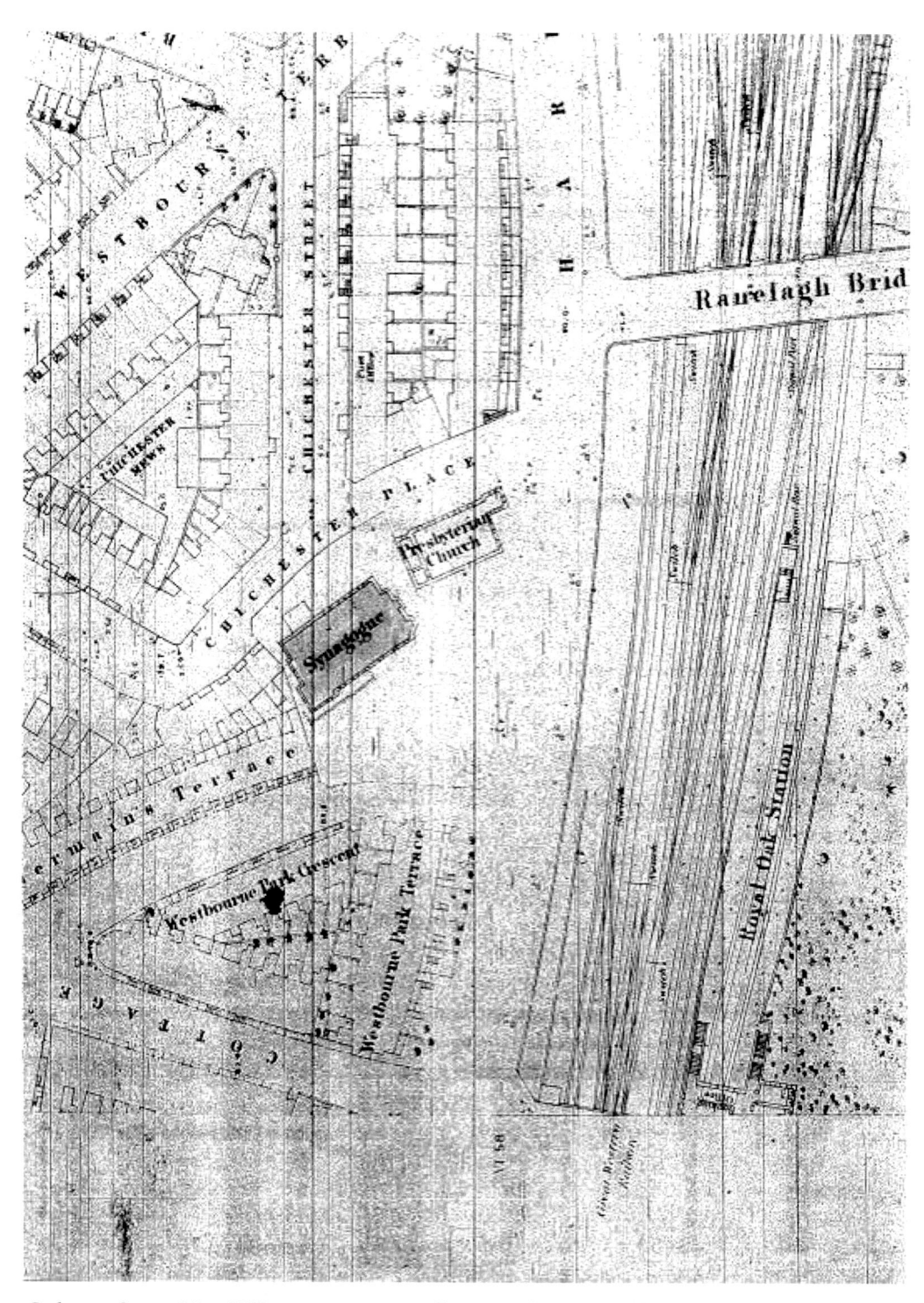

Ordnance Survey Map 1873
5ft. to a mile
[1]

Bayswater Synagogue W2
1863-1966 (demolished 1966 to make way for West Way)

LOCATION	CHAPTER	SITE	DATE ESTABLISHED	IN USE TO	DATE OF VISIT	GAZETTEER NUMBER
CITY OF LONDON	4.1.2	BEVIS MARKS SYNAGOGUE EC3	1701	still in use	2009	[2]

ADDITIONAL NOTES

Bevis Marks, 4 Heneadge Lane, EC3 (Grade I)

Spanish and Portuguese (Sephardi)

1657 First synagogue established post-readmission in Creechurch Lane, EC3

1701 Second synagogue Bevis Marks:
First purpose-built synagogue post-readmission (still in use)

BIBLIOGRAPHY

Kadish, S. 2006 *Jewish Heritage in England: an Architectural Guide*

Roth, C. 1978 *A History of the Jews in England*

Samuel, E. 2006 *A Service to Celebrate the 350th Anniversary of The Readmission of the Jews to Britain at the Spanish and Portuguese Jews'*

Synagogue Bevis Marks EC3

OTHER SOURCES

Archives of The Spanish and Portuguese Congregation

FIGURE NUMBERS   4.6-4.8

MEMBERSHIP

Date	Members	
1701	400	men
	160	women

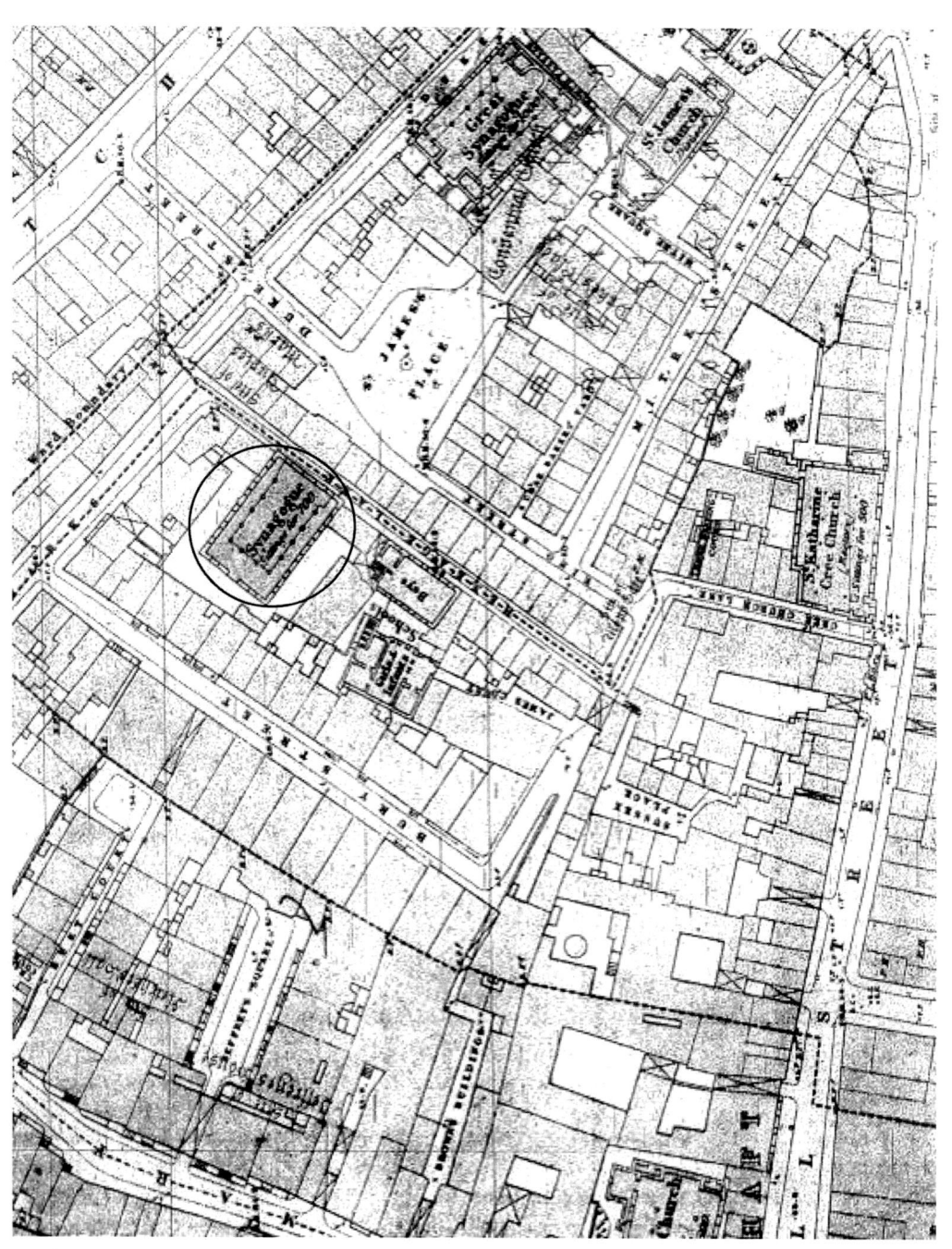

Ordnance Survey Map 1895
5ft. to a mile
[2]

Bevis Marks Synagogue
1701-still in use

LOCATION	CHAPTER	SITE	DATE ESTABLISHED	IN USE TO	DATE OF VISIT	GAZETTEER NUMBER
LONDON WEST END	4.1.3	CENTRAL SYNAGOGUE W1	1855 1870 1958	1870 1941* still in use	2009	[3]

ADDITIONAL NOTES

1855 — First synagogue built in Great Portland Street W1

1870-1941 — Second synagogue Great Portland Street
One of the original five synagogues of the United Synagogue formed in 1870. *Destroyed in the Blitz 1941

1958 — Third synagogue in same street still in use

BIBLIOGRAPHY

Black, G. 2003 *Jewish London: an Illustrated History*

Newman, A. 1976 *The United Synagogue 1870 - 1970*

Renton, P. 2000 *The Lost Synagogues of London*

OTHER SOURCES

FIGURE NUMBERS 4.9

MEMBERSHIP

Date	Male Members
1870	260
1880	380

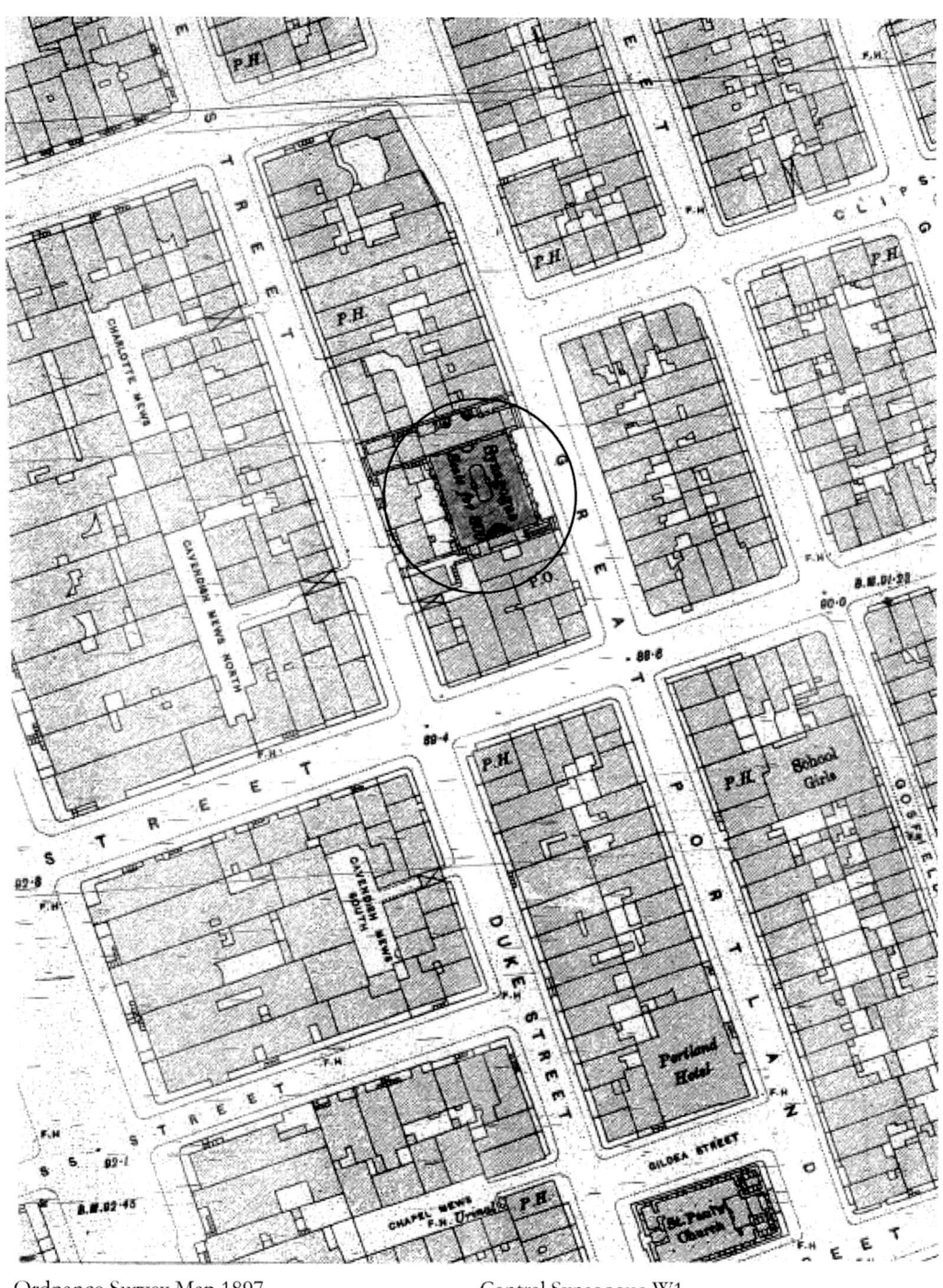

Ordnance Survey Map 1897
5ft. to a mile

Central Synagogue W1
1855-1941 (destroyed in Blitz)

[3]

LOCATION	CHAPTER	SITE	DATE ESTABLISHED	IN USE TO	DATE OF VISIT	GAZETTEER NUMBER
CITY OF LONDON	4.1.4	CREECHURCH LANE SYNAGOGUE EC3	1657	1701	no longer exists*	[4]

ADDITIONAL NOTES

1657 First Meeting Room of Sephardi Community in Creechurch Lane

1674 Enlarged

1701 The community moved to Bevis Marks Synagogue, 4 Heneadge Lane, EC3

Plaque in Creechurch Lane commemorating original synagogue

BIBLIOGRAPHY

Black, G. 2003 *Jewish London: an Illustrated History*

Renton, P. 2000 *The Lost Synagogues of London*

Samuel, E. 1924 *The First London Synagogue of the Resettlement*

Samuel, E. 2006 *A Service to Celebrate the 350th Anniversary of the Readmission of the Jews to Britain at the Spanish and Portuguese Synagogue Bevis Marks Synagogue*

OTHER SOURCES

Archives Spanish and Portuguese Congregation

FIGURE NUMBERS   4.10-4.11

MEMBERSHIP

Date	Members	
1657	85	men
	24	women

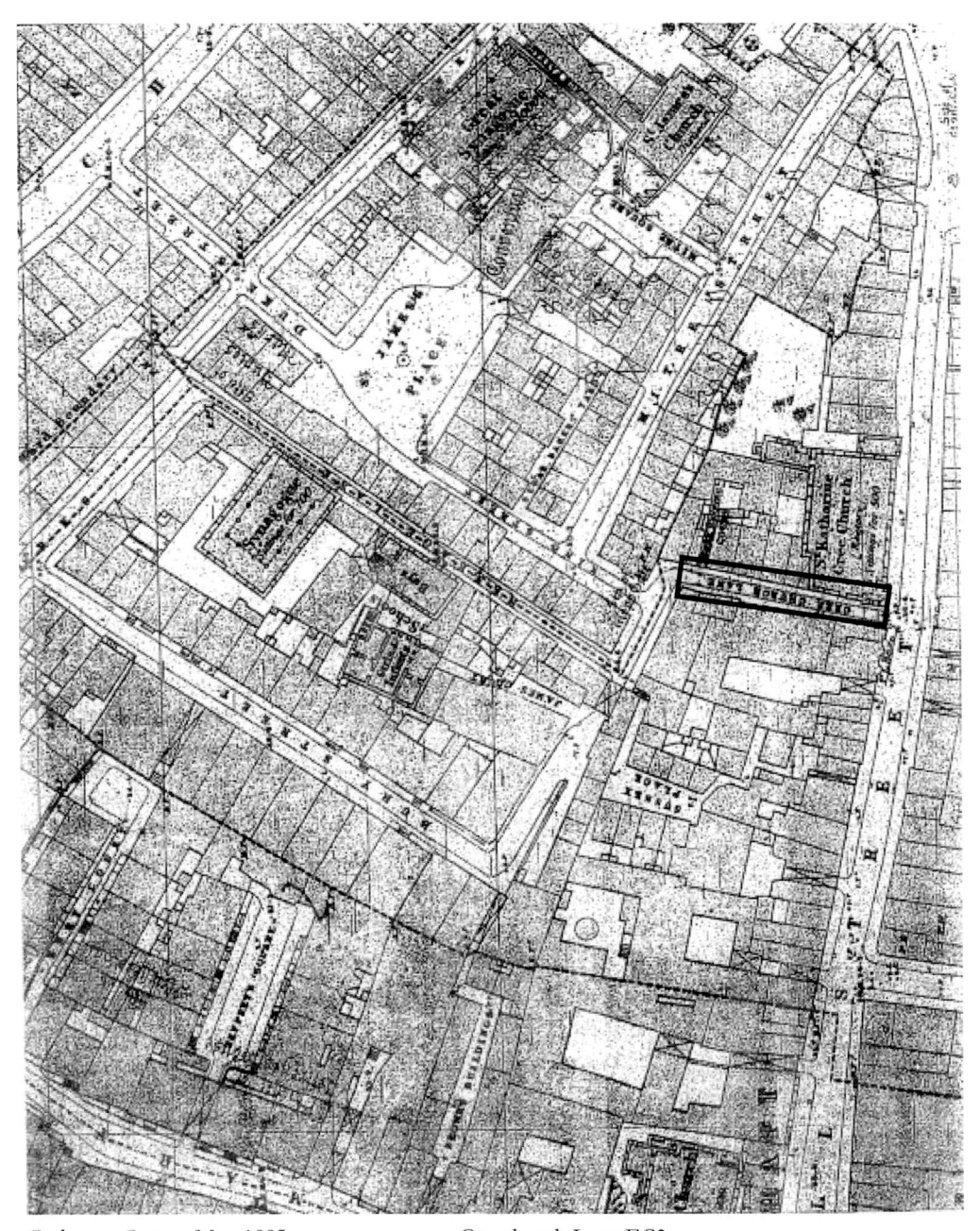

Ordnance Survey Map 1895
5ft. to a mile

Creechurch Lane EC3
1657-1701(synagogue not marked)

[4]

LOCATION	CHAPTER	SITE	DATE ESTABLISHED	IN USE TO	DATE OF VISIT	GAZETTEER NUMBER
CITY OF LONDON	4.1.5	THE GREAT SYNAGOGUE EC3	1690 1722 1766 1790 1943	1722 1766 1790 1941* 1958*	no longer exists	[5]

ADDITIONAL NOTES

      Duke's Place, EC3

      Earliest Ashkenazi synagogue following the Resettlement in 1656

1690 First Synagogue

1722 Second Synagogue

1766 Third Synagogue

1790 Fourth Synagogue (enlarged)

1941 *Destroyed in the Blitz

      Plaque in Duke's Place to commemorate the destroyed synagogue

1943 *Hut erected on bomb site

BIBLIOGRAPHY

    Kadish, S. 1996 (ed.) *Building Jerusalem, Jewish Architecture in Britain*

    Newman, A. 1976 *The United Synagogue 1870 - 1970*

    Renton, P. 2000 *The Lost Synagogues of London*

    Roth, C. 1941 *A History of the Jews in England*

    Roth, C. 1950 *The Great Synagogue*

OTHER SOURCES

FIGURE NUMBERS   4.13-4.21

MEMBERSHIP

Date	Male Members
1870	324
1880	400

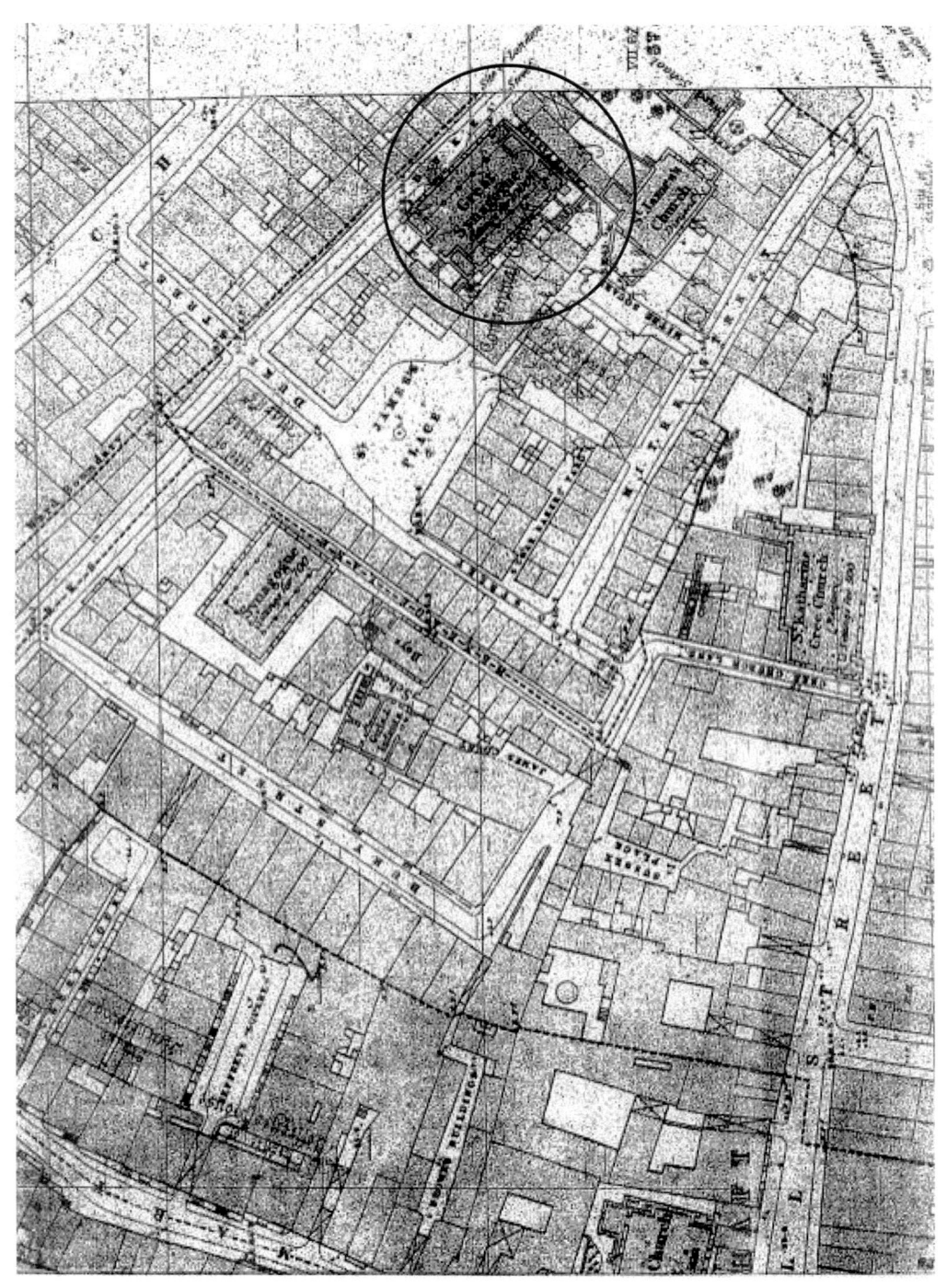

Ordnance Survey Map 1895 The Great Synagogue EC3 [5]
5ft. to a mile 1620-1941 (destroyed in the Blitz 1941)

LOCATION	CHAPTER	SITE	DATE ESTABLISHED	IN USE TO	DATE OF VISIT	GAZETTEER NUMBER
CITY OF LONDON	4.1.6	THE HAMBRO SYNAGOGUE EC3	1707 1720 1893 1899	1720 1892 1899 1936*	no longer exists	[6]

ADDITIONAL NOTES

	Magpie Alley, Fenchurch Street, EC3
1707-1720	Marcus Hamburger establishes a synagogue in his own house
	seating for 218 men and 55 women (Lindsay, 1993)
1720	Synagogue enlarged
1892	*Demolished*
1893-1899	*Services held in Vestry of Great Synagogue, Dukes Place, EC3*
1707	Hoxton Burial Ground acquired
	no longer exists
	*Closed in 1936 when it amalgamated with The Great Synagogue
1870	One of the original 5 Synagogues that formed The United Synagogue in 1870

BIBLIOGRAPHY

Lindsay, P. 1993 *The Synagogues of London*

Renton, P. 2000 *The Lost Synagogues of London*
Roth, C. 1941 *A History of the Jews of England*
Roth, C. 1950 *The Great Synagogue*

OTHER SOURCES

Bluer et al. Molas 30
Guildhall Library: Corporation of London
Newman, A. 1976 *The United Synagogue*

FIGURE NUMBERS   4.22-4.24

MEMBERSHIP

Date	Male Members
1870	161
1880	162
1890	*102*

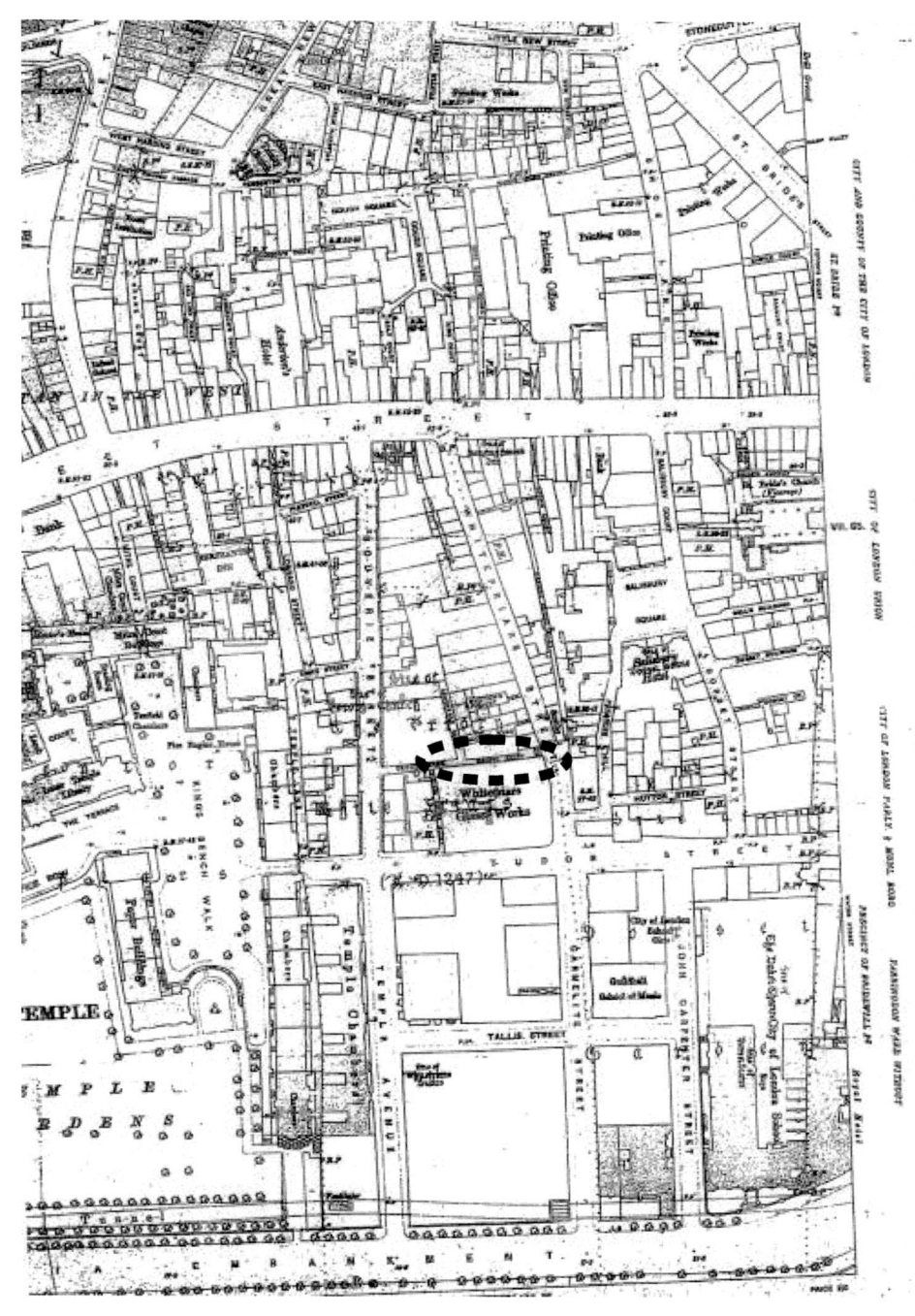

Ordnance Survey Map 1895   The Hambro Synagogue Magpie Alley EC3   (not marked)
5ft. to a mile   1707-1936   **[6]**

LOCATION	CHAPTER	SITE	DATE ESTABLISHED	IN USE TO	DATE OF VISIT	GAZETTEER NUMBER
CITY OF LONDON	4.1.7	THE NEW SYNAGOGUE EC3	1760/1 1838 1915	1838 1911 still in use	no longer exists no longer exists	[7]

ADDITIONAL NOTES

	Leadenhall Street, EC3
1760/1-1838	first synagogue built in Leadenhall Street, EC3
1838-*1911*	moved to Great St. Helen's, EC3
	no longer exists
1915	Egerton Road N16
	(still in use)
	One of the original 5 synagogues of The United Synagogue formed in 1870
1761	Brady Street Cemetery established

BIBLIOGRAPHY

Lindsay, P. 1993 *The Synagogues of London*
Newman, A. 1976 *The United Synagogue 1870 - 1970*
Renton, P. 2000 *The Lost Synagogues of London*
Roth, C. 1941 *A History of the Jews in England*

OTHER SOURCES

1999 The Jewish Chronicle

FIGURE NUMBERS   4.25 - 4.27

MEMBERSHIP

Date	Male Members
1870	283
1880	358
1910	*204*
1920	*654*
1950	*c.1000*
1960	*c.1,100*
1970	*729*

Ordnance Survey Map 1895
5ft. to a mile

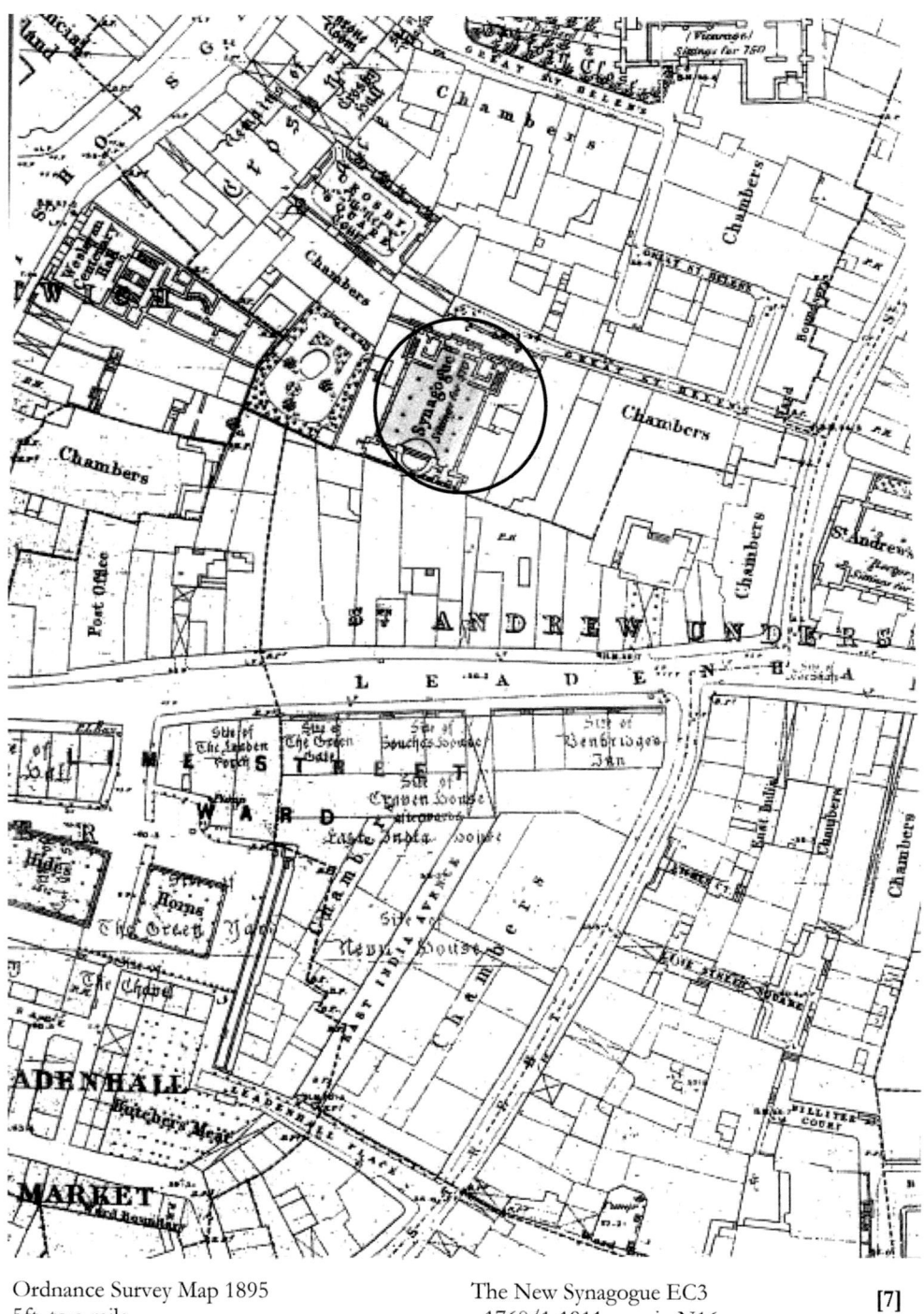

The New Synagogue EC3
1760/1-1911 now in N16

[7]

LOCATION	CHAPTER	SITE	DATE ESTABLISHED	IN USE TO	DATE OF VISIT	GAZETTEER NUMBER
LONDON WEST END	4.1.8	NEW WEST END SYNAGOGUE W2	1878/9	still in use	2010	[8]

ADDITIONAL NOTES

New West End Synagogue, St. Petersburgh Place, Bayswater W2

Grade I (2008)

BIBLIOGRAPHY

Jamilly E., 1996 *All Manner of Workmanship: Interior Decoration in British Synagogues* in *"Building Jerusalem". Jewish Architecture in Britain.* Edited and introduced by Kadish, S.

Kadish, S. 2006 *Jewish Heritage in England: An Architectural Guide*

OTHER SOURCES

1878 The Builder

FIGURE NUMBERS 4.28-4.31

MEMBERSHIP

Date	Male Members
1879	179
1880	202
1900	322

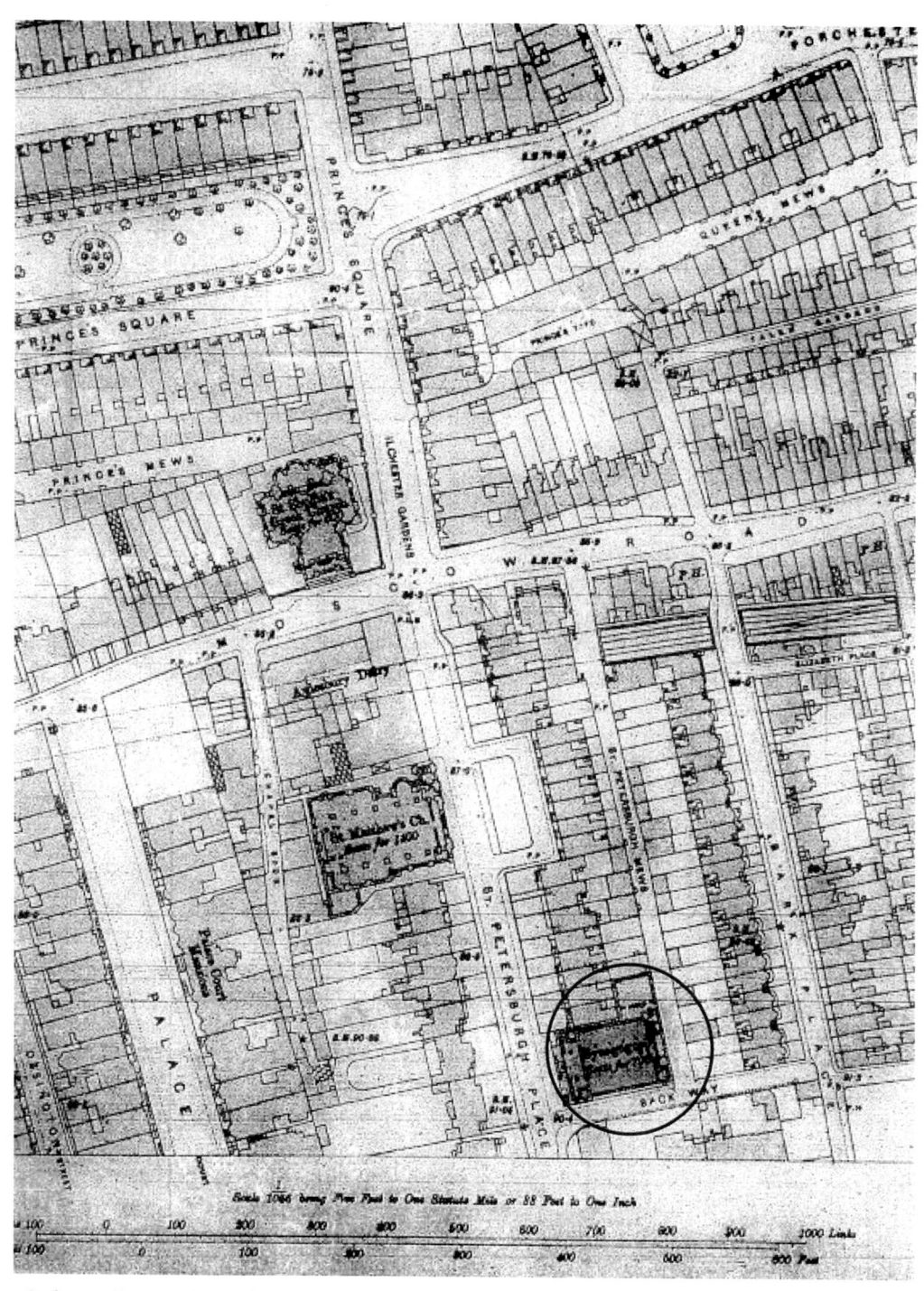

Ordnance Survey Map 1985
5ft. to a mile
[8]

New West End Synagogue W2
1878/9-still in use

Reproduced from 1985 O.S. map with the permission of the Controller of H.M. Stationary Office, Crown Copyright 2013

LOCATION	CHAPTER	SITE	DATE ESTABLISHED	IN USE TO	DATE OF VISIT	GAZETTEER NUMBER
LONDON	4.1.9	PRINCELET STREET SYNAGOGUE E1	1870	1962 closed 1983	2010	[9]

ADDITIONAL NOTES

19 Princelet Street, Spitafields, E1 (Grade II*)

now Museum of Immigration

BIBLIOGRAPHY

Kadish, S. 2006 *Jewish Heritage in England: An Architectural Guide*

Lindsay, P. 1993 *The Synagogues of London*

Lipman V. 1954 *Social History of The Jews in England 1850-1950*

Renton, P. 2000 *The Lost Synagogues of London*

OTHER SOURCES

Jewish Year Book 1896

FIGURE NUMBERS   4.32- 4.33

MEMBERSHIP

Date	Male Members
1870	120
1896	80

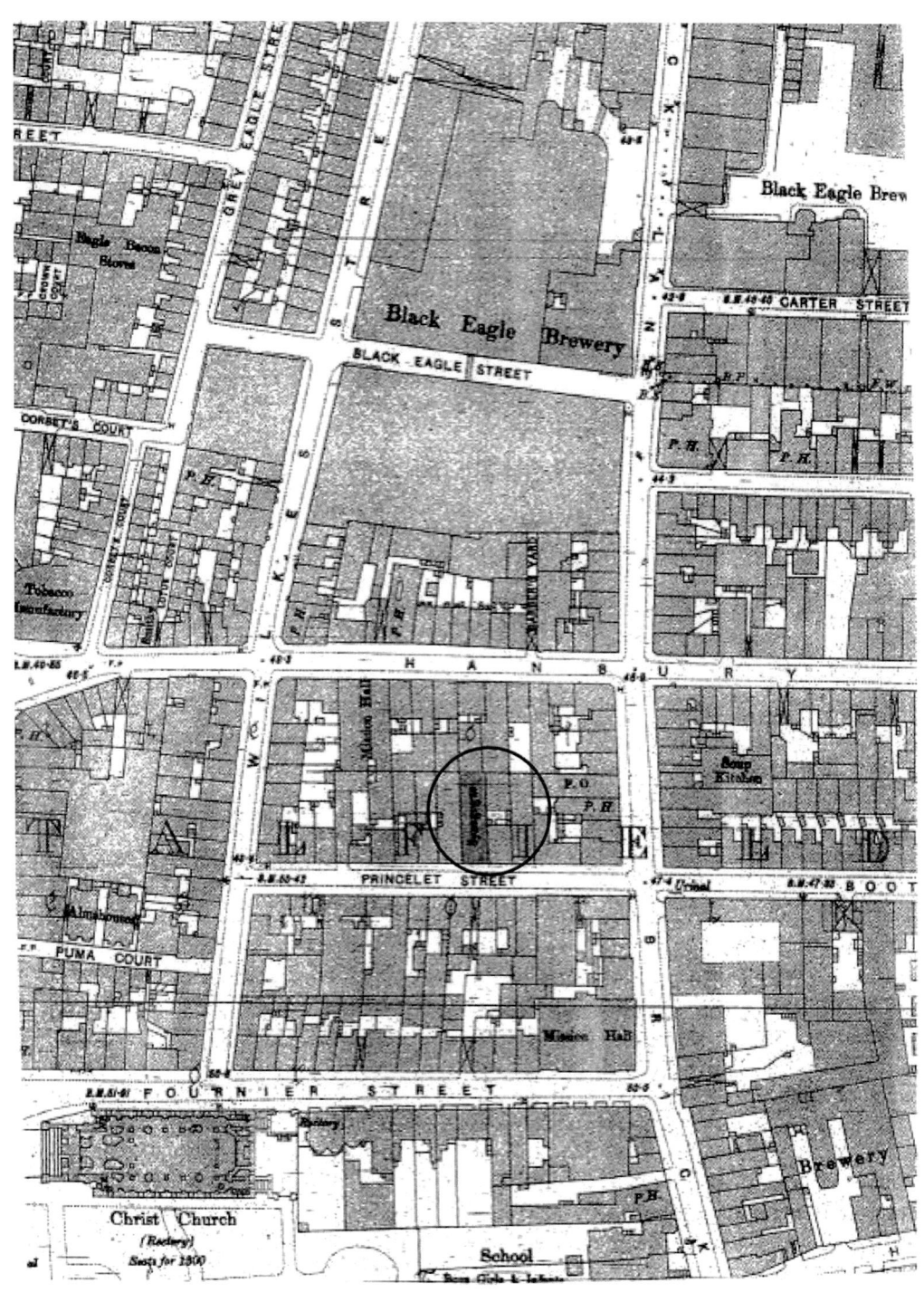

Ordnance Survey Map 1895
5ft. to a mile

Princelet Street Synagogue E1
1870-1962

[9]

LOCATION	CHAPTER	SITE	DATE ESTABLISHED	IN USE TO	DATE OF VISIT	GAZETTEER NUMBER
LONDON	4.1.10	SANDY'S ROW SYNAGOGUE EC1	c.1870	still in use	2009	[10]

ADDITIONAL NOTES

Sandy's Row Synagogue, Bishopsgate EC1 (Grade II)
c.1854 Community established a room in White's Row Spitalfield, E1
c.1870 Synagogue established in Sandy's Row
(originally a Huguenot Church dating from 1766)
Oldest Ashkenazi Congregation in London
The original congregation was comprised of Dutch Jews who set up their own synagogue independent of The United Synagogue

BIBLIOGRAPHY

Kadish, S. 2006   *Jewish Heritage in England. An Architectural Guide*
Lindsay, P. 1993   *The Synagogues of London*
Renton, P. 2000   *The Lost Synagogues of London*

OTHER SOURCES

Jewish Year Book 1896

FIGURE NUMBERS   4.34

MEMBERSHIP

Date	Male Members
1896	318

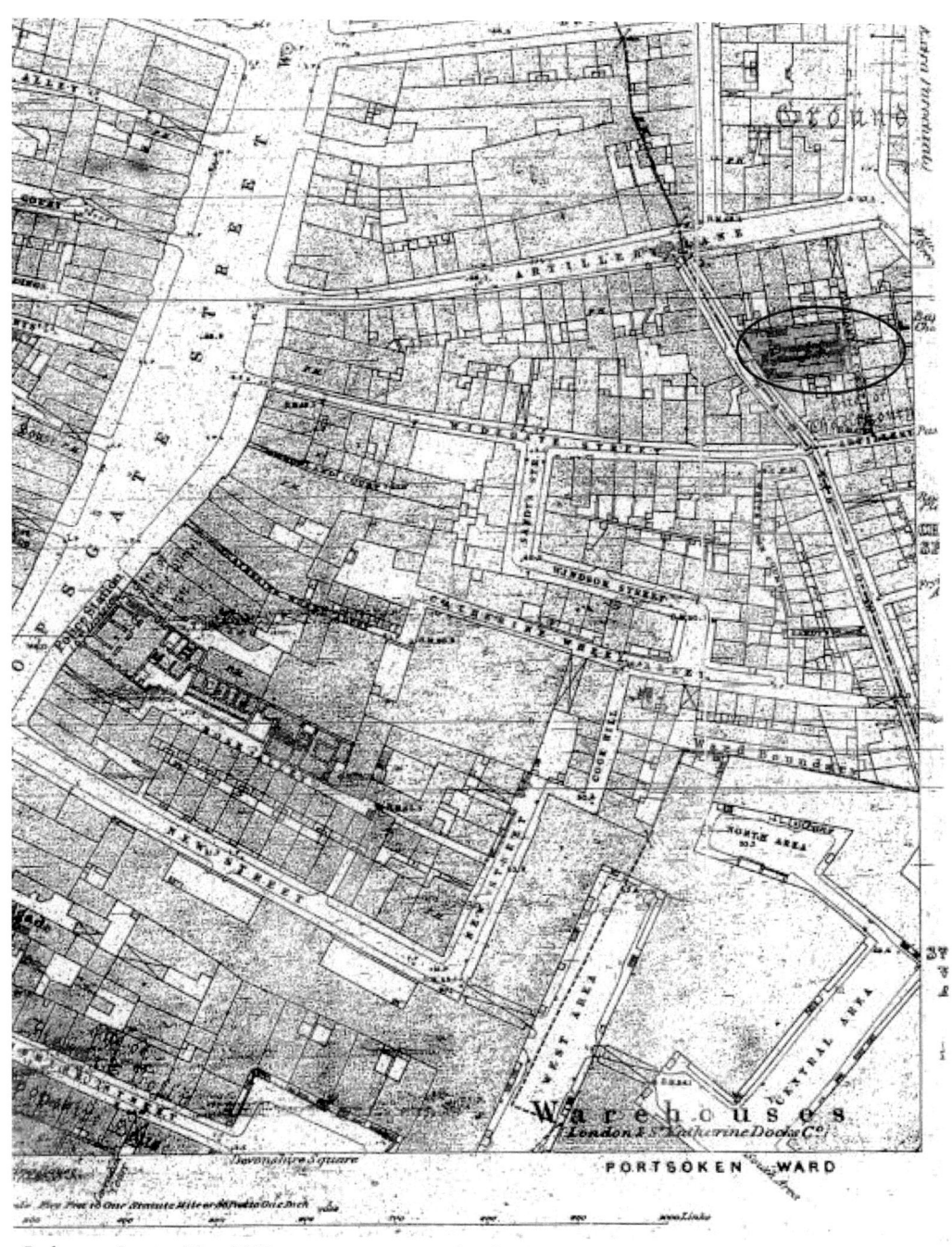

Ordnance Survey Map 1895
5ft. to a mile

Sandy's Row Synagogue EC1
c.1870-still in use

[10]

LOCATION	CHAPTER	SITE	DATE ESTABLISHED	IN USE TO	DATE OF VISIT	GAZETTEER NUMBER
LONDON	4.1.11	WESTERN SYNAGOGUE W1	1761	see below	*	[11]

ADDITIONAL NOTES

1761-1765	Room of Prayer: Great Pulteney Street W1
1765-1774	Back Alley, Denmark Court, Strand WC2
1774 -1826	Bedford Row, Denmark Court, Strand WC2
1810	A breakaway secessionist community was established in Dean Street, Soho W1 *later re-established in Maiden Lane (closed in 1907)*
1826-*1914*	St. Alban's Place SW1 no longer exists
1915- *1941*	Alfred Place WC1 (destroyed in the Blitz)
1957-1991*	Crawford Street W1 no longer exists
	Community amalgamated with the Marble Arch Synagogue

BIBLIOGRAPHY

Barnet, A. 1961 *The Western Synagogue Through Two Centuries 1761-1961*

Levy, M. 1897 *History of The Western Synagogue*

Lindsay, P.1993 *The Synagogues of London*

Renton, P. 2000 *The Lost Synagogues of London*

Roth, C. 1932 *Records of The Western Synagogue 1761-1932*

OTHER SOURCES

FIGURE NUMBERS 4.35-4.38

MEMBERSHIP

Date	Male Members
1954	*58*
1960	*341*
1970	*467*

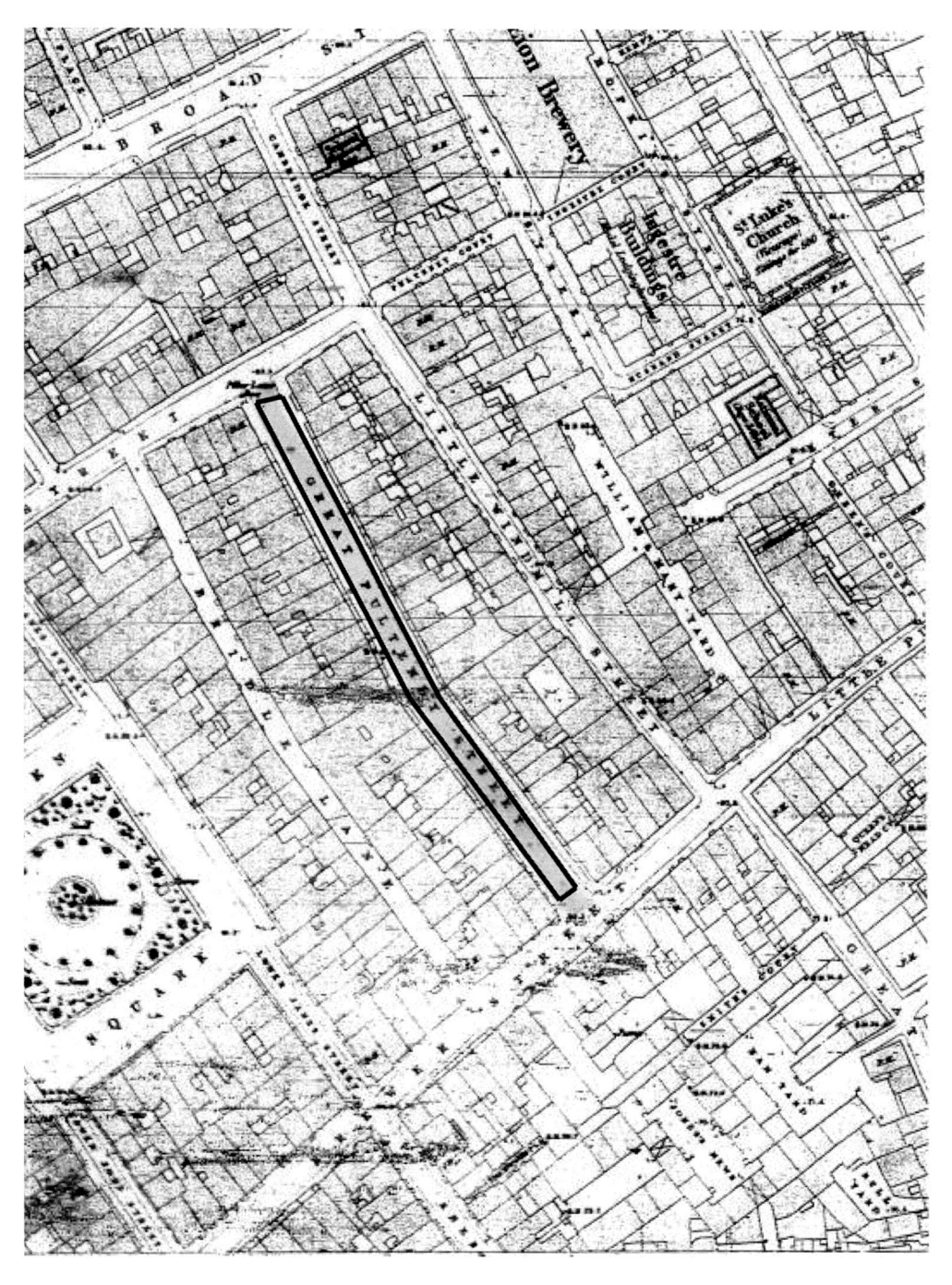

Ordnance Survey Map 1895   Western Synagogue Great Pulteney Street W1
5ft. to a mile   1761-1765 (not marked)   [11]

LOCATION	CHAPTER	SITE	DATE ESTABLISHED	IN USE TO	DATE OF VISIT	GAZETTEER NUMBER
LONDON WEST END	4.1.12	WEST LONDON SYNAGOGUE W1	c.1841 1849 1870	1848 1870 still in use	2010	[12]

ADDITIONAL NOTES

West London Synagogue, 34 Upper Berkeley Street W1 (Grade II)

First and largest Reform Congregation in Great Britain

c.1841-1848   Burton Street, St. Pancras WC1 *no longer exists*

1849-1870   Cavendish Square W1 *no longer exists*

1870   Upper Berkeley Street W1 *still in use*

BIBLIOGRAPHY

Black, G. 2003 *Jewish London: An Illustrated History*

Kadish, S. 2006 *Jewish Heritage in England: An Architectural Guide*

Lindsay, P. 1993 *The Synagogues of London*

Lipman, V. 1954 *Social History of The Jews in England 1850 - 1950*

OTHER SOURCES

1872   Illustrated London News

FIGURE NUMBERS   4.39-4.41

MEMBERSHIP

Date	Male Members
1965	2,500 families
2006	3,500 members

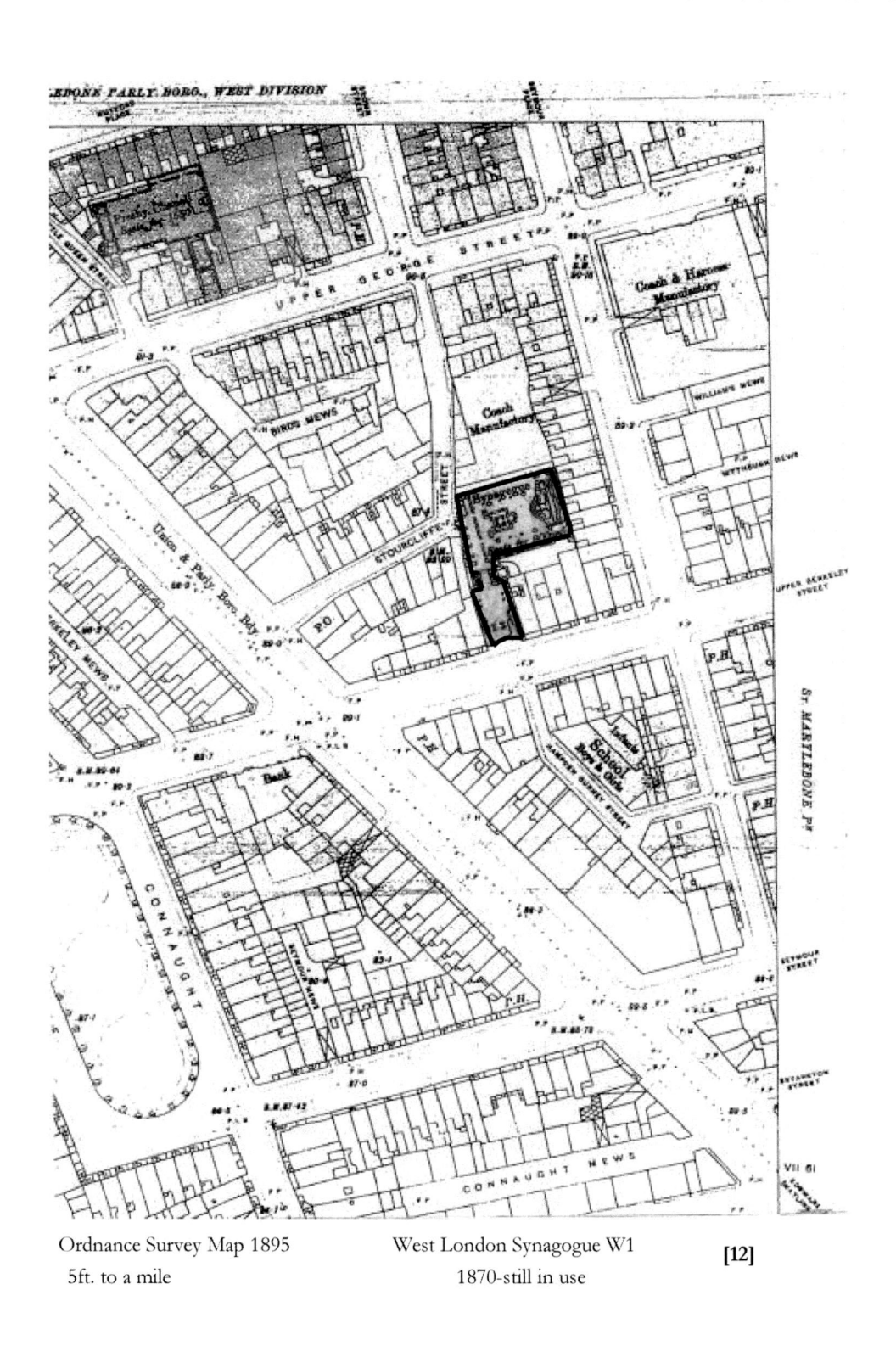

Ordnance Survey Map 1895 West London Synagogue W1 [12]
5ft. to a mile 1870-still in use

LOCATION	CHAPTER	SITE	DATE ESTABLISHED	IN USE TO	DATE OF VISIT	GAZETTEER NUMBER
LONDON	5.1.1	*VELHO* (OLD) CEMETERY OF THE SPANISH AND PORTUGUESE JEWS E1 (Sephardi)	1657	.1742	2007	[48]

ADDITIONAL NOTES

Mile End Road, E1 (Grade II listed)

The oldest resettlement Jewish cemetery in Britain

Grave of Antonio Carvajal d.1659, founder of the Sephardi Community in London

Grave of Doctor Fernando Mendez d.1724, physician to King John IV of Portugal

The Great Plague: numerous children's graves marked *"L. Angelito"* (little angel)

BIBLIOGRAPHY

Black, G. 2003 *Jewish London: An Illustrated History*

Diamond, A. 1955 *The Cemetery of The Re-settlement in TJHSE**

*Transactions of The Jewish Historical Society of England

Hyamson, A. 1951 *The Sephardim of England*

Kadish, S. 2006 *Jewish Heritage in England: An Architectural Guide*

Magoliouth, M. 1851 *The History of The Jews in Great Britain*

Roth, C. 1978 *A History of The Jews in England*

OTHER SOURCES

Bevis Marks IV (Spanish and Portuguese Synagogue Archives)

FIGURE NUMBERS   5.3-5.6

NUMBER OF BURIALS

1100: of which c.700 are children

Ordnance Survey Map 1871   *Velho* (old) Cemetery of Spanish and Portuguese E1   **[48]**
5ft. to a mile   1657-c.1742

LOCATION	CHAPTER	SITE	DATE ESTABLISHED	IN USE TO	DATE OF VISIT	GAZETTEER NUMBER
LONDON	5.1.2	*NUEVO* (NEW) CEMETERY OF THE SPANISH AND PORTUGUESE JEWS E1 (Sephardi)	1733	1918	2007	[49]

ADDITIONAL NOTES

Mile End Road, E1

BIBLIOGRAPHY

Hyamson, A. 1951 *The Sephardim of England*

Kadish, S. 2006 *Jewish Heritage in England: An Architectural Guide*

OTHER SOURCES

Maloney, C. 2009 *London Field Work and Publications*

Round Up 2008 in London Archaeology Vol. 12

Bevis Marks V (Spanish and Portuguese Synagogue Archives)

FIGURE NUMBERS

5.7

NUMBER OF BURIALS

Original Cemetery held over 10,000 burials

Remains of 7,500 who died before 1813 re-interred in Brentwood in 1974

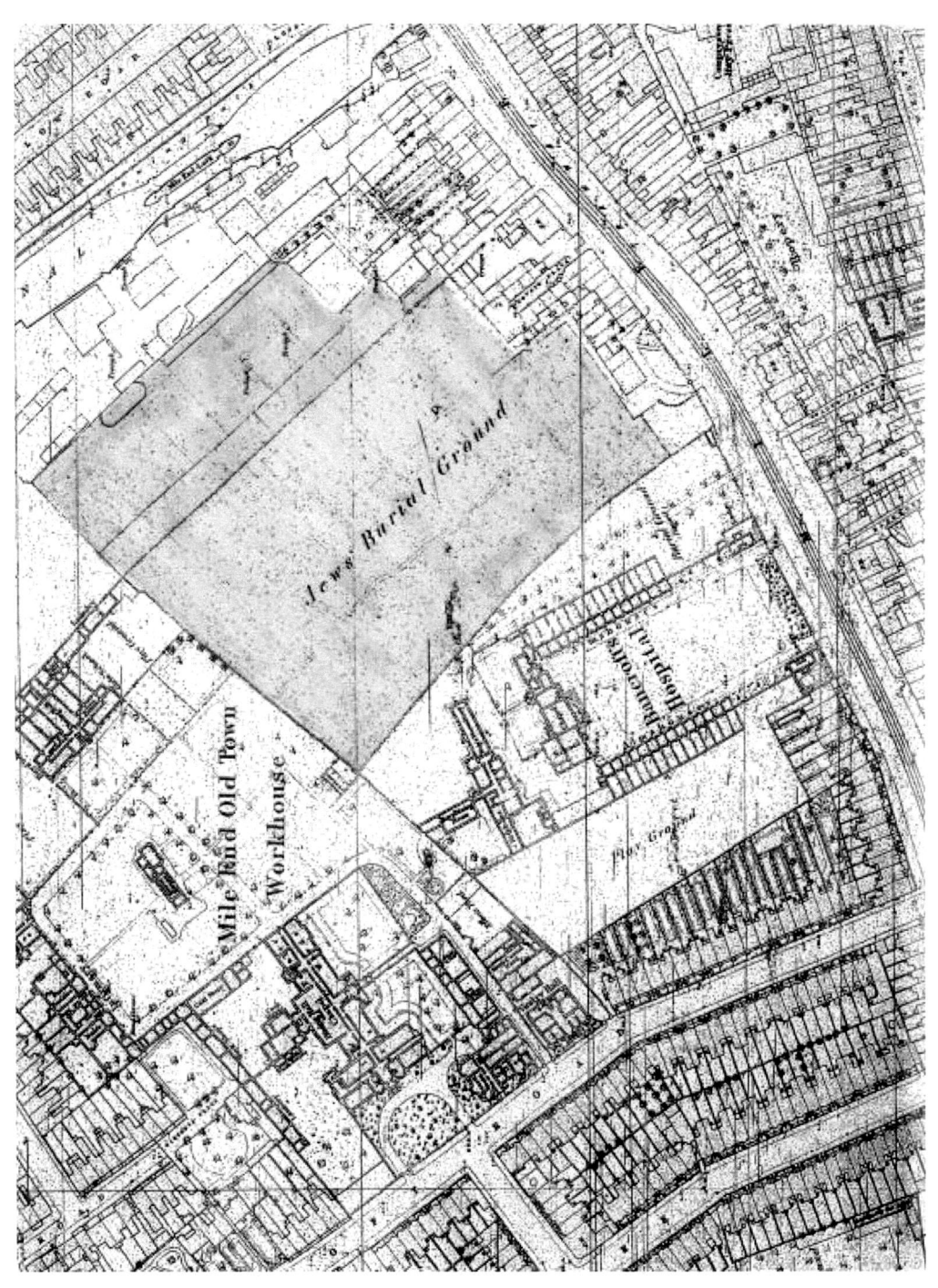

Ordnance Survey Map 1875
5ft. to a mile

Nuevo (new) Cemetery of Spanish and Portuguese
1733-1918

[49]

LOCATION	CHAPTER	SITE	DATE ESTABLISHED	IN USE TO	DATE OF VISIT	GAZETTEER NUMBER
LONDON	5.1.3	BRENTWOOD CEMETERY OF THE SPANISH AND PORTUGUESE JEWS (SEPHARDI)	1974		2010	[50]

ADDITIONAL NOTES	Coxtie Green, Brentwood, CM14 Mass Burial in 1974 of 7500 who died before 1813 Re-internment from *NUEVO* Cemetery
BIBLIOGRAPHY	Kadish, S. 2006 *Jewish Heritage in England: An Architectural Guide*
OTHER SOURCES	Spanish and Portuguese Synagogue Archives
FIGURE NUMBERS	5.8-5.9
NUMBER OF BURIALS	7,500 re-interred remains in four mass graves

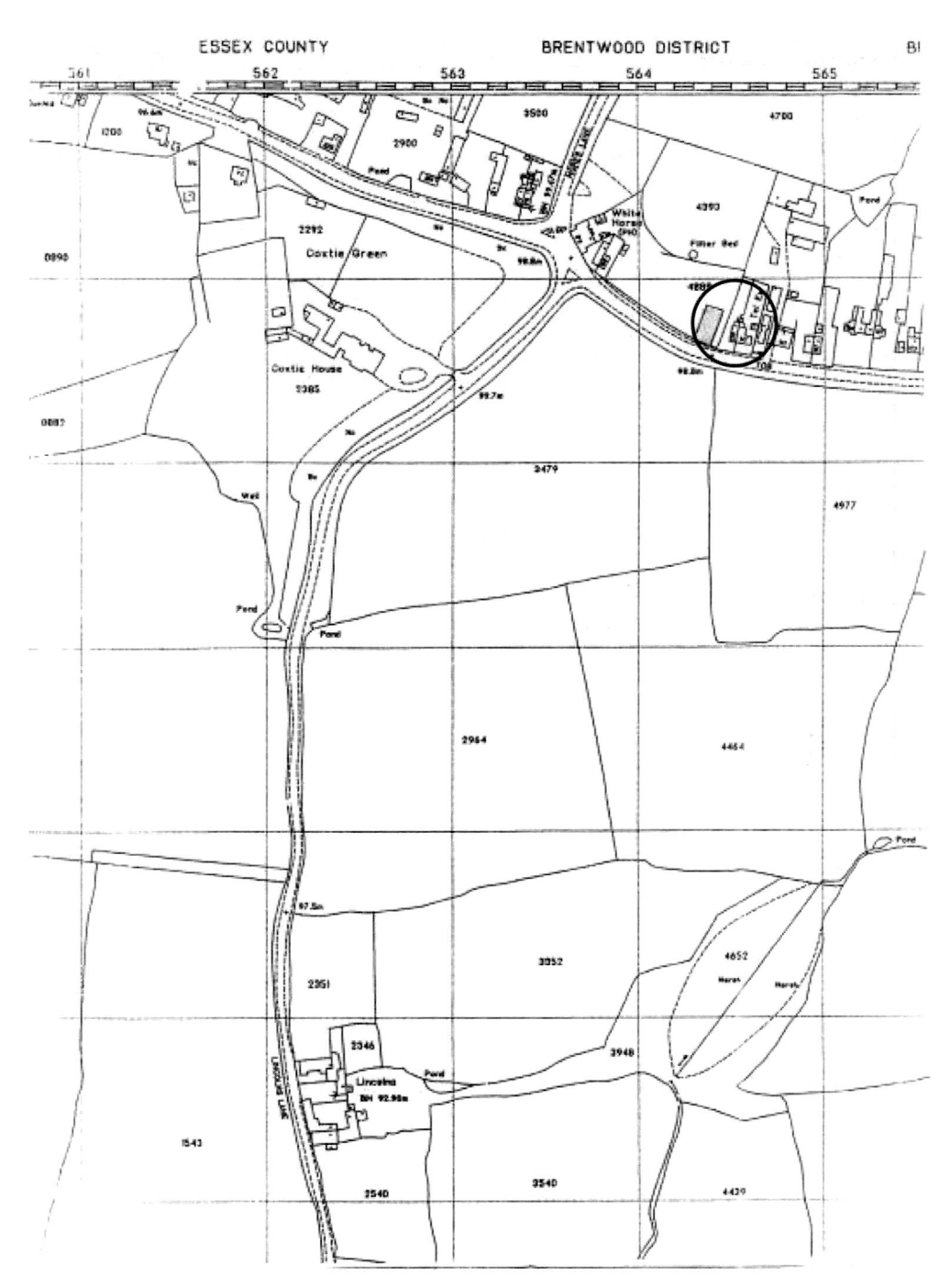

Ordnance Survey Map 1995   Brentwood Cemetery of Spanish and Portuguese
25 inches to a mile   1974, re- interred remains from *Nuevo* Cemetery CM14   **[50]**

Reproduced from 1995 O.S. map with the permission of the Controller of H.M. Stationary Office, Crown Copyright 2013

LOCATION	CHAPTER	SITE	DATE ESTABLISHED	IN USE TO	DATE OF VISIT	GAZETTEER NUMBER
LONDON	5.1.4	ALDERNEY ROAD E1 JEWISH CEMETERY E1 (Ashkenazi)	c.1696	c1852	2007	[51]

ADDITIONAL NOTES

Cemetery enlarged in 1733/1749

NOTABLE GRAVES

Rabbi Samuel Falk: Kabbalist & Ultra Orthodox "miracle-working" Rabbi
Rabbi Aaron Hart: First Chief Rabbi
Rabbi Tevele Schiff: Second Chief Rabbi

BIBLIOGRAPHY

Kadish, S. 2006 *Jewish Heritage in England: An Architectural Guide*
Roth, C. 1978 *A History of The Jews in England*
Susser, B. (ed.) 1997 *Aldeney Road Jewish Cemetery, London E1, 1697-1853*

OTHER SOURCES

Charles Tucker United Synagogue Archivist
United Synagogue Burial Society

FIGURE NUMBERS   5.10-5.14

NUMBER OF BURIALS

No register exists
Possibly over 4,000 graves, of which 40% are children's unmarked

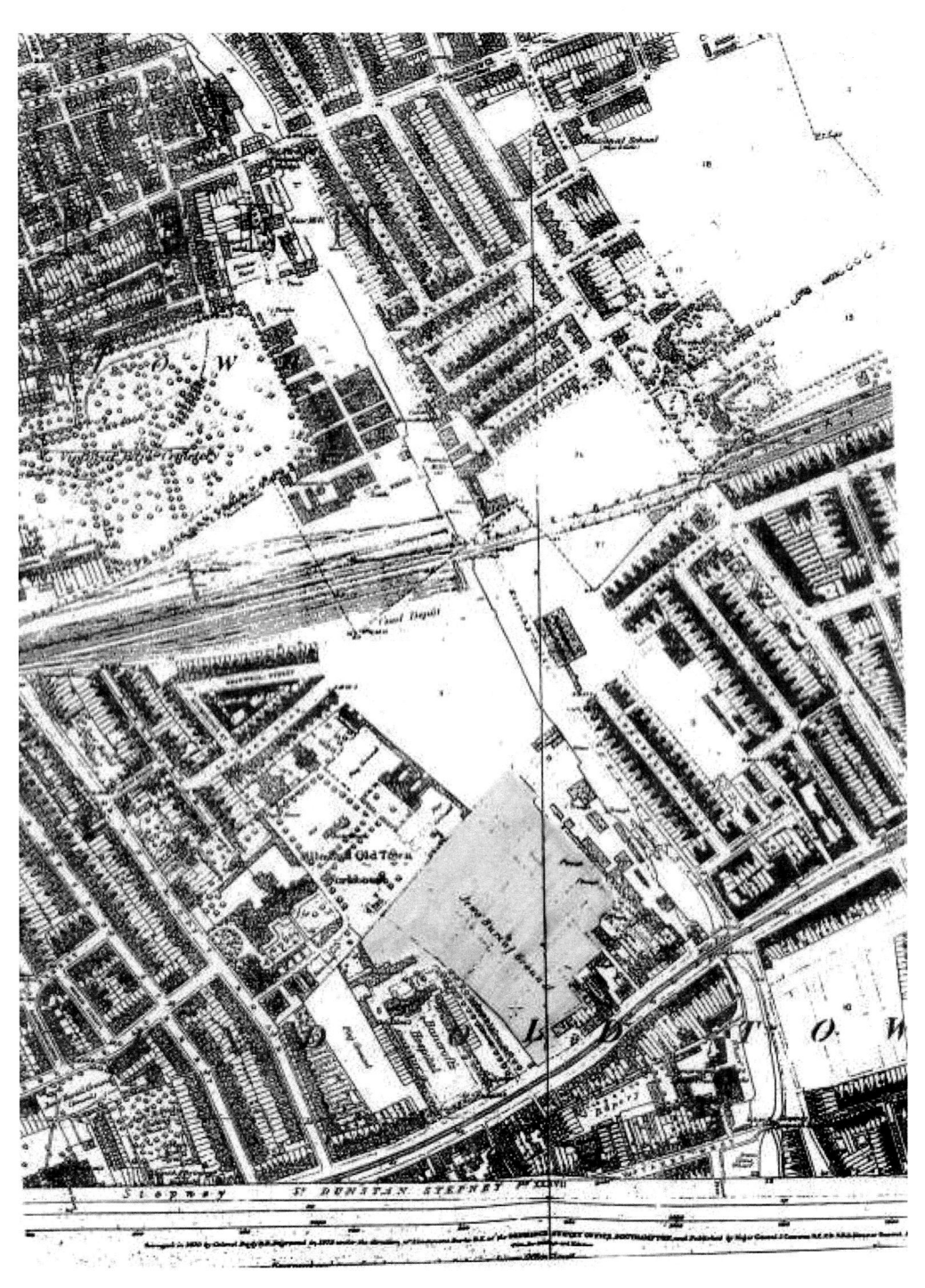

Ordnance Survey Map 1870
25 inches to a mile
[51]

Alderney Road Cemetery E1
1696-1852/3

LOCATION	CHAPTER	SITE	DATE ESTABLISHED	IN USE TO	DATE OF VISIT	GAZETTEER NUMBER
LONDON	5.1.5	BANCROFT ROAD JEWISH CEMETERY E1 (Ashkenazi)	1810	1895	2009	[52]

ADDITIONAL NOTES

Cemetery partly destroyed by bombing in 1941

All records destroyed when Western Synagogue destroyed in 1941

BIBLIOGRAPHY

Kadish, S. 2006 *Jewish Heritage in England: An Architectural Guide*

Roth, C. 1978 *A History of The Jews in England*

OTHER SOURCES

Charles Tucker United Synagogue Archivist

United Synagogue Burial Society

FIGURE NUMBERS   5.15

NUMBER OF BURIALS

600-700

No records survive

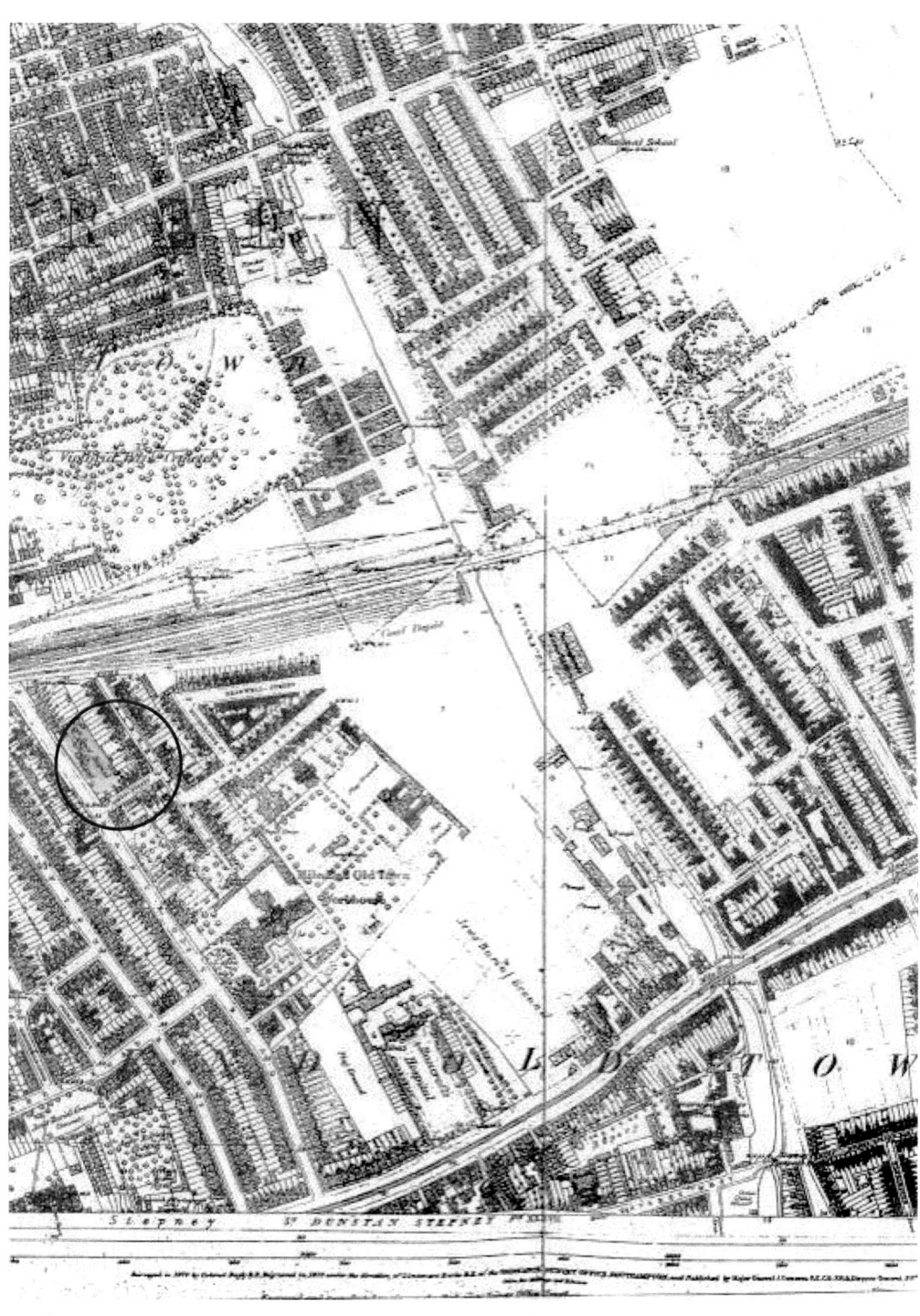

Ordnance Survey Map 1895
25 inches to a mile
[52]

Bancroft Road Cemetery E1
1810-1895

LOCATION	CHAPTER	SITE	DATE ESTABLISHED	IN USE TO	DATE OF VISIT	GAZETTEER NUMBER
LONDON	5.1.6	BRADY STREET JEWISH CEMETERY (Ashkenazi) E1	1761	1858	2009	[53]

ADDITIONAL NOTES

Burial Ground of London New Synagogue
and later shared with The Great Synagogue, Duke's Place
Contains layered burials on large central mound & back-to-back tombstones

NOTABLE GRAVES

Nathan Rothschild d.1836
Hannah Rothschild d.1850
Bust of Miriam Levy d.1856 (welfare worker)
Solomon Hirschel: Chief Rabbi 1802 - 1842

BIBLIOGRAPHY

Beach, D. 2006 *London's Cemeteries*
Black, G. 2003 *Jewish London: An Illustrated History*
Kadish, S. 2006 *Jewish Heritage in England: An Architectural Guide*

OTHER SOURCES

Charles Tucker: United Synagogue Archivist
United Synagogue Burial Society

FIGURE NUMBERS 5.16-5.19

NUMBER OF BURIALS

Several thousand in double / triple tiers and children's graves unmarked
No records survive

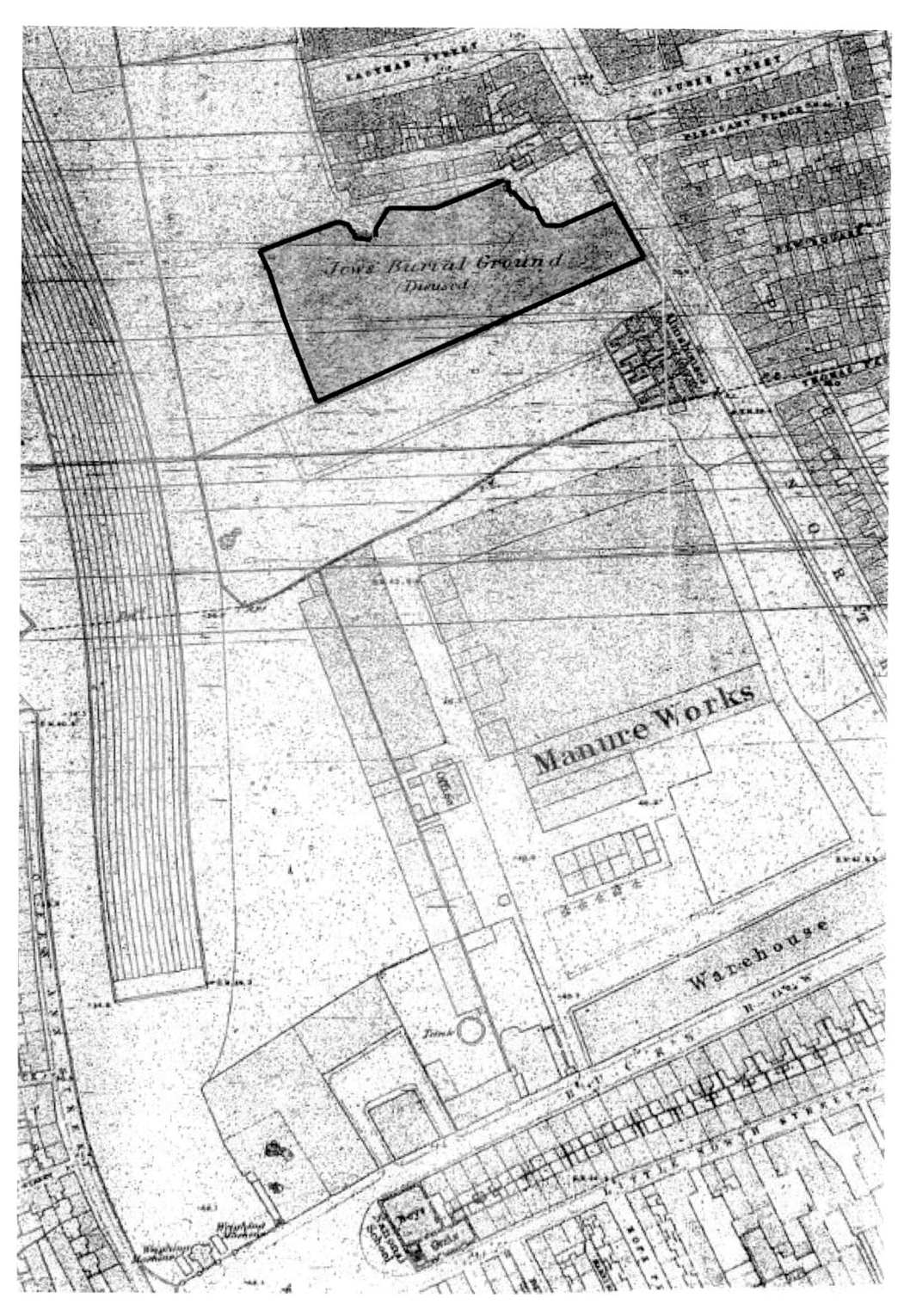

Ordnance Survey Map 1895
5ft. to a mile

Brady Street Cemetery E1
1761-1858

[53]

LOCATION	CHAPTER	SITE	DATE ESTABLISHED	IN USE TO	DATE OF VISIT	GAZETTEER NUMBER
LONDON	5.1.7	FULHAM ROAD THE WESTERN SYNAGOGUE CEMETERY (SW3) (Ashkenazi)	1815	1886	2008	**[54]**

ADDITIONAL NOTES	The Western Synagogue Cemetery, Queen's Elm Parade, Fulham Road SW3
	Adjoining The Royal Marsden Hospital
	Closed by order of the Home Office 1886
NOTABLE GRAVES	
	Solomon Hart RA, Professor of Painting Royal Academy d.1881
	Sir David Salomons, First Jewish Lord Mayor of London d.1873

BIBLIOGRAPHY	Kadish, S. 2006 *Jewish Heritage in England: An Architectural Guide*
	Levy, M. 1897 *The Western Synagogue: some materials for its History*
	Roth, C. 1933 *Records of The Western Synagogue 1761-1932*

OTHER SOURCES	Garcia M. Western Charitable Foundation

FIGURE NUMBERS	5.2

NUMBER OF BURIALS	c.750 (personal observation in 2010)

GAZETTEER 309

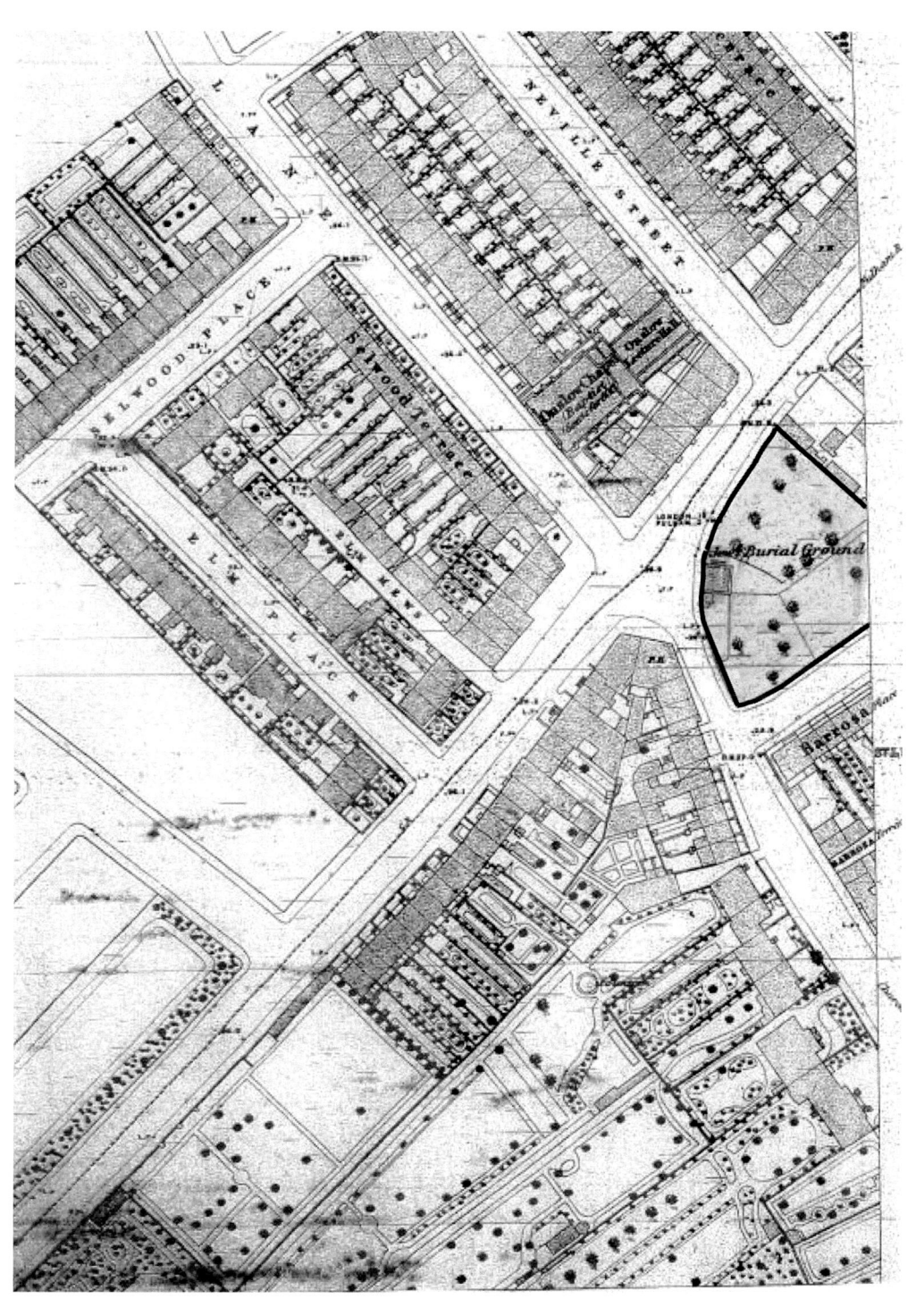

Ordnance Survey Map 1895 Fulham Road Cemetery SW3 **[54]**
5ft. to a mile 1815-1886

LOCATION	CHAPTER	SITE	DATE ESTABLISHED	IN USE TO	DATE OF VISIT	GAZETTEER NUMBER
LONDON	5.1.8	LAURISTON ROAD HACKNEY JEWISH CEMETERY E9 (Ashkenazi)	1788	1886	2009	[55]

ADDITIONAL NOTES	Hackney Jewish Cemetery, Lauriston Road, E9
	The Second Cemetery of the former Hambro Synagogue (1707), Magpie Alley, Fenchurch Street

BIBLIOGRAPHY	Kadish, S. 2006 Jewish Heritage in England: An Architectural Guide
	Lipman, V. 1962 / 7 The Rise of Jewish Suburbs: TJHSE* vol.21
	*Transactions of The Jewish Historical Society of England
	Robinson, W. 1842 The History of Antiquities of Hackney

OTHER SOURCES	Charles Tucker: United Synagogue Archivist
	United Synagogue Burial Society (Ilford Branch)

FIGURE NUMBERS	5.21-5.22

NUMBER OF BURIALS	400- 500

GAZETTEER 311

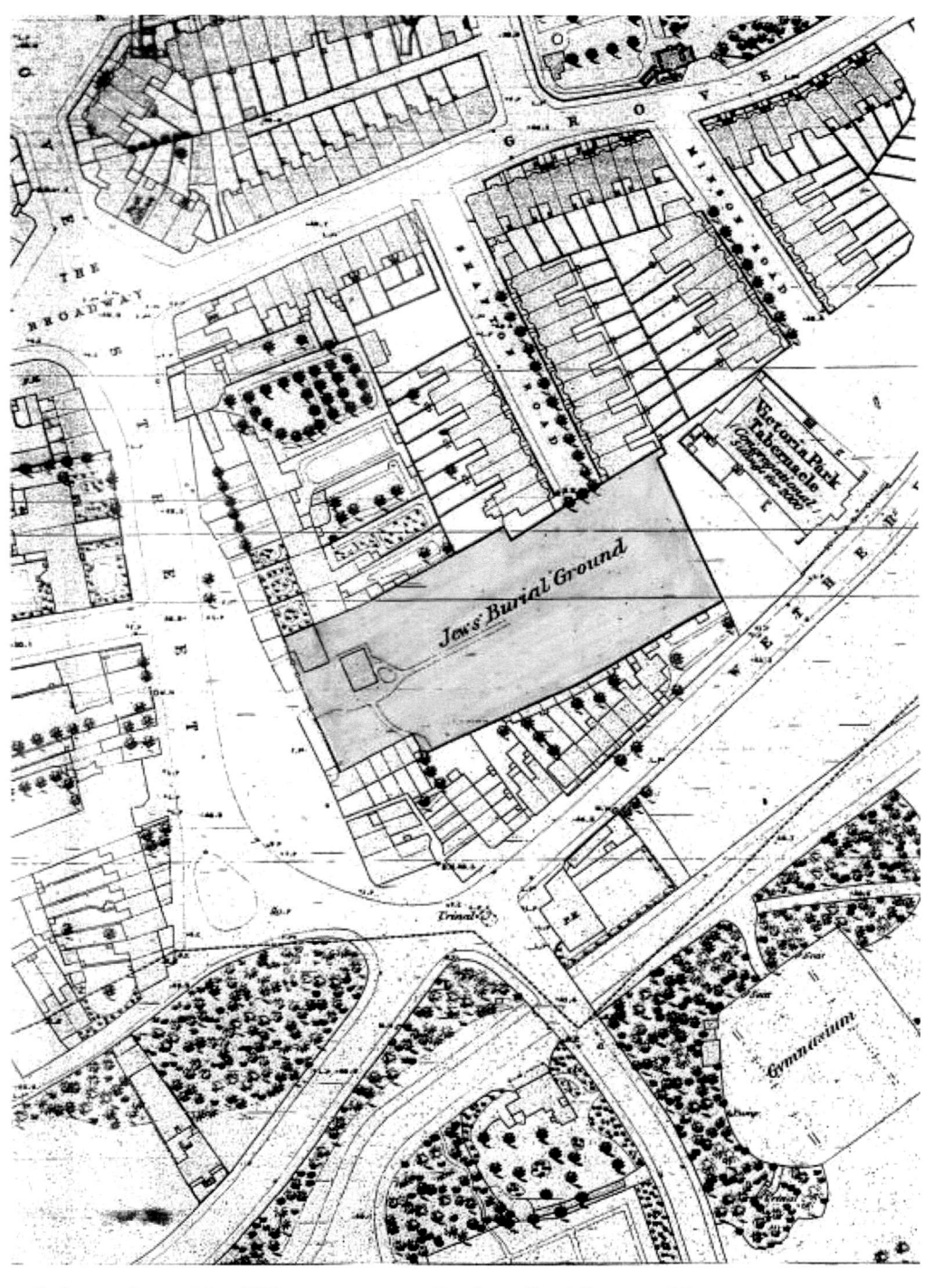

Ordnance Survey Map 1895　　　Lauriston Road Cemetery E9　　　[55]
5ft. to a mile　　　　　　　　　　1788-1886

LOCATION	CHAPTER	SITE	DATE ESTABLISHED	IN USE TO	DATE OF VISIT	GAZETTEER NUMBER
LONDON	5.1.9	WEST HAM CEMETERY E15 (Ashkenazi)	1856	c.1973	2009	[56]

ADDITIONAL NOTES

Acquired by New Synagogue Great St. Helen's and shared with
The Great Synagogue, Duke's Place
Contains re-interred remains (1960) from Hoxton Cemetery (1707 - 1878)

NOTABLE GRAVES

Rothschild Mausoleum containing:
Ferdinand de Rothschild d.1898 and Evelina de Rothschild d.1866
David Solomons d. 1873: Lord Mayor of London

BIBLIOGRAPHY

Kadish, S. 2006 *Jewish Heritage in England: An Architectural Guide*

OTHER SOURCES

Charles Tucker: United Synagogue Archivist
United Synagogue Burial Society

FIGURE NUMBERS   5.23 - 5.27

NUMBER OF BURIALS

c. 15,000

GAZETTEER 313

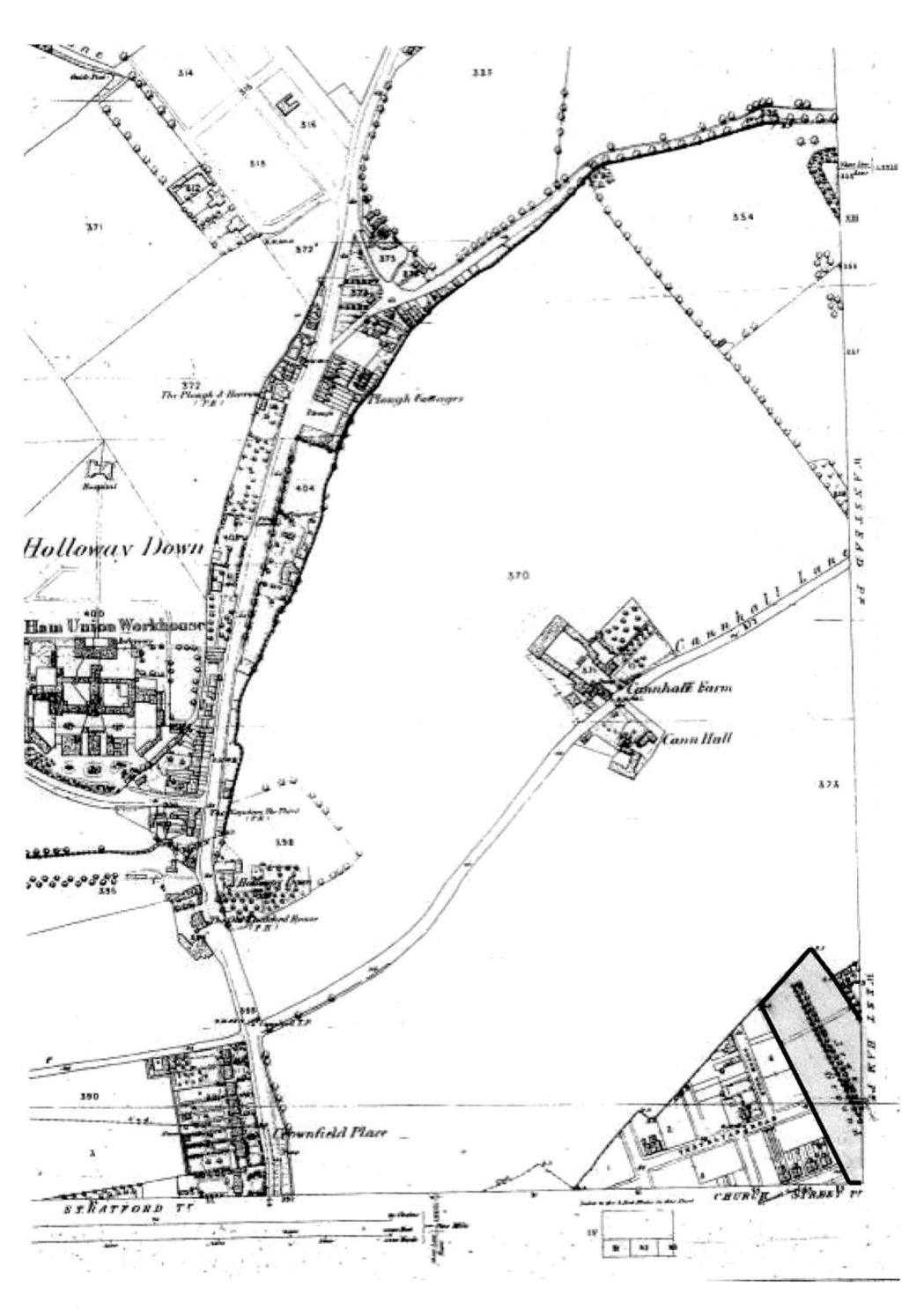

Ordnance Survey Map 1880　　　West Ham Cemetery E15　　　**[56]**
5ft. to a mile　　　　　　　　　1856-c.1973

LOCATION	CHAPTER	SITE	DATE ESTABLISHED	IN USE TO	DATE OF VISIT	GAZETTEER NUMBER
LONDON	5.1.10	WEST LONDON REFORM CEMETERY (Ashkenazi) N1	1843	1937	2009*	[57]

ADDITIONAL NOTES	West London Reform Cemetery, Balls Pond Road, corner of Kingsbury Road, N1
	* Reserved spaces until 1952
	First Cemetery of the Reform Movement of Great Britain
	Upright and Flat gravestones cultural mix of the early founders of the Reform Movement
NOTABLE GRAVES	
	Joseph Levy-Lawson, founder of The Daily Telegraph
	Sir Isaac Goldsmid, One of the founders of University College London
	Rabbi Wolf Marks 1840-1895
BIBLIOGRAPHY	
	Kadish, S. 2006 *Jewish Heritage in England: An Architectural Guide*
OTHER SOURCES	
	West London Synagogue Burial Society
FIGURE NUMBERS	5.28-5.29
NUMBER OF BURIALS	c.900

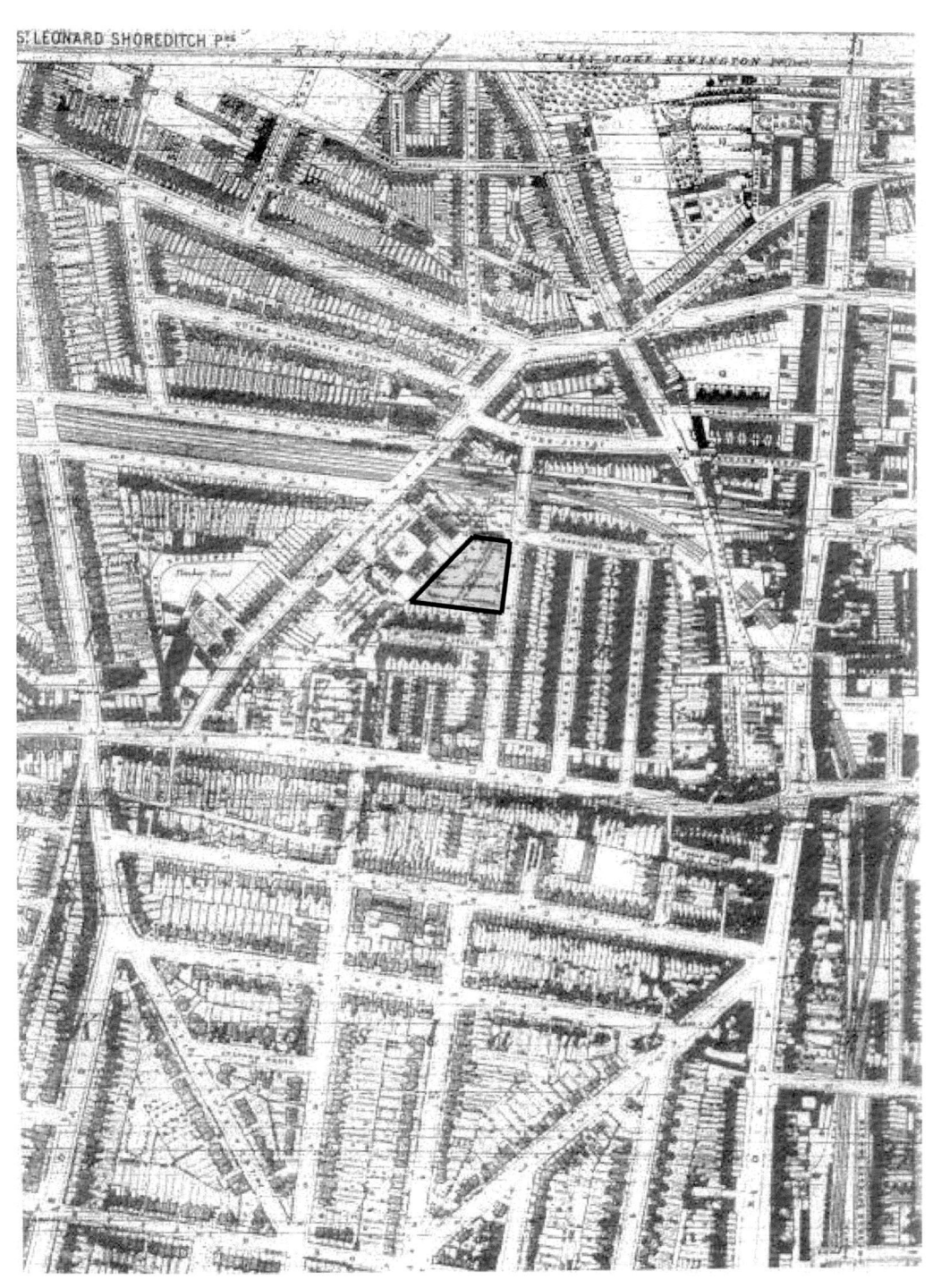

Ordnance Survey Map 1890
5ft. to a mile

West London Reform Cemetery N1
1843-1897 (reserved places till 1952)

[57]

LOCATION	CHAPTER	SITE	DATE ESTABLISHED	IN USE TO	DATE OF VISIT	GAZETTEER NUMBER
LONDON	5.1.11	WILLESDEN JEWISH CEMETERY (Ashkenazi) NW10	1873	still in use	2009	[58]

ADDITIONAL NOTES

NOTABLE GRAVES

First Cemetery of the newly formed (1870) United Synagogue

Chief Rabbis Nathan and Herman Adler
Chief Rabbi J. Hertz
Chief Rabbi Israel Brodie
Rothschild family enclosure
(Nathan Mayer Rothschild d.1915)

BIBLIOGRAPHY

Kadish, S. 2006 *Jewish Heritage in England: An Architectural Guide*

OTHER SOURCES

Charles Tucker, Archivist of The United Synagogue

FIGURE NUMBERS 5.30-5.31

NUMBER OF BURIALS

c. 20,000
still in use

GAZETTEER 317

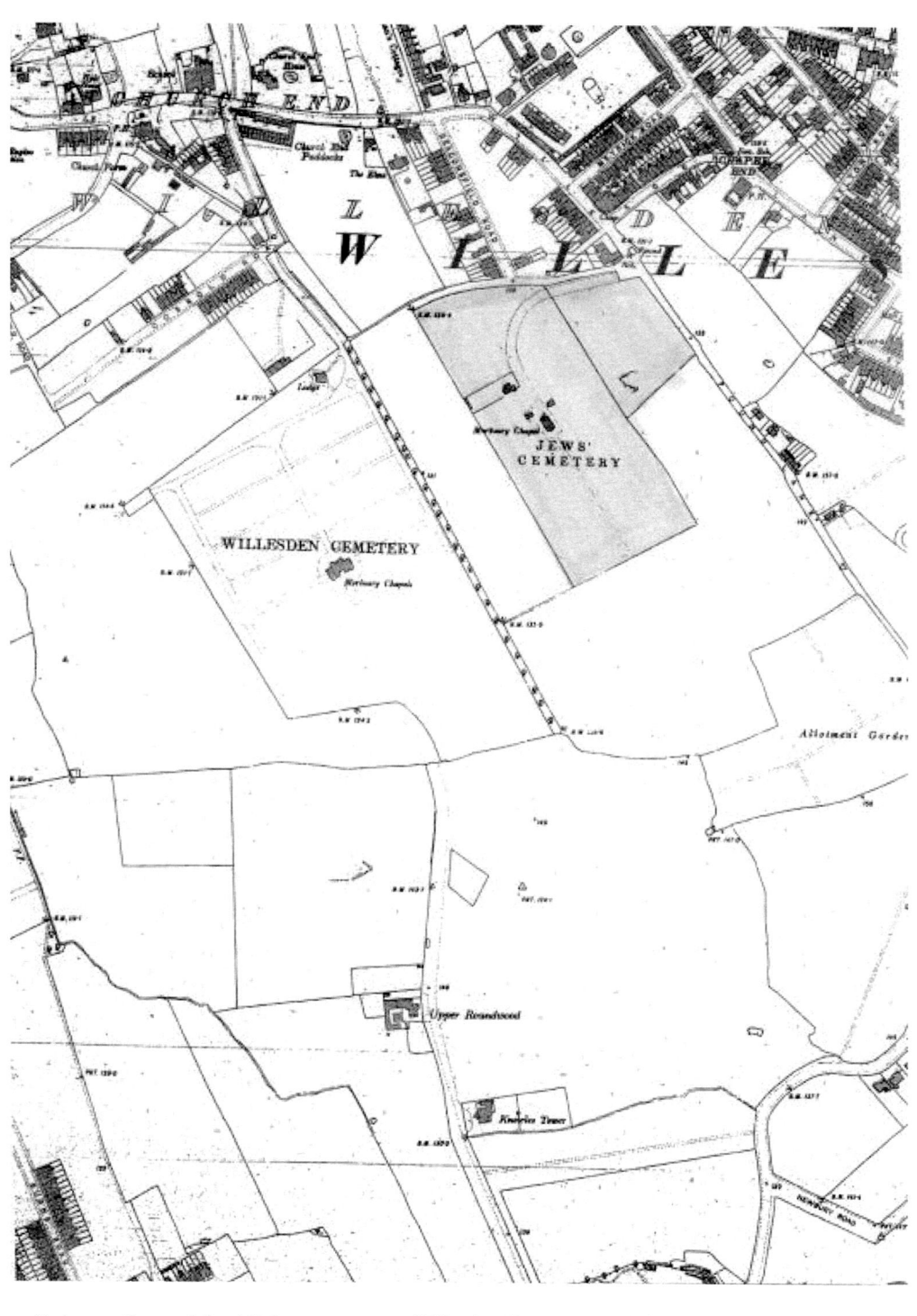

Ordnance Survey Map 1896　　　Willesden Cemetery NW10　　　[58]
25 inches to a mile　　　　　　1873-still in use

LOCATION	CHAPTER	SITE	DATE ESTABLISHED	IN USE TO	DATE OF VISIT	GAZETTEER NUMBER
BATH	4.2.1　5.2.1	SYNAGOGUE　CEMETERY	1841/2　1812	1901*　1921	2008	[13]　[59]

ADDITIONAL NOTES		
	c.1800	Traditional date of the foundation of the community (Roth 1950)
	c.1736	First mention of Jews in Bath (Roth, 1950)
	*1938	*Synagogue site demolished*
		There is no longer a Jewish Community in Bath
SYNAGOGUE		First prayer room Orchard Street (private house)
		Two further rooms / halls used for prayer
	1841/ 2-1901	Synagogue established in Corn Street

FIGURE NUMBERS	4.42	

CEMETERY	1812-1921	Coombe Down Cemetery, Bradford Road
		Ohel (Grade II)

FIGURE NUMBERS	5.32-5.35	

CONTACT INFORMATION	Alex Schlesinger:　Chairman of Friends of Coombe Down Jewish Cemetery　Richard Sermon:　Archaeological Officer: Bath and North East Somerset Council
BIBLIOGRAPHY	Brown, M. & Samuel. J. *The Jews of Bath. Transactions of Jewish Historical Society* Vol. 29 1982/1986　Kadish, S. 2006 *Jewish Heritage in England. An Architectural Guide*　Roth, C. 1950 *The Rise of Provincial Jewry*　Samuel, J. 1986 *The Jews of Bath in Bath History* Vol.1 pp 160/164

OTHER SOURCES	
	Bath Records Office
	Ordnance Survey Maps: 1895,1905,1950
	Statistical Account of the Congregations of the British Empire 1845

PLACE NAMES WITH JEWISH CONNECTIONS	none

COMMUNITY SIZE	Date	Community Size
	1847	50 persons
	1850	50

GAZETTEER 319

Ordnance Survey Map 1895 Bath: Corn Street (synagogue not marked) [13]
25 inches to a mile 1841/2-1901

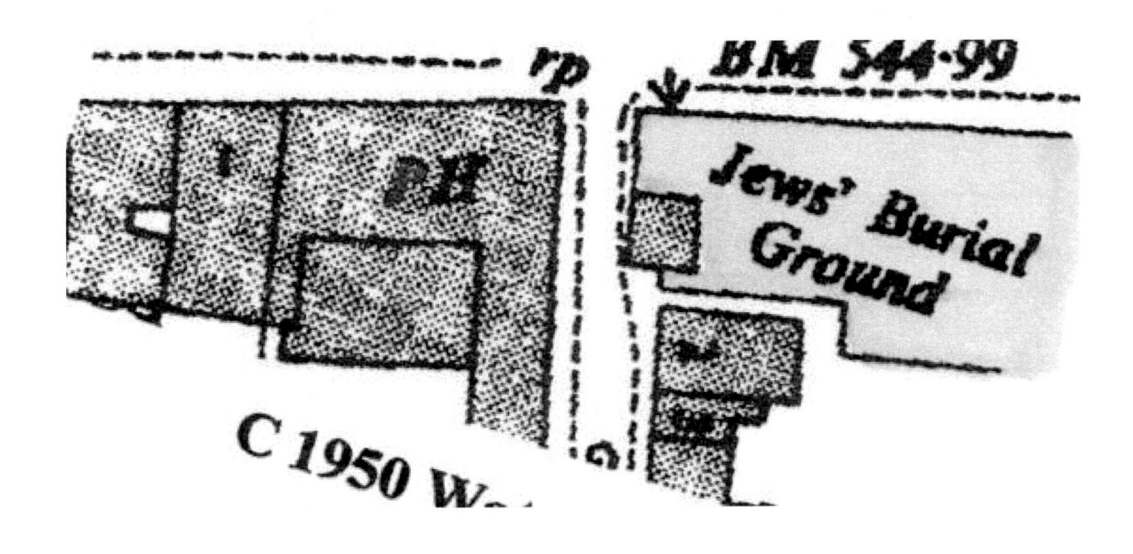

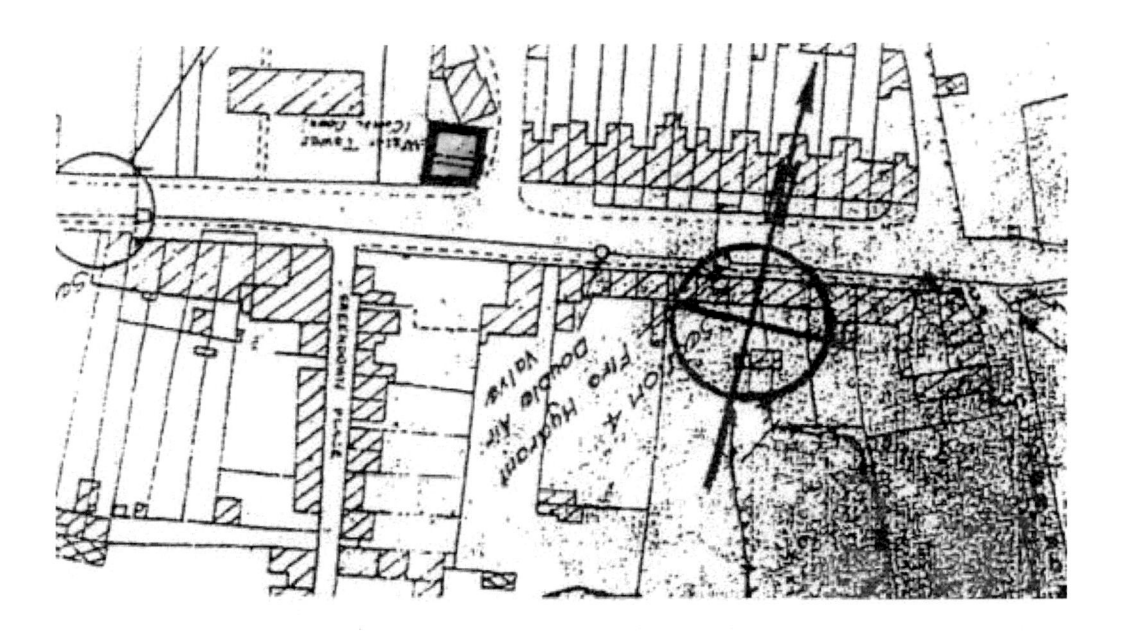

Ordnance Survey Maps 1904/1950 Bath: Bradford Road Cemetery BA2 [59]
5ft to a mile 1812-1921

LOCATION	CHAPTER	SITE	DATE ESTABLISHED	IN USE TO	DATE OF VISIT	GAZETTEER NUMBER
BIRMINGHAM					2010	
	4.2.2	SYNAGOGUES	1809	1856		[14]
			1856	still in use		
	5.2.2	CEMETERIES (2)	1766	1872		[60]
		WITTON OLD	1869	1937		

ADDITIONAL NOTES

1730 Traditional foundation of the Community (no evidence / records)
1718 First mention of Jews in Birmingham (Roth 1950)

SYNAGOGUES

c.1780   First two synagogues in private houses in area known as "The Froggery" *(no longer exists)*
1809-1856   Severn Street Synagogue: now a Masonic Hall
1856   Singers Hill, Blucher Street B1 (Grade II*) *(still in use)*

FIGURE NUMBERS 4.43 - 4.45

CEMETERIES

c.1766 - 1825   Granville Street

1823 - 1872*   Bethlehem Row, Edgbaston
*section survives: not examined

1869 - 1937   Witton Old Jewish Cemetery
(containing reinterred remains from Granville Street)

FIGURE NUMBERS 5.36

CONTACT INFORMATION

Rabbi S. Arkush: Rabbi of Birmingham Jewish Community Care
Stanley Busby: Photographer
Bernard Gingold: Administrator Singers Hill Synagogue
Lionel Singer: Community historian

BIBLIOGRAPHY

Chesses, A. 2003 *A History of Birmingham Jewry*
Josephs, Z. 1980 *Birmingham Jewry 1749 – 1914*
Kadish, S. 1996 *Building Jerusalem*
Kadish, S. 2006 *Jewish Heritage in England. An Architectural Guide*
Levine, H. 1956 *History of Birmingham Hebrew Congregation*
Margoliouth, M. 1851 *The History of The Jews in Great Britain*
Roth, C. 1950 *The Rise of Provincial Jewry*

OTHER SOURCES

Statistical Account of the Congregations of the British Empire 1845
Birmingham Reference Library
Hanson Map: 1781
Ordnance Survey Maps: 1888, 1889, 1904
Unpublished Minutes of Synagogue Meetings 1749-1914
Birmingham Hebrew Congregation Minutes 1825-1880

PLACE NAMES WITH JEWISH CONNECTIONS   none

COMMUNITY SIZE

Date	Community Size
1807	c.500 persons
1845	c.700
1850	c.800
1871	c.2,350
1900	c.4,000
1909	5,000
1934	6,000
1990	3,500
2004	c.2,700 Birmingham & Solihull

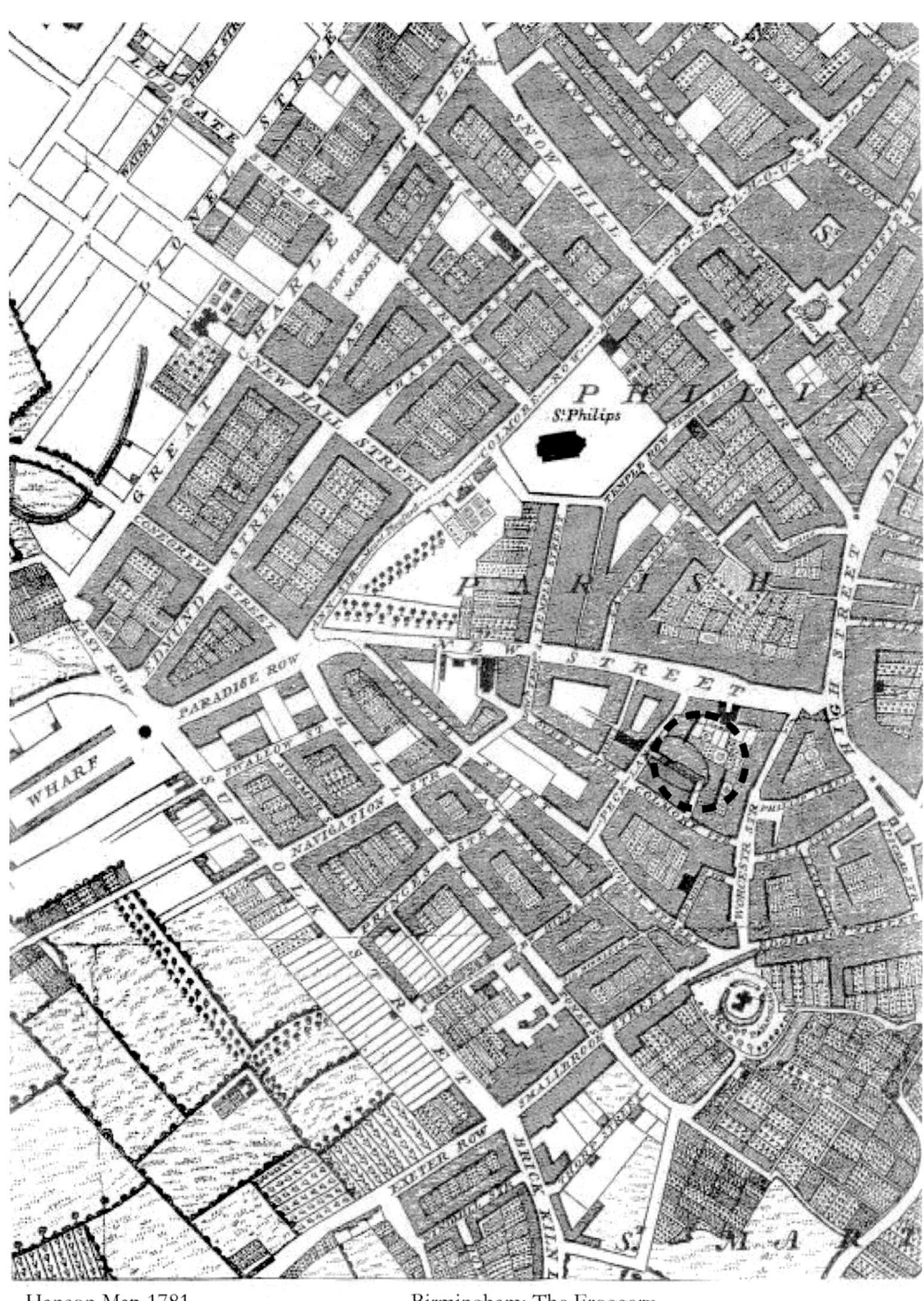

Hanson Map 1781
25 inches to a mile

Birmingham: The Froggery
c.1780 first synagogues

[14]

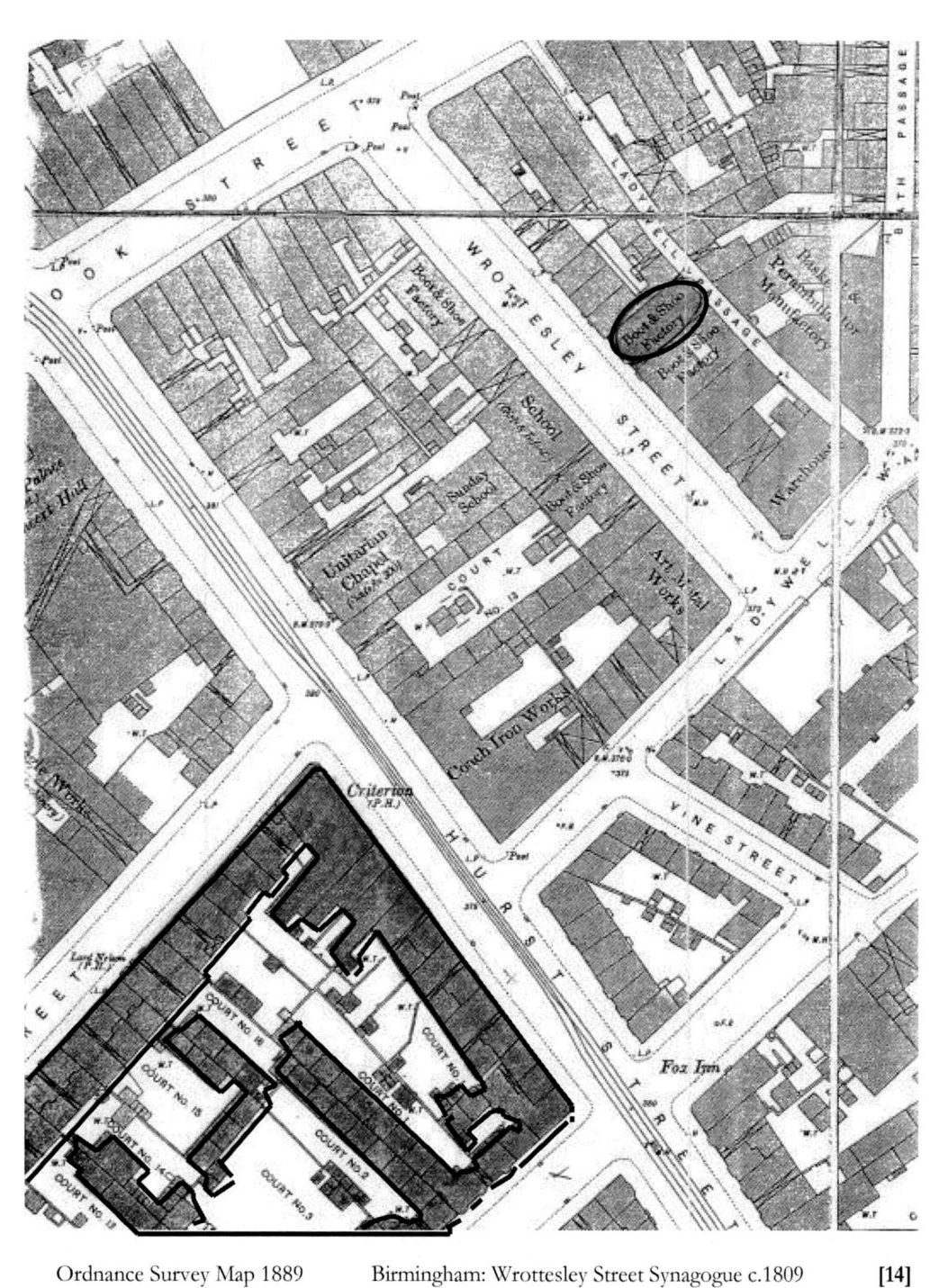

Ordnance Survey Map 1889 Birmingham: Wrottesley Street Synagogue c.1809 [14]
25 inches to a mile (shown as Boot and Shoe Factory)
Hurst Street: Section of the Courts (immigrant area)

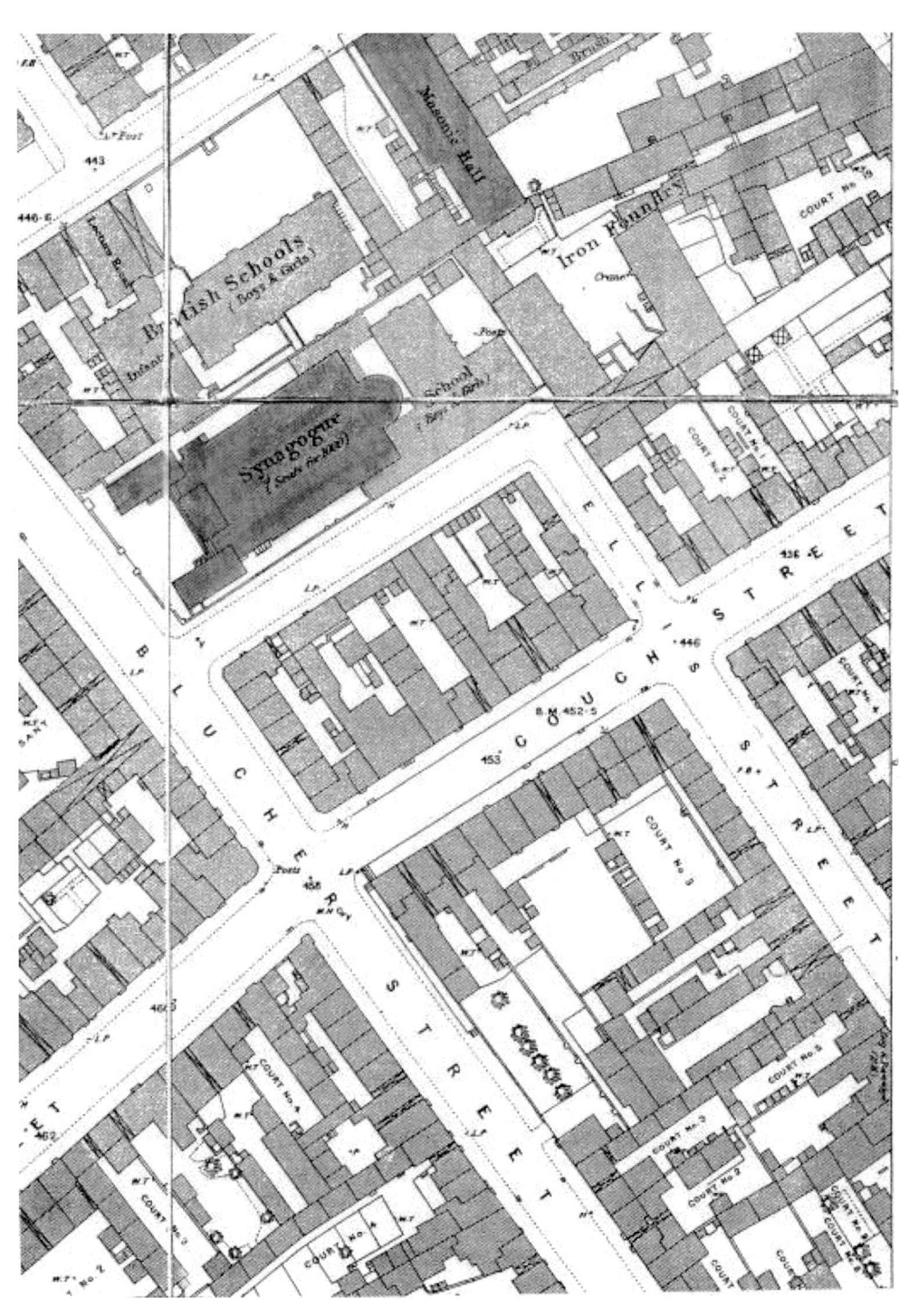

Ordnance Survey Map 1888 Birmingham: Severn Street Synagogue 1809-1856 [14]
25 inches to a mile (now Masonic Hall)
Singers Hill Synagogue, Blucher Street B1.1856-still in use

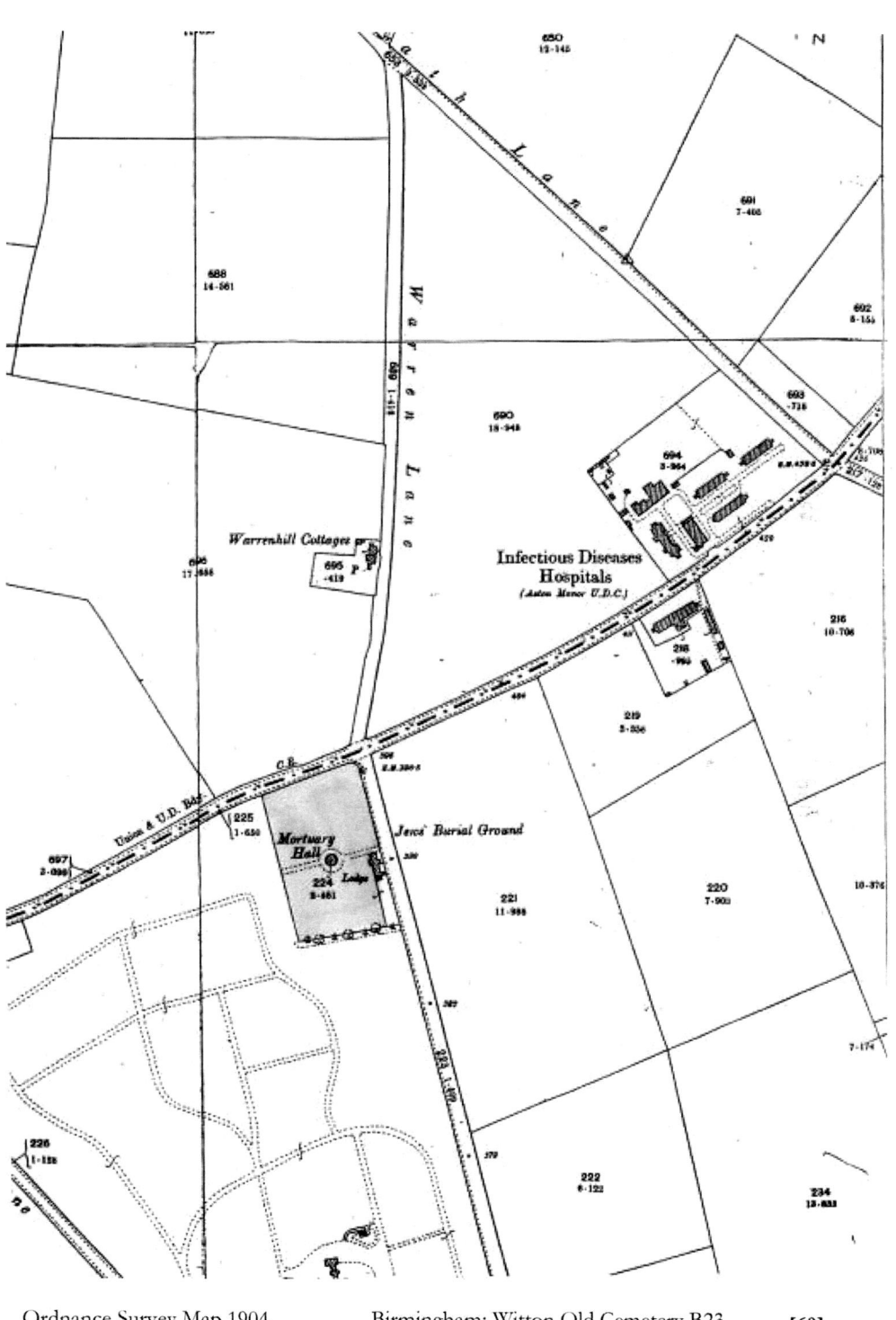

Ordnance Survey Map 1904 Birmingham; Witton Old Cemetery B23 [60]
1:2500 1869-1937

LOCATION	CHAPTER	SITE	DATE ESTABLISHED	IN USE TO	DATE OF VISIT	GAZETTEER NUMBER
BRADFORD					2010	
	4.2.3	SYNAGOGUE	1880 / 1	still in use		[15]
	5.2.3	CEMETERIES	1877	still in use		[61]

ADDITIONAL NOTES	
	c.1873 Traditional foundation of the Community (Grizzard 1984)
SYNAGOGUE	1880 / 1881 Bowland Street, BD 1 (Grade II) Reform Synagogue
	Bradford Hebrew Congregation (Orthodox) established 1888/1890 (synagogue closed 2013)
FIGURE NUMBERS	4.46-4.47
CEMETERIES	1877 Scholemoor Cemetery, Jewish Sections
	Necropolis Road, Scholemoor Road, Lidget Green BD7
	Parks and Gardens Register (Grade II)
	1912 Orthodox Cemetery
FIGURE NUMBERS	5.37- 5.38
CONTACT INFORMATION	N. Grizzard . Local historian
	M. Sender: Archivist and Historian Leeds Community
BIBLIOGRAPHY	Binns, K. 2008 *Bradford and West Yorkshire Local History*
	Rabbi Heilbron 1948 *Bradford Jewry*
	Grizzard, N. 1984 *Jewish Bradford*
	Kadish, S. 2006 *Jewish Heritage in England. An Architectural Guide*
OTHER SOURCES	Bradford Reference Library
	Ordnance Survey Maps: 1888,1923
	Jewish Community Records 2010 (J.C.R. UK)
PLACE NAMES WITH JEWISH CONNECTIONS	Moser Avenue (named after Jacob Moser 1839-1922) Lord Mayor
COMMUNITY SIZE	Date Community Size
	1895 c.300
	1900 500
	1934 750
	1955 800
	1994 c.450
	2011 c.300

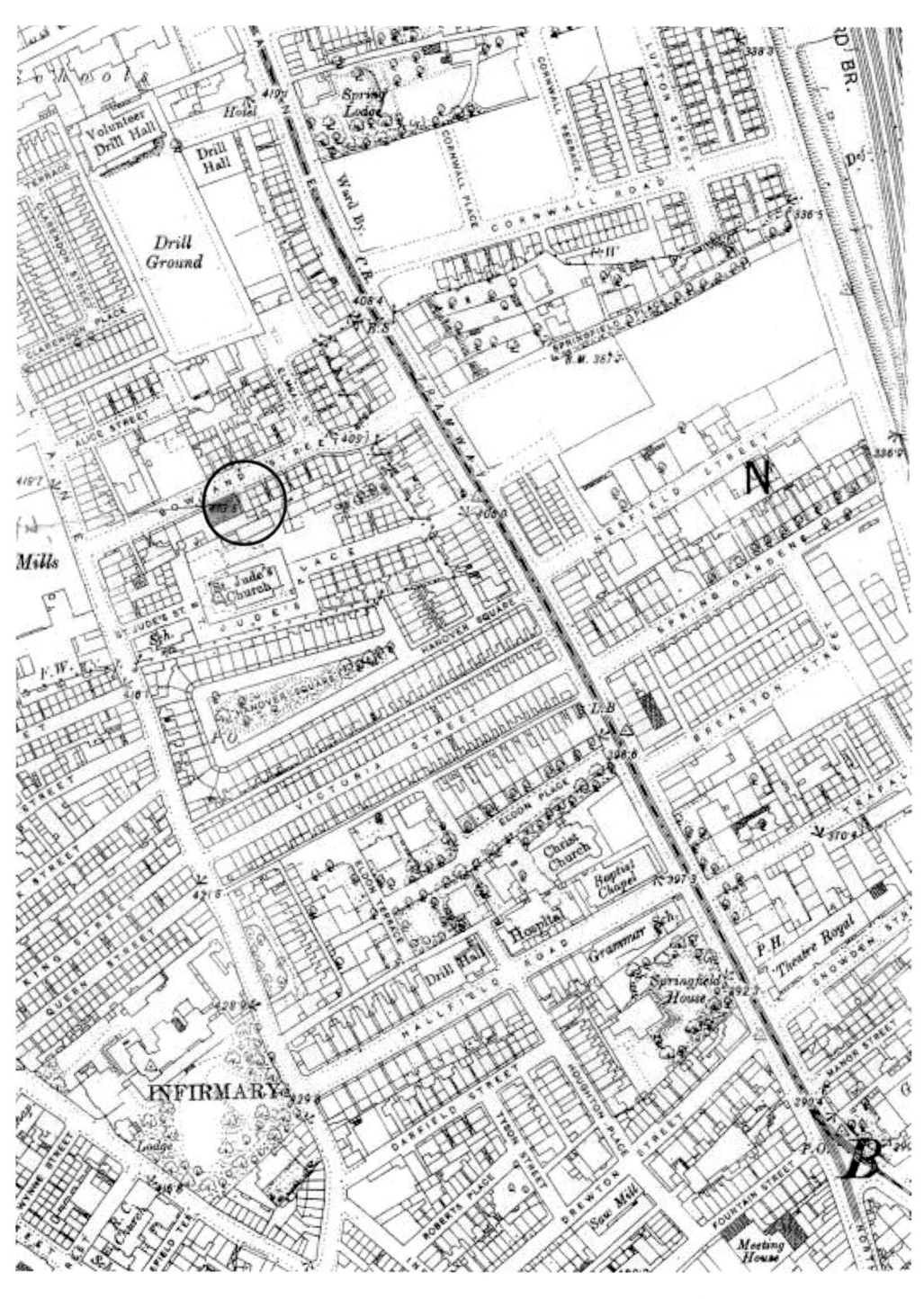

Ordnance Survey Map 1888　　Bradford: Bowland Street Synagogue BD1　　　[15]
25 inches to a mile　　　　　　　　1880/1- still in use

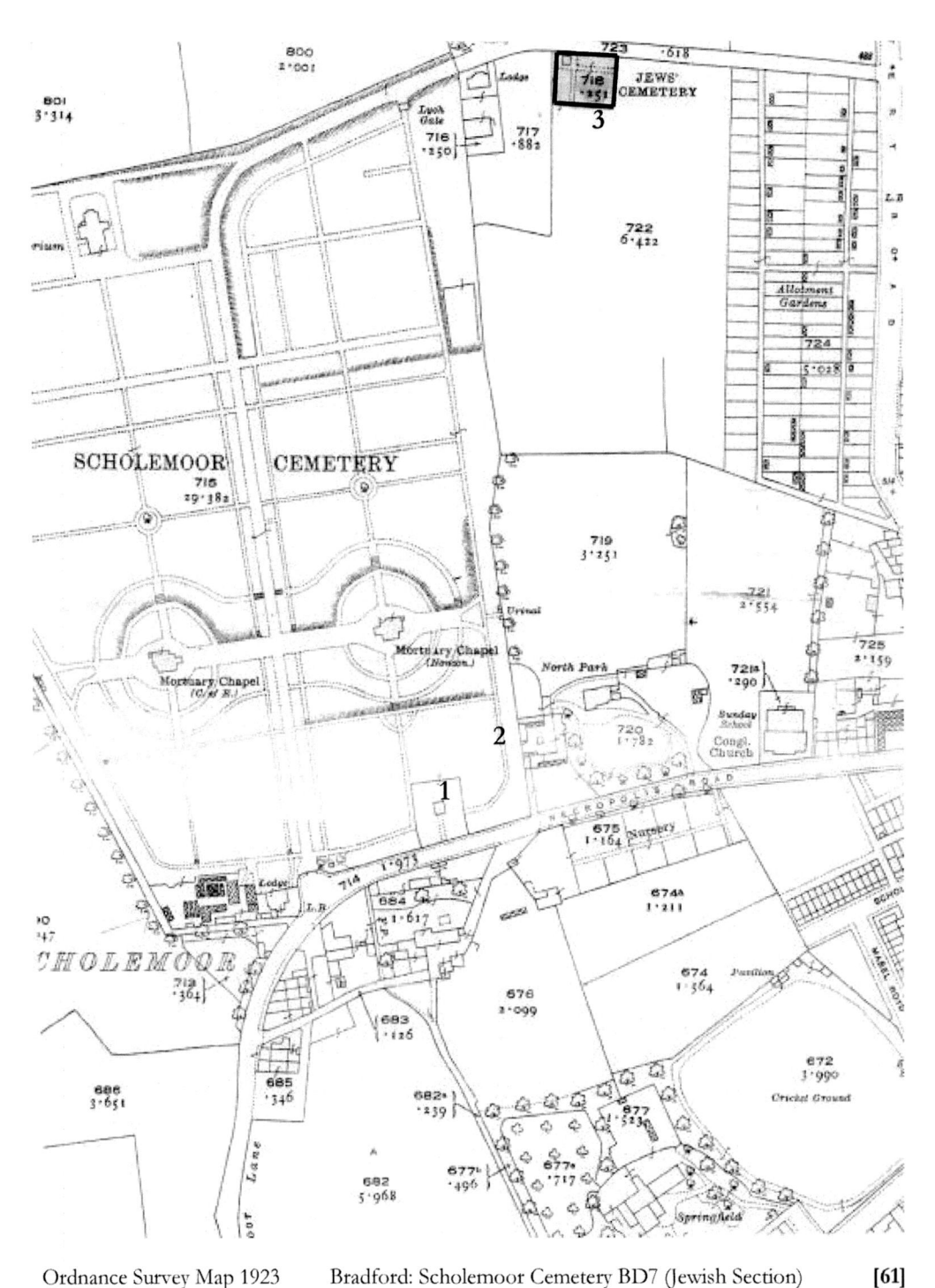

Ordnance Survey Map 1923 Bradford: Scholemoor Cemetery BD7 (Jewish Section) [61]
25 inches to a mile 1877-still in use

1. *1877 Reform Cemetery*
2. *New reform Plot currently in use*
3. *Orthodox Cemetery from 1912*

LOCATION	CHAPTER	SITE	DATE ESTABLISHED	IN USE TO	DATE OF VISIT	GAZETTEER NUMBER
BRIGHTON and HOVE	4.2.4	SYNAGOGUE	1874	still used	2011	[16]
	5.2.4	CEMETERY	1826	c.1920		[62]

ADDITIONAL NOTES	1800 Traditional foundation of the Community (Roth 1950)
	1766 First mention of Jews in Brighton (Roth 1950)

SYNAGOGUES	c.1792 First Synagogue in Jew Street
	1808 Second Synagogue in Poune's Court, West Street
	1813-1831 Community dissolved (lack of numbers)
	1821 Third Synagogue in West Street
	1825 Fourth Synagogue in Devonshire Place
	1874 Fifth Synagogue in Middle Street
	(still in use)
FIGURE NUMBERS	4.48-4.54

CEMETERY	1826- c.1920	Florence Place Old Jewish Burial Ground Ditchling Road, Brighton BN1
FIGURE NUMBERS	5.39-5.40	

CONTACT INFORMATION	Gordon Franks: senior member of community
BIBLIOGRAPHY	Kadish, S. 2006 *Jewish Heritage in England. An Architectural Guide*
	Lipman, V. 1954 *Social History of The Jews in England 1850 - 1950*
	Roth, C. 1950 *The Rise of Provincial Jewry*
	Spector, D. 1970 *The Jews of Brighton, 1770 - 1900*
OTHER SOURCES	East Sussex Records Office
	Statistical Account of the Congregations of the British Empire 1845
	Ordnance Survey Maps: 1897
	Saunders New Map: 1867
STREET AND PLACE NAMES WITH JEWISH CONNECTIONS*	Jew Street: site of first synagogue
	D'Avigdor Road
	Goldsmid Road
	Montefiore Road
	Julian Road (after Sir Julian Goldsmith
	Osmond Road (Sir Osmond Elim D'Avigdor Goldsmid
	Palmeira Square/Avenue (after the Portuguese title of Sir Isaac Goldsmid)
	Somerhill Road / Avenue / Court
	(after The Somerhill Estates of the D'Avigdor Goldsmids)
	* Brighton and Hove have more streets named after prominent Jews than any other city in Britain

COMMUNITY SIZE	Date	Community Size
	1819	9 families
	1850	150 persons
	1900	*c.100 persons*
	1934	*100*
	1935	*1525*
	1990	*10,300*
	1999	*8,000*
	2003	*3,300*

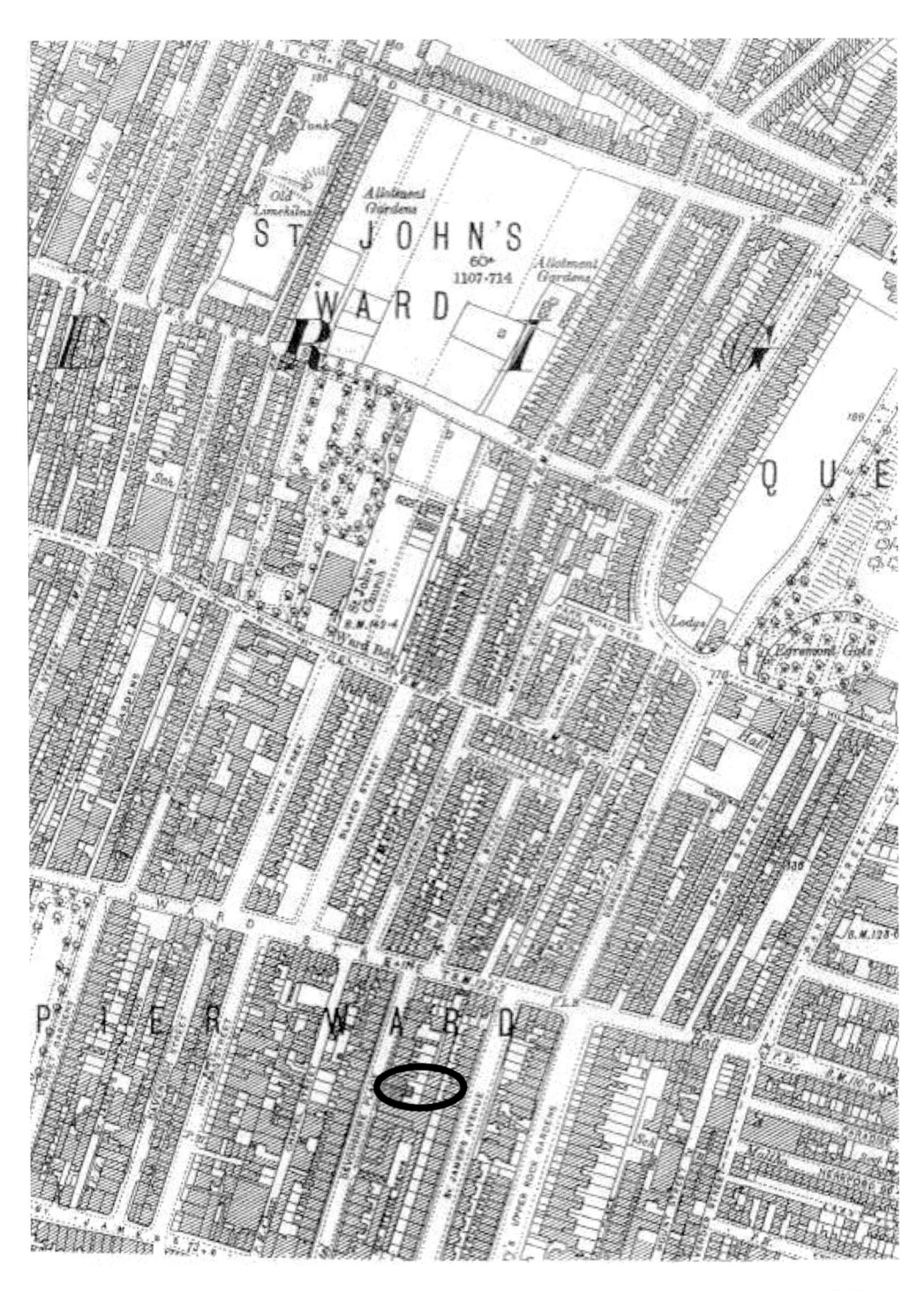

Ordnance Survey Map 1897 Brighton: Devonshire Place Synagogue BN2 [16]
25 inches to a mile 1825-1874

Ordnance Survey Map 1897　　　Brighton: Poune's Lane Synagogue c.1808-c.1813　　**[16]**
25 inches to a mile　　　　　　Middle Street Synagogue BN1 1874-still used

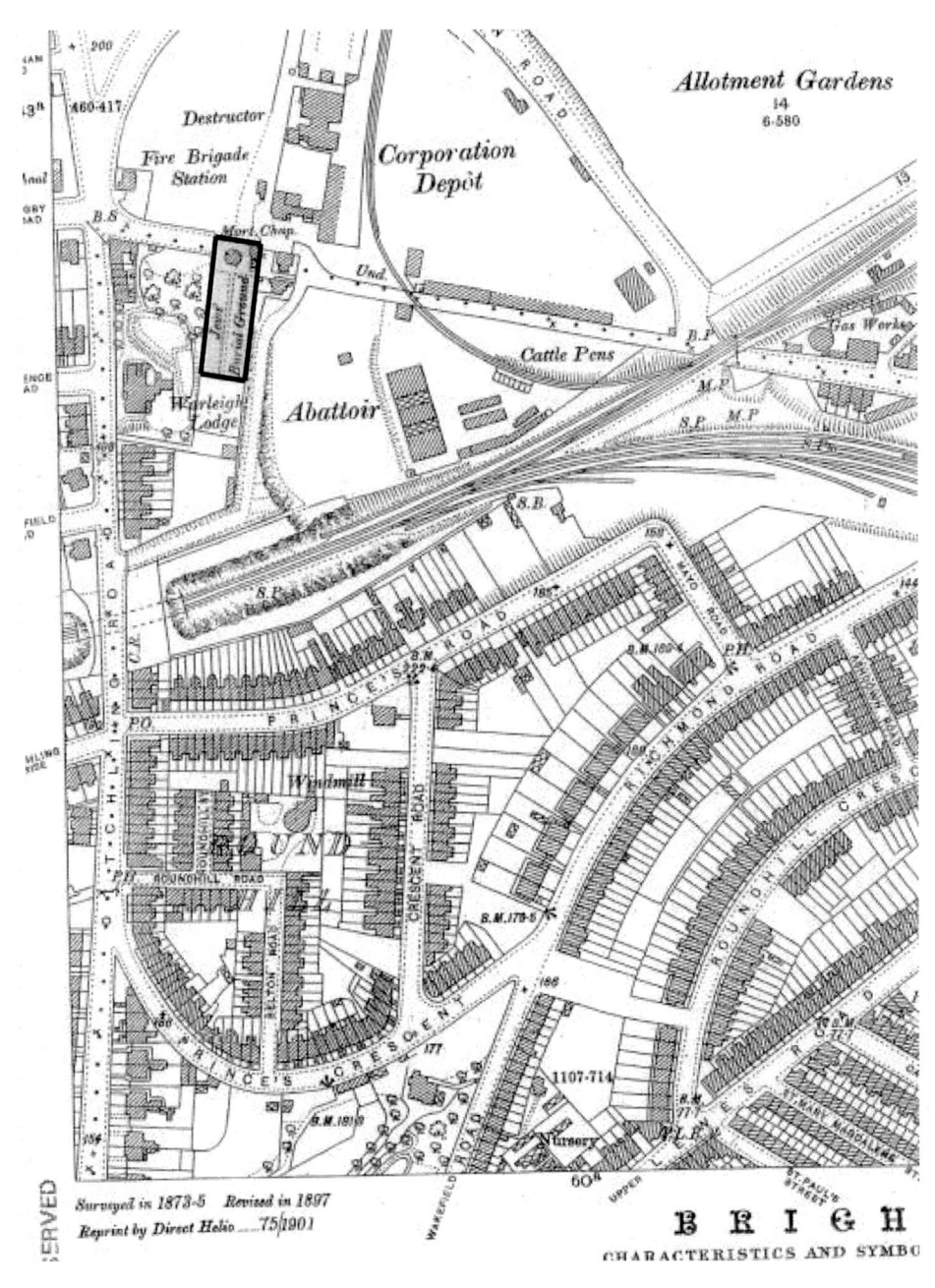

332   THE ARCHAEOLOGY OF ANGLO-JEWRY IN ENGLAND AND WALES 1656–C.1880

Ordnance Survey Map 1897　　Brighton: Florence Place Cemetery BN1　　**[62]**
25 inches to a mile　　　　　　1826-c.1920

LOCATION	CHAPTER	SITE	DATE ESTABLISHED	IN USE TO	DATE OF VISIT	GAZETTEER NUMBER
BRISTOL	4.2.5	SYNAGOGUE	PARK ROW 1870	still in use	2010	[17]
	5.2.5	CEMETERY	BARTON Rd. 1744	1944		[63]
			ROSE St. 1811	1880		

ADDITIONAL NOTES
1753 Traditional foundation of the Community (Margoliouth's History 1881)
1753 First mention of Jews in Bristol (Margoliouth's History 1881)

SYNAGOGUES
c.1756-1786   Temple Street (Old Ale House)
1786-1868   Weavers Hall, Temple Street
c.1870   Park Row
              still in use

FIGURE NUMBERS   4.55-4.60

CEMETERIES
1744-1944   Barton Road

1814-1880   Rose Street*
            * *no longer exists.*

1890   27 remains removed to the later Ridgeway Cemetery
            (not discussed)

FIGURE NUMBERS   5.41- 5.44

CONTACT INFORMATION
Alex Schlesinger: local historian
Sam Silverman: President of Park Row Synagogue

BIBLIOGRAPHY
Lipman, V. 1954 *Social History of the Jews in England 1850 – 1950*
Kadish, S. 2006 *Jewish Heritage in England. An Architectural Guide*
Roth, C. 1950 *The Rise of Provincial Jewry*
Samuel J. 1997 *Jews in Bristol*
Tobias A & S. et al.1997 *A catalogue of the Burials
in the Jewish Cemeteries in Bristol*

OTHER SOURCES
Ordnance Survey Maps: 1880, 1897,1903
Statistical Account of the Congregations of The British Empire 1845
Bristol Reference Library

PLACE NAMES WITH JEWISH CONNECTIONS   none

COMMUNITY SIZE

Date	Community Size
1800	150 persons
1850	c.300
1861	c.2000

Ordnance Survey Map 1903 Bristol: Park Row Synagogue BS1 [17]
25inches to a mile 1870-still in use

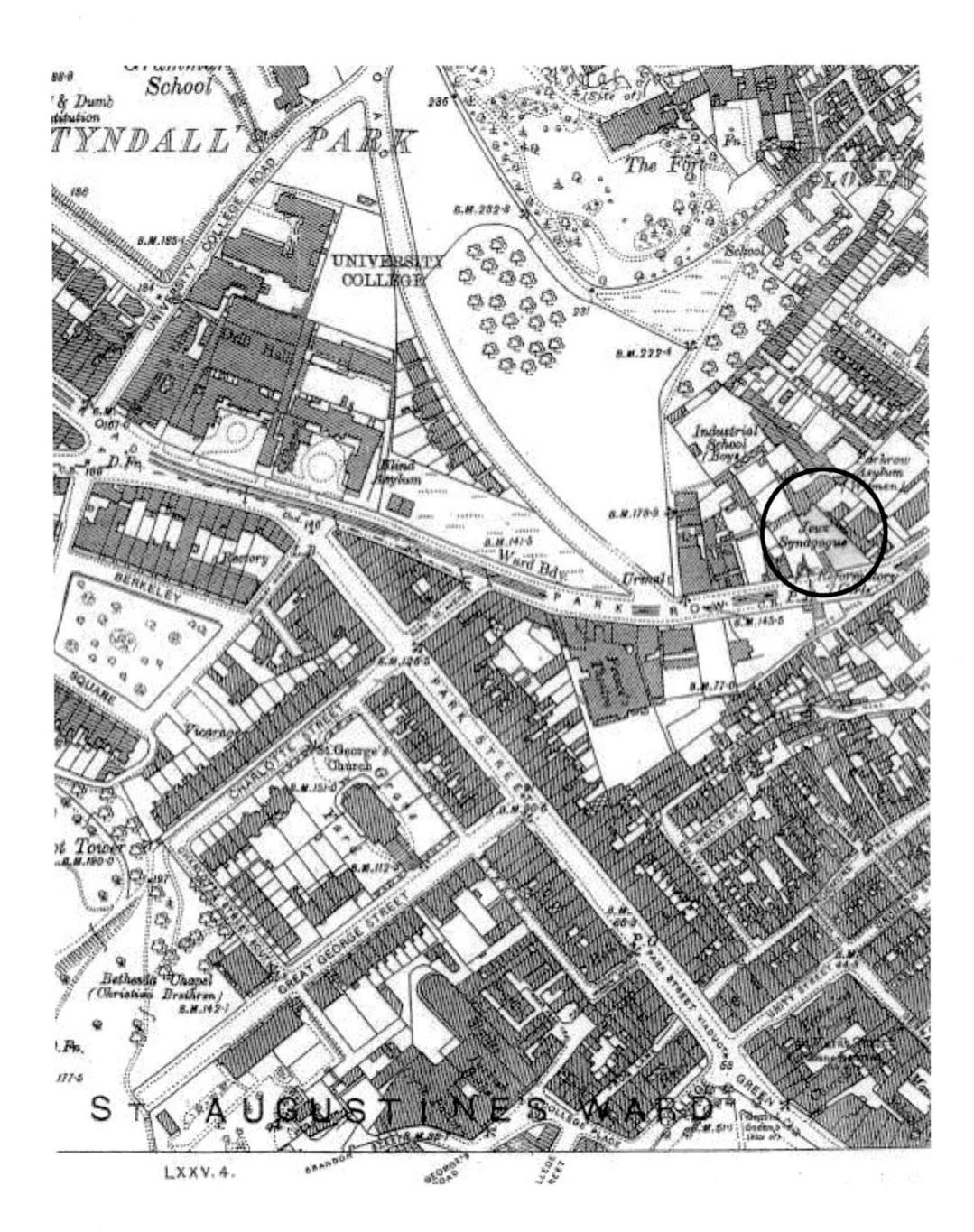

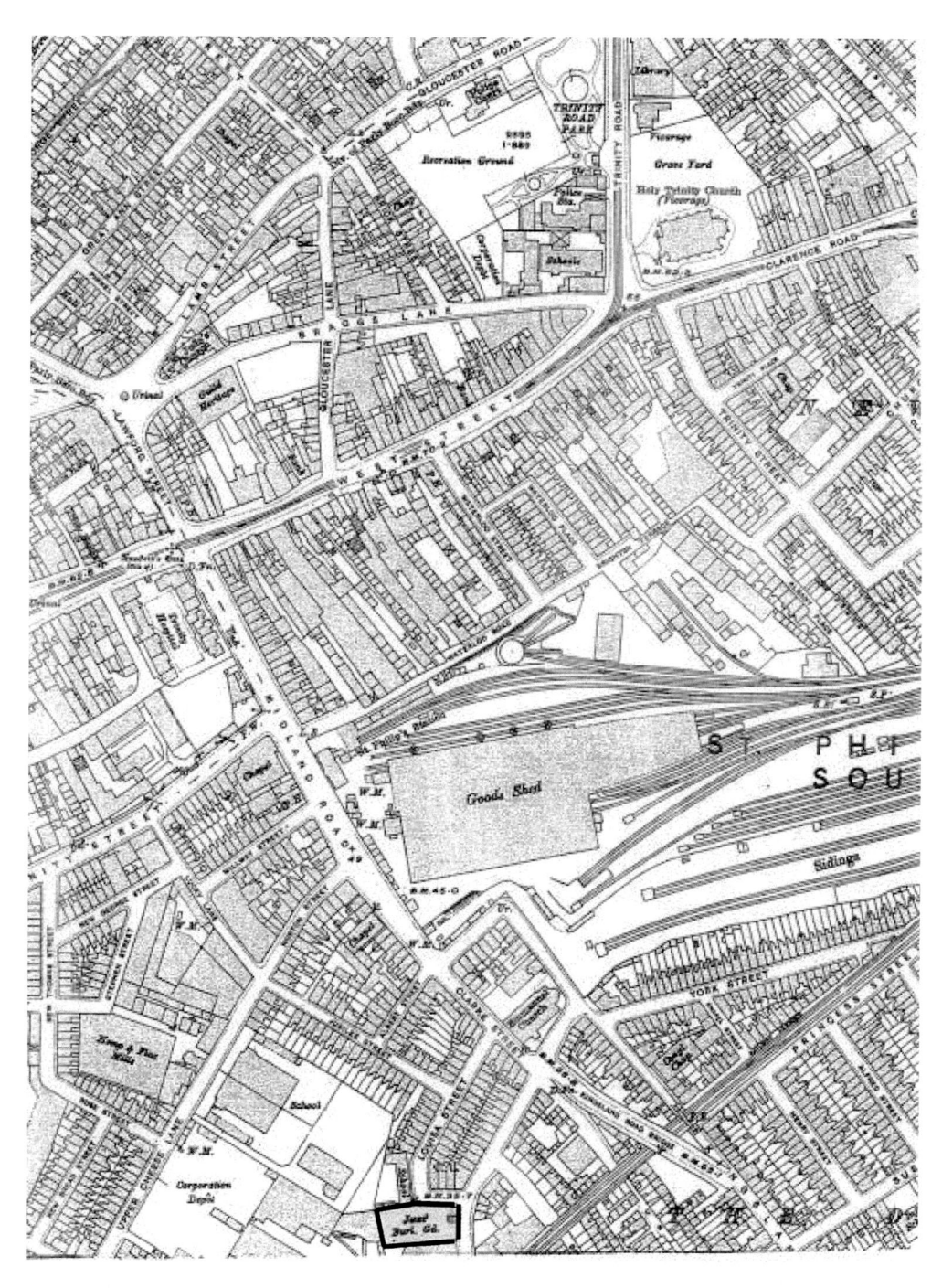

Ordnance Survey Map 1880 Bristol: St. Philips Cemetery Barton Road BS2 [63]
25 inches to a mile 1744-1944

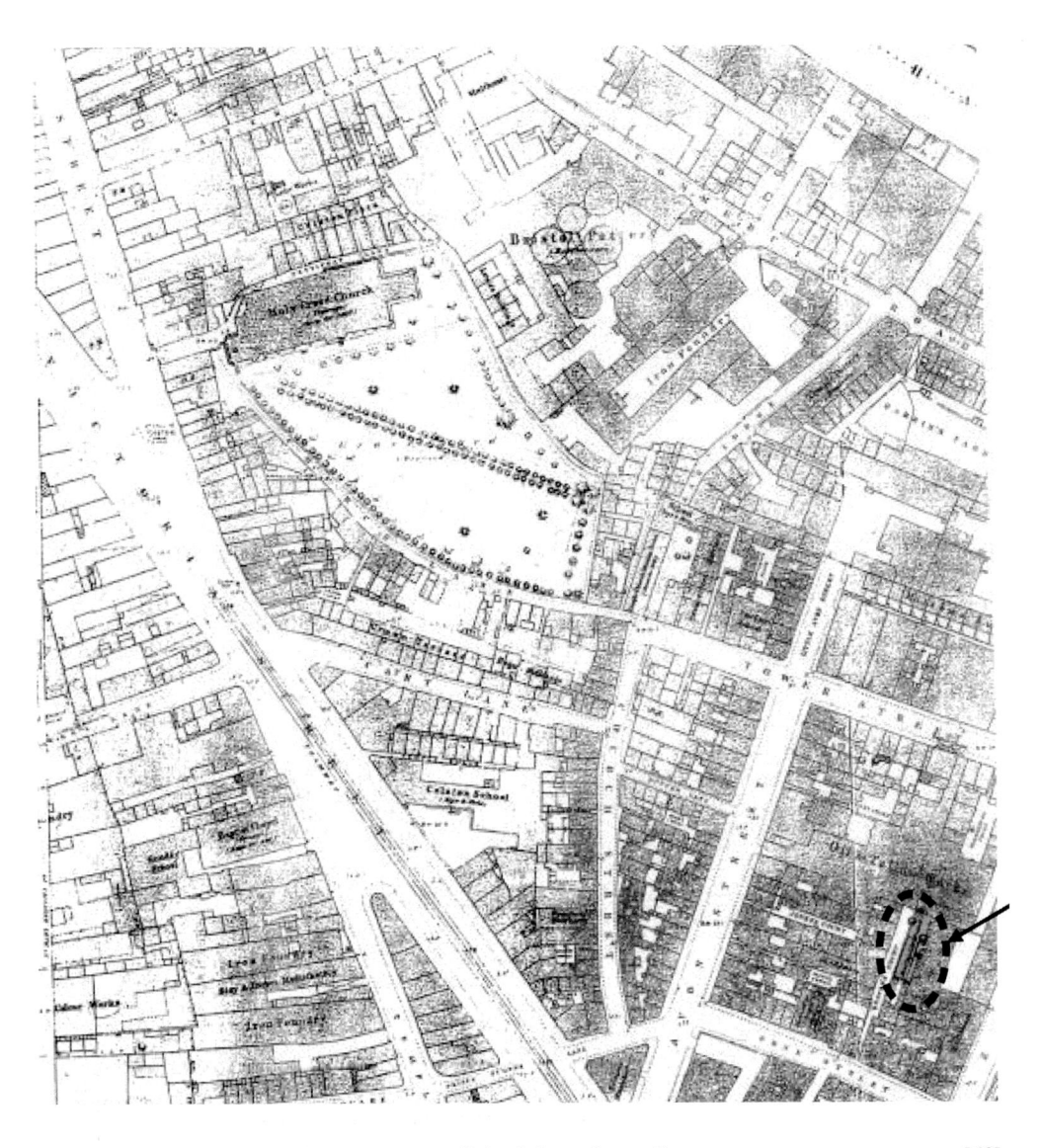

Ordnance Survey Map 1897　　　Bristol: Rose Street Cemetery　　　[63]
25 inches to a mile　　　　　　1814-1880

LOCATION	CHAPTER	SITE	DATE ESTABLISHED	IN USE TO	DATE OF VISIT	GAZETTEER NUMBER
CANTERBURY	4.2.6	SYNAGOGUES	c.1762 1847/8	1847 1931	2011	[18]
	5.2.6	CEMETERY	1760	1870*		[64]

ADDITIONAL NOTES	
	1760 Traditional foundation of Community (Roth 1950)
	c.1750 First mention of Jews in Canterbury (Roth 1950)
	*One burial in 1916

SYNAGOGUES		
	c.1750	Room of Prayer in St Dunstan's area
	c.1762-1846	First Synagogue in St. Dunstan's Street
	1847/8-1931	Second Synagogue in King Street
FIGURE NUMBERS	4.61-4.64	

CEMETERY		
	1760-1870	Whitstable Road CT2 (partial records 1831 - 1870) number of burials c.250
FIGURE NUMBERS	5.45-5.46	

CONTACT INFORMATION	
	Canterbury City Council Conservation Officer

BIBLIOGRAPHY	
	Rabbi Cohn-Sherbok 1984 *The Jews of Canterbury 1760 – 1931*
	Kadish, S. 2006 *Jewish Heritage in England. An Architectural Guide*
	Lipman, V. 1954 *Social History of The Jews in England 1850 - 1950*
	Roth, C. 1950 *The Rise of Provincial Jewry*

OTHER SOURCES	
	Kent County Archives Service
	Ordnance Survey Maps:1898
	Statistical Account of the Congregations in the British Empire 1845

PLACE NAMES WITH JEWISH CONNECTIONS	
	Jewry Street (medieval street in the heart of the Jewish community)

COMMUNITY SIZE		
	Date	Community Size
	1842	30 persons
	1845	106

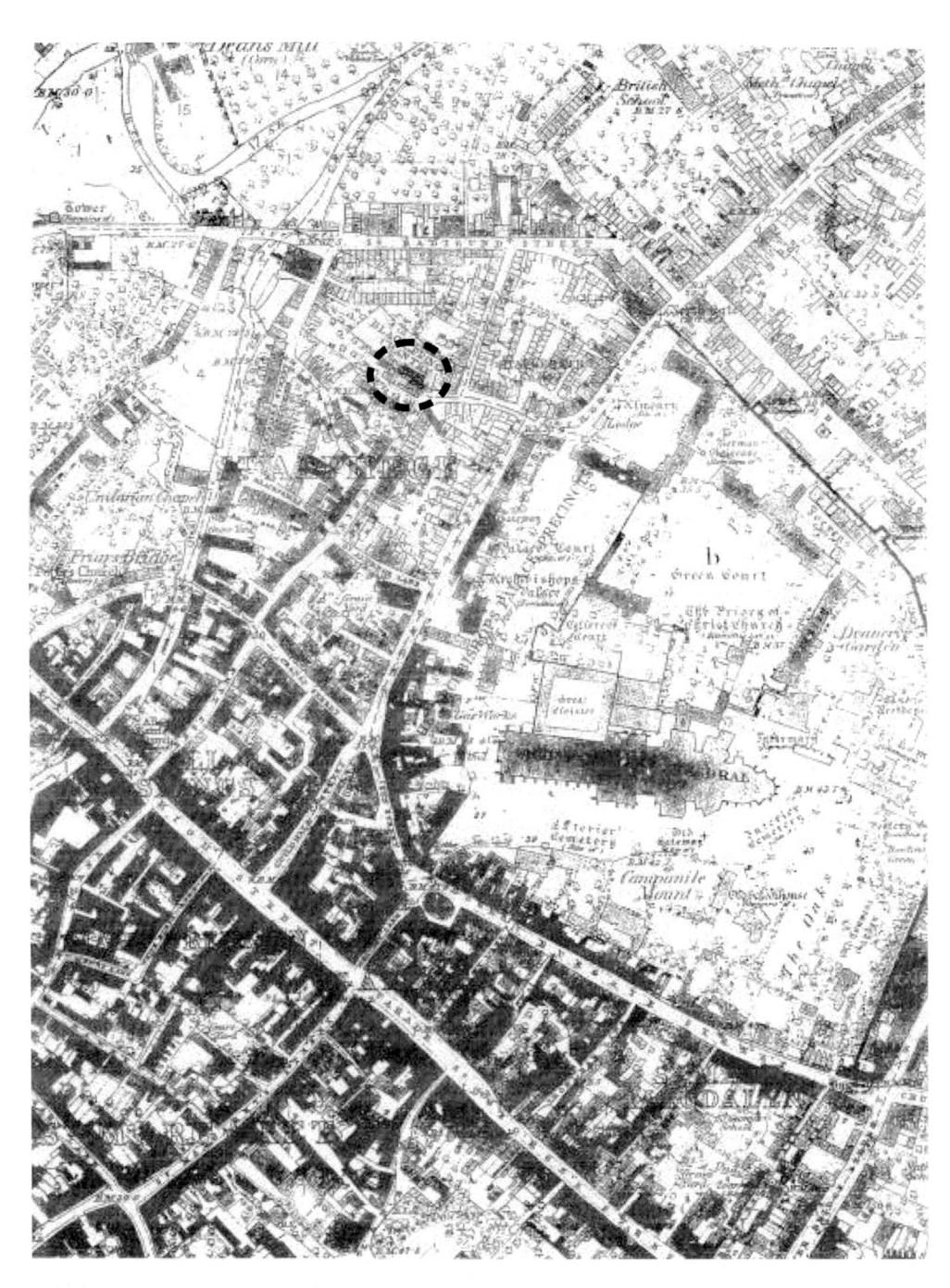

Ordnance Survey Map 1898
25 inches to a mile

Canterbury: King Street Synagogue CT1
1847/8-1931

[18]

GAZETTEER 339

Ordnance Survey Map 1898   Canterbury: Whitstable Road Cemetery CT2   **[64]**
25 inches to a mile   1760-1870

LOCATION	CHAPTER	SITE	DATE ESTABLISHED	IN USE TO	DATE OF VISIT	GAZETTEER NUMBER
CARDIFF					2009	
	4.2.7	SYNAGOGUES	1858	1949		[19]
	5.2.7	CEMETERY	1841	still in use		[65]

ADDITIONAL NOTES	
	c.1840 Traditional Foundation of the Community
	1797 First mention of Jews in Cardiff (Roth 1950)

SYNAGOGUES	
	First prayer room in Trinity Street: private house
	1858 Second Synagogue: East Terrace.
	1949 *Demolished*
FIGURE NUMBERS	nil

CEMETERY	
	Highfield Road Old Jewish Cemetery, Roth Park, CF 14 (still
	1841 occasionally used)
FIGURE NUMBERS	5.47-5.50

CONTACT INFORMATION	Rabbi Wellenburg
BIBLIOGRAPHY	Alderman, G., 1974/78 *The Jew as Scapegoat? The Settlement and Reception of Jews in South Wales before 1941*
	Dennis, M., 1951 *The Jewish Community in Wales, The Early Days*
	Henriques, U., ed. 1993 *The Jews of South Wales, Historical Studies*
	Kadish, S., 2006 *Jewish Heritage in England. An Architectural Guide*
	Lipman, V., 1954 *Social History of the Jews of England 1850-1950*
	Roth, C.,1950 *The Rise of Provincial Jewry*

OTHER SOURCES	The Glamorgan Archives
	Ordnance Survey Map: 1852
	Statistical Account of the Congregations in the British Empire 1845

PLACE NAMES WITH JEWISH CONNECTIONS	none

COMMUNITY SIZE	Date	Community Size
	1850	50/100 persons
	1900	1250
	1914	2000

GAZETTEER 341

Ordnance Survey Map 1852   Cardiff: Highfield Road Cemetery CF14
[65]
5ft. to a mile (photograph extract)   1841-still in use

LOCATION	CHAPTER	SITE	DATE ESTABLISHED	IN USE TO	DATE OF VISIT	GAZETTEER NUMBER
CHATHAM	4.2.8	SYNAGOGUES	1750 1869	1865 still in use	2010	[20]
	5.2.8	CEMETERY	1780	1940		[66]

ADDITIONAL NOTES	
	c.1750 Traditional foundation of the Community (Roth, 1950)

SYNAGOGUE(S)		
	1750-1865	First Synagogue: High Street Rochester
	c.1865	Second Synagogue On same site still in use
FIGURE NUMBERS	4.65-4.67	

CEMETERY		
	1789-1940	Only Jewish Cemetery in Britain adjacent to the Synagogue
FIGURE NUMBERS	5.51- 5.52	

CONTACT INFORMATION	David Herling: Vice Chairman, Chatham Memorial Synagogue
BIBLIOGRAPHY	Green, G., 1982 / 6 *Anglo Jewish Trading Connections with Officers and Seamen of the Royal Navy 1740-1820* Kadish, S., 2006 *Jewish Heritage in England. An Architectural Guide* Lancaster, G., 1998 *A Venerable Community in Kent.* Roth, C.,1950 *The Rise of Provincial Jewry*
OTHER SOURCES	Jewish Community Records 2010 (J.C.R. UK) Chatham Records Office Ordnance Survey Map: 1858 Statistical Account of the Congregations of the British Empire 1845

PLACE NAMES WITH JEWISH CONNECTIONS	none

COMMUNITY SIZE	Date Community Size 1850 200 1905 *103* 1915 *100* 1965 *150* 2004 *50*

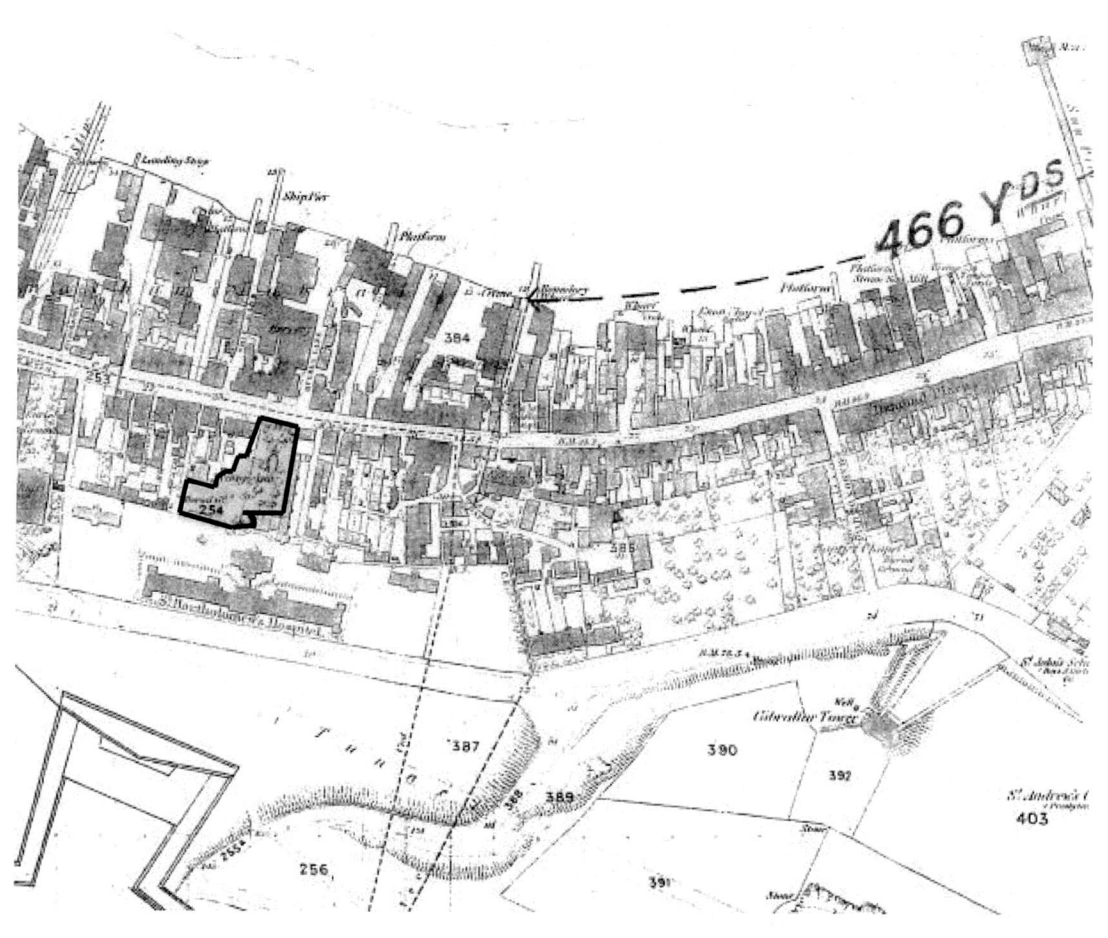

Ordnance Survey Map 1858   Chatham; High Street ME1 Synagogue and Cemetery   [20] [66]
25 inches to a mile   Cemetery 1780's-1940, synagogue c.1865-still in use

LOCATION	CHAPTER	SITE	DATE ESTABLISHED	IN USE TO	DATE OF VISIT	GAZETTEER NUMBER
CHELTENHAM	4.2.9	SYNAGOGUE	1837/9	still in use	2009	[21]
	5.2.9	CEMETERY	1824	still in use		[67]

ADDITIONAL NOTES	
	1824 Traditional foundation of the community (Roth 1950)
	c.1749 First mention of Jews in Cheltenham (Roth 1950)

SYNAGOGUE(S)	1826 First synagogue in private house
	1837 St. James' Square, GL50
FIGURE NUMBERS	4.68-4.69

CEMETERY(S)	1824 Burial Ground, Elm Street, GL51
FIGURE NUMBERS	5.53-5.54

CONTACT INFORMATION	Stone, A. : Chairman Cheltenham Jewish Community
	Webber, M. : Member of the community

BIBLIOGRAPHY	
	Kadish, S. 2006 *Jewish Heritage in England. An Architectural Guide*
	Lipman, V. 1954 *Social History of the Jews in England*
	Roth, C. 1950 *The Rise of Provincial Jewry*
	Tarode, B. 1989 *The Hebrew Congregation of Cheltenham, Gloucester and Stroud*

OTHER SOURCES	
	Ordnance Survey Maps: 1898

PLACE NAMES WITH JEWISH CONNECTIONS	Synagogue Lane, off St James' Square, GL50*
	* entrance to synagogue is in Synagogue Lane

COMMUNITY SIZE		
	Date	Community Size
	1845	c.100 persons
	1850	c.100 including Gloucester
	1896	17
	1909	6
	1955	120
	2004	133

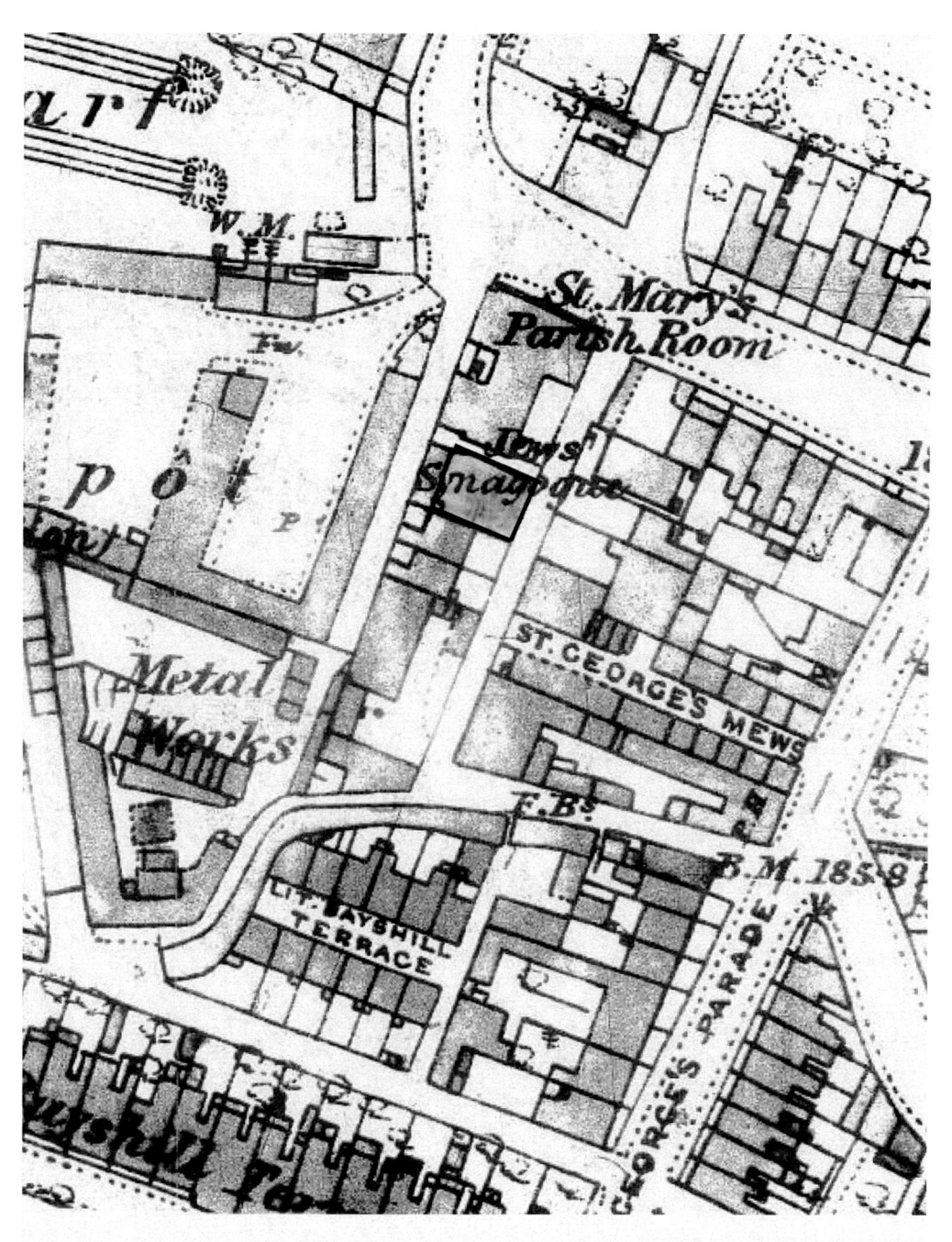

Ordnance Survey Map 1898   Cheltenham: St. James's Square Synagogue GL50   [21]
5ft. to a mile   1837/9-still in use

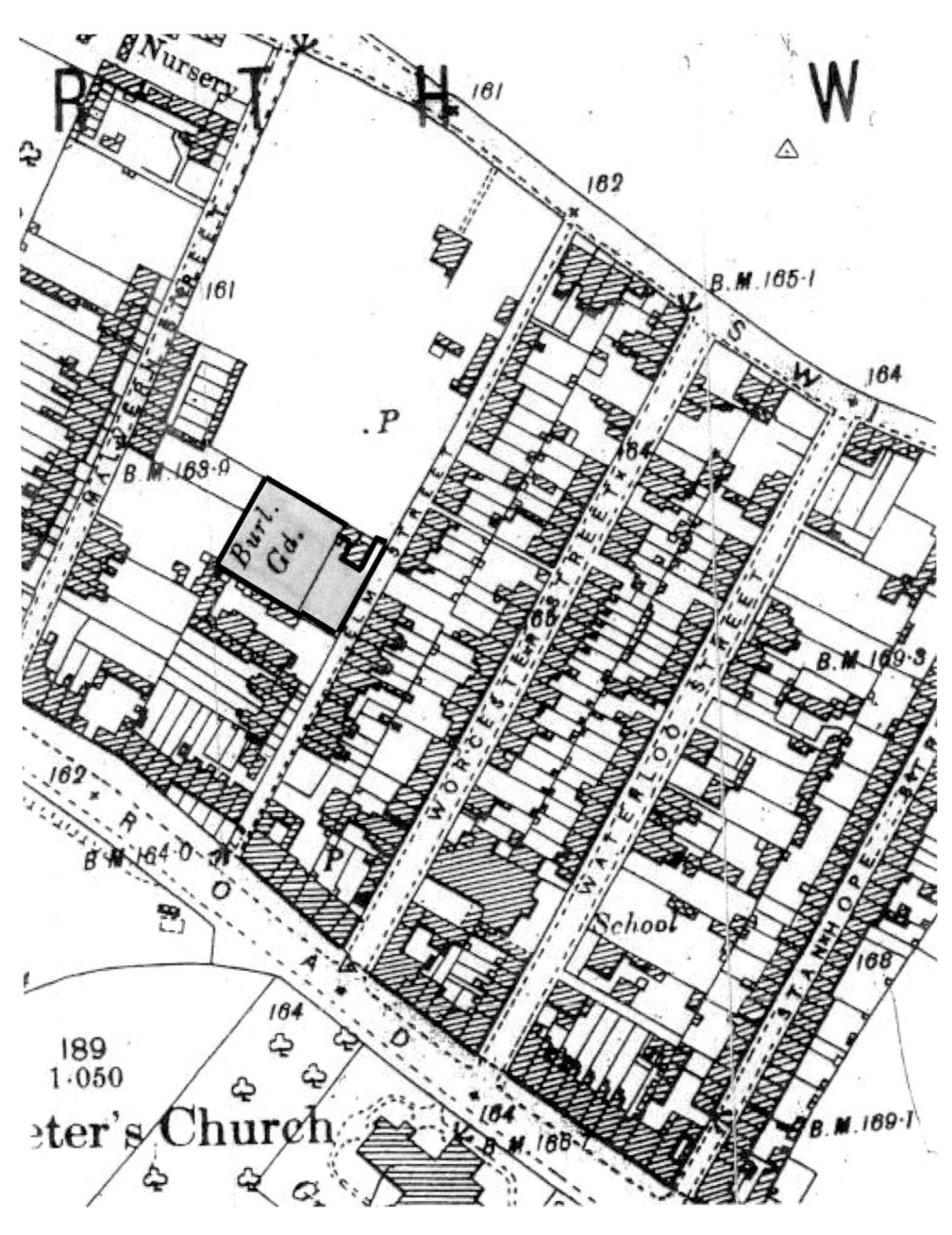

Ordnance Survey Map 1898 Cheltenham: Elm Street Burial Ground GL51 [67]
5ft to a mile 1824-still in use

LOCATION	CHAPTER	SITE	DATE ESTABLISHED	IN USE TO	DATE OF VISIT	GAZETTEER NUMBER
COVENTRY					2011	
	4.2.10	SYNAGOGUE	1870	c.2008		[22]
	5.2.10	CEMETERY	1864	still in use		[68]

ADDITIONAL NOTES		
	c.1800	Traditional foundation of the community (Roth 1950)
	c.1775	First mention of Jews in Coventry (Roth 1950)

SYNAGOGUE		
	1870-c.2008	Barras Lane CV1
		(now closed. The congregation moved to Solihull)
	2011	*Small Reform Community c.30 persons in a room of prayer*
FIGURE NUMBERS	4.70	

CEMETERY		
	1864	London Road Cemetery, Jewish Section, Whitley CV3
FIGURE NUMBERS	5.55 - 5.56	

CONTACT INFORMATION	Barry Deitch: President of Coventry Reform Community
BIBLIOGRAPHY	Kadish, S., 2006 *Jewish Heritage in England. An Architectural Guide*
	Lipman, V. 1954 *Social History of The Jews in England 1850 - 1950*
	Roth, C., 1950 *The Rise of Provincial Jewry*

OTHER SOURCES	Coventry History Centre
	Ordnance Survey Maps: 1902, 1903

PLACE NAMES WITH JEWISH CONNECTIONS	none

COMMUNITY SIZE	Date	Community Size	
	1842	111	families
	1850	50-100	persons
	1870	50	
	1902	c.25	
	2011	30	

Ordnance Survey Map 1903　　Coventry: Barras Lane Synagogue CV1　　[22]
25 inches to a mile　　　　　　1870-c.2008

GAZETTEER 349

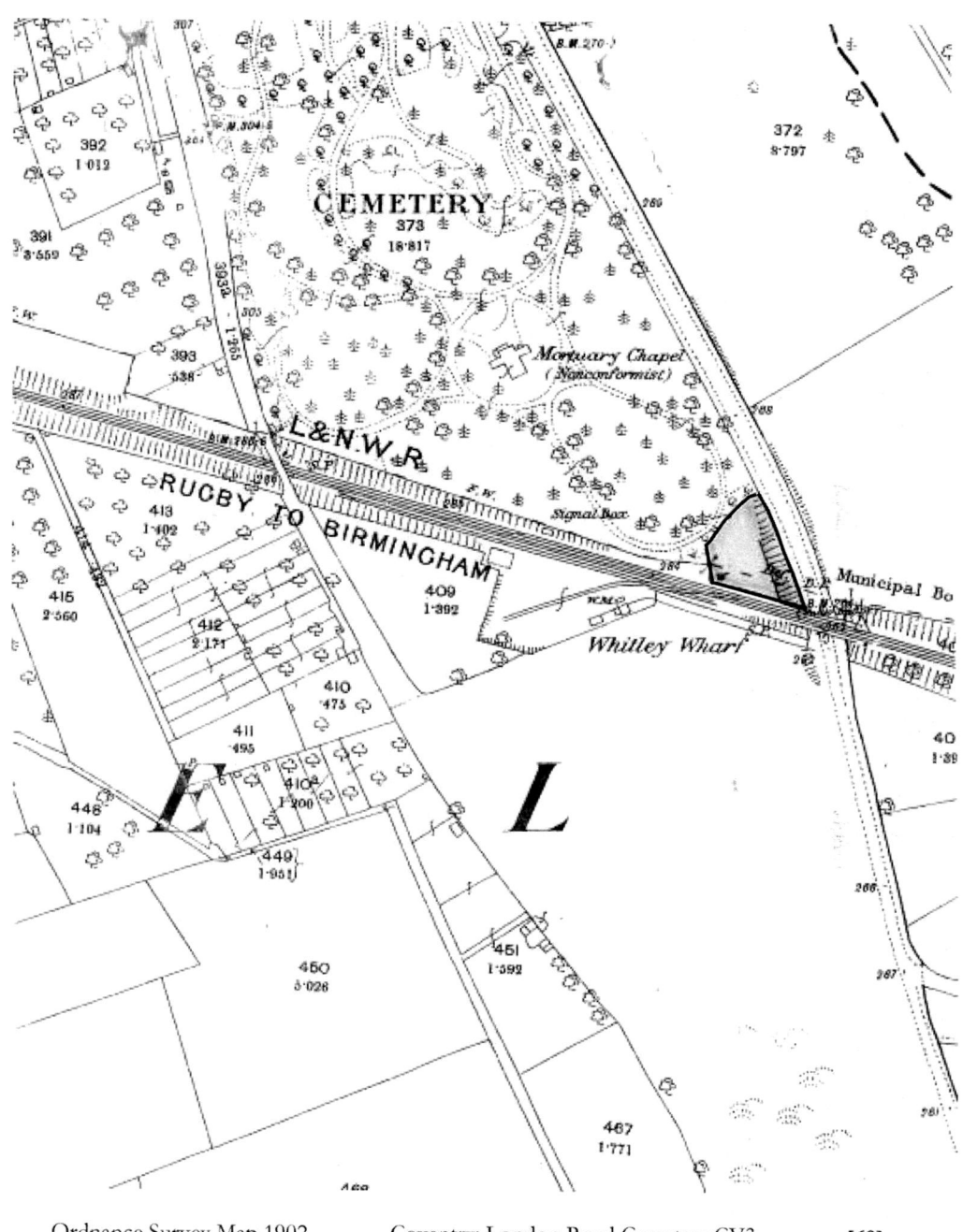

Ordnance Survey Map 1902　　Coventry: London Road Cemetery CV3　　[68]
25 inches to a mile　　1864-still in use

LOCATION	CHAPTER	SITE	DATE ESTABLISHED	IN USE TO	DATE OF VISIT	GAZETTEER NUMBER
DOVER	4.2.11	SYNAGOGUE	1863	1941*	2009	[23]
	5.2.11	CEMETERY	1863**	still in use		[69]

ADDITIONAL NOTES	
c.1770	Traditional foundation of the community (Roth 1950)
1762	First mention of Jews in Dover (Roth 1950)
	*synagogue badly damaged by bombing 1941, demolished 1950
	**First burial 1868
	There is no longer a Jewish Community in Dover

SYNAGOGUE(S)		
	1835	First synagogue: Hawkesbury Street
	1863	Second synagogue: Northampton Street (designed to hold a congregation of 250 people) (no longer exists)
FIGURE NUMBERS	4.71-4.72	

CEMETERY(S)		
		Early burials in Canterbury before establishment of cemetery
	1864	Old Charlton Road, Copt Hill, CT16
FIGURE NUMBERS	5.57-5.58	

CONTACT INFORMATION	Hambrooke & Johns: Funeral Directors
BIBLIOGRAPHY	Jones, B.J. 1916 *The History of Religion in the Annals of Dover*
	Kadish, S. 2006 *Jewish Heritage in England. An Architectural Guide*
	Lipman, V. 1954 *Social History of the Jews of England 1850 - 1950*
	Roth, C. 1950 *The Rise of Provincial Jewry*

OTHER SOURCES	Dover Records Office, Map 2010
	Ordnance Survey Map 1908
	Statistical Account of the Congregations of the British Empire 1845

PLACE NAMES WITH JEWISH CONNECTIONS	none

COMMUNITY SIZE	Date	Community Size
	1845	c.30 persons
	1850	c.50
	1880	c.200

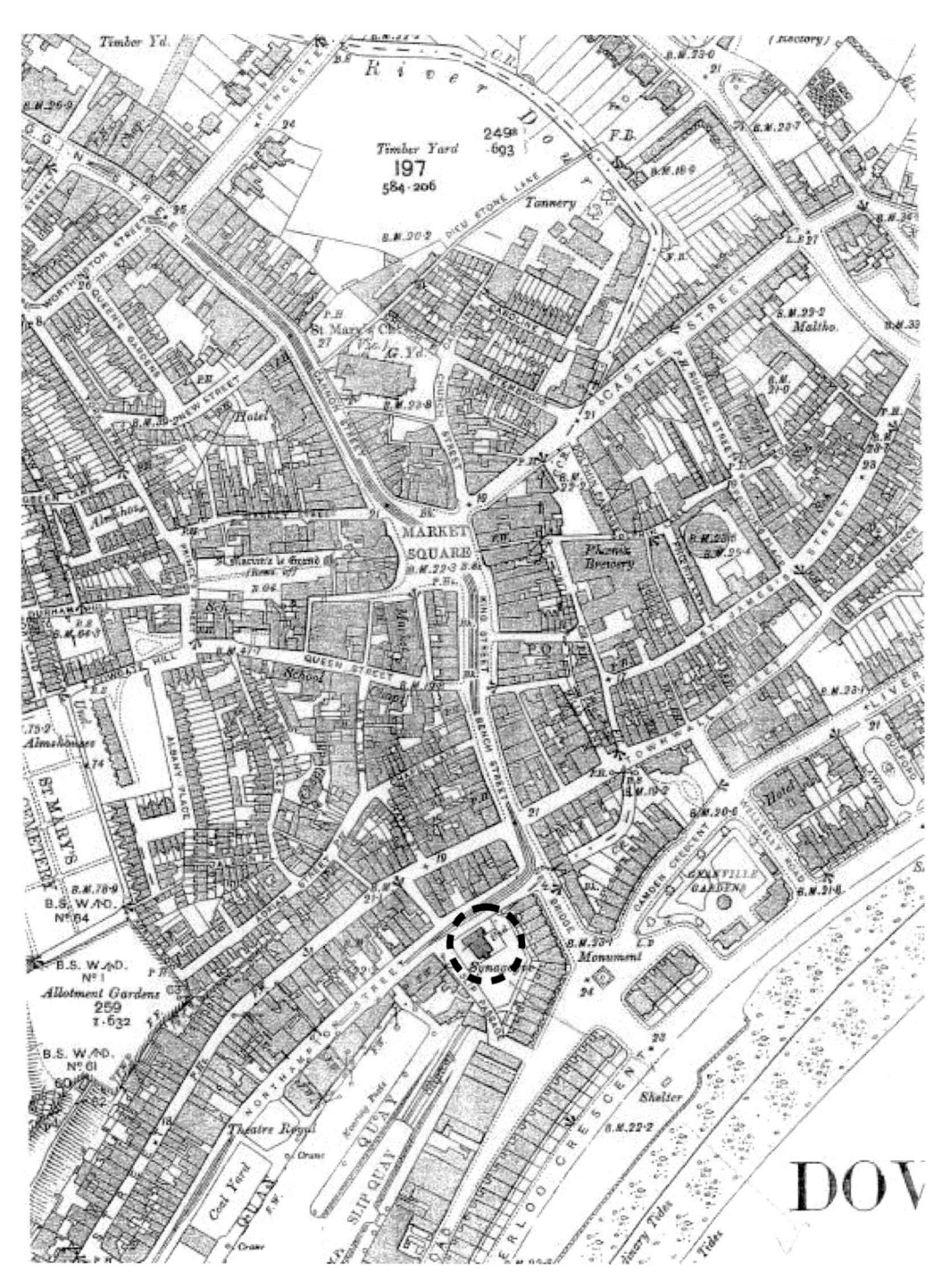

Ordnance Survey Map 1908   Dover; Northampton Street Synagogue   **[23]**
25 inches to a mile   1863-1941 (damaged and closed in World War II, demolished 1950)

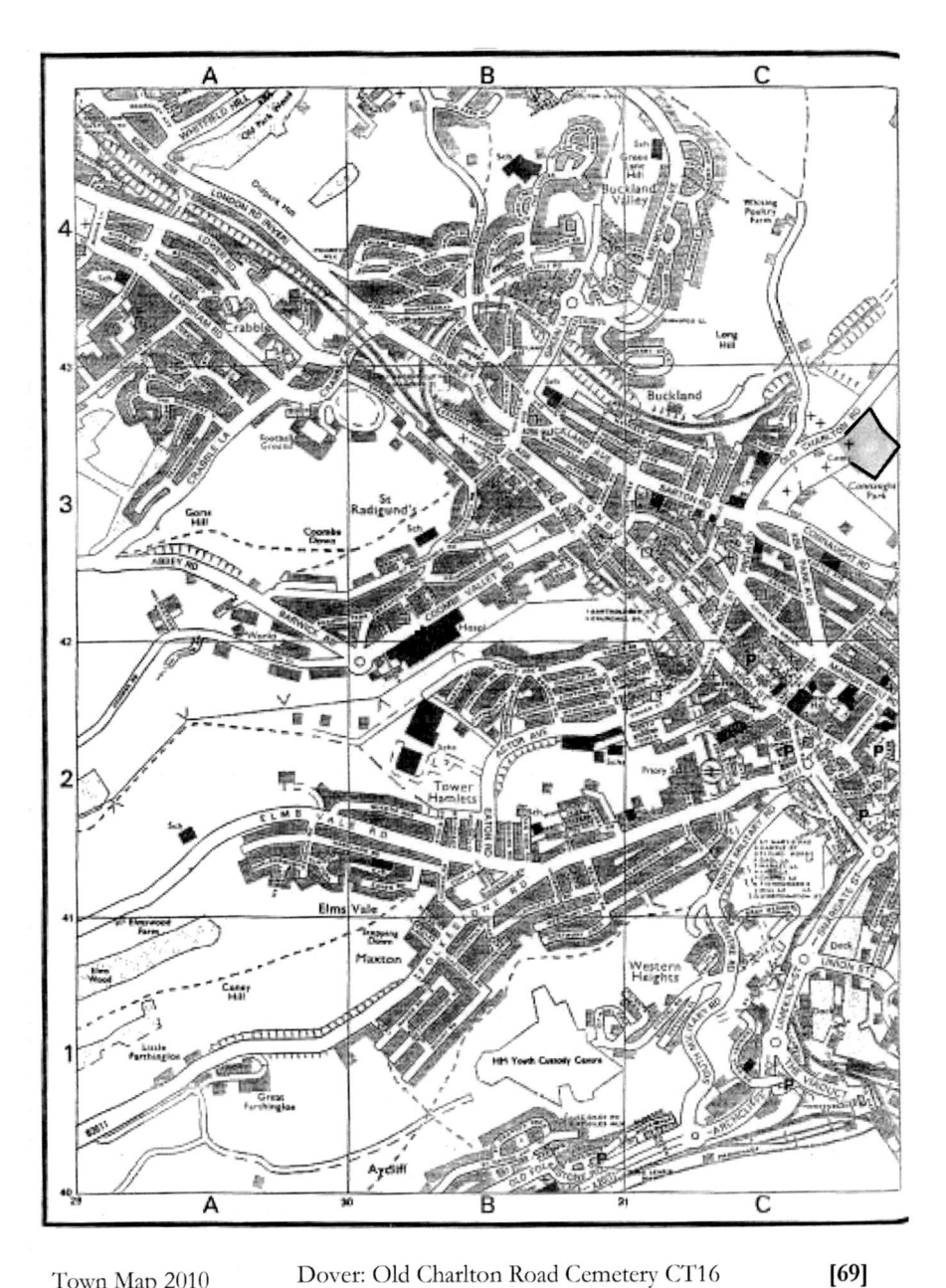

352 THE ARCHAEOLOGY OF ANGLO-JEWRY IN ENGLAND AND WALES 1656–c.1880

Town Map 2010　　Dover: Old Charlton Road Cemetery CT16　　[69]
(no scale)　　　　1864- occasionally used

LOCATION	CHAPTER	SITE	DATE ESTABLISHED	IN USE TO	DATE OF VISIT	GAZETTEER NUMBER
EXETER	4.2.12	SYNAGOGUE	1763	still in use	2009	[24]
	5.2.12	CEMETERY	1757	still used occasionally		[70]

ADDITIONAL NOTES

1763 Traditional foundation of the community (Margoliouth's History 1851)
1735 First mention of Jews in Exeter (Margoliouth's History 1851)

SYNAGOGUE(S)

1763   Exeter Synagogue
Synagogue Place, Mary Arches Street, EX4
(Grade II*)

FIGURE NUMBERS   4.73 - 4.74

CEMETERY(S)

1757   Bull Meadow Jews' Burial Ground
Magdalen Street, Bull Meadow, EX2
(Grade II - boundary wall)

FIGURE NUMBERS   5.59 - 5.60

CONTACT INFORMATION

Dr. Paul Newgass: President of Exeter Synagogue

BIBLIOGRAPHY

Kadish, S. 2006 *Jewish Heritage in England. An Architectural Guide*
Lipman, V. 1954 *Social History of the Jews of England 1850-1950*
Roth, C. 1950 *The Rise of Provincial Jewry*

OTHER SOURCES

Devon Records Office
Ordnance Survey Maps: 1896, 1898
Jewish Community Records
Statistical Account of the Congregations of the British Empire 1845

PLACE NAMES WITH JEWISH CONNECTIONS

Synagogue Place (side street entrance of synagogue)

COMMUNITY SIZE

Date	Community Size	
1842	30	families
1850	c.175	persons
2010	c.120	adults

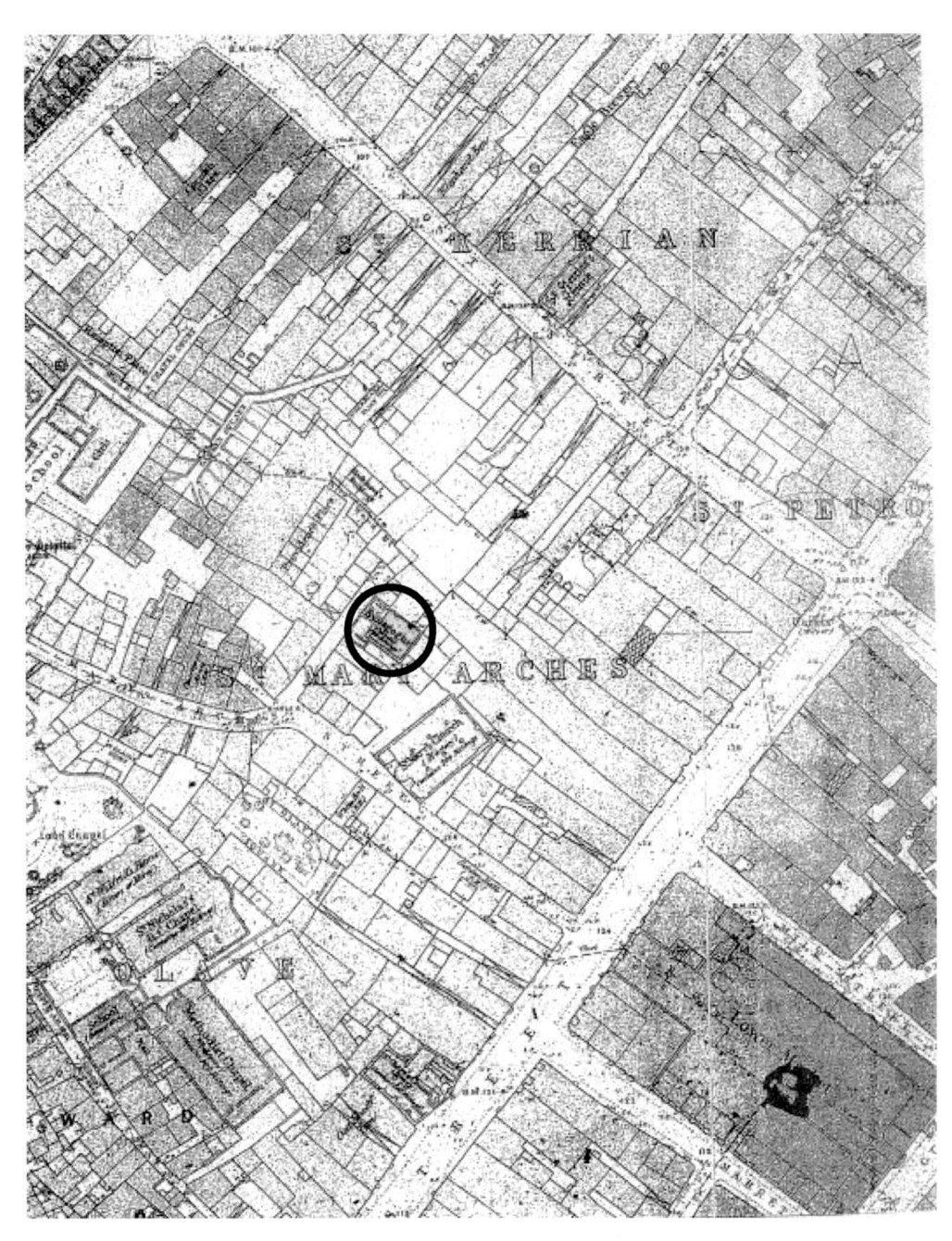

Ordnance Survey Map 1898 Exeter: Synagogue in Synagogue Place, Mary Arches EX4 [24]
10.56 inches to a mile 1763 still in use

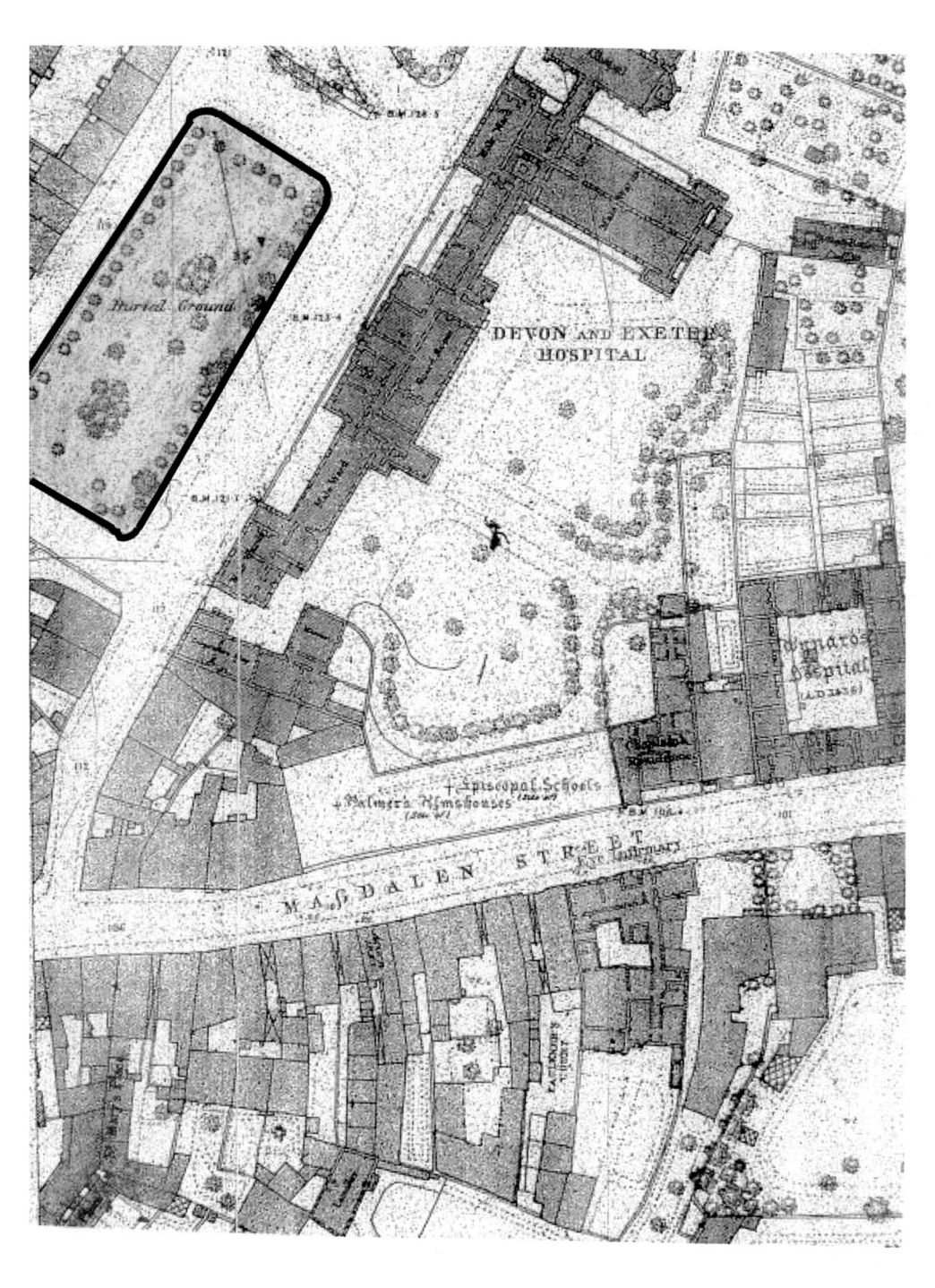

Ordnance Survey Map 1896　　　Exeter: Bull Meadow Cemetery EX2　　**[70]**
5ft. to a mile　　　　　　　　1757-still in use

LOCATION	CHAPTER	SITE	DATE ESTABLISHED	IN USE TO	DATE OF VISIT	GAZETTEER NUMBER
FALMOUTH	4.2.13	SYNAGOGUES	1766	1808	2009	[25]
			1808	1880		
	5.2.13	CEMETERY	1740/1750	1868		[71]

ADDITIONAL NOTES		
	1740	Traditional Foundation of the Community (Roth 1950)
	1720	First mention of Jews in Falmouth (Pearce, K. 2000)
		There is no longer a Jewish Community in Falmouth

SYNAGOGUES	
	1766-1808 First synagogue: established (no longer exists)
	1808-1880 Second synagogue: Smithick Hill, TR11 (Grade II)
FIGURE NUMBERS	4.75 - 4.77

CEMETERY	
	1740/1750-1868 Falmouth Jews' Burial Ground: Penryn Road, Ponsharden, TR11 Scheduled Ancient Monument: two memorial stones (Grade II)
FIGURE NUMBERS	5.61 - 5.63

CONTACT INFORMATION	Keith Pearce: Local Historian
	Eric Dawkins: Local Historian and Cemetery caretaker
BIBLIOGRAPHY	Jamilly, E. 1953 / 5 *Anglo Jewish Architects and Architecture in the 18th & 19th Centuries Transactions of the Jewish Historical Society* Vol.18, 127-141
	Pearce, K.& Fry, H. Ed. 2000 *The Lost Jews of Cornwall from The Middle Ages to the 19th Century*
	Kadish, S. 2006 *Jewish Heritage in England. An Architectural Guide*
	Lipman, V. 1954 *Social History of the Jews of England 1850 - 1950*
	Roth, C. 1950 *The Rise of Provincial Jewry*

OTHER SOURCES	
	Ordnance Survey Maps: 1882, 1896
	Falmouth & Penryn Directory & Guide: 1864
	Statistical Account of the Congregations of the British Empire 1845

PLACE NAMES WITH JEWISH CONNECTIONS	none

COMMUNITY SIZE		
	Date	Community Size
	1842	14 families
	1850	c.100 persons
	1880	no longer a community

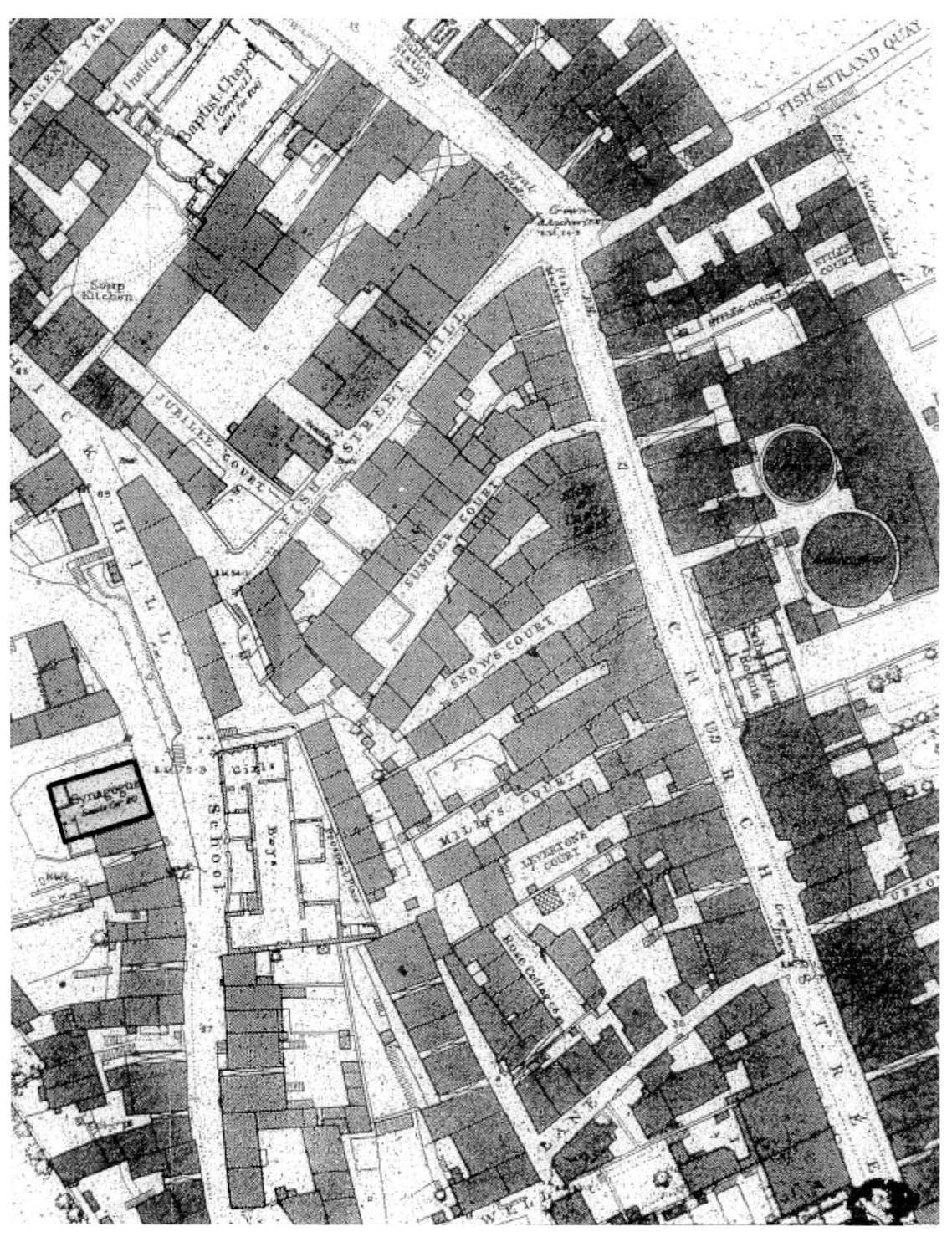

Ordnance Survey Map 1896　　　　　Falmouth: Smithick Hill Synagogue TR11　　[25]
10.56 inches to a mile　　　　　　　　　　　1808-1880

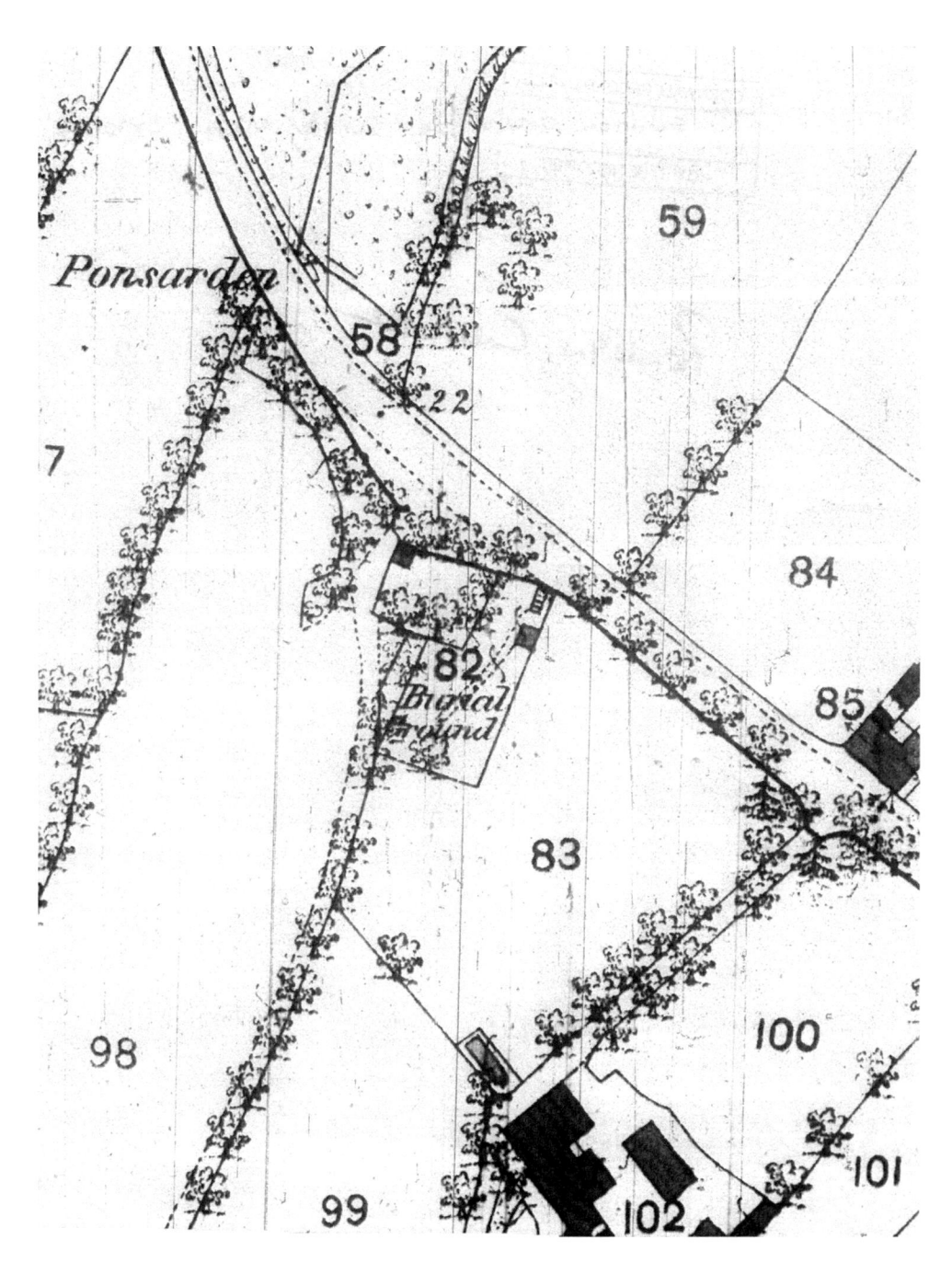

Ordnance Survey Map 1882 Falmouth: Ponsharden Jewish Cemetery (82) TR11
[71]
25 inches o the mile   c.1780-1868

LOCATION	CHAPTER	SITE	DATE ESTABLISHED	IN USE TO	DATE OF VISIT	GAZETTEER NUMBER
GLOUCESTER	4.2.14	SYNAGOGUE	c.1780-1784	1850	2009	[26]
	5.2.14	CEMETERY	c.1780-1887	*		[72]

ADDITIONAL NOTES	
	c1784 Traditional foundation of the community (Kadish 2006)
	1765 First mention of Jews in Gloucester (Margoliouth's History 1851)
	*Remains reinterred in Coney Hill Cemetery
	There is no longer a Jewish Community in Gloucester

SYNAGOGUE	c.1780 - 1784 Mercy Place, Lower Southgate Street
	(no longer exists)
FIGURE NUMBERS	nil

CEMETERIES	
	c.1780 - 1887 Mercy Place
	opposite Infirmary: Organs Passage /
	Gardeners Lane off Barton Street
	Coney Hill Cemetery, Jewish Section
	reinterred remains from Organs Passage
FIGURE NUMBERS	5.64 - 5.66

CONTACT INFORMATION	Gloucester Archives Office
BIBLIOGRAPHY	Kadish, S. 2006. *Jewish Heritage in England. An Architectural Guide*
	Lipman, V. 1954 *Social History of the Jews of England 1850 - 1950*
	Roth, C. 1950 *The Rise of Provincial Jewry*
	Torode, B. 1999 *The Hebrew Community of Cheltenham, Gloucester & Stroud*

OTHER SOURCES	Gloucester Archives Office
	Ordnance Survey Map: 1882
	Statistical Account of the Congregations of the British Empire 1845

PLACE NAMES WITH JEWISH CONNECTIONS	none

COMMUNITY SIZE	No records
	Community amalgamated with Cheltenham from 1850

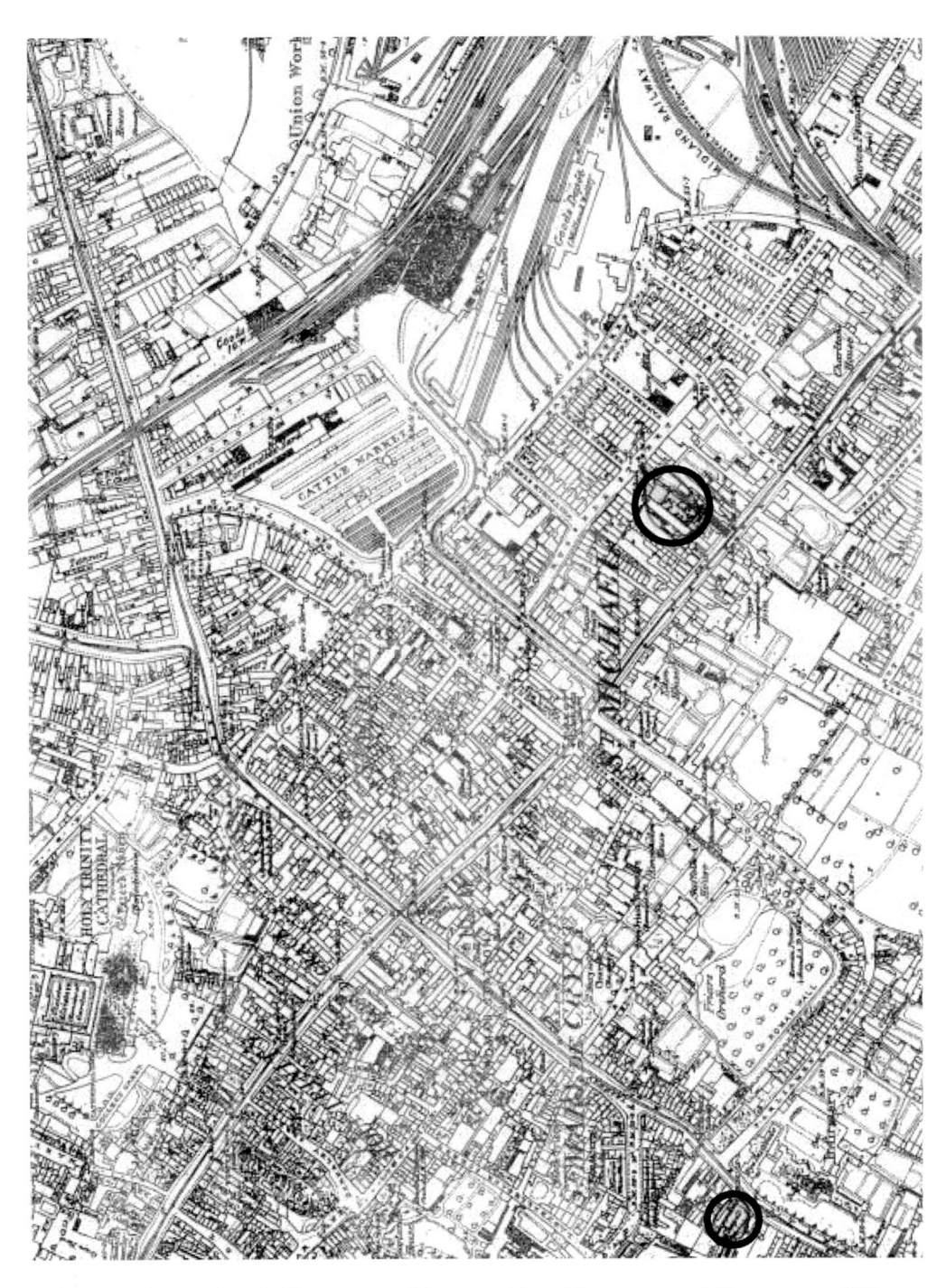

Ordnance Survey Map 1882 Gloucester: Site of Synagogue c.1784 [26]
25 inches o the mile Barton Street Cemetery c.1780-1887 [72]

LOCATION	CHAPTER	SITE	DATE ESTABLISHED	IN USE TO	DATE OF VISIT	GAZETTEER NUMBER
HULL	4.2.15	SYNAGOGUE	1780 1809 1826 / 7	1809 1826 1902	2010	[27]
	5.2.15	CEMETERY	1780 1812 1858	1812 1858 still in use		[73]

ADDITIONAL NOTES

1810 Traditional foundation of the community (Margoliouth's History 1851)
1770 First mention of Jews in Hull (Margoliouth's History 1851)

SYNAGOGUES

1780-1809   Postern Gate in Catholic Church
1809-1826   Parade Row Synagogue in Princess Dock
1826-1902   Robinson Row *(demolished 1928)*
Note: there were 16 Synagogues in Hull 1780-1995

FIGURE NUMBERS   4.78 - 4.80

CEMETERIES

1780-1812   Villa Place, HU3
1812-1858   Hessle Road, HU3
1858   Dehli Street, HU9 *(still in use)*
Note: 3 further Jewish Cemeteries in Hull established post 1880 (not discussed)

FIGURE NUMBERS   5.67 - 5.72

CONTACT INFORMATION   Dr. David Lewis: community Archivist

BIBLIOGRAPHY

Finestein, I. 1996/8 The Jews in Hull between 1766 & 1880
Transactions of the Jewish Historical Society of England
Vol.35, pages 33-91
Kadish, S. 2006   *Jewish Heritage in England. An Architectural Guide*
Lewis, D. 2002   *Hull's Six Jewish Cemeteries*
Lipman, V. 1954   *Social History of the Jews of England 1850 - 1950*
Oppel, E. 2000   *The History of Hull Orthodox Synagogues*
(and the people connected to them)
Roth, C. 1950   *The Rise of Provincial Jewry*

OTHER SOURCES

Hull History Centre
Ordnance Survey Maps: 1853, 1856, 1891
Statistical Account of the Congregations of the British Empire 1845

PLACE NAMES WITH JEWISH CONNECTIONS   none

COMMUNITY SIZE

Date	Community Size
1793	40 persons
1815	60
1845	65
1851	c.200
1880	c.2000
1895	*1350*
1900	c.2000

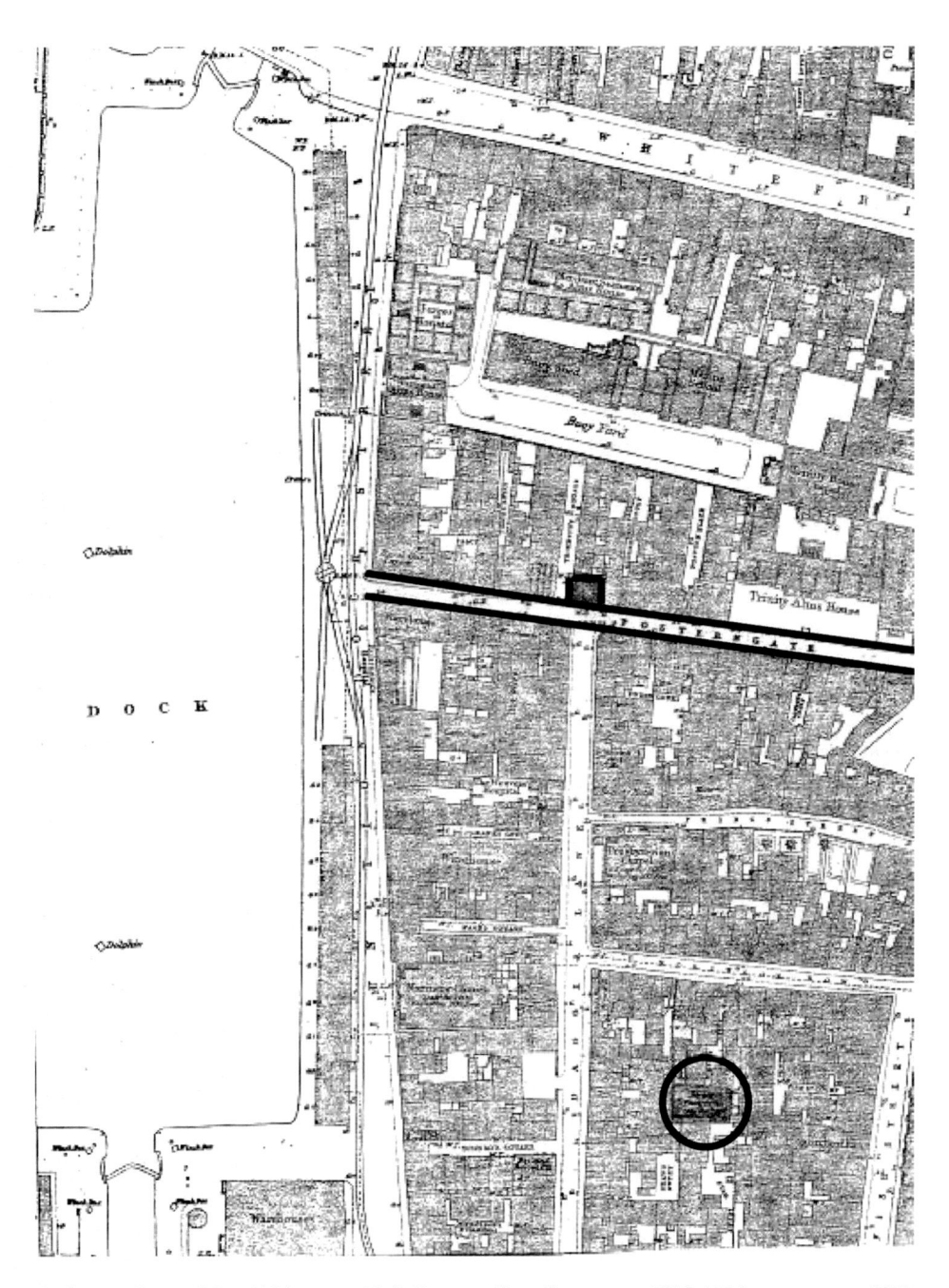

Ordnance Survey Map 1856 Hull: Postern Gate Synagogue 1780-1809 [27]
5 ft. to a mile Paradise Row Synagogue 1809-1826*
  Robinson Row Synagogue 1826-1902
  *now under docks

Ordnance Survey Map 1891 Hull: Villa Place Cemetery [73]
5 ft. to a mile (1750?) 1780-1812

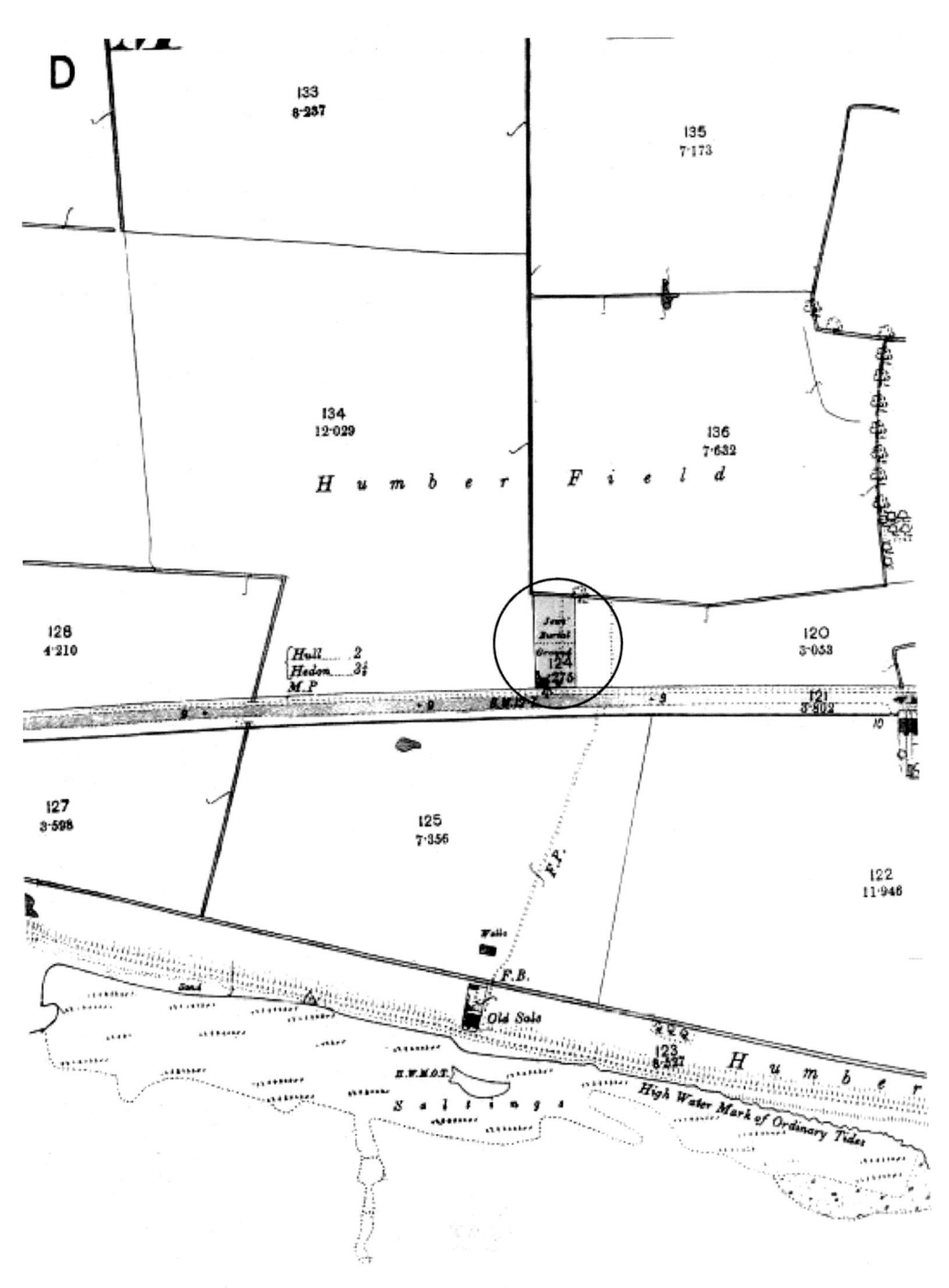

Ordnance Survey Map 1891
25 inches to a mile

Hull; Hessle Street Cemetery HU3
1812-1858

[73]

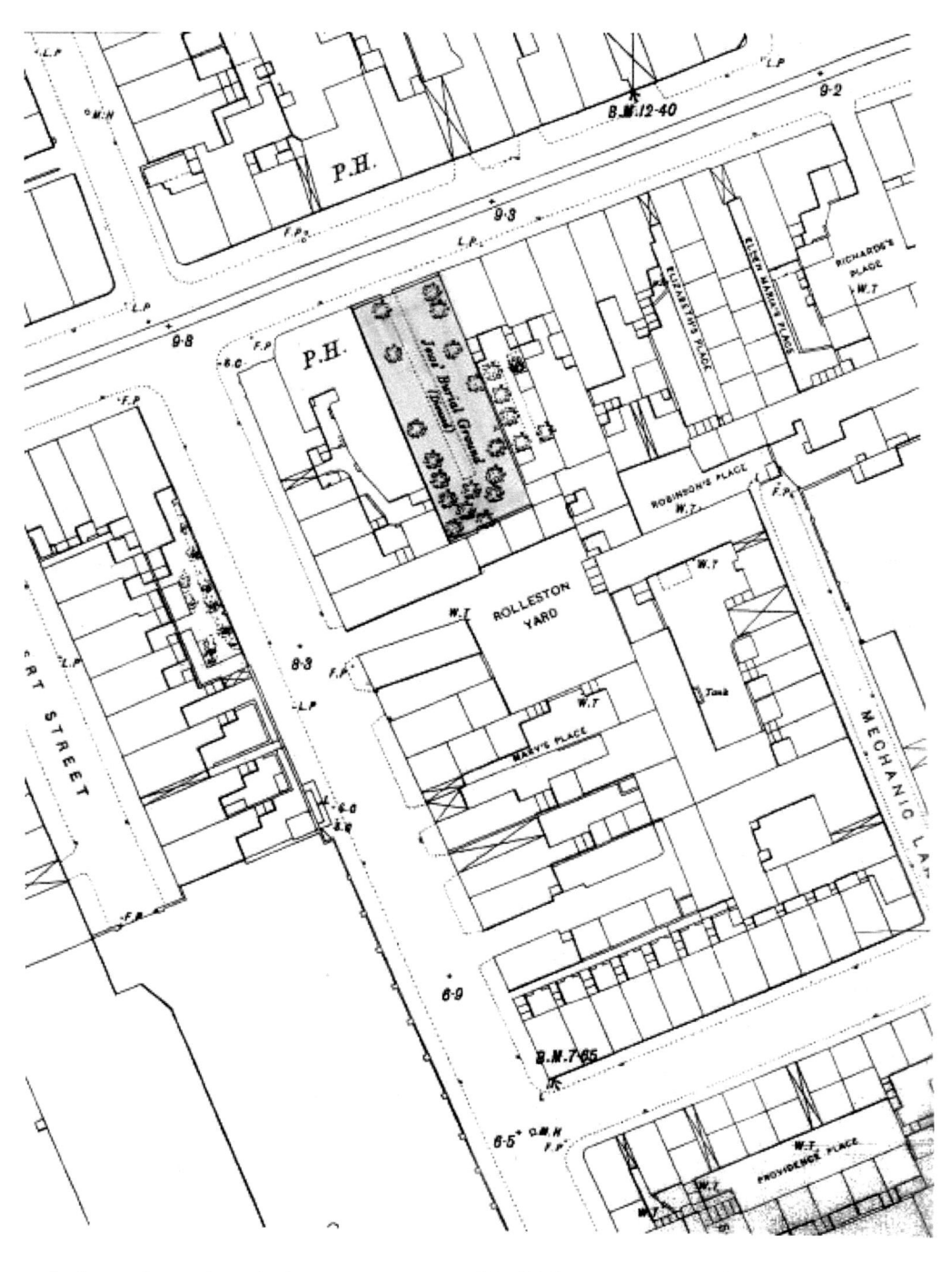

Ordnance Survey Map 1853
5ft. to a mile

Hull Delhi Street Cemetery HU9
1858-still in use

[73]

LOCATION	CHAPTER	SITE	DATE ESTABLISHED	IN USE TO	DATE OF VISIT	GAZETTEER NUMBER
IPSWICH					2010	
	4.2.16	SYNAGOGUE	1792	1877		[28]
	5.2.16	CEMETERY(S)	1796 1855	1854 1985		[74]

ADDITIONAL NOTES	
	1792 Traditional foundation of the community (Roth 1950) c.1750 First mention of Jews in Ipswich (Roth 1950) There is no longer a Jewish Community in Ipswich

SYNAGOGUE	1792-1877	Rope Lane Synagogue (demolished 1877)
FIGURE NUMBERS	4.81-4.82	

CEMETERIES	1796-1854	Salthouse Lane Jews' Burial Ground Star Lane IP4
	1855-1985	Old Cemetery, Jewish Section Cemetery Lane IP4 Last burial 1985-still in use
FIGURE NUMBERS	5.73- 5.76	

CONTACT INFORMATION	Elizabeth Sugarman: local historian
BIBLIOGRAPHY	Clark, *History of Ipswich* (unpublished) Gollancz, M. 1890/1895 *A Ramble in East Anglia* Kadish, S. 2006 *Jewish Heritage in England. An Architectural Guide* Lipman, V. 1954 *Social History of the Jews of England 1850 - 1950* Roth, C. 1950 *The Rise of Provincial Jewry*

OTHER SOURCES	Suffolk Records Office Ordnance Survey Map: 1902 Monson's Map of Ipswich: 1848 Statistical Account of the Congregations of the British Empire 1845 Ipswich Park & Gardens Register

PLACE NAMES WITH JEWISH CONNECTIONS	none

COMMUNITY SIZE	Date Community Size 1850 50 persons

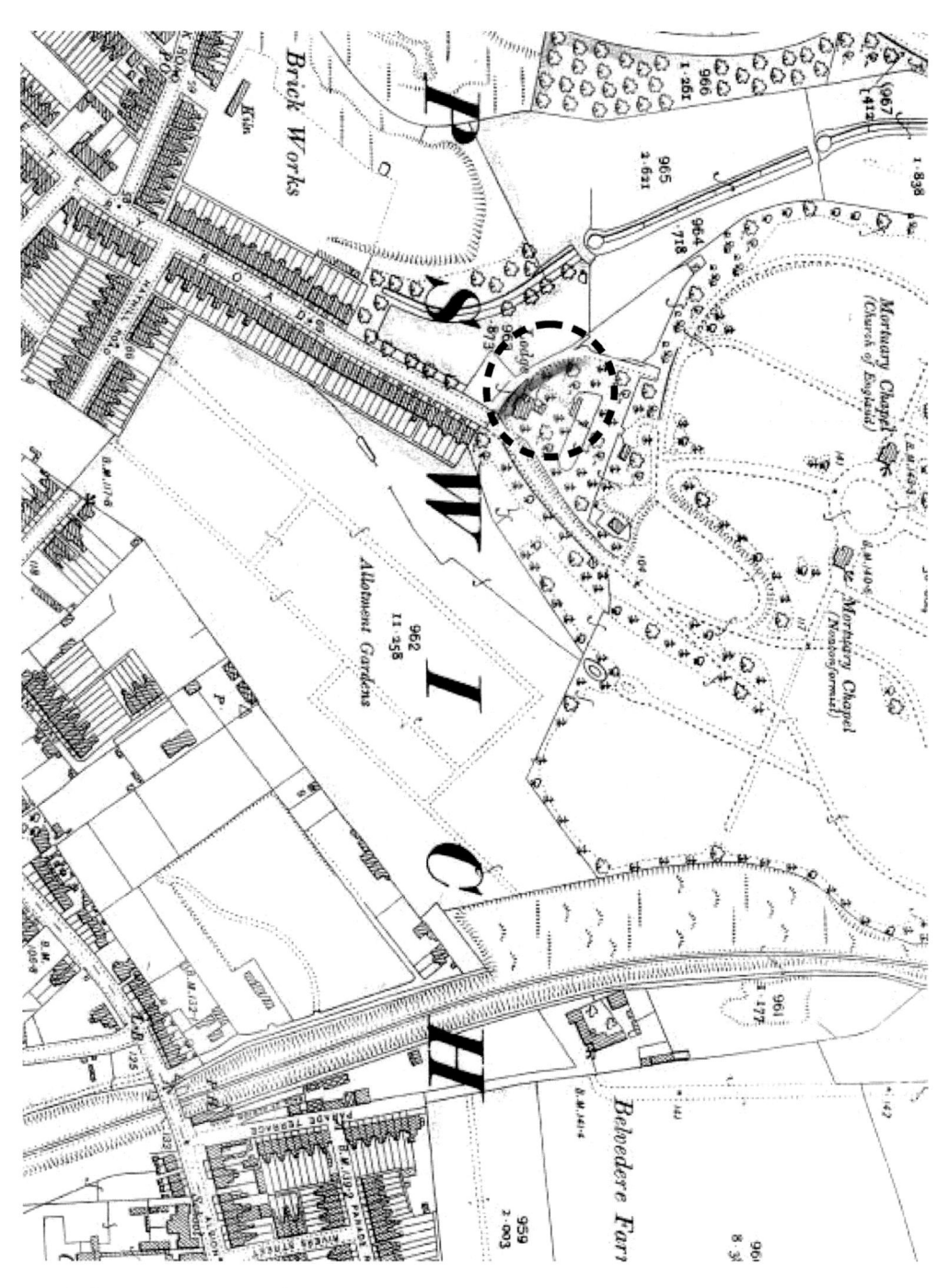

Ordnance Survey Map 1902 Ipswich: Cemetery Lane IP4 **[74]**
25 inches to a mile Jewish section 1855-1985-still in use

LOCATION	CHAPTER	SITE	DATE ESTABLISHED	IN USE TO	DATE OF VISIT	GAZETTEER NUMBER
KING'S LYNN	4.2.17	SYNAGOGUE	c.1747 1811 1826	1812 1826 1846	2010	[29]
	5.2.17	CEMETERY	1811	1846		[75]

ADDITIONAL NOTES

c.1747 — Traditional foundation of the Community (Roth 1950)
1747 — First mention of Jews in King's Lynn (Roth 1950)
There is no longer a Jewish community in King's Lynn

SYNAGOGUE(S)

c.1747-1812 Tower Street
1811-1826   Private Houses
1826-1846   9 High Street

FIGURE NUMBERS

CEMETERY(S)

1811   Millfleet Jew's Burial Ground
        Stonegate Street PE30

FIGURE NUMBERS 5.77-5.78

CONTACT INFORMATION

Dr. J. Clark: Local Historian

BIBLIOGRAPHY

Kadish, S. 2006 *Jewish Heritage in England. An Architectural Guide*
Lipman, V. 1954 *Social History of the Jews of England 1850 - 1950*
Roth, C.   1950 *The Rise of Provincial Jewry*
Tuck, W., 1987 *A Biography relating to the Jewish Sons of King's Lynn*

OTHER SOURCES

King's Lynn Records Library
Ordnance Survey Maps: 1886
Statistical Account of the Congregations of the British Empire 1845

PLACE NAMES WITH JEWISH CONNECTIONS

none

COMMUNITY SIZE

Date   Community Size
1850   25-50 persons

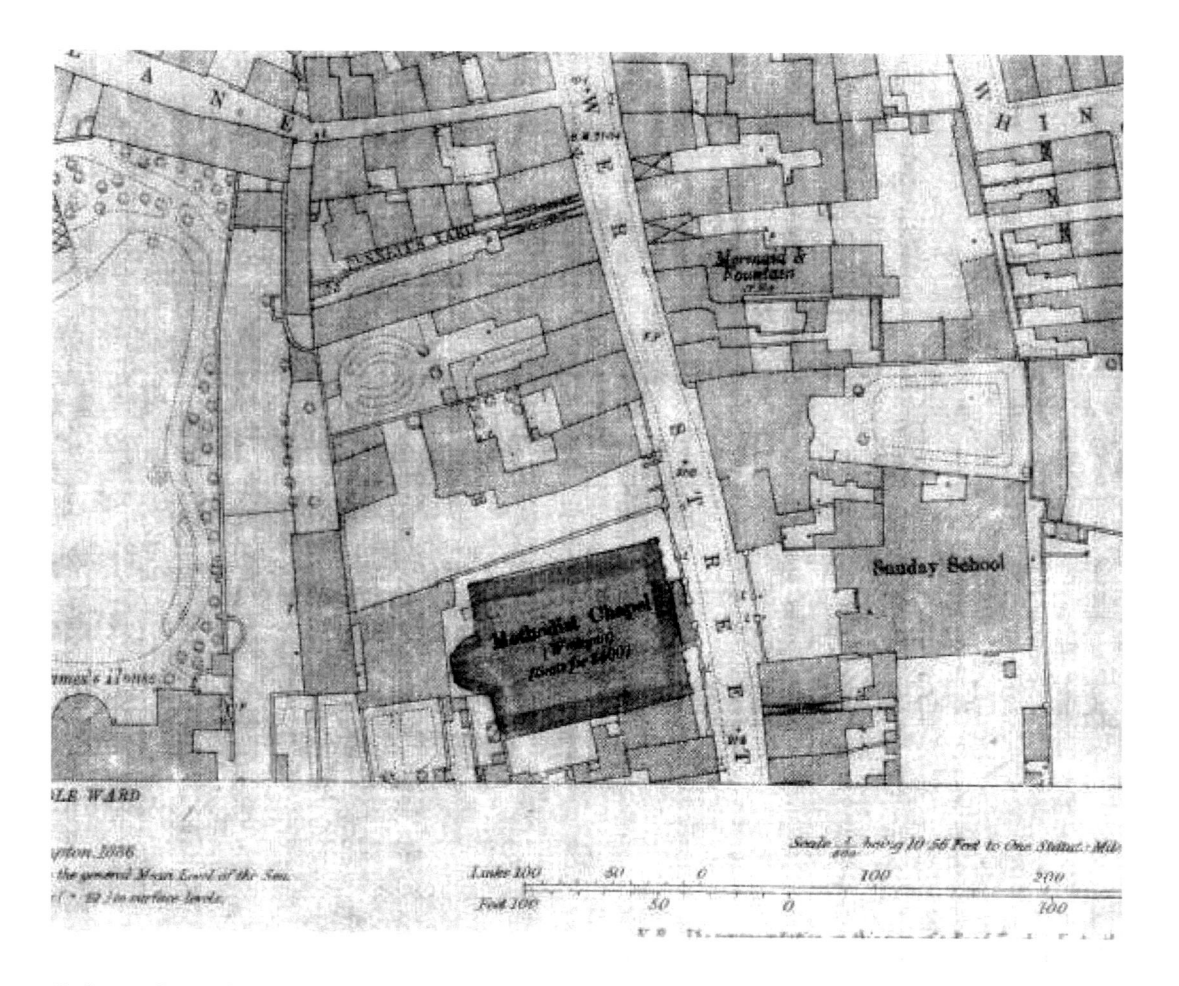

Ordnance Survey Map 1886　　King's Lynn: Tower Street (site of synagogue)　　　　　　[29]
25 inches to a mile　　　　　　　　　　1747-1812

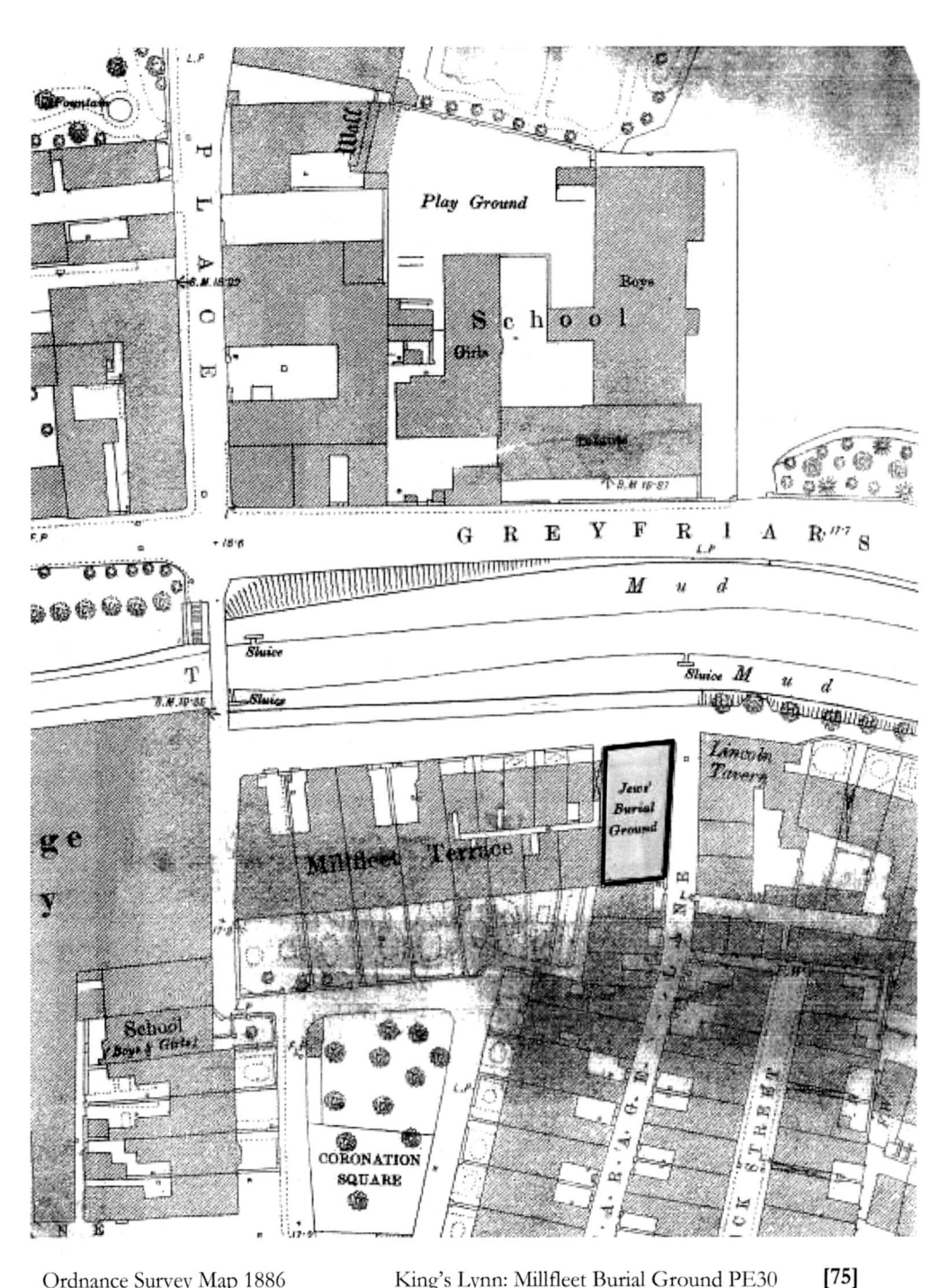

Ordnance Survey Map 1886
5ft. to a mile

King's Lynn: Millfleet Burial Ground PE30
c.1811-1846

[75]

GAZETTEER 371

LOCATION	CHAPTER	SITE	DATE ESTABLISHED	IN USE TO	DATE OF VISIT	GAZETTEER NUMBER
LEEDS	4.2.18	SYNAGOGUE	1850 1860 1869	1860 1930 1930	2010	[30]
	5.2.18	CEMETERY	1873 c.1850	1990 still in use		[76]

ADDITIONAL NOTES	
	1820 Traditional foundation of community (Roth 1950)
	c.1750 First mention of Jews in Leeds (Roth 1950)
	No evidence remaining of the synagogues from the period of discussion

SYNAGOGUES		
	1850-1860	Back Rockingham Street Synagogue
	1860-1930	Great Synagogue, Belgrade Street
	1869-1930	New Briggate's Synagogue
FIGURE NUMBERS	4.83	

CEMETERIES		
	1873-1990	Hill Top Cemetery
		Gelderd Road, LS12
	1850	Glidersome Jewish Cemetery
		Gelderd Road, LS12
		(still in use)
FIGURE NUMBERS	5.7-5.80	

CONTACT	
	Malcolm Sender: Community Archivist
	Bobby Caplin, OBE: Community Elder

BIBLIOGRAPHY	
	Freedman, M. 1995 *Leeds Jewry - A History of its Synagogues*
	Kadish, S. 2006 *Jewish Heritage in England. An Architectural Guide*
	Krausz, E. 1964 *Leeds Jewry - Its History and Social Structure*
	Roth, C. 1950 *The Rise of Provincial Jewry*
	Vaughan, L. 2003 *The Jewish Ghetto - Formation and spatial structure*

OTHER SOURCES	
	Leeds Records Library
	Ordnance Survey Maps: 1896, 1897, 1906, 1908,
	Statistical Account of the Congregations of the British Empire 1845

PLACE NAMES WITH JEWISH CONNECTIONS	none

COMMUNITY SIZE			
	Date	Community Size	
	1841	60* persons	Freedman, M.
			*(9 families & 28 male lodgers)
	1850	c.100	Freedman, M.
	1861	c.100	
	1871	c.500 / 600	The Jewish Chronicle
	1881	c.2500	
	1891	c.6000	
	1895	10,000	The Jewish Year Book 1896
	1930	15,000	The Jewish Year Book 1936
	1935	c.20,000	
	2011	7,000	

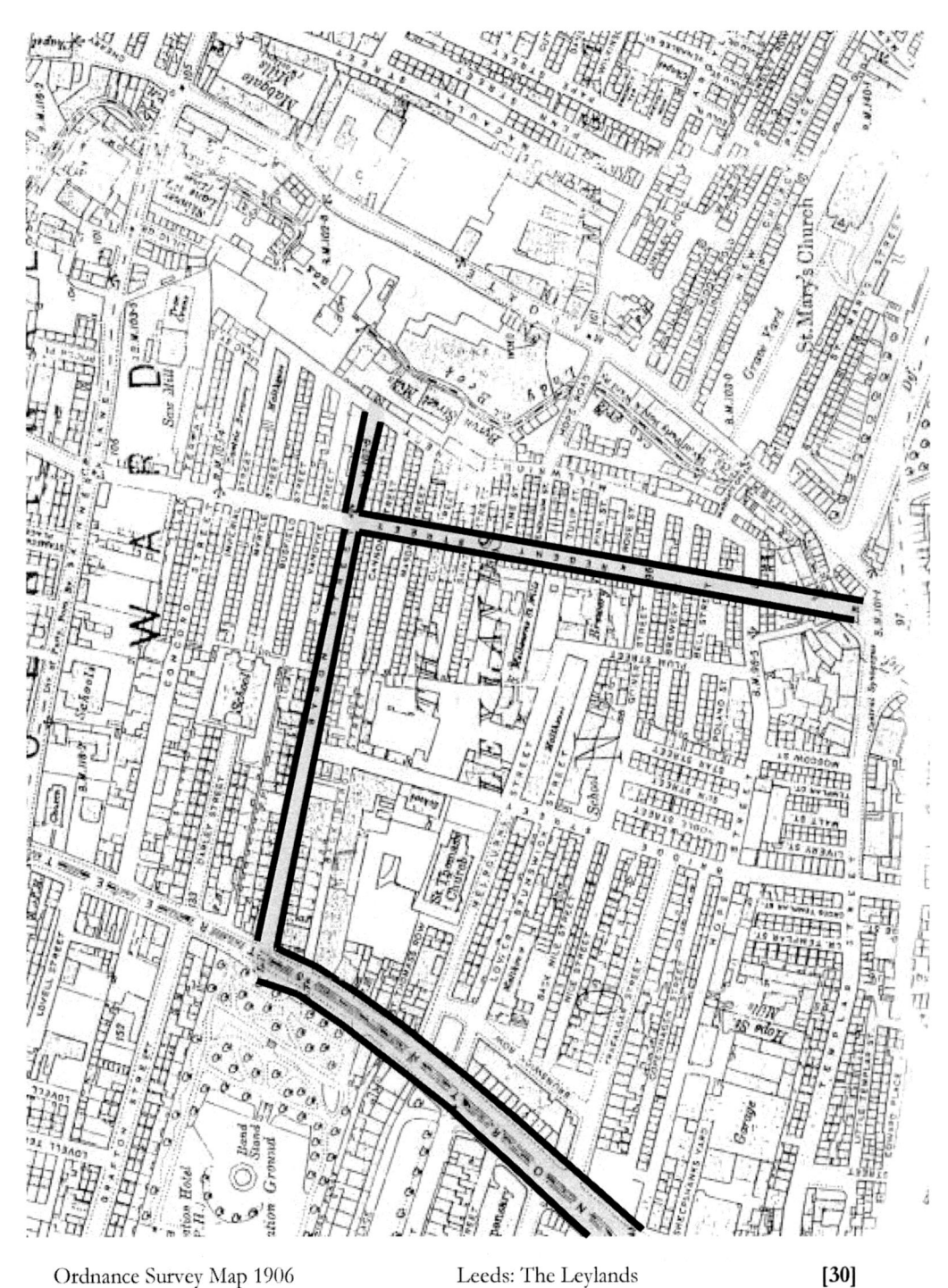

Ordnance Survey Map 1906　　　　　　Leeds: The Leylands　　　　　　[30]
25 inches to a mile　　　　mid 19th century area of Jewish settlement

Ordnance Survey Map 1896 Leeds: Back Rockingham Street Synagogue [30]
5ft. to a mile 1850-1860

374   The Archaeology of Anglo-Jewry in England and Wales 1656–c.1880

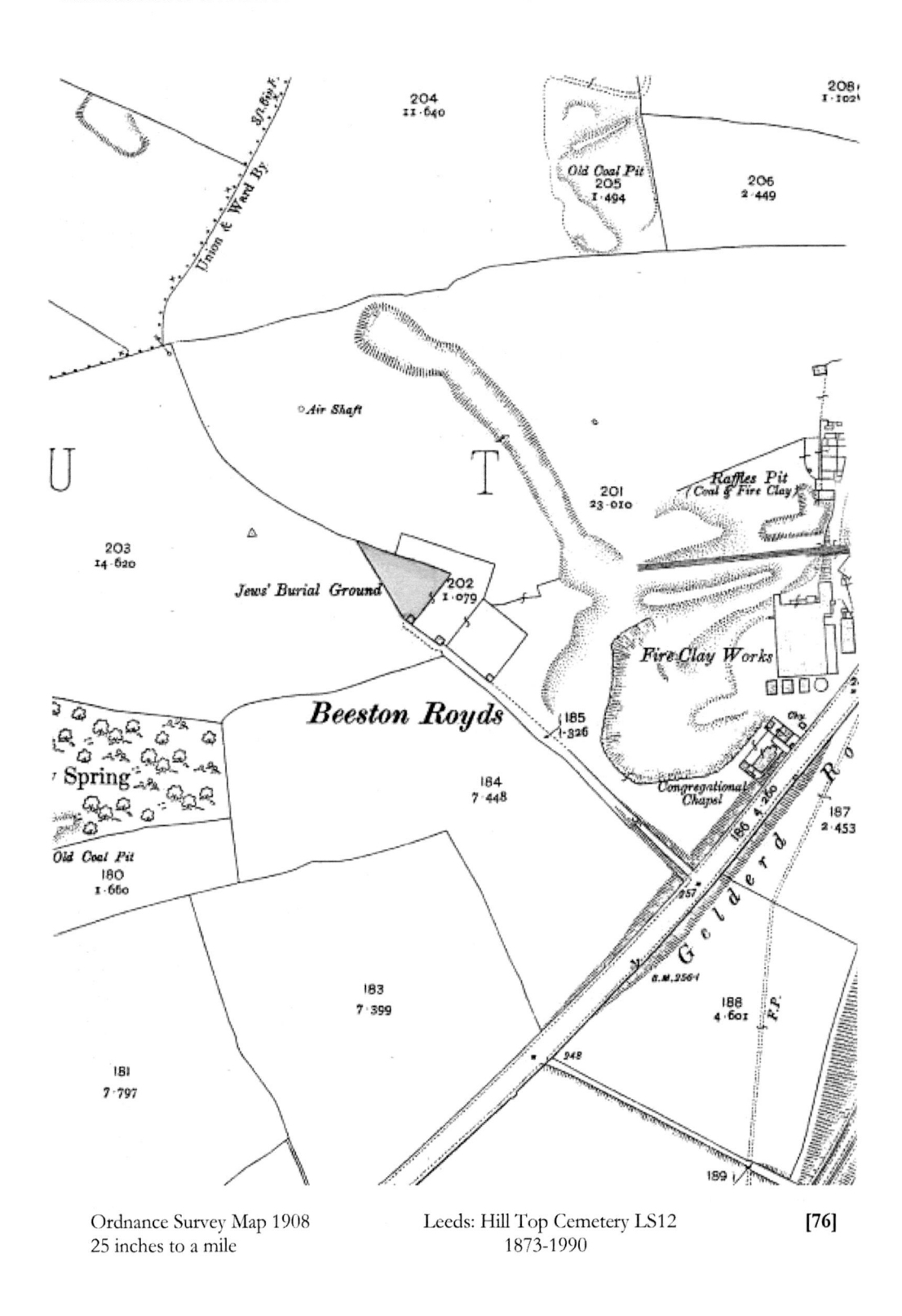

Ordnance Survey Map 1908 Leeds: Hill Top Cemetery LS12   [76]
25 inches to a mile 1873-1990

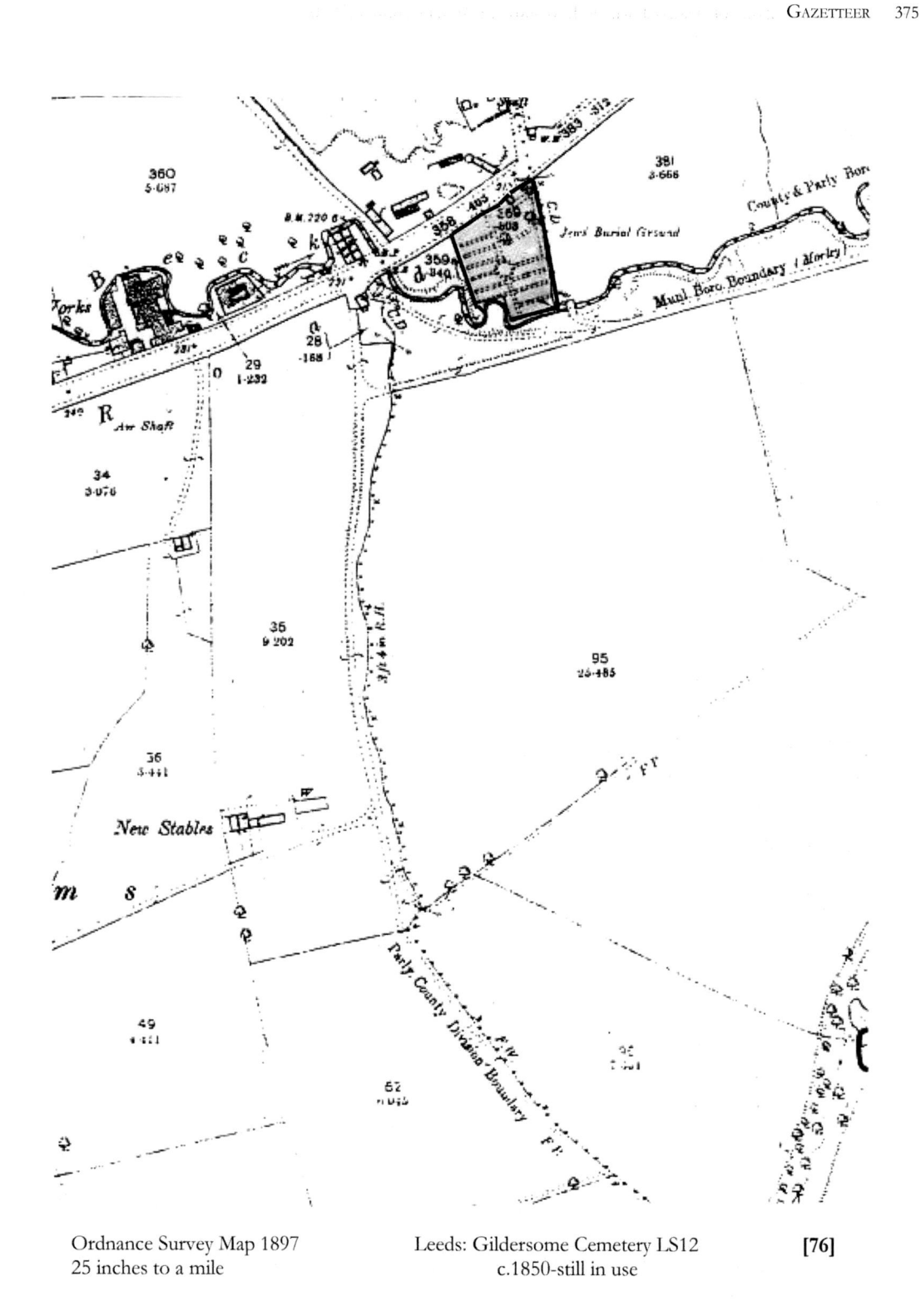

Ordnance Survey Map 1897
25 inches to a mile

Leeds: Gildersome Cemetery LS12
c.1850-still in use

[76]

LOCATION	CHAPTER	SITE	DATE ESTABLISHED	IN USE TO	DATE OF VISIT	GAZETTEER NUMBER
LIVERPOOL	4.2.19 5.2.19	SYNAGOGUES CEMETERY	1753-1874 1837	still in use 1904	2009	[31] [77]

ADDITIONAL NOTES		
	c.1750	Traditional date of foundation of the community (Roth 1950)
	c.1750	First mention of Jews in Liverpool (Roth 1950)

SYNAGOGUE(S)		
	1753-1775	Cumberland Street Synagogue (converted house)
	1775-1789	Canning Place Synagogue (converted house)
	1789-1807	Frederick Street Synagogue (converted house)
	1807-1870	Seel Street Synagogue
	1857-1874	Hope Place Synagogue
	1874	Princes Road Liverpool Old Hebrew Congregation Toxteth L8. (Grade I) updated from Grade II in 2009
		(still in use)
FIGURE NUMBERS	4.83-4.93	

CEMETERY(S)		
	1837-1904	Deane Road, Fairfield L7
	1839-1921	Green Lane, Tue Brook L13.
	1904 -	Broad Green, Thomas Drive L14
		(still in use)
FIGURE NUMBERS	5.81-5.88	

CONTACT INFORMATION	
	Arnold Lewis: Community Archivist
	Saul Marks: Deane Road Cemetery
	Liverpool Records Office
BIBLIOGRAPHY	Ainsworth, R. 2009/10 *A Century of Wurst-The Origins of Liverpool's Jewish Heritage*
	Benas, B.L. 1899 *Records of The Jews in Liverpool*
	Endelman, T. 2002 *The Jews of Britain 1656 – 2000*
	Ettinger, P. 1930 *Hope Place in Liverpool Jewry*
	Kadish, S. 2006 *Jewish Heritage in England. An Architectural Guide*
	Marks, S. 2007 *Deane Road Cemetery*
	Picton, J. 1873 *Memorials of Liverpool*
	Roth, C. 1950 *The Rise of Provincial Jewry*
	Williams, B. 1987 *Liverpool Jewry - A Pictorial History*
	Woolfman, J. 1989 *Liverpool Jewry in The Eighteenth Century*

OTHER SOURCES	
	Liverpool Records Office
	Ordnance Survey Maps: 1893
	Statistical Account of the Congregations in the British Empire 1885
	London Metropolitan Archives ACC / 2805 / 1 / 1 / 107

PLACE NAMES WITH JEWISH CONNECTIONS	
	Balm Street: named after "The Balm" created by Dr. S. Solon
	Shalom Court: street leading to Greenback Synagogue
	Solomon Street: named after Dr. S. Solomon d. c.1819
	Synagogue Court: location of first synagogue
	later known as Cumberland Street *(no longer exists)*

COMMUNITY SIZE		
	Date	Community Size
	1750	c.50 persons
	1789	100
	1810	400
	1825	1000
	1850	2,500
	1895	5,000
	1965	7,500
	2004	2,500

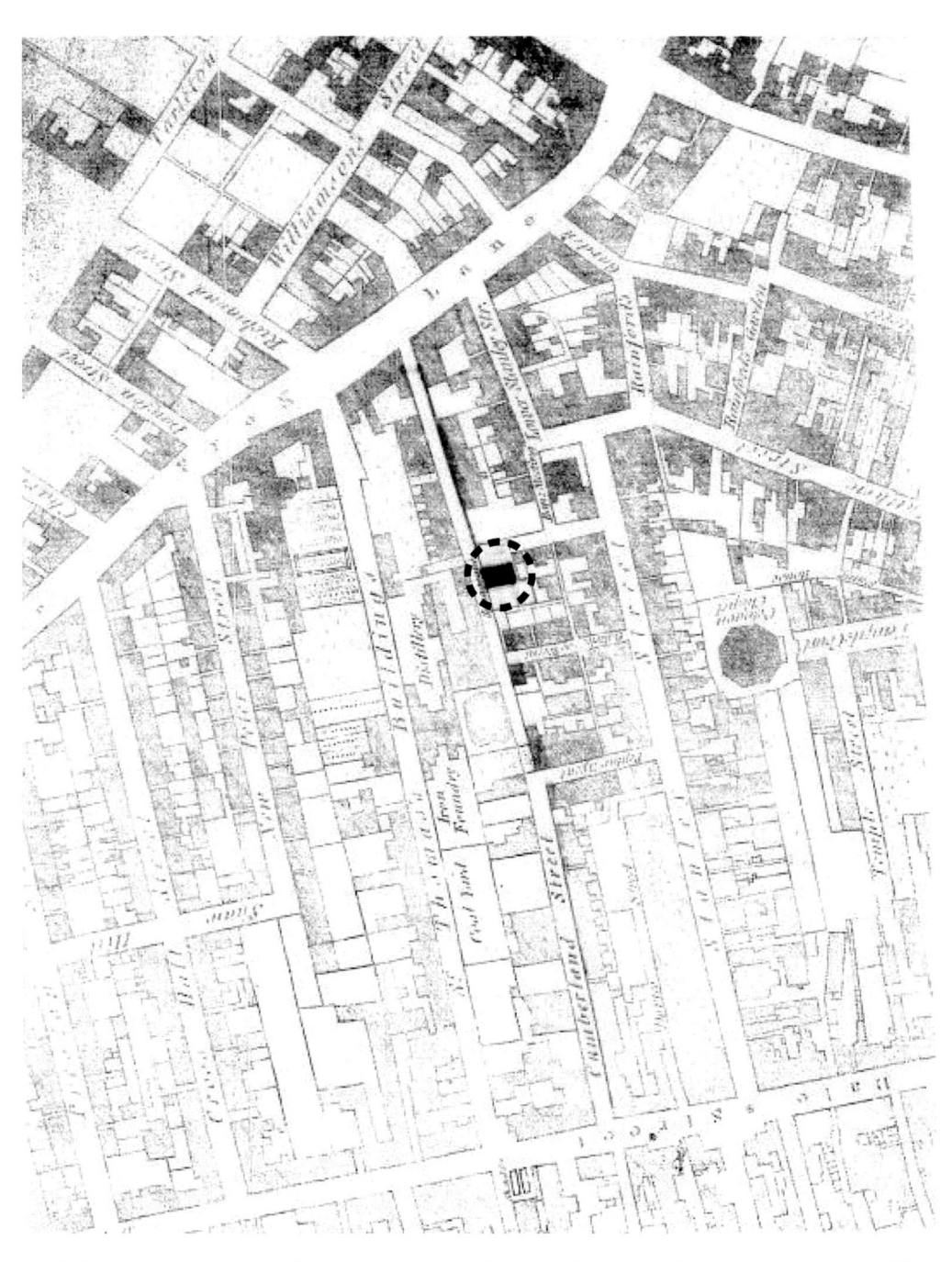

Ordnance Survey Map 1893 Liverpool: Cumberland Street Synagogue [31]
25 inches to a mile 1753-1775

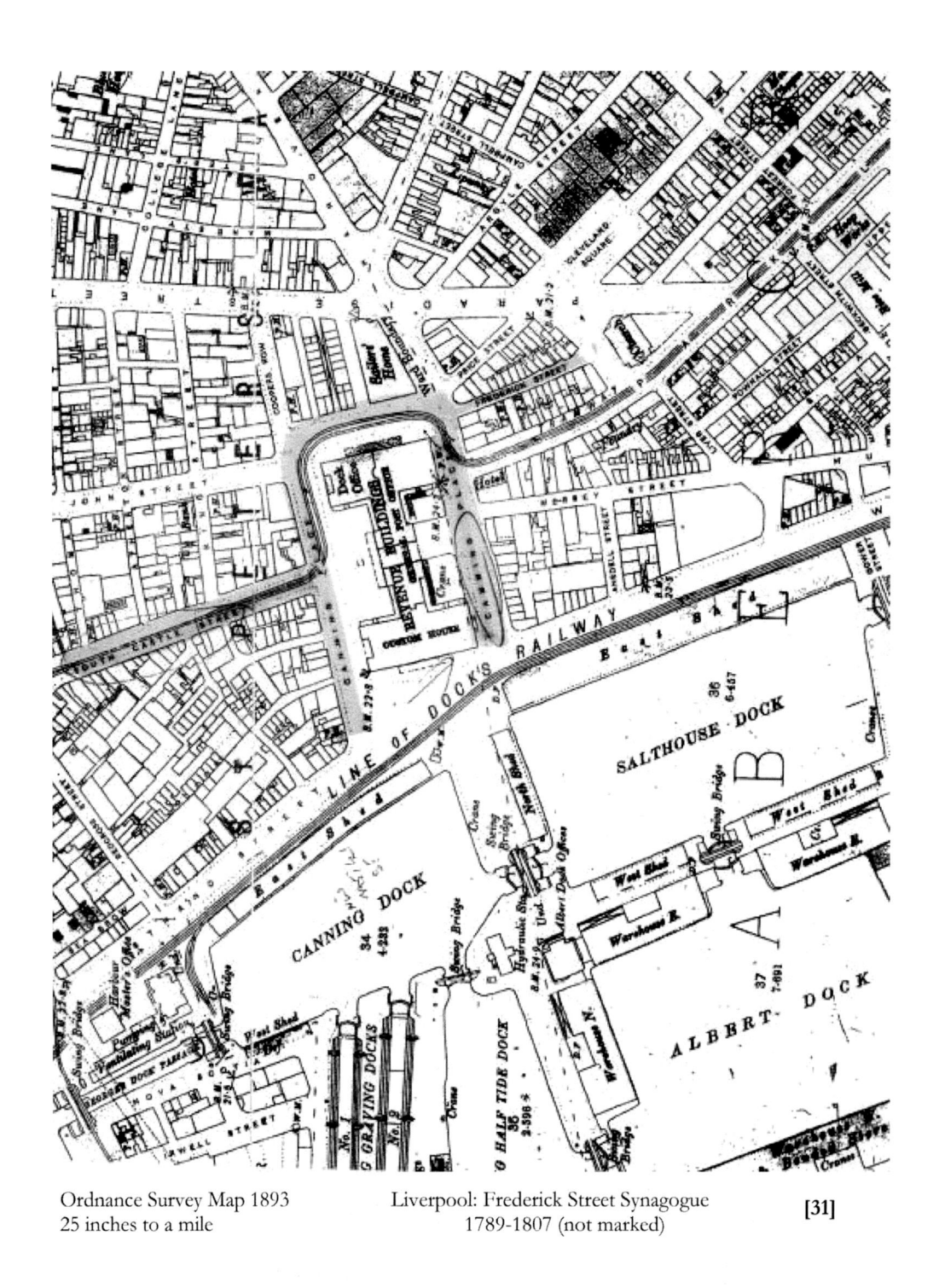

Ordnance Survey Map 1893
25 inches to a mile

Liverpool: Frederick Street Synagogue
1789-1807 (not marked)

[31]

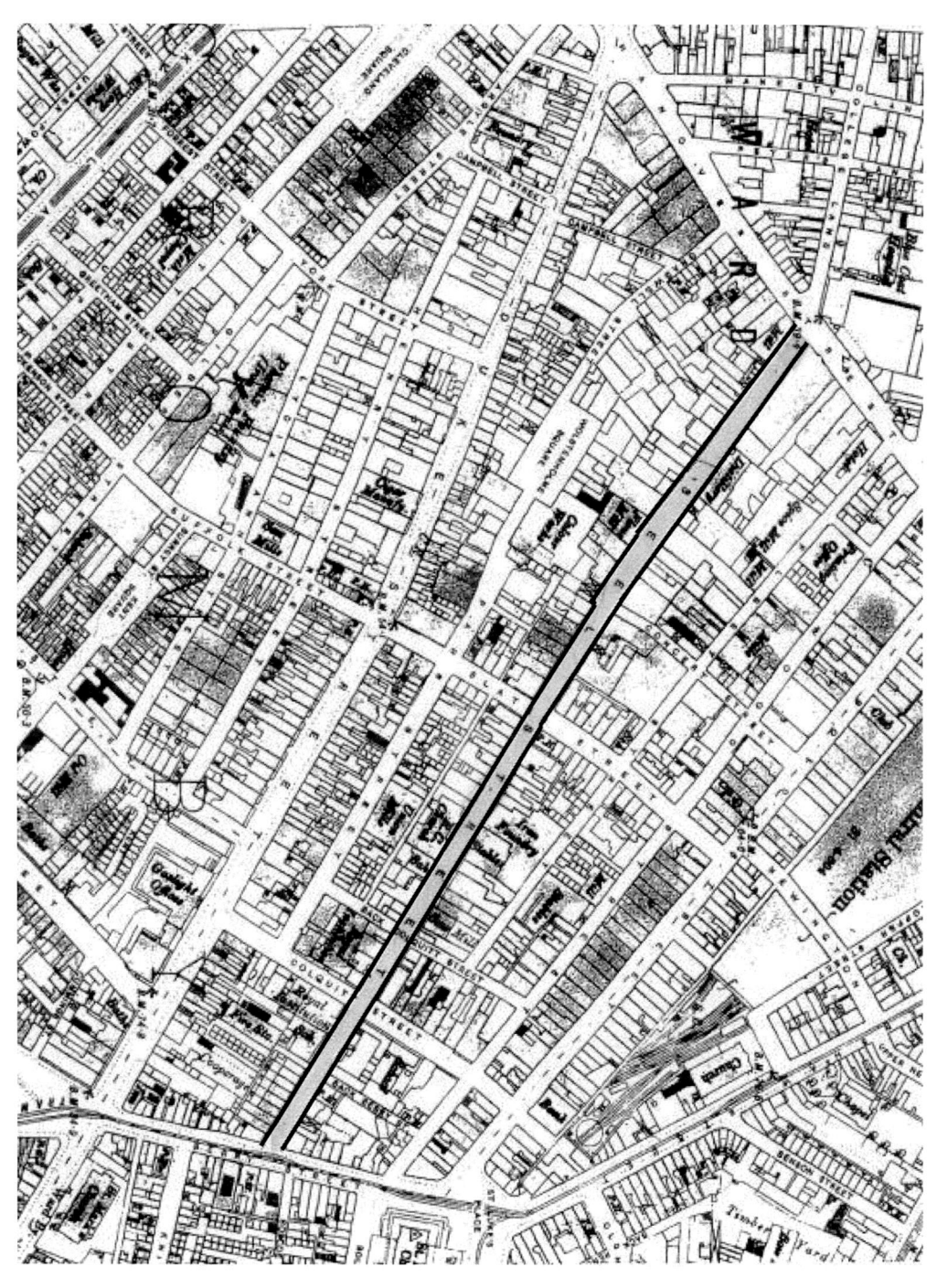

Ordnance Survey Map 1893 Liverpool: Seel Street Synagogue
25 inches to a mile 1807-1870 (not marked)

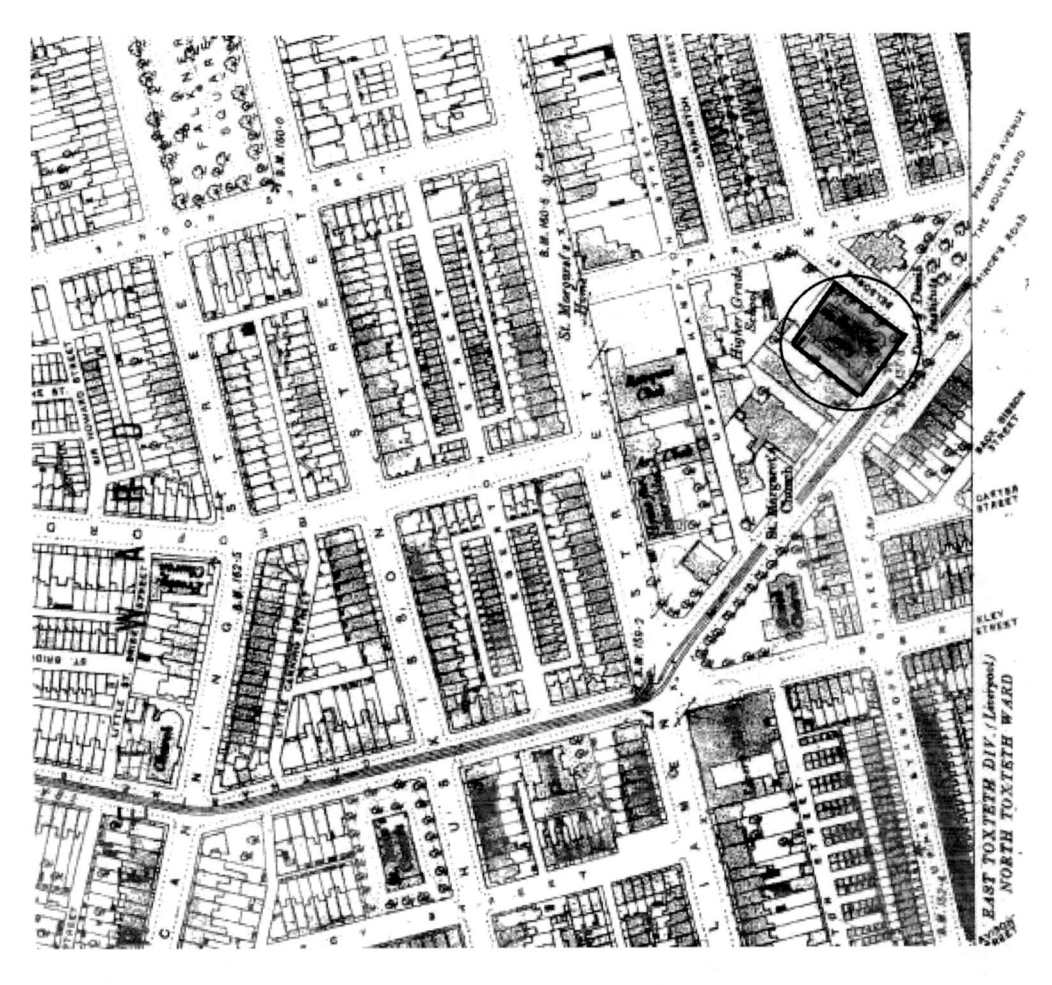

Ordnance Survey Map 1893 Liverpool: Princes Road Synagogue L8 [31]
25 inches to a mile 1874-still in use

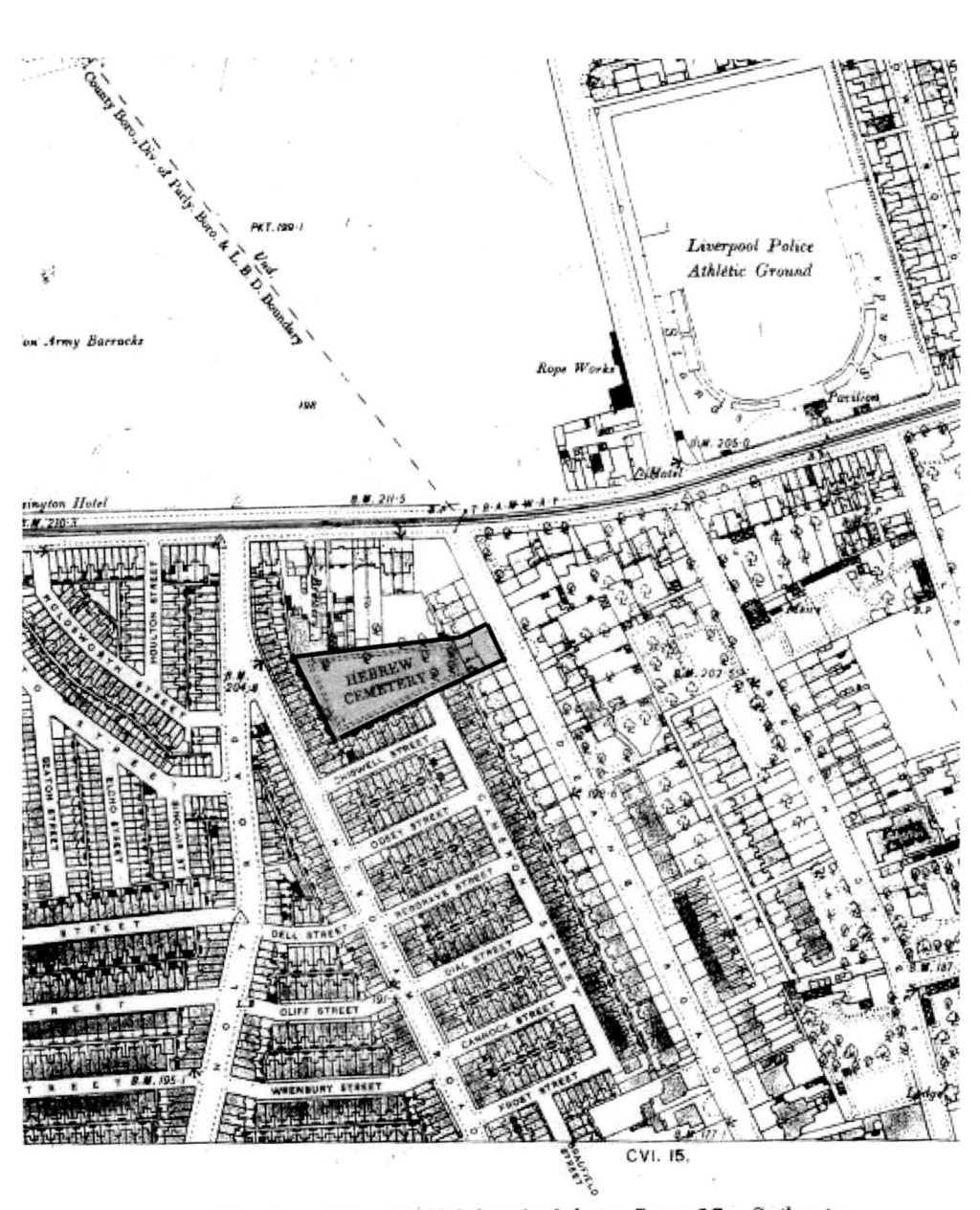

Ordnance Survey Map 1893 Liverpool: Dean Road Cemetery L7
25 inches to a mile 1837-1904 [77]

LOCATION	CHAPTER	SITE	DATE ESTABLISHED	IN USE TO	DATE OF VISIT	GAZETTEER NUMBER
MANCHESTER	4.2.20	SYNAGOGUES	1780	1984	2009	[32]
	5.2.20	CEMETERIES	1794	1953		[78]

ADDITIONAL NOTES	c.1780 Traditional foundation of the Community (Roth 1950, 111)

SYNAGOGUES	1780-c.1794	Long Millgate
	c.1800-1848	Halliwell Street
	1858-1974	Great Synagogue, Cheetham Hill Road. 1986 demolished
	1858-1941**	The Reform Synagogue, Cheetham Hill Road
	1941	** destroyed by bombing
	1874-1984*	The Spanish & Portuguese Synagogue, Cheetham Hill Road
		*now The Jewish Museum
FIGURE NUMBERS	4.94 -4.101	

CEMETERIES	1794-1840	Brindle Heath, Pendleton
	1841-1914	Prestwich Village
	1858-1905	Whitefield Old Reform Cemetery (still in use)
	1865-1953	Phillips Park, Miles Platting
FIGURE NUMBERS	5.89- 5.97	

CONTACT INFORMATION	Manchester Jewish Museum Bill Williams: Life President of The Jewish Museum and Manchester Historian Dr. Sharman Kadish: Jewish Heritage UK

BIBLIOGRAPHY	Kadish, S. 2006 *Jewish Heritage in England. An Architectural Guide* Roth, C. 1950 *The Rise of Provincial Jewry* Williams, B. 1976 *The Making of Manchester Jewry* Williams, B. 2008 *Jewish Manchester, An Illustrated History*

OTHER SOURCES	Jewish Heritage UK Ordnance Survey Maps: 1849, 1888,1892, 1893 Statistical Account of the Congregations in the British Empire 1845

PLACE NAMES WITH JEWISH CONNECTIONS	Torah Street: adjacent to Manchester Talmud Torah School 1894

COMMUNITY SIZE	Date	Community Size
	1794	c.60 persons
	1796	250 - 300
	1841	c.600
	1851	c.1,000
	1858	c.2,000
	1871	3,400
	1881	*7,000*
	2010	*c.35,000*

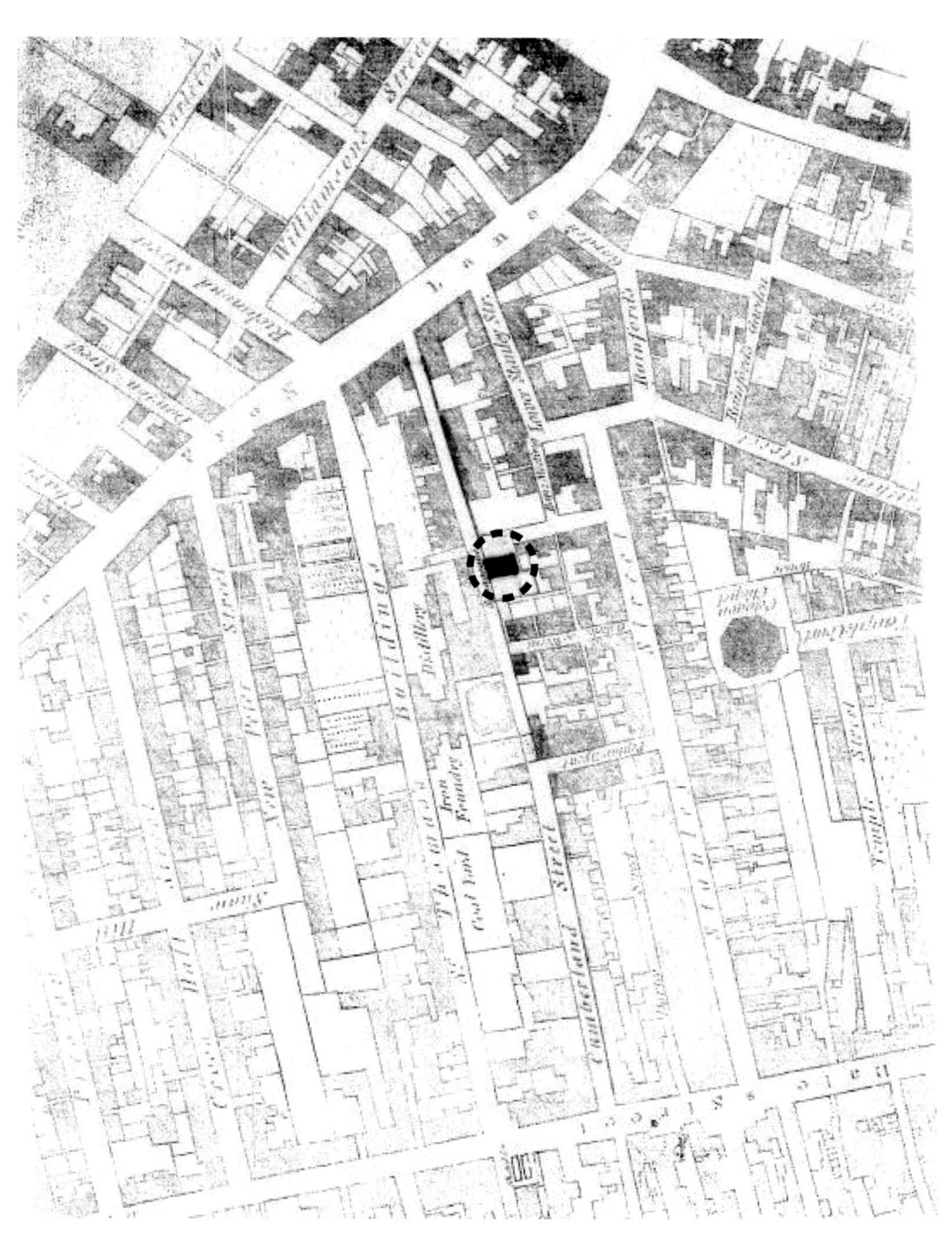

Ordnance Survey Map 1893 Liverpool: Cumberland Street Synagogue [31]
25 inches to a mile 1753-1775

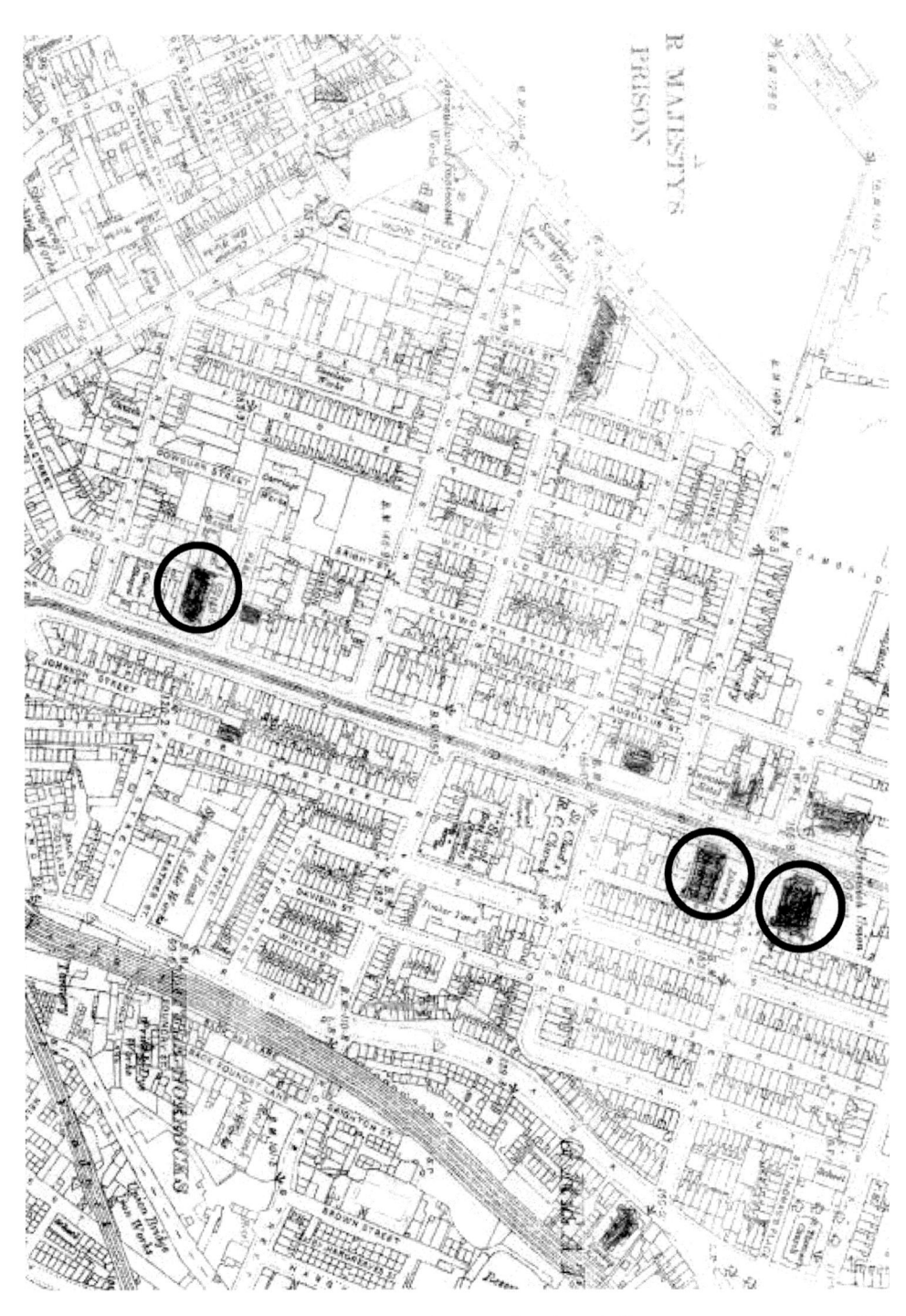

Ordnance Survey Map 1888 Manchester: Cheetham Hill Synagogues
25 inches to a mile from 1858

GAZETTEER 385

Ordnance Survey Map 1849　　Manchester: Brindle Heath Cemetery　　[78]
25 inches to a mile　　　　　　　　　　1794-1840

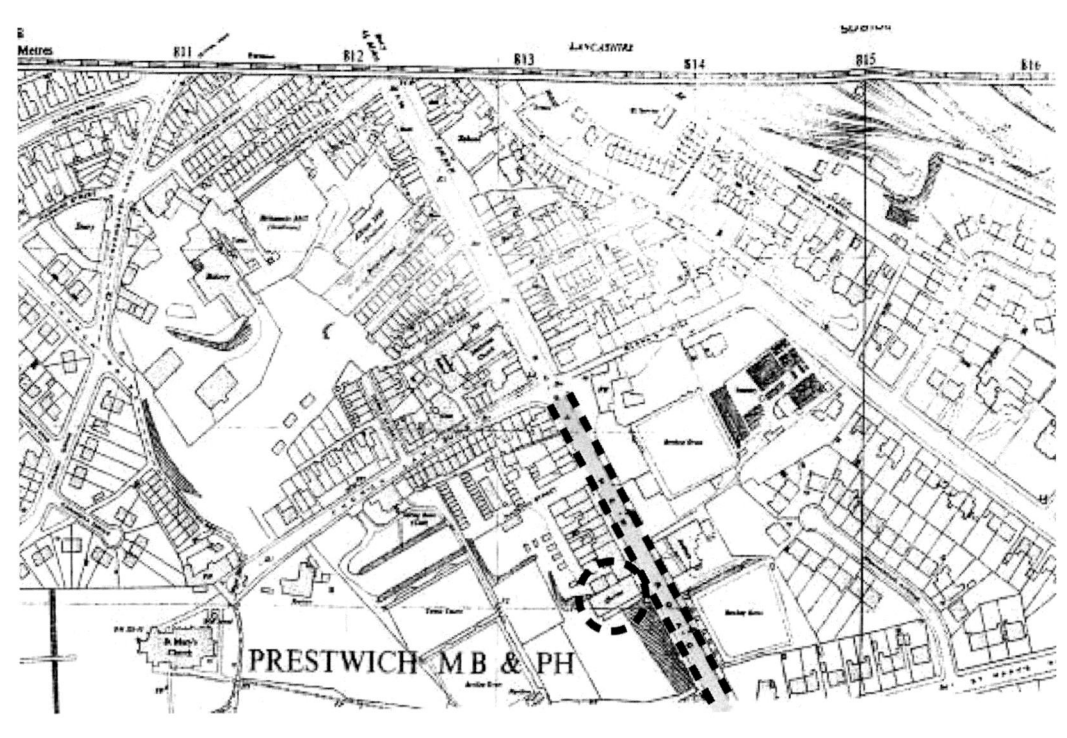

Ordnance Survey Map 1893 Manchester: Prestwich Village Cemetery [78]
25 inches to a mile 1840-1914

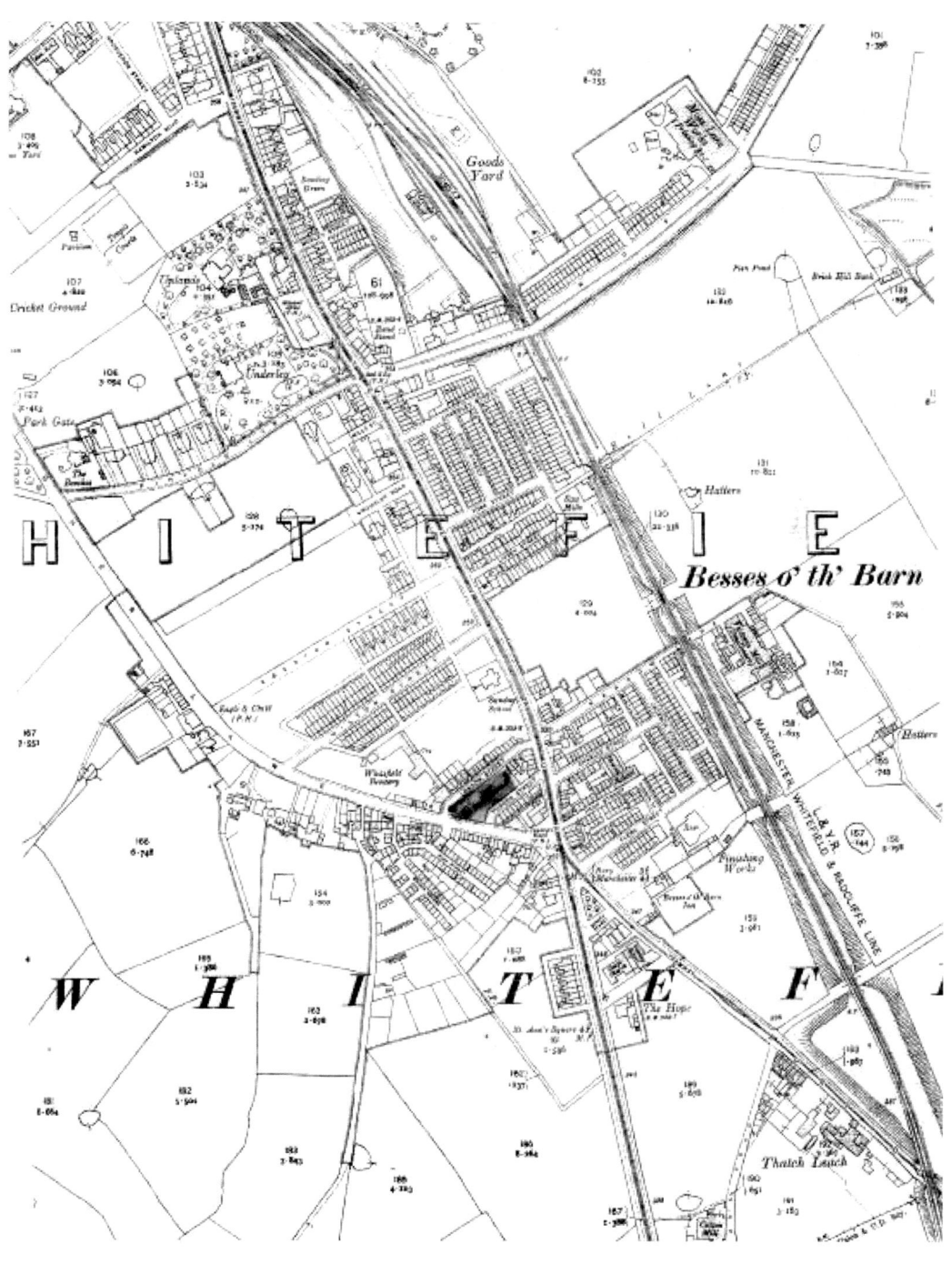

Ordnance Survey Map 1893 Manchester: Whitefield (Reform) Cemetery [78]
25 inches to a mile 1858-2005 (still occasionally used)

LOCATION	CHAPTER	SITE	DATE ESTABLISHED	IN USE TO	DATE OF VISIT	GAZETTEER NUMBER
METHYR TYDFIL	4.2.21 5.2.21	SYNAGOGUE CEMETERY	1852 1865	1980's 1999*	2010	[33] [79]

ADDITIONAL NOTES	
	1848 First mention of Jews in Merthyr Tidfil (Henriques 1993) * Burial of last Jewish Resident George Black There is no longer a Jewish Community in Merthyr Tydfil

SYNAGOGUES	1842	First Synagogue in a private house
	c.1852	Second Synagogue, John Street *demolished in the 1990s*
	1872-1983	Bryntirion Road, Thomas Town CF47 (Grade II)
FIGURE NUMBERS	4.102-4.104	

CEMETERY(S)	1865-1999	Jew's Burial Ground, Brecon Road, Cefn Cowed CF48
FIGURE NUMBERS	5.98- 5.100	

CONTACT INFORMATION	David Jacobs: Director of Reform Synagogues Partnership
BIBLIOGRAPHY	Alderman, G. 1974/78 *The Jew as Scapegoat? The Settlement and reception of Jews in South Wales before 1941* Endelman, T. 2002 *The Jews of Britain 1656-2000* Henriques, U. ed. 1993 *The Jews of South Wales, Historical Studies* Kadish, S. 2006 *Jewish Heritage in England. An Architectural Guide* Lipman, V. 1954 *Social History of the Jews of England 1850-1950* Roth, C. 1950 *The Rise of Provincial Jewry*

OTHER SOURCES	West Glamorgan Archives and Welsh Public Health Map 1852 Ordnance Survey Maps: 1898

PLACE NAMES WITH JEWISH CONNECTIONS	none

COMMUNITY SIZE	Date	Community Size
	1850	c.100 persons
	1934	400
	1946	175
	1999	nil

GAZETTEER 389

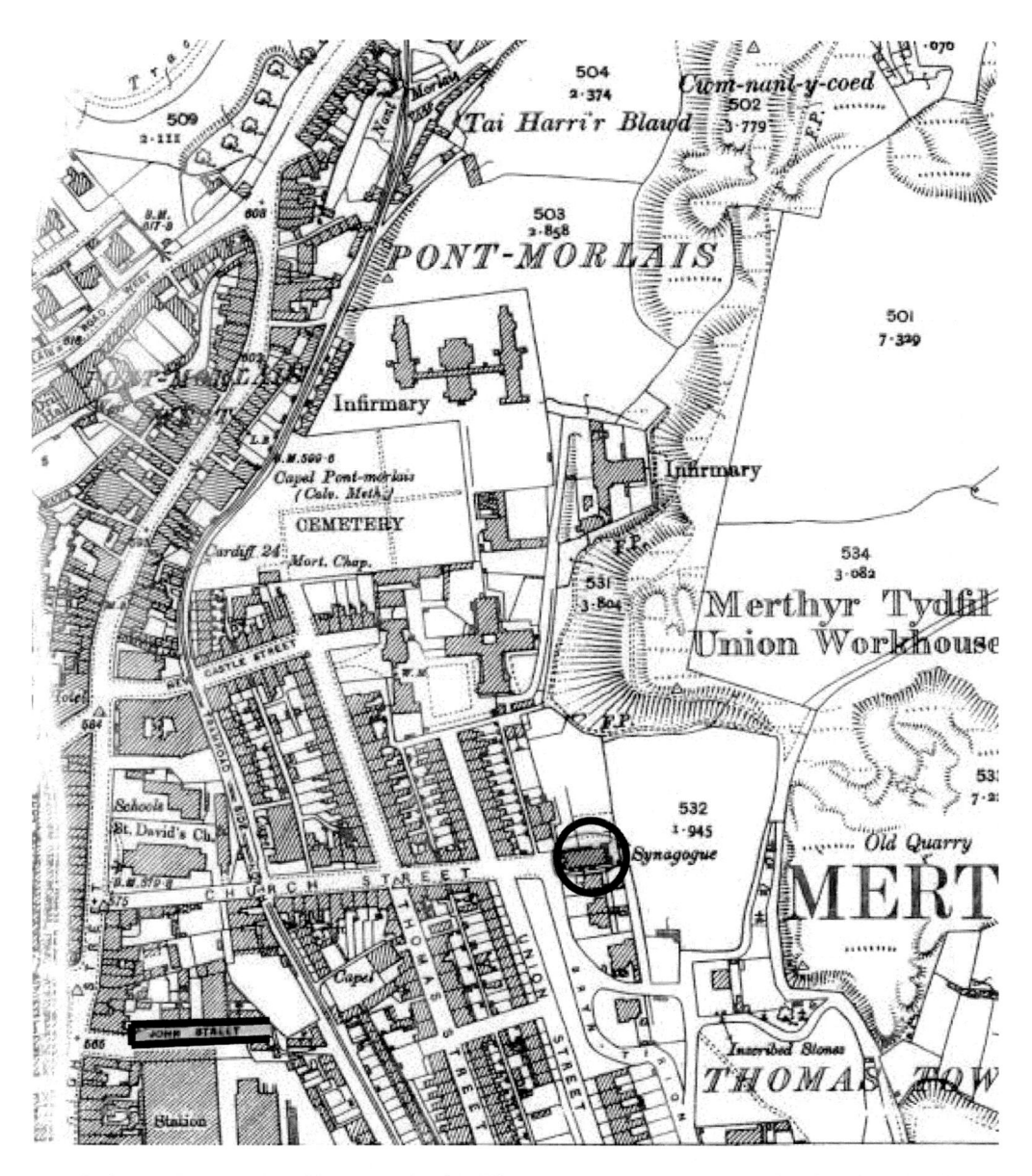

Ordnance Survey Map 1898   Merthyr Tydfil: John Street Synagogue c.1852 (demolished)   **[33]**
25 inches to a mile   Bryntiron Road Synagogue CF47 1872-1983

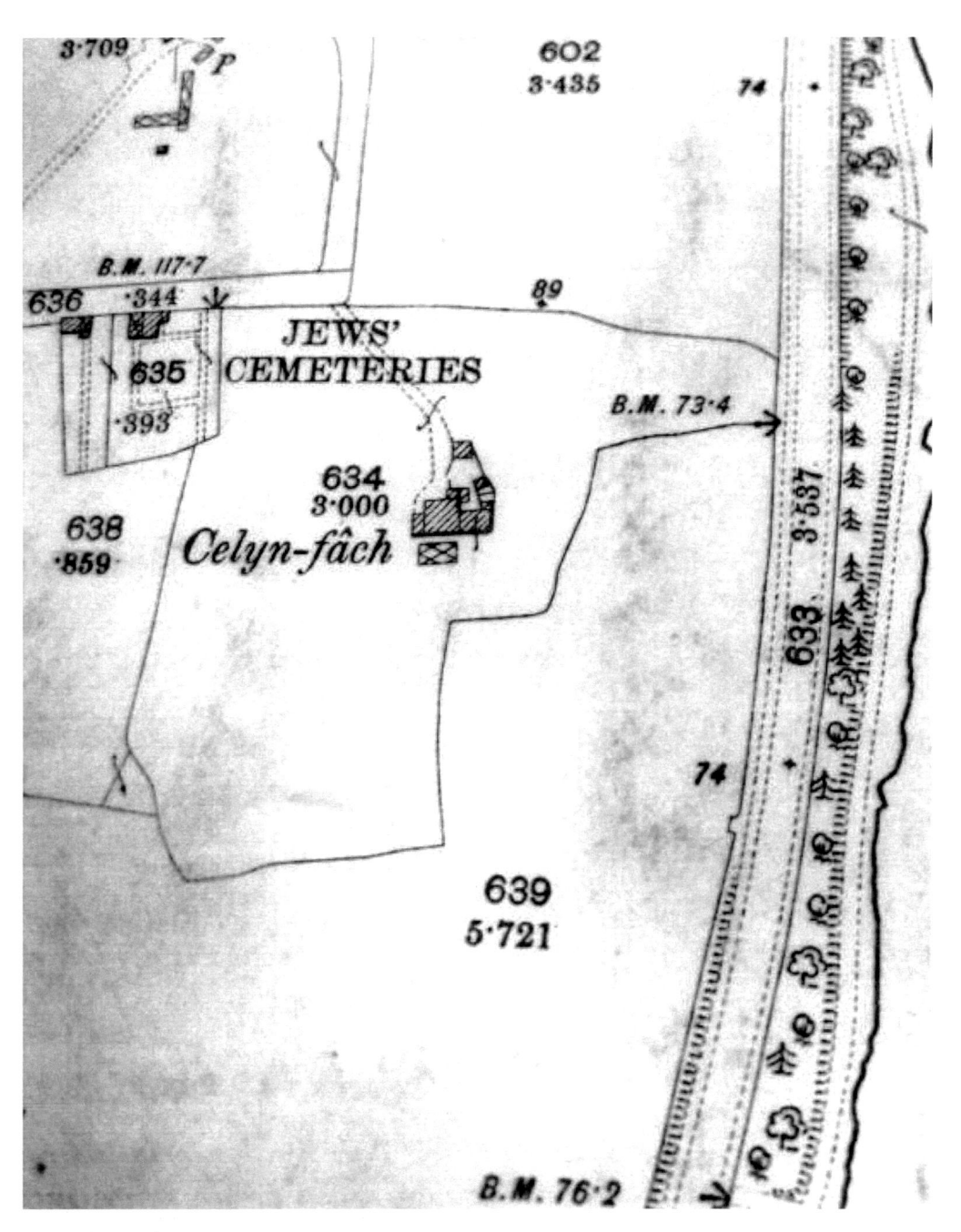

Public Health Map 1852
(photograph extract)

Merthyr Tydfil: Brecon Road Jews' Cemetery CF48 **[79]**
1865-1999

LOCATION	CHAPTER	SITE	DATE ESTABLISHED	IN USE TO	DATE OF VISIT	GAZETTEER NUMBER
NEWCASTLE	4.2.22	SYNAGOGUES	1838 1867 1879	1867 1879 1978	2010	[34]
	5.2.22	CEMETERY	1835 1857	1853 1950		[80]

ADDITIONAL NOTES		
	1775	First mention of Jews in Newcastle (Roth 1950)
	1830	Traditional date of foundation of the community (Roth 1950)

SYNAGOGUES	
	1838-1867 First Synagogue, Temple Street
	1867-1879 Second Synagogue, Charlotte Square
	1879-1978 Leazes Park Synagogue, NE1
FIGURE NUMBERS	4.105 - 4.107

CEMETERIES	
	1835-1853 First Cemetery, Thornton Street
	1857-1950 Second Cemetery, St. John's Cemetery Jewish Section Elswick Road
FIGURE NUMBERS	5.101- 5.103
CONTACT INFORMATION	Dorothy Sadlik: Chairwoman of various communal activities Joe Gellert: Communal Archivist, Jewish Cemeteries
BIBLIOGRAPHY	Guttentag, G., 1973 *The Beginnings of the Newcastle Jewish Community* Kadish, S., 2006 *Jewish Heritage in England. An Architectural Guide* Lipman, V., 1954 *Social History of the Jews of England 1850-1950* Allsover, L., 1980 *The Jewish Communities of Northeast England, 1755 – 1980* Roth, C.,1950 *The Rise of Provincial Jewry*

OTHER SOURCES	Newcastle Records Office Ordnance Survey Maps: 1850, 1898 Statistical Account of the Congregations in the British Empire 1845

PLACE NAMES WITH JEWISH CONNECTIONS	none

COMMUNITY SIZE	Date Community Size 1850 100 persons 1880 750 1900 c.2,000

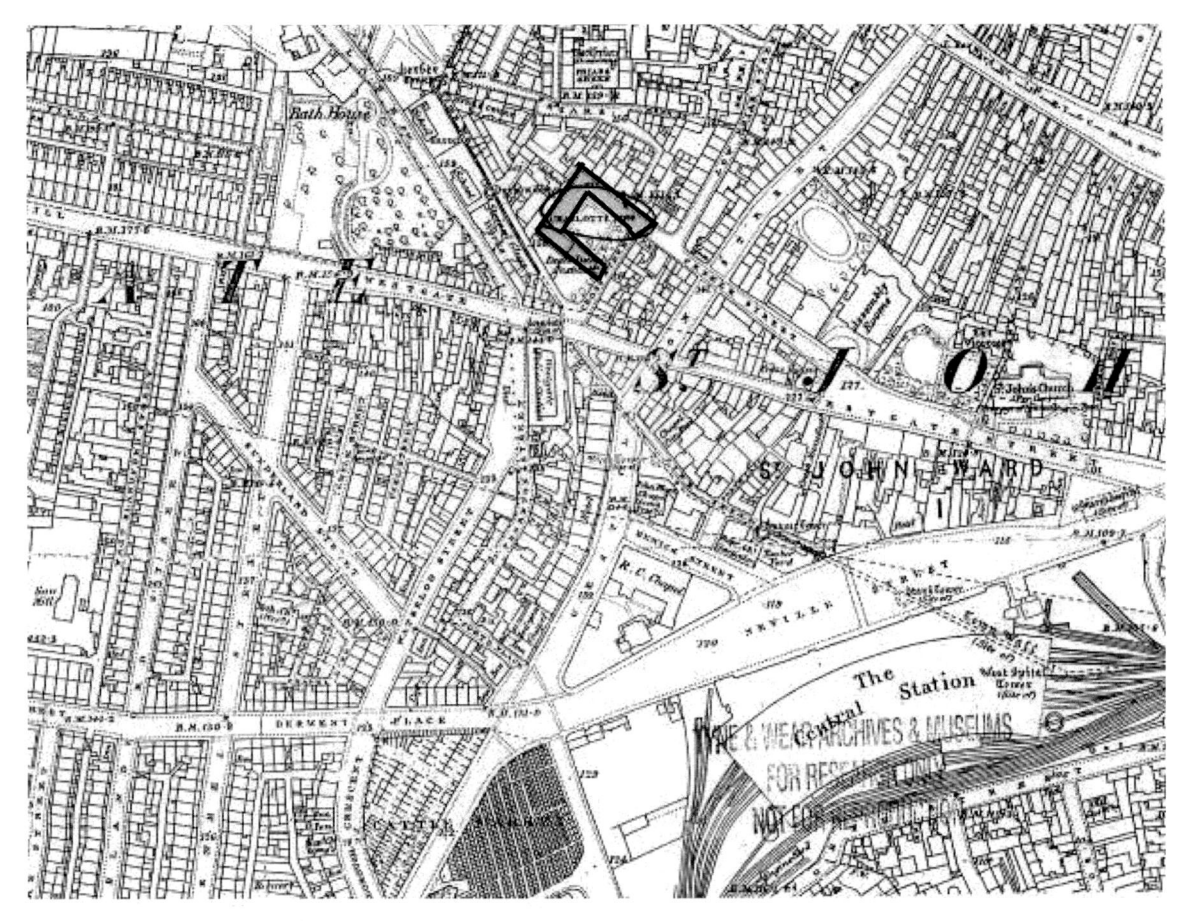

Ordnance Survey Map 1898　　　Newcastle: Charlotte Square Synagogue
[34]
25 inches to a mile　　　　　　　　　　1867-1879

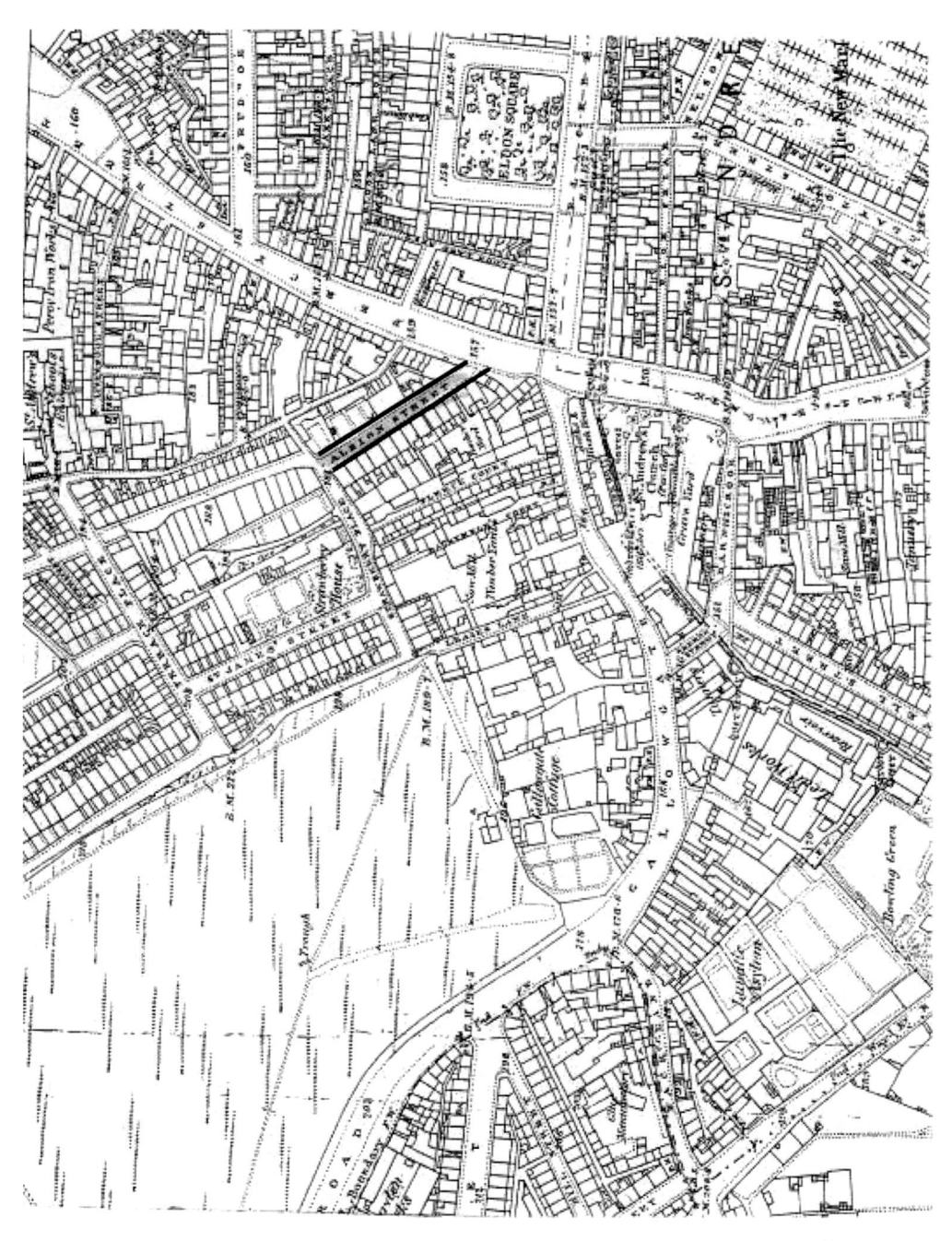

Ordnance Survey Map 1898   Newcastle: Leazes Park Synagogue Albion Street, NE1   [34]
25 inches to a mile   1879-1978 (not marked)

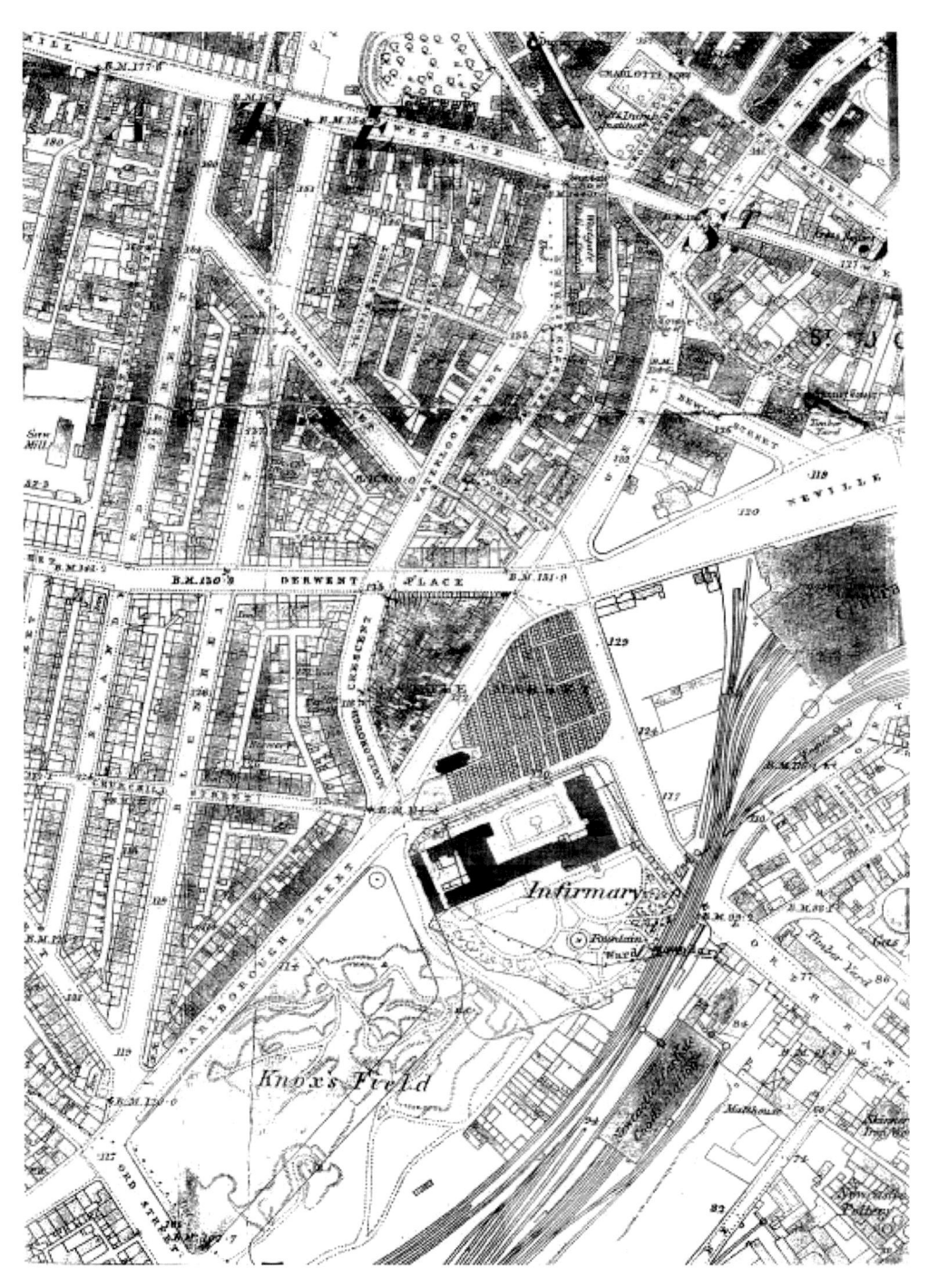

Ordnance Survey 1898
25 inches to a mile

Newcastle: Temple Street Synagogue
1838-1867

[34]

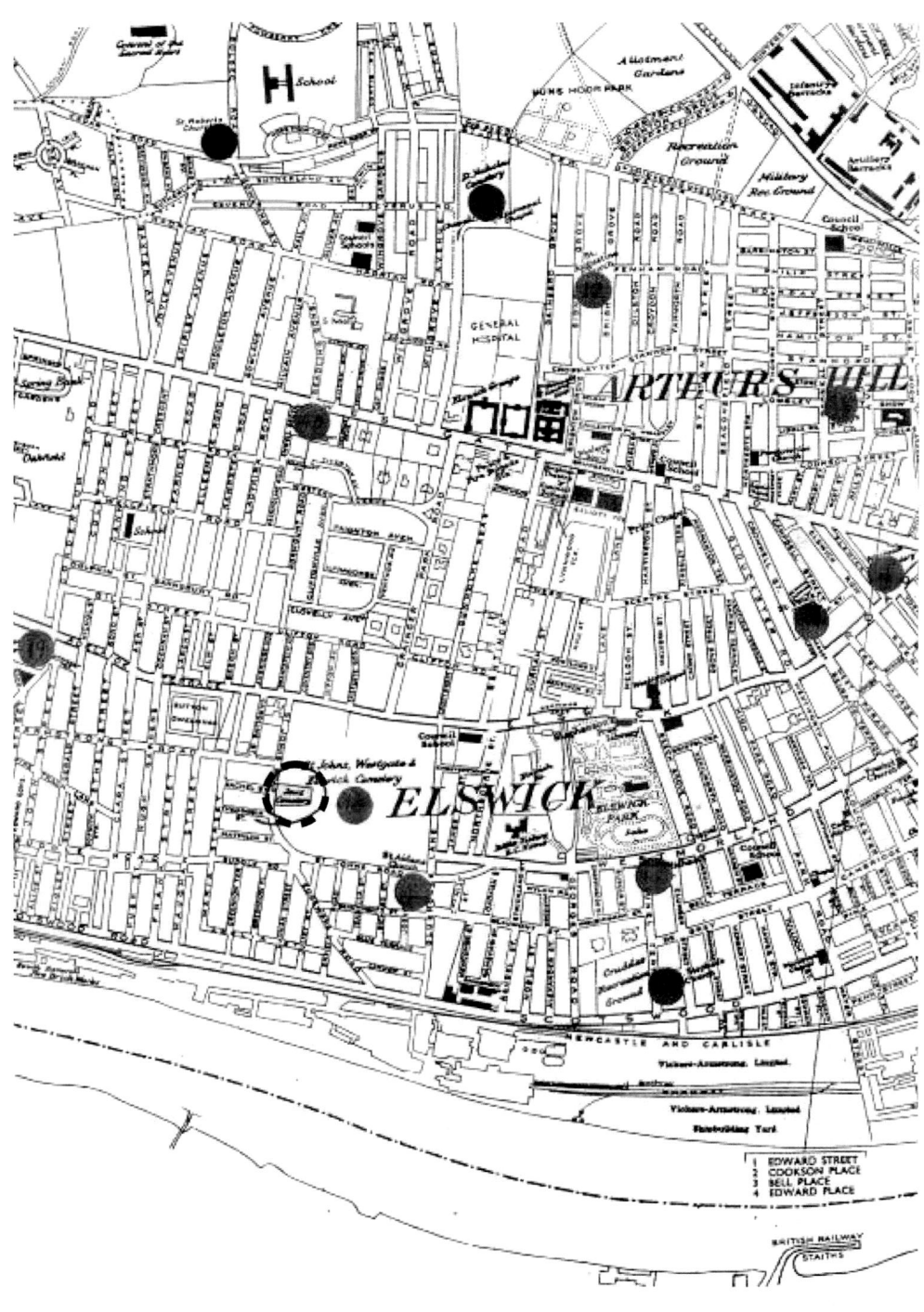

Ordnance Survey Map 1850 Newcastle: St. John's Cemetery NE4 [80]
25 inches to a mile 1857-1950

LOCATION	CHAPTER	SITE	DATE ESTABLISHED	IN USE TO	DATE OF VISIT	GAZETTEER NUMBER
NORWICH	4.2.23	SYNAGOGUES	1828 1835	1835 1942*	2010	[35]
	5.2.23	CEMETERIES	1750 1813	1826 1854		[81]

ADDITIONAL NOTES	
	1813 Traditional date of the Foundation of the Community (Roth, 1950 111) c.1750 First mention of Jews in Norwich (Roth, 1950) * destroyed by bombing

SYNAGOGUES	1828-1835 1835-1942	Tombland Alley (private house) St. Faith's Lane, later Synagogue Street
FIGURE NUMBERS	4.108-4.111	

CEMETERIES	1750-1826 1813-1854 1856**	Mariner's Lane Quaker's Lane Jews Burial Ground Jewish Section Bowthorpe Road **still in use
FIGURE NUMBERS	5.104-5.110	

CONTACT INFORMATION	Maureen and Barry Leveton: local historians and archivists
BIBLIOGRAPHY	Brown, M. 1990/ 92 The Jews of Norfolk and Suffolk before 1840 Kadish, S. 2006 Jewish Heritage in England. An Architectural Guide Leveton, M. 2009 The Jews in Norwich: 11th to 21st Century Lipman, V. 1954 Social History of The Jews in England 1850 - 1950 Roth, C. 1950 *The Rise of Provincial Jewry*

OTHER SOURCES	Norfolk and Norwich Millennium Library Ordnance Survey Maps:1850,1885 Statistical Account of the Congregations in the British Empire 1845

PLACE NAMES WITH JEWISH CONNECTIONS	Synagogue Street (location of former synagogue destroyed in 1942)

COMMUNITY SIZE	Date	Community Size
	1752	20 families
	1828	75 persons
	1850	75
	1895	50
	1935	133
	1945	150
	1990	170
	2004	239

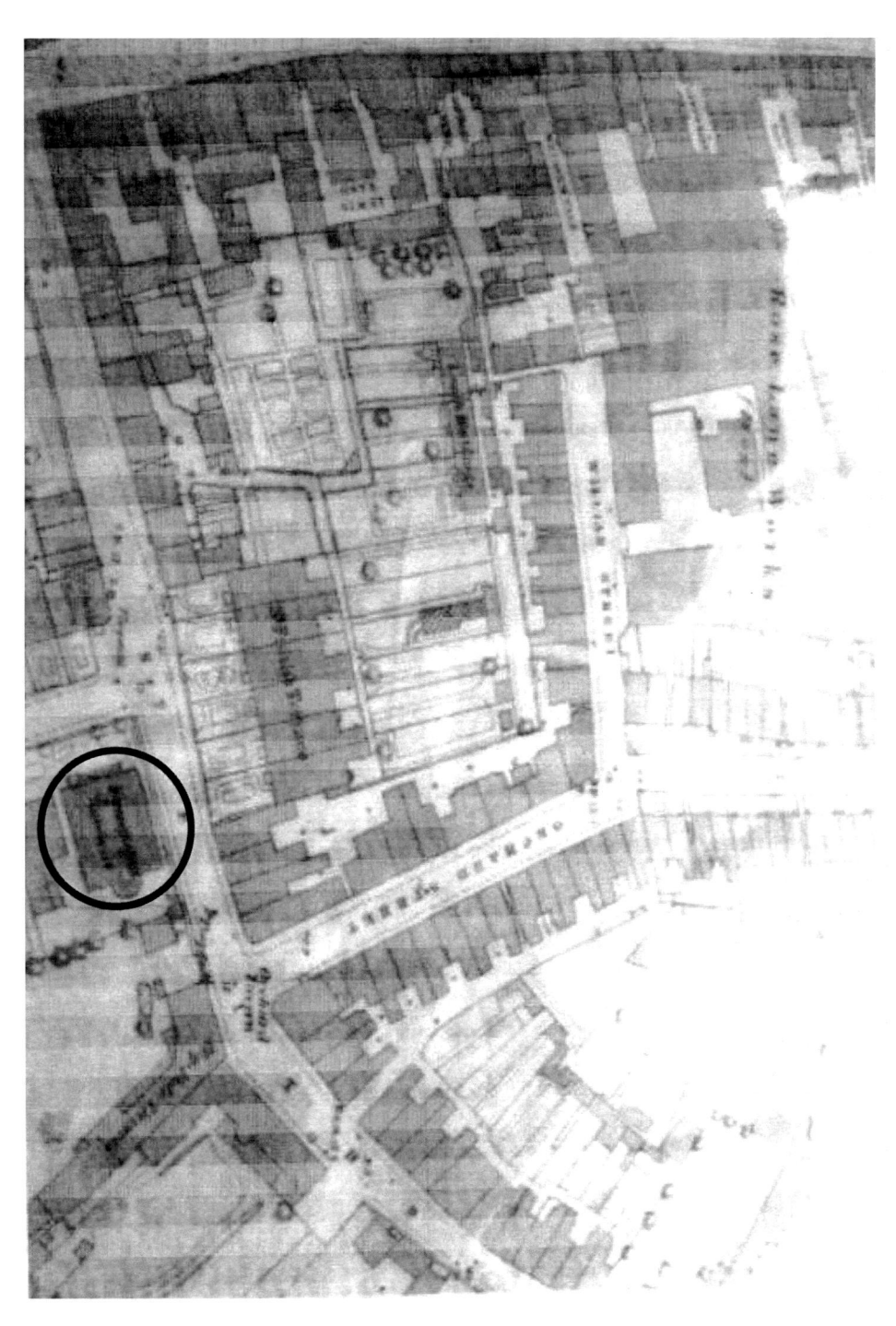

Ordnance Survey Map 1850　　　Norwich: St. Faith's Lane Synagogue　　[35]
5 inches to a mile　　　　　　　1835-1942 (photo only available)

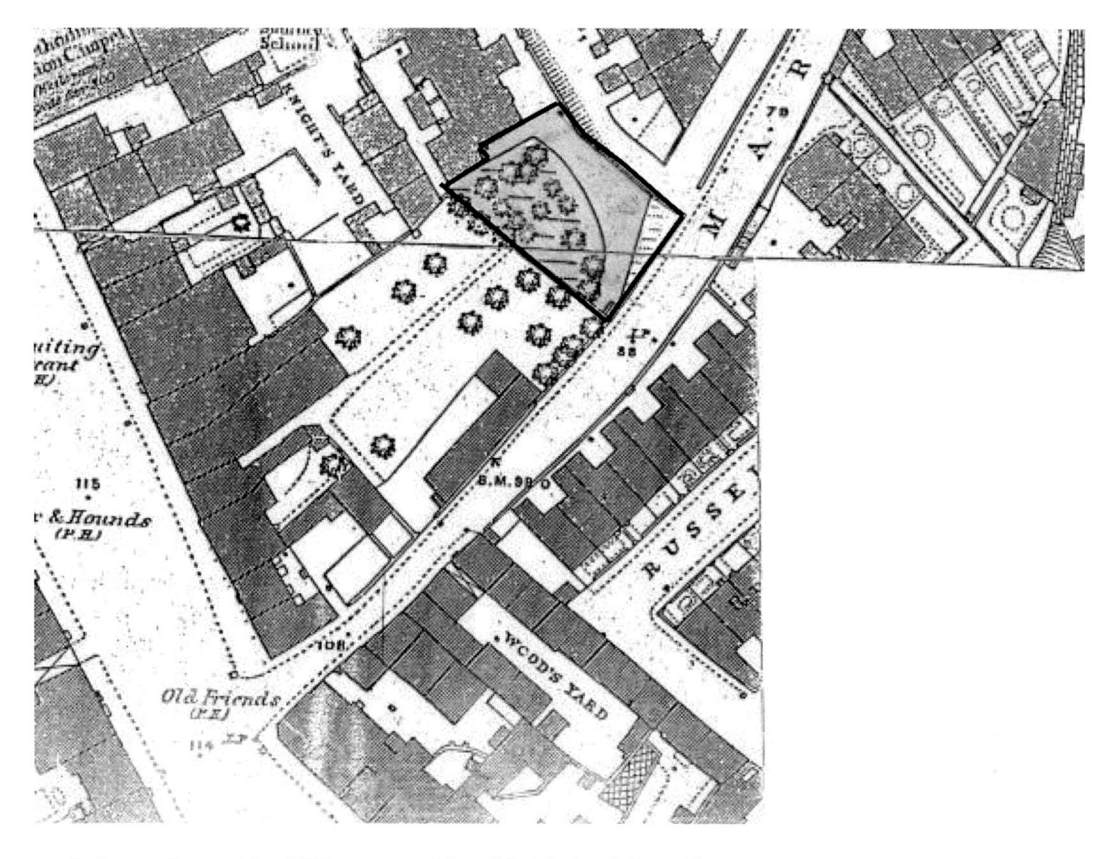

Ordnance Survey Map 1885 Norwich: Mariner's Lane Cemetery [81]
5 inches to a mile 1750-1826

LOCATION	CHAPTER	SITE	DATE ESTABLISHED	IN USE TO	DATE OF VISIT	GAZETTEER NUMBER
NOTTINGHAM	4.2.24	SYNAGOGUES	1890 1954	1954 still in use	2010	[36]
	5.2.24	CEMETERIES	1823 1869	1869 1947		[82]

ADDITIONAL NOTES		
	1822	Traditional date of the Foundation of the Community (Roth, 1950)
	1763	First mention of Jews in Nottingham (Roth, 1950)

SYNAGOGUES	Before the establishment of Synagogues, services were held in private houses and rented rooms:
	1820 — Barker Gate
	1836 — Clare Street
	1840 — Friar Lane
	1855 — Broad Street
	1863 — Clare Street
	1868 — Beck Lane
	1869 — Balloon Court
	1873 — Lincoln Street
	1883-1890 — Colin Street
	1890-1954 — Chaucer Street Synagogue
	Shakespeare Villas Synagogue, NG1
	1954 — Grade II-still in use
FIGURE NUMBERS	4.112-4.114

CEMETERIES	1823-1869	North Sherwood Street Jew's Burial Ground NG1
	1867-1947	Hardy Street Jewish Cemetery, Radford NG7
FIGURE NUMBERS	5.111-5.117	
CONTACT INFORMATION	David Snapper: 6th generation Nottingham resident Rolf Noskwith: Industrialist	

BIBLIOGRAPHY	
	Fisher, N. 1998 *800 Years: The Story of Nottingham's Jews*
	Kadish, S. 2006 *Jewish Heritage in England. An Architectural Guide*
	Lassman, A. 1944 *History of the Jews of Nottingham (unpublished)*
	Lipman, V. 1954 *Social History of The Jews in England 1850 - 1950*
	Roth, C. 1950 *The Rise of Provincial Jewry*

OTHER SOURCES	
	Nottingham Archives
	Ordnance Survey Maps: 1881
	Statistical Account of the Congregations in the British Empire 1845

PLACE NAMES WITH JEWISH CONNECTIONS	none

COMMUNITY SIZE	Date	Community Size
	1842	100 persons
	1845	50-100
	1865	80-100
	1880	c.350
	1896	500
	1934	650
	1965	1,500
	2004	627

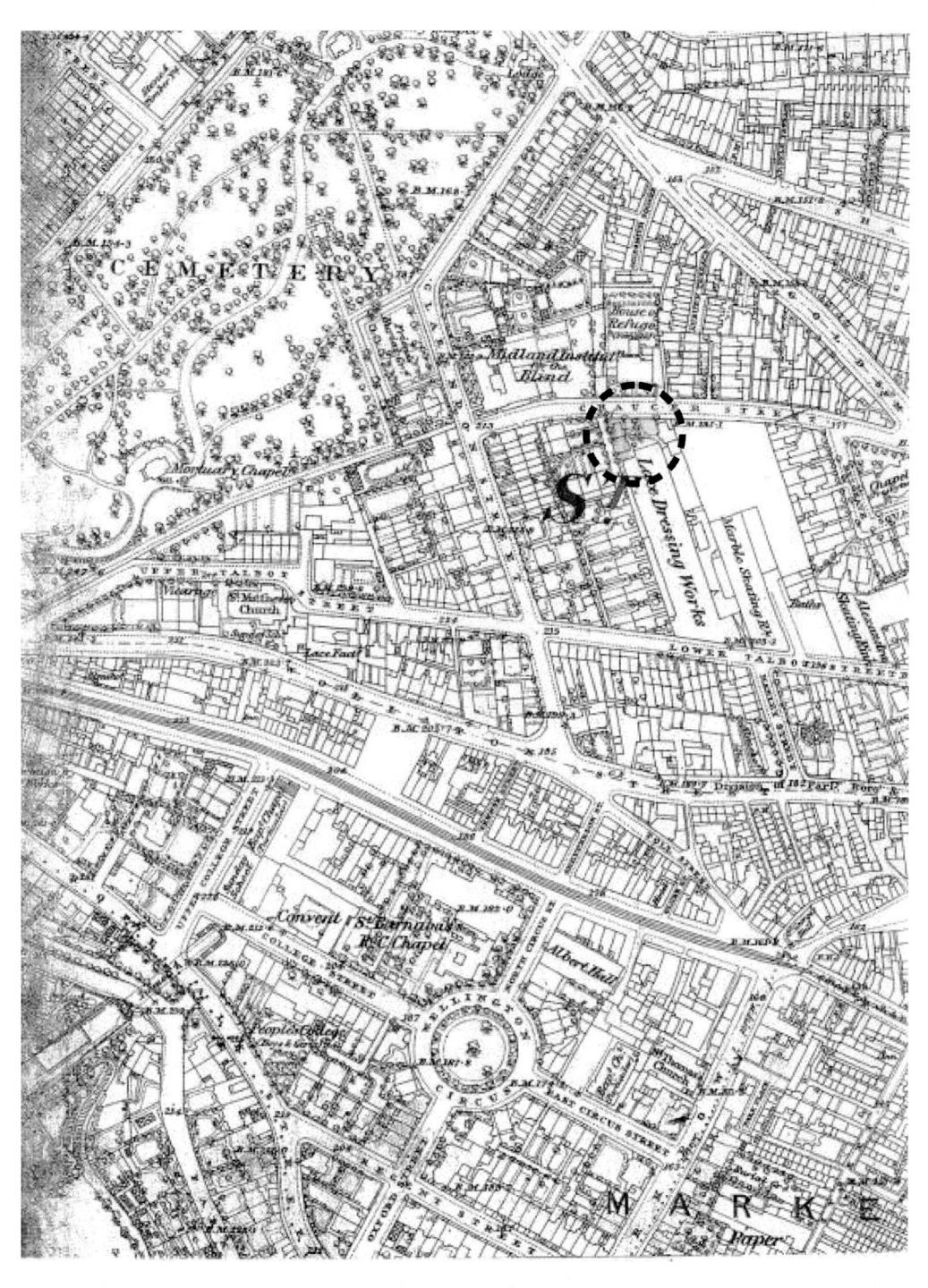

Ordnance Survey Map 1881 Nottingham: Chaucer Street Synagogue [36]
25 inches to a mile 1890-1954

GAZETTEER 401

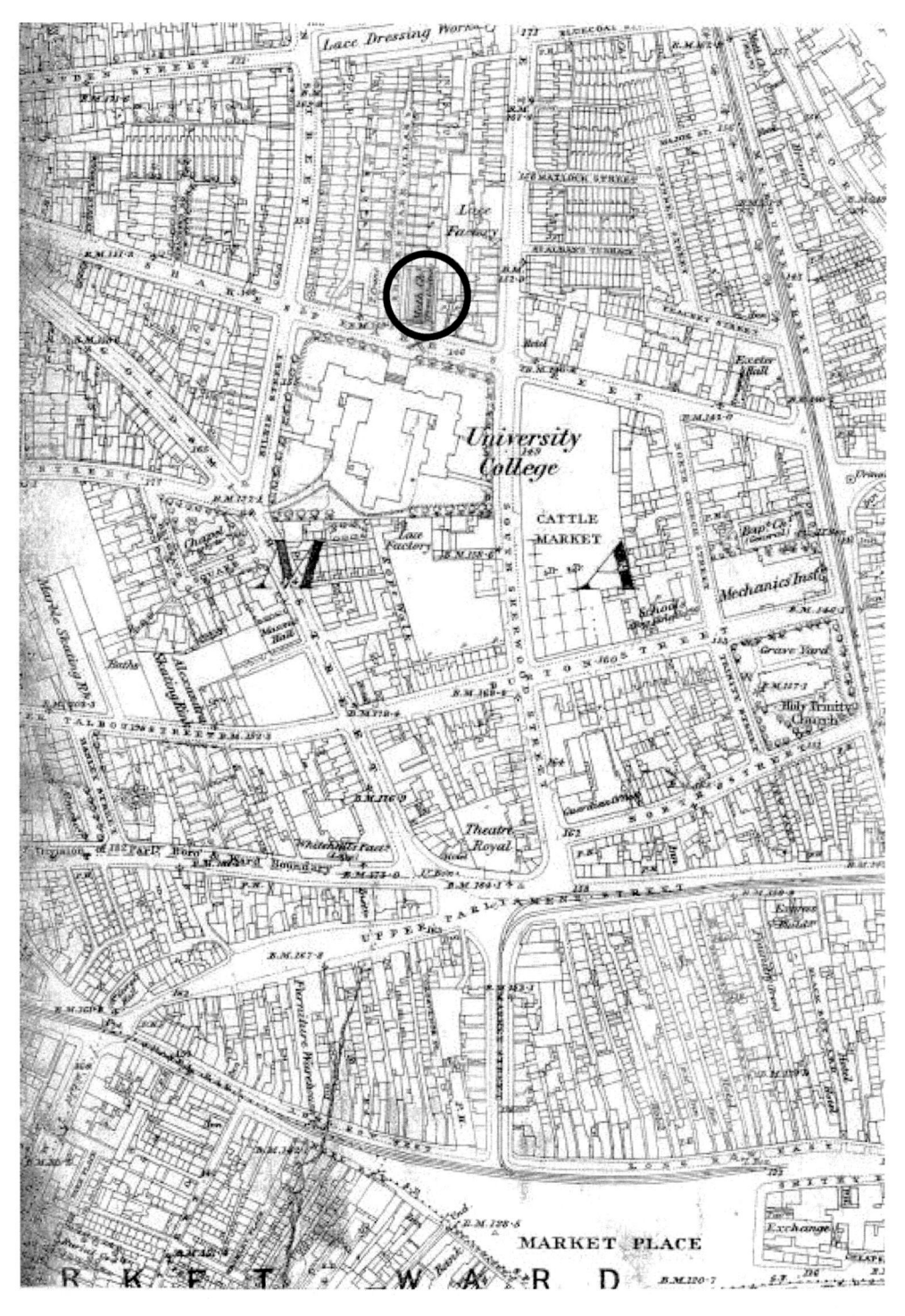

Ordnance Survey Map 1881 Nottingham: Shakespeare Villas Synagogue NG1 [36]
25 inches to a mile 1854 Methodist Chapel.-1954 Synagogue-still in use

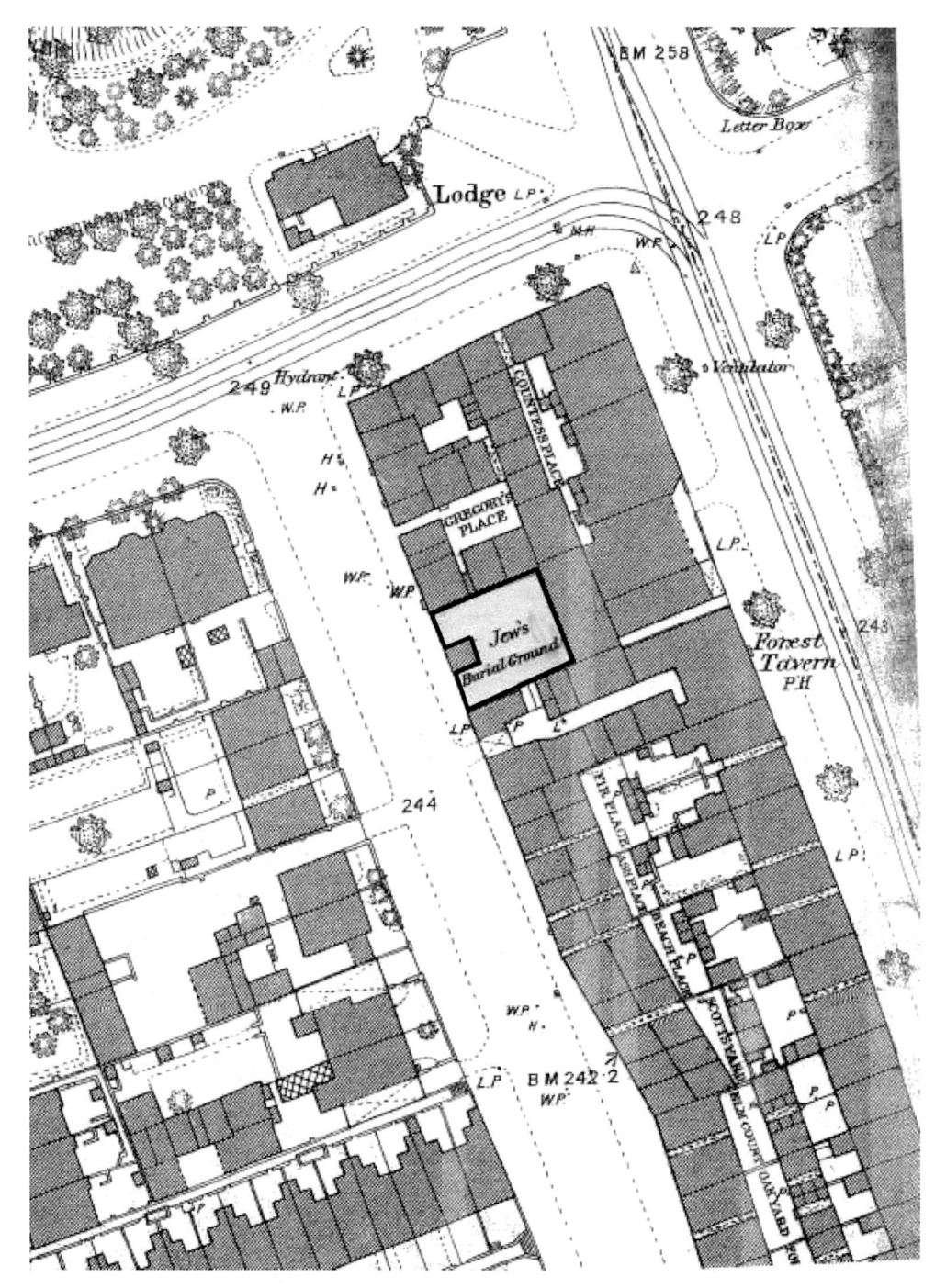

Ordnance Survey Map 1881 Nottingham: North Sherwood Street Cemetery NG1   [82]
5 inches to a mile   1823-1869

GAZETTEER 403

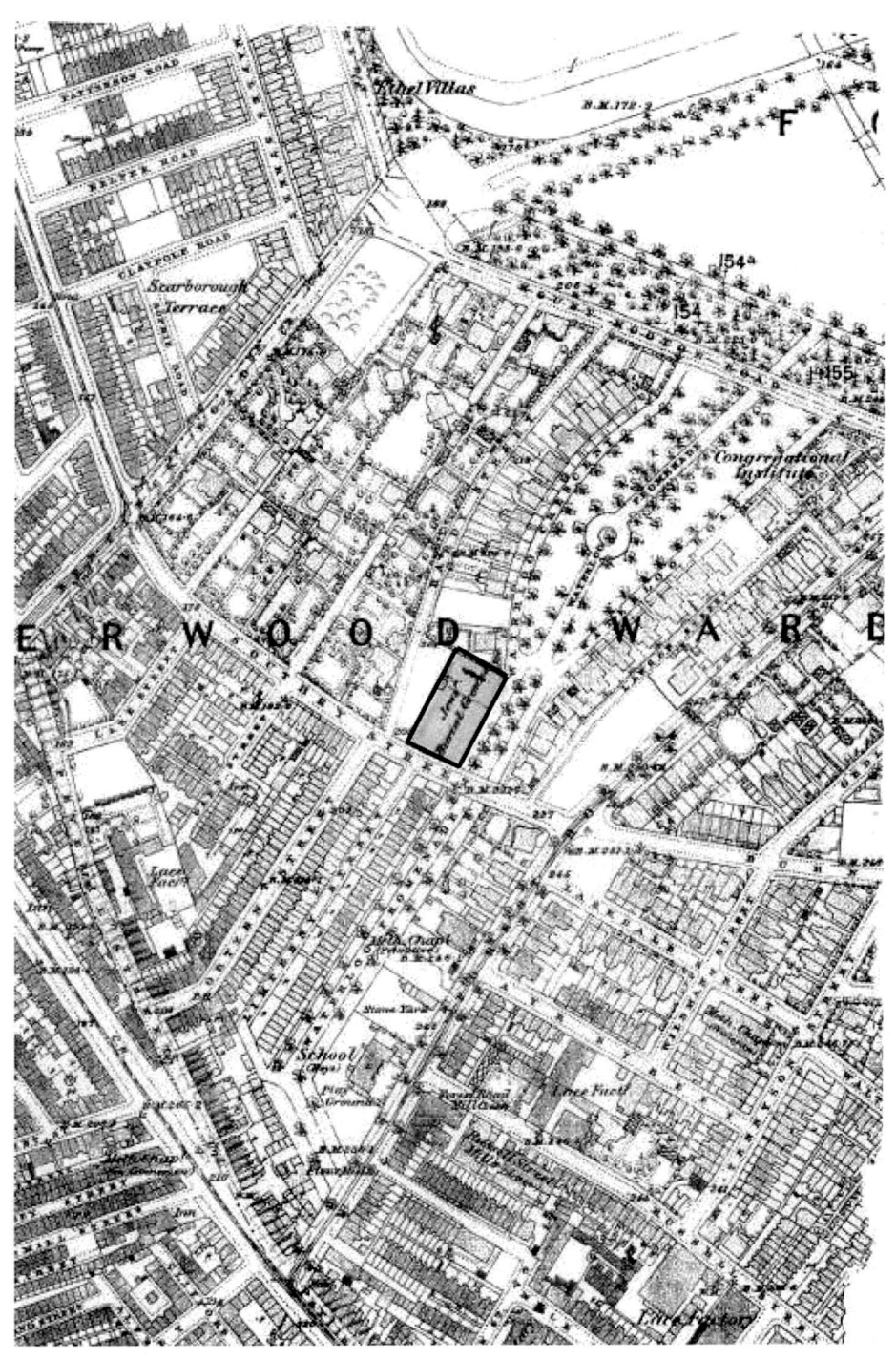

Ordnance Survey Map 1881	Nottingham; Hardy Street Cemetery NG7
25 inches to a mile	1869-1947 **[82]**

LOCATION	CHAPTER	SITE	DATE ESTABLISHED	IN USE TO	DATE OF VISIT	GAZETTEER NUMBER
OXFORD	4.2.25	SYNAGOGUES	1847 1871	1861 1878*	2010	[37]
	5.2.25	CEMETERIES	none	**		nil

ADDITIONAL NOTES

1841/2   Traditional date of the Foundation of the Community (Roth, 1950)
1733   First mention of Jews in Oxford (Roth, 1950)
*demolished 1878

** 1894 Wolvercote Cemetery established outside Oxford, Banbury Road OX2

SYNAGOGUES

1847   Frist Synagogue in Paradise Square
1871-1878   Second Synagogue in St. Aldates
1878-1884   Third Synagogue in George Street

FIGURE NUMBERS   4.115

CEMETERIES

1894   First establishment of Jewish Cemetery in Wolvercote
Earlier burials held in Birmingham, Cheltenham and London

FIGURE NUMBERS   nil

CONTACT INFORMATION

Marcus Roberts: Local Resident (JTrails - Jewish Site Tours)

BIBLIOGRAPHY

Endelman, T. 2002 *The Jews in Britain 1656 - 2000*
Lewis, D. 1992 *The Jews of Oxford*
Lipman, V. 1954 *Social History of The Jews in England 1850 - 1950*
Newman, A. 1976 *The United Synagogue 1870 - 1970*
Roth, C. 1950 *The Rise of Provincial Jewry*

OTHER SOURCES

Oxfordshire Studies Central Library
Ordnance Survey Maps: 1900
Statistical Account of the Congregations in the British Empire 1845

PLACE NAMES WITH JEWISH CONNECTIONS

Old Jewry   (medieval street)
Jew's Mount   (medieval fort?)

COMMUNITY SIZE

Date	Community Size
1841	3 families
1845	50 persons
1861	40
1878	50

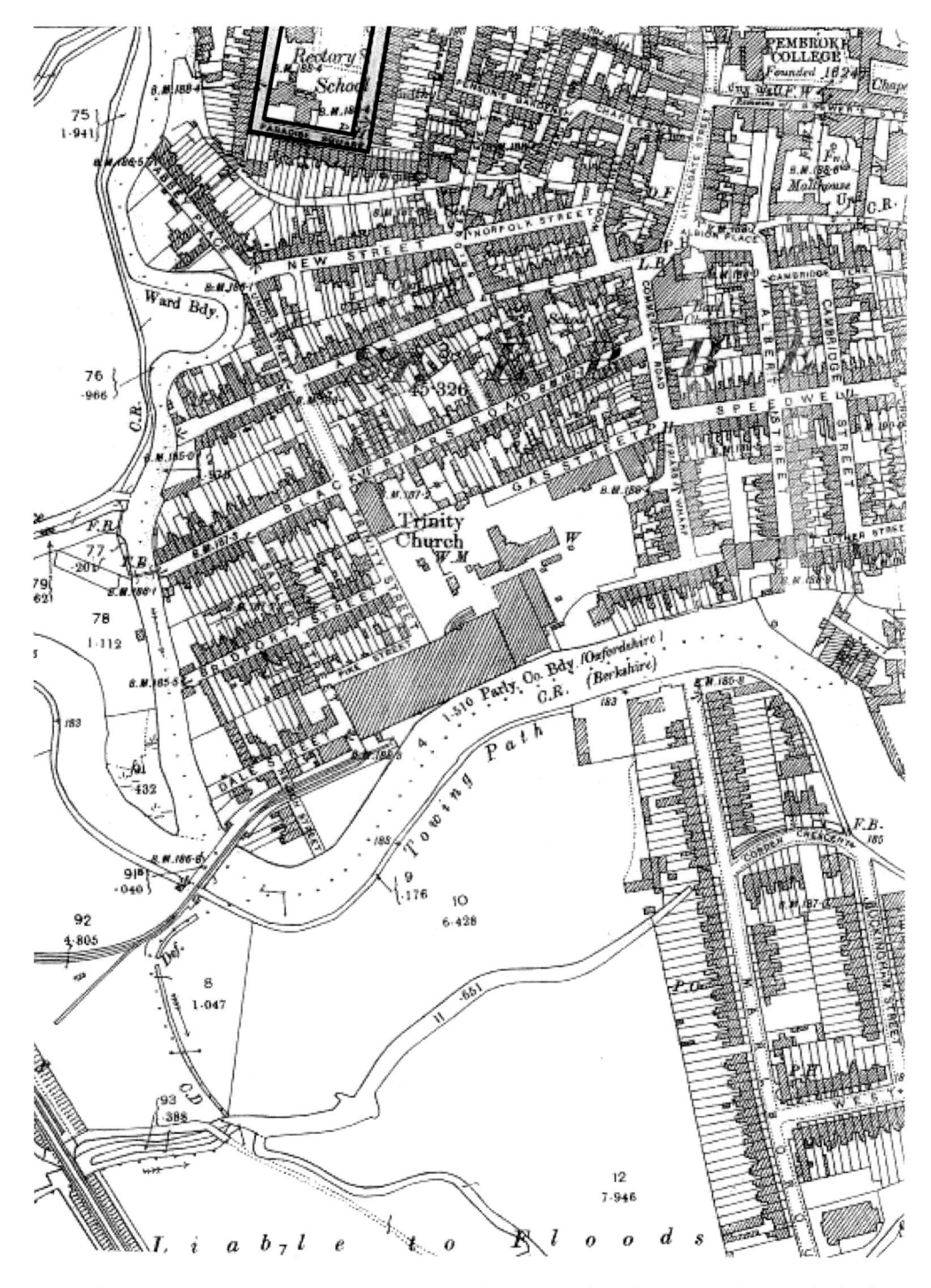

Ordnance Survey Map 1900
25 inches to a mile

Oxford: Paradise Square, site of Synagogue (not marked) **[37]**
1847?

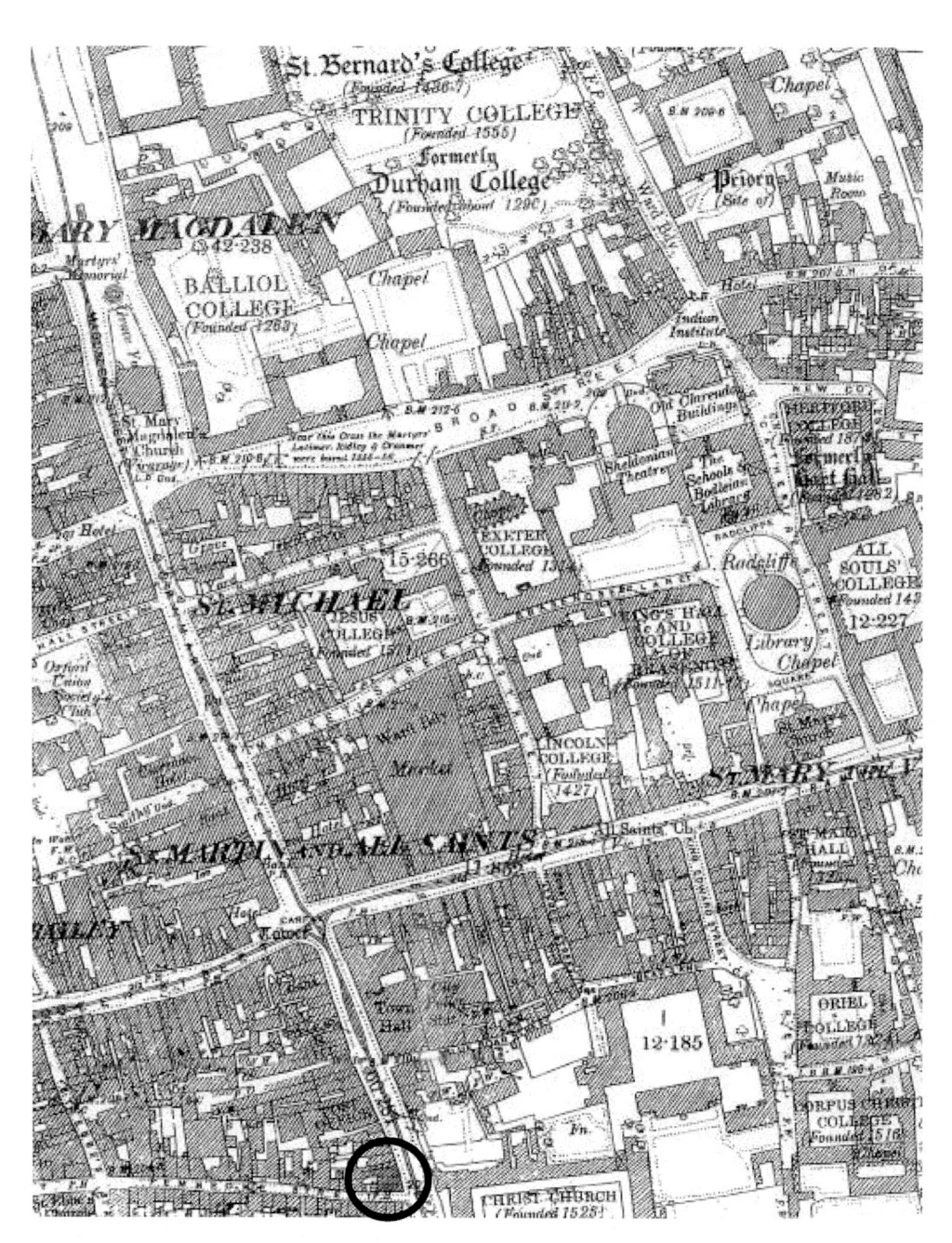

406   THE ARCHAEOLOGY OF ANGLO-JEWRY IN ENGLAND AND WALES 1656–C.1880

Ordnance Survey Map 1900   Oxford: St Aldate's, site of synagogue (not marked)   [37]
25 inches to a mile   1871-1878

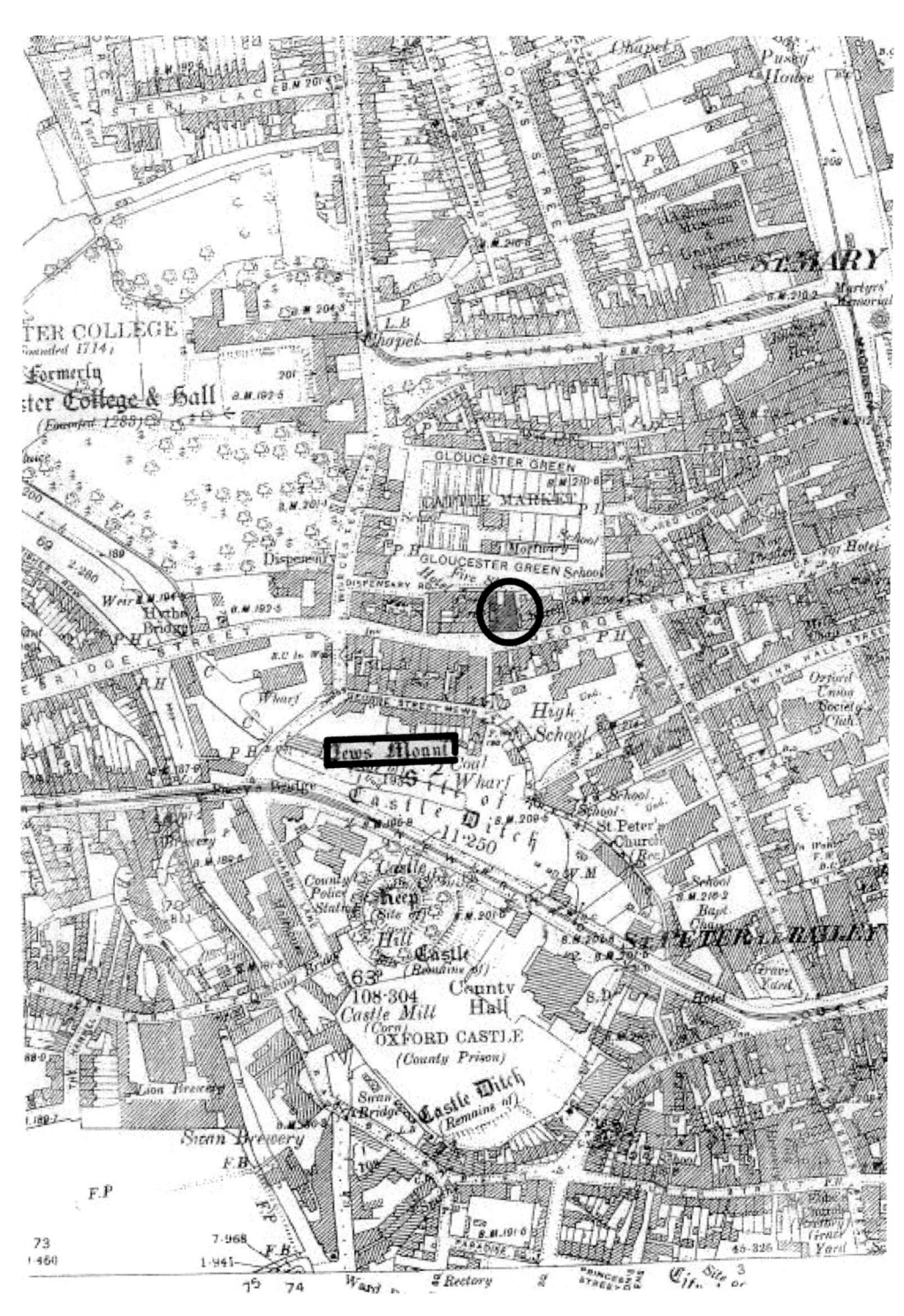

Ordnance Survey Map 1900　　　Oxford: George Street Synagogue　1878-1884　　**[37]**
25 inches to a mile　　　　　　&　　Medieval Jews' Mount

LOCATION	CHAPTER	SITE	DATE ESTABLISHED	IN USE TO	DATE OF VISIT	GAZETTEER NUMBER
PENZANCE	4.2.26	SYNAGOGUES	1768 1807	1807 1906	2009	[38]
	5.2.26	CEMETERY	earliest headstone 1791 1740/1750?	2000		[83]

ADDITIONAL NOTES	
	1807 Traditional date of the Foundation of the Community (Roth, 1950) 1740 First mention of Jews in Penzance (Margoliouth 1851) There is no longer a Jewish Community in Penzance

SYNAGOGUES	1768-1807	First Synagogue in private house in Jennings Street converted into temporary synagogue
	1807-1906	Second Synagogue in Jennings Street TR18
FIGURE NUMBERS	4.116-4.119	

CEMETERY	1791*-2000	Leskinnick Terrace, TR18 (Grade II) comprising boundary wall and four tombstones
	*earliest headstone	
FIGURE NUMBERS	5.118-5.122	

CONTACT INFORMATION	Keith Pearce: Historian of Cornish Jewish Communities and custodian Penzance Jewish Cemetery
BIBLIOGRAPHY	Lipman, V. 1954 *Social History of The Jews in England 1850 - 1950* Pearce, K. & Fry, H. 2000 *The Lost Jews of Cornwall* Roth, C. 1950 *The Rise of Provincial Jewry*

OTHER SOURCES	Ordnance Survey Maps: 1898 Statistical Account of the Congregations in the British Empire 1845

PLACE NAMES WITH JEWISH CONNECTIONS	Jews' Fields (cemetery) Market Jew Street* *This appears to be a Cornish Name: (no evidence of any connection to the Jewish Community)

COMMUNITY SIZE	Date Community Size 1768 c.25 persons 1815 50 1845 50 1892 less than 10 c.1900 no Jewish Community remaining

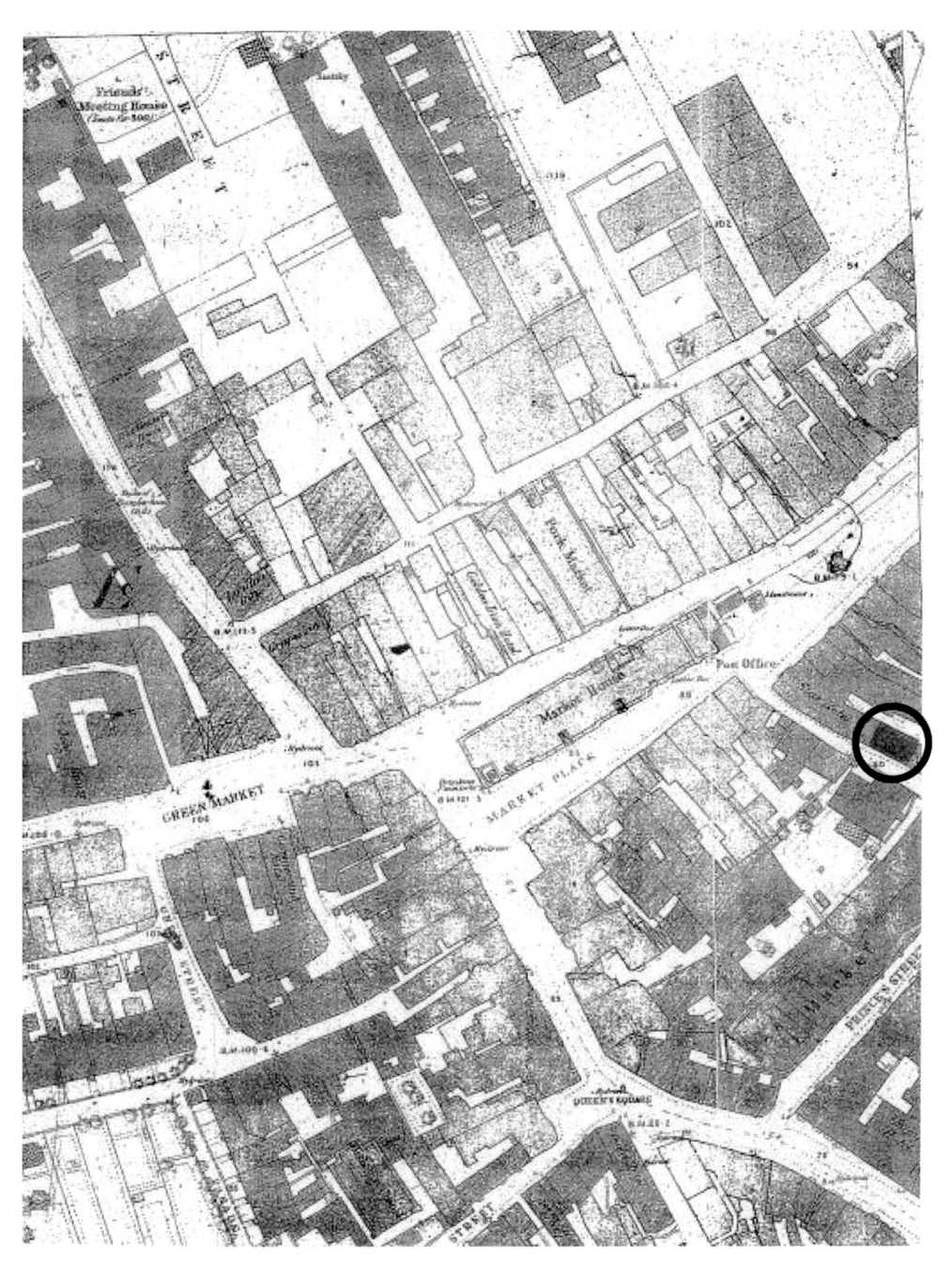

Ordnance Survey Map 1898   Penzance: Jennings Street, site of Synagogue TR18 (not marked)
5 inches to a mile   1768-1906   [38]

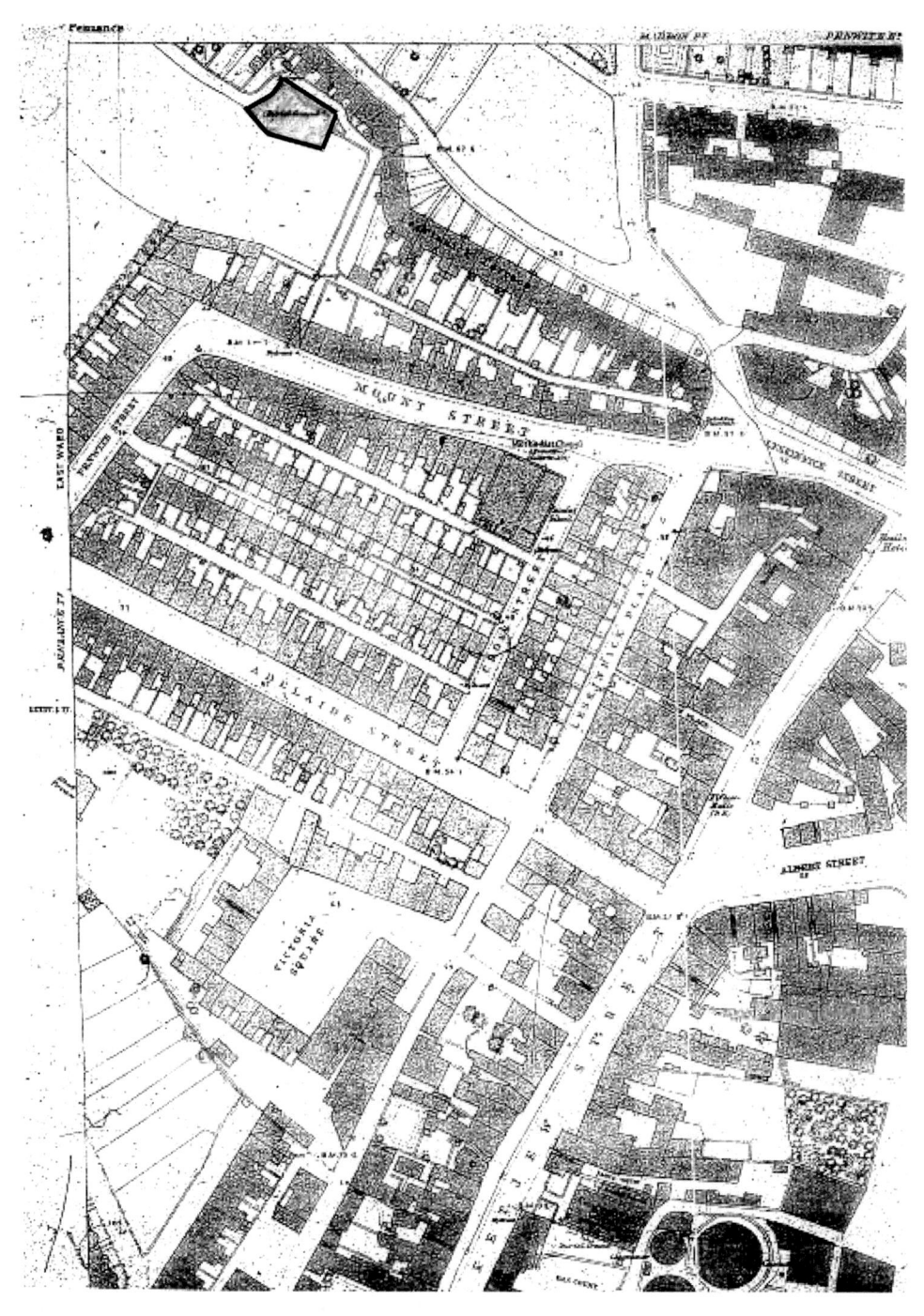

Ordnance Survey Map 1898 Penzance: Lestinick Terrace Cemetery TR18   [83]
25 inches to a mile   1791-2000

LOCATION	CHAPTER	SITE	DATE ESTABLISHED	IN USE TO	DATE OF VISIT	GAZETTEER NUMBER
PLYMOUTH	4.2.27 5.2.27	SYNAGOGUE CEMETERY*	1761 / 2 1744	still in use c.1860	2009	

ADDITIONAL NOTES		1888 ordnance survey maps in British Library too scratched and faded to include.
	c.1752	Traditional date of the Foundation of the Community (Roth, 1950)
	1740	First mention of Jews in Plymouth (Roth 1950)
		*A second smaller Jewish Cemetery in Gifford Place not discussed (see below)
		Plymouth Synagogue is the oldest Ashkenazi Synagogue still in regular use in the English speaking world.

SYNAGOGUE	1761 / 2	Synagogue in Catherine Street PL1 (Grade II*)
		still in use
	1874	Vestry House; site of *Mikvah* (ritual bath)
		Oldest surviving Synagogue in the Provinces
FIGURE NUMBERS	4.120-4.121	

CEMETERY	1744-c.1860	Plymouth Hoe Old Jew's Burial Ground
		Lambhay Hill PL1
		First burial 1744; documented from 1758
		Gifford Place Jewish Cemetery:
		first burial 1873 (not discussed)
FIGURE NUMBERS	5.123- 5.125	

CONTACT INFORMATION	Dr. Peter Lee: Honorary Treasurer of Plymouth Hebrew Congregation
BIBLIOGRAPHY	Kadish, S. 2006 *Jewish Heritage in England: an Architectural Guide*
	Lipman, V. 1954 *Social History of The Jews in England 1850 - 1950*
	Roth, C. 1950 *The Rise of Provincial Jewry*
	Susser, B. 1972 *An Account of The Old Jewish Cemetery on Plymouth Hoe*
	Susser, B. undated. *The Plymouth Synagogue (internet article)*

OTHER SOURCES	Statistical Account of the Congregations in the British Empire 1845
	Ordnance Survey Maps: 1888
	Working Party Jewish Monuments in UK and Ireland 1999
	"Plymouth's Orthodox Synagogue"

PLACE NAMES WITH JEWISH CONNECTIONS	Synagogue Lane

COMMUNITY SIZE	Date	Community Size
	1761	35 persons
	1762	c.150
	1845	c.200
	1915	260
	1945	400
	2005	200

LOCATION	CHAPTER	SITE	DATE ESTABLISHED	IN USE TO	DATE OF VISIT	GAZETTEER NUMBER
PORTSMOUTH & SOUTHSEA	4.2.28	SYNAGOGUE	1780 1936	1936* still in use**	2009	[39]
	5.2.28	CEMETERY	1749	still in use		[84]

ADDITIONAL NOTES

c.1730s Traditional date of the Foundation of the Community (Roth, 1950)
1742 First mention of Jews in Portsmouth (Roth 1950)
Portsmouth was the earliest Jewish Provincial Community
* Portsmouth
**Southsea

SYNAGOGUE

1746 First Room of Prayer in Oyster Street (off High Street)
1780-1936 First Synagogue in White's Row, Portsea
1936 Portsmouth & Southsea Synagogue
(contains the Ark and Plaques from White's Row Synagogue)

FIGURE NUMBERS 4.122-4.128

CEMETERY

1749 Old Jew's Burial Ground
Fawcett Road (previously Jew's Lane)
still occasionally used

FIGURE NUMBERS 5.126-5.127

CONTACT INFORMATION

Richard Sotnick: Former Lord Mayor of Portsmouth

BIBLIOGRAPHY

Green, G. 1982 *Anglo-Jewish Trading Connections with Officers and Seamen of The Royal Navy 1740 - 1820*
Kadish, S. 2006 *Jewish Heritage in England: an Architectural Guide*
Lipman, V. 1954 *Social History of The Jews in England 1850 - 1950*
Roth, C. 1935 *The Portsmouth Community and its Historical Background*

Roth, C. 1950 *The Rise of Provincial Jewry*

Weinberg, A. 1998 *Portsmouth Jewry 1730's to 1980's*

OTHER SOURCES

Ordnance Survey Map: 1898
Statistical Account of the Congregations in the British Empire 1845

PLACE NAMES WITH JEWISH CONNECTIONS

Jew's Lane (now Fawcett Street - location of cemetery)

COMMUNITY SIZE

Date	Community Size
1740	7 families
1770	150 / 200 persons
1812*	400 / 500
1850	300
1896	500
1919	800
1934	800
2004	235

* largest Provincial community in 1812

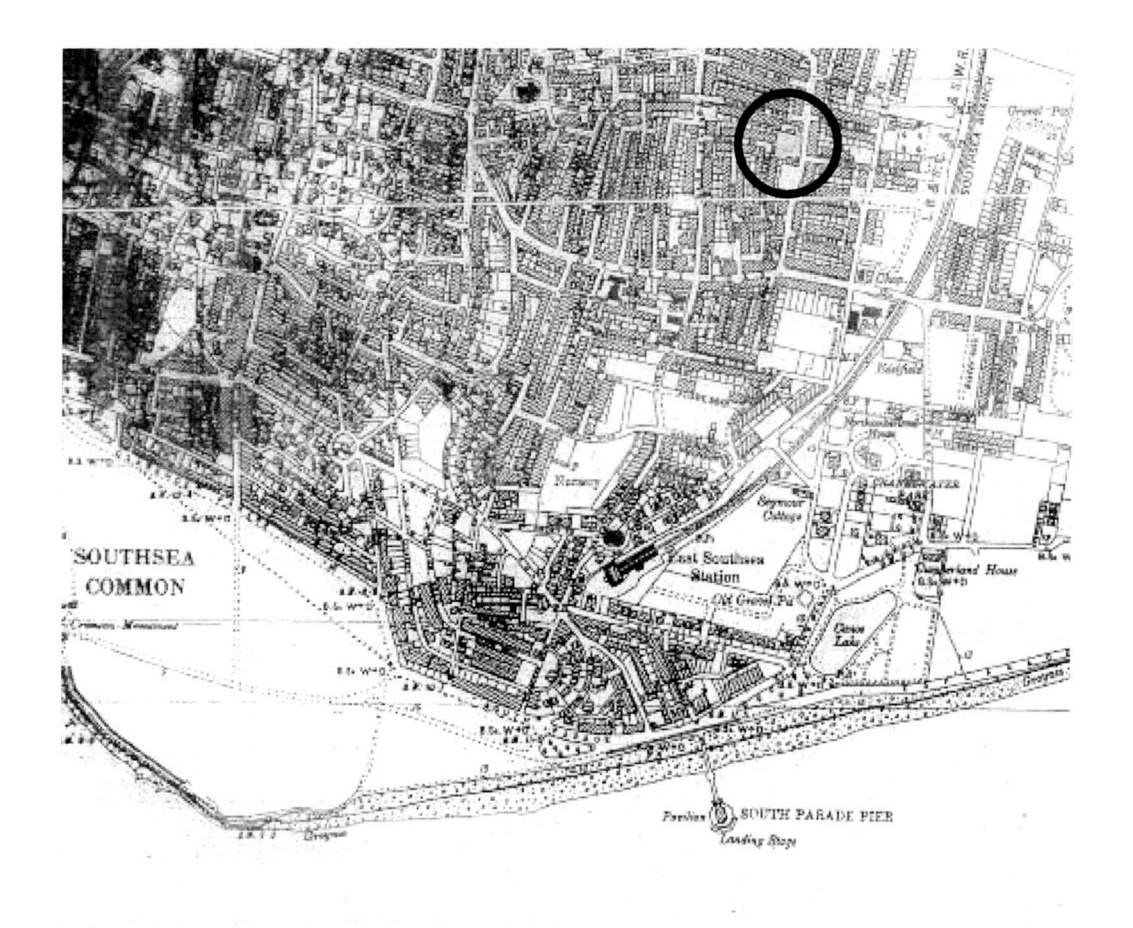

Ordnance Survey Map 1898
25 inches to a mile

Portsmouth and Southsea Cemetery
1749-still in use

[84]

LOCATION	CHAPTER	SITE	DATE ESTABLISHED	IN USE TO	DATE OF VISIT	GAZETTEER NUMBER
RAMSGATE					2011	
	4.2.29	SYNAGOGUE*	1833	still in use		[40]
	5.2.29	CEMETERY	1872	still in use		[85]

ADDITIONAL NOTES

Traditional date of the Foundation of the Community 1833 (Roth 1950)
c.1780 First mention of Jews in Ramsgate (Roth 1950)
c.1780 First mention of Jews in Ramsgate (Rodrigues-Pereira, M. 1984)
* Synagogue & Mausoleum

SYNAGOGUE
1833 Honeysuckle Road, Ramsgate CT11
1862 Mausoleum (Grade II*)

FIGURE NUMBERS 4.129-4.134

CEMETERY
1872 Upper Dumpton Park Road, Ramsgate CT11

FIGURE NUMBERS 5.128

CONTACT INFORMATION
Miss Miriam Rodrigues-Pereira: Honorary Archivist Spanish & Portuguese Congregation

BIBLIOGRAPHY

Hyamson, A. 1951 *The Sephardim of England*
Kadish, S. 2006 *Jewish Heritage in England: an Architectural Guide*
Lipman, V. 1954 *Social History of The Jews in England 1850 - 1950*
Rodrigues-Pereira, M. 1984 *Sir Moses Montefiore's Religious Foundations at Ramsgate*
Roth, C. 1950 *The Rise of Provincial Jewry*

OTHER SOURCES

Kent County Archive Service
Ordnance Survey Maps:1886,1898
Spanish & Portuguese Congregational Archives

PLACE NAMES WITH JEWISH CONNECTIONS
Montefiore Avenue, leading to East Cliff Lodge, home of Sir Moses Montefiore

COMMUNITY SIZE

Date	Community Size
1842	9 families
1850	45 persons
1880	350 including Margate
1898	60
1900	100
1946	50
1975	65
1985	300 (Margate only)
1990	200 (Margate only)

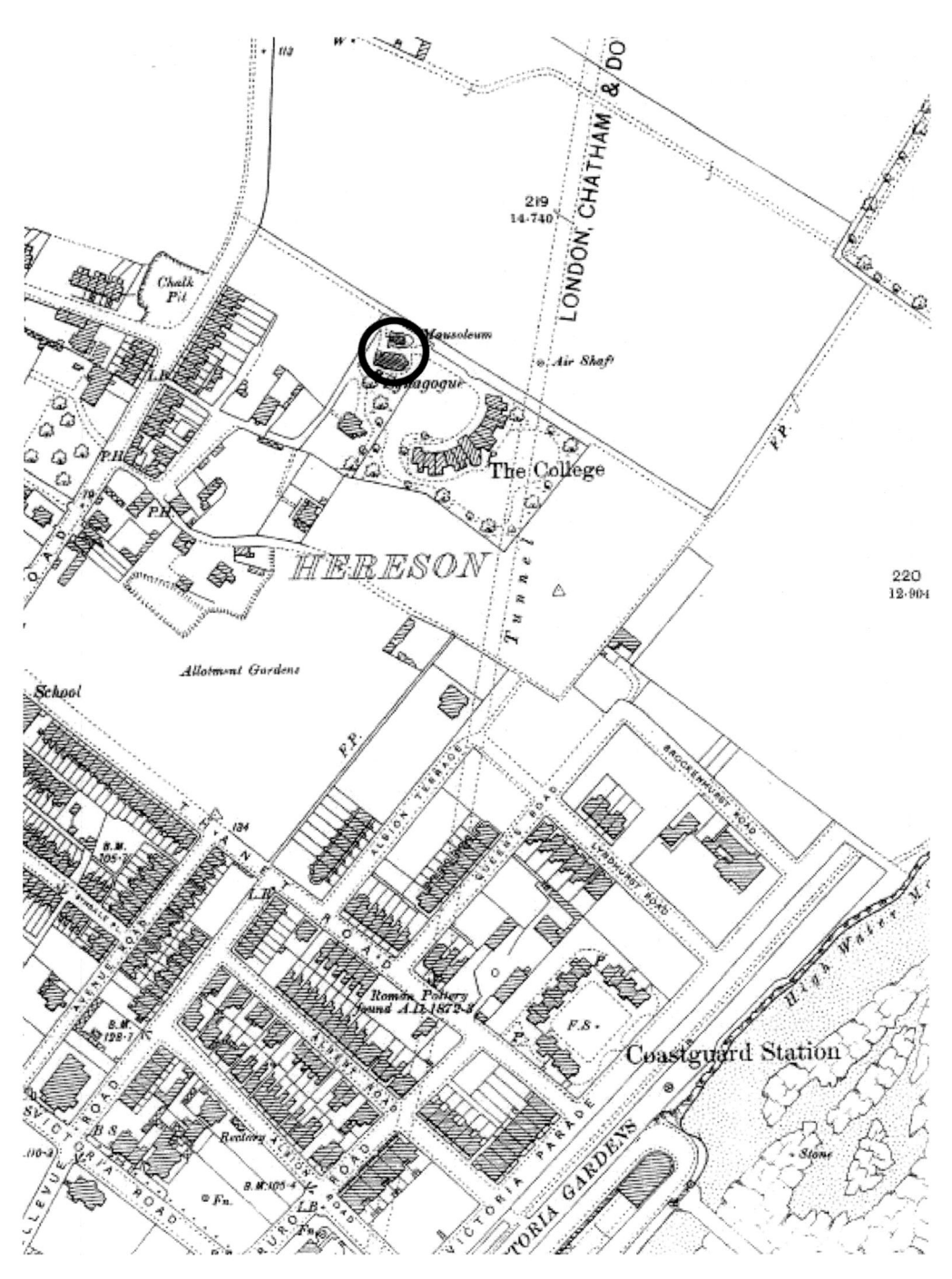

Ordnance Survey Map 1898　　　Ramsgate: Montefiore Synagogue and Mausoleum CT11　**[40]**
25 inches to a mile　　　　　　　　　Synagogue 1833-still in use

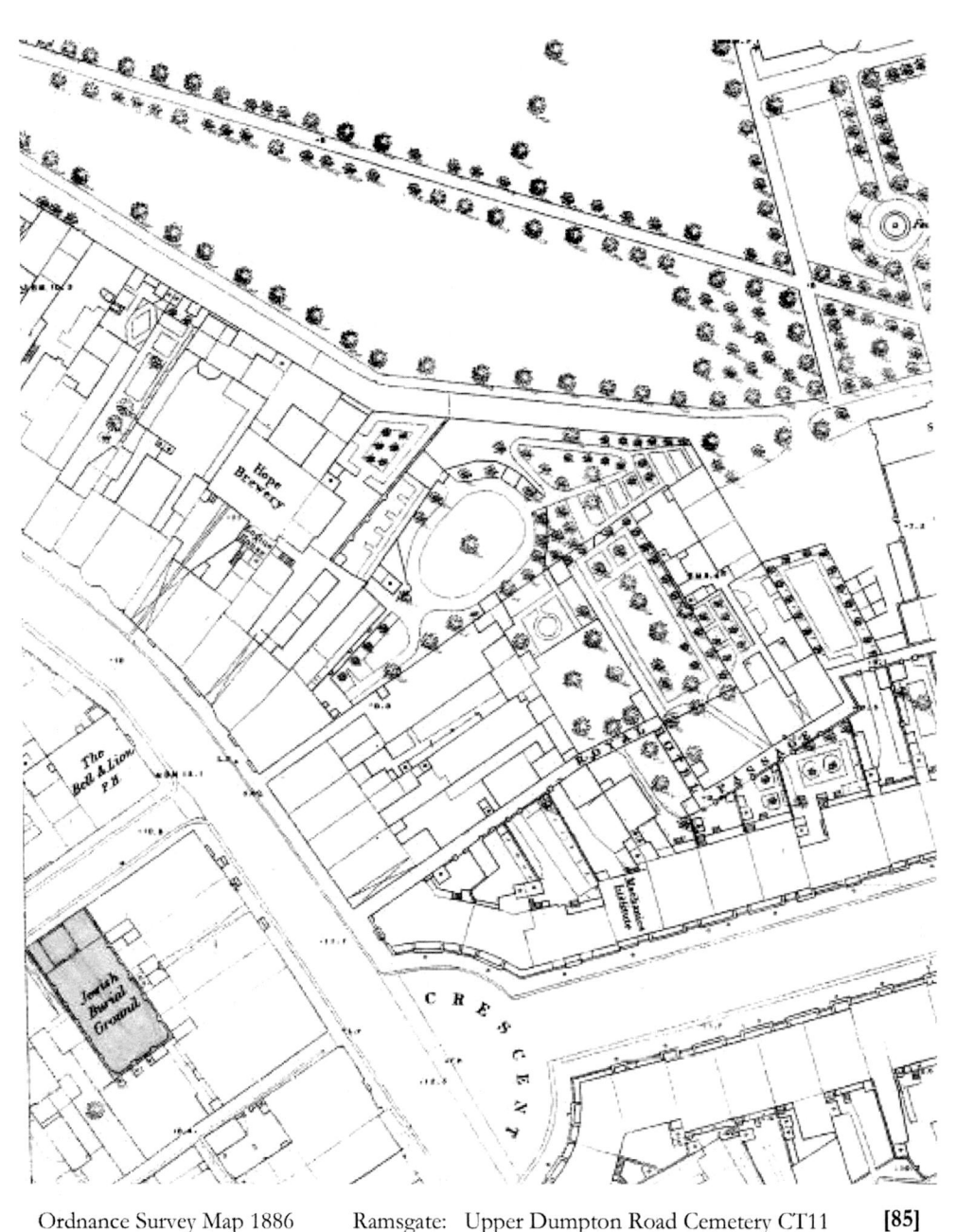

Ordnance Survey Map 1886 Ramsgate: Upper Dumpton Road Cemetery CT11   **[85]**
5 inches to a mile   1872-still in use

LOCATION	CHAPTER	SITE	DATE ESTABLISHED	IN USE TO	DATE OF VISIT	GAZETTEER NUMBER
SHEERNESS & ISLE of SHEPPEY	4.2.30	SYNAGOGUE	1811	1887	2010	[41]
	5.2.30	CEMETERIES	c.1804 1859*	1855 1899		[86]

ADDITIONAL NOTES		
	1790	Traditional date of the Foundation of the Community (Roth 1950)
	1790	First mention of Jews in Sheerness (Roth 1950)
		Community declined at the end of the Napoleonic Wars 1815
		*Possibly the smallest Jewish Cemetery in England with 11 headstones all belonging to two families
		There is no longer a Community in Sheerness or on the Isle of Sheppey

SYNAGOGUE	1811-1887	Synagogue in Kent Street, Bluetown, Isle of Sheppey demolished 1935
FIGURE NUMBERS	4.135	(Isle of Sheppey only)

CEMETERY	c.1804-1855	Sheerness Old Jews Burial Ground 2–4 Hope Street ME12
	1859-1899	Isle of Sheppey Cemetery Jewish Section Half Way Road ME12
FIGURE NUMBERS	5.129- 5.130	(Sheerness)
	5.131	(Isle of Sheppey)

CONTACT INFORMATION	Isle of Sheppey Heritage Centre Maidstone Records Office
BIBLIOGRAPHY	Kadish, S. 2006 *Jewish Heritage in England: an Architectural Guide* Lipman, V. 1954 *Social History of The Jews in England 1850 - 1950* Roth, C. 1950 *The Rise of Provincial Jewry*

OTHER SOURCES	Kent County Archive Ordnance Survey Maps: 1904 (Sheerness), 1908 (Isle of Sheppey) Statistical Account of the Congregations of The British Empire 1845

PLACE NAMES WITH JEWISH CONNECTIONS	Henry Russell Street** Henry Russell: Jewish composer of *"A Life on The Ocean Waves"*

COMMUNITY SIZE	Date	Community Size
	1842	5 families
	1850	75 persons
	1853	c.60
	1887	none

Ordnance Survey Map 1904
25 inches to a mile

Sheerness: Hope Street Cemetery ME12
c.1804-1855

[86]

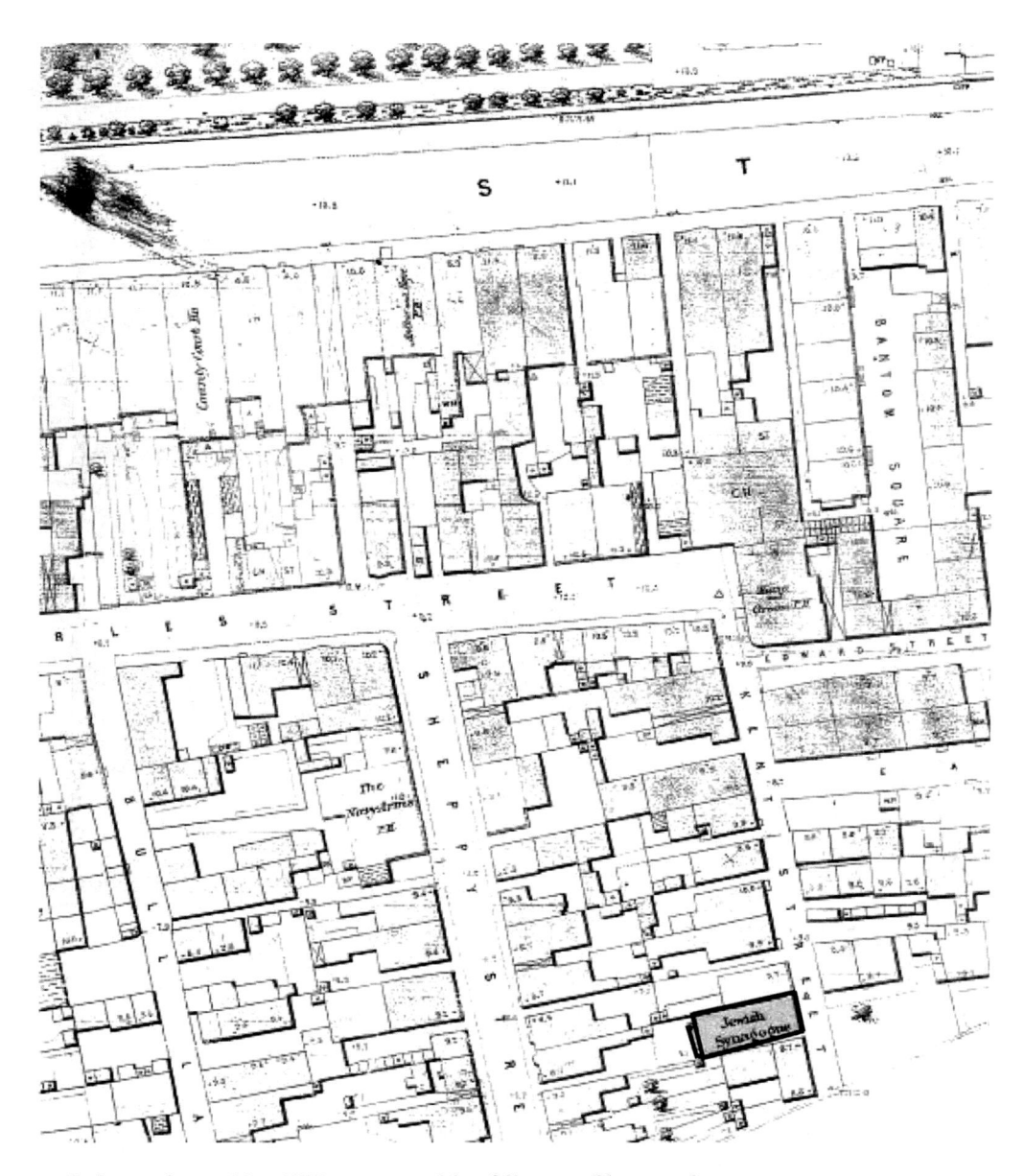

Ordnance Survey Map 1908　　　Isle of Sheppey; Bluetown Synagogue　　**[41]**
5 inches to a mile　　　　　　　1811-1887

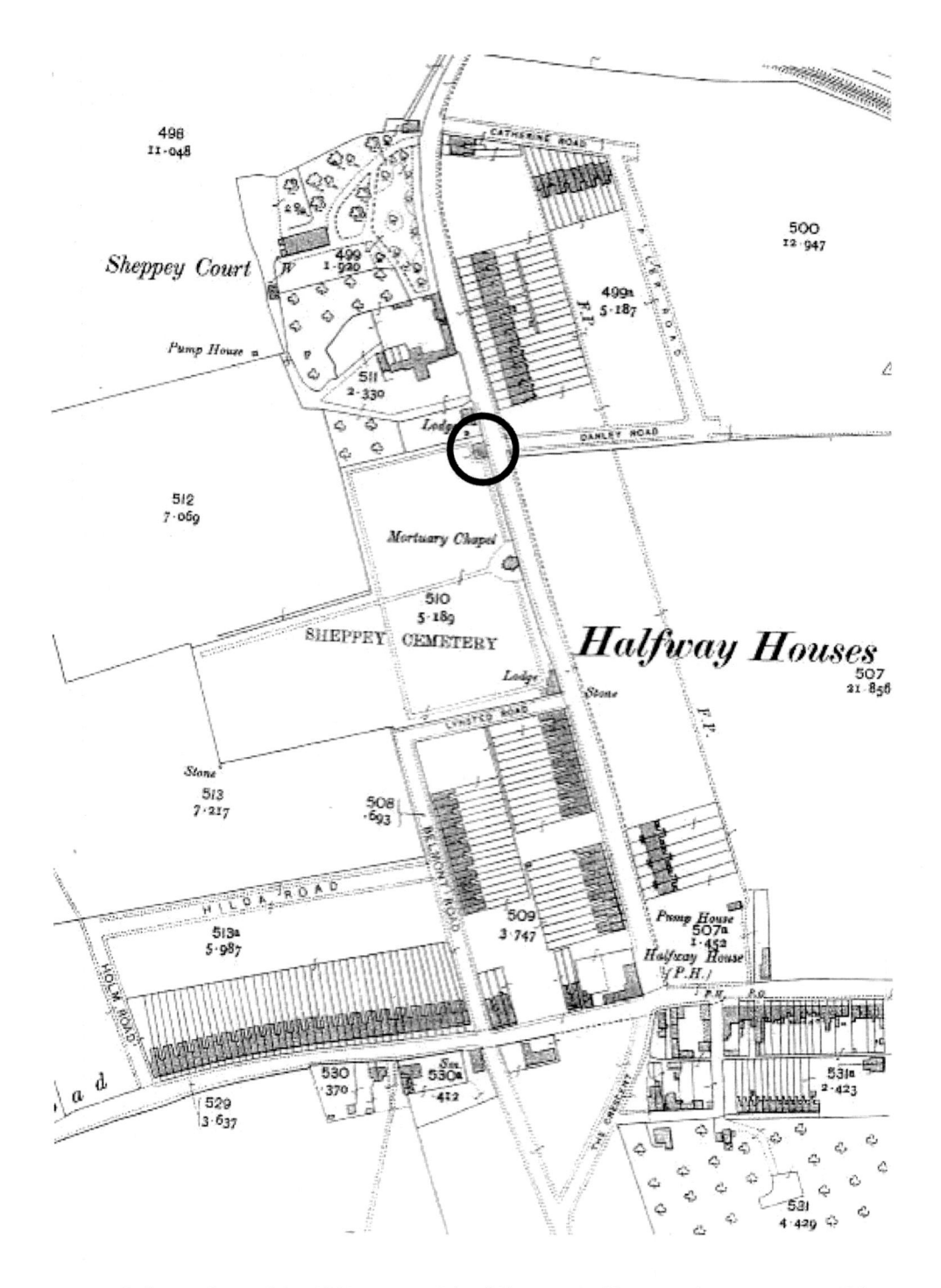

Ordnance Survey Map 1908 Isle of Sheppey; Halfway Road Cemetery [86]
25 inches to a mile 1859-1899

LOCATION	CHAPTER	SITE	DATE ESTABLISHED	IN USE TO	DATE OF VISIT	GAZETTEER NUMBER
SHEFFIELD	4.2.31	SYNAGOGUES	1851	?	2011	
			1872	1930		[42]
	5.2.31	CEMETERIES	1831	1880		[87]
			1873	1900		
			1872	still in use		

ADDITIONAL NOTES	
	1838 Traditional date of the Foundation of the Community (Roth 1950)
	c.1774 First mention of Jews in Sheffield (Ballin 1986)

SYNAGOGUE		
	1817	First Room of Prayer in Furnival Gate
	c.1820	Room of Prayer in Pinstone Street
	from 1842	Further Rooms of Prayer in Selly Street
	1851 - ?	First Synagogue in Figtree Lane
		(In use to: unknown)
	1872-1930	Second Synagogue in North Church Street*
		*Bombed in World War II
FIGURE NUMBERS	4.136-4.138	

CEMETERY		
	1831 – 1880	Bowden Street Burial Ground*
		Destroyed for redevelopment: compulsory purchase. *Site is now a car-park*
	1872	Ecclesfield Jewish Cemetery
		Colley Road S5
		Still in use (with remains from Bowden Street Burial Ground)
	1873-1900	Walkley Jewish Cemetery, Waller Rd. S6
FIGURE NUMBERS	5.132- 5.135	

CONTACT INFORMATION	Eric Sayliss: Elder of Sheffield Community
BIBLIOGRAPHY	Ballin, N. 1986 *Sheffield Jewry 1760 - 1900*
	Kadish, S. 2006 *Jewish Heritage in England: an Architectural Guide*
	Lipman, V. 1954 *Social History of The Jews in England 1850 - 1950*
	Roth, C. 1950 *The Rise of Provincial Jewry*

OTHER SOURCES	
	Sheffield Reference Library
	Ordnance Survey Maps:1889,1890,1903
	Statistical Account of the Congregations of The British Empire 1845

PLACE NAMES WITH JEWISH CONNECTIONS	none

COMMUNITY SIZE		
	Date	Community Size
	1845	c.50 persons
	1895	400
	1900	c.600
	1934	c.2,500
	1944	c.2,200
	1955	1850
	1965	1600
	1990	920
	1999	650
	2011	c.400

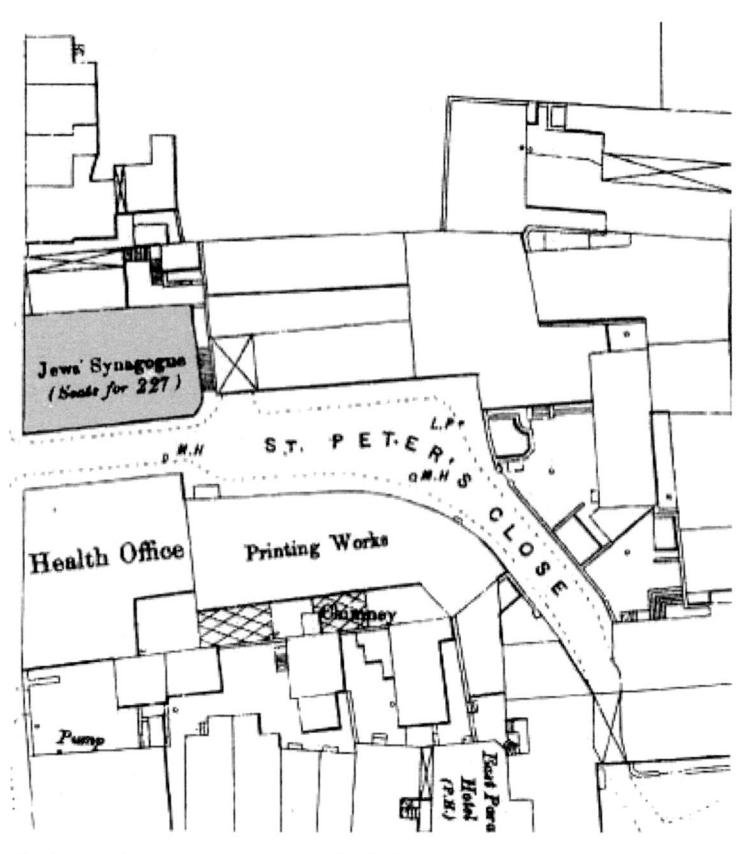

Ordnance Survey Map 1890   Sheffield: North Church Street Synagogue S1
5 inches to a mile   1872-1930

[42]

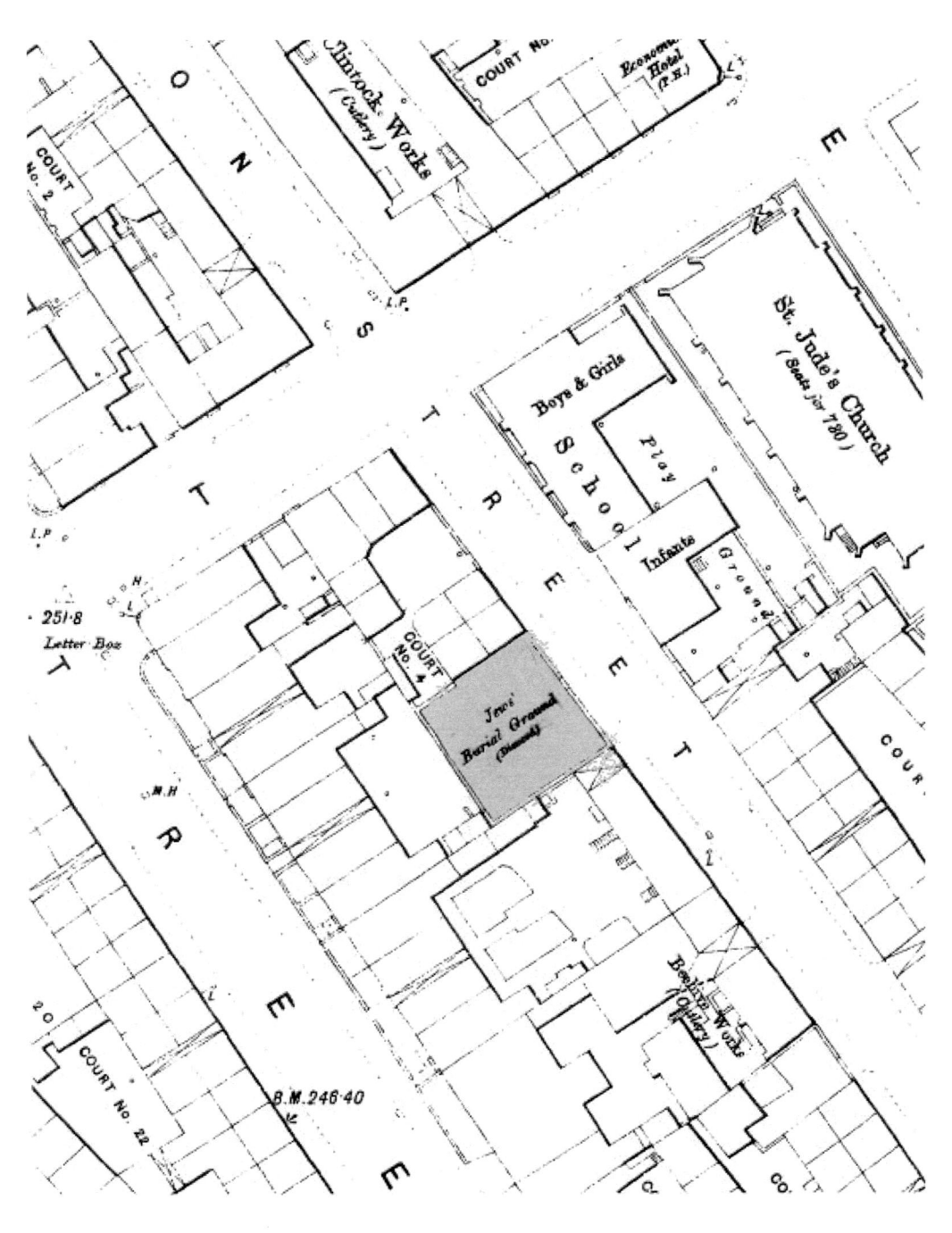

Ordnance Survey Map 1889 Sheffield: Bowden Street Cemetery
[87]
5 inches to a mile 1831-1880

Ordnance Survey Map 1903　　Sheffield: Walkley Jews' New Cemetery　　　　　　[87]
5 inches to a mile (extract)　　　　　　　1873-1900

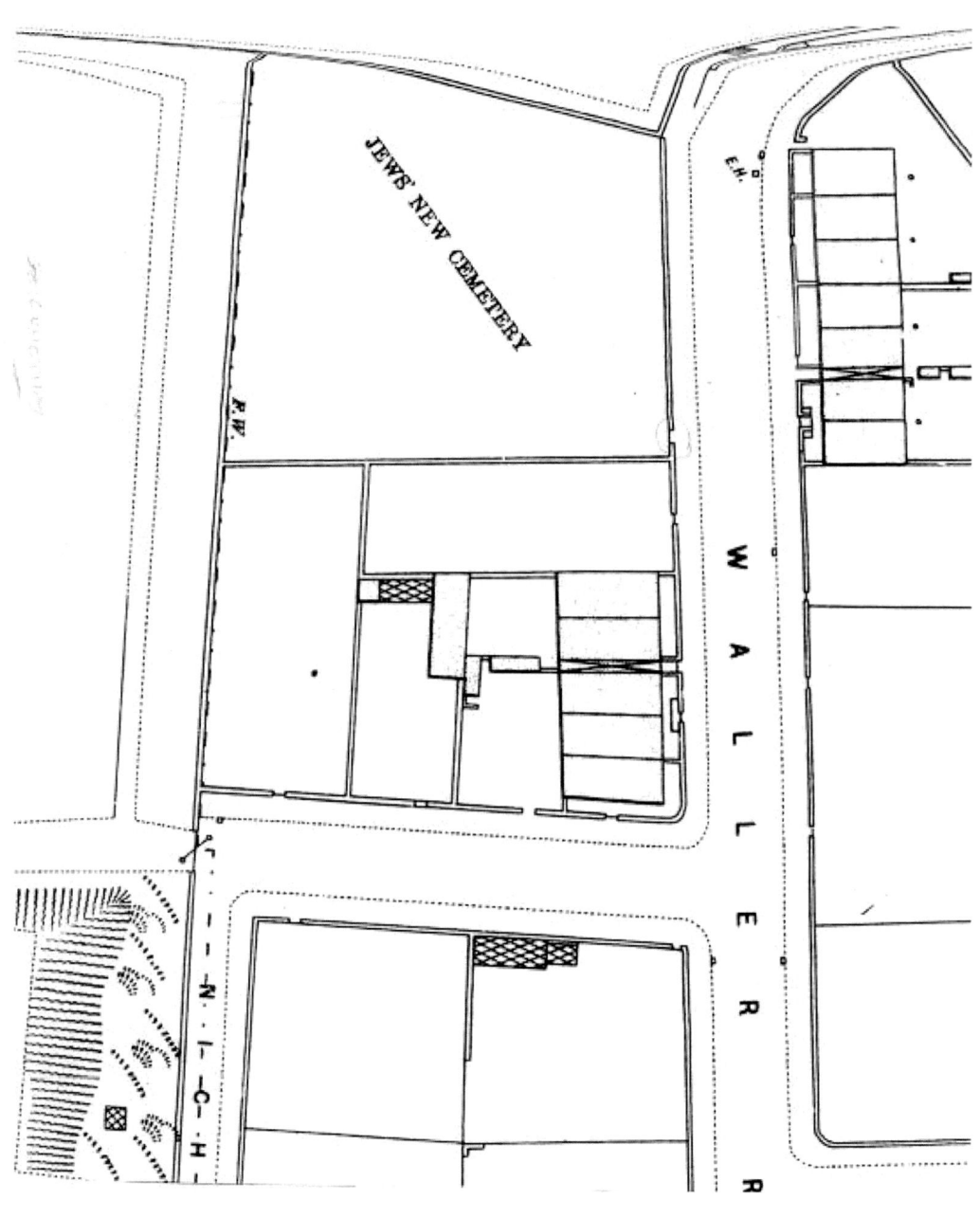

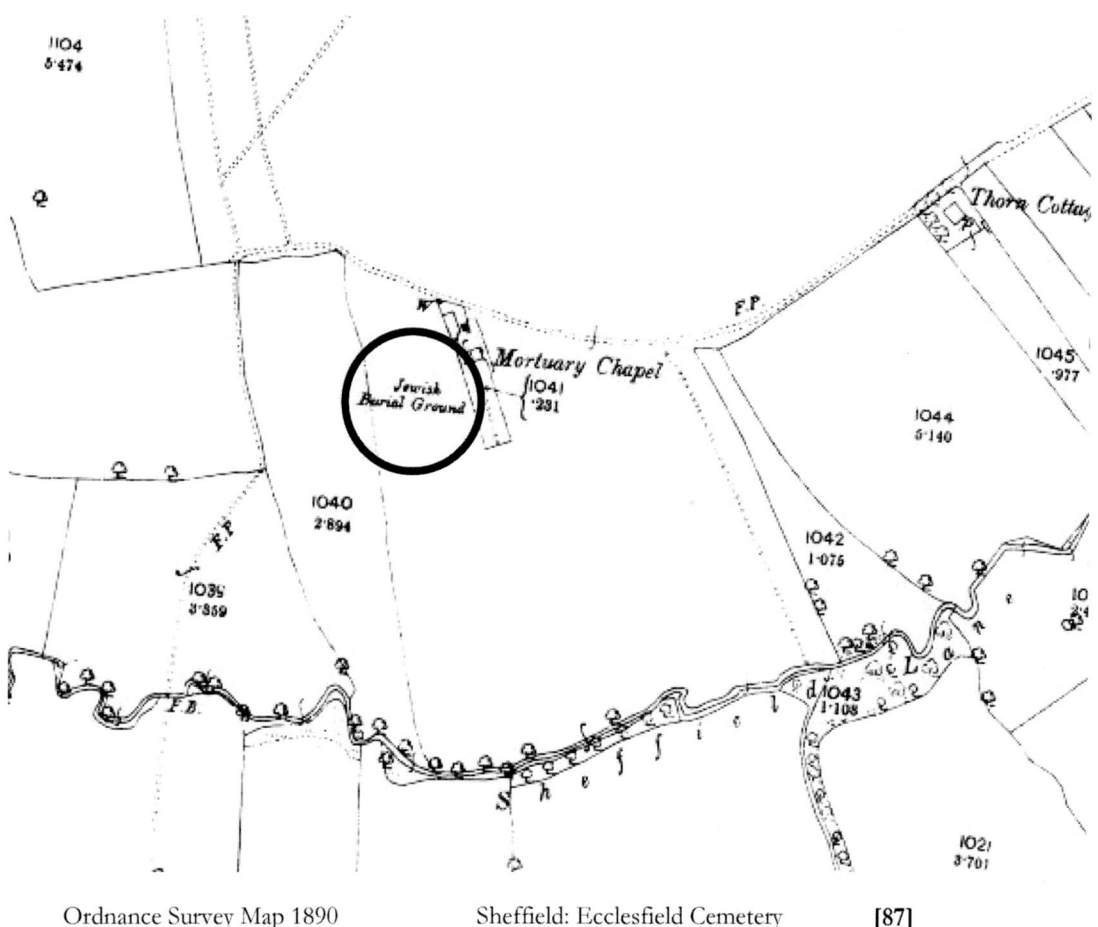

Ordnance Survey Map 1890 Sheffield: Ecclesfield Cemetery **[87]**
5 inches to a mile 1872-still in use

LOCATION	CHAPTER	SITE	DATE ESTABLISHED	IN USE TO	DATE OF VISIT	GAZETTEER NUMBER
SOUTHAMPTON	4.2.32	SYNAGOGUES	1864 1964	1964 still in use	2011	[43]
	5.2.32	CEMETERY	1846	still in use		[88]

ADDITIONAL NOTES		
	1833	Traditional date of the Foundation of the Community (Roth 1950)
	1782	First mention of Jews in Southampton (Roth 1950)

SYNAGOGUES	c.1833	Room of Prayer in East Street
	1864-1964	Synagogue: in Albion Street**
		**acquired by Southampton Council. *knocked down for car-park*
	1964	Synagogue: Mordaunt Road (former Methodist Chapel)
		still in use
FIGURE NUMBERS	4.139	

CEMETERY	1846	Southampton Common (Old) Cemetery Jewish Section Cemetery Road, SO15 Ohel (prayer hall) (Grade II)
FIGURE NUMBERS	5.136- 5.139	

CONTACT INFORMATION	Martyn Rose: President Southampton Hebrew Congregation Professor Tim Slotkin: Honorary Treasurer Southampton Hebrew Congregation
BIBLIOGRAPHY	Kadish, S. 2006 *Jewish Heritage in England: an Architectural Guide* Kushner, T. 2002 *A Tale of Two Port Jewish Communities: Southampton and Portsmouth compared.* In Cesarani, D. (ed.) *Port Jews* Lipman, V. 1954 *Social History of The Jews in England 1850 - 1950* Roth, C. 1950 *The Rise of Provincial Jewry*

OTHER SOURCES	Southampton City Archive Ordnance Survey Maps: 1898 Statistical Account of the Congregations of The British Empire 1845

PLACE NAMES WITH JEWISH CONNECTIONS	none

COMMUNITY SIZE	Date Community Size 1850 75 persons 1900 100 1934 266 2004 293

Ordnance Survey Map 1898 Southampton: Albion Street Synagogue
25 inches to a mile 1864-1964 **[43]**

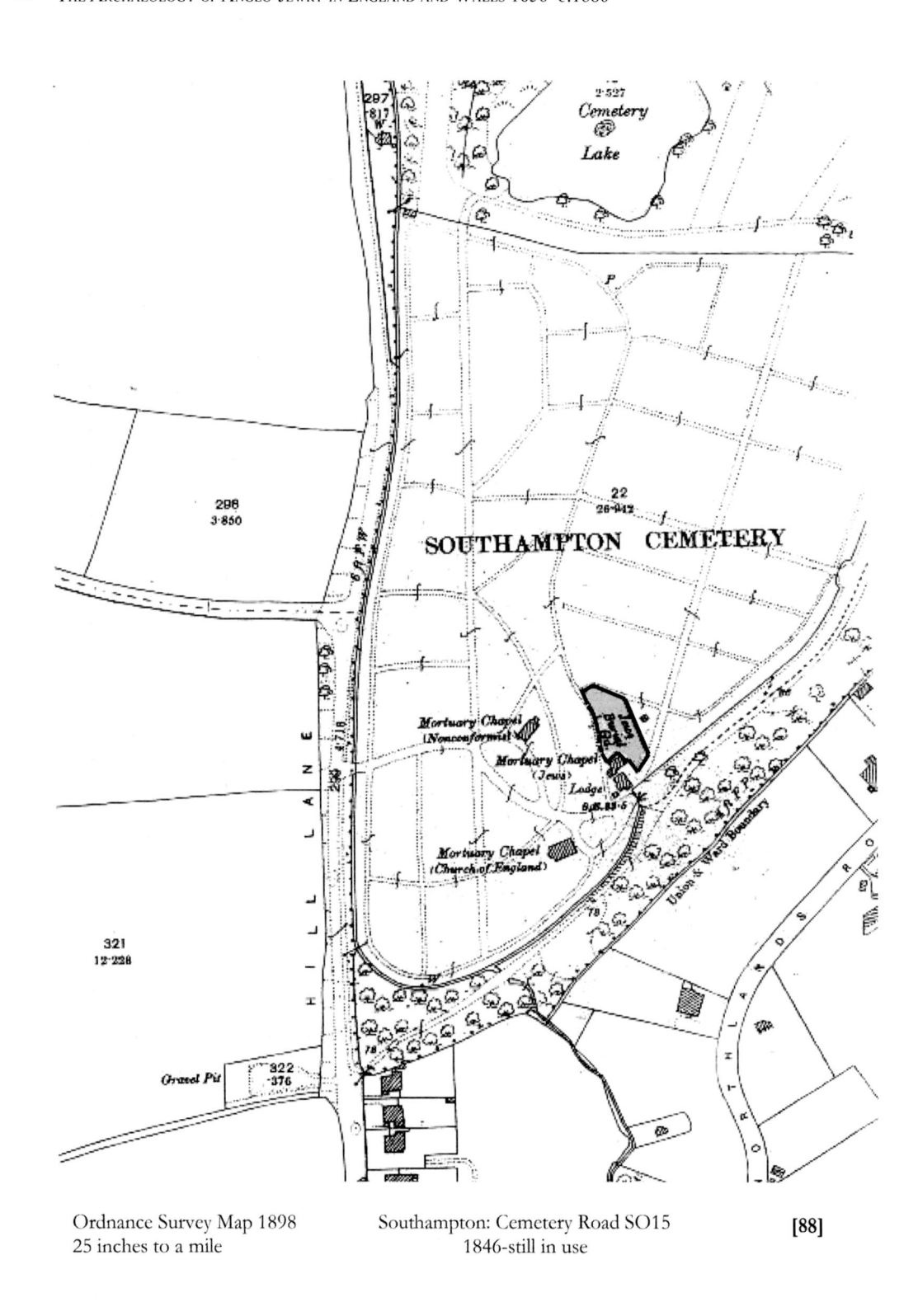

Ordnance Survey Map 1898
25 inches to a mile

Southampton: Cemetery Road SO15
1846-still in use

[88]

LOCATION	CHAPTER	SITE	DATE ESTABLISHED	IN USE TO	DATE OF VISIT	GAZETTEER NUMBER
SUNDERLAND	4.2.33	SYNAGOGUES	1781 1862 1928	1860 1928 no longer in use	2010	[44]
	5.2.33	CEMETERIES	c.1780 1856	1856 still in use		[89]

ADDITIONAL NOTES		
	c.1781	Traditional date of the Foundation of the Community (Roth 1950)
	c.1768 / 1781	First mention of Jews in Sunderland (Roth 1950)
		The Sunderland Community from a peak of over 2,000 in 1934 now has only 16 individuals

SYNAGOGUES		
	1781-1860	First Synagogue: Private House in Vine Street
	1862-1928	Second Synagogue: in Moor Street
	1928	Third Synagogue: Rhy Hope Road (Grade II) no longer in use
FIGURE NUMBERS	Nil	

CEMETERY		
	c.1780-1856	Ayres Quay Jewish Cemetery Ayres Quay Road, Ballast Hill SR1
	1856	Bishopswarmouth Cemetery: Jewish Sections Hylton Road SR4 *still in use*
FIGURE NUMBERS	5.140-5.145	

CONTACT INFORMATION	Dorothy Sadlik: Member of the Newcastle Community (born in Sunderland)
BIBLIOGRAPHY	Kadish, S. 2006 *Jewish Heritage in England: an Architectural Guide* Levy, A. 1956 *A History of Sunderland's Jewish Community 1755 – 1955* Lipman, V. 1954 *Social History of The Jews in England 1850 - 1950* Roth, C. 1950 *The Rise of Provincial Jewry*

OTHER SOURCES	Sunderland Records Office Ordnance Survey Maps: 1897

COMMUNITY SIZE	Date	Community Size
	1790	150 - 200 persons
	1851	150
	1866	c.300
	1876	600
	1893	*c.600*
	1902	1000
	1934	2000
	2001	*114*
	2010	*16*

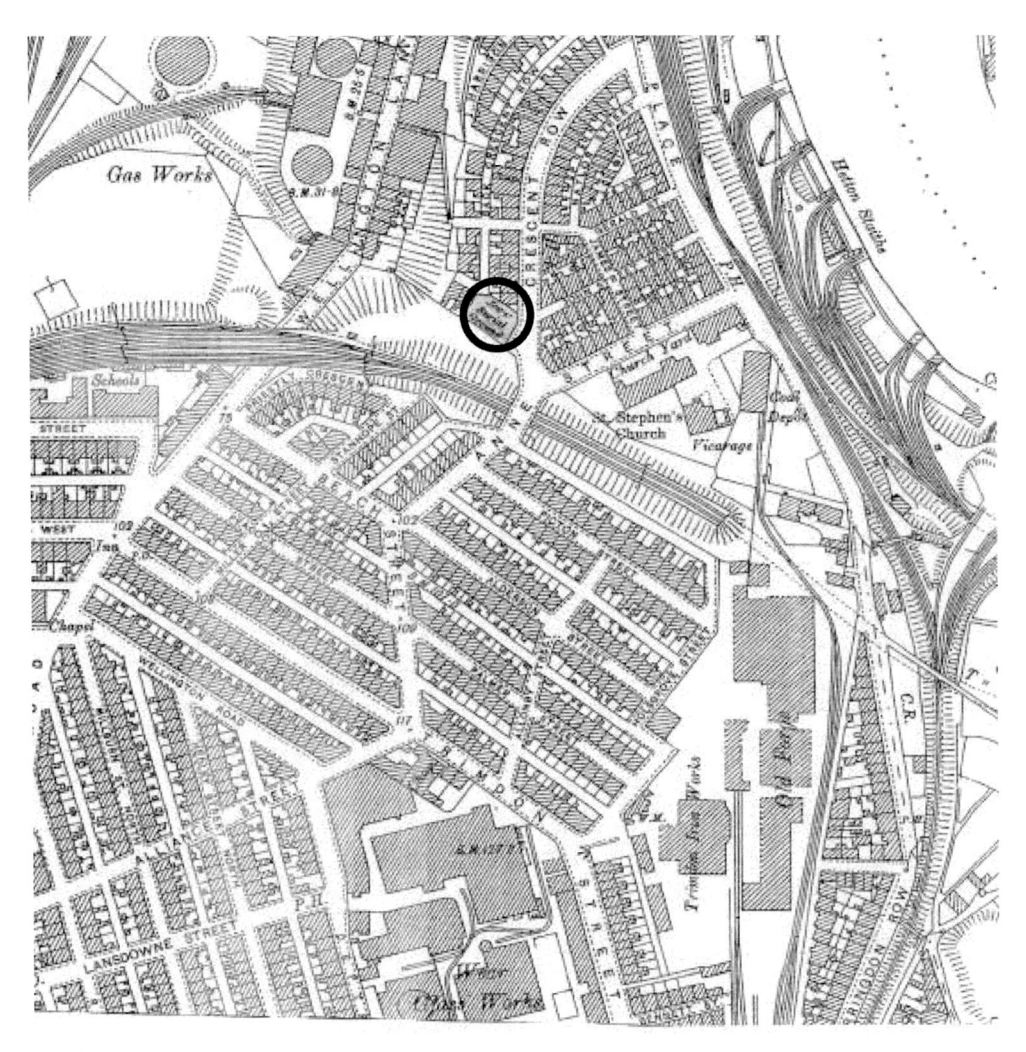

Ordnance Survey Map 1897
25 inches to a mile

Sunderland: Ayre's Quay Cemetery SR1 c.1780-1856

[89]

Ordnance Survey Map 1897 Sunderland: Bishopwearmouth Cemetery SR4 [89]
25 inches to a mile 1856-still in use

LOCATION	CHAPTER	SITE	DATE ESTABLISHED	IN USE TO	DATE OF VISIT	GAZETTEER NUMBER
SWANSEA	4.2.34	SYNAGOGUES	1740 1788 1818 1859	1788 / 9 1818 1857 1941*	2010	[45]
	5.2.34	CEMETERY	1768	1965		[90]

ADDITIONAL NOTES		
	1768	Traditional date of the Foundation of the Community (Roth 1950)
	1741	First mention of Jews in Swansea (Roth 1950)

SYNAGOGUES	1740-1788 / 9 1788-1818 1818-1857 1859-1941*	First Synagogue: Wind Street Second Synagogue: The Strand Third Synagogue: Waterloo Street Fourth Synagogue: Goat Street Coat Street *destroyed by bombing
FIGURE NUMBERS	4.140-4.142	

CEMETERY	1768-1965	Old Jews' Burial Ground High View, Mayhill SA1
FIGURE NUMBERS	5.146-5.147	

CONTACT INFORMATION	Norma Glass MBE: Member of Swansea Jewish Community David Factor: Chairman Swansea Hebrew Jewish Congregation
BIBLIOGRAPHY	Alderman, G. 1974/8 *The Jews as Scapegoats. The Settlement and reception of Jews in South Wales before 1914* Glass, M. (unpublished) *Swansea Hebrew Congregation 1730 - 1930* Henriques, U. 1993 *The Jews of South Wales - Historical Studies* Kadish, S. 2006 *Jewish Heritage in England: an Architectural Guide* Lipman, V. 1954 *Social History of The Jews in England 1850 - 1950* Roth, C. 1950 *The Rise of Provincial Jewry*

OTHER SOURCES	Swansea Records Office Board of Health Mapo: 1079 Statistical Account of the Congregations of The British Empire 1845

PLACE NAMES WITH JEWISH CONNECTIONS	None

COMMUNITY SIZE	Date Community Size 1768 40 persons 1818 60 / 70 1850 150 1901 300 / 400 1912 1,000 1939 500 1980 200 / 250 2010 50

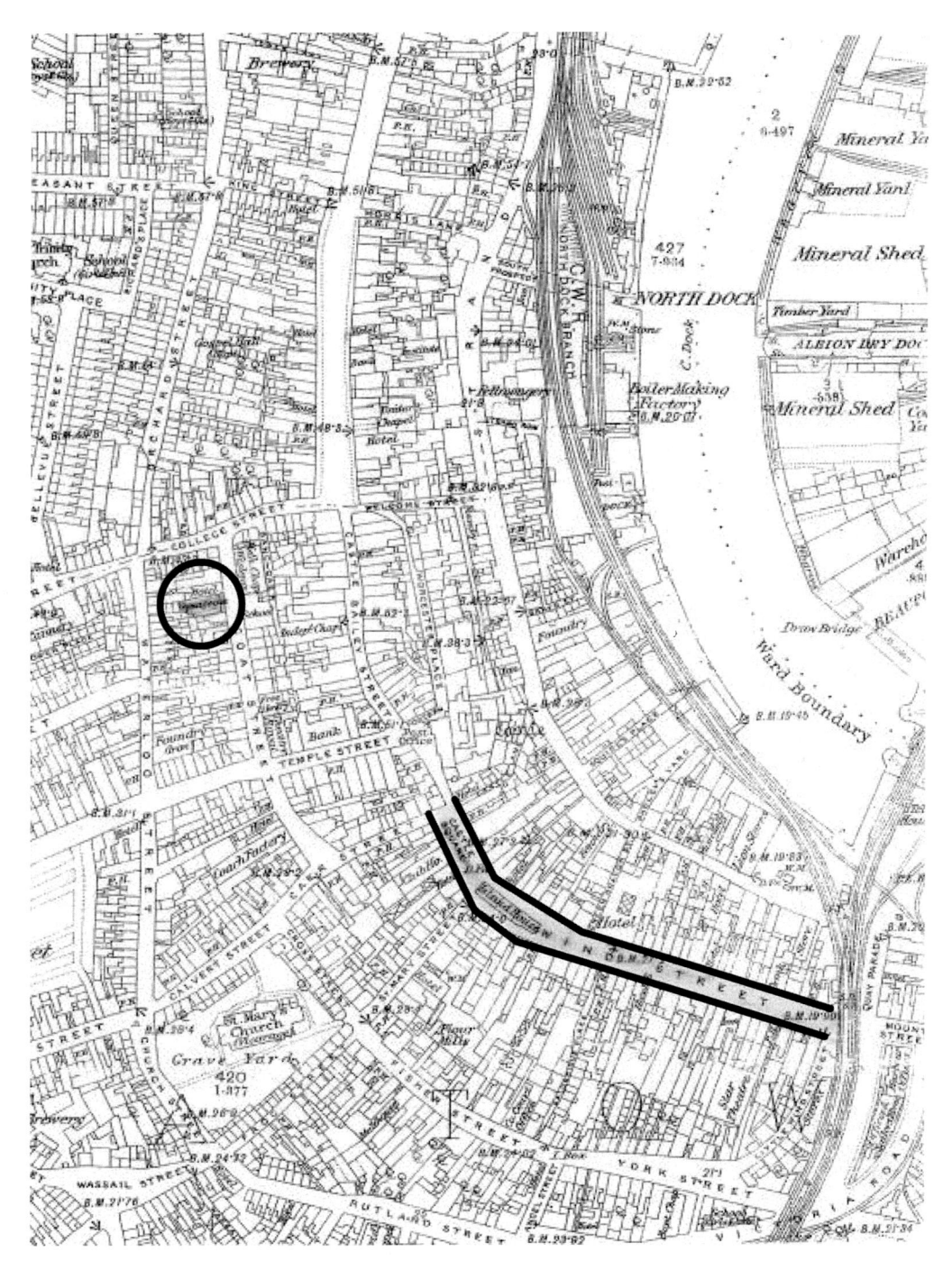

Public Health Map 1879　　　Swansea: Wind Street Synagogue 1740-c.1788 (not marked)
25 inches to a mile　　　　　　Goat Street Synagogue 1859-1941　　　　　　　　**[45]**

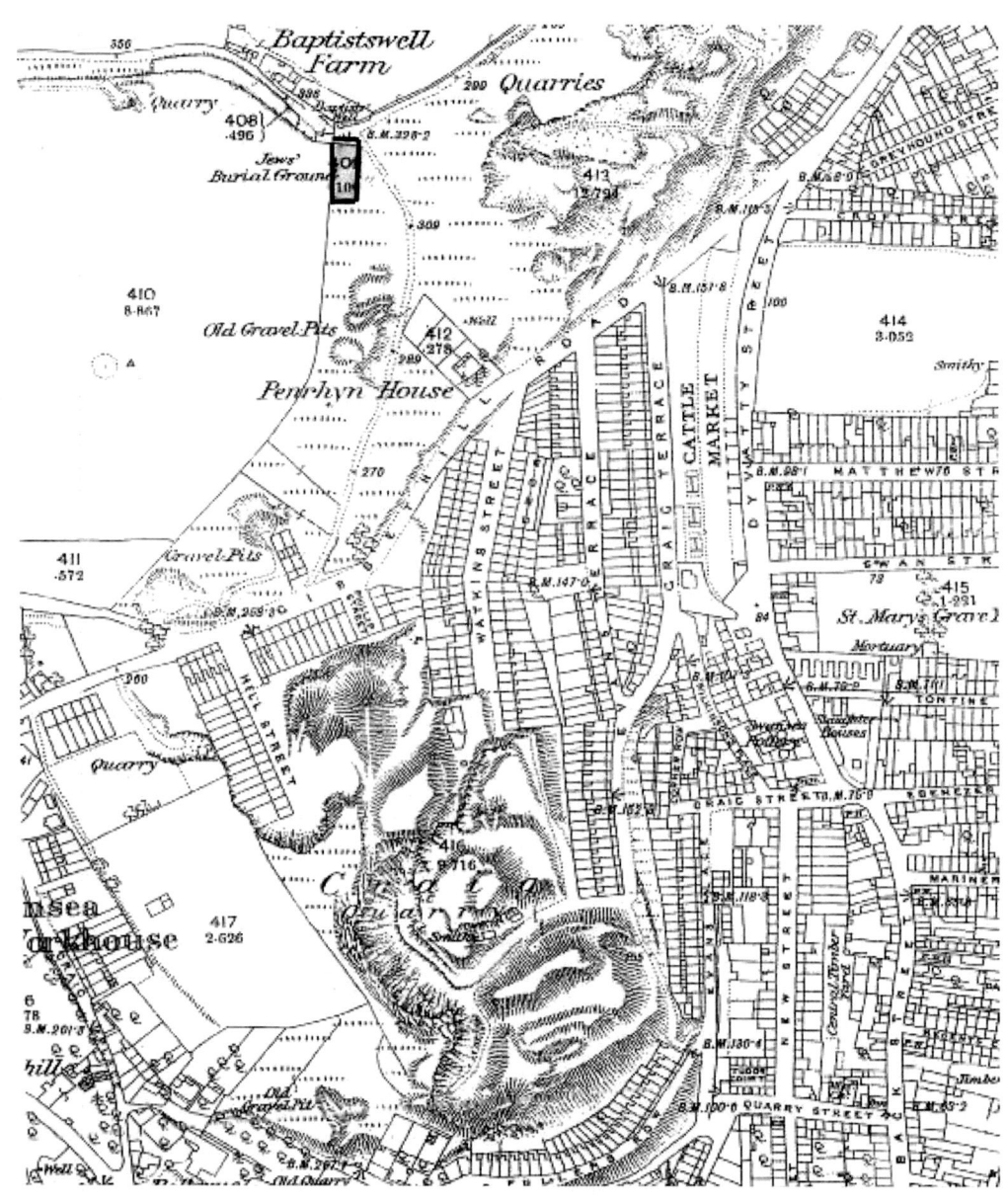

Public Health Map 1879 Swansea: High View and Long Ridge Mayhill Cemetery
25 inches to a mile 1768-1965
[90]

LOCATION	CHAPTER	SITE	DATE ESTABLISHED	IN USE TO	DATE OF VISIT	GAZETTEER NUMBER
YARMOUTH (GREAT)	4.2.35	SYNAGOGUE	1846	1892	2010	[46]
	5.2.35	CEMETERIES	1801 1858	1885 1936		[91]

ADDITIONAL NOTES	
	c.1760 First mention of Jews (Roth,1950)
	1801 Traditional date of the Foundation of the Community (Roth 1950)
	There is no longer a Jewish Community in Yarmouth (Great)

SYNAGOGUE	c.1801 – 1847	Rooms of Prayer in Chapel Street (
	1847 – 1892	First Synagogue in George Street
		(also known as Jews' Row or Synagogue Row)
FIGURE NUMBERS	Nil	

CEMETERIES	1801-1885	The Old Jews' Burial Ground
		Alma Road NR30
	1858-1936	Great Yarmouth Old Cemetery Jewish Section
		Kitchener Road NR30
FIGURE NUMBERS	5.148-5.152	

CONTACT INFORMATION	Yarmouth (Great) Town Hall & Reference Library
BIBLIOGRAPHY	
	Kadish, S. 2006 *Jewish Heritage in England: an Architectural Guide*
	Lipman, V. 1954 *Social History of The Jews in England 1850 - 1950*
	Roth, C. 1950 *The Rise of Provincial Jewry*

OTHER SOURCES	
	Yarmouth (Great) Records Office
	Ordnance Survey Maps: 1994
	Statistical Account of the Congregations of The British Empire 1845

PLACE NAMES WITH JEWISH CONNECTIONS	Jews' Row or Synagogue Row

COMMUNITY SIZE	Date	Community Size
	1845 - 1847	48 persons
	1850	c.75
	1872	no longer a community

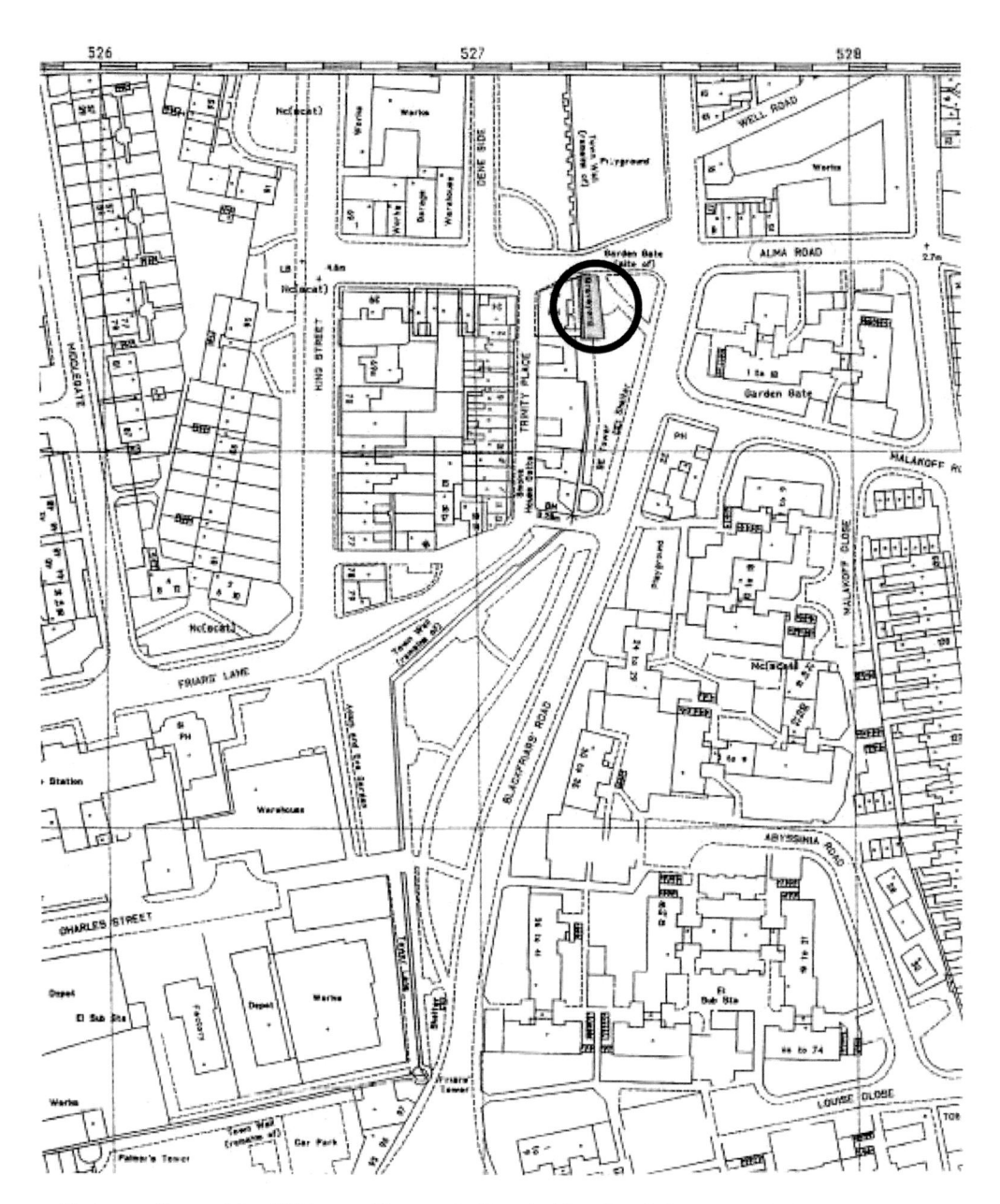

Ordnance Survey Map 1994   Yarmouth (Great): Alma Road Cemetery NR30
25 inches to a mile   1801-1885   [91]

Reproduced from 1994 O.S. map with the permission of the Controller of H.M. Stationary Office, Crown Copyright 1994

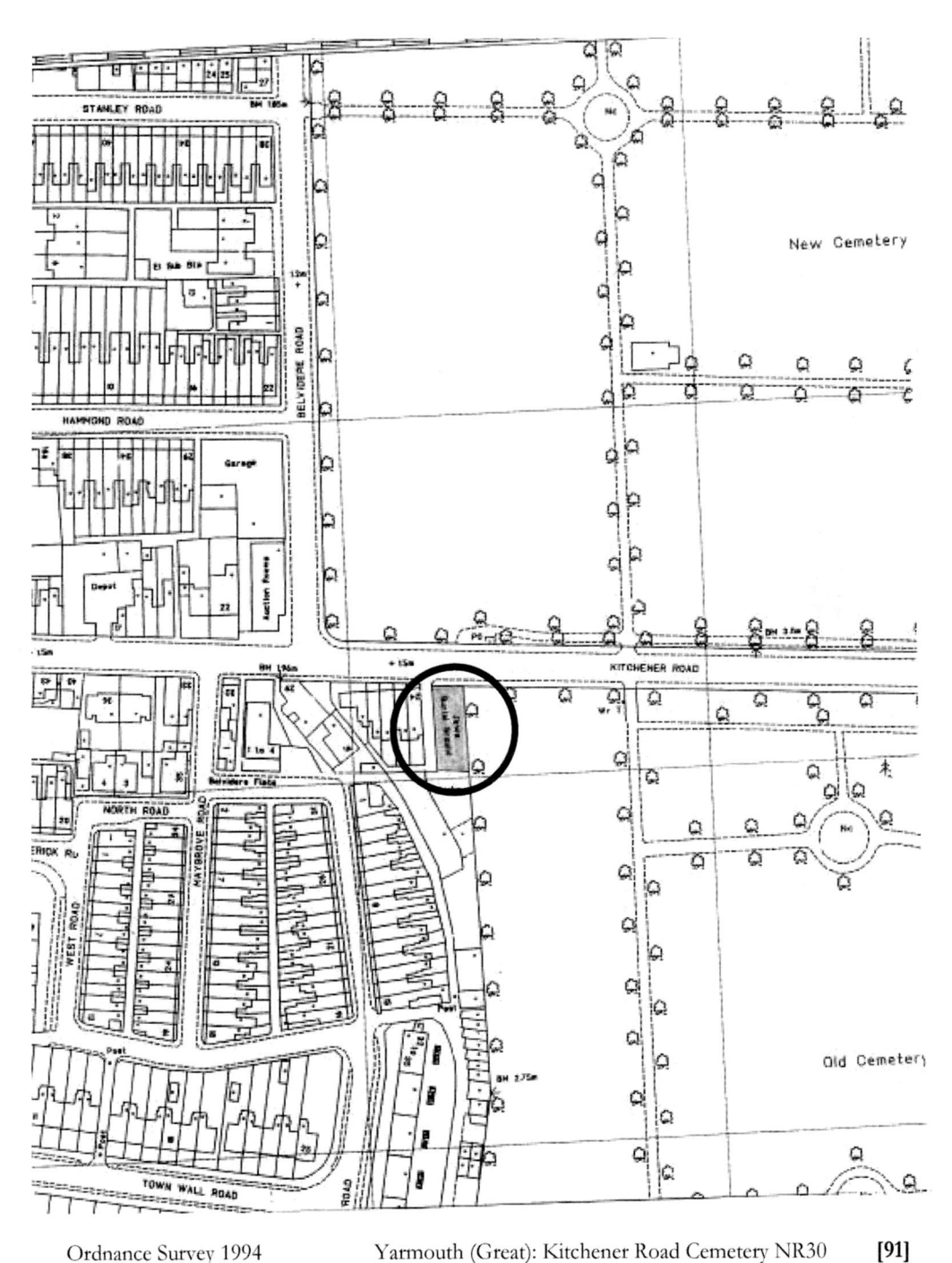

Ordnance Survey 1994 Yarmouth (Great): Kitchener Road Cemetery NR30 [91]
25 inches to a mile 1858-1936

Reproduced from 1994 O.S. .map with the permission of the Controller of Her Majesty's Stationary Office, Crown Copyright 2013